The Undivided Heart

The Undivided Heart

*Law, Morality, Human Nature, and Ethical Theory
in Ancient Israel and Second Temple Judaism*

Zachary Alan Starr

WIPF & STOCK · Eugene, Oregon

THE UNDIVIDED HEART
Law, Morality, Human Nature, and Ethical Theory in Ancient Israel and Second Temple Judaism

Copyright © 2025 Zachary Alan Starr. All rights reserved. Except for brief quotations in critical publications or reviews, no part of this book may be reproduced in any manner without prior written permission from the publisher. Write: Permissions, Wipf and Stock Publishers, 199 W. 8th Ave., Suite 3, Eugene, OR 97401.

Wipf & Stock
An Imprint of Wipf and Stock Publishers
199 W. 8th Ave., Suite 3
Eugene, OR 97401

www.wipfandstock.com

PAPERBACK ISBN: 979-8-3852-4422-5
HARDCOVER ISBN: 979-8-3852-4423-2
EBOOK ISBN: 979-8-3852-4424-9

VERSION NUMBER 07/23/25

Reprinted from the *Tanakh: The Holy Scriptures* by permission of the University of Nebraska Press. Copyright 1985 by The Jewish Publication Society.

I will give them a single [or undivided] heart and a single [or undivided] nature . . . and it shall be well with them and their children after them.

—Jeremiah 32:39

I will give them one [undivided] heart . . . that they may follow My laws and faithfully observe My rules.

—Ezekiel 11:19–20

Teach me your way, O Lord . . . let my heart be undivided in reverence for Your name.

—Psalms 86:11

As to my son Solomon, give him a whole [or undivided] heart to observe your commandments.

—1 Chronicles 28:19

Be mindful of the Lord in goodness, and seek him in singleness of heart.

—Wisdom of Solomon 1:1

Proceed in singleness of heart, in the fear of the Lord, [by] exerting yourselves in good deeds.

—Testament of Reuben 4:1

Blessed are the pure in heart, for they will see God.

—Matthew 5:8

Contents

Abbreviations | ix

Introduction | 1

1 The sages of the ancient Israelite wisdom tradition precipitated a moral change in Israelite society by extolling qualities and conduct having cooperative value, claiming that they were conducive to a prosperous society. | 14

2 The secular law collections mandated qualities and conduct having cooperative value justified on the grounds that they were beneficial for the Israelite nation, but later justified on the grounds that Yahweh commanded them. | 50

3 The priestly law collections associated qualities and conduct having cooperative value with the holiness Yahweh demanded from the Israelites. | 77

4 The prophets condemned the Israelites for disobeying Yahweh's moral commands, and Jeremiah concluded that obedience required giving human beings an undivided heart. | 96

5 Job and Qoheleth questioned the traditional doctrine that Yahweh rewards the righteous and punishes the wicked, but Ben Sira defended the doctrine; other texts posited a postmortem reward and punishment. | 123

6 The Hellenized Jews of the Diaspora intertwined Jewish law and morality with Greek philosophy, accepting the Platonic notion of a soul which is rewarded or punished in an afterlife. | 157

CONTENTS

7 Philo of Alexandria subsumed all the Greek virtues within biblical law and justified both on the basis that they were conducive to individual and societal well-being. | 194

8 The Tannaim and their predecessors, the Pharisees, promulgated and developed new rules of conduct that were handed down from generation to generation and eventually collected and organized in the Mishnah and the Tosefta. | 228

9 The Tannaim changed biblical law to achieve desirable communal ends and claimed that torah study could control the evil *yetzer*. | 265

10 Jewish apocalyptic works emphasized the influence of demonic forces on human conduct, the irremediable evil nature of human beings, the need for the righteous to separate themselves from the wicked, the promise of an individual reward and punishment, and the transformation of human nature at an end time. | 308

11 The Essenes and the followers of Jesus of Nazareth criticized the tradition of the fathers on the grounds that its rules of conduct were man-made, not divine; and they believed that an end-time was imminent. | 344

Bibliography | 391

Abbreviations

1QS	Community Rule
Abraham	Philo, *On the Life of Abraham*
Acad. post.	Cicero, *Academica posteriora*
Alleg. Interp.	Philo, *Allegorical Interpretation*
Ag. Ap.	Josephus, *Against Apion*
Ant.	Josephus, *Jewish Antiquities*
m. ʿAbod. Zar.	Mishnah, Avodah Zarah
m. ʾAbot	Mishnah, Avot
ʾAbot R. Nat.	*The Fathers According to Rabbi Nathan*
b. B. Bat.	Babylonian Talmud, Bava Batra
2 Bar.	2 Baruch (Syriac Apocalypse)
m. Ber.	Mishnah, Berakhot
y. Ber.	Jerusalem Talmud, Berakhot
Canticles Rab.	*Canticles Rabbah*
CD	Damascus Document
Contempl. Life	Philo, *On the Contemplative Life*
Creation	Philo, *On the Creation of the World*
Decalogue	Philo, *On the Decalogue*
Diog. Laert.	Diogenes Laertius, *Lives of Eminent Philosophers*
m. ʿEd.	Mishnah, Eduyyot
1 En.	1 Enoch

ABBREVIATIONS

Ep. Men.	Epicurus, *Letter to Menoeceus*
Eth. nic.	Aristotle, *Nichomachean Ethics*
Exod. Rab.	*Exodus Rabbah*
Euthyphr.	Plato, *Euthyphro*
Fin.	Cicero, *De finibus*
Gen. Rab.	*Genesis Rabbah*
m. Giṭ.	Mishnah, Gittin
b. Giṭ.	Babylonian Talmud, Gittin
Gorg.	Plato, *Gorgias*
m. Hag.	Mishnah, Hagigah
Heir	Philo, *Who Is the Heir?*
Hypothetica	Philo, *Hypothetica*
J.W.	Josephus, *Jewish War*
Joseph	Philo, *On the Life of Joseph*
Jub.	Jubilees
Leg.	Cicero, *De legibus*
Leg.	Plato, *Laws*
Let. Aris.	Letter of Aristeas
Life	Josephus, *The Life*
b. Mak.	Babylonian Talmud, Makkot
m. Mak.	Mishnah, Makkot
m. Maʿas. Š.	Mishnah, Maʿaser Sheni
Mek. of Rabbi Ishmael	*Mekilta of Rabbi Ishmael*
b. Men.	Babylonian Talmud, Menahot
b. B. Meṣiʿa	Babylonian Talmud, Bava Metsiʿa
m. B. Meṣiʿa	Mishnah, Bava Metsiʿa
t. B. Meṣiʿa	Tosefta, Bava Metsiʿa
Migration	Philo, *On the Migration of Abraham*
Moses	Philo, *On the Life of Moses*
m. Ned.	Mishnah, Nedarim
Num. Rab.	*Numbers Rabbah*

ABBREVIATIONS

Off.	Cicero, *De officiis*
Phaed.	Plato, *Phaedo*
Phaedr.	Plato, *Phaedrus*
m. Peʾah	Mishnah, Peʾah
b. Pesaḥ.	Babylonian Talmud, Pesahim
y. Pesaḥ.	Jerusalem Talmud, Pesahim
t. Pisha	Tosefta, Pisha
Pol.	Aristotle, *Politics*
Posterity	Philo, *On the Posterity of Cain*
Prob.	Philo, *Quod omnis probus liber sit*
Prot.	Plato, *Protagoras*
Providence	Philo, *On Providence*
Ps.-Phoc.	Pseudo-Phocylides, *Sentences*
m. B. Qam.	Mishnah, Bava Qamma
b. Qidd.	Babylonian Talmud, Quiddushin
Qoh	Qoheleth (Ecclesiastes)
Resp.	Plato, *Republic*
Rewards	Philo, *On Rewards and Punishments*
b. Roš. Haš.	Babylonian Talmud, Rosh HaShanah
b. Šabb.	Babylonian Talmud, Shabbat
t. Šabb.	Tosefta, Shabbat
Sacrifices	Philo, *On the Sacrifices of Cain and Abel*
b. Sanh.	Babylonian Talmud, Sanhedrin
m. Sanh.	Mishnah, Sanhedrin
t. Sanh.	Tosefta, Sanhedrin
m. Šeb.	Mishnah, Sheviʿit
Sifre Deut.	Sifre Deuteronomy
Some Precepts	*Some Precepts of the Torah*, a Qumran document
b. Soṭah	Babylonian Talmud, Sotah
Spec. Laws	Philo, *On the Special Laws*
b. Sukk.	Babylonian Talmud, Sukkah

ABBREVIATIONS

t. Sukk.	Tosefta, Sukkah
T. Ash.	Testament of Asher
T. Benj.	Testament of Benjamin
T. Dan	Testament of Dan
T. Gad	Testament of Gad
T. Iss.	Testament of Issachar
T. Jud.	Testament of Judah
T. Levi	Testament of Levi
T. Naph.	Testament of Naphtali
T. Reu.	Testament of Reuben
T. Sim.	Testament of Simeon
T. Zeb.	Testament of Zebulun
t. Ter.	Tosefta, Terumot
m. Tem.	Mishnah, Temurah
Tim.	Plato, *Timaeus*
Tusc.	Cicero, *Tusculanae disputationes*
Unchangeable	Philo, *That God Is Unchangeable*
m. ʿUq.	Mishnah, Uqtzin
Virtues	Philo, *On the Virtues*
Wis	Wisdom of Solomon
m. Yad.	Mishnah, Yadayim
t. Yad.	Tosefta, Yadayim
b. Yebam.	Babylonian Talmud, Yevamot
m. Yebam	Mishnah, Yevamot
b. Yoma	Babylonian Talmud, Yoma
m. Yoma	Mishnah Yoma

Introduction

THE UNDIVIDED HEART CONTINUES the work begun by *Toward a History of Jewish Thought: The Soul, Resurrection, and the Afterlife*,[1] in that it presents a history of Jewish legal and moral thought from the earliest times until shortly after the Mishnah was compiled in about 200 CE. Regarding moral norms and laws, *The Undivided Heart* describes a major change in the type of conduct and qualities of character that were extolled or prescribed in ancient Israel, and it describes changes in the way in which the extolled or prescribed conduct and qualities of character were justified by various communities existing in ancient Israel and during the Second Temple period. It also explains the reasons for these changes.

Regarding human nature, *The Undivided Heart* considers how the relevant communities understood the failure of people to adhere to the moral norms and laws that were extolled or prescribed and what they believed was required to get transgressors to comply. In ancient Israelite thought, decision-making was believed to take place in the heart, so the book's discussion of human nature relates to the ancient Israelite understanding of the heart.

Philosophers distinguish two basic ethical theories used to justify normative judgments: teleological theories and deontological theories. A teleological, or consequentialist, ethical theory justifies moral norms on the basis of advantageous consequences that result from the qualities of character or conduct prescribed. Put differently, teleological theories hold the morally right is what produces, or is intended to produce, the greatest amount of a particular good. Teleological ethical theories are subdivided on the basis of whether the consequences that result (or the

1. Starr, *Toward a History*.

good that is produced) are beneficial for the individual actor (a position called "ethical egoism") or beneficial for the larger community of which the individual actor is a member (a position called "utilitarianism").[2] A deontological, or non-consequentialist, ethical theory justifies moral norms on the basis of conformity to some standard other than the advantageous consequences that result from, or the amount of the relevant good that is produced by, the moral norms. Qualities and conduct which conform to the relevant standard are justified regardless of whether or not the resulting consequences are advantageous and regardless of whether any particular good is produced.[3] Of relevance for present purposes is the deontological position called the Divine Command Theory. The Divine Command Theory justifies qualities and conduct on the basis of conformity to what are perceived to be the commands of God, holding that the standard of what is morally right is "the will or law of God."[4]

Although the book recounts a history of legal and moral thought in Jewish civilization that is consistent with the consensus of scholarly opinion, it also presents a number of new understandings of that history. Three ways in which the history recounted here deviates from more traditional understandings of the same history are of particular note. First, the book describes a significant moral development that occurred in ancient Israel after the monarchy was established, a movement away from esteeming qualities of character and conduct having competitive value and toward esteeming qualities of character and conduct having cooperative value. Until now, this moral development has gone virtually unnoticed.

Second, the book demonstrates that the ethical theory that justified the moral norms and laws advocated after the monarchy was established was a teleological ethical theory, not a deontological one. So, contrary to what is widely assumed to be true, the Divine Command Theory was not the original ethical theory justifying moral norms and laws. The book also demonstrates that a rise in individualism in the Second Temple period resulted in a change in the teleological position used to justify moral norms and laws. An initial utilitarianism gave way to ethical egoism, and this led to the problem of moral evil. The problem of moral evil led, in turn, to people shifting the beneficial consequences

---

2. See Frankena, *Ethics*, 14–16, 17–23, 34–43.
3. See Frankena, *Ethics*, 16–17, 23–28.
4. See Frankena, *Ethics*, 28–30.

an individual was assumed to derive from righteousness from the here and now to a future time and place, an afterlife.

Third, the book explains that the Hebrew phrase "*lev 'echad*," usually translated "single heart," is better translated "undivided heart," and it offers a new understanding of why moral rectitude was thought to require one to have such a heart. It is argued that in ancient Israel a heart was considered to be divided, or defective, when human desires and emotions prevented a person from choosing what righteousness requires. Conversely, a heart was considered to be *un*divided, or whole, when all human passions were fully integrated, enabling the righteous act to be chosen.

Regarding the first mentioned deviation from traditional understandings, chapter 1 of *The Undivided Heart* explains that throughout the patriarchal period and during the period of the Israelite conquest of Canaan and the period of the judges, the qualities of character and conduct esteemed by the ancient Israelites were those having competitive value. Qualities and conduct having competitive value are those which are useful when societies and persons are engaged primarily in competitive activities, activities in which success is of paramount importance. Qualities having competitive value include being strong, courageous, and cunning, and conduct having competitive value includes lying, stealing, and cheating.

As described in the book of Genesis, the patriarchal period was a time of fierce competition for limited resources among small family units, and success in acquiring the resources needed to sustain life was of paramount importance. Accordingly, under the extreme, life-threatening circumstances of famine in Canaan, Abram was forced to go to Egypt where he had to tell falsehoods to remain alive. Similarly, during the period of the conquest of Canaan, Israelite tribes were in competition with the tribes of other people for control of the land and its resources, and Israelite survival depended on success in this endeavor. So, qualities and conduct having competitive value are also extolled in the books of Joshua and Judges.

Chapter 1 goes on to explain that only after the establishment of the monarchy in the tenth century BCE did social, political, economic, and religious conditions change in a way that led the sages of the ancient Israelite wisdom tradition to extol qualities and conduct having cooperative value. Qualities of character and conduct having cooperative value are those which are useful when societies and persons are engaged primarily in cooperative activities, activities in which people cooperate with one another to achieve a common end. Such qualities include being honest, just, and patient, and such conduct includes being fair and not oppressing the defenseless. Chapter 1 explains that qualities and conduct having cooperative value were the ones extolled in the book of Proverbs and identified therein with being "righteous."

With respect to the second deviation from traditional understandings, chapter 1 also explains that qualities and conduct having cooperative value were associated in the ancient Israelite wisdom tradition with qualities and conduct in accord with the moral order ordained by God at the time of creation. Being in accord with the moral order God created—being righteous—was justified by the sages of the Israelite wisdom tradition because it resulted in receiving God's favor and, hence, in achieving well-being. Therefore, the book of Proverbs teaches that the consequences of righteousness are advantageous for both the individual actor and the Israelite community, and this was claimed to be known through wisdom (that is, through human experience and reason). In short, the new moral norms extolled in Proverbs were chosen on the basis of human experience and reason (they were not divinely revealed) and were justified by their beneficial consequences (not because they were commanded by God). Nowhere in Proverbs is it stated that God had commanded the qualities and conduct the proverbs extol.

Chapters 2 and 3 discuss Israelite law collections. It is demonstrated that these law collections, no less than Proverbs, extol qualities and conduct having cooperative value. Such qualities and conduct were understood by the sages in the Israelite wisdom tradition to be enforced by God only in the sense that those who acted within the moral boundaries fixed at the time of creation achieved favorable results and those who acted outside those boundaries suffered unfavorable results. Moreover, as mere instruction to devotees of wisdom, qualities and conduct having cooperative value could be humanly enforced only by the approval given to them by the community. Enforcement of the new morality was enhanced, however, by the ancient Israelite legists who instituted laws mandating qualities and conduct having cooperative value, and who, by mandating specific punishments for prohibited conduct, created mechanisms to ensure that the laws were obeyed. These laws, originally part of an oral tradition created by lay leadership in tribal clans and villages, were eventually committed to writing at various times from the tenth to the sixth centuries BCE. Once committed to writing, the laws took on an aura of divinity conferred on them by the writing process itself.

Chapter 2 focuses on the secular, or non-cultic, law collections found in the books of Exodus and Deuteronomy. It is demonstrated that the various laws in these collections, such as the moral exhortations of the Decalogue and the laws requiring protection of the disadvantaged members of Israelite society, unquestionably extolled qualities and conduct having cooperative value. Moreover, the chapter discusses that these laws were justified because they were believed to bring the beneficial consequences of peace, order, harmony, and prosperity to Israelite society. Therefore, the ethical theory justifying the normative judgments in the secular law collections is utilitarianism.

Chapter 3 focuses on the priestly law collections in the book of Leviticus, especially the Holiness Code. It is explained that the Holiness Code was promulgated by a new priestly school formed at the end of the eighth century BCE, and that this school extended the concept of holiness from a sacred sphere (the sanctuary) and its officiants (the priests) to the entire land of Israel and its Israelite occupants. The priestly authors of the Holiness Code saw the nation's holiness to be central to the moral order God ordained at the time of creation, evidencing a link to Israel's wisdom tradition. And the essence of Israel's holiness entailed adhering to qualities and conduct having cooperative value. Chapter 3 also explains that the ethical theory justifying the moral norms extolled in the Holiness Code is, again, utilitarianism because the Code argues that the well-being of the nation depended on Israel's holiness. Conversely, it was believed that the people's collective unholiness would lead to the exile of the nation from the land and to its complete destruction.

Chapters 2 and 3 also explain that at some time before the various law collections were incorporated into the Torah's narrative material, the laws contained in these collections came to be accepted as commands of God. This may have been due to the aura of divinity that resulted from having been committed to writing or may have developed out of the belief that the laws reflected demands placed on humanity by the moral order God ordained at the time of creation. The Torah's narrative that God had revealed these laws to Moses before the conquest of Canaan is not a historical account but a myth. Indeed, it was only well after the conquest of Canaan that the new morality advocated in Proverbs and in the Torah's law collections first appeared.

Nevertheless, it could now be claimed that the laws and moral exhortations of the Torah were justified because they were the commands of God that had been made known to humanity through revelation. The new morality was thus transferred from the realm of wisdom to the realm of prophecy, and the ethical theory used to justify the new morality was correspondingly transferred, in part, from a teleological theory to a deontological theory. The ethical theory was only partly transferred because the revelation took the form of a covenant or suzerainty treaty between an overlord and his vassal, with God envisioned as a tribal chief who rules his vassal Israel pursuant to the terms of an agreement. The covenant detailed the specific benefits that God would grant the Israelite nation for obedience to divine law, as well as the specific punishments God would impose for transgressions, so beneficial consequences for obeying God's commands were still promised, and nowhere in the law collections is it stated that consequences are irrelevant to a decision to obey God's commands. Therefore, the teleological, utilitarian justification of these law collections remained clearly visible beneath a deontological veneer.

The third above-mentioned deviation from traditional understandings of the relevant history is encountered in chapter 4. This chapter recounts that from the mid-eighth to the sixth centuries BCE the Israelite literary prophets reasserted the importance of qualities and conduct having cooperative value, equating them with what was required pursuant to the terms of the covenant God had made with the Israelite nation. It is explained that, since the Israelites' covenant with God was understood to contain curses intended to punish the Israelite nation for violations of the covenant, the prophets preached that the military defeats suffered by Israel and Judah, and the people's exile from the land, had resulted from the people's disobedience of their covenant obligations. Although some prophets prophesized that a remnant of the people would repent, be restored to the land, and then faithfully fulfill their obligations under the covenant, Jeremiah believed that obedience to God's moral commands could only occur if human nature were radically altered, if human beings were, so to speak, remade by God.

Chapter 4 further recounts that Jeremiah attributed the people's moral failure to a defective condition of the human heart, which he described as a "thickening" around the heart. Jeremiah called such a heart "uncircumcised." According to Jeremiah, human beings could not be righteous unless given by God non-defective, or circumcised, hearts. Jeremiah called a non-defective, circumcised heart a *lev ʾechad*, which is a heart that has had the thickening around it removed. The Hebrew phrase *lev ʾechad* is traditionally translated "single heart," and Jeremiah is traditionally interpreted as envisioning the elimination of free will. But this chapter explains that the traditional translation is inadequate, and the traditional interpretation is erroneous. In order to show why this is so, the chapter discusses how the human heart was viewed in ancient Israelite thought. With this understanding, it is argued that a better translation of *lev ʾechad* is "undivided heart," and that a more accurate interpretation of what Jeremiah envisioned is the creation of a human heart that is at one with what God wills because it is not divided by competing desires and emotions but integrates all desires and emotions into a harmonious whole which freely follows God's moral commands. The concept of an undivided heart is repeatedly used throughout the Second Temple period in almost all Jewish texts to describe a person who is righteous, although it may be referred to in different ways, such as a pure heart, a whole heart, a faithful heart, or a heart that can control evil inclinations.

In the book's fifth chapter, attention is turned to the Second Temple period. What is most significant at the beginning of this period is the increasing individualism that occurs. The increased emphasis on the fate of the individual, as opposed to the fate of the nation, is clearly seen in Ps 37, a wisdom psalm. This psalm echoes the priestly notion that unrighteousness leads to exile from the land, but whereas the priests taught that unrighteousness by *some* Israelites led to exile from the land of *all* Israelites, Ps 37 teaches that only the unrighteous Israelites will be exiled from the land. The fate of the righteous Israelites is different; it is said that they shall "inherit the land, and abide forever on it."[5] The belief that righteousness is justified because righteous individuals are rewarded while unrighteous individuals are punished corresponds to the ethical theory called ethical egoism.

As a consequence of the increased emphasis on the fate of the individual (rather than the fate of the nation), the problem of moral evil arises—that is, the problem that wicked individuals prosper and righteous individuals suffer. Some Second Temple texts, including Ps 37, deny that this is the case. According to Ps 37, righteousness is always instrumentally good—the righteous are always rewarded with material

5. Ps 37:29.

well-being, and the wicked are always punished, *in this life*. This is the point of view found in traditional Israelite wisdom literature, and it is the position taken in the apocryphal book called the Wisdom of Ben Sira (dated to about 180 BCE), which chapter 5 discusses at length. Ben Sira is noteworthy in two other ways as well. First, it links the Israelite wisdom found in Proverbs—that which is known through human experience and reason—with the Mosaic covenant found in the Torah—that which is known through revelation. Second, it echoes Jeremiah's understanding that a divided heart prevents obedience to the Torah, teaching that to be righteous one must control their evil desires and emotions—what Ben Sira calls the *"yetzer,"* or "inclinations." And Ben Sira specifically argues that controlling one's desires and emotions is a matter of exercising free will and choosing correctly, supporting a nontraditional interpretation of *lev 'echad*. Therefore, Ben Sira supports the position taken in chapter 4 that Jeremiah was not envisioning the end of free will.

Chapter 5 also discusses the biblical books of Job and Qoheleth (both probably written in the third century BCE). These books challenge the conventional wisdom that righteousness is always rewarded and wickedness always punished, and this challenge leads their authors to consider the problem of moral evil (the problem that the wicked prosper and the righteous suffer). Finally, chapter 5 mentions texts such as the biblical book of Daniel (written in about 160 BCE) which postulate for the first time the idea of resurrection, and, in order to resolve the problem of moral evil, claim that individual reward and punishment are meted out to resurrected individuals in an afterlife.

Chapters 6 and 7 focus on Jewish Hellenistic texts written in the diaspora during the Second Temple period. The authors of these texts were well versed in Greek philosophical thought and argued that Jewish teaching was consistent with, if not superior to, such thought. It was easy to argue that Jewish moral norms were equivalent to Greek moral norms because both civilizations had experienced the same moral development—from esteeming qualities and conduct having competitive value to esteeming qualities and conduct having cooperative value. The author of the Wisdom of Solomon, for example, identified the biblical concept of righteousness with the Greek cardinal virtues of justice, temperance, courage, and prudence, and the author of 4 Maccabees claimed that Mosaic law was actually the source for the Greek cardinal virtues. Similarly, the author of the Letter of Aristeas demonstrated that Jewish law and morality were equivalent to the moral principles of the

Stoics, and the author of the *Sentences* of Pseudo-Phocylides, assuming the persona of an ancient Greek moralist, had no trouble espousing the moral principles found in the Torah. The Hellenized Jews did, however, adopt some Greek views that were without biblical parallels. To resolve the problem of moral evil they adopted the Greek metaphysical notion of an immortal soul which is rewarded or punished in an afterlife. The acceptance of this belief meant that the Hellenized Jews were also adopting the ethical theory of ethical egoism.

Also discussed are the Hellenized Jews' efforts to show that acting in accord with Mosaic law was consistent with Stoic teaching that proper conduct entailed acting in accord with nature. In fact, Philo of Alexandria argued that the laws of Moses were in the truest sense laws in accordance with nature because only Mosaic laws were modeled after laws implanted by God into the natural world. Scholars invariably claim that, in so arguing, Philo was imposing an alien Stoic view of the world onto the biblical view. According to these scholars, the laws of Moses are arbitrary, changeable, and often irrational dictates derived through revelation, not universal, unalterable, and rational truths derived from human reason, which is how the Stoics characterized the laws of nature. But chapter 7 argues that Philo realized that, biblically speaking, the moral norms commanded by God are derived from the rational and eternal moral order that God ordained at the time of creation. Indeed, *physis* (the Greek word for nature) is understood by the author of 4 Maccabees to actually be the world order built into creation by God.

Then, too, chapters 6 and 7 discuss the view of human nature found in Jewish Hellenistic texts. This discussion reveals that the Greek views adopted by the Hellenized Jews were essentially in agreement with the view of Jeremiah. The Greek philosophers had argued that the acquisition of virtue required that the rational part of the soul control the nonrational parts of the soul—the irrational appetites and desires—so that the entire soul acted in harmony. The integrated soul of Greek philosophy may readily be compared to the undivided and integrated heart envisioned by Jeremiah. In fact, the authors of the Wisdom of Solomon and the Testaments of the Twelve Patriarchs describe the harmony required for virtuous conduct using the phrase "singleness of heart," and Philo associates immoderate desire with a thickening of the heart and a heart that is "uncircumcised." However, whereas Jeremiah wanted *God* to transform human nature, the Jewish Hellenists believed that there are practices inherent in biblical law that enable a person to transform *themselves* without the need for divine intervention. Specifically, Philo said that the law of Moses provides the training or practice (*askesis*) that enables one to acquire the self-control (*enkrateia*) needed to restrain the emotions and achieve the virtue the Greeks called temperance (*sophrosune*).

Chapters 8 and 9 consider legal and moral developments occurring in Judea *after* Ben Sira, from the middle of the second century BCE to the third century CE. During this period, the Jews of Judea were divided by a variety of divergent points of view that led to the formation of separate "sects." These disagreements concerned, in large part, how to incorporate extrabiblical traditions and teachings into the legal system, how to justify them theologically, and who had authority to do so. Chapters 8 and 9 focus on the sect that was the precursor to what is called Rabbinic Judaism—the Pharisees and their successors, the Tannaim. This sect promulgated extrabiblical laws that they claimed had been handed down to them by their ancestors (called "the tradition of the fathers") and which were collected into the Mishnah in around 200 CE.

Chapters 8 and 9 explain that the laws collected into the Mishnah were not derived from biblical law in any obvious way. In fact, the Tannaim often set aside biblical law, or altered it, to achieve what they believed to be desirable communal ends. In other words, the ethical theory underlying Tannaitic moral laws was utilitarianism; they were based on what human experience and reason indicated were beneficial consequences for the community. It was not originally said that any new law was divinely revealed or constituted a divine command. Only centuries later, in the tractate Avot (added to the Mishnah generations after the Mishnah was first compiled), is the claim explicitly made that all the rules of conduct collected in the Mishnah had been divinely revealed to Moses and handed down orally in an uninterrupted chain of tradition. The rabbis came up with this myth (the "Oral Torah myth") not because they believed the socially advantageous consequences of the moral laws was an inadequate justification for them, but because they wanted to respond to polemical attacks claiming that the rules of conduct they advocated (being man-made, not divine) were inferior to those of their opponents (claimed to be divinely revealed), and to, thereby, legitimize their own authority to determine the law.

Chapter 9 also focuses attention on the fact that the Tannaim and subsequent rabbis viewed torah study, *tzedakah* (charity), *gemilut hasidim* (acts of lovingkindness), and repentance as especially important moral norms, and that they reduced the moral teaching of the Torah to the single principle of loving your neighbor as yourself. Attention is also paid to the rabbinic concept of the "evil *yetzer*." This concept, a modification of Ben Sira's use of the word *yetzer*, was introduced to explain disobedience of the Torah's divine laws. Most typically, the rabbis understood the evil *yetzer* to be an internal force, located in the human heart, which was part of a person from birth. It was explicitly associated by some with human passions and decision-making. The understanding that there exist opposing forces residing in and affecting the human heart when a person is deciding what action to take, and that evil passions needed to be controlled, is, of course, reminiscent of Jeremiah's vision of the undivided heart. Moreover, at times the rabbis agreed with Jeremiah that the problem of a divided heart could be resolved only through divine intervention, and the rabbis composed prayers petitioning God to remove their evil *yetzer*. But more typically the rabbinic viewpoint accorded with Philo's view that a person could transform themselves without the need for divine intervention. Specifically, the rabbis claimed that the evil *yetzer* could be controlled through torah study.

Consideration of Jewish apocalyptic texts occurs in chapter 10. The authors of these texts were far less sanguine than the Tannaim about the ability of human beings to control evil inclinations, although they agreed that the cause of human wickedness was a hardened or defective heart. Specifically, they saw little, if any, possibility for gentiles or wicked Jews to cure their defective hearts because they believed them to be controlled by powerful external demonic forces. This was in keeping with their dualistic worldview which saw the distinction between good and evil to be part of the basic structure of the cosmos. The human condition is described in the apocalypses as hopelessly wicked and corrupt, and they envision no improvement in this condition until the coming of a messiah and a day of judgment sometime in the future when, it was said, God would destroy the demonic forces (and the wicked human beings) and create a new world order, including a transformed humanity without defective hearts. The apocalypses instructed righteous Jews to segregate themselves from gentiles and from wicked and apostate fellow Jews. Although a utilitarian teleological position is sometimes expressed, the ethical theory justifying the normative judgments of the apocalyptic authors is best described as ethical egoism, with the beneficial consequences being delayed to a future time and place. They maintain that righteous individuals will be rewarded at the end time.

The book's last chapter discusses two sects which opposed the Tannaim's reliance on legal traditions handed down by their ancestors and which shared many of the viewpoints found in the apocalypses. These sects—the Essenes and the followers of Jesus of Nazareth—asserted their own independent authority to incorporate extrabiblical traditions and teachings into the legal system. The Essenean sectarian community of Khirbet Qumran (associated with the Dead Sea Scrolls) was founded in about the middle of the second century BCE and existed until 68 CE. The members of the sect shared the apocalyptic view that contemporary Jewish society was divided into two parts, the righteous and the wicked. They viewed themselves as the righteous, an elect community constituting the true Israel, aligned with God and obedient to God's law. They viewed the rest of Jewish society as transgressors of God's law, steeped in wickedness. They believed that they lived in a predetermined period of wickedness that was to end *imminently* with the arrival of a messianic age.

The Essenes derived law *entirely* on the basis of biblical exegesis. Adiel Schremer argues that this constituted a "revolution," asserting that, prior to the revolution, "it was not customary to appeal to the written text of the Torah in order to draw halakhic guidance from it."[6] As explained in chapter 11, the Essenes considered the *halakhot* [laws] of the Tannaim and their predecessors to be based on "false legal exegesis," and they considered such *halakhot* to be "lies or falsehoods."[7] So, they called the Tannaim and their predecessors "*dorshei halakot*" ("lying interpreters"). In sharp contrast to the *halakhot* of the Tannaim, the Essenes claimed that their *halakhot* had been derived exclusively from divinely revealed biblical exegesis. A distinction was made, however, between laws that were "revealed" in the biblical text and laws that were "hidden" in the biblical text, called, respectively, "*niglot*" and "*nistarot.*"

Jesus of Nazareth similarly rejected *halakhot* derived from "the tradition of the fathers." And despite employing the same exegetical techniques used by the Tannaim, he sometimes arrived at *halakhot* that were substantively different from theirs, including *halakhot* regarding Sabbath observance and divorce. In such instances, Jesus' followers believed that only Jesus' interpretations were authoritative. Moreover, Jesus based several of his differing interpretations and modifications of biblical law

---

6. Schremer, "'[T]he[y] Did Not Read,'" 111–15.
7. See chapter 11, sec. A, 2.

on a concept of natural law not used by the Tannaim but used by the Essenes. And although Jesus recognized that wickedness was caused by an undivided heart, Jesus never expressed agreement with the Tannaim that righteousness could be achieved through torah study.

Finally, while all three sects extolled qualities of character and conduct having cooperative value and reduced their moral teaching to the single maxim of loving your neighbor as yourself, the ethical theory employed by both the Essenes and Jesus to justify these moral norms differed from that of the Tannaim. Jesus, as the Essenes, preached the imminent arrival of the kingdom of God, when righteous individuals would be rewarded and wicked individuals punished. So, the ethical theory justifying their normative judgments is best characterized as ethical egoism, the same theory that justifies the normative judgments in Ps 37. However, while both Jesus and the Essenes allude to Ps 37, they interpret the psalm's language that righteous individuals "shall inherit the land" to refer to righteous individuals inheriting the kingdom of God at the end time. In other words, they transferred the beneficial consequences promised to righteous individuals in Ps 37 from the here and now to the afterlife. In contrast, the Tannaim were more focused on the well-being of the entire Jewish community in the here and now, so the ethical theory justifying their normative judgments is best characterized as utilitarianism.

CHAPTER 1

The sages of the ancient Israelite wisdom tradition precipitated a moral change in Israelite society by extolling qualities and conduct having cooperative value, claiming that they were conducive to a prosperous society.

A BRIEF SUMMARY OF what a leading expert on ancient Greek civilization says about the development of moral values in that civilization is instructive for understanding the development of moral values in ancient Israel. Arthur Adkins distinguishes between qualities and conduct having "competitive value" and qualities and conduct having "cooperative value."[1] He contends that societies and persons engaged primarily in competitive activities (activities in which success is of paramount importance) value qualities and conduct different than the qualities and conduct valued by societies and persons engaged primarily in cooperative activities (activities in which people cooperate with one another to achieve a common end). The qualities and conduct valued by societies and persons engaged primarily in competitive activities are said by Adkins to have competitive value, and the qualities and conduct valued by societies and persons engaged primarily in cooperative activities are said by Adkins to have cooperative value.

1. See Adkins, *Moral Values*, 12–14; Adkins, *Merit*, 6–7.

According to Adkins, since the society depicted in the epic poems attributed to Homer is a society of small family units (*oikoi*) in competition with each other for scarce resources, competitive activities dominated, and the qualities and conduct which that society believed it needed most, and thus valued most highly, were those having competitive value. These competitive qualities were those possessed by the warrior-chieftain, such as strength, courage, shrewdness or cunning, and skill in warfare. The warrior-chieftain sought to obtain as much material wealth for himself and his *oikos* as he could, by any means possible—just or not. It was only success in acquiring material wealth that brought the warrior-chieftain praise and honor, and his use of deceit and plunder was not met with disapproval by his *oikos* if it resulted in the acquisition of additional wealth.[2] Qualities having cooperative value—such as honesty and fairness—took an inferior position because it was not evident to the *oikos* that its well-being depended, to any great extent, upon qualities having cooperative value.

Then, beginning in about the late eighth century BCE with the development of city-states and increased commerce, cooperation gradually came to be viewed as more conducive to the well-being of the individual and the city-state than competition. Accordingly, qualities and conduct having cooperative value came to be considered superior to qualities and conduct having competitive value. Hesiod and Theognis, in the late eighth and sixth centuries BCE, respectively, and Socrates and Plato, in the fifth and fourth centuries BCE, respectively, argued that it was individually and collectively more beneficial for one to be just and truthful than for one to unfairly and dishonestly acquire material goods (that is, to acquire material goods in excess of one's fair share).[3] Hesiod, for example, advises his brother Perses to "do what is just" because the "more *agathe* (beneficial to oneself) road is to go past on the other side toward justice"; and he opines that, for those who are just, "their city flourishes, and the people prosper in it."[4]

---

2. See Adkins, *Moral Values*, 10–21; Adkins, *Merit*, 31–57. Cf. Hume, *Inquiry*, 17–18 (where society is ready to perish from extreme necessity, every man may provide for himself by all the means which prudence can dictate, without regard to justice); Hobbes, *Leviathan*, 108 (where men live in a "state of war," the "notions of right and wrong, justice and injustice, have there no place").

3. See generally Adkins, *Moral Values*, 22–146; Adkins, *Merit*, 70–79, 259–315. For Hesiod, to seek more than your fair share constitutes *hubris* which is not beneficial because it leads to reprisals. Adkins, *Moral Values*, 27–28.

4. Hesiod, *Works and Days*, 213, 225. See Adkins, *Moral Values*, 27–28. See also

It seems certain that some such development took place in ancient Israelite society.⁵ The biblical narratives depict the patriarchs as nomads, existing in small family units, who were both competing with other family units for scarce resources and subject to the power of foreigners for survival. These narratives also depict Joshua and the judges (the pre-monarchal tribal leaders and warrior-chieftains) as living in a time of disunity, the Israelite tribes each struggling for their individual survival. Indeed, prior to the establishment of the Israelite monarchy the Israelite tribes were constantly engaged in warfare for control of the land of Canaan, as well as engaged in intertribal strife and rivalry. Nor were the Israelite tribes unified by devotion to Yahwism; rather, most Israelites continued to worship the Canaanite gods. The disuniting, harsh, and competitive conditions existing during the patriarchal and pre-monarchal periods explain why the patriarchal and pre-monarchal leaders appearing in biblical narratives possessed qualities and engaged in conduct having primarily competitive value.

In opposition to these narratives, the biblical wisdom tradition and biblical law extol qualities and conduct having cooperative value.⁶ Clearly, a moral change had occurred in ancient Israel, a change from esteeming qualities and conduct having competitive value to extolling qualities and conduct having cooperative value. Why did this moral change occur? Probably for the same reasons why a similar moral change occurred in ancient Greece—new political, social, and economic conditions made cooperation more conducive to individual and collective well-being than competition.⁷ The moral norms expressed

---

Adkins, *Merit*, 71–73.

5. See generally Daube, *Studies in Biblical Law*, 201 (Certain customs are likely to develop at a "certain stage of political and economic development"; customs, that is, are "determined less by the specific characteristics of a race than by material environment").

6. Daube interprets the opposition as two "strikingly divergent tendencies" within Israelite wisdom itself. See Daube, *Law and Wisdom*, 85 ("There is an idealistic [type of wisdom], which would inculcate a very high standard of nobility and selflessness; at the other end stands a distinctly lower [type of wisdom] recommending . . . all sorts of devices to attain a desirable object: deceit, cunning, and so forth"), 86 ("It cannot be accidental that while we come across many narratives in which the lower wisdom is represented, it is utterly absent from wisdom literature proper"), 91 (We find "the lower philosophy . . . permeating the narratives of the Bible").

7. See n5 of this chapter. See generally Henrich, *WEIRDest People*, 103–4 (asserting that humanity's cultural evolution from "mobile networks to sedentary or semi-sedentary communities capable of controlling territory increasingly favored dense, intensive networks formed by community-level cooperative institutions").

in biblical wisdom will be discussed in this chapter; the moral norms expressed in biblical law will be discussed in chapter 2 (focusing on the law collections constituting the Covenant Code and the Deuteronomic Code) and chapter 3 (focusing on the priestly law collections in Leviticus, especially the Holiness Code).

The biblical wisdom tradition begins around the time of king Solomon (reigning ca. 961–922 BCE). By that time, the fiercely independent Israelite tribes had finally been converted into members of a common empire having common objectives, and the tribal confederacy had ceased to exist. This conversion was due in part to David's success in unifying the empire around a revitalized Yahwism, with the ark of the covenant given a permanent location in Jerusalem. In addition, society had developed from a seminomadic to a sedentary culture, from sheep herding to a horticultural and agricultural economy.[8] Then too, under king Solomon, there was an economic boom—individual wealth increased, and the building of crude cities, urbanization, domestic trade, and foreign commerce all began. As a consequence of these changed political, social, economic, and religious conditions, it may justifiably be presumed, the authors of biblical wisdom literature realized that cooperation was more beneficial to individuals and to the community at large than competition, and they associated qualities and conduct having cooperative value with the concept of "righteousness" (*tzedakah*), much as Greek thinkers such as Hesiod, Socrates, and Plato associated qualities and conduct having cooperative value with the concept of "justice" (*dikaiosune*).

Moreover, qualities and conduct having cooperative value blended well with the monotheism of Yahwism. Unlike pagan religion, Yahwism viewed God as the creator of both a natural order and a moral order. Violation of the moral boundaries Yahweh imposed upon all humanity (by committing wicked acts such as murder or adultery)[9] was understood to occasion Yahweh's destruction of the violator's entire community, but adherence to those boundaries (by righteous conduct) gained Yahweh's favor for the entire community. So, Yahweh was believed to enforce qualities and conduct having cooperative value.[10] The book of Proverbs

---

8. See Lipschits, "History," 2110; Scheindlin, *Short History*, 8.

9. In Proverbs, the wicked (*rishaim*) are contrasted with the righteous (*tzadikim*). See, e.g., Prov 4:18–19; 10:3, 7; 12:5, 7, 10.

10. Although the Greek god Zeus created neither the natural order nor a moral order, Hesiod taught that Zeus would enforce qualities and conduct having cooperative value. See Hesiod, *Works and Days*, 225, 238 (Zeus never decrees war or famine

emphasizes that wisdom—knowledge of the moral boundaries imposed on humanity by Yahweh—is the means by which to gain Yahweh's blessing and achieve success and prosperity for the nation.[11]

A. The biblical narratives extol qualities and conduct having competitive value such as strength, courage, cunning, and skill in warfare.

The narratives found in the book of Genesis describe a time when there was fierce competition for limited resources among small family units.[12] It is, therefore, unsurprising that these narratives indicate that success in acquiring the means to survive was of paramount importance, and persons blessed by God are depicted as possessing qualities and exhibiting conduct having competitive value. For example, under the extreme, life-threatening circumstances of famine in Canaan, Abram is forced to go to Egypt where he must tell falsehoods, passing his wife off as his sister, in order that "it may go well with [him] . . . [and that he] may remain alive."[13] Here, and elsewhere, lying is depicted as a perfectly proper weapon when one is in a position of weakness vis-à-vis

---

upon those who are just but ordains punishment for those who practice "harsh deeds"); Adkins, *Moral Values*, 28–29. See generally Henrich, *WEIRDest People*, 123–39 (discussing the cultural evolution from a belief in gods who were "not particularly moral" to a belief in supernatural beings who punish or reward for "proper behavior," i.e., adherence to moral norms "beneficial to the community"). Cf. Assmann, *Mind of Egypt*, 130–31 (The Egyptians assumed that *maat*, the Egyptian concept of "connective justice," which included moral norms having cooperative value, could not exist "without the state and its coercive rods").

11. See Blenkinsopp, *Wisdom and Law*, 24–29 (arguing that "an early corpus of gnomic material, embodying the kind of prudential, religiously neutral, and sometimes even opportunistic ethic found, for example, in Egyptian instructions, [was] given a Yahwistic 'baptism'"; that "collections of proverbs expressing the common ethos of the scribal schools were modified and supplemented by religious teachers in the later period of the Judean monarchy"; and that one of the characteristic features of "this more explicitly religious phase [is] . . . the belief in Yahweh as sustainer of the moral order").

12. See, e.g., Gen 13:5–9 (Abraham and Lot must separate because "the land could not support them staying together" and "there was quarreling between the herdsman of Abram's cattle and those of Lot's cattle"); 36:6–7 (Esau had to separate from Jacob because "their possessions were too many for them to dwell together, and the land . . . could not support them").

13. Gen 12:13. See Barton, *Old Testament Ethics*, 25 (discussing "the 'ancestress in danger' story (Gen 12, 20, and 26)," asserting that "the logic of the story . . . is that the patriarch is deliberately deceiving a foreign king," and asking, "Did the Israelites in this period . . . regard lying as justified for the attainment of a good end?").

a foreigner and when telling the truth would result in death, and lying in such situations did not render one unworthy of divine protection.[14] Even theft is regarded as justifiable when one is under foreign control and there are pressing circumstances.[15] Perhaps most surprisingly, Jacob is characterized as one who repeatedly subverts justice pursuant to the principle of *summa ius summa iniuria*.[16]

Closer to the time period depicted in the Homeric poems is when, according to the biblical account, the Israelite tribes were in competition with the tribes of other people for control of the land of Canaan and its resources and when Israelite survival depended on success in this endeavor.[17] This time is depicted in the book of Judges as "one of unrest and disorder," when the people failed to obey Yahweh and worshiped the baals, and when "rampant individualism" prevailed rather than "a concern for the common good."[18] It is again not surprising, therefore, that the relevant narratives evidence that qualities and conduct having competitive value were still much more highly esteemed than those having cooperative value.

The narratives concerning the conquest of Canaan begin with God's thrice-repeated admonition to Joshua to be "strong and very resolute" (*hzak v'emetz miode*).[19] This expression is a "military exhortation"

---

14. See Gen 12:13; 20:2–12; 26:7; Exod 1:19. See also Gen 34:1–29 (Guile was used to slay all the males in a Hivite city and take all their material goods). Deceit seems to have been commonly employed during the patriarchal period even when no truly exigent circumstances were present. See Gen 27:1–30 (Jacob and Rebekah contrive to deceive Isaac and rob Esau of Isaac's blessing); 29:21–27 (Jacob is deceived by Laban); 30:31–43 (Jacob obtains prosperity by tricking Laban); 31:19–35 (Rachel steals Laban's property and deceives him about it).

15. See Exod 3:22; 11:2; 12:35–36. See generally Eichrodt, *Theology*, 2.323. But see Daube, *Studies in Biblical Law*, 49–50; Tigay, "Exodus," 104.

16. See Daube, *Studies in Biblical Law*, 190–220. The maxim may be translated as "The greatest right is the greatest injury," and it means that granting a party the maximum extent of rights may actually do the party an extreme injustice.

17. Although archaeological evidence does not support the biblical account of Israel's early history, it does support the existence of "refugees" joining "nomadic/outlaw elements," a process of settlement (including some settlements exhibiting "significant foreign traits"), and a movement from a "seminomadic to a sedentary culture." Lipschits, "History," 2109–11.

18. Rodd, *Glimpses*, 290–91. See Judg 17:6; 21:25 ("Every man did what was right in his own eyes").

19. Josh 1:6, 7, 9. See also Deut 3:28 ("imbue [Joshua] with strength and courage [*ḥazkahu ve emetzehu*]"); 31:7, 23; Josh 1:18.

signifying "the courage necessary for all difficult endeavors."[20] The very next chapter relates that the capture of Jericho was achieved through deceit. The harlot Rahab hides two spies sent by Joshua to reconnoiter the region, and when the king of Jericho ordered her to produce the spies, Rahab lies. She tells the king of Jericho that the spies have left when, in fact, she had hidden them on the roof.[21] Other instances of victory by means of cunning or stealth include the assassination of King Eglon of Moab (by the Benjaminite Ehud)[22] and the assassination of the Canaanite military commander Sisera (by Jael, wife of Heber, who feigned friendship with Sisera and then, when he was asleep, drove a tent pin through his temple).[23] In addition, there are countless instances where courage, bravery, military adeptness, and skill in warfare are all favorably described.[24] The importance of strength is extolled in the exploits of Samson,[25] and the importance of courage is highlighted in the account of young David's willingness to fight the well-armed giant Goliath although David was carrying only a slingshot.[26]

Finally, there are several stories depicting Israelite conduct during the period as "unrighteous," that is, lacking qualities and conduct having cooperative value. These include Achan's theft of silver and gold during the capture of Jericho,[27] the tribe of Dan's theft of Micah's sacred objects and callous confiscation of territory from "a tranquil and unsuspecting people,"[28] the disloyalty of the homeless Levite taken in by Micah,[29] and a woman's brutal rape, abuse, and murder by a gang of depraved Benjaminites.[30] In the last three of these cases the narrative is preceded by the statement that "in those days there was no king in

---

20. Meyers, "Joshua," 465.
21. Josh 2:1–8.
22. Judg 3:15–30.
23. Judg 4:17–23.
24. See, e.g., Judg 3:31 (Shamgar slew six hundred Philistines with an oxgoad); 2 Sam 23:8–23 (describing the courageous and brave military exploits of David's warriors).
25. Judg 14:1—16:31.
26. 1 Sam 17:1–55.
27. Josh 7.
28. Judg 18.
29. Judg 17:7—18:20.
30. Judg 19:22–29.

Israel," suggesting that without a central authority general lawlessness was inevitable, and prevailed.

Eichrodt asserts that in about the mid-eighth century BCE there was a movement away from qualities having competitive value (which he refers to as "warlike virtues") and toward qualities having cooperative value (which he refers to as "passive virtues"). He associates this shift in moral norms with the "effect of the prophetic movement," which, he says, emphasizes God's "ethical will."[31] In Eichrodt's view:

> There now occurs an *important shift within the moral norms themselves*. Emphasis is laid on points quite different from those previously stressed, and, in conjunction with this, areas of conduct so far overlooked are brought within the realm of moral obligation. *Much less value is attached to warlike virtues*. . . . The path of external expansion . . . is utterly condemned by the prophets as open rebellion against Yahweh.
>
> In these circumstances there was bound to be less and less justification for the warlike spirit in religion and ethics. Only in a very qualified way did military boldness, and the courageous hazarding of life and limb against the enemies of the land, retain moral value.
>
> Within this approach to social morality, *the so-called passive virtues* take on quite [a] new force in the determination of individual conduct. No longer do a proud sense of independence, and enthusiasm for war, knightly daring and self-confident contempt for one's opponent form the dominant ideal of moral conduct, but humility and self-restraint, patience and love of peace, which best reflect inward solidarity with one's fellow countrymen.[32]

Although Eichrodt is correct in emphasizing a shift in moral norms, Eichrodt's analysis of the cause of the shift (attributing it to the "prophetic movement") and his dating of the shift (mid-eighth century) are inaccurate.[33] Rather, the increased emphasis on those qualities hav-

---

31. Eichrodt, *Theology*, 2.326–27.

32. Eichrodt, *Theology*, 2.329, 331 (emphasis original). See Barton, *Old Testament Ethics*, 25 ("We can hardly ignore the possibility that stories in Genesis, as also in Judges, are *stories of the remote past*, in which different ethical standards were believed to be appropriate from those that obtained in the author's own day" [emphasis original]). See also n6 and n48 of this chapter.

33. See Bright, *History of Israel*, 264 (The classical prophets were "not innovators, but men who stood in the mainstream of Israel's tradition"); Hillers, *Covenant*, 140–42 (The prophets "drew on a conventional stock of ideas and phrases with deep roots in

ing cooperative value was more likely the result of changes in economic, religious, social, and political circumstances that had occurred earlier. As smaller family units began to live less seminomadic—more agrarian and urban—ways of life, and as tribal units gradually coalesced into a national entity or entities, the need for people to cooperate with each other in order to achieve common ends gradually began to increase.[34]

To be sure, there always had been some degree of cooperation among the Israelite tribes—minimal cooperation was required to fight common enemies—and this is well described in the books of Joshua and Judges. However, during the entire period dealt with by those books, "tribes, clans, families, and individuals enjoyed the maximum freedom of action";[35] and "[except] for brief, emergency alliances, Israelite tribes maintained complete autonomy."[36]

Due to each tribe's complete autonomy, as well as their collective failure to fully embrace devotion to, and practice of, Yahwism,[37] intertribal controversy was common, and each tribal chieftain sought what he believed to be in the best interests of his tribe, irrespective of the common good of the tribal league. As explained by Orlinsky:

> On several occasions the tribes of Reuben and Gad and the half tribe of Manasseh had to be ordered to help their

Israel's history").

34. See generally Bright, *History of Israel*, 167 (The tribes maintained "a precarious existence surrounded by foes, but without organized government of any sort"), 177–78 (The earliest Israelite towns were "exceedingly crude" and devoid of "material culture" but "the period of the Judges witnessed a gradual but marked improvement in Israel's economy"; skills were learned, trade through camel caravans was introduced, seaborne commerce expanded, "numerous towns were built," land was "secured for cultivation by clearing the forests," and the use of baked lime plaster for cisterns enabled "an increased density of population"); Lipschits, "History," 2109–11 (Beginning in the late thirteenth century BCE, Egyptian military campaigns destroyed all the major urban centers of Canaan, and much of the population became refugees who joined existing "seminomadic/outlaw elements"; then, during the Iron Age I (1200–1000/950 BCE), "tiny settlements appeared . . . moving from seminomadic to a sedentary culture, from sheep herding to a horticultural and agricultural economy").

35. Hillers, *Covenant*, 95.

36. Orlinsky, *Ancient Israel*, 50. See Judg 17:6 ("In those days there was no king in Israel; every man did as he pleased"); Bright, *History of Israel*, 166, 181 (The tribal system was "exceedingly loose" and "had none of the apparatus of state"; it could neither "restrain the centrifugal forces that operated . . . [nor] prevent intertribal rivalries from flaring into war"); Hillers, *Covenant*, 147 ("In the days of the judges . . . [each] village community and each tribal group had freedom . . . to regulate its own affairs").

37. See Rodd, *Glimpses*, 291 ("Israel was guilty of worshipping the baals and was disobedient of Yahweh").

fellow tribesmen secure their allotments in western Palestine [Josh 1:12–18]. When the crucial struggle between the Israelites and the Canaanites came to a head in the battle near Taanach in the valley of Jezreel [about 1125 BCE], an event made famous in the song of Deborah [Judg 5], several tribes refused to join in the battle and accordingly were cursed. A whole century of indecision and wavering passed before the reluctant tribes, faced with a common danger, were able to bring themselves to make a common cause. The individualism and desert way of these tribes died hard.

The same process is reflected in the religious picture painted by the Book of Judges. The complete devotion to the Lord advocated by Moses and Joshua ran into dire opposition. The Israelite population at large, even the newcomers in the land, conveniently adapted their way of life to the Canaanite practices, especially those which were aimed at the maintenance and improvement of their [individual] well-being. . . . Such heroes as Saul and David [about 1,000 BCE], it should be noted, gave some of their children names which included the element "Baal."[38]

The prevalence of tribal independence and resulting intertribal conflict is well reflected in the account of the refusal of the tribe of Benjamin to give up those of its members who had raped and killed the concubine of the Levite from Ephraim staying in Gibeah (in the territory of Benjamin). The other Israelites demanded that the wrongdoers be handed up, but the Benjaminites persisted in their refusal. There followed several days of fighting, resulting in the death of 40,000 Israelites on the first two days. On the third day, the other Israelites employed a cunning strategy which enabled them to kill 25,000 Benjaminites, and then "put to the sword . . . everything that remained [in Gibeah]" and "set fire to all the towns that were left."[39]

---

38. Orlinsky, *Ancient Israel*, 48–49. See Bright, *History of Israel*, 181 (The tribal league could not enforce the purity of Yahwism, "nor at any time persuade all Israel to act concertedly").

39. Judg 20. See Hillers, *Covenant*, 96–97 ("Where a tribe was willing to harbor rapists and murderers, the only recourse was to a blood-feud which hurt the innocent along with the guilty and threatened to destroy all Israel"). Cf. Falk, *Hebrew Law*, 24 (Under conditions of semi-nomadism the tribal chief was responsible for any crime committed by a member of his clan against a stranger, and failure to punish the wrongdoer or turn him over "gave rise to war against the whole clan; thus collective responsibility for the deed of the individual was put on the group as a whole").

Even after the monarchy was established and Saul was able to realize "a measurable degree of unification among the individualistic tribes of Israel,"[40] tribal conflict persisted. When Saul summoned the Israelites to respond to the Ammonite siege of Jabesh-Gilead, "the response of the tribes was still far from unanimous," and in battle against the Philistines at Michmash, "part of Saul's army deserted."[41] It was not until the reign of David that Israel ceased to be a tribal confederacy and became "a complex empire organized under the crown."[42] It was also during the reign of David that the Israelites finally defeated the Philistines and established a new shrine in Jerusalem "where the Ark was housed as an official institution of the state."[43]

It seems reasonable to assume that three primary factors—(1) a new political and social reality (moving from competition among the tribes toward a national identity and consciousness), (2) the revitalization of Yahwism (promoting mutual bonds of fellowship and uniting the secular and the religious community under the crown), and (3) an increase in population, density, economic prosperity, and urbanization (brought by Solomon)[44]—simultaneously fostered cooperation and made cooperation more important than competition for everyone's well-being.[45] People began to see themselves not as members of a clan or tribe that had to compete with other clans or tribes for scarce resources but as members of a united Israelite nation, the success of which depended upon all members of the nation working together for the common good.

It may have also been realized by some that, with more people living in closer proximity and with increasing economic interdependence, the economic success of the nation depended on fair dealings and harmonious relations among all Israelites. This would explain why the use of

40. Orlinsky, *Ancient Israel*, 54–55.
41. Orlinsky, *Ancient Israel*, 55.
42. Bright, *History of Israel*, 205.
43. Bright, *History of Israel*, 198–201, 206.
44. Bright, *History of Israel*, 217–24 ("Many individuals grew rich," existing cities expanded, many new cities were built, increased productivity enabled "an increased density of population," and "the population may have doubled since the days of Saul"). See also Henrich, *WEIRDest People*, 128 (Religious beliefs and practices "have fostered trade by increasing trust").
45. See generally Henrich, *WEIRDest People*, 103–4 ("Scaling up" required that "existing kin-based institutions [be modified] . . . to forge tighter and more cooperative communities"), 128 (Religious beliefs and rituals "expanded people's conceptions of their communities by shifting their focus from their own clans or tribes to larger imagined communities").

false weights and measures is repeatedly and universally condemned—in wisdom literature, law collections, and prophetic utterances.[46] Such a deceptive practice undermined the commercial interaction vital for Israelite society to prosper. Accordingly, the prestige of those qualities having cooperative value increased, and some people sought to instill those qualities in the people through instruction, law, and prophetic utterance.

Whatever the cause, however, beginning in about the late tenth century BCE, a shift in moral norms unquestionably occurred. It was then, during the reign of King Solomon (the person purported to have authored the book of Proverbs), that the biblical wisdom tradition had its genesis.[47] And, in sharp contrast to the competitive focus of the moral norms found in biblical narrative, the moral norms advanced by the authors of biblical wisdom, such as may be found in the book of Proverbs, consist of qualities and conduct having cooperative value.[48]

B. The book of Proverbs extols qualities and conduct having cooperative value, understood as constituting righteousness, for these were seen to be in accord with God's moral order and, consequently, in the interests of the Israelite nation.

Proverbs extols righteousness and understands righteousness to mean possessing qualities and exhibiting conduct having cooperative value.

---

46. For example, Deut 25:13–16 warns the Israelites, "You must have completely honest weights and completely honest measures, if you are to endure long on the soil that the Lord your God is giving you." See Milgrom, *Leviticus*, 245; Boström, *Sages*, 201–2 (The use of false weights is condemned four times in Proverbs as an "abomination to the Lord"; the use of false weights and scales "seems to have been a common problem to the ancient Near East").

47. See Collins, *Jewish Wisdom*, 5 ("The wisdom tradition had its origin in the time of Solomon"); Gordis, *Koheleth*, 20 ("There is every reason to believe that [the reign of King Solomon] marked the first Golden Age of Wisdom literature"); Von Rad, *Wisdom in Israel*, 75–76 (What can be deduced concerning the social and economic situation underlying the book of Proverbs corresponds "to the circumstances of the pre-exilic monarchical period and indeed, on the whole, to those of an urban cultural milieu"); Bright, *History of Israel*, 219–20 (Wisdom "was fostered at Solomon's court"), 438 ("The wisdom tradition in Israel is exceedingly old, reaching back at least to the tenth century," although the book of Proverbs was not compiled until the postexilic period).

48. Daube's distinction between a "lower philosophy . . . permeating the narratives of the Bible" and the "idealistic wisdom of Proverbs" seems roughly equivalent to the distinction made herein between the narratives' esteem for qualities having competitive value and Proverbs' esteem for qualities having cooperative value. See Daube, *Law and Wisdom*, 85–97.

Being righteous is synonymous with being in accord with a moral order ordained by God at the time of creation. It is unclear, however, whether righteousness was viewed as primarily intrinsically good—good in itself because it constituted being in accord with God's moral order—or as primarily instrumentally good—good as the means to the material benefits that are a consequence of being in accord with God's moral order. If it is accepted, as seems to be the case, that Proverbs placed more value on the good of the materially beneficial consequences of righteousness than on the good of simply being in accord with God's moral order, righteousness is most appropriately classified as an instrumental good.

Classifying righteousness as an instrumental good, the ethical theory justifying the normative judgments in Proverbs is best characterized as teleological. But it is then unclear whether the teleological approach in Proverbs is best characterized as utilitarianism or ethical egoism—that is, it is unclear whether the consequences of righteousness were seen to be beneficial primarily for the Israelite nation as a whole or for the righteous individuals themselves. Proverbs clearly asserts that righteousness has beneficial consequences for the individual, but this seems to be primarily because the righteous individual receives community approval (is honored) and the wicked individual receives community disapproval (is shamed).[49] And the righteous individual is honored and the wicked individual is shamed because righteousness was believed to be beneficial for the Israelite nation as a whole. Accordingly, the ethical theory justifying the normative judgments in Proverbs is best characterized as utilitarianism.

1. "Righteousness" denotes qualities and conduct having cooperative value.

According to Rodd, "righteousness" is "an empty concept" denoting "conformity to [whatever are] the prevailing norms of society."[50] He claims that "righteousness" originally represented "the customary ethic

---

[49]. See Daube, *Law and Wisdom*, 99–104 (discussing "the shame element in wisdom").

[50]. Rodd, *Glimpses*, 49, 51. But see Falk, *Hebrew Law*, 8 (The term "righteous" was originally used to describe the successful party in a secular, legal case; it was later used by religionists to describe persons living according to divine law because such persons are acquitted when subjected to divine judgment); Koehler, *Theology*, 166–67 (finding the origin of "righteous" in "legal parlance" with the sense of "innocent"). See also Rodd, *Glimpses*, 47n12 (describing what Rodd thinks are unsatisfactory attempts by biblical scholars to provide meaning to the term "righteousness").

of the peasant society" but was then "filled out in different ways."⁵¹ Although Rodd nowhere clearly specifies what he takes to be "the customary ethic of the peasant society," in the book of Proverbs "righteousness" (*tzedakah*) is "filled out" by, and denotes, qualities and conduct having cooperative value delineated in that work.

One is admonished to seek peace and avoid strife or discord;⁵² to be kind and truthful and not to lie or bear false witness;⁵³ to be temperate (in control of one's passions) and slow to anger;⁵⁴ to be honest and fair in dealings with your neighbor;⁵⁵ not to have sexual relations with your neighbor's wife;⁵⁶ not to use false weights;⁵⁷ to have humility;⁵⁸ to have patience;⁵⁹ to avoid oppressing the defenseless;⁶⁰ to be generous and compassionate, not envious;⁶¹ not to kill or commit acts of violence;⁶² not to steal;⁶³ not to pervert justice;⁶⁴ and not to reveal secrets or be a tattletale.⁶⁵ In addition, Proverbs teaches that one should take counsel, correction, and instruction, including punishment as a means of correction;⁶⁶ accept

---

51. Rodd, *Glimpses*, 51.

52. Prov 3:30; 6:19b; 17:1, 19; 19:11; 14:17, 29; 26:17. Proverbs 11:29 famously claims that one "who makes trouble for his household shall inherit the wind," and it is repeatedly claimed that contentious women should be avoided. Prov 21:9, 19; 25:24.

53. Prov 6:17b, 19a; 11:17; 12:17, 22; 13:5a; 19:9; 20:28; 25:18.

54. Prov 16:32; 21:17; 22:24.

55. Prov 3:27–29; 29:7.

56. Prov 5:1–23; 6:20–35; 7:1–27. See Fox, "Proverbs," 1442, 1445.

57. Prov 11:1; 20:10, 23.

58. Prov 6:17a; 8:13; 11:2; 14:3; 22:4.

59. Prov 14:17, 29.

60. Prov 14:31; 21:13; 22:16, 22–23.

61. Prov 21:26; 22:9.

62. Prov 1:11, 16; 6:17; 21:7.

63. Prov 30:9. But see Prov 6:30 ("A thief is not held in contempt for stealing to appease his hunger").

64. Prov 17:15, 23; 24:23–25.

65. Prov 11:13; 20:19; 25:9.

66. Prov 12:1, 15; 13:24; 15:15, 19, 22; 19:20; 20:18, 30; 21:15; 23:13–14; 29:15. Cf. Plato, *Gorg.* 472 (Socrates claims that wrongdoers would be less happy [less well-off] "if they are not punished and do not meet retribution for their crimes").

the discipline of God;⁶⁷ never return evil for evil;⁶⁸ be prudent;⁶⁹ and be diligent and industrious, not slothful.⁷⁰

2. Righteousness was believed to be instrumentally good, the means to achieving material well-being.

As Kaufmann sees it, an "unmistakable utilitarianism pervades Proverbs."⁷¹ Proverbs teaches that one should be "righteous" because being righteous results in one's "flourishing," and, conversely, the wicked are said to "vanish from the land."⁷² Proverbs 11:28 specifically states that "the righteous [*tzedikim*] shall flourish like foliage."⁷³ In addition, it is suggested that one must be righteous to receive God's blessing.⁷⁴ More specifically, Proverbs states that the righteous can only desire the good, and that if you are a good person (that is, if you only desire the good), you obtain God's blessing.⁷⁵ Therefore, all those material goods associated with being blessed by God—life, prosperity, inheritance of the land

---

67. Prov 3:11.

68. Prov 20:22; 24:29. Socrates, according to Plato's early dialogues, taught that justice (*dikaiosune*) primarily entails never inflicting an injury, not even in retaliation. Plato, *Crito* 49c–d ("There is no difference between injuring people and doing them an injustice"). Cf. Matt 5:38–39; Lam 3:30.

69. Prov 21:16.

70. Prov 6:6–11; 12:24, 27; 19:15; 20:4; 21:25; 22:29; 24:30–31.

71. Kaufmann, *Religion*, 324. See Gordis, *Koheleth*, 33 ("The *morality* inculcated in Wisdom literature is utilitarian. . . . Basic to its world-view is the idea that virtue leads to well-being and vice leads to poverty and disaster" [emphasis original]). But see Von Rad, *Wisdom in Israel*, 80.

72. Prov 2:22. See n9 in this chapter. Cf. Adkins, *Moral Values*, 27 (Regarding the emergence of cooperative values like justice in Greece, Adkins states: "If prosperity is the goal, then the most effective way of commending the less-valued justice is to ensure that the unjust do not prosper, or at all events that it is believed that the unjust do not prosper").

73. See also Prov 14:11 ("The tent of the upright shall flourish"). Cf. Ps 1:1–6. See Tirosh-Samuelson, *Happiness*, 66–68; Boström, *Sages*, 219–23 (discussing sayings in Proverbs which place an emphasis on the Lord "as the one granting success and well-being to the righteous man").

74. See generally Boström, *Sages*, 101–2 (In Prov 10:1—22:16 "the Lord is actively involved in supplying the needs of righteous people and in the destruction of the wicked [and] . . . actively provides for the success and well-being of the righteous person . . . [leading to their] safety, honour and happiness").

75. Prov 11:23; 12:2. See also Prov 14:19 (equating "the good" with "the righteous"). See generally Von Rad, *Wisdom in Israel*, 75–79 (discussing "goodness" and "the good man" in Israelite wisdom literature).

eternally, deliverance from trouble, reward, etc.—are, according to Proverbs, achieved by the good person through their righteousness and lost by the evil person through their wickedness.[76]

That the righteousness of the good person led to their receipt of God's blessing and that the wickedness of the evil person led to their inevitable destruction were understood to be inherent in the moral order created by God.[77] Rodd, relying upon the analysis of Von Rad, states:

> In ancient Israel life was understood as lived within a universe in which goodness led to blessing and evil to weakness and disaster. This meant that "the good man is the one who knows about the constructive quality of good and the destructive quality of evil and submits to this pattern which can be discerned in the world."[78]

The view that there is a moral order in the world that one must discern and submit to, as well as an order in the natural world, is supported by the narratives in the book of Genesis, discussed below. Being "righteous" is depicted in these narratives as acting in accord with the moral order that God has imposed on the world and, therefore, as the means to receiving God's favor, while acting wickedly is depicted as violating God's moral order and, therefore, as the cause of God's wrath. Although these narratives do not fully specify the qualities and conduct constituting "righteousness," they do depict righteousness in general terms as avoiding violent acts that threaten the fabric of society, such as murder and rape.

---

76. See Prov 2:21–22; 10:2–3, 30; 11:4, 8, 18–20, 30; 12:3, 7, 28; 21:21 (equating "righteousness" and striving "to do good" with life (or being saved from death), longevity, what is pleasing to God, success, honor, and having "true reward").

77. See Boström, *Sages*, 136–37 (Proverbs "believes in a world which is characterized by regularity, order and harmony (established and upheld by God). The correspondence between character and consequence underline this worldview and is an indication . . . that the world of men was regarded as being marked by justice"). See also Blenkinsopp, *Wisdom and Law*, 20 ("A particular society's stock of proverbs represents . . . a distillation of collective experience based on the observation of order, regularity, and causality in nature and in human affairs"), 25 (A moral consensus is built up in ancient Israel "on conclusions drawn from repeated observations, e.g., of the kinds of situations calculated to generate anger, resentment, and dissension").

78. Rodd, *Glimpses*, 275 (quoting Von Rad, *Wisdom in Israel*, 78).

3. The Israelites saw the natural world as being well ordered.

The dominant, overarching view expressed in the Hebrew Bible is that the world is well ordered. Regarding the natural world, the Israelites recognized that there is stability and regularity in natural phenomena. This stability and regularity includes the establishment of boundaries. Creation, for example, involves separating the water above the expanse from the water below it, separating the land from the water, separating the day from the night, separating light from darkness, and separating each animal and plant species from each other.[79] It is this notion of Yahweh's creation of order in the natural world by means of setting boundaries that informs Yahweh's response to Job (a work in the Israelite wisdom tradition):

> Where were you when I laid the earth's foundation? . . .
>
> When I closed the sea behind doors.
>
> When it gushed forth out of the womb,
>
> Swaddled it in dense clouds,
>
> When I made breakers My limit for it [or, "put *bounds* upon it"],
>
> And set up its bars and doors,
>
> And said, "You may come so far and no further;
>
> Here your surging waves will stop?"[80]

The prophet Jeremiah goes so far as to speak of the "laws of the moon and stars" and to imply that their regularity is, for all intents and purposes, permanent.[81] He compares the permanence of these natural limits to the permanence of the Israelite people—both are due to divine activity.[82] God's creative activity was seen as continual, not restricted to

---

79. Gen 1:4–19. See also Lev 19:19 (prohibition against mixtures, such as mating different kinds of cattle and sowing fields with different seeds). See generally Milgrom, *Leviticus*, 236 (The most favored explanation of the prohibition against mixtures "is that it is a violation of the order God brought into the world by separating the species [in Gen 1]").

80. Job 38:4–11. See Pope, *Job*, 247 (alternate translation). See also Prov 8:29 (God "assigned the sea its limits, So that its waters never transgress His command"); Ps 104:5–9 (God "set bounds" for the oceans).

81. Jer 31:35. Cf. Jer 33:25 ("laws of heaven and earth"); 5:22 (God "set the sand as a boundary for the sea" as "a limit for all time"); Job 38:33 ("laws of heaven").

82. Jer 31:36. Cf. Jer 33:25–26.

God's initial acts which brought the world and the people of Israel into existence. As Eichrodt puts it, it was possible

> to portray natural events, which elsewhere might have been given an anthropomorphic life of their own, as *a direct act of God*, who controls both Nature and history by the omnipotence with which he fills all things. Thus the bestowal of rain and fertility is the direct gift of Yahweh; in the rain he blesses the field, causes the plants to grow, and gives animals their food.... The earthquake comes from the blow of his fist, the smoking volcanoes have felt his touch.... The regular return of the seasons of the year with their gifts of harvest and the comforting light of day after the dark of night spring from the paternal care of the Creator.[83]

It is precisely because God's creative activity was perceived to be ongoing that the regularity and normal boundaries experienced in natural phenomena could be violated when God determined to do something different, such as when God determined to part the waters of the Sea of Reeds.

4. According to the Israelites, God established a moral order as well as a natural order.

Just as natural phenomena were experienced as orderly and regular due to boundaries established and maintained by divine activity, so too were social phenomena experienced as orderly and regular due to boundaries, or limits, established and maintained by divine activity. It was believed that, if these moral boundaries or limits were not respected, dire consequences would occur. These dire consequences were seen to follow either automatically or, as with unusual natural phenomena, upon God's direct intervention.[84] According to Kaufmann, "The general notion throughout

---

83. Eichrodt, *Theology*, 2.153–54 (emphasis original). See also Buber, *Moses*, 77 ("It is irrelevant whether 'much' or 'little,' unusual things or usual, tremendous or trifling events happened; what is vital is only that what happened was experienced, while it happened, as the act of God"); Kaufmann, *Religion*, 73 ("Typical is the notion that the order of the cosmos is a covenant which God has imposed on it.... The blessings of fertility, the regularity of nature, the order of the times and seasons have all been ordained by God"); Tirosh-Samuelson, *Happiness*, 71 ("The teleological structure of the universe is ascribed in the Bible not to necessity, but to a purposeful creative act that brings everything into existence 'in wisdom'").

84. See generally Barton, *Ethics in Ancient Israel*, 211–226; Boström, *Sages*, 90–140.

the Bible is that there is a universal moral law that even the gentiles are obliged to obey."[85] The notion of a moral order appears early in the book of Genesis, in the story of the first murder.[86] In this story, Cain is unable to control the passion generated by his jealousy of his brother Abel, and Cain kills Abel. This action exceeds the limits for human conduct established by God, and it is, thus, immediately followed by God's punishment of Cain. Sarna writes: "The culpability of Cain rests upon an unexpressed assumption of the existence of a moral law operative from the beginning of time. That is why God intervened, for no man can hope to escape His all-embracing sovereign rule."[87]

The idea that a moral order exists next appears in the flood story. In this story, God determines "to put an end to all flesh" because "the earth is filled with lawlessness [*hamas*] because of them."[88] The Hebrew word *hamas* is a technical legal term that implies lawlessness, injustice, and social unrighteousness, as well as violence.[89] As with the story of Cain and Abel, God intervenes because violent, lawless, unjust, and

---

Similarly, ancient Greeks and Egyptians accepted that a moral and physical order is imbedded into the very structure of the universe. See, e.g., Winston, "Philo's Ethical Theory," 381–82 (The pre-Socratic philosopher Anaximander "intimated that human justice is rooted in the very structure of the cosmos"; the pre-Socratic philosopher Heraclitus explicitly stated that "the underlying and controlling unity of the universe is a divine Logos, to which human action must conform"; and the Egyptians accepted the concept of *maat*). *Maat* represented the cosmic and social order initiated by the god Re at creation. *Maat* was the "generic term for the totality of all social norms" and was "the principle that forms individuals into communities and gives their actions meaning and direction by ensuring that good is rewarded and evil punished." Assmann, *Mind of Egypt*, 127–28. The goddess Maat, the daughter of Re, personified order, harmony, justice, and truth; her counterpart was the god of disorder and chaos, Seth, who opposed communal relations and isolated himself from the other gods. See Assmann, *Mind of Egypt*, 133–34. See also Von Rad, *Wisdom in Israel*, 144–57 (comparing the biblical concept of "wisdom" as a "personified entity immanent in creation" to the Egyptian goddess Maat and commenting that, while Israelite teachers were "dependent on the idea of the Egyptian goddess of order," in the process of "transference . . . to the Hebrew thought-world," the "foreign ideas . . . become completely different"); Assmann, *Mind of Egypt*, 124–25 (comparing Egyptian and Israelite wisdom traditions). See generally Morenz, *Egyptian Religion*, 113–30.

85. Kaufmann, *Religion*, 296. See Kaufmann, *Religion*, 233 ("The Bible . . . recognizes the existence of a universal law from primeval times, to which all men are subject"); Sarna, *Understanding Genesis*, 145–46.

86. See Gen 4:1–13.

87. Sarna, *Understanding Genesis*, 31. See also Novak, *Natural Law*, 31–36 (The story assumes that Cain knew that the murder of Abel was prohibited by God).

88. Gen 6:13.

89. Sarna, *Understanding Genesis*, 52; Speiser, *Genesis*, 51.

unrighteous conduct upset the moral order imposed on man by God's sovereign rule, and perforce reaped undesirable consequences. Noah is spared, however, because Noah was "a righteous man" (*ish tzedik*) who was "without blame" (*tamim*) and "walked with God."[90] Thus, "righteousness" (*tzedakah*) entails "walking with God" and describes conduct that is in accord with God's moral order.[91] Sarna comments:

> The story of the Flood, like that of Sodom and Gomorrah, presupposes the existence of a moral law governing the world for the infraction of which God, the Supreme Judge, brings men to account. It asserts, through the medium of the narrative, that man cannot undermine the moral basis of society without endangering the very existence of civilization. In fact, society, by its own corruption, actually may be said to initiate a process of inevitable retribution.[92]

Chapters 15 and 16 of Genesis describe God's covenant with Abraham and his offspring.[93] God's obligations pursuant to the agreement are spelled out with a fair degree of detail. God will make Abraham "the father of a host of nations," will cause Abraham "to be exceedingly fertile, and [will] make nations of [him]; and kings shall stem from [him]."[94] God will also give Abraham and his descendants the whole land of Canaan "as an everlasting possession."[95] Yet, the obligations of Abraham and his descendants pursuant to the agreement are not clearly specified. God tells Abraham only: "Follow my ways and be blameless [*tamim*]."[96] What this means can be better understood when it is remembered that it was precisely because Noah was blameless and

---

90. Gen 6:9.

91. That *tzedakah* and *mishpat* (justice) are antonyms of *hamas* is supported by Ezek 45:9 and Job 19:7. Under the doctrine of collective responsibility, discussed below, individual righteousness would not necessarily protect you from harm if your community, including ancestors, were unrighteous. See Gen 18:16–33.

92. Sarna, *Understanding Genesis*, 52. See also Sarna, *Understanding Genesis*, 145–46 ("As with the Flood, the Sodom and Gomorrah narrative is predicated upon the existence of a moral law of universal application for the infraction of which God holds all men answerable.... The theme receives full expression in the oracles of Amos [1:3–2:3] and thereafter dominates the prophetic consciousness").

93. See generally Hayes, *Introduction*, 78–79.

94. Gen 17:5–6.

95. Gen 17:8.

96. Gen 17:1. See generally Hillers, *Covenant*, 100–6 (The covenants with Noah and Abraham bind only God).

walked with God that God saved Noah from destruction. Clearly, then, walking with God (or in God's ways) and being blameless were understood to mean adhering to the norms of conduct approved of by God and built into the world order.⁹⁷

That this is the case is supported by the justification the Hebrew Bible offers for giving Abraham and his descendants the land belonging to the Canaanites. The Canaanites were removed from the land because their "iniquity" (*avon*)—that is, their violation of the moral norms established by God—caused the land to "spew them out."⁹⁸ This is to say that the removal of the Canaanites from the land, just as the destruction of the generation of the Flood, was pursuant to a regular process (a moral order) akin to regular processes found in nature. Sarna writes: "The universally binding moral law had been flouted [by the Canaanites], just as in the days of Noah, and with the same inevitable consequences. The pre-Israelite inhabitants of Canaan had been doomed by their own corruption."⁹⁹

Sarna makes this point even clearer in his discussion of the conduct which caused the annihilation of Sodom and Gomorrah. He says:

> As with the Flood, the Sodom and Gomorrah narrative is predicated upon the existence of a moral law of universal application for the infraction of which God holds all men answerable. *The idea that there is an intimate, in fact, inextricable connection between the socio-moral condition of a people and its ultimate fate is one of the main pillars upon which stands the entire biblical interpretation of history.* The theme is central to the Flood story, basic to the Sodom and Gomorrah narrative and fundamental to the understanding of the Book of Jonah. It constitutes the Torah's vindication of God's action in destroying the inhabitants of Canaan before the invading Israelites. . . . The theme receives full expression in the oracles of Amos and thereafter dominates the prophetic consciousness. . . .

---

97. See also Gen 18:19 ("To keep the way of Yahweh" is achieved by "doing what is just and right [*tzedakah v'mishpat*]"); chapter 4, n28 (discussing the hendiadys *mishpat v'tzedakah*).

98. See Gen 15:16; Lev 18:28; Sarna, *Understanding Genesis*, 124–25. See also Speiser, *Genesis*, 113 ("Amorites" is sometimes used as "the collective term for the pre-Israelite population of Canaan"); 1 Kgs 14:24.

99. Sarna, *Understanding Genesis*, 124–25. See generally Sarna, *Understanding Genesis*, 142–46 (discussing the annihilation of Sodom and Gomorrah, as well as the conduct which caused it).

> The Bible declares tacitly, but unequivocally, through the medium of our narrative, that all socially approved actions and all societal patterns must take second place to the higher obligations which the moral order of the universe imposes upon men.[100]

These "higher obligations" seem to consist of, in the earliest periods of Israelite civilization, primarily the avoidance of uncontrolled passion and violent acts that threaten the fabric of society, such as murder and rape. Later, beginning in about the late tenth century BCE, the sages of the Israelite wisdom tradition expanded the range of these "higher obligations" demanded by God's moral order—the expansion included all those qualities and acts having cooperative value denoted by the concept of righteousness, described above.[101]

5. Righteousness was seen to be intrinsically good, good in itself, as well as instrumentally good.

Although righteousness was said to be instrumentally good, the way to receive material well-being, the book of Proverbs also includes passages which suggest that righteousness was to be chosen without consideration of materially beneficial consequences, and even at the expense of one's material well-being.[102] The very teaching that associates righteousness with flourishing states in full:

> He who trusts in his wealth shall fall,
> But the righteous shall flourish like foliage.[103]

Thus, "trusting in wealth" does not result in "flourishing" but in its opposite—"falling."

If righteousness should be chosen in preference to wealth, in preference to material well-being, then being righteous is not desirable primarily because it is the means required to attain material well-being. Rather, to be righteous is itself to flourish, to attain well-being. In other words,

---

100. Sarna, *Understanding Genesis*, 145–46 (emphasis original).

101. See sec. B, 1 in this chapter. Although the biblical book of Proverbs was not created until "some time during the period of the Second Temple . . . the book represents the effort of a Second Temple editor to bring together a cross-section of scribal wisdom covering a long period of time." Blenkinsopp, *Wisdom and Law*, 18–19.

102. See Prov 11:4, 28; 16:8; 28:6. Cf. Prov 3:14–15; 8:10–11, 19.

103. Prov 11:28.

in some passages of Proverbs being righteous is seen to be intrinsically good, not merely instrumentally good.[104] Perhaps some saw righteousness as instrumentally good while others saw righteousness as intrinsically good; perhaps there was simply confusion and inconsistency about this; or perhaps it was understood that righteousness *generally* leads to the actor's receiving God's blessing and material well-being but, in instances in which it does not, the righteous act should still be chosen because righteous behavior is always beneficial to society, if not always directly beneficial to the individual actor.[105]

6. Righteousness was seen to benefit the individual primarily because of the community approval it was given.

According to Von Rad, in ancient Israelite thought, righteous behavior is good not primarily because such behavior is in one's individual interest but because such behavior is in the interest of one's community. If this is correct—if righteousness was believed to be justified primarily because of its materially beneficial consequences for the Israelite nation as a whole—then the ethical theory justifying normative judgments in ancient Israelite thought is utilitarianism. At the same time, the individual Israelite may have been *motivated* to be righteous because the community approved of righteous conduct and disapproved of wicked conduct.[106]

According to Von Rad, a man "was considered to be 'righteous'" only if he "lived up to what the community expected of him."[107] So, righteous conduct was in one's *individual* interest primarily because the consequences of such conduct benefited the community, and an

---

104. Of course, a good can be intrinsically good *and* instrumentally good—it can be chosen for its own sake as well as for the sake of something else; but, if it is chosen for the sake of something else, then it is that something else which is "most complete" and the "best good." See Aristotle, *Eth. nic.* 1097a25–35.

105. See Prov 11:10–11; Boström, *Sages*, 120 (The outlook found in Proverbs "is not entirely individualistic.... The character-consequence relationship [in Prov 11:10–11] is ... depicted as relating not only to the individual, but also to the community").

106. See generally Frankena, *Ethics*, 114 (distinguishing justification and motivation).

107. Von Rad, *Wisdom in Israel*, 78. See Rodd, *Glimpses*, 275 ("Goodness is a matter of living in such a way that it brings blessing to the community"), 276 ("Primarily the proverbs present an ethics which is essentially an attempt to maintain the well-being of society"). See also Daube, *Law and Wisdom*, 103 ("A member of a group . . . has the duty to consider how his doings will affect the group's standing.").

individual was judged "with regard to their effect on society."[108] This is to say that Israelite society was a "shame culture," a culture in which people are motivated to act in ways that win community approval (honor) and avoid community disapproval (shame or disgrace).[109] Von Rad explains that the righteous persons were the ones who lived up to what the community expected of them and fulfilled the claims the community made upon them.[110]

Von Rad adds that in an "established social community" experience confirmed that "righteousness will always have the effect of promoting the community and will always then raise the prestige [or honor] of the person concerned."[111] Conversely, because wicked behavior always has the effect of damaging the community, wickedness always brings shame upon the person concerned.[112] In other words, righteous behavior by all members of the community may have been recognized to lead to the community's collective prosperity and well-being but not necessarily to each community member's individual prosperity and well-being except to the extent that each community member believed that their individual prosperity and well-being was inextricably linked to the prosperity and well-being of the entire community or were motivated by the fear of being shamed by unrighteousness and the hope of being honored by righteousness.[113]

Many didactic sentences in Proverbs support the understanding that the moral norms taught in Proverbs were enforced by means of shame.[114]

108. Von Rad, *Wisdom in Israel*, 78. See Boström, *Sages*, 120, 124 ("Through their ill considered speech . . . the wicked expose their true character, ruining their positions in society"), 134 ("Fellow-men were seen as playing an active role in the realization of the consequences of certain types of behaviour"). Cf. Assmann, *Mind of Egypt*, 127–29 (*Maat* required that the individual do something for others, for the well-being of society, but presumed that such "self-sacrifice" or "altruism" would be remembered by others and rewarded "as a function of social action").

109. See Adkins, *Moral Values*, 12n1 ("A shame-culture is one whose sanction is overtly 'what people will say'"); Adkins, *Merit*, 48–49. See also n49 in this chapter. See generally Henrich, *WEIRDest People*, 34–36 (describing the distinction between shame and guilt and explaining why shame dominates in "regulated-relational societies").

110. Von Rad, *Wisdom in Israel*, 78–79.

111. See Von Rad, *Wisdom in Israel*, 130.

112. See, e.g., Rodd, *Glimpses*, 278 (Adultery brings shame upon the adulterer).

113. As Frankena might analyze this situation, the desire to be honored and not shamed *motivated* people to do that which was deemed to be morally right but did not *justify* it. See Frankena, *Ethics*, 114.

114. See, e.g., Prov 6:30, 33; 25:7c–10. See also Boström, *Sages*, 103 (It may be presumed that the sages responsible for Proverbs believed that "society will acknowledge

In particular, Proverbs teaches that a good name "is preferable to great wealth,"[115] that the conduct of a member of a family will affect the reputation of the entire family,[116] and that punishment and/or condemnation for violation of moral norms is appropriate and should be welcomed by the person being reproved.[117] Similar norms in priestly sources are also enforced, in part, by means of shame.[118]

Rodd emphasizes that behavioral norms and the justification for these norms were not critically examined in Israelite society. In discussing the book of Proverbs, he asserts:

> In Israelite society the individual conformed unthinkingly to the norms and values that derive from the communities in which he or she lived. "The community life has its ethical atmosphere; it compels the individual to live up to specific expectations which people have of him, it provides him with long established examples and values. As a rule, the individual conforms unthinkingly to these community-determined factors."[119]

But how were the norms and values of Israelite society arrived at in the first place? How did men originally come to know what conduct was beneficial for the community—what conduct should be honored and what conduct should be shamed? It was *not* through divine revelation.

C. According to Proverbs, knowledge of what is righteous is achieved through wisdom, not revelation.

Proverbs teaches that righteousness results from being guided by wisdom.[120] Boström claims that because the term "righteous" designates a man who knows how to avoid evil and live correctly, "righteous" is synonymous with "wise."[121] This claim is supported by the fact that the differing justifications found in Proverbs for being righteous are found,

---

the righteous person while unrighteousness will face spite, repulsion and judgment"). See generally Rodd, *Glimpses*, 19–27 (citing the work of Daube and Bechtel); Daube, *Law and Wisdom*, 32–34, 49–55, 99–101.

115. Prov 22:1.
116. See Prov 12:4; 17:6; 28:7; 29:15; Daube, *Law and Wisdom*, 103.
117. Prov 9:8; 29:15, 18.
118. See, e.g., Lev 19:17 ("Reprove your kinsman").
119. Rodd, *Glimpses*, 273–74 (quoting Von Rad, *Wisdom in Israel*, 75).
120. See Prov 8:20.
121. Boström, *Sages*, 213.

as well, for being wise. This is to say that wisdom is depicted as being both intrinsically good and instrumentally good. Wisdom is intrinsically good because the wise man has knowledge of the moral order created by God, and such knowledge is good in itself. Yet precisely because he has knowledge of the divinely created moral order, the wise man can act in accord with that order and, as a consequence, obtain happiness (material well-being) for himself and the nation. As the means to happiness, wisdom is instrumentally good. Proverbs places most emphasis on the beneficial consequences of wisdom (and righteousness) for the Israelite nation,[122] and, thus, the ethical theory justifying its normative judgments is best characterized as utilitarianism.

Wisdom is seen as being obtained through human experience and reasoning, that is, from observing the consequences that result from particular actions and reasoning that similar actions will result in the same kind of consequences. Knowledge that some sorts of actions result in beneficial consequences and other sorts of actions result in deleterious consequences constitutes knowledge of the moral order ordained by God. This knowledge enables one to act in accord with that order, to act in accord with God's will, and to, therefore, be righteous.[123]

1. The book of Proverbs offers instruction based upon popular morality, not divine revelation.

Scholars distinguish the morality of biblical wisdom literature from the morality of the Torah. The latter, according to Kaufmann, "is prophetic, given by God in a revelation"; the former "grounds morality on prudence and 'God-fearing,' rather than on a historical covenant."[124] The source of

---

122. See Barton, *Ethics in Ancient Israel*, 178 ("Wisdom is focused on happiness and success, but for society as a whole, not simply for the individual"; the goal of good conduct is "the maintenance of good order and harmony in society").

123. See Blenkinsopp, *Wisdom and Law*, 21 ("One of the basic goals of the sages in Israel [was] . . . to bring human conduct into line with a cosmic law of regularity and order. . . . To be wise is, in a word, to live in conformity with the law of nature . . . [and] a moral consensus is built . . . on conclusions drawn from repeated observations, e.g., of the kinds of situations calculated to generate anger, resentment, and dissension").

124. Kaufmann, *Religion*, 322-23. See Eichrodt, *Theology*, 2.313 (emphasizing the importance of norms which possess "a certain independent validity"); Barton, *Ethics in Ancient Israel*, 94-126 (presenting evidence in the Hebrew Bible "for an ethic based on a perception of a moral order in the world . . . [which derives from God] by way of God's character as creator rather than as a result of his . . . commands").

biblical wisdom, says Kaufmann, "is not a prophetic revelation, but the teaching of reason,"[125] and the nature of biblical wisdom, he says, "stands out clearest in the book of Proverbs," which is "a counterpart to the Torah, the book of divine commands."[126]

Although many of the didactic sentences found in Proverbs admonish the reader to heed the "commandments" contained therein,[127] the teachers of biblical wisdom are not referring to divine commandments revealed by God to Moses and set forth in the Torah. Rather, what is meant is "always the instruction and commands of father, mother, sage, or of wisdom personified."[128] Similarly, when the reader is taught, "Hear, my son, the instruction of thy father, and forsake not the teaching of thy mother,"[129] the moral norms taught by the father and mother were those of the established convention or popular morality, not those divinely commanded.[130]

According to Eichrodt:

> Even within a morality ... strongly determined by religious factors, importance still attaches to the *acknowledgement of such norms* as possess a certain independent validity for the control

---

125. Kaufmann, *Religion*, 326. See Blenkinsopp, *Wisdom and Law*, 20 (The Proverbs represents "a deposit of the accumulated wisdom of the past, a distillation of collective experience based on observation of order, regularity, and causality in nature and human affairs").

126. Kaufmann, *Religion*, 323.

127. See, e.g., Prov 3:1; 6:23; 7:1; 10:8.

128. Kaufmann, *Religion*, 325 ("The first chapters of Proverbs are full of the image of a father instructing his son, exhorting him to obey wisdom and get understanding"); Fox, "Proverbs," 1448.

129. Prov 1:8.

130. See Collins, *Jewish Wisdom*, 2 (The instruction in Proverbs addresses "the individual person, typically 'my son.' The address is authoritative, but it has neither the force of law nor the vehemence of the prophetic oracle. The authority to which it lays claim is that of the accumulated wisdom of parents and tradition"); Boström, *Sages*, 125 ("The sentences in Proverbs 10:1—22:16 ... appear to be based mainly on traditional views and observations"), 134 ("A large number of sayings in [Proverbs] are best interpreted as simple expressions of common sense built on observation and traditional views"). See generally Eichrodt, *Theology*, 2.316–19; Barton, *Ethics in Ancient Israel*, 77–93 (identifying a morality of "custom and convention" and concluding that "on many moral issues there were widely held conventional beliefs").

of conduct, and do not require the citation of a divine command to support them in every instance.[131]

The awareness of moral norms possessing an independent validity and obligatory on all, argues Eichrodt, is voiced in Israel in phrases that are used for socially unacceptable behavior—"do not do this folly" and "such things are not done in Israel."[132] For example, when Tamar objects to her brother Amnon's attempt to have sexual relations with her, she says: "Don't brother. Do not force me. Such things are not done in Israel! Don't do such a vile thing! Where will I carry my shame?"[133]

2. The popular morality taught in the book of Proverbs is based upon knowing the boundaries or limits that God sets for man and acting in accord with those boundaries or limits.

If the moral norms taught in Proverbs are based on the instruction of parents, or conventional or popular morality, not on divine commandments, how was that conventional morality arrived at in the first place and why was it taken to be authoritative, to have independent validity? The answer to the first part of the question is that conventional morality was derived from "wisdom" (*hokhmah*), a term that is virtually identical to knowledge (*daʾat*), understanding (*bina*), or prudence (*mezimmah*).[134] The knowledge or understanding that wisdom provided was knowledge of the moral order God ordained at the time of creation—knowledge of the boundaries or limits God wills human beings to respect—and the prudence that wisdom provided concerned how to prudently adjust your behavior to act within the limits that God wills for human beings to respect. So, the wise man was believed to be the one who not only grasped the nature of God's moral order (the

131. Eichrodt, *Theology*, 2.316 (emphasis original). See also Von Rad, *Wisdom in Israel*, 87–88.

132. Eichrodt, *Theology*, 2.317 (citing biblical passages). See Barton, *Ethics in Ancient Israel*, 88, 96, 100; Rodd, *Glimpses*, 44–47; Gen 20:9; 29:26; 34:7.

133. 2 Sam 13:12–13. See Blenkinsopp, *Wisdom and Law*, 108 (When Tamar warns Amnon "that 'such a thing is not done in Israel' [she is] implying that this outrage would be a gross violation of the traditional law and ethos of the kinship group").

134. Wisdom, knowledge, understanding, and prudence are all "intertwined almost to the point of synonymity." Von Rad, *Wisdom in Israel*, 53. See also Fox, "Wisdom," 116–17 (The sages treat the "complex of faculties and knowledge" associated with *hokhmah* "as a unity, though the language was able to distinguish different facets thereof").

nature of the limits imposed on humanity) but lived in accord with that order—who, in other words, abided by God's will.

Having knowledge of and living in accord with God's moral order meant that the wise man (*hokem*) was capable of making the right practical decisions, so he may be compared to the man who, in Aristotelian terms, possesses the virtue of good judgment or prudence (*phronesis*).[135] Standing in contrast to the wise man is the fool (*kisel* or *'avil*).[136] The fool is the "disorderly" person who, possibly through some inner weakness, is unable to adapt himself to that moral order which God imposes on all humanity and thus unable to exercise good practical judgment.[137]

3. Wisdom begins with the fear of Yahweh.

Having the "fear of Yahweh" means having knowledge of Yahweh,[138] and having knowledge of Yahweh, in turn, means having knowledge of that which Yahweh wills, i.e., knowledge of that which is "right, just, and equitable,"[139] and this is virtually identical to knowledge of the moral order (with its boundaries and limits) that God imposes on humanity. Therefore, because wisdom is associated with the ability to grasp the structure of the universe created by God, and, thus, is associated with knowledge of God's will, wisdom is said to begin with the "fear of Yahweh." Proverbs 1:7 teaches: "The fear of Yahweh is the beginning of knowledge; but the foolish despise wisdom and discipline."

Von Rad calls this verse "one of the most characteristic didactic sentences in the whole book of Proverbs" and points out that substantially

---

135. See Fox, "Wisdom," 115–19 (discussing the broad range of the Hebrew word *hokhmah*, including the potential ability "to make right decisions and act correctly in new situations" and noting that when Proverbs insists that *hokhmah* yields ethical behavior "it is making new and bold assertions about the validity of human intelligence"); Aristotle, *Eth. nic.* Book 6.

136. As many different terms, in addition to *hokhmah*, are used to refer to wisdom, so are many different terms used to refer to foolishness or stupidity. See Rodd, *Glimpses*, 274n9.

137. Von Rad, *Wisdom in Israel*, 83. See also Rodd, *Glimpses*, 274 ("The pair of terms 'wise' and 'fool' refer not to intellectual knowledge and learning but to practical understanding of right and wrong").

138. Prov 2:5; 9:10. See generally Eichrodt, *Theology*, 2.268–77.

139. See Prov 2:5–9; Fox, "Proverbs," 1441 (Knowledge of God "is not theological knowledge, namely an understanding of the nature of God, but rather a constant awareness of God's will").

the same verse occurs in Prov 9:10; 15:33; Ps 111:10; and Job 28:28.[140] According to Von Rad, in saying that the fear of Yahweh is the beginning of wisdom, Israel was "of the opinion that effective knowledge about God is the only thing that puts a man in a right relationship with the objects of his perception, that it enables him to ask questions more pertinently, to take stock of relationships more effectively and generally to have a better awareness of circumstances."[141]

Having effective knowledge about God means that one is able to discern the beneficial quality of that which is good and the harmful quality of that which is bad and to submit to the pattern discerned.[142] Thus, paradoxically, the fear of God is not only the starting point of wisdom but, because knowledge that there is a moral order leads to knowledge of what that order requires—knowledge of what God wills—the fear of God is also the ultimate objective of wisdom.[143]

4. The ultimate source of wisdom is human experience of act-consequence occurrences.

Von Rad argues that the ultimate basis of the instruction constituting popular morality is "experience."[144] He writes: "We are dealing with experiences of orders, indeed of laws, of the truth of which men have become convinced in the course of generations. Here, then, human behaviour is determined . . . by the experience of inherent natural laws."[145]

In other words, the moral norms of popular morality were based on the well-established experience of the community as to the sorts of conduct that led to life, prosperity, and success, and the sorts of conduct

---

140. Von Rad, *Wisdom in Israel*, 65–66.

141. Von Rad, *Wisdom in Israel*, 67–68.

142. Von Rad, *Wisdom in Israel*, 78.

143. See Sir 1:14, 16, 18 (The "fear of the Lord" is the "beginning," the "fullness," and the "crown" of wisdom). See also Fox, "Wisdom," 115 ("Proverbs . . . sets wisdom as both the goal and the reward of human effort"). Cf. Morenz, *Egyptian Religion*, 113 (*Maat* was not only the task to which Egyptians were to dedicate themselves; it was also their reward).

144. See Von Rad, *Wisdom in Israel*, 88–90.

145. Von Rad, *Wisdom in Israel*, 90. See Barton, *Ethics in Ancient Israel*, 112 (The "moral advice in Proverbs" rests on "observation of the regularities of the world"); Blenkinsopp, *Wisdom and Law*, 20 (Proverbs "represents a deposit of the accumulated wisdom of the past, a distillation of collective experience based on the observation of order, regularity, and causality in nature and in human affairs").

that led to the opposite results. Elsewhere, concerning the source of the instruction found in Proverbs, Von Rad writes:

> In the first instance we encounter . . . the paramount significance accorded to experience. If a sentence originated from the experience of the fathers, then it could already of itself claim by itself normative significance. . . . But in these instructions for correct behaviour there are included also experiences which men have had directly of Yahweh, that he proves to be the [defender] of those who are without legal rights, that he quite personally "complements" a good deed with his blessing. Again, we must not forget the characteristic concept of reality as a force which continually has its effects upon men. This concept will now need to be amplified only in this respect, that in these effects, orders can be discerned, from which a man can deduce norms for his behaviour. In these effects of reality Yahweh was at work, ordering and directing.[146]

Included in the type of experience generating the didactic sentences of Proverbs is the experience of an order in the "succession of phenomena" whereby certain types of human action (or actions performed by people possessing certain character traits) seem to be regularly followed by certain events, an "act-consequence relationship."[147] For example, when Proverbs teaches, "He who sows injustice shall reap misfortune,"[148] the implication is that misfortune follows injustice just as surely as reaping of the grain follows the sowing of the seed.[149] These

---

146. Von Rad, *Wisdom in Israel*, 94 (emphasis original). See also Rodd, *Glimpses*, 281–82 ("Sometimes the results of righteousness and wickedness come directly from Yahweh, but more commonly they are the result of what has been built into an orderly world").

147. See Von Rad, *Wisdom in Israel*, 124; Collins, *Jewish Wisdom*, 3–4 ("Proverbial wisdom posits a chain of act and consequence, which is set in motion by the creator"); Blenkinsopp, *Wisdom and Law*, 46 (referring to "an intrinsic connection between act and consequence"); Barton, *Ethics in Ancient Israel*, 112 (Proverbs "seems to think of wrong actions bringing about bad consequences in a quasi-automatic way"). See also Boström, *Sages*, 90–91 ("One of the dominant thought patterns in the book of Proverbs is that quality of life runs closely parallel to conduct. This view, which is often referred to as the 'act-consequence relationship,' is in our opinion more accurately designated by 'the character-consequence relationship' since the relationship reflected in the texts pertains more to life-style than to individual actions"), 131 ("The consequences of certain acts were viewed as 'natural' . . . [in that] a particular kind of action leads to certain consequences," but this does not prove "that actions have *built-in* consequences" [emphasis added]).

148. Prov 22:8.

149. See Collins, *Jewish Wisdom*, 4.

THE SAGES OF THE ANCIENT ISRAELITE WISDOM TRADITION

teachings suggest to some scholars that unrighteous actions *of their own accord* bring about harmful consequences, and righteous actions *of their own accord* bring about beneficial consequences—without extraordinary divine intervention.[150] That this order of an act-consequence relationship was seen to correspond to the order of cause and effect experienced in natural phenomena is made evident by such sentences as the one just quoted and by Prov 26:20: "Where no wood is, the fire goes out; And where there is no whisperer, contention ceases."

Von Rad suggests the process by which experience of act-consequence occurrences led to a belief in a moral order when he writes:

> Daily, incessantly, man encounters contingent events (chance events) whose meaning and inner necessity are at first hidden from him. Only occasionally does he succeed in recognizing behind the contingent event a clear, inner necessity. Then the experience loses its contingent character, and its place is taken by the awareness of an order which is at work behind the experiences.[151]

Yet, the order of an action followed by a regular consequence is not always experienced; sometimes the usual and expected consequence does not follow the action. This could be explained by the belief that in social phenomena, no less than in natural phenomena, Yahweh's creative activity is ongoing; Yahweh could always intervene to alter what would otherwise have been the normal course of events, as when Pharaoh's heart was hardened.[152] But it could also be explained by the belief that Yahweh has built a certain indeterminacy into the order

---

150. For example, if you are cruel or pursue ill-gotten gains, you will bring about trouble for yourself and your household (Prov 11:17; 15:27), but, if you are diligent, you can become rich (Prov 10:4; 21:25). See also Blenkinsopp, *Wisdom and Law*, 46 ("The observation that pride leads to disaster (e.g. Prov 11:2; 16:18; 18:12), or that laziness generally leads to poverty (e.g. Prov 10:4; 20:13; 21:25), made on the basis of experience, was intended to suggest obvious consequences for the moral life"). See generally Barton, *Ethics in Ancient Israel*, 112, 211–26. Cf. Adkins, *Moral Values*, 27–31. To say that consequences follow actions automatically pursuant to God's moral order does not preclude God's direct intervention. Blenkinsopp, *Wisdom and Law*, 47, 49.

151. Von Rad, *Wisdom in Israel*, 124.

152. See generally Von Rad, *Wisdom in Israel*, 107 ("The statements of the teachers move in a dialectic which is fundamentally incapable of resolution, speaking on the one hand of valid rules and, on the other, of ad hoc divine actions"), 191–94 (Events were always part of direct divine intervention); Boström, *Sages*, 104 (Even if God "was regarded as responsible for the correspondence between a man's life and his fate, we also note an emphasis on God's freedom to work out his purposes").

itself. In other words, it was experienced that "human activity is not equally successful and meaningful on every occasion, that its success and meaningfulness . . . is tied to specific times."[153] Therefore, "the aim of wisdom instruction was, in large measure, the recognition of the right time, the right place and the right extent for human activity."[154] This teaching is reflected in the book of Qoheleth at 3:1–8.

5. It was believed that a life guided by wisdom leads to happiness.

It was an accepted belief that one who guides his or her life in accord with wisdom achieves "happiness," or a state of well-being.[155] As one proverb puts it:

> Happy [*ashrei*] is the man that finds wisdom,
> And the man that obtains understanding . . .
> Her ways are ways of pleasantness,
> And all her paths are peace [*shalom*].[156]

The connotation of the Hebrew word *ashrei*, translated "happy," is similar to the connotation of the classical Greek word *eudaimonia*. *Eudaimonia* is also typically translated as "happiness" but actually refers to the entire condition of a person, not to a mental state. To achieve *eudaimonia* is to flourish as a human being—to achieve a condition of complete well-being. Similarly, *ashrei* "pertains to the quality of life as a whole rather than to a momentary sensation of pleasure."[157] Likewise, the Hebrew word

---

153. Von Rad, *Wisdom in Israel*, 139.

154. Von Rad, *Wisdom in Israel*, 139. Cf. Aristotle, *Eth. nic.* 1106b21–24 (Virtuous character entails having feelings "at the right times, about the right things, toward the right people, for the right end, and in the right way").

155. See Prov 8:36 (Those who achieve wisdom find life and obtain the favor of the Lord); Tirosh-Samuelson, *Happiness*, 58 ("The ancient Israelite wisdom tradition . . . was concerned with ordering life so as to maximize success and prosperity"). Cf. Assmann, *Mind of Egypt*, 125–26 (Ancient Egyptian wisdom literature was concerned with teaching the "prevailing norms" that were the "criterion for success").

156. Prov 3:13, 17. See Prov 3:2 (Wisdom bestows on one "years of life and well-being [*shalom*]"; 8:32, 34 ("Happy [*ashrei*] are they who listen to wisdom and follow its ways").

157. Tirosh-Samuelson, *Happiness*, 64. See generally Tirosh-Samuelson, *Happiness*, 55–100 (discussing the use of *ashrei* in biblical literature). See also Janzen, "'AŠRÊ," 221–22 ("The basis of the *'ašrê*-ascription consists of . . . descendants; fertility of fields, flocks and herds; and security from enemies"), 223 (To receive that which is bestowed by being blessed "qualifies a person or group to be called 'AŠRÊ").

shalom has a much broader connotation than "peace." As *ashrei*, it refers to a state of "wholeness," or complete "well-being."[158] Therefore, the two words—*ashrei* and *shalom*—complement each other,[159] and their use in the above-quoted passage indicates that it was believed that a life guided by wisdom led to complete well-being. On this understanding, wisdom is *instrumentally* good—good as the means to complete well-being.

Tirosh-Samuelson writes:

> The ancient Wisdom tradition . . . maintained that the moral order and in turn, human well-being, are located in the very structure of the universe. Only the wise man—he who grasps the structure and lives in accordance with it—can flourish, i.e., experience happiness.
>
> The Israelite sapiential tradition presupposed that reality is meaningfully ordered and that human intelligence is capable of deciphering that order so as to orient human life in accord with it.[160]

On Tirosh-Samuelson's account, grasping the nature of (that is, the boundaries and limits of) the moral order that God has imposed on humanity and integrating one's conduct into that order was seen to be the means for individuals and societies to attain God's blessing, the means to achieve life, prosperity, and success.[161] Similarly, Kaufmann claims that the phrase "the fear of Yahweh" provides a religious basis for Proverbs' exhortations, and he says that this "religious basis," just as the secular basis, "is tinged with a certain utilitarianism."[162] This is to say that, since

---

158. See Eichrodt, *Theology*, 2.358 (*Shalom* "is used in the widest sense to include every divine blessing"); Tirosh-Samuelson, *Happiness*, 63–64 (To have God's blessing "includes whatever the Israelite understood by the term *shalom*, 'wholeness,' 'welfare,' 'harmony,' or 'peace' as it is usually translated").

159. See Janzen, "'AŠRÊ,'" 221 (The content of ascribing *shalom* to something is the same as ascribing to it *ashrei* or *baruch*).

160. Tirosh-Samuelson, *Happiness*, 55–56, 58. See also Tirosh-Samuelson, *Happiness*, 71 (Since the order in the universe is due to a purposeful creative act, "creation itself is intelligible to those who possess the wisdom to discern its internal order"); Von Rad, *Wisdom in Israel*, 80–81 (One must achieve "integration into a divine order that is imposed upon man and in which alone he can find blessing").

161. See Von Rad, *Wisdom in Israel*, 79 ("Good conduct and prosperity are two sides of one and the same thing"). Cf. Assmann, *Mind of Egypt*, 133 (The ancient Egyptians saw the aim of the individual to be not "individual self-fulfillment" but "the development of social connection," the maintenance of an orderly, harmonious, and prosperous society from which the individual reaps benefits.).

162. Kaufmann, *Religion*, 324.

"God oversees all the acts of men and knows their innermost thought, doing good will benefit man, while doing bad will harm him."[163]

But here one encounters the same ambivalence encountered with the concept of "righteousness."[164] Notwithstanding that wisdom is good because it leads to material well-being, wisdom is also said to be good even when it does not lead to material well-being—wisdom is said to be even "better than silver" and "greater than gold."[165] Teaching of this type suggests that wisdom is primarily *intrinsically* good.[166] The tension between wisdom as primarily instrumentally good and as primarily intrinsically good is clearly manifest in chapter 8 of Proverbs, which states:

> It is Wisdom calling . . .
> Riches and *honor* belong to me,
> *Enduring* wealth and success.
> My fruit is better than gold, fine gold,
> And my produce better than choice silver.
> I walk on the way of righteousness,
> On the paths of justice.
> I endow those who love me with substance;
> I will fill their treasuries.[167]

Commenting on this passage, Fox says: "Wisdom promises material rewards but she emphasizes that she is superior to gold and silver . . . and that she bestows wealth only in honest ways."[168] Unfortunately, Fox's comment does not directly address the issue of whether wisdom is viewed in this passage as primarily instrumentally good or as primarily intrinsically good.

Perhaps the author is extolling wisdom as primarily instrumentally good but is distinguishing increases in wealth which are "enduring"

---

163. Kaufmann, *Religion*, 324. See, e.g., Prov 24:12 (God "shall render every man according to his work"). See also Boström, *Sages*, 213–14 ("The fear of the Lord bears the function of promoting wisdom" and designates "the correct attitude of the wise man towards God and life"), 219 (The fear of the Lord is used in reference to the person who "puts his trust in [the Lord] as his personal god and is rewarded with protection and safety").

164. See sec. B, 5 in this chapter. Coherence between the concepts of "wisdom" and "righteousness" is to be expected since, in Proverbs, being righteous inevitably results from being guided by wisdom. See Prov 8:20; Boström, *Sages*, 213.

165. Prov 3:14. See also Prov 8:10–11, 19; 16:16.

166. Cf. n102 in this chapter and accompanying text.

167. Prov 8:1, 17–21 (emphasis added).

168. Fox, "Proverbs," 1450–51.

from those that are fleeting. To act dishonestly may enable you to obtain "fine gold" and "choice silver," but, if your dishonesty is discovered, the community will disapprove of your conduct, your reputation will be ruined, and, consequently, your wealth will not be *enduring*. It is for this reason, arguably, that both "enduring wealth" and "honor" are claimed to "belong" to wisdom.[169] On this interpretation of the passage, one who acts righteously (i.e., one who is guided by wisdom) is like Kant's shopkeeper, who gives the customer the correct change only because it is good for business.[170]

Yet, the passage may be extolling wisdom as primarily intrinsically good. A life in conformity with God's will, achieved through wisdom, may have been seen to be a good in itself. To act in accord with the moral order that confronts you may have been seen as more important for an individual than amassing material well-being. Von Rad argues:

> If one were to suggest that [Proverbs'] "success thinking" was utilitarianism or eudemonism, one could hardly misunderstand it more. Behind this concept of life there lies not the dispassionate utilitarian standpoint of the man who has taken his life into his own hands, but the action, which has to be constantly repeated, of pious integration into a divine order that is imposed upon man and in which alone he can find blessing.[171]

In the final analysis, however, the weight of the evidence supports the view that the ethical theory justifying the normative judgments in Proverbs is utilitarianism. The moral norms of conventional morality were derived on the basis of what human experience and reason demonstrated to be the sorts of conduct that led to life, prosperity, and success, as well as the sorts of conduct that led to the opposite results, and they were accepted as authoritative precisely for that reason—they were believed to result in the nation's material well-being. And these moral norms all had cooperative value.

---

169. See also Prov 22:1 ("Repute is preferable to great wealth, Grace is better than silver and gold"); Fox, "Proverbs," 1470 (Grace is said to mean the esteem which others have for you).

170. See Kant, *Groundwork*, 8–9.

171. Von Rad, *Wisdom in Israel*, 80. See also Perdue, *Wisdom and Cult*, 11 ("The wise person [believed] that there existed an all embracing 'order' to the components of reality" and "the wise man's task was to uncover his place, function and time within the structure of this order which permeated the spheres of the cosmos, society, man, and the realm and nature of the holy. By successfully integrating himself within these spheres of reality, or 'order,' the wise man . . . achieves harmony within himself.").

CHAPTER 2

The secular law collections mandated qualities and conduct having cooperative value justified on the grounds that they were beneficial for the Israelite nation, but later justified on the grounds that Yahweh commanded them.

As explained in the first chapter, in about the late tenth century BCE, the sages of the Israelite wisdom tradition began to compose proverbs extolling qualities and conduct having cooperative value, justifying them on the basis that they were beneficial for the well-being of the Israelite nation, if not always the individual Israelite. However, as mere instruction to devotees of wisdom, such qualities and conduct were humanly enforced only by the community approval given to them and the community disapproval given to their opposites.[1] Righteousness was also enforced by God in that God created the moral order responsible for an act-occurrence relationship, so righteous acts were believed to result in beneficial consequences and wicked acts in adverse consequences.[2]

Human enforcement of the new morality was enhanced, however, by the ancient Israelite legists who developed laws, including those

---

1. See Daube, *Law and Wisdom*, 87 ("Except in one or two very specific cases . . . legal sanctions were nonexistent [for enforcement of the moral norms espoused in wisdom literature]").

2. See chapter 1, sec. C, 4. Proverbs 6:32–34, for example, teaches that adulterers, perforce, subject themselves to disease and reprisal by angry husbands.

preserved in the Torah's several law collections dated from about the eighth to the late seventh centuries BCE.[3] These laws do not merely extol qualities and behavior having cooperative value, they *mandate* them. And the specific qualities and conduct mandated are essentially the same as those commended by wisdom.[4] Moreover, the legists justified these qualities and conduct in the same way as the sages—on the grounds that they promoted the well-being of the Israelite nation. Thus, the ethical theory of the legists was also utilitarianism.

Later, when in the exilic and postexilic periods the Torah (Pentateuch) was created, several ancient law collections were inserted into the Torah's narrative, "tied to the prophetic tradition, with Moses as the prophet par excellence," and said to constitute commands that God revealed to his prophet Moses.[5] Then, the ethical theory justifying the qualities and conduct mandated could be said to be the Divine Command Theory. The view that the qualities and conduct mandated by the laws constituted divine *commands* was consistent with the understanding that having such qualities and exhibiting such conduct put you in accord with the moral order God had created and continually maintained. As Sarna explains this development:

> The Bible presumes that God operates by an order which man comprehends, and that a universal moral law had been decried for society.... [This means] that the same universal sovereign will that brought the world into existence continues to exert itself thereafter making absolute ... demands upon man, expressed in categorical imperatives—"thou shalt," "thou shalt not."[6]

Kaufmann's understanding is that the moral admonitions which the Torah purports to be divinely revealed commands constituted a

---

3. See Daube, *Law and Wisdom*, 57 (The difference between the law collection in Exodus and wisdom is that the rules in the law collection "are enforceable, wisdom is not enforceable"). See generally Halberstam, "Law in Biblical Israel," 20–22 ("It is probable . . . that ancient Israelite societies had some measure of a 'legal enterprise'"). See also Moore, *Judaism in the First Centuries*, 1.18 ("It must be assumed that the elders of the town or village . . . administered the law in accordance with custom and precedent, a consuetudinary law in essence older than the written law and underlying it").

4. Cf., e.g., (1) Prov 24:23–25; Exod 23:28; Deut 16:19; (2) Prov 20:23; Deut 20:13–16; and (3) Prov 22:28; Deut 19:14. See Kaufmann, *Religion*, 324; Weinfeld, "Origin of Humanism," 243; Daube, *Law and Wisdom*, 34–35.

5. See Halberstam, "Law in Biblical Israel," 22–23.

6. Sarna, *Understanding Genesis*, 17.

"transference" of the moral norms found in the wisdom tradition to the realm of prophecy. He writes:

> For the first time morality was represented as a prophetic revelation, an expression of the supreme will of God. The idea was expressed in an unparalleled legend: God revealed himself not to a visionary, a priest, or a sage, but to a whole people. Men heard the command from the mouth of God. Morality was thus transferred from the realm of wisdom to the realm of prophecy, the realm of the absolute divine command.[7]

In any case, the new morality that first appeared beginning in about the late tenth century BCE came to be crystallized in two parallel but distinct traditions: Torah and prophecy on the one hand and wisdom on the other.[8] To justify the new morality, the wisdom tradition appealed to the experience and observation that adherence to the new moral norms had beneficial consequences for the individual actor and the nation, while the tradition of Torah and prophecy appealed to the novel idea that the new moral norms constituted divine commands that had been revealed to the people at the time of the exodus from Egypt. Yet, the tradition of Torah and prophecy never abandoned the original justification for these new moral norms since the prophetic tradition consistently and repeatedly claimed that divine commands should be obeyed because obedience had beneficial consequences for the individual actor and the nation.

In this chapter, the origin and nature of the major secular law collections found in the Torah are described. Then the moral norms set forth in Decalogue are analyzed to show that they each had the greatest cooperative value and, therefore, constituted the most fundamental norms. Next, other secular laws found in the Torah's law collections are discussed to demonstrate that they, too, mandate qualities and conduct having cooperative value. Finally, it is argued that the ethical theory the Torah offers to justify the moral norms espoused in the secular law collections is best characterized as utilitarianism, not the Divine Command Theory.

---

7. Kaufmann, *Religion*, 233–34. See Barton, *Ethics in Ancient Israel*, 226 ("There are two major models for ethics attested in ancient Israelite literature: a concept of 'moral order' in the world, and a divine command theory").

8. See Kaufmann, *Religion*, 316–17. To assert that there were two distinct traditions is not meant to deny that there is a close relationship between the content of ancient Israelite law and wisdom, as discussed below.

THE SECULAR LAW COLLECTIONS

A. The Hebrew Bible's major secular law collections were incorporated into the Torah's narrative account of Israelite liberation well after their period of fixation.

In addition to the moral norms articulated in the Decalogue,[9] there are two major secular law collections in the Hebrew Bible: the Covenant Code (Exod 20:23—23:19) and the Deuteronomic Code (Deut 12—26).[10] The Covenant Code is the earliest, dated to the eighth century BCE, and is "possibly a revision or adaptation of the Code of Hammurabi."[11] The Deuteronomic Code is dated to the late seventh century BCE, close to or during the reign of King Josiah, and is thought to have grown out of "a revision and transformation of the Covenant Code."[12]

The civil and criminal laws contained in these law collections were not originally part of Israelite *religion*.[13] Although the Torah relates the myth that they were received through divine revelation after the exodus from Egypt, in reality they came from judicial precedents, customs, and popular morality, and were arrived at, like the instruction found in the Israelite wisdom tradition, through human experience and reason.[14] According to Daube, even though the Covenant Code is said to be "given by God," it lacks an "authentication" [such as "I am the Lord your God"] because it "approaches wisdom in the sense that these rules have proved themselves, have been gradually worked out by the elders, by the courts," and constitute "rational rules."[15] Similarly, he says, "If you take a little code in the book of Numbers [chapter 35] that gives the criteria by which you can distinguish accidental killing from murder . . . again we find no authentication, because this is a collection of rules that have rationally proved themselves, just like the wisdom rules and the [Covenant Code rules]."[16]

---

9. There are two versions of the Decalogue. See Exod 20:2–17; Deut 5:6–21.

10. See generally Hayes, *Introduction*, 128; de Vaux, *Ancient Israel*, 1.143–44. Although the biblical law collections are referred to as "codes," this terminology is inaccurate. See Hayes, *Introduction*, 133 (Law codes "are generally systematic and exhaustive and intended for use by courts," and the biblical law collections do not share all these characteristics); Blenkinsopp, *Wisdom and Law*, 97.

11. Halberstam, "Law in Biblical Israel," 28.

12. Halberstam, "Law in Biblical Israel," 28.

13. Daube, *Studies in Biblical Law*, 1.

14. See Falk, *Hebrew Law*, 11.

15. Daube, *Law and Wisdom*, 58.

16. Daube, *Law and Wisdom*, 58.

Blenkinsopp makes essentially the same point as Daube when he states that the "typical form of case law," such as is found in the Covenant Code, "is really a case of group experience applied to the solution of a particular problem," and, in this respect, "is analogous to [the] proverbial sayings . . . in which, as experience teaches, certain consequences are seen to flow from certain behaviours."[17] Put differently, "a good deal of what is commonly described as the religious character of Biblical law was not from the beginning inherent in that law," and the view that Hebrew law was never distinguished from religion is "something of a simplification."[18] Judges who resolved disputes were, however, likely seen to be guided by God in rendering their decisions.[19]

Initially, there probably were no written laws in ancient Israel; rather "there was, most likely, [only] a body of [oral] tradition that provided the basis for social justice," and this "oral tradition was likely a broad one, consisting of law, narrative, song, advice, and prophesy."[20] Halberstam claims that when these rules were written down, the writing down itself gave the law collections "an aura of the Sacred."[21] Alternatively, Blenkinsopp speculates that "the writing down of the laws, and especially the provision of motivation for their observance, was intended as another form of moral guidance and instruction, comparable to the collection of aphoristic material in the Book of Proverbs."[22] It is precisely because the writing down of the laws may have been intended for moral guidance and instruction that many of the biblical "laws" are actually moral admonitions, like the material found in Israelite wisdom.

17. Blenkinsopp, *Wisdom and Law*, 92.

18. Daub, *Studies in Biblical Law*, 2–3.

19. See Exod 18:13–27; Num 11:16–17. See also 2 Chr 19:5–7 (King Jehoshaphat charged the judges: "Consider what you are doing, for you judge not on behalf of man, but on behalf of [Yahweh], and He is with you when you pass judgment"); Halberstam, "Law in Biblical Israel," 22 (In resolving disputes the king "would be seen . . . as imitating or even channeling the justice of God"). See generally Levinson, "Deuteronomy," 384–85 (discussing the centralization of the courts set forth in Deut 17:8–13); de Vaux, *Ancient Israel*, 1.150–57 (discussing the king's judicial powers, judges, courts of law, and legal procedure); Eichrodt, *Theology*, 1.74–76.

20. Halberstam, "Law in Biblical Israel," 20–21.

21. Halberstam, "Law in Biblical Israel," 22.

22. Blenkinsopp, *Wisdom and Law*, 97. See generally Halberstam, "Law in Biblical Israel," 23 ("Some scholars have argued that the nature of [the biblical law collections] are entirely theoretical: educational texts that convey ideals of justice," but "Bruce Wells . . . argues that this position is too extreme"), 24 ("While some laws strongly appear to reflect actual practice, others most likely 'reflect the idiosyncratic ideals of a particular code's authors'" [quoting Wells]).

THE SECULAR LAW COLLECTIONS

Recognizing this fact, two general forms of biblical law have been distinguished: conditional or case law and absolute or apodictic law.[23] Conditional law is the usual type of law found in ancient Near Eastern legal collections and is similar in form to much of modern tort, contract, and property law. It features a characteristic "if-then" pattern—if a person does X, or if X happens, then Y will be the legal consequence—and is developed on the basis of casuistry.[24] It was this kind of law "which formed the basis for the daily administration of justice in Israel, as elsewhere in the Near East."[25] Absolute or apodictic law is an unconditional statement of prohibition or command, such as "You shall not murder." Apodictic law functions as a type of moral admonition (or instruction, such as occurs in wisdom literature) in that no penalties are imposed. Apodictic law is not found in other ancient Near Eastern legal collections.[26]

With specific reference to the Deuteronomic Code, Blenkinsopp states, "There can be no doubt . . . that [its] legal and sapiential traditions flow together."[27] He notes that the pattern of an "imperative or prohibitive accompanied by motivation" which occurs in the Decalogue "and other types of legal enactment" is typical of the type of instruction used by the Israelite sages and provides "a further indication of the link between legal and sapiential-didactic genres."[28] Similarly, Daube claims that

23. Hayes, *Introduction*, 129; Blenkinsopp, *Wisdom and Law*, 94–95. These two forms of biblical law may be usefully compared to the two distinct ways of discussing ethical issues analyzed by Jonsen and Toulmin. See Jonsen and Toulmin, *Abuse of Casuistry*, 23 ("We inherit two distinct ways of discussing ethical issues. One of these frames these issues in terms of principles, rules, and other general ideas; the other focuses on the specific features of particular kinds of moral cases").

24. See Halberstam, "Law in Biblical Israel," 30–31 ("Biblical law is primarily casuistic" and is aimed at persuading rather than commanding). See also Hayes, *What's Divine*, 32 (The casuistic formulations of laws reinforces the conception of divine law "as wise instruction rather than bald commandment").

25. Blenkinsopp, *Wisdom and Law*, 101.

26. See de Vaux, *Ancient Israel*, 1.147.

27. Blenkinsopp, *Wisdom and Law*, 118. See also Blenkinsopp, *Wisdom and Law*, 111 (Deuteronomy must have been "drafted by scribes at the Judean court educated in much the same way as those for whom the aphoristic literature in Proverbs was put together; another indication, therefore, of the close connections between the legal and sapiential-didactic traditions").

28. Blenkinsopp, *Wisdom and Law*, 32. See also Blenkinsopp, *Wisdom and Law*, 50 ("Deuteronomy abounds in the kind of moralizing and educational language associated with the sages"). See also Daube, *Law and Wisdom*, 5–9 (concluding that the use of the imperative in the Decalogue's fifth commandment is evidence that it "descends from, has its original setting in, wisdom"), 40–49 (discussing a "form of instruction" in Deuteronomy which, like the use of the imperative, is expressive of a connection with wisdom).

Deuteronomy "stands midway between legislation and a wisdom book."[29] He goes on to state:

> Deuteronomy describes its laws as wisdom: "And ye shall keep and do the statutes, for this is your wisdom (the technical term ḥokhma) and understanding in the sight of the nations" [Deut 4:6].[30] . . . I have never heard any nation say this. It could not be made clearer, however, that these laws are for Israel what wisdom is for the neighboring world. . . . No doubt in the course of translation into law the material would be considerably modified, and here and there the theology of Deuteronomy might lead to straight opposition. But this does not detract from the basic phenomenon: the dominant, determinant role of wisdom in the composition of this code.[31]

The fact that the specific qualities and conduct mandated by Israelite secular laws are the very same qualities and conduct extolled in Israelite wisdom provides substantial evidence of the close connection between Israelite secular law and wisdom. Put differently, that the secular laws mandate qualities and conduct having cooperative value is a consequence of, and reflects, that "little care was taken to expressly separate legal precedent from authoritative legislation, or from wise advice . . . [and that the] practice of law in ancient Israel was . . . to promote a moral vision that would lead to harmony within Israelite families, clans, and communities."[32]

It was only after "the period of the fixation" of the biblical law collections that the Torah was formed; when that happened the law collections were "incorporated into the Torah book as finished entities and neither edited, revised, nor stylized."[33] The people responsible for creating the To-

---

29. Daube, *Law and Wisdom*, 26–27.

30. See Blenkinsopp, *Wisdom and Law*, 86 ("*Torah* . . . [now] used for the first time not of an individual stipulation of law . . . but of a collection or corpus of laws . . . is for Israel the counterpart of the intellectual traditions, the 'wisdom,' of other nations"), 114 (In Deuteronomy the law is understood "as the peculiarly Israelite embodiment of wisdom").

31. Daube, *Law and Wisdom*, 27. See Weinfeld, "Origin of Humanism," 245 ("Deuteronomy represents the fusion of law and wisdom"), 246 (" Deuteronomy drew on or was directly influenced by wisdom literature"). See also Daube, *Law and Wisdom*, 3–25 (arguing that the fifth commandment of the Decalogue descends from wisdom and discussing the blend between legislation and instruction (or wisdom) in Deuteronomy).

32. Halberstam, "Law in Biblical Israel," 24.

33. Kaufmann, *Religion*, 172. See also Hayes, *Introduction*, 127–28 ("Later editors inserted law collections from various periods and authorships into the [biblical]

rah placed the several law collections in the Torah's narrative account of the Israelite nation "as the climax of a story of liberation, revelation, and the forging of a divine-human relationship."[34] In this narrative account, Israelite law is described as commands that God revealed to Moses and the Israelite nation at Mount Sinai (or Horeb).[35] The revelation of the law takes the form of a covenant or suzerainty treaty between an overlord and his vassal, with God envisioned as a tribal chief who rules his vassal Israel pursuant to the terms of an agreement.[36] God's relationship with Israel also takes the form of a relationship between an owner and his slaves, paralleling Akkadian deeds of liberation.[37] Israelites, as liberated slaves acquired and adopted by God, are obligated to obey God's commands.[38] Accordingly, the covenant proposed in Exod 19:4–6 specifically refers to the people's liberation from slavery by God, and states that God requires, in return, that Israel obey God and keep God's covenant.[39]

---

narrative . . . [and represented them] as having issued from [the] time of intimate contact between Yahweh and Israel at Sinai—a claim that imbued the nation's legal traditions with an air of high antiquity and conferred upon them divine sponsorship"); Blenkinsopp, *Wisdom and Law*, 94 (The Covenant Code "existed independently prior to its incorporation into the Sinai narrative").

34. See Halberstam, "Law in Biblical Israel," 28.

35. See Blenkinsopp, *Wisdom and Law*, 94 (Although the earliest collection of biblical laws, the Covenant Code, "is presented [in the Torah] as given to Moses at Sinai," it is "widely agreed" that, "since it presupposes an agrarian economy, it cannot be earlier than the settlement in Canaan").

36. Falk, *Hebrew Law*, 7 (citing Exod 6:7; 19:5; 24). Cf. Gen 17:7–8; Lev 26:12. See Bright, *History of Israel*, 150–52; Holtz, "Reading Biblical Law," 2206–7. See also Tigay, "Exodus," 136 (The covenantal relationship is "modeled on ancient royal covenants" and on "suzerainty treaties"); Hayes, *Introduction*, 118–23. See generally Hillers, *Covenant*, 25–71 (comparing the form and execution of suzerainty treaties to Exod 20 and Josh 24, which deal with the form and execution of the Sinai covenant).

37. Falk, *Hebrew Law*, 7.

38. Milgrom, *Leviticus*, 177–78 (The people of Israel are Yahweh's tenants and slaves; hence "they must obey Yahweh's laws.").

39. See also Daube, *Studies in Biblical Law*, 50–51 (God was metaphorically conceived as redeemer under Israelite social legislation, and, in accordance with such legislation, when God redeemed the Israelites from Egyptian bondage, the Israelites became God's property or slaves).

B. The most fundamental laws of Israelite society, found in the Decalogue, mandate qualities and conduct having cooperative value.

The most fundamental moral values underlying the obligations imposed by biblical secular law may be ascertained by identifying those obligations which impose the penalty of death for noncompliance. In some cases, the biblical legists not only impose the penalty of death but prescribe a particular mode of death, usually death by stoning.[40] This mode of death is significant; it constituted a ritual which carried with it "features of communal participation and religious solemnity."[41] As Greengus explains:

> Death by stoning, in the biblical tradition and elsewhere in the ancient Near East, is reserved for crimes of a special character. In those cases there is no special "executioner," for the community assembled is the mass executioner of the sentence. Offenses that entail this mode of execution must therefore in theory or in fact, "offend" the corporate community or are believed to compromise its most cherished values to the degree that the commission of the offense places the community itself in jeopardy.[42]

This notion that some offenses are so detrimental to community values (and, thus, to the well-being of the entire community) that everyone must be involved in its eradication brings to mind the priestly notion that sins adversely affect the *entire* community by polluting the sanctuary and driving Yahweh out of the sanctuary and the land.[43] In any event, when the penalty prescribed for prohibited conduct is death by stoning, it may

---

40. See de Vaux, *Ancient Israel*, 1.158–60 (discussing penalties and stating that stoning "was the normal method of execution and . . . must . . . be presumed when the text does not state it precisely").

41. Greengus, *Laws in the Bible*, 176.

42. Greengus, *Laws in the Bible*, 176. See Levinson, "Deuteronomy," 376 (Stoning was reserved for "offenses regarded as violating the community's fundamental values" and "compelled the entire community to act collectively to repudiate the offense").

43. See chapter 3, sec. B, 1, 3. In fact, some scholars contend that the phrase "you shall purge evil from your midst," which is included in every instance of death by stoning, "almost certainly belongs to the purity system" and most probably refers "to the removal of the uncleanness that attaches to the notorious sinner." Rodd, *Glimpses*, 13. See also Falk, *Hebrew Law*, 5, 58 (Certain crimes, such as murder, were specifically said to pollute the land and the community felt bound to "purge the evil from among them, lest they [all] be held collectively responsible for the sin of the individual").

be presumed that the prohibited conduct was deemed to undermine one or more of the community's most cherished values.

It is unsurprising, therefore, that biblical law provides that anyone who pronounced the name of Yahweh in blasphemy or otherwise deviated from allegiance to Yahweh was to be stoned to death.[44] Allegiance to Yahweh constituted the community's most fundamental value. Stoning those who subverted this value both removed the offending person and deterred others from similar subversive conduct. These objectives are made clear; the punishment of stoning is said to be necessary to "sweep out evil from your midst"[45] and to make certain that "all Israel will hear and be afraid, and such evil things will not be done again in your midst."[46]

Given the supreme value placed on allegiance to Yahweh, it is easily understood why persons disloyal to Yahweh were condemned to death by stoning, but other persons for whom biblical law prescribes death by stoning include a "wayward and defiant son";[47] a woman who "commits fornication while under her father's authority";[48] and a man who lies with a woman engaged to another man, together with the engaged women with whom he lies.[49] Why were these behaviors deemed to violate the Israelites' most cherished values? The answer is that the moral values these prescriptions seek to protect are the essential cooperative values of order, peace, and harmony, without which human society is imperiled.

Regarding the first two cases of death by stoning (the disobedient son and disrespectful daughter), order, peace, and harmony are compromised if children disobey, and are disrespectful of, their parents, for such children will likely become adults who neither obey nor respect any political or societal authority, much less any conventional norms of

---

44. See Deut 13:1–19; 17:2–7; Lev 20:27; 24:11–17, 23. Cf. Exod 22:19; Lev 18:21; 1 Kgs 21:8–14. See also Falk, *Hebrew Law*, 71 ("Idolatry and other forms of insurrection against the suzerainty of God were the most serious crimes").

45. Deut 13:6.

46. Deut 13:12. See Daube, *Law and Wisdom*, 30 ("Deuteronomy supplies the earliest example in world literature of . . . the deterrent purpose of punishment"), 32 (It is intended that the victim of the death penalty serve as an example deterring others).

47. Deut 21:18–21. Cf. Exod 21:15 ("He who strikes his father or his mother shall be put to death"), 17 ("He who insults his father or mother shall be put to death"); Lev 20:9 ("If anyone insults his father or his mother, he shall be put to death"); Deut 27:16 ("Cursed be he who insults his father or mother").

48. Deut 22:20–21.

49. Deut 22:23–24. Cf. Deut 22:22; Lev 18:20; 20:10.

behavior.⁵⁰ Therefore, having respect for one's parents constituted a *"sine qua non* in ancient Israel, and elsewhere."⁵¹ Indeed, all the cooperative values encouraged in the wisdom tradition are predicated upon respect for one's father and mother. Proverbs begins with the passage:

> My son, heed the discipline of your father,
> And do not forsake the instruction of your mother.⁵²

The third case of death by stoning (sexual relations between a man and a woman *engaged* to someone else, which is a form of adultery)⁵³ likewise compromises order, peace, and harmony as such relations often result in disorder, strife, and disunity.⁵⁴ Disorder, strife, and disunity are also the likely result of sexual relations between a *married* woman and a man other than her husband, and, though not explicitly punished by stoning, such relations were certainly considered a danger to fundamental cooperative values.⁵⁵ It is noteworthy that the wisdom tradition condemns illicit sexual relations specifically because such relations cause strife. Proverbs 6:32–34 could hardly be more graphic; it warns one not to sleep with

---

50. During the period of the tribal confederacy, rebellious sons and disrespectful daughters were punished by their father or by the chief of the clan, who could put them to death or sell them into slavery. It was only after the establishment of a centralized system of justice that a rebellious son or disrespectful, adulterous daughter had to be committed for trial before the local court. See Falk, *Hebrew Law*, 25, 27 (citing Gen 38:24; 42:37; Exod 21:7; Deut 21:19).

51. Milgrom, *Leviticus*, 221. See Daube, *Law and Wisdom*, 9 ("Respect of the child for the parent . . . is one of the most prominent themes—perhaps the most prominent theme—in ancient Oriental and Old Testament wisdom"), 13–15 (discussing "Deuteronomy's deep concern for the right relations within the family and the preservation of [the family's] continuity," and commenting that the rebellious son, who Deuteronomy considers "a glutton and a drunkard" [Deut 21:20], "wastes the [family's] existing substance instead of preserving and building on to it" and breaks "family ties").

52. Prov 1:8. See also Prov 6:20; 23:22. See generally Daube, *Law and Wisdom*, 3–25 (The Decalogue's fifth commandment, to honor one's parents, derives from ancient wisdom and is further evidence of the close relationship of wisdom and law).

53. See Tigay, "Exodus," 142 ("In the Bible, adultery means voluntary sexual relations between a married or engaged woman and a man other than her husband"); Schwartz, "Leviticus," 244.

54. See Rodd, *Glimpses*, 278 (Adultery "destroys marriages . . . and [poses] a threat to comfortable relations between men within the community"). Other effects of adultery, such as creating questions about parentage and property rights, also cause disorder, strife, and disunity.

55. See Deut 22:22; Lev 20:10. Cf. Deut 22:28–29. See also Exod 22:15–16. See generally Greengus, *Laws in the Bible*, 48–59; Rodd, *Glimpses*, 28–43.

someone else's wife because the "fury of the husband will be passionate" and the husband will "show no pity on his day of vengeance."

All the above-mentioned behaviors that were punished by stoning offenders to death, and which were thus viewed as egregiously compromising fundamental values (viz., disloyalty to Yahweh, disrespect for parents, and adultery), are prohibited by the Decalogue.[56] This fact supports Weinfeld's opinion that the Decalogue constitutes a "fundamental set of regulations" constituting the behaviors incumbent upon all Israelites for their very membership into Israelite society.[57] Arguably, therefore, the other behaviors prohibited by the Decalogue were also viewed as compromising fundamental values and detrimental to the well-being of society. These prohibited behaviors include bearing false witness, murder, stealing, and coveting.[58] Significantly, the first three of these behaviors subjected the wrongdoer to death, which probably meant death by stoning.[59] The fundamental values compromised by such behaviors are, again, order, peace, and harmony, and, thus, prosperity and well-being.[60]

The giving of false testimony, for example, undermines an orderly, peaceful, and harmonious society because such a society requires that disputes be resolved by means of a nonviolent procedure recognized as fair, and fairness cannot be achieved when false testimony is permitted. The giving of false testimony was especially repugnant to the biblical authors because in ancient times "the possibility of obtaining alternative, forensic evidence was limited," and so the justice system was "fatally compromised when witnesses ... committed perjury and gave false

---

56. (1) Disloyalty to Yahweh, Exod 20:3; Deut 5:7; (2) disrespect to parents, Exod 20:12; Deut 5:16 (see also Exod 21:15, 17; Lev 19:3; 20:9; Deut 27:16; Prov 30:17); (3) adultery, Exod 20:13; Deut 5:17.

57. Weinfeld, "Uniqueness of the Decalogue," 8. See Weinfeld, "Uniqueness of the Decalogue," 4, 8–11; Miller, "Place of the Decalogue," 230–31 (The Decalogue consists of "the fundamental principles"); Bright, *History of Israel*, 146 (The Decalogue "represents a central feature in the covenant that brought Israel into being as a people"). But see Rodd, *Glimpses*, 80–92. See also Hillers, *Covenant*, 50 (The Decalogue constitutes "an obvious parallel" to the stipulations of a suzerainty treaty and sets forth those acts which "are intolerable if there is to be any covenant with God, or any higher life together as his people.").

58. Exod 20:13–14; Deut 5:17–18.

59. See n40 in this chapter.

60. See Bright, *History of Israel*, 152 ("The stipulations of the Decalogue forbid such actions as would encroach upon the rights of fellow Israelites and destroy peace in the community").

testimony."[61] Under biblical law, therefore, anyone who falsely testified had to be punished without mercy. According to Deut 19:16–21:

> If a man appears against another to testify maliciously and gives false testimony against him, the two parties to the dispute shall appear before the Lord, before the priests or magistrates in authority at the time, and the magistrates shall make a thorough investigation. If the man who testified is a false witness, if he has testified falsely against his fellow, you shall do to him as he schemed to do to his fellow. Thus you will sweep out evil from your midst; others will hear and be afraid, and such evil things will not again be done in your midst. Nor must you show pity.[62]

So, one who attempted to use the judicial apparatus of the community to cause the death of another by giving false testimony had themselves to be put to death.[63]

A system of justice is also compromised if the rulings of those charged with resolving disputes are disregarded. Consequently, Deut 17:8–13 states that those who act "presumptuously" by disregarding the verdict in a case "shall die," adding: "Thus you will sweep out evil from Israel: all the people will hear and be afraid and will not act presumptuously again." Additionally, the biblical law collections establish a "professionalized local judiciary,"[64] and the judges appointed were required to "govern the people with due justice," show no partiality, and accept no bribes.[65] The expressed objective of these provisions is to have a just system of dispute resolution, and because such a system of dispute resolution is essential for order, peace, and harmony in any society, these provisions support the contention that the qualities and conduct promoted by biblical secular law are those having cooperative value. Significantly, a form of the term *tzedakah* (righteousness), used in Proverbs to commend qualities and conduct having cooperative value, is used in the Deuteronomic Code to commend the general objectives of

---

61. Greengus, *Laws in the Bible*, 274.

62. See Daube, *Studies in Biblical Law*, 110 ("The conclusion that we have before us a law ordaining literal retribution is unavoidable"). Cf. Exod 23:1–3. See generally Greengus, *Laws in the Bible*, 274–78.

63. See Daube, *Deed and Doer*, 156–57.

64. Levinson, "Deuteronomy," 383. See Blenkinsopp, *Wisdom and Law*, 116 ("State-appointed judges . . . were taking over the functions of the elders and the local head of household").

65. See Deut 16:18–20; 27:25; Exod 23:8. See generally Greengus, *Laws in the Bible*, 278–81.

the legal system. The Israelites are commanded: "Justice, justice [*tzedek*] shall you pursue, that you may thrive."[66]

The Decalogue's prohibition of "murder," which "covers murder and manslaughter,"[67] expresses the understanding "that killing outside what is permitted by law or custom is . . . 'contrary to the will and best interests of the community.'"[68] Illicit killing is contrary to the best interests of the community because it is inconsistent with the peace and stability required for the community to achieve well-being and prosperity. For this reason, the murderer must be removed from society by putting him or her to death and must be shown "no pity."[69] In the thinking of priestly authors, murder "defiles" or "pollutes" the land, and unless and until the murderer is put to death (and thus the evil or pollution swept away) all Israelite society is adversely affected.[70] The authors of the Deuteronomic Code put it this way: it is necessary to "purge Israel of the blood of the innocent" so that "it will go well with you [that is, go well with Israelite society]."[71]

The prohibition against murder provides particularly compelling evidence of the change to moral norms having cooperative value. This is because during the time of the tribal confederacy, when conduct having competitive value was more highly esteemed, killing was not condemned as a public wrong subject to punishment by recognized authorities.[72] Rather there existed a system of self-help—a system of private, tribal revenge, or "blood vengeance." The killing of any member of a clan (whether intentional, unintentional, accidental, or criminally negligent) was viewed as an attack against the entire clan, and the blood of the victim had to be avenged by the victim's kindred.[73] Such blood vengeance likely led to unrelenting family feuds, irreconcilable with an orderly, peaceful, and harmonious community. After the social and economic changes described in the first chapter led to the increasing importance of cooperative values, murder became condemned as a

---

66. Deut 16:20. Cf. chapter 1, n4 and accompanying text (quoting Hesiod).

67. Rodd, *Glimpses*, 98. See also Daube, *Deed and Doer*, 46–47 (distinguishing *ratzaḥ*—"to murder"—which implies moral condemnation, from *haragh*—"to slay").

68. Rodd, *Glimpses*, 98 (quoting Hyatt, *Exodus*, 214).

69. See Exod 21:12–13; Lev 24:21; Num 35:16–18, 30; Deut 19:11–13.

70. See Num 35:34.

71. Deut 19:13.

72. Falk, *Hebrew Law*, 72.

73. See Falk, *Hebrew Law*, 56–57.

public rather than a private wrong, and the system of blood vengeance was ended.[74] It was only then that distinctions between intentional, unintentional, accidental, and criminally negligent killing began to be made.[75] This is because such distinctions are almost irrelevant when competitive values hold sway, but become important when cooperative values are more highly esteemed.[76]

The prohibition against stealing probably included the stealing and enslavement of persons (that is, kidnapping) as well as the stealing of property.[77] Kidnapping obviously poses a serious threat to an orderly, peaceful, and harmonious society. That kidnapping was viewed as such in ancient Israel is evidenced by Deut 24:7. This law provides that a kidnapper must die in order to "sweep evil out of your midst."[78] Although specific laws pertaining to the stealing of property impose penalties of only compensatory and punitive damages, not death,[79] the prohibited behavior was, nevertheless, viewed as extremely detrimental to the well-being of society. This is evidenced by the fact that the punitive damages imposed on the thief could be severe, with one law imposing penalties of four and five times the value of the item stolen.[80] Nonlegal material

---

74. See Halberstam, "Law in Biblical Israel," 24–27. Nevertheless, after public judgment had been passed, a convicted murderer was still handed over to the kinsman of the victim for execution of the judgment, and, in certain circumstances, the kinsman could even put the murderer to death "upon encounter." See Num 35:19–21; Deut 19:11–13; Falk, *Hebrew Law*, 27.

75. See Num 35:11, 15, 22–24; Exod 21:12–14; 22:1–2. See also Daube, *Law and Wisdom*, 58 (The rules in Num 35 giving the criteria by which to distinguish accidental killing from murder are "secular rational rules" which require "no authentication," in contrast to the rule prohibiting the taking ransom from a murderer for which "authentication" is added because it is not one of the "secular rational rules"). See generally Greengus, *Laws in the Bible*, 147–83.

76. See Adkins, *Moral Values*, 13 (Where competitive activities are the most highly valued, only results matter and intentions are unimportant); Adkins, *Merit and Responsibility*, 46–47 (In a system of values like the Homeric system, based on competitive standards, "intentions are almost irrelevant").

77. See Weinfeld, "Uniqueness of the Decalogue," 2; Miller, "Place of the Decalogue," 240. See also Rodd, *Glimpses*, 94–95; b. Sanh. 86a ("Thou shalt not steal [Exod 20:13] . . . refers to the stealing of human beings").

78. Cf. Exod 21:16. See generally Greengus, *Laws in the Bible*, 183–87; Daube, *Studies in Biblical Law*, 95–96 (discussing how the law relating to theft of persons developed from originally applying only to the case where a man was stolen and sold to later including the case where a man is stolen but not, or not yet, sold).

79. See Exod 21:37—22:3. See generally Greengus, *Laws in the Bible*, 211–30; Daube, *Studies in Biblical Law*, 89–96.

80. See Exod 21:37.

suggests that penalties imposed for theft might have even been as high as seven times the value of the item stolen.[81] In addition, the victim of a potential property theft was given license to kill the would-be thief in certain circumstances.[82] Finally, relying upon 2 Sam 12:5, among other things, Daube convincingly argues that originally all kinds of theft was punishable by death.[83]

The last of the fundamental obligations in the Decalogue is the prohibition against coveting anything that belongs to your neighbor.[84] This commandment is quite different from the other commandments in the Decalogue in that it does not concern one's outward behavior but one's "inner desires."[85] According to Miller, this commandment is "a guard against an internal, private attitude or feeling that tends to erupt into public and violent acts against one's neighbor," as when David's lust for Bathsheba led to adultery and the murder of Uriel, or when Ahab's desire for Naboth's vineyard led to Jezebel's subornation of perjury and the murder of Naboth.[86] Miller further claims that this prohibition explicitly recognizes "the connection between internal feelings and external acts, between private attitudes and public deeds."[87] Miller concludes: "The point [of the prohibition against coveting] is clear. The inner attitudes and feelings potentially also have to do with the well-being and security of one's neighbor, and they are subject to a degree of control for the good of the community."[88]

If Miller is correct, then the prohibition against coveting clearly has cooperative value; it maintains a just, peaceful, and harmonious society by guarding against "public and violent acts against one's neighbor." But this commandment cannot be humanly enforced. There are not, and cannot be, laws with humanly enforced punishments for coveting since "no law can legislate for mental attitudes or could be enforced in the

---

81. See Prov 6:30–31.

82. See Exod 22:1. See also Greengus, *Laws in the Bible*, 215–18.

83. Daube, *Studies in Biblical Law*, 94n30.

84. See generally Rodd, *Glimpses*, 94–98, 104–8.

85. Rodd, *Glimpses*, 94. See also Rodd, *Glimpses*, 94–97 (Rejecting arguments that the Hebrew word translated as "covet" includes "both the plotting to obtain what was coveted and its actual seizure").

86. Miller, "Place of the Decalogue," 241 (relying on 2 Sam 11 and 1 Kgs 21).

87. Miller, "Place of the Decalogue," 242.

88. Miller, "Place of the Decalogue," 242.

courts."[89] Of course, since all the commandments are subject to divine enforcement, and since it was believed to be possible for God to know one's inner desires,[90] infractions of the prohibition against coveting could be punished by God. The prohibition against coveting is, therefore, of fundamental importance not only because of its cooperative value in preventing murder, adultery, and theft, but because of its related insight that divine punishment follows upon evil desires and intentions, not just evil actions. In addition, the recognition that divine punishment exists for evil thoughts that could not possibly be known by human courts heightened awareness that divine punishment exists for evil actions that *could* be known by human courts but which go unnoticed or otherwise escape human punishment.[91] One is reminded of the claim made by the Athenian politician Critias (460–403 BCE) that some "shrewd man," seeing that the law established by men, though preventing sinners from deeds of "open violence," did not prevent sinners from committing evil deeds "in secret," invented the "fear of Gods" in order to "frighten sinners should they sin ... secretly in deed, or word, or thought."[92]

In sum, the qualities and conduct encouraged by the Decalogue were those qualities and conduct having cooperative value.[93] So, by the time the Decalogue was formulated, qualities and conduct having cooperative value were recognized as essential for an orderly, peaceful, harmonious, and prosperous society—that is, essential for the well-being of Israelite society and all Israelites. And the specific qualities and conduct required by the Decalogue (to respect your parents, not to pervert justice by giving false testimony, not to murder, not to steal, not to commit adultery, and not to covet your neighbor's wife or property) were considered

---

89. Rodd, *Glimpses*, 94.

90. See Johnson, *Vitality*, 84 ("Yahweh is primarily concerned, not with a man's outward appearance, but with his heart.... In fact it is He alone who knows the heart of man for what it really is"); Jer 17:10 (God probes the heart to repay everyone according to their true intentions); 1 Sam 16:7 ("The Lord sees into the heart").

91. See Milgrom, *Leviticus*, 228 (Although furtive crimes "escape the notice of authorities, they are known by God, who will exact retribution from the offender"), 229, 244 (Even if the blind, deaf, and aged cannot enforce the dignity they merit, "God will punish those who deny it").

92. Critias, *Sisyphus*, fragment 25 (preserved in the works of Sextus Empiricus).

93. See Levinson, "Deuteronomy," 355 ("The intent [of the Decalogue] is to transform society by creating a moral community" where there is "active respect for the integrity of the neighbor"). See also Eichrodt, *Theology*, 1.76 ("The [Decalogue's] prohibition of murder, adultery and theft, and the inculcation of respect for parents, comprise ... the elementary bases of communal human life.").

those qualities and conduct that were *most* essential for the Israelites' well-being. However, as discussed in the next two sections of this chapter, the other provisions of biblical secular law are no less associated with the advancement of qualities and conduct having cooperative value.[94]

C. Secular laws required that the disadvantaged members of Israelite society, including debtors, widows, orphans, and resident aliens, be protected from oppression and helped to survive.

Being in debt in ancient times could lead to the enslavement of the debtor and/or members of the debtor's family. As Greengus explains:

> In ancient times when a person borrowed money, the debt obligation fell not only upon the borrower and his worldly goods but also upon the members of his family. In the absence of sufficient assets, the debtor or members of his family could be taken into debt slavery in order to repay the obligation through their labor.[95]

People desirous of fostering a peaceful, orderly, and harmonious society, and of advancing the well-being of all the members of society, would naturally wish to establish more equitable economic conditions in which strong and wealthy people were prevented from oppressing and enslaving those who were weak and impoverished. Thus, in early Israel "there is a deliberate rejection of the rigid order [existing elsewhere in Syria and Palestine] that oppressed the poor to maintain an elite, and this rejection, we may assume, is nourished on the one hand by the history of state-slavery in Egypt and wilderness wandering, and on the other hand by the history of oppression remembered by those Canaanite serfs who came to be numbered among the Israelites."[96]

The laws of the Holiness Code, discussed in the next chapter, if put into effect, might have provided some measure of relief for the debtors in Israelite society but did not prevent an Israelite and/or a member of

---

94. See generally Milgrom, *Leviticus*, 2 ("A case can be mounted that all of the Torah's codes are compilations of traditions comprising interpretations and applications of Mosaic principles").

95. Greengus, *Laws in the Bible*, 86. See also Falk, *Hebrew Law*, 93–97 (The debtor could be seized by the creditor and made to pay his debt by laboring for him, and the debtor's dependents "could be surrendered by the debtor in the same way as goods").

96. Hillers, *Covenant*, 80 (citing Song of Hannah, 1 Sam 2:4–8).

his family from becoming the debt slave of another Israelite. In 2 Kings, for example, the wife of one of Elisha's disciples cried out to him that her husband was dead and that a creditor was coming to seize her two children "as [debt] slaves."[97] To help such people, laws in the Covenant Code and the Deuteronomic Code limit the duration of servitude for debt slaves to no more than six years.[98]

According to these provisions, in the seventh year the debt slave had to be released "without payment."[99] Furthermore, the debt slave was not to be released "empty-handed" but had to be "furnished" out of the creditor's "flock, threshing floor, and vat."[100] No judicial sanctions are specified for those who failed to comply with the law's requirements to release debt slaves, remit their debts, and furnish those released with supplies, but Israelites are told that they should not "feel aggrieved" when they set debt salves free because compliance is rewarded by Yahweh—Yahweh "will bless you in all you do."[101] This language demonstrates that the underlying justification for the manumission of debt slaves, and, in general, for possessing qualities and adhering to conduct having cooperative value, is individual and/or collective self-interest. The creditor who releases a debt slave in the seventh year is promised a reward from Yahweh—if not a direct reward, then an indirect one, obtained as a result of the benefit that would accrue to Israelite society collectively. A further motivation for a creditor to release a debt slave was the honor that the community would bestow on the creditor for compliance with the law and the shame the creditor would experience for noncompliance.

Another mechanism the law establishes for the relief of debt slaves is the *shemitah*, which is like the jubilee (*yovel*) except that the *shemitah* occurs every seven years. The law states:

> Every seventh year you shall practice remission of debts. This shall be the nature of the remission: every creditor shall remit the due that he claims from his fellow; he shall not dun [demand money from] his fellow or kinsman, for the remission

---

97. 2 Kgs 4:1. See also Prov 22:7.

98. Deut 15:12; Exod 21:2–4. See generally Greengus, *Laws in the Bible*, 86–112; Levinson, "Deuteronomy," 379–80.

99. Exod 21: 2. See Deut 15:1–3 (In the seventh year "you shall practice remission of debts").

100. Deut 15:13.

101. Deut 15:18.

proclaimed is of the Lord. You may dun the foreigner; but you must remit whatever is due you from your kinsman.[102]

That the law forbids pressing your kinsman for payment of a debt owed, but not a foreigner, is significant. It shows that the aim of the law is the establishment of a peaceful, orderly, and harmonious *Israelite* society. Relations with an outsider need not be as harmonious as relations with a kinsman. As Levinson puts it: "By providing specific mechanisms to eliminate poverty and financial inequality every seven years, Deut. seeks to prevent economic injustice from becoming entrenched in [Israelite] society."[103]

It was, of course, immediately seen that creditors would be unwilling to extend credit as the *shemitah* approached, knowing that the loan would soon have to be remitted. Therefore, the law states that you must never "harden your heart and shut your hand against your needy kinsman"; rather, you "must [always] open your hand and lend sufficient for whatever he needs."[104] There follows a specific warning against the failure to lend when the *shemitah* approaches: "Beware lest you harbor the base thought, 'The seventh year, the year of remission, is approaching,' so that you are mean to your needy kinsman and give him nothing."[105] Understandably, there are no judicial sanctions imposed for failing to lend as the *shemitah* approached; reliance is placed on divine enforcement. If you fail to lend, the needy kinsman "will cry out to the Lord against you, and you will incur guilt. Give to him readily and have no regrets when you do so, for in return the Lord your God will bless you in all your efforts and in all your undertakings."[106] So, the motivation to obey the law, and to lend to needy kinsmen, is self-interest.

The law does not stop there. There are also laws against usury. The laws against usury, like the laws requiring the remittance of debt, distinguish between Israelites and non-Israelites. The law prohibits the taking of interest from fellow Israelites (especially from the poor) but permits

---

102. Deut 15:1–3. See Greengus, *Laws in the Bible*, 102 (suggesting that the *shemitah* and the jubilee "were constructions based upon social ideals of justice, but not necessarily realized or realizable in actuality"); Levinson, "Deuteronomy," 379 (This "blueprint for social justice is highly idealistic"); Weinfeld, *Social Justice*, 11, 177 (During the monarchial period, the laws of *shemitah* and *yovel* "remained utopian").

103. Levinson, "Deuteronomy," 379.

104. Deut 15:7–8.

105. Deut 15:9.

106. Deut 15:9–10.

Israelites to take interest from non-Israelites.[107] Again, there is only divine enforcement of the usury law.[108] Moreover, Israelites are restricted in the type of item that may secure the creditor's loan, and the creditor may hold security for only a very limited time.[109] To enforce the restriction on the holding of a security, the law asks the creditor to sympathize with, and to have compassion for, the desperate situation of the borrower.[110] Not content to rely solely on human sympathy, the law threatens divine intervention as well. The Covenant Code commands:

> If you lend money to My people, to the poor among you, do not act toward them as a creditor; exact no interest from them. If you take your neighbor's garment as a pledge, you must return it to him before the sun sets; it is his only clothing, the sole covering of his skin. In what else shall he sleep? Therefore, if he cries out to Me, I will pay heed, for I am compassionate.[111]

A peaceful, orderly, and harmonious society requires that, in addition to impoverished debtors, other disadvantaged people be protected from oppression and injustice. And so biblical law frequently admonishes the protection of widows, orphans, and resident aliens. Like the restriction on holding the borrower's garment overnight, laws protecting other disadvantaged members of Israelite society urge sympathy for them but also threaten divine punishment for noncompliance. For example, the Covenant Code commands:

> You shall not wrong a stranger or oppress him, for you were strangers in the land of Egypt. You shall not ill-treat any widow or orphan. If you do mistreat them, I will heed their outcry as soon as they cry out to Me, and My anger shall blaze forth and

---

107. Exod 22:24; Deut 23:20–21; Lev 25:36–37. See Falk, *Hebrew Law*, 93 ("Hebrew law recognized the lending of money . . . as a kind of charity toward kinsmen rather than as a form of investment bearing interest").

108. Greengus, *Laws in the Bible*, 103 ("Its reward or punishment came from Heaven, not from the courts"). See Deut 23:21 ("Do not deduct interest from loans to your countrymen, so that the Lord your God may bless you in all your undertakings"). Cf. Prov 28:8.

109. See Deut 24:6, 10–13, 17–18; Exod 22:25–26. See also Greengus, *Laws in the Bible*, 102–6.

110. David Hume claims that sympathy, not self-interest, is the foundation of morality. See Hume, *Principles of Morals*, sec. 5, part 1, 40–46.

111. Exod 22:24–26.

I will put you to the sword, and your own wives shall become widows and your children orphans.[112]

Relying once again on both sympathy and self-interest for motivation, the disadvantaged are also protected by the commandment to pay a laborer's wages immediately and not to hold the wages overnight, "for [the laborer] is poor and urgently depends upon [the wages], else he will cry against you to the Lord, and you will incur sin."[113] Finally, the disadvantaged are protected by the commandments requiring landowners to leave something in their fields at harvest time and during the sabbatical year for the less fortunate to take.[114]

D. Most of the remaining secular laws also promote qualities and conduct having cooperative value.

There do exist certain laws which do not readily appear to promote qualities and conduct having cooperative value. These include laws prohibiting homosexuality and bestiality under pain of death, and laws prohibiting certain intergenerational unions.[115] It is probable, however, that the concerns underlying these laws are related to ritual purity, not to any strictly moral concern.[116] For the most part, moral laws all promote conduct and qualities having cooperative value. Some, such as

---

112. Exod 22:20–23. See also Exod 23:9; Lev 19:33–34; Deut 5:12–15; 10:17–19; 15:12; 24:17–22; 27:19. See generally Levinson, "Deuteronomy," 355 (The Decalogue "employs a singular form of 'you,' rather than the expected plural form, to stress that God directly addresses each former slave as an individual human being"), 370 (Punishments and rewards "are predominately addressed to a plural 'you,' stressing communal rather than individual responsibility").

113. Deut 24:14–15. See also Lev 19:13. See generally Falk, *Hebrew Law*, 99–100.

114. See Deut 24:19–22; Lev 19:9–10; 23:22; Exod 23:11. Concern for the poor is also evidenced in the sacrificial system which allowed for a cereal offering to be made by those who were too poor to afford the required burnt offerings of an entire animal (Lev 1:10) or of birds (Lev 1:14). See Lev 2:1–14; Milgrom. *Leviticus*, 16, 23, 25–26, 224 ("YHWH is the protector of the defenseless, and only those who follow his lead can achieve holiness.").

115. See Exod 22:18; Lev 18:12–14, 22–23; 20:13, 15–16; Deut 27:21. See generally Greengus, *Laws in the Bible*, 26–28, 80–85.

116. See Milgrom, *Leviticus*, 196–97 (The concern with homosexuality is the spilling of the life force); Schwartz, "Leviticus," 239 (The Holiness Code "views certain sexual acts that are not potentially procreative as aberrant"). Other laws unrelated to strictly moral concerns include Lev 19:19 and Deut 22:9 (attempting to maintain boundaries established by God in the created order).

laws against rape, clearly seem to promote the peace, order, and harmony required to achieve common goals of prosperity and well-being.[117] Also clearly promoting peace, order, and harmony are laws requiring that if one sees their neighbor's ox, sheep, or ass gone astray, they take the animal back;[118] laws prohibiting the use of false weights;[119] and laws prohibiting the spreading of false rumors.[120]

Many of the secular laws, however, are comparable to modern-day tort, contract, and property law in that they promote peace, order, and harmony by providing rules and mechanisms to resolve disputes fairly, including providing that reasonable compensation be paid to persons damaged by another's negligence. So, for example, the Covenant Code contains rules and mechanisms to resolve disputes that arise among herders, or between herders and farmers. If a herder, through indifference or negligence, allowed his livestock to graze on a farmer's field or vineyard and the land was "grazed bare," the herder was required to "make restitution for the impairment of that field or vineyard."[121] If a herder hired a laborer to herd his animals and one of the animals died, was injured, or was "carried off" by force of arms with no witnesses, then, if the hired laborer swore "an oath before the Lord" that he was not responsible for what happened, the laborer was not required to make restitution; nor was restitution required if the animal was torn apart by wild beasts and the damaged or dead animal was produced; but, if the animal was stolen while in the custody of the laborer, the custodian was deemed to have been negligent and was required to make restitution.[122]

In addition to disputes arising from overgrazing or custodial negligence, there were also disputes arising when animal owners failed to protect others from damage caused by dangerous livestock. Rules addressing these disputes are set forth in Exod 21:29–36:

> When an ox gores a man or woman to death, the ox shall be stoned and its flesh shall not be eaten, but the owner of the ox

---

117. In the case of rape, the harm was not necessarily viewed as the physical assault against the woman attacked but the damage to her male relatives. See Rodd, *Glimpses*, 263–69. See generally Greengus, *Laws in the Bible*, 60–69.

118. See Deut 22:1–3. Cf. Exod 23:4. See Greengus, *Laws in the Bible*, 232–35.

119. See Deut 25:13–15.

120. See Exod 23:1.

121. Exod 22:4. See generally Greengus, *Laws in the Bible*, 247–51.

122. Exod 22:9–12. See Greengus, *Laws in the Bible*, 193–99, 218–19; Falk, *Hebrew Law*, 100. On the swearing of oaths, see Falk, *Hebrew Law*, 50–52.

is not to be punished. If, however, that ox has been in the habit of goring, and its owner, though warned, has failed to guard it, and it kills a man or a woman—the ox shall be stoned and its owner, too, shall be put to death. . . . So, too, if it gores a minor, male or female, [the owner] shall be dealt with according to the same rule. But if the ox gores a slave, male or female, he shall pay thirty shekels of silver to the master, and the ox shall be stoned. . . . When a man's ox injures his neighbor's ox and it dies, they shall sell the live ox and divide its price; they shall also divide the dead animal. If, however, it is known that the ox was in the habit of goring, and its owner failed to guard against it, he must restore ox for ox, but shall keep the dead animal.[123]

E. The ethical theory that best characterizes the way in which the legists justified the qualities and conduct mandated by the secular law collections is utilitarianism.

Motive clauses in many of the biblical secular laws show that the qualities and conduct mandated were justified, in the eyes of their authors, on the basis of their beneficial consequences.[124] A justification based on beneficial consequences shows that the authors held a teleological (or consequentialist) ethical theory. In certain instances, the advantageous consequences were realized by an individual actor, showing that the type of teleological ethical theory held by the author was ethical egoism. But more often, the advantageous consequences were realized by the entire community, showing that the author accepted the type of teleological ethical theory called utilitarianism.

The fifth commandment of the Decalogue is a clear instance of a motive clause evidencing a utilitarian justification of the conduct prescribed. As it appears in Exodus, the fifth commandment directs the Israelites: "Honor your father and your mother, that you may long endure on the land that the Lord your God is assigning to you."[125] Commenting on the motive clause—*that you may long endure on the land*—Tigay states:

---

123. See Greengus, *Laws in the Bible*, 172–79, 231–32; Falk, *Hebrew Law*, 76, 116; Rodd, *Glimpses*, 220; Greenberg, "Some Postulates," 24–25 (explaining why an ox that kills a human must be put to death and its flesh not eaten).

124. See also Halberstam, "Biblical Law," 31–32.

125. Exod 20:12.

> This does not refer to personal longevity. Ancient Near Eastern legal documents make children's right to inherit their parents' property contingent on honoring them by providing and caring for them. Here God applies this condition on a national scale: the right of future generations of Israelites to inherit the land of Israel from their parents is contingent on honoring them.[126]

In other words, it was believed that the conduct involved in honoring one's parents—providing and caring for them—was justified because, as a consequence of acting in this way, the nation would long endure on the land. The relationship between the act—Israelites honoring their parents—and the occurrence—Israelites long enduring on the land—is the same type of act-occurrence relationship underlying the instructions given in Proverbs,[127] and the underlying ethical theory justifying the act is also the same—utilitarianism.

The authors of the deuteronomic version of the fifth commandment expanded on the wording in Exodus, writing: "Honor your father and your mother, as the Lord your God has commanded you, that you may long endure, *and that you may fare well*, in the land that the Lord your God is assigning to you."[128] Apparently, the authors of the expanded version believed that a beneficial consequence of honoring parents was, in addition to the nation enduring on the land, the nation faring well, that is, achieving material well-being. According to Daube, the language of this motive clause is evidence of the commandment's connection with wisdom because it "promises a reward," and this, he says, "is typical of wisdom."[129] Daube adds that "wisdom is keen on precisely this kind of reward: long life and . . . well-being."[130] According to Levinson, the "motivational phrase" contained in the fifth commandment "is typical" of the book of Deuteronomy's "exhortations to obedience."[131] These exhortations repeatedly, frequently, and adamantly proclaim that obedience brings "life" (prosperity and well-being), while disobedience brings "death" (disaster and utter destruction).

The emphasis on the beneficial consequences of the secular laws contained in some of their motive clauses is also found in the narrative

---

126. Tigay, "Exodus," 142.
127. See chapter 1, sec. C, 4.
128. Deut 5:16 (emphasis added).
129. Daube, *Law and Wisdom*, 10.
130. Daube, *Law and Wisdom*, 10.
131. Levinson, "Deuteronomy," 359 (citing Deut 4:40; 5:26; 6:3, 18; 12:25, 28; 22:7).

setting in which the secular law collections were placed, showing a continuing utilitarian justification was maintained by the redactors of the Torah and its component parts. In the deuteronomic account of the giving of the law at Mount Sinai/Horeb, for example, after God speaks the words of the Decalogue to the whole congregation, the tribal heads and elders ask that the people no longer be required to hear the voice of the Lord. They tell Moses: "You go closer and hear all that the Lord our God says, and then you tell us everything that the Lord our God tells you, and we will willingly do it."[132] Yahweh is pleased with the people's willingness to obey, and Moses tells the people that the Lord said:

> May they always be of such a mind, to revere Me and follow all My commandments, *that it may go well with them and with their children forever!* Go, say to them, "Return to your tents." But you remain here with Me, and I will give you the whole instruction—the laws and the rules—that you shall impart to them, for them to observe in the land that I am giving them to possess.[133]

Then Moses cautions the people:

> Be careful, then, to do as the Lord your God has commanded you. Do not turn aside to the right or to the left: follow only the path that the Lord your God has enjoined upon you, *so that you may thrive and that it may go well with you, and that you may long endure in the land you are to possess.*[134]

Similar promises of well-being for obedience to God's law and threats of complete destruction for disobedience repeatedly appear throughout the book of Deuteronomy.[135] Because chapter 28 of Deuteronomy (like chapter 26 of Leviticus)[136] functions "in the same way as do the blessings and curses in [suzerainty] treaties, to encourage [national] obedience to a code of behavior which has just been set forth,"[137] its

---

132. Deut 5:24.
133. Deut 5:25–28 (emphasis added).
134. Deut 5:29–30 (emphasis added).
135. Deut 4:40; 5:16; 6:3, 14–15, 18–19; 7:9–15; 8:1; 11:8–9, 13–17, 22–26; 12:28; 28:1–68; 30:1–20.
136. See chapter 3, sec. B, 6.
137. Hillers *Covenant*, 54. See Hillers, *Covenant*, 136–37; Levinson, "Deuteronomy," 406, 408.

promises of national well-being for obedience and threats of complete national destruction for disobedience are extensive.[138]

Less extensive promises are found in chapter 7 which states that obedience results in an abundance of food and in good health:

> And if you obey these rules and observe them carefully, the Lord ... will bless the issue of your womb and the produce of your soil, your new grain and wine and oil, the calving of your herd and lambing of your flock.... The Lord will ward off from you all sickness; He will not bring upon you any of the dreadful diseases of Egypt.[139]

Similarly succinct is chapter 11, which clearly links obedience to prosperity and material well-being:

> If, then, you obey the commandments ... I will grant the rain for your land in season, the early rain and the late. You shall gather your new grain and wine and oil—I will also provide grass in the fields for your cattle—and thus you shall eat your full.[140]

Perhaps most succinct is chapter 30:

> I set before you this day, life and prosperity, death and adversity ... life and death, blessing and curse. Choose life ... by loving the Lord your God, heeding His commands, and holding fast to Him.[141]

Of course, after the law collections were incorporated into a narrative account of Israelite liberation and claimed to be the commandments of God, some may have believed that the laws were to be obeyed simply because they were commanded by God, *regardless of consequences*. But this is never explicitly stated in the narrative accounts of the giving of the law, and it seems unlikely to have been the dominant point of view of the Torah's redactors.[142]

---

138. See also Daube, *Law and Wisdom*, 30–31.
139. Deut 7:12–15.
140. Deut 11:13–17.
141. Deut 30:15–20.
142. See chapter 5, sec. A.

CHAPTER 3

The priestly law collections associated qualities and conduct having cooperative value with the holiness Yahweh demanded from the Israelites.

THE BIBLE'S CULTIC LAWS are found mainly in Leviticus and in parts of Numbers.[1] In Leviticus, scholars distinguish between two traditions referred to as "P" and "H." P, a designation for "priestly material," includes chapters 1 to 16. These chapters deal with laws of sacrifice and ritual purity. More specifically, chapters 1 to 7 detail the sacrificial system (including burnt offerings, cereal offerings, well-being offerings, purification offerings, and reparation offerings); chapters 8 to 10 describe the installation of Aaron and his line as priests, as well as the priestly sacrificial duties; chapters 11 to 15 contain the dietary laws and laws of ritual purity and impurity; and chapter 16 prescribes the ritual for Yom Kippur (the Day of Atonement).[2] H, a designation for "Holiness Code," consists of chapters 17 to 26.[3] The Holiness Code was likely compiled during the Babylonian exile, but is based on oral and written priestly

---

1. Hayes, *Introduction*, 148. See generally Hayes, *Introduction*, 148–64; Blenkinsopp, *Wisdom and Law*, 120–29 (discussing the origin and development of the priestly narrative and law designated as P).
2. Hayes, *Introduction*, 148; Blenkinsopp, *Wisdom and Law*, 129–30.
3. See Blenkinsopp, *Wisdom and Law*, 130–32 (discussing the Holiness Code).

teachings going back to the late eighth century BCE.[4] It is the portion of Leviticus most relevant for present purposes.

The ethical teaching of the priestly tradition centers around the concept of holiness.[5] The Israelite nation is admonished to be holy and told that, if it were holy, it would prosper, but if a sufficient number of individuals in the nation were unholy, the entire nation would be exiled from the land. In other words, the priestly materials emphasize the idea of collective responsibility, teaching that the wickedness of certain individuals adversely affected *everybody*. Accordingly, before turning to the priestly materials themselves, a brief history of collective responsibility in ancient Israel is offered. Then, after the ethical components of priestly materials are discussed (viz., the moral norms advanced and the ethical theory used to justify those norms), the importance of Ps 37 is mentioned. This psalm accepted the priestly view that unholiness resulted in exile from the land, but rejected the priestly idea that the conduct of the wicked affected the well-being of the righteous, and is evidence of individualism that increasingly developed throughout the Second Temple period.

A. In ancient Israel there was collective and intergenerational responsibility.

The Hebrew patriarchal society, as other primitive societies, was based on the idea of collective or communal responsibility.[6] The entire community was held collectively responsible for the conduct of any one of its individual members. Moral responsibility was seen to be collective because members of the various households saw themselves as acting

---

4. See Halberstam, "Law in Biblical Israel," 28; Milgrom, *Leviticus*, 175. See also Hayes, *Introduction*, 148 (Although the priestly materials "reached their final form in the exilic and post-exilic periods, they preserve older cultic and priestly traditions"). But see Klawans, *Impurity and Sin*, 22 (assuming both P and H "stem from the pre-exilic period").

5. See Blenkinsopp, *Wisdom and Law*, 130–31 ("The demand that the people be holy in conformity with the holiness of their God occurs for the first time at the beginning and end of the [section of H comprised of Leviticus chapters 19 and 20] . . . a self-contained unit which could more properly be called the Holiness Code than the larger composition to which that title is generally applied").

6. Falk, *Hebrew Law*, 67. See Greengus, *Laws in the Bible*, 182–83 (providing examples of ancient Near Eastern use of the principle of community responsibility, including Hammurabi Laws §§23–24). See generally Daube, *Studies in Biblical Law*, 155–60 (distinguishing communal responsibility from communal merit).

as part of the household rather than as separate agents.[7] The idea of collective and intergenerational responsibility underlies the account of the execution of Achan together with his sons and daughters for the misdeed of Achan alone.[8] Collective responsibility may also be seen in certain ancient practices mentioned by Falk, including blood vengeance (where the blood of a slain person had to be avenged by his kindred).[9]

The works of biblical wisdom, however, which are even "more ancient than the morality of Torah and prophets," are said Kaufmann to deal largely with individual responsibility, and, he says, by the time that the morality of the biblical wisdom tradition was transferred to the prophetic tradition "the cultural environment of Israel had long since passed the stage of collective morality."[10] Conformity to the principle of individual responsibility is attributed to King Amaziah of Judah (r. 798–769 BCE) who killed those of his servants who had slain his father, King Jehoash, "but did not put to death the children of the assassins in accordance with what is written in the Book of the Teaching of Moses."[11]

Despite a new emphasis on individual responsibility, the concept of collective responsibility did not disappear; rather, individual responsibility and collective responsibility coexisted.[12] According to Kaufmann,[13] although a man is requited for his own deeds, he is not conceived to be an isolated entity, but, rather, is conceived to be inextricably bound up with his family, tribe, people, city, and land. And since his life extends in effect beyond his own person, the scope of his reward and punishment

---

7. See Barton, *Ethics in Ancient Israel*, 54 (Biblical scholars have "argued that in ancient Israel ... people did not distinguish the individual from the group," and moral responsibility "was assigned to the community as a whole ... because the idea of individual responsibility had not yet arrived").

8. Judg 7. See also 1 Sam 22:19. But see Greenberg, "Some Postulates," 31 (arguing that the death of Achan's household was not a matter of "vicarious or collective punishment pure and simple, but a case of collective contagion of a taboo status," incurred because Achan stored the misappropriated devoted objects in his tent).

9. Falk, *Hebrew Law*, 24–25.

10. Kaufmann, *Religion*, 234. See also Eichrodt, *Theology*, 1.78, n3 (arguing that "it seems certain that in the Book of the Covenant ... the principle had already been firmly established, that children are not to be punished in place of their parents" even though the principle "is not found in so many words until Deut 24:16").

11. 2 Kgs 14:5–6 (referring to the language of Deut 24:16).

12. Daube provides two examples evidencing the transition from the communal responsibility of the household to the individual responsibility of the offender alone. See Daube, *Studies in Biblical Law*, 211–14, 235–45.

13. Kaufmann, *Religion*, 330–31.

may also extend beyond his own person. Thus, although various laws of the Torah reflect the concept of individual requital, a belief in collective retribution and in collective responsibility, especially between members of the same family, endured, and "the collective responsibility of the family before God remained fundamental."[14] Moreover, "The people of Israel constitute[d] a special sphere of collective responsibility. The basis of this responsibility is not natural, like that of the family or tribe, but artificial; it is the covenant that God made with the people. . . . Every sin committed by part of the people is counted against Israel and [explained] the fate of the entire people."[15]

Falk similarly states that even though biblical law established individual liability of every member of the nation, it still preserved various remnants of the ancient system of collective responsibility, as when in Deut 21:1–9 the elders of a village near which a man had been murdered were held "collectively responsible to the divine overlord" for the murder.[16] Collective responsibility attached to the community closest to the area where the crime occurred when the identity of the criminal was not known. In this situation, the elders of the relevant town had to perform an expiatory ritual which involved breaking the neck of a heifer. The death of the heifer, in effect, atoned for the spilt blood of the murder victim which violated one of Yahweh's most important commands—to reject death and choose life.[17] It therefore appears that the expiatory ritual performed by the elders was akin to the purification ritual typically performed by the priests at the Temple.[18]

Falk agrees with Kaufmann that, although "ordinary law" may have, to a great extent, moved beyond the notion of collective responsibility, "divine retribution was still imposed upon the community as a whole."[19] The belief in the collective and intergenerational responsibility of Israel before God is clearly stated at various places in the Torah, including in

14. Kaufmann, *Religion*, 330–31.

15. Kaufmann, *Religion*, 331.

16. Falk, *Hebrew Law*, 67. See also Barton, *Ethics in Ancient Israel*, 55 ("Throughout the Old Testament, both individual and corporate responsibility for sin can be encountered").

17. See Greengus, *Laws in the Bible*, 179–83; Milgrom, *Leviticus*, 13.

18. See Milgrom, *Leviticus*, 15–16, 31–32, 69. See also Greengus, *Laws in the Bible*, 181 (Nahmanides describes the ritual performed by the elders "as a kind of sacrifice . . . and relates it to two others, which likewise take place away from any temple or shrine; their common function is expiation").

19. Falk, *Hebrew Law*, 6.

the Decalogue of Exod 20, where it is famously stated that God visits "the guilt of the parent upon the children, upon the third and upon the fourth generations of those who reject Me, but showing kindness to a thousandth generation of those who love Me and keep My commandments."[20]

The collective responsibility of the nation to adhere to the commandments is related to the terms of the covenantal relationship, which takes the form of a suzerainty treaty, obligating God (the overlord) to give Israel (the vassals) the land of Canaan as an everlasting possession only if Israel obeyed God's law. As Falk describes it:

> Israel's vassalage made any individual trespass against the Law an act of rebellion, for the person concerned might in this way cause the annulment of the divine promises and the basis of Israel's existence. It was therefore the responsibility of the whole community to prevent such an act or to exclude the offenders from its midst.[21]

If offenders did not atone for their sins or were not excluded from the community, the land would become polluted. For priestly sources, it is the pollution of the land that matters. If the cause of the pollution were not remedied, the nation would be banished from the land. The land would "spew out" the Israelites as it had previously "spewed out" the Canaanites for their defilement of the land.[22] Responsibility thus fell on the children of the guilty to purge the pollution caused by the sins of their parents.[23]

Complaints against collective responsibility may be found.[24] These include Abraham's protest against the innocent of Sodom and Gomorrah being wiped out together with the guilty[25] and the protest of Moses and Aaron against God's announced intention to wipe out the whole people for Korah's revolt.[26] Ultimately, Deut 24:16 restricted punishment to the

20. Exod 20:5–6. See also Exod 34:6–7; Num 14:18; Lev 26:39; Deut 5:9–10; Lam 5:7.

21. Falk, *Hebrew Law*, 7. Cf. Falk, *Hebrew Law*, 24 (In seminomadic society, the failure of a tribal chief to extradite a member of his clan who has injured an outsider, or to punish him to the satisfaction of the plaintiff clan, gave rise to war against his whole clan).

22. See Lev 18:24–30. Cf. Prov 2:20–22 ("The wicked will vanish from the land").

23. Milgrom, *Leviticus*, 177.

24. Kaufmann, *Religion*, 331.

25. Gen 18:22–32.

26. Num 16:19–23. See Daube, *Studies in Biblical Law*, 155–56 (distinguishing the protest of Moses and Aaron, claiming that communal responsibility should be replaced

responsible individual in civil and criminal law, but "collective responsibility for wrongdoing [continued to operate] in the realm of offenses against God" until the time of the prophet Ezekiel, if not longer.[27]

B. The cultic code required that all Israelites be holy (i.e., possess qualities and do acts having cooperative value) in order for Israel is to receive the providence and protection of Yahweh.

Although Leviticus primarily concerns cultic regulations, it is also "replete with ethics."[28] The details of the cultic regulations are well addressed in Milgrom's *Leviticus* and, for the most part, will not be described here. Important for present purposes, however, are the cultic regulations concerning purification and reparation offerings. After the ethical ideas underlying these regulations are described, the moral norms advanced in the Holiness Code and the ethical theory used in the Holiness Code to justify these norms are discussed.

1. The purification offerings prove that every individual's conduct was believed to impact the well-being of the whole nation.

In discussing the purification offerings, Milgrom builds upon an understanding of biblical religion advanced by Kaufmann. Kaufmann had argued that the religion of Israel was radically different than pagan religion.[29] The latter was premised on the idea that there exists a primordial realm of being prior to the gods and above them upon which the gods depend and whose decrees they must obey. Pagan gods were subject to evil forces inherent in the primordial realm, and paganism considered impurity, or demonic evil, as an autonomous, baleful realm feared by the gods as well as by human beings. In sharp contrast to paganism, in Israelite religion there was no primordial demonic realm above God to

---

by individual responsibility, from the protest of Abraham, claiming that it should be replaced by communal merit).

27. See Levinson, "Deuteronomy," 401. See also Greenberg, "Some Postulates," 31–33 (Collective punishment remained but only as the prerogative of God; biblical criminal law "foregoes entirely the right to punish any but the actual culprit in all civil cases").

28. Milgrom, *Leviticus*, 6 ("Ethical values are buried in recondite rituals and in misunderstood (and mistranslated) commandments").

29. See Kaufmann, *Religion*, 21–149.

which God was subject, and which was the source impurity and evil. Thus, cultic rites in Israel, unlike pagan rites, were not a means of combating or propitiating harmful spirits but were directed solely toward the domain of Yahweh.

Building upon Kaufmann's work, Milgrom argued that with the demise of the world of demons, only one creature remained with "demonic" power—the human being. Endowed with free will, "human power ... can [not only] defy God, but, in Priestly imagery ... can drive God out of his sanctuary."[30] Humans can do this by polluting the sanctuary with their moral and ritual sins.[31] To avoid the pollution of the sanctuary the priests had to influence the people to confess and atone for their wrongs and had to periodically purge the sanctuary. Even unintentional violations of prohibitive conduct, if severe enough, polluted the sanctuary from afar, necessitating a purification sacrifice. As Milgrom explains it:

> While sin may not scar the face of the sinner, it does scar the face of the sanctuary. This image graphically illustrates the Priestly version of the old doctrine of collective responsibility: When evildoers are punished, they bring down the righteous with them. Those who perish with the wicked are not entirely blameless, however. They are inadvertent sinners who, by having allowed the wicked to flourish, have also contributed to the pollution of the sanctuary. Thus, in the Priestly scheme, the sanctuary is polluted (read: society is corrupted) by brazen sins (read: the rapacity of the leaders) and also by inadvertent sins (read: the acquiescence of the "silent majority"), with the result that God is driven out of his sanctuary (read: the nation is destroyed).... Israel, having expunged the demons from its beliefs, attributes impurity to the rebellious and inadvertent sins of humans instead.[32]

This is to say that the priestly authors believed that the well-being of the Israelite nation was affected by the conduct of each of its

---

30. Milgrom, *Leviticus*, 9.

31. See generally Hayes, *Introduction*, 152–57 (discussing ritual and moral impurity in Leviticus); Klawans, *Impurity and Sin*, 21–42 (same).

32. Milgrom, *Leviticus*, 15. See also Milgrom, *Leviticus*, 30–33, 177 (Responsibility "falls on the children to make amends for the pollution caused by sin that their forebears left behind. In H what matters is that the land is still polluted; if the parent has not remedied the pollution, someone else must take over responsibility or the land will become polluted and the people and then God will be banished").

members.[33] More particularly, the conduct of an individual member could corrupt the whole nation and, if unchecked, would ultimately lead to the nation's destruction. Milgrom asserts that, because the purification offerings taught that the moral sin of the individual adversely affected the entire society, Israel's priesthood made moral rectitude "an indispensable factor in determining Israel's destiny."[34]

The ritual purging of the sanctuary of the moral impurity caused by the accidental violation of prohibitive conduct involved the sacrifice of specified animals, the daubing of blood from the sacrificed animal on the horns of the altar, and, in certain cases, the eating of some of the sacrificed animal by the priest who offered that animal as a purification offering.[35] According to Milgrom, "When the priest consumes the purification offering he is making a profound theological statement: holiness has swallowed impurity; life can defeat death."[36] Holiness symbolized life (and prosperity); impurity symbolized death (and destruction).[37]

2. Reparation offerings show a step toward a guilt culture.

Milgrom comments that the reparation offerings provided a mechanism to atone for a deliberate crime against God, usually irremediable, provided that the person, having a sense of guilt, repented before they were apprehended and made restitution to the person victimized.[38] Repentance was the important factor; it "convert[ed] an intentional sin into an unintentional one, thereby making it eligible for sacrificial expiation."[39] Because the sinner's repentance issued from feelings of guilt, the reparation offering (in addition to becoming the vehicle for an incipient doctrine of repentance) represented a step toward a

---

33. See Klawans, *Impurity and Sin*, 40 ("The ultimate result of the accumulation of moral impurity—the exile of the people from the land of Israel—is a punishment that affects everyone. Men and women, the children and the elderly, the innocent and the guilty—all will suffer equally the terror of exile"). Cf. Daube, *Law and Wisdom*, 103 (In the wisdom tradition it is recognized that what a member of a group does affects the entire group). Klawans restricts his use of the term "moral impurity" to certain specific acts. See Klawans, *Impurity and Sin*, 26.
34. Milgrom, *Leviticus*, 43.
35. Lev 4:1—5:13; 6:17–23.
36. Milgrom, *Leviticus*, 99.
37. See Milgrom, *Leviticus*, 120.
38. Milgrom, *Leviticus*, 15. See Lev 5:14–26; Num 5:5–8.
39. Milgrom, *Leviticus*, 15. See also Milgrom, *Leviticus*, 50–51.

guilt culture in what was predominately a shame culture. Other priestly materials similarly emphasize that confession, or acknowledgement of guilt, is needed to attain expiation of sin.[40]

3. The Holiness Code radically extended the notion of holiness.

Milgrom claims that the priestly tradition represented by H (which he identifies with a new priestly school formed at the end of the eighth century BCE)[41] differed from the priestly tradition represented by P in that H radically extended holiness from a sacred sphere (the sanctuary) and its officiants (the priests) to the entire land of Israel and all its Israelite occupants.[42] Since "holiness" implied "separateness," the holiness of the nation of Israel meant that Israel had to separate itself from all other nations of the world.[43] According to Milgrom, H envisions that Israel's separateness from the other nations of the world and its *imitatio Dei* (that is, its godliness or holiness) would result in "a universal *imitatio Israel*," a universal adherence to "justice and righteousness."[44] Put differently, in H's view, when the other nations of the world witnessed how God rewarded Israel with life, prosperity, and security for its justice and righteousness (i.e., its godliness or holiness), the other nations of the world would be induced to behave similarly.[45]

Noting that H was well aware of the antediluvian legends concerning God's creation of a moral order as well as an order in the natural world, Milgrom maintained that Israel's separateness from the other nations of the world was seen by H to be as central to the order God created in the human world as the separateness of differing physical substances was to the order God created in the natural world.[46] Moreover, just as the priests, because they are innately holy, "are qualified to enter into Yahweh's presence, so if Israel obeys Yahweh's commands (19:37), it will

---

40. See Lev 26:40–41.
41. Milgrom, *Leviticus*, 175.
42. Milgrom, *Leviticus*, 5, 181, 213.
43. See Hayes, *Introduction*, 151.
44. Milgrom, *Leviticus*, 180 (citing Gen 18:18–19; 22:18). Cf. Deut 4:5–8.
45. Milgrom, *Leviticus*, 180–81 (citing Lev 26:3–13).
46. Milgrom, *Leviticus*, 179–80. See also Schwartz, "Leviticus," 242 (Leviticus 19:19 should be understood as commanding Israelites to observe the boundaries God has fixed in the natural order).

attain holiness (19:2) and qualify for admission into the presence—that is, the providence and protection—of Yahweh."[47]

In keeping with H's extension of holiness to all Israelites, H applies the teaching of P that the priest's holiness can defeat impurity—that life can defeat death—to the people at large: "As long as [the people] live a life of holiness and serve God by obeying God's commandments, they can overcome the forces of impurity—death. 'You shall heed my statutes and my rules, which if one does them, he shall live by them [Lev 18:5].'"[48]

Thus, the overriding view of H concerning the qualities the Israelites should possess and the conduct they should exhibit was that they should be holy and act holy. Milgrom asserts that holiness "means *imitatio Dei*—the life of godliness."[49] The life of godliness, the life of purity and holiness, entails moral achievement; the ungodly life, the life of impurity and unholiness, entails moral failure.[50] Life and death (prosperity and destruction) are not caused by outside demonic forces but rather are set loose by the people themselves through their holiness or impurity. To the priestly mind, sins against God defiled the land and holiness sanctified the land.[51]

4. The qualities and conduct required for Israel to achieve holiness were qualities and conduct having cooperative value.

H's position as to the specific conduct that holiness required is best seen in chapter 19 of Leviticus, which Milgrom takes to be a central turning point in the entire book.[52] The chapter begins by admonishing Israel to be holy ("You shall be holy, for I, the Lord your God, am holy")[53] and ends by admonishing Israel to obey all of God's commandments ("You shall faithfully observe all My laws and all My rules"). These admonitions

---

47. Milgrom, *Leviticus*, 182 (citing Lev 19). See Milgrom, *Leviticus*, 220.
48. Milgrom, *Leviticus*, 99.
49. Milgrom, *Leviticus*, 107. See Milgrom, *Leviticus*, 120–21; 213–15.
50. See Milgrom, *Leviticus*, 123.
51. Milgrom, *Leviticus*, 139.
52. Milgrom, *Leviticus*, 17. See also Milgrom, *Leviticus*, 212–19; Weinfeld, "Uniqueness of the Decalogue," 11–15 (stating that chapter 19 is "the only place in the priestly code where we encounter an intermingling of cultic and ethical laws such as we find in the Ten Commandments").
53. See Harvey, "Love," 6 (The "focal text for the connection of *imitatio Dei* with holiness is of course Leviticus 19:2, 'Ye shall be holy for I the Lord your God am holy'").

constitute the main thrust of Lev 17 to 27. In between these two admonitions chapter 19 sets forth what H considered to be the most important of God's commandments.[54] Included among these commandments, which were chosen "for their aptness to be subsumed under the rubric of holiness or its negation, impurity and desecration . . . [and thus provide] the prescription to effect a transformation to holiness"[55] are commandments which require for their fulfillment the very same qualities and conduct having cooperative value extolled in Proverbs—don't steal;[56] don't deal deceitfully or falsely with one another;[57] don't defraud or rob your fellow Israelite;[58] be sure to pay the wages of a laborer promptly;[59] don't render an unfair opinion which favors the poor or shows deference to the rich, but judge your kinsman fairly;[60] honor your father and mother;[61] respect your elders;[62] don't spread false rumors to have unjust charges brought against your countryman or otherwise pervert the cause of fair judicial proceedings;[63] don't falsify measures of length, weight, or capacity, but have an honest balance;[64] care for the poor and the stranger;[65] don't abuse or harm the defenseless;[66] don't bear a grudge against your countryman;[67] and, most famously, don't hate your kinsfolk,

---

54. Milgrom, *Leviticus*, 212 ("Unlike all other priestly pericopes . . . which expound a unified theme, this chapter comprises a miscellany of laws (ritual and ethical, apodictic, and casuistic, directed to the individual and to the collective)"). See also Rodd, *Glimpses*, 5–18 (noting that chapter 19 of Leviticus fails to make any distinction between ethical and cultic precepts, commenting that "both actions which break ethical precepts and those which infringe cultic and ritual purity equally affect Israel's holiness," and asserting that ethics in the Hebrew Bible "cannot be divorced from the question of purity").

55. Milgrom, *Leviticus*, 213.

56. Lev 19:11.

57. Lev 19:11.

58. Lev 19:13.

59. Lev 19:13.

60. Lev 19:15.

61. Lev 19:3.

62. Lev 19:32.

63. Lev 19:16. See Schwartz, "Leviticus," 241.

64. Lev 19:35.

65. Lev 19:9–10, 33–34.

66. Lev 19:14. See Milgrom, *Leviticus*, 216 (Commenting on verse 14, Milgrom states that "deaf" and "blind" are metonyms for all the helpless, and "curse" and "stumbling block" stand for abuse and harm). Cf. Deut 27:18.

67. Lev 19:17.

but love your fellow as yourself.⁶⁸ All of these commandments emphasize that human beings must possess the divine attributes of justice and/or compassion which are essential to God's holy nature, and which Israel must emulate if it is to also become holy.⁶⁹ Requiring special mention is verse 19:16b which Milgrom renders, "You shall not stand aloof by the blood of your fellow," and interprets as forbidding one "to remain on the sidelines of one's endangered fellow."⁷⁰

Milgrom sees chapter 19 and other H material discussed in the next subsection as reflecting the priestly response to the indictment of Israel's moral failings by the prophets of the eighth century BCE, especially Isaiah of Jerusalem.⁷¹ Isaiah condemned Israel's corrupt judicial leaders who perverted justice by taking bribes, and he condemned the rich who robbed the poor and seized their land. The priestly authors of H adopted Isaiah's teaching that Israel's holiness implies "that Israel must be ethical," and they prescribe "specific commandments (Leviticus 19) by which holiness can be attained."⁷² These priests saw that moral purity was just as important as ritual purity.⁷³

5. The priestly concern with qualities and conduct having cooperative value is further evidenced by the jubilee legislation aimed at providing some measure of protection for the impoverished farmer.

The priestly authors offer legislation to protect impoverished farmers from the permanent loss of their land. Such protection would have had the effect of mitigating the hostility and violence that destitute farmers, without any hope of improved economic circumstances, could have been expected to unleash against the wealthy. This legislation,

---

68. Lev 19:17–18. See Milgrom, *Leviticus*, 218 (The verb "love" (*ahavta*) with the preposition *le* implies doing, not feeling). Cf. Hillers, *Covenant*, 152–53 (In Deuteronomy, love of Yahweh is "linked inseparably" with service to Yahweh); Eichrodt, *Theology*, 2.297 ("Close link between love [of God] and the demand for obedience and the fulfillment of the law"). See also Kaufmann, *Religion*, 322n10 ("The plain meaning of [this passage] is national in scope"; it is "limited to the Israelite"). Cf. chapter 2, sec. C (The secular law collections prohibit pressing your kinsman for payment of a debt owed or charging him interest, but not a foreigner).

69. See Milgrom, *Leviticus*, 213, 219–20.

70. Milgrom, *Leviticus*, 217.

71. Milgrom, *Leviticus*, 214.

72. Milgrom, *Leviticus*, 214–15.

73. Milgrom, *Leviticus*, 215. Cf. chapter 4, sec. E.

in chapter 25 of Leviticus, concerns the "jubilee (*yovel*) year."[74] In the jubilee, every fiftieth year, anyone who had sold part of their land to a creditor to relieve their debt had to be allowed to return to their land and have their debt cancelled.[75] The legislation also provided that any seller of land had to be given the opportunity to redeem the land sold at any time before the jubilee year.[76]

It is specifically stated that the debtor's "nearest kinsman shall come and redeem what his kinsman has sold."[77] But, if the forced seller, even with the aid of his kinsman, was unable to redeem the land, when the year of the jubilee occurred the land had to be "released" and returned to the forced seller; and, similarly, if anyone had been forced to sell his dwelling house, and the house was outside of a walled city, at the time of the jubilee the house had to be "released through the jubilee" and returned to the forced seller; and in both cases the related debt was cancelled.[78]

If a debtor forced to sell part of their land became further impoverished and took out a new loan from the creditor, and then defaulted on the new loan, the debtor was required to become a "tenant farmer" for the creditor (he fell under the creditor's authority). In these circumstances,

---

74. "Jubilee" is the translation of the Hebrew *yovel*, derived from the root "y-b-l," "to bring," and seems to mean "sending forth, home-bringing" or "liberation." Schwartz, "Leviticus," 257. See also Weinfeld, *Social Justice*, 160.

75. Lev 25:8–13, 28, 31. See generally Schwartz, "Leviticus," 257 ("The basic postulate of the jubilee ... is that the Israelites have entered Canaan, the land is divided up (by lot, see Num 33:54) in perpetuity. The land of Canaan is not the Israelites' property; it is rather a 'holding.' ... So are the plots of land held by each tribe, clan, and family. ... The Israelites are mere leaseholders, tenants on the divine estate, and the holdings God has parceled out to them are inalienable. ... The jubilee ... is an assertion of God's exclusive proprietorship and dominion, designed to keep the Israelites constantly aware that they are His indentured servants"); Falk, *Hebrew Law*, 86 (The jubilee illustrates the "divine ownership of all property"); Milgrom, *Leviticus*, 298–302 ("Each Israelite clan has been assigned a plot of land (Num 26) that must always remain in its possession. Even when it is sold it can be reclaimed, a process called 'redemption,' and every fiftieth year [the jubilee year] it must be restored to its original owner"). See also Weinfeld, *Social Justice*, 175–78 (Jubilee is of ancient origin and was "inherent in tribal society of the pre-monarchical period"); Greengus, *Laws in the Bible*, 101–2 ("Some scholars have argued that the jubilee was an institution of pre-monarchal times. ... But others see it as a never actualized, utopian program. The latter position is more likely"); Milgrom, *Leviticus*, 301 ("As far as we know, these antislavery laws remained utopian; there is no hard evidence they were ever enacted"); Falk, *Hebrew Law*, 118 (The rules of the jubilee "were ... seldom enforced").

76. Lev 25:23 ("The land must not be sold beyond reclaim").

77. Lev 25:25.

78. Lev 25:28, 31. See Weinfeld, *Social Justice*, 176 (Dwelling houses *in* walled cities had to be exempted for practical reasons).

the creditor was required to lend the debtor such additional funds as the debtor required without charging the debtor interest on those funds.[79] If the debtor/tenant farmer still could not repay his loans and could not support himself and his family, he was forced, with his family, to enter the household of the creditor.[80] The law provided, however, that the debtor's status would not be that of a chattel slave but had to be that of a debt slave (a "hired or bound laborer");[81] that the debtor only had to serve the creditor up until the time of the jubilee year, at which time the debtor could "return to his ancestral holding"; and that the creditor could not rule over the debtor slave "ruthlessly."[82]

Milgrom emphasizes the moral aspect of the jubilee. He asserts that the jubilee was "a socioeconomic mechanism to prevent latifundia (the loss of the debtors' land to the creditor-rich) and the ever-widening gap between the rich and the poor."[83] The jubilee, as well as the right to redeem and the prohibition against enslaving impoverished farmers, may be compared to the social reforms enacted in ancient Greece by Solon (ca. 630–560 BCE) referred to as the *seisachtheia*.[84] Solon was faced with socioeconomic problems virtually identical to the those that the jubilee law is designed to address, namely latifundia, wealth inequality, and the indentured servitude or enslavement of impoverished farmers who had lost their inherited land.

As described by Adkins, "Many of the smaller farmers of early sixth-century Attica were in debt, whether to larger farmers or to other wealthy individuals, and many had been forced into the position of bondmen to their creditors."[85] Latifundia was rampant in Attica, and many smaller farmers had been enslaved as a result of their debt.[86] In addition, the

---

79. See Lev 25:35–37; Milgrom, *Leviticus*, 300.

80. See Milgrom, *Leviticus*, 301 (The debtor "no longer enjoys the usufruct of his forfeited land," but "he receives wages, all of which pay off his debt").

81. See Greengus, *Laws in the Bible*, 86 (distinguishing chattel slave from debt slave and noting that "the same Hebrew terms are used to describe both kinds of slaves"). See also Tigay, "Exodus," 144 (distinguishing Hebrew slaves, "who are really indentured servants," from "full, permanent slaves, who were foreigners").

82. Lev 25:39–43. See Milgrom, *Leviticus*, 301.

83. Milgrom, *Leviticus*, 302. The jubilee also had a clear theological aspect. See n75 in this chapter.

84. See generally Weinfeld, *Social Justice*, 168–74 (comparing the reforms of Solon to the remission of debts in the time of Nehemiah).

85. Adkins, *Moral Values*, 47.

86. See generally Lewis, "Solon's Agrarian Legislation," 144–50 (describing the social

wealthier citizens were engaged in factionalism and competition for power. These conditions had led to revolution in other Greek states, and Solon warned that Athens would soon be destroyed if the wealthy citizens did not restrain their greed and unjust deeds.[87] He urged Athenians to accept what he termed *"eunomia"* ("good order") as the way to end discord and strife. *Eunomia* included good laws, having the laws well obeyed, and an appropriate distribution of wealth, power, and resources.[88] To advance *eunomia*, Solon introduced a new and more humane law code intended to remove economic injustice and hardship, protect the impoverished farmers, and allow for the redemption of land. The measures taken by Solon had significant cooperative value, and the measures set forth in chapter 25 of Leviticus, if put into practice, similarly would have had significant cooperative value.

6. Being holy was justified, according to the H source, by the material well-being that holiness brought to Israelite society.

The qualities and conduct extolled by the sages of the Israelite wisdom tradition were those qualities and conduct that human experience suggested had cooperative value. This is to say that such qualities and conduct were seen to be the means required for the nation to achieve collective well-being—an orderly, harmonious, and prosperous society—and, as such, were viewed as being instrumentally good. To the extent that these qualities and conduct served to integrate a person into the divine moral order, they may also have been seen (at least by some) to be intrinsically good, but the sages of Israelite wisdom never based the intrinsic worth of these qualities and conduct on the grounds that they were commanded or authenticated by Yahweh.

Subsequently, when these moral norms were transferred to the realm of prophecy, the priestly authors of the Holiness Code *did* base the intrinsic worth of these qualities and conduct on the grounds that they were commanded and authenticated by Yahweh. Additionally, these priests taught that Yahweh required the nation to be holy, and taught that holiness meant possessing the qualities and displaying the conduct specified in chapter 19 of Leviticus. Commenting on chapter 19 of Leviticus,

---

and economic conditions leading to the crises that Solon was called upon to resolve).

87. See Adkins, *Moral Values*, 48–50.
88. Adkins, *Moral Values*, 50–53.

Schwartz writes that the separate paragraphs are punctuated with the repeated refrain, "I am the Lord" or "I the Lord am your God," which "is approximately equivalent to 'because I, the Lord, say so.'"[89] Schwartz also writes: "Only through faithful observance of God's commandments can the Israelite fulfill the sacred charge of being holy."[90]

Thus, it might appear that the priestly authors viewed the commended qualities and conduct as being *intrinsically* good. They were justified, irrespective of consequences, because Yahweh commanded them as required for Israel to be holy. But this appearance is undermined by the fact that compliance with the commands, being holy, was understood as necessary to avoid pollution of the land; and avoiding pollution of the land was understood as necessary to avoid expulsion from the land and destruction, as necessary, that is, for the well-being of the nation. This is made clear by chapter 26 of Leviticus. Hillers explains that chapter 26 of Leviticus serves as the last of the six principal parts of a typical suzerainty treaty, the part which sets forth the blessings and curses for, respectively, honoring or breaching the terms of the treaty.[91]

In setting forth these blessings and curses chapter 26 provides evidence of what its priestly authors understood to be the ultimate basis upon which qualities and conduct having cooperative value were justified, which is to say why one was justified in obeying Yahweh's commandments. Obedience is said to bring life, peace, and material well-being.[92] Disobedience is said to bring the opposite; it will drive Yahweh from the sanctuary and from the community, and the Israelites will be bereft of Yahweh's blessing and protection. If Yahweh is not obeyed, Yahweh will spurn the Israelites, lay their cities in ruin, drive them from their land, and cause their land to become desolate.[93]

It thus seems reasonable to suppose that the priestly authors of the Holiness Code, no less than the sages of Proverbs, viewed qualities and conduct having cooperative value as justified because they were required for the nation to achieve collective well-being—required, that is, for the

---

89. Schwartz, "Leviticus," 240. See also Daube, *Law and Wisdom*, 56–57 (distinguishing "authentication or legitimation of a law" from "the motivation of a law: the reasons for a law").

90. Schwartz, "Leviticus," 240.

91. See Hillers, *Covenant*, 29, 37–39, 53–54.

92. See Lev 26:3–13; 18:5 (By obedience "man shall live"); 25:18 (Observe laws "that you may live upon the land in security"). See also Milgrom, *Leviticus*, 318 (Leviticus 26:4–5 refers to "plenty"; and Lev 26:6 refers to economic and political security).

93. See Lev 26:27–33.

THE PRIESTLY LAW COLLECTIONS

Israelites to remain on the land and achieve an orderly, harmonious, and prosperous society. Therefore, they viewed qualities and conduct having cooperative value as justified primarily, if not entirely, because they were believed to be *instrumentally* good. This type of justificatory position is consistent with the ethical theory of utilitarianism. The teaching that God commanded the desired qualities and conduct, arguably, served to reinforce the existing utilitarian justification rather than to provide a justification that was theretofore lacking. Nowhere in the H material is it stated that one should obey God's commands, should be holy, regardless of consequences, which is what would be required if a deontological ethical theory truly underlay the H material.

C. Psalm 37 adopted the priestly emphasis of remaining on the land as the consequence of qualities and conduct having cooperative value but differentiated the fate of the righteous from the fate of the wicked.

In the "Pentateuchal system," says Rivkin, the "ultimate punishment is to be driven from the land" and "the ultimate reward [is] to gather in overabundant harvests in peace and tranquility," but "there is no provision made for that individual who, though law-abiding himself, is swept into exile along with the majority who have sinned."[94] Thus, an individual's salvation was ultimately not dependent on what that individual did himself or herself.[95] This "flaw" in the Pentateuchal system, asserts Rivkin, "distressed the psalmist who strained to reassure the individual that God's justice somehow extended to the individual as well."[96]

Psalm 37, composed in the Second Temple period, supports Rivkin's assertion. Psalm 37 is an alphabetical acrostic psalm "whose themes, structure, and vocabulary are characteristic of [Proverbs]. 'Wisdom' is mentioned explicitly in v. 30, and thus the psalm should be considered a wisdom psalm, written by someone who was part of the wisdom movement or heavily influenced by it."[97] Psalm 37, like wisdom

---

94. Rivkin, *Hidden Revolution*, 244.
95. Rivkin, *Hidden Revolution*, 244.
96. Rivkin, *Hidden Revolution*, 244.
97. Berlin and Brettler, "Psalms," 1307.

literature in general, identifies righteousness with wisdom and with qualities and conduct having cooperative value.[98]

The psalmist addresses the concern that many of the righteous were "*ʾanavim*" ("lowly"),[99] not reaping the material rewards that righteousness was supposed to bring. Many righteous were also "vexed" because they saw that the wicked were not only prosperous but schemed against, and even slaughtered, the righteous.[100] The psalmist cautions the righteous not to be "incensed by wrongdoers," to be "patient," and to "wait for the Lord."[101] He assures them that the Lord blesses them[102] and that "He will cause [their] vindication to shine forth like the light, the justice of [their] case, like the noonday sun."[103]

Particularly relevant for present purposes, the psalmist sees the vindication of the righteous to be that they would "inherit the land, and abide forever on it,"[104] while the wicked would be "cut off," i.e., separated from the land.[105] In fact, that the righteous would inherit the land is repeated six times and has been called the "major theme" of the psalm.[106] Thus, the psalmist adopted the priestly notion that moral impurity had the effect of causing the people's removal from the land but applied it only to the wicked, not to the righteous. In other words, while the priestly authors of Leviticus maintained a collective approach to reward and punishment, teaching that the fate of righteous individuals was adversely affected by misdeeds of the wicked, Ps 37 maintained an individual approach to reward and punishment, teaching that the fate of righteous individuals would *not* be adversely affected by misdeeds of the wicked, that the fates of the righteous and the wicked would be different.

What is also noteworthy about Ps 37 is that the psalmist claims that the righteous always receive divine protection. He states: "I have never

---

98. See Ps 37:21, 26 (The righteous man "is always generous and lends" in contrast to the wicked man who "borrows and does not repay").

99. Ps 37:11. The Hebrew word *ʾanavim*, translated in the most recent JPS version as "the lowly," has the connotation of being poor, humble, and afflicted. So, they might be called the downtrodden. The King James version translates *ʾanavim* as "the meek."

100. Ps 37:7, 12, 14.

101. Ps 37:1, 7.

102. Ps 37:22.

103. Ps 37:6.

104. Ps 37:29. Upon inheriting the land, they will "delight in abundant well-being [*shalom*]." Ps 37:11.

105. Ps 37:9, 28, 38. See Berlin and Brettler, "Psalms," 1308. Cf. Prov 2:21–22.

106. Berlin and Brettler, "Psalms," 1307.

seen a righteous man abandoned, or his children seeking bread."[107] Conversely, according to the psalmist, eventually, the wicked are always punished. He states:

> I saw a wicked man, powerful, well-rooted like a robust native tree.
> Suddenly he vanished and was gone;
> I sought him, but he was not to be found.[108]

That the righteous are *always* rewarded and the wicked are *always* punished *in this life* is the point of view of traditional Israelite wisdom. This point of view is still maintained by Ben Sira as late as 180 BCE, despite being seriously challenged by the authors of Job and Qoheleth.[109] Later in the Second Temple period, the Essenes and the followers of Jesus of Nazareth invest Ps 37 with sectarian eschatology, reinterpreting it to mean that *in a new world to come* the righteous will be rewarded with eternal life and the wicked will be punished with eternal punishment.[110]

---

107. Ps 37:25.
108. Ps 37:35–36.
109. See chapter 5, secs. B, 1, 2, and C.
110. See chapter 11, secs. A and B, 6.

CHAPTER 4

The prophets condemned the Israelites for disobeying Yahweh's moral commands, and Jeremiah concluded that obedience required giving human beings an undivided heart.

UPON THE DEATH OF Solomon in 922 BCE, the dynastic state created by David precipitately fell apart, replaced by "two rival states of second-rate importance."[1] These two states—Israel in the north and Judah in the south—coexisted with each other, sometimes at war and sometimes in friendly alliance, until the northern state was destroyed by Assyria in 722 BCE.[2] The internal political condition of the northern kingdom had been unstable until the reign of Omri, who established a dynasty that held power for three generations. The southern kingdom maintained a Davidic line of succession until the reign of King Zedekiah (r. 597–586 BCE) which was when Judah suffered ultimate defeat and destruction at the hands of the Babylonians, marking the beginning of the Babylonian exile.[3] In addition to having battled external enemies who

---

1. Bright, *History of Israel*, 229.

2. Bright, *History of Israel*, 229. See generally Bright, *History of Israel*, 229–66 (providing a history of Israel and Judah up to the mid-eighth century BCE); Scheindlin, *Short History*, 8–23 (same).

3. A first deportation to Babylon occurred in 597 BCE, ending the reign of King Jehoiachin. See Botta, "Babylonian and Persian Period," 530–31. See generally Nickelsburg, *Jewish Literature*, 8–11 (summarizing the relevant history and its import on postexilic Jewish literature).

defeated and destroyed them, both Israel and Judah also experienced internal strife and discord, and many of their inhabitants experienced material hardships.

Thus, in neither Israel nor Judah had the laws and moral norms described in the previous chapters achieved their intended goal. These laws and moral norms required that one act with compassion for the poor and disadvantaged members of society, avoid strife and discord, be honest and fair in dealing with others, resolve disputes through just proceedings, make non-usurious loans to kinsmen, and, in general, possess qualities and act in ways having cooperative value. The legists and sages believed that adherence to these laws and moral norms would bring the community harmony, prosperity, and well-being. The prophets agreed. They attributed the failure to achieve the desired outcomes to the inability of the people to follow the laws and moral norms God had commanded, not to any inadequacy with the laws and moral norms.

Some contemporary biblical scholars have claimed that many of the laws found in the Hebrew Bible were never intended to be followed, and were, in fact, never put into practice.[4] For example, in discussing the biblical imposition of the death penalty for adultery, Rodd mentions McKeating's claim that "there is no evidence that [the death penalty] was actually applied."[5] Rodd continues:

> McKeating concludes from this that society's ethical values cannot be read off from the law.... While the law may have value in revealing the ideals held by [certain] members of Israelite society, even describing how people were supposed to behave, the study of ethics must begin with the actual behaviour recorded in the narratives.... [McKeating] adds that the ethics of the Old Testament and the ethics of ancient Israelite society do not necessarily coincide.[6]

Rodd goes on to summarize the views of Wenham who argues that

---

4. See generally Hillers, *Covenant*, 88–89 ("In fact, there is no evidence that any collection of Near Eastern laws functioned as a written code that was applied by a strict method of exegesis to individual cases. As far as we can tell, these bodies of laws served educational purposes and gave expression to what was regarded as just in typical cases, but they left considerable latitude to local courts for determining the right in individual cases").

5. Rodd, *Glimpses*, 39.

6. Rodd, *Glimpses*, 39.

> scholars have misrepresented biblical ethics by failing to distinguish between (1) the world of the writers themselves, (2) the world of law, and (3) the ethical world of the actors.... The actors behave in accordance with certain ethical principles which may not be congruent with those enshrined in the laws or held by the biblical writers.[7]

Rodd concludes "that a large gap exists between law, ethical norms, and actual behaviour."[8] With specific reference to laws providing relief to debt slaves (the laws of the *shemitah* and the *yovel*), many scholars have claimed these laws were "utopian" or "highly idealistic" and never actually enacted or put into practice.[9]

But even if the biblical laws had all been enacted and put into practice, neither these laws nor the moral norms promulgated by the sages were widely followed. For the most part, wealthy and powerful Israelites sought to advance their own individual material well-being at the expense of the poor and disadvantaged members of society, and they were willing to employ unjust means to achieve their unjust ends. For example, in the northern kingdom, despite evidence that the House of Omri achieved a considerable degree of material prosperity, the lot of its peasantry was miserable. According to Bright:

> [There was] a progressive disintegration of the structure of Israelite society, and a harsh system that tended to place the poor at the mercy of the rich. The former, forced in hard times to borrow from the latter at usurious rates of interest, mortgaging their land, if not their own persons or those of their children, in security, faced—and, one gathers, not infrequently (2 Kgs 4:1)—the prospect of eviction, if not slavery. We may suspect, if we cannot prove, that the great drought in Ahab's reign (1 Kgs, chs. 17f.) . . . caused many small farmers to lose all they had. Although we cannot say how many great landowners enlarged their estates by highhanded injustice, we may suppose that . . . Israel was full of people who, like Jezebel, had no conception of covenant law or, like Ahab, little concern for it.[10]

It fell to the prophets to decry unrighteous conduct and to reassert the importance of qualities and conduct having cooperative value,

---

7. Rodd, *Glimpses*, 40.
8. Rodd, *Glimpses*, 43.
9. See chapter 2, n102; chapter 3, n75.
10. Bright, *History of Israel*, 244–45.

associated by them with adherence to the moral commands of a covenant, or treaty, that they imagined God (Yahweh) had made with the nation of Israel. The nonliterary prophets of the tenth and ninth centuries BCE spoke out against moral lapses of the rulers, but never issued wholesale condemnations of the people or proclaimed that unrighteousness would lead to the utter destruction of the nation. But precisely such condemnations and proclamations issued from the literary prophets whose words were set down in the books of the Hebrew Bible that bear their names. Literary or classical prophecy begins with Hosea and Amos in the middle of the eighth century BCE and ends with Malachi in the fifth century BCE. The prophets interpreted the defeats of the northern and southern kingdoms to be punishments inflicted by God for the idolatry and moral failings of the people, pursuant to the terms of the covenant they said existed between God and the Israelites.

A. The political and socioeconomic conditions that served as the impetus for classical prophecy include the oppression of the poor and weak by the wealthy and powerful.

Von Rad sees the emergence of classical prophecy as connected with four factors, two of which are most relevant for present concerns. The first factor relates to economic and social developments. Von Rad writes:

> The state with its taxation and its civil service had brought about a further disintegration of the old social order within the tribes of Israel. In this connection, the transference of the focal point of the economy to the towns was a particular blow. The great landowners, who already lived in the towns, gained control over country people, and the result was severe social injustice. Because of the burden of taxation, the peasant, economically weak, became less and less able to remain a free man on his own land—his old influential and honourable status in the time of the ancient Israelite [tribal league] as a free man liable for military service dwindled away, and ownership of land came more and more into the hands of a small number of capitalist town-dwellers. The country people became increasingly part of a proletariat.[11]

---

11. Von Rad, *Message of the Prophets*, 10.

Von Rad's view of the relevant socioeconomic conditions is supported by Bright. Bright describes an economic resurgence of Israel and Judah in the eighth century BCE but contrasts it with a picture of "social disintegration."[12] Relying on accounts from the book of Amos, Bright describes the situation in the northern kingdom as follows:

> Israelite society [in the eighth century BCE] was marked by egregious injustices and a shocking contrast between extremes of wealth and poverty. The small farmer . . . found himself often at the mercy of the moneylender and, at the slightest calamity . . . liable to foreclosure and eviction, if not bond service. The system, which was itself harsh, was made harsher by the greed of the wealthy, who took unmerciful advantage of the plight of the poor in order to enlarge their holdings, often resorting to the sharpest practices, the falsification of weights and measures, and various legal dodges to achieve their ends. . . . But though dishonest practices obtained everywhere, since the judges were venal . . . the poor had no redress. In increasing numbers they were robbed and dispossessed.[13]

While the social deterioration in Judah was not as great as it was in Israel, and the concentration of wealth in the hands of a few was not as extensive, "Judahite society was not free of the [social] disease that had destroyed Israel," and the wealthy class in Judah "was clearly no better than its counterpart in Israel."[14] According to Milgrom, in the eighth and seventh centuries BCE, the poor existed in Judah in large numbers as a result of "the loss of landed property due to its inability to support growing families; the increased latifundia . . . and, above all, the massive influx of homeless and landless refugees as a result of the destruction of the northern kingdom."[15]

The second relevant factor to which Von Rad attributes the emergence of classical prophecy is "the rise of Assyria to the summit of her power and the threat which she directed against Palestine from the eighth century onwards."[16] After the second millennium BCE, when

12. See Bright, *History of Israel*, 255–60.
13. Bright, *History of Israel*, 260.
14. Bright, *History of Israel*, 278.
15. Milgrom, *Leviticus*, 177. See also Milgrom, *Leviticus*, 225 ("Increasing latifundia and urbanization led to the dissolution of family and clan structure, leaving the widow and orphan open prey to exploitation" which was condemned by Jeremiah and Ezekiel).
16. Von Rad, *Message of the Prophets*, 10.

Assyria had been a major player in world politics, Assyria reached a low point in its fortunes but began to recover by the eighth century. From the middle of the eighth century until the end of the seventh century Assyria was a constant threat to both Israel and Judah.[17] From at least 738 BCE Israel began paying tribute to Assyria. Shortly thereafter, Israel formed a coalition with Aram for the purpose of resisting the Assyrians. In 734 BCE Assyria attacked the Aramean-Israelite coalition forces and destroyed them. All Israelite lands in Galilee and Transjordan were overrun, portions of the population were deported, and numerous cities were destroyed. Following a subsequent attempt by Israel to resist Assyrian domination, Assyria attacked again. Samaria, the capital of the northern kingdom, fell to the Assyrians in 722 BCE. Thousands of its citizens were deported to Upper Mesopotamia and Media, "there ultimately to vanish from the stage of history."[18]

Under the rule of Ahaz, the southern kingdom began paying tribute to Assyria at the time of the Aramean-Israelite coalition, making Judah a vassal state of the Assyrian empire. Ahaz's son and successor, Hezekiah, reversed his father's policy and sought to get Judah free of Assyria. In 704 BCE Hezekiah formally refused tribute to Assyria and took steps toward Judah's independence from Assyria. Most significantly, Hezekiah formed a coalition with the king of Tyre and other Phoenician cities seeking to revolt against Assyria. In 701 BCE Assyria attacked and crushed the kingdom of Tyre, and the revolt fell apart. Based on Assyrian documents, Assyria "reduced forty-six of Judah's fortified cities and deported their population, while shutting Hezekiah and the remnant of his troops up in Jerusalem 'like a bird in a cage.'"[19]

Hezekiah was forced to agree to harsh terms of surrender, including a drastically increased tribute, and he was forced "to strip the Temple and the royal treasury" in order to pay it.[20] Hezekiah's son Manasseh, who ruled from 687 to 642 BCE, gave up the rebellion and declared himself a loyal vassal of Assyria. By 622 BCE, however, Assyria was under pressure from the Babylonians and Medes, leaving Judah free to temporarily regain its independence. Assyria fell to the Babylonians and their allies in 610 BCE.

---

17. See Bright, *History of Israel*, 269–316.
18. Bright, *History of Israel*, 275.
19. Bright, *History of Israel*, 286.
20. Bright, *History of Israel*, 286.

Judah came under Egyptian control at about the same time that Babylonia defeated Assyria. The Egyptians deposed Jehoahaz, who was then king of Judah, placing his brother, Jehoiakim, on the throne as an Egyptian vassal.[21] Jehoiakim was "a petty tyrant unfit to rule."[22] He squandered resources building a new and finer palace, using forced labor to do so. Judah remained a vassal of the Pharaoh until 603 BCE when, after the Egyptians were defeated by the Babylonians at Carchemish, Jehoiakim transferred his allegiance to the Babylonian ruler Nebuchadnezzar. Not long afterward, Jehoiakim rebelled. In 597 BCE, after Jehoiakim had died and his eighteen-year-old son Jehoiachin had been placed on the throne, Jerusalem surrendered to the Babylonians. "The king, the queen mother, the high officials, and leading citizens, together with an enormous booty, were taken to Babylon."[23] The king's uncle, Zedekiah, was installed as ruler. Following further rebellion, the Babylonians placed Jerusalem under blockade, and in 587 BCE breached the walls of the city. The city was destroyed in 586 BCE, and a further group of the population was deported to Babylonia.

B. The literary prophets denounce social injustice—the oppression of the poor and weak by the wealthy and powerful—and all other forms of unrighteousness.

From as early as the time of David, prophets had denounced action by members of the ruling class that violated the moral norms and laws set forth in wisdom literature and in the several biblical law collections. One such denouncement is Nathan's condemnation of David for his adultery with Bathsheba and murder of Bathsheba's husband Uriah after David caused Bathsheba's pregnancy.[24] Then there is Elijah's condemnation of Ahab and his wife Jezebel for the treachery they used to acquire the vineyard of Naboth.[25] After Naboth refused to sell his vineyard to Ahab, Jezebel, in Ahab's name, instructed the elders and nobles in Naboth's town to get "two scoundrels" to falsely testify that Naboth had "reviled God and king," and to then, on the bases of the false testimony, stone Naboth

---

21. See generally Bright, *History of Israel*, 324–33.
22. Bright, *History of Israel*, 325.
23. Bright, *History of Israel*, 327.
24. See 2 Sam 11–12.
25. See 1 Kgs 21.

to death.²⁶ The elders and nobles did as they were told, and, after Naboth was stoned to death, Ahab went to take possession of Naboth's vineyard. Elijah confronted Ahab at the vineyard with these words: "Thus said the Lord: Would you murder and take possession? Thus said the Lord: In the very place where the dogs lapped up Naboth's blood, the dogs will lap up your blood too. . . . Because you have committed yourself to doing what is evil in the sight of the Lord, I will bring disaster upon you."²⁷

Whereas the nonliterary prophets denounced the immorality of the nation's rulers for isolated acts of wrongdoing, the literary prophets primarily denounced the immorality of *all* the people. Moreover, when the literary prophets did denounce the rulers, it was not for isolated moral lapses but for the failure to do what is "just and right" (*mishpat v'tzedakah*), that is, for the failure to establish a just society by rescuing the weak and the poor from exploitation by the strong and the wealthy.²⁸ For example, Jeremiah goes to the palace of the king of Judah and demands of the king and his courtiers: "Do what is just and right; rescue from the defrauder him who is robbed; do not wrong the stranger, the fatherless, and the widow; commit no lawless act, and do not shed the blood of the innocent in this place."²⁹

Jeremiah tells his audience that, if they did not heed his demands, "this place shall become a ruin."³⁰ He accuses King Jehoiakim of using forced labor to build his palace and of caring only about "ill-gotten gains," "shedding the blood of the innocent," and "committing fraud and violence."³¹ Jeremiah tells Jehoiakim that "all went well" with Jehoiakim's father, King Josiah, because Josiah "upheld the rights of the poor and needy."³² Similarly, Ezekiel condemns the "princes of Israel"

---

26. 1 Kgs 21:10.

27. 1 Kgs 21:19.

28. Jer 22:3; Ezek 45:9–12. See Weinfeld, *Social Justice*, 17–18, 34–36 (The Hebrew phrase *mishpat v'tzedakah* is a hendiadys signifying "the concept of social justice," and "implicitly refers to kindness and mercy"), 45–56 (discussing *mishpat v'tzedakah* as the task of the king), 219–20. Weinfeld claims that the doing of justice and righteousness by the ruling class means the enactment of social legislation "on behalf of the poor and less fortunate classes of people" so that "equality and freedom prevails." Weinfeld, *Social Justice*, 5, 8–9.

29. Jer 22:3. See Rom-Shiloni, "Jeremiah," 958 (Jeremiah makes a legal demand that the king keep specific moral laws as part of his "particular responsibility").

30. Jer 22:5.

31. Jer 22:13–17.

32. Jer 22:15–16. But see Weinfeld, *Social Justice*, 55.

because they failed to do what is "right and just"—they failed to stop people's eviction from their inherited land, failed to stop "lawlessness and rapine," and failed to establish just and standardized measures for commercial transactions.[33] Then too, Isaiah of Jerusalem indicts judicial leaders for taking bribes to pervert justice and wealthy civic leaders for robbing the poor and seizing their land.[34]

Just as a ruler must do justice and righteousness toward his people, "so, according to the Israelite perception, the individual must do justice and righteousness to his neighbor."[35] Doing justice and righteousness to one's neighbor means behaving in a "proper and correct" manner.[36] Ezekiel proclaims:

> Thus, if a man is righteous and does what is just and right . . . if he has not defiled another man's wife . . . if he has not wronged anyone; if he has returned the debtor's pledge to him and has taken nothing by robbery; if he has given bread to the hungry and clothed the naked; if he has not lent at advance interest or exacted accrued interest; if he has abstained from wrongdoing and executed true justice between man and man; if he has followed My laws and kept My rules and acted honestly—he is righteous. Such a man shall live—declares the Lord God.[37]

The other prophets make similar proclamations but, unlike Ezekiel, they do not typically provide a listing of specific behaviors that are deemed to be righteous. Rather, they speak generally. Micah, for example, says:

> He has told you, O man, what is good,
>
> And what the Lord requires of you:
>
> Only to do justice [*mishpat*]
>
> And to love goodness [*hesed*],
>
> And to walk modestly with your God;
>
> Then will your name achieve wisdom.[38]

---

33. Ezek 45:9–12. See Ezek 22:6–13 (condemning every one of the "princes of Israel"); 46:18 (The princes must not "take property away from any of the people and rob them of their holdings"); Weinfeld, *Social Justice*, 55–56; Weinfeld, "Uniqueness of the Decalogue," 16–18. See also Mic 3:1–3, 9–11 (rebuking rulers "who detest justice and make crooked all that is straight," who "build Zion with crime," and who "judge for gifts").

34. Isa 3:14; 5:8, 20, 23. See Milgrom, *Leviticus*, 214.

35. Weinfeld, *Social Justice*, 17.

36. Weinfeld, *Social Justice*, 17n26.

37. Ezek 18:5–9. See also Isa 58:6–7.

38. Mic 6:8. See Weinfeld, *Social Justice*, 1, 29 ("*Hesed*" is often found in the

THE PROPHETS CONDEMNED THE ISRAELITES

The "distinctive feature of classical prophecy is its vehement denunciation of social corruption."[39] Amos, Isaiah, Micah, and Hosea all "accuse the wealthy and aristocratic class of dispossessing and impoverishing the masses, of living wantonly and luxuriously."[40] In general, the prophets accused the people of not "knowing" Yahweh, which is to say not adhering to the stipulations of the covenant which they envisioned existed between Yahweh and the nation of Israel—not obeying God's will.[41] They envision Yahweh initiating a lawsuit against the people for their breach of the covenant, a so-called covenant lawsuit.[42]

One of the earliest of the literary prophets, Amos, preached in the northern kingdom around 750 BCE. He condemned those "who devour the needy, annihilating the poor of the land," and who used "an ephah that is too small, and a shekel that is too big, tilting a dishonest scale, and selling grain refuse as grain."[43] Hosea, a contemporary of Amos who also preached in the northern kingdom, focused more on the people's idolatry than on their disobedience of moral commands, but still Hosea condemned the latter, envisioning a covenant lawsuit:

> Hear the word of the Lord,
> O people of Israel!
> For the Lord has a case
> Against the inhabitants of the land,
> Because there is no honesty and no goodness
> And no obedience to [knowledge of] God in the land.
> [False] swearing, dishonesty, and murder,

Bible in conjunction with justice or with righteousness), 35–36 (*Hesed* is translated as "kindness" and "is identical with goodness and mercy"; it is not a characteristic that is congruous with "strict justice" but is found in conjunction with *mishpat* and *tzedakah*, or in parallelism with them); Heschel, *Prophets*, 1.201 ("Righteousness implies benevolence, kindness, generosity," and "is associated with a burning compassion for the oppressed" (citing Deut 24:10–13)); Jer 9:23 (Yahweh acts "with kindness (*hesed*), justice (*mishpat*), and equity (*tzedakah*)"). Cf. Prov 21:21 ("He who strives to do good and kind deeds (*tzedakah v'hesed*) attains life, success, and honor.").

39. Kaufmann, *Religion*, 347.
40. Kaufmann, *Religion*, 347. See, e.g., Amos 6:1, 4–7.
41. See Hillers, *Covenant*, 120–24.
42. See Hillers, *Covenant*, 124–31.
43. Amos 8:4–6. See Von Rad, *Message of the Prophets*, 106 ("Amos shows us a society whose social life is cleft in two—a property-owning and therefore economically self-sufficient upper class lived at the expense of the 'little people' [Amos 5:11; 8:6], and ... slaves, foreigners, orphans, and widows had no one to uphold their just claims [as bribery] was the order of the day [Amos 5:7, 12].").

> And theft and adultery are rife;
> Crime follows crime![44]

Isaiah was also a contemporary of Amos who prophesied in the southern kingdom of Judah. Isaiah saw and condemned the same things in the south that Amos saw and condemned in the north. According to Von Rad, Isaiah "carries forward Amos's indictments of every form of miscarriage of justice and exploitation of the weak."[45] Also in the south, Jeremiah accused the people of ignoring the plight of the needy.[46] He also condemned them for failing to execute justice between one man and another; oppressing the stranger, the orphan, and the widow; shedding the blood of the innocent; stealing; murdering; committing adultery; and falsely swearing.[47] Micah is another Judean who criticized the people for their socioeconomic abuses, "particularly the oppression of peasant landholders by the wealthy nobles of Jerusalem."[48] Micah saw in Jerusalem "greedy men dispossessing the poor [Mic 2:1–2, 8–9]; corrupt rulers who did not dispense justice but were themselves guilty of cruel oppression [Mic 3:1–3, 9–11]; and a clergy that uttered no rebuke because its only concern was its living [Mic 3:5, 11]."[49]

C. The prophets attributed the military defeats of Israel and Judah to the people's unrighteousness, and proclaimed that such unrighteousness would ultimately result in total devastation and ruin.

The prophets reinterpreted the "Day of Yahweh," which in ancient Israel referred to a day of triumph when Yahweh would intervene on Israel's behalf, to a day of destruction when Yahweh would call Israel to account for its unrighteousness.[50] Toward this end, Yahweh was seen to be directing

---

44. Hos 4:1–2.

45. Von Rad, *Message of the Prophets*, 120. See Barton, *Old Testament Ethics*, 146–47 ("Isaiah shared many of the concerns of other eighth-century prophets," focusing especially "on the expropriation of ancestral land (5:8–10) and on miscarriage of justice (1:23; 3:9; 5:23; 10:1–2; 29:21)").

46. See Jer 5:28.

47. Jer 7:5–10.

48. Bright, *History of Israel*, 293.

49. Bright, *History of Israel*, 293.

50. See Amos 5:18–20; 8:9–12; Joel 1:15–20; 2:1–2; Zeph 1:7–15; Zech 14:1. See also Hayes, *Introduction*, 258–59.

THE PROPHETS CONDEMNED THE ISRAELITES

the aggression of Assyria and Babylonia. In other words, Assyria and Babylonia were seen as instruments used by Yahweh to punish the Israelites for their unrighteousness. Hosea, for instance, interpreted the military defeats suffered by the northern kingdom at the hands of Assyria as having been brought upon that kingdom by Israel herself, "that is to say, by her evil deeds."[51] Hosea says that because Israel rejects what is good, "an enemy shall pursue him";[52] that because "they went their own way ... Assyria is their king";[53] and because "they refuse to repent ... [a] sword shall descend upon their towns [and] consume their limbs."[54]

Similarly, Isaiah interpreted Judah's military defeats as punishment inflicted by Yahweh because of the injustices and iniquities in Judean society. A parable is presented in chapter 5 of the book of Isaiah which depicts God as a farmer of a vineyard. God is said to have done everything possible for the vineyard to yield grapes but, instead, the vineyard yielded only "wild grapes."[55] The parable continues with God's determination to destroy the vineyard, now revealed to be the House of Israel and the men of Judah:

> Now I am going to tell you
> What I will do to My vineyard:
> I will remove its hedge,
> That it may be ravaged;
> I will break down its wall,
> That it may be trampled.
> And I will make it a desolation;
> It shall not be pruned or hoed,
> And it shall be overgrown with briers and thistles.
> And I will command the clouds
> To drop no rain on it.
> For the vineyard of the Lord of Hosts
> Is the House of Israel,
> And the seedlings he lovingly tended
> Are the men of Judah.

51. Von Rad, *Message of the Prophets*, 115.
52. Hos 8:3.
53. Hos 11:1–5.
54. Hos 11:5–6.
55. Isa 5:2.

And He hoped for justice [*mishpat*],
But behold, injustice [literally, "annexation" (*mishpach*)];[56]
For equity [*tzedakah*],
But behold, inequity [literally, "a cry" (*tzahkah*)]![57]

The prophets viewed the Israelites' breaches of their covenant with Yahweh as comparable to a vassal's breaches of a treaty with a suzerain. Indeed, the prophets' conception of a covenant between God and the nation of Israel may very well have been derived from their knowledge of such suzerainty treaties. And just as a suzerainty treaty contained curses intended to punish a vassal for any violation of the treaty,[58] the prophets understood the Israelites' covenant with Yahweh to contain curses intended to punish the Israelites for any violation of the covenant. In fact, according to Hillers, the prophets repeatedly "frame their oracles of woe in terms echoing the curses associated with [suzerainty] treaties."[59] A good example of such framing, according to Hillers, is contained in chapter 5 of the book of Jeremiah which "depicts the prophet, like an Israelite Diogenes, searching through Jerusalem for one righteous man."[60] When he can find no righteous man, he announces the devastation that will follow:

Therefore,
The lion of the forest strikes them down,
The wolf of the desert ravages them.
A leopard lies in wait by their towns;
Whoever leaves them will be torn in pieces.
For their transgressions are many,

---

56. See Weinfeld, *Social Justice*, 218 (*Mishpach* is "usually translated 'violence' or 'bloodshed' [but] could also have the meaning 'annexation' and here refers to the annexation of the property of the poor to the property of the rich").

57. Isa 5:5–7. See Weinfeld, *Social Justice*, 218 (The word *tzahkah* "means the cry of the oppressed"). For Weinfeld, the point of the parable is that justice and righteousness is the appointed task of the people of Israel. The vineyard (the people of Israel) ought to have brought forth justice and righteousness but produced instead the annexation of the poor people's property and the cry of the oppressed. Weinfeld, *Social Justice*, 218–19. See also Mic 3:12 ("Jerusalem shall become heaps of ruins"); Jer 4:22–28 ("The whole land shall be desolate"); 8:13–17; Zeph 1:15–18.

58. See Hillers, *Covenant*, 37–45.

59. Hillers, *Covenant*, 132.

60. Hillers, *Covenant*, 132. See Jer 5:1–5.

THE PROPHETS CONDEMNED THE ISRAELITES

Their rebellious acts unnumbered.[61]

Hillers contends that Jeremiah's words are comparable to the "wild animal" curses found in suzerainty treaties, including the first and second Sefire treaties and Esarhaddon's treaty with Baal of Tyre, as well as to curses contained in chapter 26 of Leviticus.[62] Other suzerainty treaty curses used by the prophets are curses about "breaking a man's weapon—most often the bow" and about being "compelled by famine to eat [one's] own sons and daughters."[63] Not only are the words and imagery used by the prophets in their curses comparable to the words and imagery used in suzerainty treaty curses, but the function of the curses is the same. According to Hillers, the threats made by the prophets are meant to work in the same way as the threats contained in the treaties, but the threats of the prophets "appear at a later stage, after the treaty is already broken."[64] Hillers elaborates as follows:

> It is not just that a treaty says the gods will send wild animals and that the prophets say that Yahweh will do so, but that in the treaty the curse is invoked as the consequence for rebellion and that the prophetic doom is announced for the same reason—as the consequence of rebellion. The significant thing is that Jeremiah says "Therefore a lion from the forest shall smite them." We need an adequate explanation for this "therefore." What framework is there that makes the coming of predators the just and normal course of the people's sin? There seems to be no escape from seeing the treaty relation in a special way as the foundation for this "therefore." Only if we presuppose a relation binding Israel to God on pain of curses do the prophets seem logical.[65]

Understanding that the prophets viewed Israel as having a covenant with Yahweh comparable to a vassal's treaty with his suzerain explains why the prophets proclaimed that Israel's breaches of the covenant were

---

61. Jer 5:6.

62. See Hillers, *Covenant*, 132–33. Hillers finds further instances of the "wild animal" curse in Jer 8:17 and Hos 13:7–8. Hillers, *Covenant*, 133–34.

63. Hillers, *Covenant*, 135–37 (noting "that these parallels are not occasional and scattered, but frequent and striking"). See Hos 1:5; Jer 19:9; 49:35; Ezek 5:10; 39:3.

64. Hillers, *Covenant*, 138.

65. Hillers, *Covenant*, 138–39. Although the particular imagery used by Jeremiah to describe the consequence of transgressions and rebellious acts may be explained only in terms of the breach of a suzerainty treaty, the belief that wicked conduct results in adverse consequences may, of course, also be explained in terms of the moral order ordained by God and the holiness God demanded of the Israelites.

not only the cause of defeats it suffered but would, ultimately, result in its total devastation.[66] This is because the curses in suzerainty treaties "aim at total destruction of the offender, all he is and all he has."[67] The curse "is not limited to the vassal king but is spread, in widening circles, over his wife and children, to the third generation, his possessions and his country."[68] In this regard, treaty terms are significantly different than ancient law. As Hillers explains:

> In law, whether in Mesopotamia or Israel or elsewhere, the penalty for a man's wrongdoing was inflicted on his own person, with very few exceptions, and the punishments fit the crime. The *lex talionis* (law of retaliation), "an eye for an eye" and the rest of it, was intended to limit the damages exacted to the extent of the injury done. But the punishment for breach of this oath by the gods [i.e., the oath taken upon execution of a suzerainty treaty] is neither limited nor proportionate.[69]

The idea that the fall of Israel to the Assyrians and the fall of Judah to the Babylonians were brought about by God as a result of the Israelites' unrighteousness is not an idea found solely in the prophetic books. The same idea undergirds the thinking of the deuteronomistic historian, the redactor who compiled the material from the book of Deuteronomy through the book of 2 Kings.[70] The Deuteronomist was responding to the defeat of Israel in 722 BCE and the defeat of Judah in 586 BCE. As explained by Hayes:

> Yahweh had promised the patriarchs that their descendants would live in his land. He had promised that the house of David would stand forever. But here the monarchy had collapsed, and the people were defeated and in exile.... How could the disasters of 722 and 586 be reconciled with the convictions that Yahweh controlled history and that he had an eternal covenant with Israel and David? ... The Deuteronomistic historian's basic idea is that Yahweh's unconditional and eternal covenants with the patriarchs and David do not preclude the possibility of

---

66. See Jer 7:3-15; 19:1-14; Mic 3:9-12. See also Kaufmann, *Religion*, 397 ("While Jeremiah and Ezekiel combine the religious with the moral factor in their prophesies of destruction, Micah insists that it will come for moral sins alone").

67. Hillers, *Covenant*, 38.

68. Hillers, *Covenant*, 38.

69. Hillers, *Covenant*, 38. See generally Daube, *Studies in Biblical Law*, 102-47 (discussing *lex talionis*).

70. See Hayes, *Introduction*, 230-31 (discussing the Deuteronomistic historian).

punishment or chastisement for sin, as specified in the conditional Mosaic covenant.[71]

The classic expression of this point of view is in the book of 2 Kings:

> In the ninth year of Hoshea, the king of Assyria captured Samaria. He deported the Israelites to Assyria and settled them in Halah, at the [river] Habor.... This happened because the Israelites sinned against the Lord their God.... The Lord warned Israel and Judah by every prophet [and] seer, saying: "Turn back from your wicked ways, and observe My commandments and My laws, according to all the Teaching that I commanded your fathers."... But they did not obey.... The Lord was incensed at Israel and He banished them from His presence; none was left but the tribe of Judah alone.... Nor did Judah keep the commandments of the Lord their God.... So the Lord spurned all the offspring of Israel, and He afflicted them and delivered them into the hands of plunderers, and finally He cast them out of His presence.[72]

D. Jeremiah and Ezekiel conclude that unless human nature were radically transformed, human beings would continue to disobey God's moral commands.

Many of the prophets, including Amos, Hosea, Isaiah, and Zephaniah, envisioned that a remnant of the people would survive the destruction brought upon the Israelites by violation of their covenant with God. Moreover, these prophets envisioned that this chastised remnant would repent, be restored to the land of Israel, and thereafter faithfully observe God's moral commands.[73] Isaiah also envisioned the restoration of the Davidic line of rulers.[74] But not all the prophets were sanguine about the ability of the people to repent and then obey God's moral commandments faithfully. Neither Jeremiah nor Ezekiel, both of whom were alive when Jerusalem fell in 586 BCE, believed that the people could ever obey God's moral commandments—could ever be righteous—unless God brought about a radical transformation of human nature.

71. Hayes, *Introduction*, 231–32.

72. 2 Kgs 17:6–20.

73. See Amos 9:8b–11, 13–15; Hos 2:16–25; Isa 6:11–13; 10:21–23; Zeph 3:11–15, 20.

74. Isa 11:1–11, 16.

Jeremiah, more than any other prophet, reflects on "whether man's disposition can or cannot be changed."⁷⁵ In one prophecy, Jeremiah expresses the opinion that the people are simply "unable to do right" because they are too "foolish" and too "stupid."⁷⁶ Presumably, the people's foolishness and stupidity referred to their inability to grasp and adapt to God's moral order—their inability to obey God's will.⁷⁷ In less theological terms, it likely referred to their inability to know what was really in their own interest and their inability to control their passions. In another prophecy, Jeremiah suggests that the force of habit had so permanently ingrained unrighteousness into human personality that it was now an unchangeable aspect of human nature. He queries:

> Can the Cushite [who is dark-skinned] change his skin,
> Or the leopard his spots?
> Just as much can you [the people] do good,
> Who are practiced in doing evil!⁷⁸

But Jeremiah's most significant statement concerning human nature appears in his prophecy of a new covenant in chapter 31. Implicit in this prophecy is a conviction that obedience to God's moral commands can only occur if human beings are "remade."⁷⁹ Jeremiah envisions a complete transformation of human nature when, after seventy years of

---

75. Von Rad, *Message of the Prophets*, 185.

76. Jer 4:22.

77. See Rom-Shiloni, "Jeremiah," 904 ("Jeremiah utilizes wisdom literature ... bringing into his prophesies wisdom conceptions"). Cf. chapter 1, sec. C, 2 and n137 (In wisdom literature the wise man is contrasted with the fool who is unable to adapt himself to the moral order God has imposed on humanity).

78. Jer 13:23. Cf. Aristotle, *Eth. nic.* 1103a25–1103b25 (A state of character results from the repetition of similar activities, that is, through habit, and the habits we acquire can make us either virtuous or vicious), 1105b10–20 (No one who fails to perform just acts has the least prospect of becoming just).

79. See Heschel, *Prophets*, 1.128. See also Kaufmann, *Religion*, 426 ("Experience teaches [Jeremiah] that mankind as now constituted cannot keep God's covenant, hence a new mankind must be created"); Levinson, "Deuteronomy," 414 (Regarding Deut 30:6—which states that God would "open up [circumcise]" the hearts of the Israelites after bringing them back from exile—Levinson comments that "God is the agent," in contrast with the previous call [in Deut 10:16] for the Israelites to themselves "cut away" the thickening about their hearts. "The change in perspective," says Levinson, "suggests skepticism about the people's ability to effect such a change of heart independently. Still more skepticism is evident in the prophetic vision of a divine 'reprogramming' of the human heart by inscribing the Torah upon it (Jer 31:31–34; Ezek 11:19–20; 36:26–27)").

exile in Babylon,[80] God makes a "new covenant" with the Israelites. In making the new covenant, Jeremiah prophesies, God would write his moral commandments upon the hearts of the people so that all men shall "heed" (literally, "know") Yahweh.[81] As explained by Von Rad, what was new in the new covenant was not different conduct that God required from man, but the ability of man to act in accordance with the conduct that God had already required:

> The content of the Sinai covenant was the revelation of the *torah*, that is to say, the revelation of Israel's election and appropriation by Yahweh and his will as expressed in law. This *torah* is also to stand in the centre of the new covenant. . . . Jeremiah neither says that the revelation given at Sinai is to be nullified in whole or part . . . nor does he in any sense suggest any alteration or expansion of its content in the new covenant. The reason why a new covenant is to ensue on the old is not that the regulations revealed in the latter have proved inadequate, but that the covenant has been broken, because Israel refused to obey it. . . . Yahweh is, as it were, to by-pass the process of speaking and listening, and to put his will straight into Israel's heart. . . . [If] God puts his will directly into their hearts, then, properly speaking, the rendering of obedience is completely done away with, for the problem of obedience only arises when a man's will is confronted by an alien will. Now, however, the possibility of such a confrontation has ceased to exist, for men are to have the will of God in their heart, and are only to will God's will. What is here outlined is the picture of a new man, a man who is able to obey perfectly because of a miraculous change of his nature.[82]

---

80. See Jer 29:10.

81. Jer 31:31–34. See Heschel, *Prophets*, 1.128–29 ("the new covenant" will accomplish "the complete transformation of every individual"); Rom-Shiloni, "Jeremiah," 982 ("In the new covenant, God's 'torah' (*Teaching*) will be internalized into the hearts and minds of the people, an internal transformation that will remove the option of disobedience"); Hayes, *Introduction*, 295 (The new covenant "will be inscribed directly upon the heart, built into human nature so that there will be no need to study and learn what Yahweh requires . . . [rather] humans will be hardwired to obey these teachings"). See also Levinson, "Deuteronomy," 414.

82. Von Rad, *Message of the Prophets*, 182. See Hayes, *Introduction*, 295–96. The idea that the heart prevents human beings from acting righteously is already present in the early biblical narrative of the flood story. See Gen 6:5 ("Every plan [or inclination, *yetzer*] devised by [man's] mind [or heart, *lev*] was nothing but evil all the time"); 8:21 ("The devisings of man's mind [or inclinations of man's heart, *yetzer levo ha-adam*] are evil from his youth"). See generally Collins, *Jewish Wisdom*, 82.

In chapter 32, Jeremiah talks of God giving the exiles who return to Jerusalem from Babylon a "single heart and a single nature" to "revere" (literally, "fear") Yahweh in order that the new covenant becomes "an everlasting" one.[83] Specifically, he declares in God's name:

> I will give them a single heart [*lev 'echad*] and a single nature [*derech 'echad*] to revere [fear] Me for all time, and it shall be well with them and their children after them. And I will make an everlasting covenant with them ... and I will put into their hearts reverence for [fear of] Me, so that they do not turn away from Me.[84]

The use of the expression "fearing Yahweh" links Jeremiah's view with wisdom literature where the fear of God is associated with having knowledge of, and adapting to, God's moral order.[85] Jeremiah places this "fear of God" in the human heart not primarily because the human heart was believed to be the organ responsible for wisdom and understanding, but because the human heart was "recognized as a governing factor in one's behaviour."[86]

According to Johnson, "It is through the instrumentality of the heart that a man decides upon one particular course of action as against another."[87] Accordingly, Yahweh is more concerned with a person's heart than with their conduct.[88] Even if your conduct is good and you do that which God commands, you might possess a defective heart. For example, you might decide to do the right thing to trick another person into believing you are trustworthy. Therefore, Yahweh "examines"

---

83. Jer 32:36–40. See also Urbach, *Sages*, 1.400–19 (analyzing love and reverence [fear] of God in rabbinic sources).

84. Jer 32:39–40.

85. See chapter 1, sec. C, 3. See also Rom-Shiloni, "Jeremiah," 904 ("Jeremiah utilizes wisdom literature ... bringing into his prophesies wisdom conceptions").

86. Johnson, *Vitality*, 79. See generally Johnson, *Vitality*, 75–87 (In ancient Israel, the heart was considered the seat or instrument of human intellectual and volitional activity).

87. Johnson, *Vitality*, 79. See also Greenstein, "The Heart," 209–10 ("The biblical 'heart' functions as the seat of emotions, will, and thought"). Hayes errs in asserting that Jeremiah is registering "dissatisfaction with the element of free will." Hayes, *Introduction*, 295–96. Rather, Jeremiah is suggesting that human beings lacked the capacity (including knowledge and self-control) to choose correctly. See generally Eichrodt, *Theology*, 1.357–58 (In prophetic thought, the divine power "does not seek from men the submission of senseless automata.... It challenges them to make their own judgments and decisions"). See also chapter 5, n151 and accompanying text.

88. See chapter 2, n90.

the heart to know the kind of person you really are.[89] When at Sinai/ Horeb the Israelites promise to Moses, "You tell us everything that the Lord our God tells you, and we will willingly do it," God says, "May they always be of such a mind [literally, *lev*, "heart"], to revere Me and follow all my commandments, that it may go well with them and with their children forever!"[90] Conversely, the Bible associates the failure to do that which God commands with a defective heart, often equating disobedience with a deceitful heart (concealing one's true intentions or misrepresenting the truth) or an arrogant heart (thinking that you are better than, or deserve more than, others).[91] Jeremiah himself accuses the Judeans of having both types of defective hearts.[92]

Johnson further states that when Jeremiah asserts about the soon-to-be-exiled men of Judah that there has been a "thickening about [their] hearts"[93] and that "all the House of Israel are uncircumcised of heart,"[94] he is implying that "if Yahweh's ideal standard of behaviour is to become an actuality, it is necessary for man to undergo a radical change of heart."[95] His uncircumcised heart must be changed to a "faithful heart"

---

89. See Johnson, *Vitality*, 84. See also Jer 17:10 (Yahweh probes the heart to repay everyone with "the proper fruit of his deeds").

90. Deut 5:24–25.

91. See Johnson, *Vitality*, 85 (citing numerous examples). See also Lev 26:41 (Pursuant to the curses of the covenant, after their disobedience causes God to spurn the Israelites and scatter them among the nations, "their obdurate [lit. "uncircumcised"] heart" shall "humble itself, and they shall atone for their iniquity").

92. See Jer 17:9; 49:16. See also Job 31:5–10 (In proclaiming his righteousness, Job says that his "heart" did not "follow after [his] eyes" and was not "ravished by the wife of [his] neighbor").

93. Jer 4:4. See also Isa 6:10 (petitioning God to make the people's heart fat [*hashmen lev ha'am*] so that they cannot repent and be saved).

94. Jer 9:25. Cf. Deut 10:16; 30:6; Lev 26:41.

95. Johnson, *Vitality*, 85–86 ("Failure to act fittingly or aright to Yahweh's demands is ascribed, on the one hand, to the 'fatty' condition of the heart or (somewhat similarly) to its need for 'circumcision,' and, on the other hand, to the fact that the heart has turned to stone or, as we should say, has become 'petrified'" [citing numerous biblical passages]). Jeremiah's reference to the "thickening [about] their hearts" seems to refer to an actual physical condition brought about by unrighteous conduct. Such an understanding implies that the radical change of heart Jeremiah desired entailed the removal of the outer part of the human heart that unrighteousness had made thick, fat, or hard. Therefore, Jeremiah analogizes this radical change of heart to the circumcision which is the sign of the covenant between God and Israel—the removal of the foreskin from the penis—and calls the heart still encased in a thickened outer part an "uncircumcised" heart. See Jer 4:4 ("Open [lit. 'circumcise'] your hearts to the Lord. Remove the thickening about your hearts"). Cf. Deut 10:16 ("Cut away [lit. 'circumcise'] . . . the thickening

THE UNDIVIDED HEART

(*lev ne'eman*),⁹⁶ a "steadfast heart" (*lev nachon*),⁹⁷ a heart that is "wholehearted with," or "at one (*shalem*) with," Yahweh, and thus he will be able "to walk in [Yahweh's] ways and keep His commandments,"⁹⁸ able to serve Yahweh "faithfully, with all [his] heart."⁹⁹

It appears from this that Jeremiah sees that human beings are conflicted, torn between competing desires, or, as we might say today, of two minds. One might love one's neighbor and desire to do that which is righteous by treating one's neighbor fairly but fail to do so because of a competing desire or emotion. The desire for wealth or power or sexual satisfaction might compete with the desire to do that which is righteous; and emotions of hate, jealousy, or fear might compete with the emotion of love for one's neighbor. When these competing desires and emotions affect the choice made,¹⁰⁰ the heart is defective, not at one with Yahweh. Thus, Jeremiah concludes, human beings will not do what is righteous unless Yahweh gives them a "single heart" (or, better translated, an "undivided heart" or an "integrated heart"),¹⁰¹ a heart that is at one with Yahweh because it is not divided by competing desires and emotions and is able to integrate all desires and emotions into a harmonious whole which chooses to follow Yahweh's moral commands.¹⁰² The problem of the heart

---

about your hearts"), 30:6 ("God will open up [circumcise] your heart"); Lev 26:41. In this way, the new covenant that Jeremiah envisions is accompanied by a new circumcision, a new sign of the covenant.

96. Neh 9:8.

97. Ps 57:8.

98. 1 Kgs 8:61; 15:3, 14. See also 1 Chr 28:9 (*lev shalem*).

99. 1 Sam 12:24; 1 Kgs 2:4. See Johnson, *Vitality*, 84–85. See also Ps 119:2, 10, 34; 1 Chr 29:17–18.

100. The Hebrew "*lev*" may usefully be compared to the Greek "*thymos*" as used during the Homeric period. In the Homeric epic poems, the *thymos* is the organ associated with intellectual activity that is charged with emotion such as when someone must deliberate and choose among competing options. When Odysseus is left alone in battle and must choose what to do, Homer writes that Odysseus spoke to his proud *thymos* and deliberated about two possibilities—two courses of action. Homer, *Iliad*, 11.403-13. See Bremmer, *Greek Soul*, 55.

101. Cf. Ps 86:11 ("Let my heart be undivided [*yachad*]"); Exod 26:6 ("And make fifty gold clasps, and couple the cloths to one another with the clasps, so that the Tabernacle becomes one whole [*mishkan echad*]"; that is, the cloths become united, a single unit); 36:13 ("Couple the units to one another . . . so that the Tabernacle becomes one whole"). The adverbial form of this root is used in Deuteronomy to describe two or more disparate things being brought together to work in harmony as a single unit. See Deut 22:10 ("You shall not plow with an ox and an ass together [*yachdav*, in harmony]").

102. See Johnson, *Vitality*, 82–83 (The heart of one who acts in conformity with God's

being affected by desires and emotions that impede one's choosing to obey God's moral commands will develop in rabbinic material into the notion of the "bad impulse" (*yetzer ha-rah*).[103]

Jeremiah's prophecy concerning the creation of a transformed human being influenced Ezekiel, and the position of Ezekiel with respect to human nature is virtually identical to that of Jeremiah.[104] Ezekiel claims that the people are totally dominated by sin and that they have been so dominated in every age of Israel's history.[105] Ezekiel understands the problem to be, as did Jeremiah, that the hearts of the people were defective. Specifically, he says that their hearts are hearts of stone.[106] Accordingly, he agrees with Jeremiah that the people cannot act righteously unless they are given new hearts, hearts that are not hearts of stone but hearts of flesh.[107] Ezekiel, as Jeremiah, describes this new heart of flesh as being "one heart" (*lev 'echad*),[108] indicating that Ezekiel, as Jeremiah, believed that disobedience to God's moral commands occurs when desires and emotions adverse to righteous conduct affect the decision-making process.

In addition to the need for "one heart," Ezekiel claims that the people need to be given a new "spirit" (*ruach*).[109] In this way, he says (declaring the word of Yahweh), "I will cause [them] to follow My laws and faithfully to observe My rules."[110] The reference to a new spirit reflects

---

moral commands is described in terms of its "integrity"); 1 Kgs 3:6 (David "walked before [God] in faithfulness and righteousness and in integrity of heart"). See also Heschel, *Prophets*, 1.211 ("Inner identification with God's will ... is the goal of the new covenant"). Cf. Wis 1:1 ("singleness of heart"); Aristotle, *Eth. nic.* 1102b15–25 (distinguishing virtuous people, whose souls are integrated in that the irrational part of the soul "agrees with reason in everything," from continent and incontinent persons, whose souls are divided in that the irrational part of the soul clashes and struggles with reason).

103. See Johnson, *Vitality*, 85n2; chapter 9, sec. C. See also Schechter, *Aspects of Rabbinic Theology*, 252 ("When a man 'loves in his heart' to do a [*mitzvah*, give charity], the *Evil Yezer* in him says, 'Why should you do a [*mitzvah*] and diminish thy property?'" [quoting *Exod. Rab.* 36:8]).

104. See Kaufmann, *Religion*, 442.

105. Von Rad, *Message of the Prophets*, 198. See Bright, *History of Israel*, 337 ("Ezekiel declared that his people had been corrupt from the beginning" [citing Ezek 20:1–31; 23]).

106. Ezek 11:19; 36:26.

107. Ezek 11:19; 18:31; 36:26.

108. Ezek 11:19.

109. Ezek 36:26. Cf. Ps 51:12.

110. Ezek 36:27. See also Klawans, *Impurity and Sin*, 30–31 (By "conjuring the image of ritual purification [in Ezek 36:25] Ezekiel may be figuratively describing the ease

the fact that, for the ancient Israelite, the heart "is ultimately regarded as specifically subject to the influence of the [*ruach*]."¹¹¹ In short, Ezekiel, no less than Jeremiah, envisions a future when "Yahweh's law, teachings, and commandments will not change" but when the Israelites will be able to follow Yahweh's law, teachings, and commandments because "human nature will [have been] transformed."¹¹² As Von Rad explains, Ezekiel's position closely parallels "Jeremiah's pericope on the new covenant (Jer 31:33ff.).... [The] purpose of God's saving activity is the re-creation of a people able to obey the commandments perfectly."¹¹³

E. The literary prophets proclaim that obedience to God's moral commands is more important than adherence to God's cultic requirements.

For the prophets, the moral requirements of the covenant are far more important than the cultic requirements, and they admonish the people for being scrupulous in obeying the latter but lax in obeying the former.¹¹⁴ In fact, the prophets rank ethics as supreme; they maintain that Israel's holiness depends on its adherence to the covenant's moral requirements, not its cultic requirements. To put it differently, for the prophets, "Yahweh's holiness is characterized mainly by ethics."¹¹⁵ Isaiah, for example, declares that Yahweh is "exalted by *mishpat*" and "proved holy by *tzedakah*."¹¹⁶ Since Yahweh's holiness is due to Yahweh being just and righteous, for Israel to be holy requires that Israel be just and

---

with which God will be able to bring about a change in the people's moral status ... [but without] God's help, the defilement of the people by sin is permanent").

111. Johnson, *Vitality*, 82.

112. Hayes, *Introduction*, 305. Hayes asserts that this transformed nature entails a loss of free will. Hayes, *Introduction*, 305. As with her similar assertion regarding Jeremiah, this assertion is inaccurate. See n87 in this chapter. But see Ganzel, "Ezekiel," 1051.

113. Von Rad, *Message of the Prophets*, 203.

114. See generally Eichrodt, *Theology*, 1.364–68; 2.326–29. According to Eichrodt, the prophetic movement creates no "new content," but it does, however, make "the authority of the moral norms more inwardly based," insisting that one be "convinced of the justice of the good" and condemning mere "external submission" to the moral commands of the covenant law. Eichrodt, *Theology*, 2.327–28, 338 ("Truly moral action is not exhausted in the external observance of incidental prescriptions, but presupposes an interior affirmation of the divine will").

115. Milgrom, *Leviticus*, 215.

116. Isa 5:16.

righteous. In this regard the prophets are to be distinguished from H, the priestly school founded at about the same time that classical prophecy began. Although H emphasizes the idea that the people must be holy and insists that moral conduct is necessary for holiness, H also insists that adherence to ritual is as important for holiness as moral conduct.[117]

Not only do the prophets consider being "just and righteous" the primary requirement for holiness but they "go beyond the early religion" in making Israel's justice and righteousness "decisive for the national destiny."[118] Kaufmann explains as follows:

> In the literature prior to classical prophecy, national doom and exile are, as a rule, threatened only for idolatry. The idea that God dooms a whole society for moral corruption is not altogether absent in the early literature, but it is for particularly heinous sins which the whole society has committed or is responsible for that the doom comes [such as in the accounts of the Flood and Sodom and Gomorrah]. . . . Violations of everyday social morality—perversion of justice, bribe-taking, exploitation of the poor, and the like—are never mentioned. These are regarded as "venial sins," subject to the regular process of God's judgment and his individual providence.
>
> Classical prophecy radically alters this view; it threatens national doom and exile for everyday social sins. . . . The new stress on morality has as its concomitant a new attitude toward the cult. It was the prophets who expressed for the first time the idea that the cult . . . has no intrinsic value. . . . Morality, on the other hand, is an absolute value. . . . [While] the cult is sacred only as a symbol, morality is essentially godlike, being a reflection of the qualities of God.[119]

Amos is the first prophet to make social morality the decisive factor in Israel's national destiny and "to conceive the idea of the primacy of morality."[120] In a first-person direct speech attributed to Yahweh, Amos says:

> I loathe, I spurn your festivals,
> I am not appeased by your solemn assemblies.
> If you offer Me burnt offerings—or your meal offerings—

---

117. See Milgrom, *Leviticus*, 215, 221–22; chapter 3, sec. B, 3–4.
118. Kaufmann, *Religion*, 365.
119. Kaufmann, *Religion*, 365–67. See also Hayes, *Introduction*, 255–58.
120. Kaufmann, *Religion*, 366, 368.

> I will not accept them;
> I will pay no heed
> To your gifts of fatlings.
> Spare Me the sound of your hymns,
> And let Me not hear the music of your lutes.
> But let justice well up like water,
> Righteousness like an unfailing stream.[121]

Other prophets are no less emphatic in urging the primacy of morality. Micah, for example, offers the following rhetorical questions about cultic observance:

> With what shall I approach the Lord,
> Do homage to God on high?
> Shall I approach Him with burnt offerings,
> With calves a year old?
> Would the Lord be pleased with thousands of rams,
> With myriads of streams of oil?[122]

He then responds that what is good (*tov*), and what God requires, is only that the people act justly and with kindness (*hesed*).[123] For Jeremiah, the national cult was an abomination. He not only censured it, but he declared that its sacrificial ritual "had never been more than peripheral to Yahweh's demands."[124]

F. For the prophets, righteousness is something that is intrinsically good as well as instrumentally good.

The prophets certainly express a belief that obedience to God's moral commands results in military success, political power, and prosperity for the nation of Israel,[125] and that disobedience of God's moral commands results in military defeat, loss of political power, and material ruin for the nation of Israel. So, it can be argued, for the prophets (no less than for

---

121. Amos 5:21–24.
122. Mic 6:6–7.
123. Mic 6:8. See n38 in this chapter ("*Hesed*" is associated with justice and righteousness). See also Isa 1:10–17; 58:2–10; Jer 7:1–12; Hos 6:6. Cf. Prov 21:2, 27.
124. Bright, *History of Israel*, 338 (citing Jer 6:16–21; 7:21–23).
125. See, e.g., Isa 48:18.

the sages and legists), kindness, justice, and righteousness are justified by their beneficial consequences for the nation; they are primarily *instrumentally* good, the means to achieving national well-being.[126] Therefore, the ethical theory that best characterizes the justification the prophets offer for their moral judgments is utilitarianism.

Yet, it can also be argued that for the prophets, kindness, justice, and righteousness are primarily *intrinsically* good. They are good not because they are the means to achieving material well-being for the nation, but because they constitute the qualities that God wants you to possess, the qualities that constitute holiness, the qualities that one needs in order to be in a state of well-being.[127] Consequently, kindness, justice, and righteousness are superior to all other goods, including wisdom, strength, and riches. Jeremiah expresses this position when he writes:

> Thus said the Lord:
> Let not the wise man glory in his wisdom;
> Let not the strong man glory in his strength;
> Let not the rich man glory in his riches.
> But only in this should one glory:
> In his earnest devotion to Me.
> For I the Lord act with kindness [*hesed*],
> Justice [*mishpat*], and equity [*tzedakah*] in the world;
> For in these I delight.[128]

According to Eichrodt, in ascribing only "relative value" to "the natural goods" the prophets represent a change from "ancient Israel."[129] He claims that to a "large extent the goods to which action is directed in ancient Israel are *the natural goods of life*, those which are indispensable for the existence of the community."[130] These natural goods are, he

---

126. National or collective well-being must be distinguished from individual well-being. The individual members of Israelite society who had achieved material well-being for themselves was the very segment that the prophets condemned for denying material well-being to everyone else through their unrighteousness.

127. Cf. Von Rad, *Wisdom in Israel*, 80 (For the authors of Proverbs "blessing" is achieved by "integration" into the divine order); Perdue, *Wisdom and Cult*, 11 (The objective of the wise man is to achieve "harmony within himself" by successfully integrating into the world order).

128. Jer 9:22–24. See Eichrodt, *Theology*, 2.355 (Jeremiah is here seeing and grasping the "higher world of spiritual and moral life in fellowship with God").

129. Eichrodt, *Theology*, 2.349–59.

130. Eichrodt, *Theology*, 2.349 (emphasis original).

says, "peace, or at least victorious war, abundance of children, worldly possessions, long life, friendship and love," and "it is to these goods that the promises and threats at the close of the Law relate."[131] Eichrodt further claims that, with changing social and economic circumstances, the prophets brought out "with unmistakable clarity *the extremely relative value of all natural goods*."[132] The prophets, writes Eichrodt,

> do not see the natural goods as either harmful in themselves or as unimportant and valueless for the loyal Yahwist; but they certainly do regard them as only of relative value. For they are measured against an absolute value, namely the destiny of Israel to be God's people. . . . Where earthly goods come into conflict with this supreme value, there they indeed lose all worth of their own, and fall under condemnation.[133]

Ultimately, Eichrodt sees the prophets as having *combined* "natural goods" and "spiritual goods."[134] He claims that this combination of natural and spiritual goods is demonstrated by the prophets' terminology, including their use of the word *shalom* (well-being), "which as early as Num 6:26 is used in the widest sense to include every divine blessing, and which now combines the supreme good of fellowship with God with the blessings of earthly life."[135]

---

131. Eichrodt, *Theology*, 2.349.
132. Eichrodt, *Theology*, 2.354 (emphasis original).
133. Eichrodt, *Theology*, 2.355.
134. Eichrodt, *Theology*, 2.358.
135. Eichrodt, *Theology*, 2.358. By "fellowship with God" Eichrodt means being in the right relationship with God by being obedient to God's commandments. See Eichrodt, *Theology*, 2.249, 254.

CHAPTER 5

Job and Qoheleth questioned the traditional doctrine that Yahweh rewards the righteous and punishes the wicked, but Ben Sira defended the doctrine; other texts posited a postmortem reward and punishment.

BABYLON FELL TO CYRUS II of Persia in 539 BCE and the following year Cyrus issued a decree liberating the Judean exiles. The first group of exiles returned immediately thereafter. The rebuilding of the temple (destroyed by the Babylonians in 587 BCE) soon commenced and the rebuilt temple was dedicated in 515 BCE. This marks the beginning of the Second Temple period, which extends until the Romans destroyed the rebuilt temple in 70 CE. During the first third of the Second Temple period (the Persian period), the Jewish community in the relatively small Persian province of Yehud or Judea enjoyed "a more or less large autonomy."[1] The Persian period ends and the Hellenistic period begins in 334 BCE when Alexander the Great conquered Persia. The Hellenistic period ends and the Roman period begins in 30 BCE when the Romans defeated the Ptolemaic Kingdom after having conquered Jerusalem in 63 BCE.[2]

---

1. Bickerman, *From Ezra*, 13.
2. See generally Scheindlin, *Short History*, 25–49 (providing a brief history of Judea and the Jewish diaspora during the Second Temple period); Cohen, *From the Maccabees*, 1–6, 8–12 (containing a chronology and summary of postexilic developments).

The most important event during the Persian period, aside from the restoration of the temple, was the activity of Ezra and Nehemiah. Nehemiah governed Judea from 445 to sometime after 433 BCE, and then for another shorter period. Following an outcry that unfair economic practices (similar to those that had been condemned by the prophets) were being employed by the wealthy and powerful against the poor, Nehemiah instituted several economic reforms described in chapter 5 of the book of Nehemiah. These reforms included the remission of debts incurred to pay the king's tax; the manumission of the debtors' sons and daughters who had been given as a pledge and then subjected to slavery on account of the debts; and the return to the debtors of their fields, vineyards, and homes that had been used as security for the debt and ultimately forfeited.[3]

Ezra, described in the Bible as "a scribe expert in the Teaching of Moses [*torat moshe*]" and as a "priest-scribe, a scholar in matters concerning the commandments of the Lord and His laws to Israel," arrived in Judea sometime during the last half of the fifth century BCE with a commission from the Persian emperor to "regulate Judah and Jerusalem according to the law of your God."[4] The Bible relates that Ezra initiated the public reading of the "Teaching of Moses" and that the entire community took "an oath with sanctions to follow the Teaching of God, given through Moses . . . and to observe carefully all the commandments of the Lord."[5] These teachings, compiled by the Judean elders in Babylonia using documents preserved from the period of the monarchy, came to be called the Torah.[6] The Torah became the object of constant study and meditation. According to Bickerman:

---

3. Neh 5:4–12. See Weinfeld, *Social Justice*, 168–69. See also Greengus, *Laws in the Bible*, 127 (Debt slavery "was increasingly recognized as injurious to the health of a society and its people," and the measures taken by Nehemiah (ca. 450 BCE) "are paralleled by the reforms of Solon in Athens (ca. 600 BCE)").

4. See Ezra 7:1–20. See also Blenkinsopp, *Wisdom and Law*, 120–21 ("The final compilation and redaction of the laws may therefore have been mandated by the [Persian] authorities as the civil and religious constitution of the province of Yehud").

5. Neh 8:1–12; 10:1–30.

6. See Scheindlin, *Short History*, 30–31 ("The Judean elders in Babylonia compiled an official national history and codification of laws, customs, and religious practices, enabling them to reorganize the national identity around religious behavior and to some extent to turn the national identity itself into a religion"); Blenkinsopp, *Wisdom and Law*, 138 ("The gradual development towards a comprehensive Torah, the Pentateuch as we have it, followed the evolving and expanding need for normative order in the postexilic community").

The democratization of the instruction in the Law in the fourth century opened the way to the coming of the scribe, and imperceptibly compromised the supremacy of the priest. From now on, the superiority of learned argument over authoritative decree prevailed.[7]

These developments are significant. The moral change from esteeming qualities and conduct having competitive value to esteeming qualities and conduct having cooperative value had previously been accepted by only a small segment of society.[8] In particular, it may only have been the intelligentsia—sages, legists, priests, and prophets—who unreservedly esteemed those qualities and that conduct having cooperative value, collectively referred to as "righteousness" (*tzedakah*).[9] When, in the postexilic period, the Torah was accepted as an authoritative text, publicly read, and widely taught, many more people would have come to esteem righteousness, even if most people still did not act righteously.

Despite more people esteeming righteousness, there had been, and continued to be, disagreement about the justification or rationale for righteousness.[10] Most often it was claimed that righteousness was instrumentally good. It was the means of achieving a prosperous society. But it was also claimed that righteousness was intrinsically good. It was justified because God commanded it. This preexilic disagreement is more fully examined in section A. Disagreements about the justification for righteousness not only persisted in the postexilic period but became

---

7. Bickerman, *From Ezra*, 17–18. See also Blenkinsopp, *Wisdom and Law*, 141 (The author of the Chronicles restricts the task of those "professionally responsible" for the interpretation of the written law "largely if not exclusively to Levites," but eventually "it would be shared by laymen," and "Ben Sira attests that the scribe was first and foremost a legal scholar with the responsibility of teaching others").

8. See chapter 4, nn6–9 and accompanying text.

9. Included among the specific qualities and conduct accepted by all as constituting righteousness were: seeking peace and avoiding strife or discord; not committing acts of violence; being temperate and slow to anger; being honest and fair in dealings with fellow Israelites; not using false weights or other deceptive business practices; not having sexual relations with someone else's wife; not oppressing the defenseless; not stealing; not bearing false witness or otherwise perverting the system of dispute resolution; not spreading false rumors or revealing secrets; not being envious of others or coveting their property; respecting and obeying one's parents; and being just, humble, patient, generous, and compassionate.

10. See generally Barton, *Old Testament Ethics*, 28–30, 45–54 (discussing what Barton takes to be the three basic models, or types of "rationales," underlying biblical ethical principles: "obedience to God's revealed will," "conformity to a pattern of natural order," and "imitation of God"); Fox, "Reflections on the Foundations," 36–39.

more compelling and varied. Increasingly people saw themselves as individuals rather than members of a community, and they began to question whether righteousness served their individual interests.

This increasing individualism led to the problem of moral evil, addressed in section B. In brief, the crucial moral problem in the centuries before the Common Era arose from the realization that righteousness did *not* result in material benefits and well-being for the righteous individual, as was thought to be required by the moral order created by God. On the contrary, righteous people suffered material deprivation and subservience while wicked people enjoyed great wealth and power. This perversion of justice is called the problem of moral evil. The problem is addressed at length in the biblical books of Job and Qoheleth [Ecclesiastes]—both believed to have been written around 250 BCE. Although the author of Job acknowledges the problem (acknowledges, that is, the existence of moral evil), questioning whether well-being is in fact the necessary consequence of righteousness, he doesn't reject the ultimate value of righteousness. But the author of Qoheleth concludes that the value of righteousness is exceeded by the value of enjoyment or pleasure.

Ben Sira, the author of the apocryphal book The Wisdom of Ben Sira [Ecclesiasticus or Sirach], written in about 180 BCE and discussed in section C, was familiar with the book of Qoheleth and accepted its conclusion that enjoyment is intrinsically good, but he did not reject the ultimate value of righteousness. Rather, he denied that there was a problem; he denied the existence of moral evil. Ben Sira insisted that eventually, and *in this life*, righteous individuals (the "godly") always prosper and unrighteous individuals (the "sinners") always suffer. This had been and continued to be the conventional teaching of the Israelite wisdom tradition.

This conventional teaching became impossible to accept after the reign of Antiochus IV (r. 175-164 BCE). Antiochus persecuted and slaughtered the most righteous Jews (those most loyal to the covenant) and granted power and wealth to the most wicked Jews (those willing to transgress the covenant).[11] The reality that unrighteous individuals lived long lives in prosperity while righteous individuals suffered persecution and were slaughtered in their youth could no longer be denied, and it

---

11. See Scheindlin, *Short History*, 36–38 (describing Antiochus's attempt to impose Hellenistic culture on the Judeans and the conflict that arose between those Judeans who supported Antiochus's attempt at Hellenization and those Judeans who resisted it); Starr, *Toward a History*, 39–41; Moore, *Judaism in the First Centuries*, 1.48–55.

could not be explained by conventional wisdom. Nevertheless, as discussed in section D, people faced with the reality of moral evil could continue to extol righteousness by adopting new beliefs. They postulated the existence of an afterlife and argued that, if righteous individuals did not prosper (and wicked individuals did not suffer) in this life, they would surely prosper (and suffer) in an afterlife.

A. Differences in ethical theories justifying righteousness.

The dominant basis upon which Proverbs and the biblical law collections justified righteousness was the type of teleological (or consequentialist) ethical theory called utilitarianism. This is to say that righteousness was believed to result in beneficial consequences (well-being) for the nation. This belief rested primarily on two grounds: that such an act-consequence relationship was inherent in the nature of the moral order Yahweh had created, and that Yahweh had covenanted with the nation, promising that, if Israelites were righteous (or, in priestly terminology, holy), Yahweh would bless the nation with prosperity.

Proverbs and the biblical law collections, however, also justified moral norms by the type of teleological ethical theory called ethical egoism. This is to say that righteousness was believed to result in beneficial consequences (well-being) for each righteous person.[12] This belief could be easily held because the people did not see themselves primarily as individuals but as part of the collective whole. Therefore, their own individual well-being was, for them, inextricably linked to the well-being of the Israelite nation. In addition, righteousness was in each person's individual interest because it was enforced through a "shame culture" and/or humanly imposed sanctions. Furthermore, actions not subject to shame or human sanctions (because they were done in secret) were believed to be enforced by Yahweh, who probes the heart. Finally, any failure of individuals to be rewarded or punished in a manner warranted by their conduct was masked by the belief in collective and intergenerational reward and punishment. Righteous individuals might be suffering, and wicked people might be prospering, due to the conduct of their ancestors.

---

12. See generally Fox, "Reflections on the Foundations," 36–37 ("Perhaps the most common mode of justification for observing the commandments is the hope for reward and the fear of punishment. . . . In Scripture this mode of justification occurs repeatedly. . . . [This] approach is taken toward individuals, not only toward the people as a corporate body").

Yet, these understandings of the Hebrew Bible's justification of righteousness, as based on a *teleological* ethical theory, are contradicted by the Bible's teaching that righteousness is to be preferred *over* material well-being. On the basis of this teaching, righteousness cannot be justified as *instrumentally* good—good as the means to collective and/or individual well-being—because righteousness is to be chosen *instead of* material well-being. In other words, righteousness is justified as itself *intrinsically* good, good because it reflects the will of Yahweh and places the individual in the right relationship with Yahweh and the moral order Yahweh created.

Such a justification of righteousness is graphically depicted in the biblical narrative of the binding of Isaac.[13] In this narrative, Abraham is praised for conforming his will with God's will even though what God willed was the death of Isaac upon whose life depended all the promises of material well-being God had made to Abraham.[14] That adverse consequences would result from conforming his will to God's will was irrelevant to Abraham's choice of conduct. For Abraham, the only relevant consideration in choosing what to do (the only justification for his choice) was whether or not he was conforming his will to God's will—whether or not he was obeying God's command and, therefore, was in the right relationship with God. This sort of justification for one's choice of conduct is the hallmark of a type of non-consequentialist (or *deontological*) justification called the Divine Command Theory.[15]

As Frankena explains, however, one who proclaims adherence to the Divine Command Theory may, in reality, be a closet teleologist:

> Sometimes, when asked why we should do what God wills, a theologian replies that we should do so because God will

---

13. Gen 22. See Sarna, *Understanding Genesis*, 163 (The divine communication to Abraham held out no expectation of reward, and tradition "has rightly seen in Abraham the exemplar of steadfast, disinterested loyalty to God"). Cf. Dan 3. See also Fox, "Reflections on the Foundations," 36–38 (contrasting a "purely prudential mode of justification" with a mode of justification "which puts the primary stress on the fact that the commandments come from God, and this alone is sufficient to make them binding on man").

14. To say that Abraham conformed his will to the will of God implies that Abraham's heart was undivided or integrated in the way that Jeremiah and Ezekiel envisioned would occur if God recreated mankind with a new heart. See chapter 4, sec. D.

15. See Frankena, *Ethics*, 16–17, 23–30 (The "Divine Command Theory" is a deontological ethical theory which holds that the standard of what is morally right is "the will or law of God"). Cf. Daube, *Law and Wisdom*, 56–65 (distinguishing what Daube calls the "authentication" of a law from the "reasons" for a law).

reward us if we do and punish us if we do not, if not in this life then in the hereafter. This reply may be meant only to motivate us to obey God, but if it is intended to justify the claim that we ought to obey God, then it presupposes a basic ethical egoism, for then the theologian is telling us that, basically, one ought to do what is to one's own interest.... For him, then, the basic normative principle is not obedience to God but doing what is for one's own greatest good. In short, he is a teleologist . . . not a deontologist at all.[16]

With Frankena's example in mind, it may reasonably be argued that biblical authors who seem to justify righteousness on the basis of the Divine Command Theory (since they claim that righteousness is commanded by God) are actually teleologists. This is because they suggest that obedience to God's commands is itself justified because of the beneficial consequences of obedience. God rewards obedience and punishes disobedience.

In response, it could be argued that the claim that God rewards obedience and punishes disobedience is not advanced as a justification for righteousness but only as a means of motivating the people to do that which is justified by the Divine Command Theory.[17] But even if this were the case, there is another problem with reliance on the Divine Command Theory as constituting the Bible's justification for righteousness. It is the so-called *Euthyphro* problem. In Plato's dialogue of that name, Euthyphro suggests, in effect, that what makes something right is that God commands it, and Socrates then asks him, "Is something right because God commands it or does God command it because it is right?"[18] It may similarly be asked of the biblical authors, "Is righteousness justified because it is commanded by God, or is righteousness commanded by God because it is right—good (beneficial) for the nation?"[19] To ask this question is to ask whether, for the biblical authors, the standard of that which is good is actually something other than that it is commanded by God.[20] If the standard is something other than that it is commanded

---

16. Frankena, *Ethics*, 28. See also Barton, *Ethics in Ancient Israel*, 127–56 (suggesting several ways in which biblical authors attempted to rationalize divine commands and show them to be reasonable).

17. See Frankena, *Ethics*, 114 (distinguishing motive from justification for doing what is morally right).

18. See Plato, *Euthyphr.* 10a.

19. See n24 in this chapter.

20. See Frankena, *Ethics*, 29–30.

by God, then, once again, an apparent deontological ethical theory may turn out to be a teleological theory.

Heschel seeks to dismiss the *Euthyphro* problem, asserting that such a problem "could only arise when the gods and the good were regarded as two different entities, and where it was taken for granted that the gods do not always act according to the highest standards of goodness and justice."[21] He claims that where "the righteousness of God is inseparable from His being" no dichotomy exists between the holy (what is commanded by God) and the good, and to inquire whether a particular act is holy because it is good, or vice versa, is "meaningless."[22] Heschel further claims that such a dichotomy was "alien to the spirit of the great prophets."[23] But to the extent that Heschel is claiming that the Hebrew Bible does not distinguish between what God commands and what is righteous, Heschel's argument falls under the weight of biblical passages which *do* so distinguish, as well as under the weight of much biblical material evidencing that a concept of what is righteous was reached by biblical authors on the bases of observation, experience, and reason, not God's commands.[24]

The most famous biblical instance of a dichotomy between the good and the holy, between what is righteous and what God commands or wills, is when God reveals to Abraham an intention to destroy all of Sodom and Gomorrah because of the great wickedness of its inhabitants, and Abraham protests: "Will You sweep away the innocent along with the guilty?," and, "Shall not the judge of all the earth deal justly?"[25] Commenting on Abraham's protest, Mittleman states that Abraham knew on the bases of reason or "natural cognition" that justice rests on the idea of desert and entails giving persons their due, and so he "does not need God to tell him this."[26] Mittleman concludes: "This story seems to assume the

---

21. Heschel, *God in Search of Man*, 17.

22. Heschel, *God in Search of Man*, 17.

23. Heschel, *God in Search of Man*, 17. But see Barton, *Ethics in Ancient Israel*, 101 ("The prophets . . . often seem to appeal to moral principles that are not presented as positive divine law").

24. See chapter 1, sec. C, 4 (The sages who initiated the new moral norms did not claim them to have been commanded by God but derived them on the basis of human experience and reason). Only later were these new moral norms said to have been commanded by God.

25. Gen 18:23, 25.

26. Mittleman, *Short History*, 25.

reality and accessibility of independent and objective moral knowledge, available both to God and man."[27]

Other biblical protests, pointing to a standard of right behavior independent of what God wills, are made by Jeremiah and the author of the book of Job, both of whom claim that God is acting contrary to this proper standard in causing or willing the wicked to prosper and the righteous to suffer.[28] Ezekiel goes as far as to state that God gave the Israelites "laws that were not good,"[29] again indicating that it is "possible to evaluate commandments given by God against some standard other than the divine will."[30]

That the Hebrew Bible recognizes a moral reality knowable to human beings independent of God's commands is also supported by the words of the prophet Amos. In Amos 1:3—2:3, Amos

> castigates non-Israelites for violating what are assumed to be generally accepted moral norms of conduct. The nations have neither been commanded by God . . . nor subject to the covenantal stipulations of biblical law. Yet they are expected to know the relevant moral norms, presumably on the basis of their own natural moral sense.[31]

For the most part, the written materials that Israelite society produced during the period of the Second Temple did not fundamentally alter or challenge the moral norms promulgated during the preexilic period, although these norms became more closely identified with God's commandments.[32] But disagreement about ethical theories

---

27. Mittleman, *Short History*, 27.
28. See Jer 12:1; Job 9:20–24.
29. Ezek 20:25.
30. Barton, *Ethics in Ancient Israel*, 155. See also Barton, *Old Testament Ethics*, 139 (arguing that the ethical teaching of the prophet Isaiah assumed an "ordered universe whose moral pattern ought to be apparent to all whose reason is not hopelessly clouded").
31. Mittleman, *Short History*, 27. See also Sarna, *Understanding Genesis*, 145–46. See generally Barton, *Ethics in Ancient Israel*, 94–126 (There was a belief in ancient Israel, as in Egypt and Mesopotamia, of a moral order "built-in to the fabric of the world," and "ethical behaviour was primarily conformity to 'order' rather than obedience to God").
32. Already at the beginning of this period the prophet Ezekiel directly equates the qualities and conduct constituting righteousness with following Yahweh's laws. See Ezek 18:5–9. Similarly, a postexilic psalm associates happiness with observing God's laws. Ps 119:1–2. See generally Eichrodt, *Theology*, 2.374–78. Eichrodt contends that "the leaders in the restoration of the Jerusalem community based their

justifying these moral norms persisted. In fact, the types of justifications that were advanced became more varied. Specifically, distinct types of teleological justifications appeared due to the increased importance of the individual and the emergence of a new belief, the belief in a postmortem reward and punishment.

In particular, disagreement arose as to whether "the good" (individual well-being), believed to be the necessary consequence of righteousness, is obtained in the present life, as Ben Sira maintained, or whether it is only obtained in an afterlife of some sort. And, for those who thought that "the good" is only obtained in an afterlife, differences arose as to the nature of that postmortem good. For some, existence in the afterlife was believed to be physical, and so the postmortem good was believed to be of a material nature. For others, existence in the afterlife was believed to be "spiritual" (or nonphysical), and so the postmortem good was believed to be of a nonmaterial nature.

B. An increasing emphasis on individuality during the Second Temple period focused attention on the problem of moral evil.

At its beginning, the Israelites had a seminomadic way of life and a patriarchal social structure in which there was a close association of the individual and the community. What Eichrodt calls "clan-thinking" is characteristic of this way of life and this social structure. As Eichrodt describes it, clan-thinking means that "the common life of the members of the clan is founded on a spiritual and psychical unity in which each individual is a representative of the whole, and in turn has his entire private attitude to life shaped by the whole."[33] This type of thinking leads to the acceptance of the notion of collective and intergenerational

---

actions decisively on the unconditional Ought of the divine will," and that because "the motive of obedience to the Law dominated [their] ethical thinking," other motives were "excluded." Eichrodt, *Theology*, 2.374-75. Yet, Eichrodt acknowledges that the motive of loyalty to the law "was unable to prevent the admixture of other motives," and that "the earthly reward for loyalty to the Law was bound to acquire enormous importance." Eichrodt, *Theology*, 2.376-77. Ultimately, says Eichrodt, the "purpose of the Divine ought" was seen to be "the good fortune of the individual and the of the nation . . . [and the 'Divine ought'] takes second-place to the cravings for earthly happiness." Eichrodt, *Theology*, 2.378.

33. Eichrodt, *Theology*, 2.233. See Cohen, *From the Maccabees*, 84 ("Israelites . . . readily accepted the fact that an individual was part of a clan and a nation, and that one's fate was indissolubly linked to that of one's ancestors, descendants, and contemporaries").

responsibility in which the clan or tribe is collectively liable for the trespasses of its members.³⁴

Clan-thinking also leads to the championing by the tribe of any member injured by an outsider. The laws of blood vengeance constitute an expression of this social structure and related way of thinking.³⁵ In addition, the "solidarity-relationship" of Israelites as members of the covenant with Yahweh "was able to build upon the solidarity association of the clan, and to be understood as an organic extension of the latter" so that "the unification of the tribes into the people of Yahweh brought about an enlargement of the circle of those linked by solidarity."³⁶ In preexilic Israel, it was accepted that the reward and punishment meted out by Yahweh was intergenerational and collective, meaning that the people of Israel were rewarded and punished by Yahweh as a group, and the group included distant ancestors.³⁷

The transition to a settled civilization brought about a significant revision in clan solidarity and clan thinking,³⁸ as did the establishment of the monarchy.³⁹ Nevertheless, the concept of collective responsibility did not disappear; rather, individual and collective responsibility coexisted.⁴⁰ Then, at around the time of the Babylonian exile, the understanding of reward and punishment as intergenerational and collective was seriously challenged.⁴¹ For example, in revising the book of Kings, the author of Chronicles, composed in the Second Temple period, abandoned the doctrine of corporate responsibility because he believed "that no one suffers

---

34. See Eichrodt, *Theology*, 2.233; chapter 3, sec. A. See generally Eichrodt, *Theology*, 2.236–40; Starr, *Toward a History*, 34–36.

35. See Greengus, *Laws in the Bible*, 152 ("Closest kinsmen had both the right and the duty to avenge a homicide; they acted in their capacity as . . . 'redeemer of the blood (of the slain victim)'").

36. Eichrodt, *Theology*, 2.238.

37. See Starr, *Toward a History*, 35–36; Gordis, *Koheleth*, 15–16 ("Concern with the group was a fundamental aspect of traditional Semitic and Hebrew thought").

38. See Eichrodt, *Theology*, 2.240–41.

39. See Eichrodt, *Theology*, 2.242–46.

40. See chapter 3, sec. A.

41. See generally Greengus, *Laws in the Bible*, 157–60 ("The concept of collective or transferred responsibility was abandoned after the time of Ezekiel"). See also Cohen, *From the Maccabees*, 9, 84, 110 (After the Babylonian exile the "entire tribal structure had been destroyed"; the "breakdown of the tribe into the clan, and the clan into the family, mirrored the breakdown of the belief in corporate responsibility and the emergence of [individual responsibility]").

for a crime committed by someone else."⁴² Similarly, the prophet Ezekiel (who delivered his prophesies while he was in the Babylonian exile) proclaims in chapter 18 that everyone is rewarded or punished for their own actions and not for the actions of their ancestors.⁴³

Chapter 18 begins with Ezekiel being told by God that the proverb "Parents eat sour grapes and their children's teeth are blunted [or set on edge]" shall no longer be said, but that only the person who sins "shall die."⁴⁴ Accordingly, Ezekiel declares in God's name that "if a man is righteous and does what is just and right," he "shall live."⁴⁵ Ezekiel next claims that if a righteous man has a son who is not righteous, the righteousness of the father does not protect the son; rather the son "shall die" on account of his own unrighteous conduct.⁴⁶ Conversely, if the father is unrighteous but the son is righteous ("He has obeyed My rules and followed My laws"), the father shall "die for his iniquity" but the son "shall not die for the iniquity of his father, but shall live."⁴⁷

Then Ezekiel stresses the importance of repentance, saying that "if the wicked one repents of all the sins that he committed and keeps all My laws and does what is just and right, he shall live; he shall not die."⁴⁸ The unrighteous acts previously done by such person shall not be counted against him.⁴⁹ Similarly, "if a righteous person turns away from his righteousness and does wrong . . . he shall die."⁵⁰ None of the righteous deeds previously done by the righteous person will be used to offset this punishment.⁵¹ Finally, Ezekiel asserts that it is possible for

---

42. Cohen, *From the Maccabees*, 85 (For example, the Chronicler attributes the destruction of the temple to the sins of Manasseh).

43. Ezek 18:1–32. Cf. Jer 31:27–30; Deut 24:16. See Starr, *Toward a History*, 36–37. See also Gordis, *Koheleth*, 25 ("A fundamental evolution in men's thinking now took place. . . . [The] collective viewpoint now gave way to a heightened interest in the individual"); Kaufmann, *Religion*, 438–39 (Ezekiel emphasizes that there is no retributive bond between generations but does not deny that "punishment comes upon society as a whole and strikes at innocent and guilty alike").

44. Ezek 18:1–4.

45. Ezek 18:5, 9.

46. Ezek 18:10–13.

47. Ezek 18:14–19.

48. Ezek 18:21. Cf. Ezek 33:14–15.

49. See Ezek 18:22.

50. Ezek 18:24. Cf. Ezek 33:13.

51. Ezek 18:24. Ezekiel claims that it is not "unfair" to punish a righteous person once he commits a wicked act and to reward a wicked person once he commits a righteous act. Ezek 18:25–28; 33:17–20. But this claim is questionable. Why is it fair to

YAHWEH REWARDS THE RIGHTEOUS AND PUNISHES THE WICKED

all Israelites to repent—to "cast away" their transgressions which have subjected them to the wrath of Yahweh—by *getting themselves* "a new heart and a new spirit."[52]

These views concerning repentance seem to contradict the views advanced by Ezekiel in chapters 11 and 36 that humans could not act righteously *by themselves*. They needed to be given a new heart and a new spirit *by God*. But it may be that Ezekiel is imagining that God had now made it possible for those in exile *to get themselves* a new heart and spirit.[53] In any event, this issue does not affect Ezekiel's point concerning individualism, that "the righteousness of the righteous shall be accounted to him alone, and the wickedness of the wicked shall be accounted to him alone."[54]

This new emphasis on individual reward and punishment served to focus attention on the problem of moral evil.[55] If God rewards or punishes each person according to their own conduct, then, if God is just and omnipotent, each righteous person should be rewarded by God and each wicked person should be punished by God. Yet, experience teaches that there are many righteous people who suffer and many wicked people who prosper. Such experience prompted Jeremiah (who, like Ezekiel, prophesized during the time of the Babylonian exile, but in Judea) to charge an omnipotent God with injustice, exclaiming: "Why does the way of the wicked prosper? Why are the workers of treachery at ease?"[56] Habakkuk (ca. 612 BCE) similarly complains that God remains silent while the wicked swallow up those who are righteous.[57] The problem of the wicked prospering and the righteous suffering (the problem of moral evil) is dealt with at length in the biblical books of Job and Qoheleth.[58]

---

punish a person for a minor transgression committed in old age, ignoring thousands of righteous acts done previously? Why is it fair to reward a person for a single righteous act committed after a lifetime of abject wickedness?

52. Ezek 18:31.

53. Cf. Bar 2:30–31 ("But in the land of their exile they will come to themselves. . . . [God]will give them a heart that obeys and ears that hear") 3:7 ("For you [God] have put the fear of you in our hearts").

54. Ezek 18:20.

55. See Starr, *Toward a History*, 34–39; Gordis, *Koheleth*, 34 (The problem of moral evil "became the central problem of Jewish theology in the Second Temple period").

56. Jer 12:1.

57. See Hab 1:13.

58. For a brief discussion of the problem of moral evil in Job and Qoheleth, see Starr, *Toward a History*, 37–39.

1. The author of the book of Job questions the conventional view that righteousness is always rewarded with material well-being.

Job, who is described as extremely pious—as one who is "blameless and upright," who "fears God and shuns evil"[59]—accepted conventional wisdom. He accepted that the moral order God made part of the world at the time of creation required that human well-being was the necessary consequence of righteousness and human misery the necessary consequence of blameworthiness. Thus, Job believed that the large family, health, and substantial wealth he enjoyed was the necessary consequence of his righteousness, and he praised God for it. Then God decided to determine if Job had acted righteously and had praised God only because God rewarded him for it. God devised a test. God took away Job's material assets, caused the death of all his children, and inflicted Job with disease.[60] Would Job still praise God, or would he curse God? Would Job still accept the conventional wisdom about the value of righteousness, or would he reject it?

Because Job knew that he was blameless and upright, Job claimed that God had "wronged" him in taking away all that was conducive to his well-being and bringing upon him great misery.[61] He began to question his belief that righteousness always leads to well-being, and he declared that God "destroys [both] the blameless and the guilty."[62] Job's interlocutors, however, insisted that Job must not be blameless; they unquestioningly accepted the traditional view that justice (the moral order) required that one who is righteous be rewarded with well-being and one who is wicked be punished with suffering.[63] Thus, the view that righteousness is instrumentally good is presented as a conventional and universally

---

59. Job 1:1, 8. See also Job 23:11–12 (Job has kept God's way without swerving, not deviating from what God commanded); 31:1–21 (In demanding that God weigh him "on the scale of righteousness [*bmizne-tzedek*]," Job says that he has never "hurried to deceit," committed adultery, or denied the needs of the impoverished or unprotected).

60. Job 1:6—2:7.

61. Job 19:6.

62. Job 9:22.

63. See, e.g., Job 4:7 ("What innocent man ever perished?"); 8:6 ("If you are blameless and upright [God] will protect you" and "grant well-being [*shilam*] to your righteous home"); 34:10–12 (God "pays a man according to his actions"). See also Collins, *Jewish Wisdom*, 13 (The "dogmatic doctrine of retribution . . . is articulated in the book by the friends of Job"). Significantly, no interlocutor suggests that Job is being punished for the wickedness of his ancestors, which evidences that the position of Ezekiel on this matter had become conventional.

accepted position.[64] Yet, the author of the book of Job, through the book's main character, questions this conventional position.[65]

In the closing chapter of Job, God asserts that Job's interlocutors "have not spoken the truth about Me" but that Job *has* spoken the truth.[66] According to Greenstein, the author's main point is that traditional views must be challenged if they fail to comport with experience. Greenstein asserts:

> Although the problem of innocent suffering . . . is the topic of discussion among the participants in the dialogues, it is not the theme of Job. Instead, Job incorporates two main themes. First, the book presents a philosophical argument about how knowledge is warranted or justified. Job's companions stubbornly cling to the claim that all worthwhile knowledge has been transmitted and learned from tradition. . . . Job, on the other hand, bases his claims on his personal observation—knowledge can be transformed by new experience, such as what has happened to him. . . .
>
> A second, and arguably even more prevalent, theme in Job is that of honesty in talking about God. . . . Job takes pride in his absolute commitment to speaking only truth. . . . Job may not have arrived at the truth, but he had reason to believe in what he was saying, as it came to him honestly, unlike the words of his companions, who merely repeated uncritically the wisdom they had received. Seen this way, the book of Job . . . rejects a blind reliance on tradition.[67]

---

64. That righteousness was universally accepted as merely an instrumental good is supported by the book's opening chapter where God decides to test whether Job was righteous only to obtain material well-being. Job 1:6–12.

65. See Collins, *Jewish Wisdom*, 13 (The book of Job "represents a reaction . . . against the more dogmatic doctrine of retribution found in one stream of Proverbs"). Collins, as many commentators, interprets the book as concluding that the ways of God are unknowable to human beings and that a righteous person who experiences suffering should accept the will of God. Collins, *Jewish Wisdom*, 14.

66. Job 42:7.

67. Greenstein, "Job," 1494.

2. Observing that the righteous are sometimes requited according to the wicked, and vice versa, and rejecting any postmortem reward and punishment, Qoheleth argues that enjoyment is the only thing intrinsically good.

The author of the book of Qoheleth (in Latin translation, Ecclesiastes), written after the spread of Greek ideas throughout the Near East had begun,[68] agrees with the author of Job in rejecting a blind reliance on tradition.[69] Qoheleth (not the author's name but a sobriquet for him)[70] has been said to "incorporate the fundamental tenet of Greek philosophy—the autonomy of individual reason, which is to say, the belief that individuals can and should proceed with their own observations and reasoning powers on a quest for knowledge and that this may lead to discovery of truths previously unknown."[71] Relying on his own observations, Qoheleth questions the traditional doctrine of retribution and ultimately rejects the belief that righteousness is instrumentally good.

He says that it is simply not the case that well-being (the good) is a necessary consequence of righteousness. Rather, he observes that "sometimes an upright man is requited according to the conduct of the scoundrel; and sometimes the scoundrel is requited according to the conduct of the upright."[72] He also rejects the Greek idea that humans have a soul that can survive the destruction of the body and be rewarded or punished after death.[73] So the problem of moral evil cannot be resolved for him on the basis of a postmortem reward and punishment. Furthermore,

---

68. See Gordis, *Koheleth*, 63–67; Collins, *Jewish Wisdom*, 14. See generally Machinist, "Ecclesiastes," 1601.

69. See Madigan and Levenson, *Resurrection*, 183 (Qoheleth "casts into grave doubt the belief in a personal and just God who providentially directs the destinies of nations and individuals.... For Koheleth, rather, 'God' refers to an inexorable and ultimate fate unresponsive to human action and thus human merit. This is indeed a frontal assault on the previous thinking").

70. See Machinist, "Ecclesiastes," 1602.

71. Fox, "Wisdom," 123. See Collins, *Jewish Wisdom*, 14–15. See also Gordis, *Koheleth*, 37 ("*Job* and *Koheleth* are distinguished by their fearless use of reason in confronting the most fundamental issues of life ... and their unswerving allegiance to truth" [emphasis original]).

72. Qoh 8:14. See also Qoh 7:15 ("Sometimes a good man perishes in spite of his goodness, and sometimes a wicked one endures in spite of his wickedness"). Cf. Prov 11:16. Even when the wicked are punished, their punishment is often long delayed, "which is why men are emboldened to do evil." Qoh 8:11–12.

73. See Qoh 3:19–21; Machinist, "Ecclesiastes," 1606; Starr, *Toward a History*, 11–12.

the traditional doctrine of retribution is predicated on the assumption that human beings can predict what God is going to do, but Qoheleth observes that one can never predict what God is going to do.[74]

Qoheleth concludes from his observations that a person should seek "enjoyment," for "the only good [*tov*] a man can have under the sun is to eat and drink and enjoy himself."[75] Significantly, enjoyment includes not only physical enjoyment but mental enjoyment (tranquility or peace of mind), and mental enjoyment is more readily available to a simple worker, "whether he has much or little to eat," than a "lover of wealth," whose abundance "doesn't let him sleep."[76] This observation leads Qoheleth to further observe that the accumulation of wealth is important only as the means to enjoyment, not as an end in itself,[77] and that, despite the value of satisfying one's physical needs, attempts to satisfy all desires only leads to frustration, not to mental tranquility, since human desires are limitless.[78]

Qoheleth does not conclude that one should be *un*righteous. He concludes only that righteousness does not necessarily lead to enjoyment, which is, for him, intrinsically good.[79] The implication is that one should (or, at least, may) be righteous so long as righteous conduct does not

---

74. Qoh 7:23–24 (One cannot fathom the secret of why things happen in life); 11:5 ("You cannot foresee the actions of God"). See Blenkinsopp, *Wisdom and Law*, 74–76, 78 (As a consequence of man's inability to know the future "the link between act and consequence . . . is called into question"). See generally Von Rad, *Wisdom in Israel*, 97–110 (discussing that there had always been a recognition of the "limits of wisdom" and a questioning of the "connection between goodness and well-being" so that the "sudden emergence" of the questioning of wisdom's conceptual scheme in Job and Qoheleth "is not something *fundamentally* new" [emphasis added]).

75. Qoh 8:15. See Tirosh-Samuelson, *Happiness*, 70 ("In Wisdom literature . . . 'tov' is . . . a life-giving force that creates 'well-being' and 'life' . . . for the wise/righteous and his community"). See also Qoh 2:24 ("There is nothing worthwhile for a man but to eat and drink and afford himself enjoyment"); 3:12 ("The only worthwhile thing there is for [people] is to enjoy themselves"); 3:22 ("There is nothing better for man than to enjoy his possessions"); 9:7–9.

76. See Qoh 5:9–13. Cf. Sir 31:1 (Anxiety about wealth "drives away sleep"); Epicurus, *Ep. Men.* 128, 131 ("Pleasure" is defined as "the lack of pain in the body and disturbance in the soul"). See Long, *Hellenistic Philosophy*, 61–62 (Epicurus "is credited with a conception of happiness which consists above all in peace of mind").

77. See Qoh 5:9–11; 6:1–9.

78. See Qoh 6:7. Gordis translates, "All a man's toil is for his wants, but his desires are never satisfied." Gordis, *Koheleth*, 170. Cf. Plato, *Gorg.* 493e.

79. See Gordis, *Koheleth*, 123 ("Koheleth's morality . . . recognizes the pursuit of happiness as the goal"). Cf. Epicurus, *Ep. Men.* 131 ("Pleasure is the goal").

substantially interfere with one's enjoyment.[80] As he states it, one should not "overdo goodness," just as one should not "overdo wickedness."[81] Although the closing lines of the book admonish the reader to observe God's commandments, this admonition, say many scholars, is probably "the work of a later orthodox editor," not Qoheleth.[82]

C. The Wisdom of Ben Sira associates the law of Moses with the moral norms of the wisdom tradition and maintains the traditional doctrine that the righteous are always rewarded and the wicked are always punished in this world at the appointed time.

The Wisdom of Ben Sira, known in its Greek translation as the Wisdom of Sirach (and in the Latin translation as Ecclesiasticus), was originally written in Hebrew around 180 BCE in Jerusalem by Joshua ben Sira.[83] Ben Sira mentions neither resurrection of the dead nor an immortal soul but accepts that all rewards and punishments are received in this life.[84] Though accepting the conventional wisdom, Ben Sira represents an important change from the wisdom literature contained in the Bible.

---

80. See Qoh 5:9–13. Cf. Epicurus, *Ep. Men.* 132 ("It is impossible to live pleasantly without living prudently, honorably, and justly"). See, Long, *Hellenistic Philosophy*, 69 (Epicurus regarded the virtues as instrumentally good, being necessary to achieve happiness, "not as ends," not as intrinsically good).

81. Qoh 7:16–17. See Machinist, "Ecclesiastes," 1610 (This terminology "recalls the Greek philosophical adage . . . to do 'nothing overmuch'"); Gordis, *Koheleth*, 57, 178–79 (Qoheleth favors the Aristotelian "golden mean," not as a "principle of ethics" but as expressing the conviction that "moderation" is wise because "both extremes of saintliness and wickedness lead to unhappiness"). Cf. Sir 31:22 ("In everything you do be moderate"); Theognis, *Theognidea*, 219–20, 335–36, 401–2, 657–58; Aristotle, *Eth. nic.* 1106b25 (Virtue is a "mean, insofar as it aims at what is intermediate"). See also Tirosh-Samuelson, *Happiness*, 78n85.

82. Machinist, "Ecclesiastes," 1618. See Gordis, *Koheleth*, 128, 200. Machinist argues that this concluding admonition *may* be "congruent with the views of the rest of the book" because the rejection of the doctrine of retribution "does not invalidate the power and sovereignty of God." Machinist, "Ecclesiastes," 1618. But Qoheleth would not observe the commands of God if they conflicted with enjoyment.

83. See generally Wright, "Wisdom of Ben Sira," 2208–9 (discussing the work's authorship and textual history); Collins, *Jewish Wisdom*, 42–44 (same).

84. See Satlow, "Ben Sira," 427 ("Ben Sira did not believe in an afterlife. He did believe that all people were justly rewarded or punished in this world"); Wright, "Wisdom of Ben Sira," 2216; Sir 17:30 ("Human beings are not immortal"); 38:21 ("Do not forget, there is no coming back").

The biblical pursuit of wisdom, as evidenced in Proverbs and Qoheleth, "is a philosophical undertaking," an "attempt to arrive at an understanding of life without recourse to prophetic revelation."[85] For Ben Sira, though, the understanding of life expressed in the wisdom tradition becomes identified with the laws of the Torah, said to be known through "prophetic revelation," previously ignored by the teachers of wisdom.[86] This is not to say, as some scholars claim, that for Ben Sira *all* wisdom is derived from divinely revealed laws.[87] Rather, Ben Sira "was defining the Mosaic covenant in terms of the well-established wisdom tradition," and so he is still able to draw on other sources of wisdom besides the Torah.[88]

At the inception of the Second Temple period the qualities and conduct constituting righteousness in the wisdom tradition had become associated with following Yahweh's laws and keeping Yahweh's rules. In addition, Ezra had "succeeded in transferring the spiritual leadership of the community . . . [to] scribes, who were the interpreters and expounders of the Law,"[89] and throughout the period there was "a sense of scripture among the Jews."[90] By the late Second Temple period, "concepts such as the rabbis' 'Torah from heaven' and 'Torah from Sinai' [had] undoubtedly began to percolate," formulations of both the Torah (that is, the Pentateuch) and the Prophets (that is, the second section of the Hebrew Bible) had been created, and there existed "a tradition of education in the Torah."[91] Thus, it is not surprising that the prologue to the book of Ben

---

85. Collins, *Jewish Wisdom*, 39.

86. See Collins, *Jewish Wisdom*, 41 ("The main innovation of [Ben Sira] in the tradition of the Jewish wisdom school was in the prominence he gave to the Torah of Moses"). See also Urbach, *Sages*, 1.287 (Whereas in Proverbs the term "Torah" does not refer to the Mosaic Torah but to "the teaching of the father, the mother, the teacher, or to the counsels of Wisdom itself, in [Ben Sira] the two concepts of Torah—that of Moses and that of Wisdom—are merged into a single idea").

87. See Satlow, "Ben Sira," 427 (Ben Sira saw wisdom as deriving not "through observation and study of nature and human mores . . . [but] from the knowledge revealed by God on Mount Sinai"); Sanders, *Paul and Palestinian Judaism*, 331 (Wisdom for Ben Sira is "represented by and particularized in the Torah given by God through Moses"); Eichrodt, *Theology*, 2.345 (For Ben Sira, "the content of all wisdom" is "knowledge of the Law").

88. See Collins, *Jewish Wisdom*, 54–55.

89. Gordis, *Koheleth*, 14–15, 24.

90. Reed, "Canon," 571–72; Miller, "Torah," 625.

91. Miller, "Torah," 625; Reed, "Canon," 571–72; Collins, *Jewish Wisdom*, 17–20, 54.

Sira notes that Ben Sira had devoted himself to "the reading of the Law and the Prophets and the other books of our ancestors."[92]

Having steeped himself in the study of the laws included in the Torah, as well in study of the Israelite wisdom tradition, Ben Sira probably realized that the moral norms the wisdom tradition espoused on the bases of observation, experience, and reason were substantially the same as the moral norms included in the laws of the Torah said to have been revealed, and commanded, by God. Accordingly, he saw the laws of the Torah as an instantiation of what observation, experience, and reason showed to be valuable to one's well-being.[93] Blenkinsopp argues that whereas in the older wisdom tradition wisdom "stood for a certain quality of life attainable by the application of reason," for Ben Sira "wisdom belonged to the divine world and was attainable only as a gift of God."[94] Hogan puts it differently. Hogan says that in Ben Sira, the Hebrew word *torah*

> is closely related to the order of creation. Probably, it was familiarity with the older view of [*torah*] as advice for living in harmony with the order of creation that prompted Ben Sira to identify the [*torah*] of Moses with Wisdom. The message of Sir 24 is that the [*torah*] of Moses is the "supreme actualization" of the divine wisdom that pervades creation.[95]

In chapter 24 of Ben Sira, Ben Sira directly equates the wisdom tradition with the idea of a Mosaic covenant. Wisdom personified describes itself, stating, "I came forth from the mouth of the Most High," was instructed by the Creator to dwell "in Jacob, and in Israel," was given a "resting place . . . in Jerusalem," "took root in an honored people," and am to be identified with "the book of the covenant of the

---

92. Sir Prologue. See also Collins, *Jewish Wisdom*, 18 ("The first clear witness to a canon, in the sense of an accepted corpus of authoritative scripture, is found in the prologue to Ben Sira," and the body of the work contains "what we might call a 'canon consciousness' with respect to the Torah"); Tirosh-Samuelson, *Happiness*, 74 ("In Ben-Sira's academy, students . . . studied Scripture along with ancient Wisdom tradition, especially the Book of Proverbs").

93. See Collins, *Jewish Wisdom*, 55 (Ben Sira "defin[ed] the Mosaic covenant in terms of the well-established wisdom tradition").

94. Blenkinsopp, *Wisdom and Law*, 171.

95. Hogan, "Meanings," 532 (quoting Collins, *Jewish Wisdom*, 58). See also Blenkinsopp, *Wisdom and Law*, 163–66 (Ben Sira, following Prov 8:22–31, "represents wisdom as first of all created things and the principle which informs the created order," and "he identifies this pre-existent Wisdom with Torah," making Torah "the supramundane principle of order as it has been made available to Israel").

Most High God, the law that Moses commanded . . . as an inheritance for the congregations of Jacob."[96]

Wisdom is also associated with God's commandments in several other passages, and the study of Torah is recommended as the way to acquire wisdom.[97] Both wisdom and the law of Moses are understood by Ben Sira to be responsible for the moral order created by God that had existed in the world since creation.[98] Wisdom is also understood as the principle that had informed the *natural* order since creation,[99] and Ben Sira explicitly associates the formation of this natural order with the setting of boundaries.[100] So, presumably, he associated the creation of the *moral* order with the setting of boundaries as well, and he saw the moral boundaries contained in the revealed laws of Moses as an instantiation of those same moral boundaries the wisdom tradition had identified without reliance on prophetic revelation. Because of his association of God's laws with the moral order God created, Ben Sira could suggest "that keeping the commandments is expected of all the descendants of Adam."[101]

A merging of moral norms taught in the wisdom schools with the moral norms dictated by the laws of the Torah may also be found in the apocryphal mixed-genre work of Baruch, which is dated by scholars to the second century BCE, shortly after the Maccabean revolt. Baruch states:

> Hear the commandments of life, O Israel; give ear, and learn wisdom!
>
> Why is it O Israel, why is it that you are in the land of your enemies,

---

96. Sir 24:3, 13–17, 23. See Hogan, "Meanings," 538 (Ben Sira is the first author "explicitly to equate the figure of personified Wisdom with 'the law that Moses commanded'"). See generally Collins, *Jewish Wisdom*, 49–53.

97. See Sir 1:26 ("If you desire wisdom, keep the commandments"); 6:34–37 (To achieve wisdom, "reflect on the statues of the Lord, and meditate at all times on his commandments"); 15:1 ("Whoever holds to the law will obtain wisdom"); 19:20 ("In all wisdom there is the fulfillment of the law"). See also Collins, *Jewish Wisdom*, 54–61. See generally Tirosh-Samuelson, *Happiness*, 73–76.

98. See generally Collins, *Jewish Wisdom*, 57–61 ("The law revealed to Moses was implicit in creation from the beginning, and so it is an actualization . . . of natural law"); Tirosh-Samuelson, *Happiness*, 71–72, 75–76.

99. See Sir 1:4 ("Wisdom was created before all other things").

100. See Sir 16:26–27.

101. Hogan, "Meanings," 538.

that you are growing old in a foreign country?

You have forsaken the fountain of wisdom.

If you had walked in the way of the Lord, you would be living in peace forever....

[*Wisdom*] *is the book of the commandments of God*, the law that endures forever.

All who hold her fast will live, and those who forsake her will die....

Happy are we, O Israel, for we know what is pleasing to God.[102]

While innovative regarding the sources of wisdom, Ben Sira accepted the conventional teaching that adherence to the moral norms extolled in Proverbs and mandated in the Torah's law collections was instrumentally good in that it led to well-being, but Ben Sira focused on the well-being of the individual rather than the community. Moreover, Ben Sira's terminology is different than the terminology used in Proverbs. In Proverbs, those who "fear the Lord" act according to what observation, experience, and reason demonstrate to be beneficial; they are the "righteous," in contrast to the "wicked."[103] For Ben Sira, those who "fear of the Lord" act in obedience to the "law of the Most High"; they are the "godly," the "devout," or the "God-fearing," in contrast to the "ungodly," or the "sinners."[104]

For Ben Sira those obedient to the law of the Most High are, *in all cases*, rewarded in this life; and those who disobey the law are, *in all cases*, punished in this life.[105] He emphasized that *not even one sin will go unpunished.*[106] Ben Sira further believed that the rewards the devout

102. Bar 3:9—4:4 (emphasis added). See Hogan, "Meanings," 532; Blenkinsopp, *Wisdom and Law*, 168 (Clearly expressed in Baruch is "the pattern of [Wisdom's] preexistence, descent, embodiment in Torah").

103. See chapter 1, sec. C, 2–3. Cf. Sir 1:14-20.

104. See Sir 2:15-16 (Those who fear the Lord are equated with those who "do not disobey [God's] words," "keep [God's] ways," and are "filled with [God's] law"); 44:10 ("Godly men" perform "righteous deeds"); 11:17 (God's favor is with the "devout"); 12:4 (contrasting the "devout" with the "sinner"); 49:4 (Those who "abandoned the law of the Most High" are "sinners"); 7:16-17 (relating "sinners" to "the ungodly"); 9:11-12 (same); 12:6 (same).

105. See, e.g., Sir 1:16-19; 2:8-14; 5:3; 9:11-12; 11:17; 12:6; 16:13-14; 49:4. See also Wright, "Wisdom of Ben Sira," 2211 (Although he recognizes that bad things affect all people, "in order to maintain his beliefs, he claims that they happen 'to sinners seven times more'" [citing Sir 40:8-11]).

106. Sir 7:8.

YAHWEH REWARDS THE RIGHTEOUS AND PUNISHES THE WICKED

receive include honor (community approval) and the punishments the sinners receive include shame or disgrace (community disapproval).[107] The reward of honor and the punishment of shame are received not only in one's life but also after one's death—that is, one's honor or shame affects the lives of one's children.[108] Anything unnoticed by the community, including one's intentions, is rewarded or punished by God, who sees all.[109]

Ben Sira recognized that there are godly people who suffer and sinners who prosper, but such cases, in his view, do not undermine the basic principle that "everyone receives [from God] in accordance with his or her deeds."[110] The godly will be rewarded, and the sinner will be punished, "at the appointed time."[111] If a sinner is prospering, this is only because "the Lord is slow to anger"; but "suddenly the wrath of the Lord will come upon [him], and . . . [he] will perish."[112] Similarly, God will eventually reward one who is devout, though he may now be suffering. This is because "it is easy . . . [for] the Lord to make the poor rich suddenly, in an instant."[113] Also, it may be that God is testing those who are devout, as God tested Abraham.[114] Therefore, Ben Sira teaches:

> Accept whatever befalls you, and in times of humiliation be patient.

---

107. Sir 1:23–24; 3:11; 5:14—6:1; 24:22; 41:14—42:8. See Collins, *Jewish Wisdom*, 34, 49; Wright, "Wisdom of Ben Sira," 2211 ("Deeply embedded in the cultural system of Second Temple Judea are the values of honor and shame").

108. Sir 41:7 ("Children will blame an ungodly father for they suffer disgrace because of him"), 12–13 ("A good name lasts forever"). See Miller, "Ben Sira," 483 ("While there is no afterlife, a good reputation does live on"); Collins, *Jewish Wisdom*, 49 (The motif that "the memory of the righteous is a blessing but the name of the wicked will rot" is "far more prominent" in Ben Sira than in Proverbs [citing Prov 10:4]).

109. Sir 1:30; 16:17–23; 23:18–21; 35:24 (God repays mortals according to both their deeds and their "thoughts"); 42:18 (God "searches out the . . . human heart"). Cf. chapter 2, n90.

110. Sir 16:14. See Cohen, *From the Maccabees*, 89–90 ("Ben Sira argues that . . . each person is responsible for his or her own deeds, and receives appropriate treatment from God" so that sinners "cannot evade responsibility for [their] deeds").

111. See Sir 39:16–17; Collins, *Jewish Wisdom*, 85–86. See generally chapter 1, sec. C, 4–5.

112. Sir 5:3–7. See also Sir 11:12 (The ungodly "will not be held guiltless all their lives").

113. Sir 11:21.

114. Sir 2:1–5; 44:20.

> For gold is tested in the fire, and those found acceptable [are tested] in the furnace of humiliation....
>
> You who fear the Lord, trust in him, and your reward will not be lost.[115]

Accordingly, Ben Sira cautions: "Call no one happy before his death."[116]

The specific qualities and conduct extolled by Ben Sira include, predictably, the same qualities and conduct extolled in Proverbs, the biblical law collections, and the books of the several prophets, with Ben Sira often indicating the rewards and punishments to be received for, respectively, adhering to or violating the conduct he recommends. To begin, Ben Sira "echoes the [moral] injunctions of the Decalogue," urging people not to steal, commit adultery, bear false witness, covet, or murder, and to honor their parents.[117] He seems especially concerned about honoring one's parents, devoting numerous verses to it. He tells his readers to honor their fathers and mothers, not only because God commands it, but because it will keep them in safety, give them a long life, avoid disgrace, atone for their sins, and repay their parents for what they have given them.[118]

He condemns adultery and all "sexual immorality," claiming that the disgrace of an adulterer "will never be blotted out," and that they "will leave behind an accursed memory."[119] Adultery is just one instance of sins related to unrestrained appetites and out-of-control passions. With regard to some passions, though, the sin is not a matter of failing to restrain it but of having it at all. In other words, some passions are "unjust," "base," "evil," or "shameless."[120] These include "gluttony," "lust," and "jealousy."[121] Ben Sira is particularly critical of unjust anger. He writes:

> Unjust anger ... tips the scale to one's ruin.
> Those who are patient stay calm until the right moment, and then cheerfulness comes back to them.

---

115. Sir 2:4–8. Cf. Ps 37.

116. Sir 11:28. Cf. Aristotle, *Eth. nic.* 1100a5–10. But see Collins, *Jewish Wisdom*, 78–79 (Ben Sira's point is not that anything can happen up until death but "that death itself can be the occasion of divine judgment").

117. Collins, *Jewish Wisdom*, 47.

118. Sir 3:1–16; 7:27–28. Cf. Exod 20:2; Deut 5:16.

119. Sir 23:16–27; 41:17. See Collins, *Jewish Wisdom*, 68–70.

120. See Sir 1:22; 6:4; 18:30; 23:4–6. Cf. Aristotle, *Eth. nic.* 1107a10–25 ("Not every action or feeling admits of the mean" but "are automatically ... base").

121. Sir 23:6; 30:24; 37:30–31.

> They hold back their words until the right moment; then the lips of many tell of their good sense.[122]

He warns that, if you "fall into the grip of passion," you "may be torn apart as by a bull," and twice says that "evil passion" and "base desire" "will make you the laughingstock of your enemies."[123] In sum, Ben Sira considers temperance (and the related quality of self-control) a primary virtue.[124]

He condemns not only stealing[125] but obtaining wealth in any dishonest manner,[126] such as by using inaccurate "scales and weights";[127] he cautions that "dishonest wealth . . . will not benefit you on the day of calamity" and "will dry up like a river."[128]

The Decalogue's prohibition against coveting is echoed by Ben Sira's teaching that one should be ashamed of "gazing at another's man wife."[129]

Ben Sira does not specifically mention the Decalogue's prohibition against bearing false witness, but he does say that lying (being "double-tongued") destroys the peace of those who are impacted by it,[130] "results in no good,"[131] brings shame, and leads to one's "downfall."[132] He admonishes that one should never "speak against the truth,"[133] and he asserts: "Fight to the death for truth, and the Lord God will fight for you."[134] He also equates honesty with pursuing justice,[135] and honesty in pursuing justice prohibits bearing false witness.

---

122. Sir 1:22–24. See also Sir 27:30; 30:24. Cf. Prov 12:16.

123. Sir 6:4; 18:31. See also Sir 5:2 ("Do not follow your inclination and strength in pursuing the desires of your heart").

124. See Tirosh-Samuelson, *Happiness*, 76; n158 in this chapter and accompanying text. Temperance (*sophrosune* in Greek) is one of the four cardinal virtues in ancient Greek culture, the other three being wisdom (or prudence), justice, and courage. See Collins, *Jewish Wisdom*, 162; chapter 6, n65.

125. Sir 41:19.

126. Sir 5:8. See also Daube, *Law and Wisdom*, 89.

127. See Sir 42:4.

128. Sir 5:8; 40:13. See also Sir 13:24.

129. Sir 41:21.

130. Sir 28:13–26.

131. Sir 7:13.

132. Sir 5:13–14. See also Sir 41:17.

133. Sir 4:25.

134. Sir 4:28.

135. Sir 27:8–9.

Similarly, the prohibition against murder finds expression in the teaching that any "injustice" is "outrageous" to "the Lord and to mortals"[136] and in the teaching that one should refrain from strife because "the sinner disrupts friendships and sows discord among those who are at peace" and because a "hasty dispute sheds blood."[137] That murder is prohibited is also indicated by the fact that ungodly behavior of various kinds is likened to murder.[138]

In addition to echoing the moral norms found in the Decalogue, many other well-established moral norms from Proverbs and the Torah are echoed by Ben Sira. For instance, he frequently mentions the importance of protecting the poor, disadvantaged, and oppressed segments of society, as well as caring for the sick and bereaved. Specific passages include Ben Sira 4:1–6 (don't cheat the poor, add to the troubles of the desperate, delay giving to the needy, or reject a supplicant in distress, for, if you give one reason to curse you, "their Creator will hear their prayer"), 4:9–10 (rescue the oppressed from the oppressor and be a father to orphans, for then God "will love you"), 7:20 (don't abuse slaves or hired laborers),[139] 7:32 ("Stretch out your hand to the poor, so that your blessing may be complete"), 7:34–35 ("Mourn with those who mourn" and "do not hesitate to visit the sick" because "for such deeds you will be loved"), 29:9 (help the poor), and 35:17–18 (God will hear the cries of widows and orphans if you oppress them). Ben Sira frequently admonishes to give alms because "almsgiving atones for sin" and "will rescue you from every disaster," and because "no good comes to one who does not give alms."[140] The Hebrew word used by Ben Sira to refer to almsgiving is *tzedakah*, used in Proverbs to refer generally to righteous behavior.[141]

Ben Sira echoes the law collections (which impose a harsh punishment upon rebellious sons) in that he advocates strict discipline for children to avoid heartache.[142] He echoes Proverbs in advising that one not betray any secrets, and adds that, if you betray secrets, you lose

---

136. Sir 10:7.
137. Sir 28:8–9, 11.
138. Sir 34:25–27.
139. See Collins, *Jewish Wisdom*, 73–74.
140. See Sir 3:30; 7:10; 12:3; 29:12.
141. See Satlow, "Ben Sira," 433. Cf. chapter 9, sec. B, 2.
142. See Sir 7:23; 30:1–13 ("He who loves his son will whip him often, so that he may rejoice at the way he turns out"); 42:5. See generally Collins, *Jewish Wisdom*, 73.

friends.¹⁴³ Losing friends is bad because "faithful" friends are a "sturdy shelter" and "beyond price."¹⁴⁴ Ben Sira discusses friendship at great length, warning that one needs to be careful in choosing friends, and, because most friends are not loyal friends (they will not "stand by you in time of trouble"), one should neither trust friends hastily nor keep them without assessing their loyalty.¹⁴⁵

Also well established in both the Torah and Proverbs is the importance of humility, and for Ben Sira as well, although you should not be afraid to "give yourself the esteem you deserve," you should show humility (and not be proud) in order to be "loved."¹⁴⁶

There is one Torah-based teaching that Ben Sira does not follow. This is the famous command to love your neighbor as yourself. Ben Sira says to adhere to this command *only if your neighbor is not a sinner*.¹⁴⁷

Ben Sira suggests that to obey the laws of the Torah, you must *not* have "a divided mind" or a heart that is "full of deceit."¹⁴⁸ This is reminiscent of the concern of Jeremiah and Ezekiel that divided or deceitful hearts (passions and emotions which conflict with doing what God wills) cause people to disobey God's commands.¹⁴⁹ Ben Sira advances the ideas of Jeremiah and Ezekiel by associating moral failure with the biblical word *"yetzer"* (meaning "human inclinations")¹⁵⁰ and by asserting that because human beings have the ability to control their *yetzer* (their inclinations), they have the ability to obey the laws of the Torah without God radically altering human nature. Adherence to the law of Moses is a matter of exercising one's free will, choosing or willing to do that which is commanded by God. In Ben Sira's own words:

---

143. Sir 22:22; 27:16-21; 42:1.

144. Sir 6:14.

145. Sir 6:5-17; 9:10. Cf. Prov 18:24; Aristotle, *Eth. nic.* 1170a15-20. See Collins, *Jewish Wisdom*, 74-75. See also Daube, *Law and Wisdom*, 97-99 (Drawing attention to the importance that wisdom attaches to "a man's association, the company he keeps").

146. Sir 3:17; 7:17; 10:12-29. Cf. Aristotle, *Eth. nic.* 1123b1-16 (Magnanimity, appropriately esteeming yourself, is a virtue).

147. Sir 12:7. Cf. chapter 10 (The authors of Jewish apocalypses teach that the righteous should separate themselves from the wicked).

148. Sir 1:28, 30. See also Sir 23:2 (praying for God to "set whips over [his] thoughts, and the discipline of wisdom over [his] mind").

149. See chapter 4, sec. D. See also chapter 9, sec. C.

150. See Gen 6:5; 8:21.

> Do not say, "It was the Lord's doing that I fell away . . ."
>
> It was he who created humankind in the beginning, and he left them in the power of their own free will [or, alternatively translated, gave them over to the power of their inclinations, *yetzer*]. If you choose, you can keep the commandments.
>
> Before each person are life and death, and whichever one chooses will be given.[151]

Ben Sira also teaches that adherence to the law of Moses is evidence that one is in control of inclinations to disobey, and he perhaps suggests that adherence to the law trains one to control any inclinations to disobey in the future.[152]

The book of Qoheleth was well known to Ben Sira,[153] and, despite Ben Sira's commitment to conventional wisdom and his equating wisdom with the laws of the Torah, Ben Sira adopts certain moral norms from Qoheleth not found in the Torah. Specifically, Ben Sira advocates enjoyment as intrinsically good. In his own words:

> My child, treat yourself well, according to your means. . . . Do not deprive yourself . . . of a day's enjoyment; do not let your share of the desired good pass by you. . . . Give, and take, and indulge yourself, because in Hades [*Sheol*] one cannot look for luxury.[154]

---

151. Sir 15:11–17. See Blenkinsopp, *Wisdom and Law*, 79. But see Collins, *Jewish Wisdom*, 83 (In Ben Sira the free choice of man "is conditioned by the inclination with which a person is fitted at creation," and there is an "unresolved tension . . . between divine determination and human free will"). Cf. Josephus, *Ant.* 13.171–73 ("The Sadducees do away with fate, holding that there is no such thing and that human actions are not achieved in accordance with her decree, but that all things lie within our power, so that we ourselves are responsible for our well-being"). See Satlow, "Ben Sira," 447. See also Fried, "4 Ezra," 345; Klawans, "Jewish Theology," 641; chapter 6, sec. E (discussing *yetzer* in the Testaments of the Twelve Patriarchs); chapter 9, sec., D (discussing *yetzer* in rabbinic material); chapter 10, sec. D (discussing *yetzer* in 4 Ezra). Kugel believes that the word *yetzer* originally designated only an *evil* inclination and is so used by Ben Sira. See Kugel, "Testaments," 1810. But see Brand, "Evil and Sin," 647 (translating *yetzer* in Ben Sira as just "inclination"). See generally Rosen-Zvi, "Two Rabbinic Inclinations," 536–39. In any event, Kugel agrees that the picture of human nature painted in Ben Sira is one of "complete free will," in which there is "an *internal*" struggle between willing the godly act and willing the ungodly act; but for Kugel the struggle is not between a man's two opposing inclinations (the good and the evil) but between "a man and his evil *yetzer*." Kugel, "Testaments," 1810 (emphasis original).

152. Sir 21:11. See Brand, "Evil and Sin," 648.

153. See Gordis, *Koheleth*, 46–48.

154. Sir 14:11–16. See also Sir 30:21–24. The reference to *Sheol* does not mean that Ben Sira believed in a meaningful postmortem existence. See Starr, *Toward a*

The phrase "according to your means" suggests Qoheleth's caution not to strive for ever greater wealth. As Ben Sira puts it, striving for wealth "leads one astray."[155] In addition, health and physical fitness are more important than, and may conflict with, striving for wealth.[156] But, again, there is nothing wrong with luxury and wealth so long as it is justly obtained; only "dishonest wealth" is condemned.[157] Nor is there anything wrong with sensual pleasures, such as fine food and wine, music and beauty, so long as they are enjoyed in moderation.[158] Ben Sira also seems to follow Qoheleth in claiming that one atones for sin not by prayer or ritual but by adhering to proper moral norms, such as honoring one's parents and giving alms.[159] He also echoes Qoheleth in mentioning that "anxiety [mental disturbance] brings on premature old age."[160]

Ben Sira offers extensive practical advice that is based solely on experience and common sense, not the law of Moses, and is justified teleologically.[161] These pragmatic maxims are, for the most part, novel in the sense that exact duplicates are not found in the book of Proverbs. Examples of Ben Sira's practical advice are:

- "Don't pick a fight with the quick-tempered and don't journey with them through lonely country, because bloodshed means nothing to them, and where no help is at hand, they will strike you down."[162]

History, 15–22.

155. Sir 31:5–7.
156. Sir 30:14–16.
157. Sir 13:24.
158. See Sir 31:27–28; 37:29–31; 40:20–21. Cf. chapter 6, n32, n40, n65 (Moderation is one of the four cardinal virtues identified by Greek philosophers).
159. See Sir 3:3, 14–15, 30; 35:1–5 ("To forsake unrighteousness is an atonement"). See also Sir 34:23. In mentioning the importance of forgiveness, Ben Sira says, "Forgive your neighbor the wrong he has done, and then your sins will be pardoned when you pray." Sir 28:2. See also Sir 28:3–7.
160. Sir 30:24.
161. See generally Collins, *Jewish Wisdom*, 62 ("Approximately half of Ben Sira's book is taken up with practical wisdom concerning relations with family members, women, rulers, servants, and friends and other aspects of social behavior . . . much of [which] is paralleled in the late Egyptian Instructions of Phibis"). See also Collins, *Jewish Wisdom*, 62–79; Daube, *Law and Wisdom*, 85–97 (distinguishing among "lower," "idealistic" and "realistic" wisdom).
162. Sir 8:16.

- "Those who repay favors give thought to the future; when they fall they will find support."[163]
- "Whoever touches pitch gets dirty, and whoever associates with a proud person becomes like him."[164]
- "When you make a deposit, be sure it is counted and weighed, and when you give or receive, put it all in writing."[165]

In sum, despite equating wisdom with the laws of the Torah, Ben Sira does not espouse the Divine Command Theory or any deontological theory. What makes something morally right for Ben Sira is not that God wills it but that it enables a person to achieve a happy life. This is a teleological theory of the egoist variety; "the good" is individual well-being or happiness. One obeys God's commandments because to disobey brings disgrace and, at the appointed time, personal disaster, while obedience brings honor and, eventually, happiness. Collins puts it this way:

> There can be no dispute that [Ben Sira's] teaching is eudaemonistic (in the sense that its goal, at least in part, is a good and happy life) and utilitarian. In this respect it stands fully in the tradition of Proverbs, which also has a strong pragmatic emphasis on results [consequences] rather than on intentions. It should be remembered however, that the covenantal relationship also appealed strongly to enlightened self-interest. The observance of the Law would result in blessing, while disobedience would bring about a curse. Even the Golden Rule . . . is not simply an appeal to altruism. Doing to others as you would wish them to do to you is also a pragmatic way to ensure one's interest.[166]

D. The belief in a postmortem reward and punishment arose to resolve the problem of moral evil.

To recap, while the authors of the books of Job and Qoheleth questioned the traditional view that God always rewards the righteous and

---

163. Sir 3:31.

164. Sir 13:1. Cf. Sir 12:13–14. See n147 and accompanying text in this chapter.

165. Sir 42:7.

166. Collins, *Jewish Wisdom*, 76 (Collins is using "utilitarian" in an ordinary, non-philosophical sense to mean being "useful," "in one's interests," "practical," or "pragmatic"). But see Hayes, *What's Divine*, 97–98 ("One keeps the commandments because it is God's will").

YAHWEH REWARDS THE RIGHTEOUS AND PUNISHES THE WICKED

punishes the wicked, Ben Sira accepted it. Ben Sira could accept the traditional view because he was among the affluent members of society, and this segment of society saw their affluence as confirming their righteousness.[167] The situation was quite different for the less affluent segments of society. For them, the return to Jerusalem after the exile had not initiated the glorious new age promised by Ezekiel and Second Isaiah,[168] and high optimism soon gave way to disillusionment. This change in attitude is reflected in the message found in chapters 54 to 66 of Isaiah (attributed by some scholars, along with chapters 40 to 53, to a so-called "Second Isaiah," but by others to a so-called "Third Isaiah") which are set in the land of Israel shortly after the return. The prophesies of Third Isaiah "display a sense of disappointment or frustration with the realities of the restoration, rather than the exuberant hope that marks the prophesies in [chapters] 40–53."[169]

Moreover, Third Isaiah reflects a split in the community between "the chosen ones" of Yahweh and the wicked of the Israelite community; "envisions an imminent judgment that will separate the righteous and wicked of Israel"; and depicts a judgment and end time "in mythic, ahistorical terms" which leads to "the creation of new heavens and a new earth."[170] Nickelsburg claims that in Third Isaiah "we have the primary ingredients for the third- and second-century apocalyptic theology of 1 Enoch and Daniel: an oppressed minority who deem themselves the righteous; the expectation of an imminent judgment to alleviate the present situation; the dawn of a new age qualitatively different from the present one; [and] the use of mythic, ahistorical language to depict these future events."[171]

In short, disillusioned, less affluent returnees, who considered themselves to be the chosen ones of Yahweh, were suffering despite their righteousness, and they saw many wicked people prospering despite

---

167. See Gordis, *Koheleth*, 34 ("The teachers of Wisdom . . . being representative of the affluent group, felt no compulsion to adopt . . . new views. The sages of the conventional school maintained unchanged the old view of retribution here and now. Indeed, they made it . . . the cornerstone of their teaching.").

168. See Nickelsburg, *Jewish Literature*, 10. See Sommer, "Isaiah," 765 (Chapters 40 to 66 of Isaiah were written by a prophet that scholars call "Second Isaiah," and many scholars say chapters 54 to 66 were written by yet another prophet whom they call "Third Isaiah").

169. Sommer, "Isaiah," 765.

170. Nickelsburg, *Jewish Literature*, 12.

171. Nickelsburg, *Jewish Literature*, 12. See chapter 10.

their transgressions. For those who were righteous but poor there was a theological problem which needed to be resolved—the problem of moral evil. This problem became acute during the reign of Antiochus IV Epiphanes, the Seleucid king of Hellenistic Syria from 175 to 164 BCE,[172] and the problem of moral evil led to widespread belief in a *postmortem* reward and punishment.[173] According to Collins,

> even before [Ben Sira's] time, some Jews argued that retribution must come after death. This belief is first attested in the Book of the Watchers [1 En. 1–36; late third or early second century BCE], and it gained ground rapidly after the persecution in the time of Antiochus Epiphanes. It is already implied in Koheleth, who rejects it with the skeptical question: "Who knows whether the human spirit goes upward and the spirit of animals goes downward to the earth?"(3:21).[174]

The new view of reward and retribution in an afterlife, which, ultimately, became normative, took two basic forms—that a resurrected physical body is rewarded or punished or that an immortal soul is rewarded or punished. The former view was more typically held by less well-off, and less Hellenized, Jews in Judea. The latter view was more typically held by the Hellenized Jews of the diaspora, discussed in the next two chapters. In either case, the problem of moral evil is resolved by postulating that righteous persons who are not rewarded by God in this life will be rewarded by God in an afterlife, and that wicked persons who are not punished by God in this life will be punished by God in an afterlife.[175]

This idea of a postmortem reward and punishment enabled those who believed that God always rewards the righteous and always punishes the wicked to adhere to this traditional belief even though many who were righteous (now associated with the chosen ones and those who meticulously observed the laws of the Torah) died without having been rewarded with material prosperity in this present life, and might, in fact, have had to endure great suffering and early death, while many who were wicked and who flagrantly and consistently transgressed the

---

172. See n11 in this chapter.

173. See Starr, *Toward a History*, 39–41; Gordis, *Koheleth*, 34 (The solution reached by the lower classes to the problem of moral evil was "the doctrine of another world where the inequalities of the present order would be rectified").

174. Collins, *Jewish Wisdom*, 92. See Starr, *Toward a History*, 11–12.

175. See Starr, *Toward a History*, 39–90.

law of Moses lived long lives during which they enjoyed luxury and power without ever being punished for their sins and unrighteousness. Widespread adoption of belief in a postmortem reward and punishment is evidence that most people accepted a teleological ethical theory in which "the good" is associated with well-being, even if they never explicitly stated such.[176]

Briefly focusing on the belief in the resurrection of the dead, chapters 7 to 12 of the book of Daniel, written at the time of the Seleucid persecution of 167 to 164 BCE, is seen as a theological response to the crises of that persecution and of the martyrdom of those who refused to violate any of the Torah's laws.[177] Daniel reflects the fact that, during that time, the most devout Jews (that is, those who observed the laws of the Torah most meticulously) were persecuted and killed by a king whose mind was "set against the holy covenant";[178] at the same time, those unfaithful Jews who acted "wickedly toward the covenant" were prospering.[179] Daniel refers to these most devout Jews as *ha-maskilim*, "the knowledgeable," and he says that they "make the many understand" and "lead the many to righteousness [*matzdikei ha-rabim*]."[180] Yet they are also among the ones who "suffer captivity and spoilation" and "fall by the sword and flame."[181]

Although Daniel envisions a time when the righteous and the knowledgeable will be rescued from the evil designs of the wicked king, many of them had already been killed without having been rewarded in this life for their righteousness. Moreover, many of the wicked, those who had "forsaken the covenant," had died without having been punished in this life. Accordingly, Daniel envisioned that the recent deceased would be resurrected in order to be given the reward or punishment they deserved, and God's justice would thus be vindicated.[182]

---

176. See generally Eichrodt, *Theology*, 2.379 (The belief in resurrection did not essentially alter the concern with "the goods of material happiness"; the hope of reward and punishment was "now concentrated on the world beyond").

177. See Starr, *Toward a History*, 41; Wills, "Daniel," 1635–36.

178. See Dan 11:28.

179. See Dan 11:32.

180. See Dan 11:33, 35; 12:3. See also Wills, "Daniel," 1636 ("The scribal visionaries who produced Daniel were strongly opposed to Antiochus IV Epiphanes . . . yet they were probably not closely aligned with the Maccabees. The group is probably to be identified with those who are 'knowledgeable'").

181. See Dan 11:33.

182. Dan 12:2–3. Commenting on Daniel 12:2–3 Wills states: "The doctrine of resurrection and judgment probably came about during the persecutions of Antiochus

Similarly, in the book of 2 Maccabees, one of the pious brothers who refused to abandon God's laws during the persecutions of Antiochus IV Epiphanes could declare before being martyred, "We are ready to die rather than transgress the laws of our ancestors," and another could say, "You dismiss us from this present life, but the King of the universe will raise us up to everlasting renewal of life, because we have died for his laws."[183] In fact, all of the substantial apocalyptic material of the Second Temple period "strains to solve the riddle of the suffering of the righteous."[184]

The apocalyptic work referred to as the Epistle of Enoch (1 En. 92 to 105), written in the second century BCE, is particularly noteworthy.[185] In 1 En. 102:6–11, the sinners ask whether righteousness is profitable, and they conclude that it is not. Specifically, the sinners ask: "As we die, the righteous have died, and what have they gained from their [good] deeds?"[186] The sinners also state that fellow sinners "have died in splendor and wealth," and that "judgment has not been executed on them in their life," and indicate that they consider this life to be the only place of reward and punishment.[187] In response to the sinners' challenge, the author envisions that the righteous will ultimately be rewarded by becoming "companions with the hosts of heaven," which Collins refers to as "the resurrection of the spirit" and Grabbe refers to as "astral immortality."[188]

IV as a means to discern justice at a time when pious people, the *knowledgeable*, were being martyred." Wills, "Daniel," 1658 (emphasis original). See also Starr, *Toward a History*, 42–44.

183. 2 Macc 7:2, 9. See generally Starr, *Toward a History*, 44–45.

184. Kaufmann, *Religion*, 438. See also Starr, *Toward a History*, 70 (The aim of all apocalyptic literature "is to address the issue of the suffering of the righteous on earth; that is, to address the problem of moral evil"). See generally chapter 10.

185. See chapter 10, sec. A, 2.

186. 1 En. 102:6b–c.

187. 1 En. 103:5d–6d.

188. Starr, *Toward a History*, 69–72.

CHAPTER 6

The Hellenized Jews of the diaspora intertwined Jewish law and morality with Greek philosophy, accepting the Platonic notion of a soul which is rewarded or punished in an afterlife.

AFTER ALEXANDER THE GREAT'S conquest of the Persian Empire and following his death in 323 BCE, a period of intense fighting among his generals led to the establishment of three separate empires: the Antigonid Kingdom in Macedonia and mainland Greece, the Ptolemaic Kingdom in Egypt, and the Seleucid Kingdom stretching from the Hellespont to Central Asia.[1] The rulers of the Ptolemaic and Seleucid Kingdoms founded new cities at strategic locations that replaced or overshadowed older Persian political centers.[2] One of these newly founded cities was Alexandria in the western Nile delta. Inhabited by an ethnically diverse population, including a large Jewish population (which had existed in Egypt since the mid-seventh century BCE), Alexandria became the cultural center of the Ptolemaic Kingdom. It gained such prominence in the arts and sciences and attracted so many distinguished men of letters and scholars that it soon surpassed even Athens in the diversity of its culture.[3] After the Roman Republic conquered the Ptolemaic Kingdom in 31 BCE, Alexandria remained an important center of arts and sciences.

1. See Kosmin, "Hellenistic Period," 535–36.
2. Kosmin, "Hellenistic Period," 536.
3. Long, *Hellenistic Philosophy*, 2.

Among the important new cities in the Seleucid Kingdom was Antioch. It was founded along the Orontes River in northern Syria. A common culture and language (a new kind of Greek known as *koinē*) gave the Seleucid Kingdom a sense of unity with the Ptolemaic Kingdom.[4] "Hellenism" is the term used to refer to this common Greek civilization, and Hellenism was the dominant world culture throughout the Second Temple period.[5]

The most influential Hellenic philosophical movements were Stoicism, Skepticism, and Epicureanism.[6] The influence of these movements continued well into the Common Era. Additionally, in the first century BCE "Platonism began a long revival and an interest in Aristotle's technical writings was also re-awakened."[7] Diaspora Jews, especially in Alexandria, read the writings of important Greek thinkers and were greatly influenced by them. The Alexandrian Jewish population produced out of its midst their own school of philosophers who consciously, deliberately, and systematically set about remaking Greek philosophy according to a Jewish pattern of belief and tradition.[8] Describing these Hellenistic Jewish writers, Wolfson states:

> In presenting the beliefs and laws and practices of Judaism to a hostile world . . . they tried to show that their God . . . is the God of the philosophers, that their laws . . . were like the ethics and politics recommended by the philosophers, and that their practices, though outlandish, could be explained as being based upon reason.[9]

Many of these Hellenized Jewish thinkers of the diaspora were as concerned about the problem of moral evil as the less Hellenized authors of Daniel and the Epistle of Enoch living in Judea. However, the solution to the problem for the Jews of the diaspora was influenced by their acceptance of the Greek idea, advanced by Plato, of an immortal soul that is subject to reward or punishment in an afterlife. This Platonic idea was adopted by the pseudonymous Jewish author of a work called the *Sentences* of Pseudo-Phocylides and by the authors of two

4. See Long, *Hellenistic Philosophy*, 2.

5. See generally Cohen, *From the Maccabees*, 26–37 (discussing conceptions of Hellenistic Judaism).

6. Long, *Hellenistic Philosophy*, 1.

7. Long, *Hellenistic Philosophy*, 1.

8. Starr, *Toward a History*, 60.

9. Wolfson, *Philo*, 1.19.

apocryphal works (the Wisdom of Solomon and 4 Maccabees), all written after 50 BCE, discussed in this chapter. Belief in an immortal soul was also accepted by the most important Alexandrian Jewish philosopher, Philo, discussed in chapter 7.[10] By contending that righteousness is justified primarily because the souls of righteous individuals are rewarded in an afterlife and the souls of wicked individuals are punished in an afterlife, the ethical theory justifying the normative judgments of these thinkers is ethical egoism.

In addition to adopting the same Platonic metaphysical concepts and the same ethical theory, the authors of these works were alike in seeking to harmonize Jewish moral norms with the moral norms they discovered in the Greek tradition. Also engaged in this task of reconciliation, though not adopting the Platonic notion of an afterlife, were the authors of two other important works by Hellenized Jews of the diaspora discussed in this chapter, the Letter of Aristeas and the Testaments of the Twelve Patriarchs. Both of these date from the second century BCE or earlier, prior to the revival of Platonism. This temporal context may account for their omission of any mention of the soul's postmortem reward and punishment.

A. The Letter of Aristeas aims to demonstrate that Jewish law and morality are essentially equivalent to the moral principles of the Stoics, and are worthy of respect and admiration.

The Letter of Aristeas purports to be a communication from a Greek named Aristeas to his brother Philocrates recounting events concerning a purported decision by Ptolemy II Philadelphus (who ruled the Ptolemaic Kingdom from 285 to 246 BCE) to arrange for the translation of the "laws of the Jews" into Greek.[11] According to this purported communication, the chief librarian in Alexandria persuaded Ptolemy to authorize this translation for the purpose of adding the laws of the Jews to the king's library.[12] Ptolemy is then said to have written a letter to Eleazar, identified as the high priest in Jerusalem,[13] delivered by Aristeas, requesting that the high priest provide translators for Ptolemy's

---

10. See generally Starr, *Toward a History*, 60–90.
11. Let. Aris. 10.
12. See Let. Aris. 9–10.
13. See Gruen, "Letter of Aristeas," 2716 (questioning historicity of Eleazar).

project.¹⁴ In response, according to the Letter, seventy-two scholars were sent by Eleazar to Alexandria, and these scholars completed the task of translating the "laws of the Jews" into Greek in seventy-two days. In addition to recounting these purported events, Aristeas describes a purported speech made by the high priest explaining certain unusual customs of the Jews, including their dietary laws, and a purported seven-day symposium in Alexandria at which occasion the seventy-two Jewish translators answered questions posed by King Ptolemy.

Scholars widely agree that the real author of this document is "a Jew with a decidedly Jewish agenda."¹⁵ The author uses Aristeas as a pseudonym. An official of Ptolemy named Aristeas never existed, and the events recounted in the purported communication never occurred. The date of the document is a matter of dispute, but it was not created during the reign of King Ptolemy II. Most scholars "opt for a date around 200 BCE or a half century or so later."¹⁶ Lacking historical veracity, the value of the Letter "lies . . . in using the work as a window upon Jewish mentality in the circumstances of a diaspora community."¹⁷

The window on Jewish mentality afforded by the Letter shows that in the two centuries before the Common Era, Hellenized Jews felt a need to demonstrate that the laws of Moses, and the values fostered by those laws, were compatible with the laws and values of the larger Hellenistic culture in which these Jews were immersed (or, at least, compatible with the laws and values of the more sophisticated aspects of that Hellenistic culture) and felt a related need to demonstrate that a life in conformity with Mosaic laws and values merited respect and admiration. This need is suggested by two related claims made by Aristeas in a conversation he has with Ptolemy recounted at the beginning of the Letter.

First, Aristeas claims that "the same God who has given [the Jews] their law guides your kingdom also . . . though we address him differently, as Zeus and Dis."¹⁸ Second, Aristeas claims that the God who has given the Jews their law is the "overseer and creator of all things" and is "he whom all men worship."¹⁹ In other words, Aristeas believes that behind different deities with different names only one God really exists,

14. See Let. Aris. 35–40.
15. Gruen, "Letter of Aristeas," 2711.
16. Gruen, "Letter of Aristeas," 2711.
17. Gruen, "Letter of Aristeas," 2712.
18. Let. Aris. 15–16.
19. Let. Aris. 16.

and that this God is not a mythological, anthropomorphic god, but a real, abstract God.

In expressing this view Aristeas is reflecting ideas that, in Hellenistic culture, had their origin with the pre-Socratic philosophers Xenophanes and Heraclitus.[20] These philosophers rejected the conception found in the epic poems attributed to Homer that there is a pantheon of Olympian gods (Zeus, Hera, Apollo, Athena, etc.) who are, essentially, powerful and immortal human beings, and instead referred to the deity in non-mythological terms such as "the one."[21] The theological ideas of Xenophanes and Heraclitus were accepted by subsequent Greek philosophers, including the Stoics. Zeno of Citium (335–262 BCE), the founder of the Stoa, said: "God is one and the same with Reason (*Logos*), Fate, and Zeus . . . ; he [is] also called by many other names."[22] Zeno's identification of God with *Logos*, the rational order inherent in the cosmos that providentially guides the cosmos for the good, was adopted by his students.[23]

In short, the Jewish author of the Letter depicts the fictional Greek narrator, Aristeas, as a philosopher who has a sophisticated, Stoic conception of God,[24] and the Jewish author wants such a person to express the idea that Jewish law and morality derive from the very same non-mythological God recognized by Stoic philosophers to be the source of reason, order, and providence in the world.[25] Because Jewish law is acknowledged by Aristeas to be derived from the same God who guides Ptolemy in ruling his kingdom, Jewish law can be presumed to be compatible with the laws of the Ptolemaic kingdom.

The Jewish author has this idea expressed by a real Greek philosopher—the person purported to have been in charge of the king's library, Demetrius of Phalerum (ca. 350–280 BCE).[26] Demetrius tells Ptolemy:

---

20. See generally Wolfson, *Philo*, 1.17–18.

21. See Schmitz, "Concept of 'God' in Aristeas," 706 (Xenophanes did not name "the one" but Heraclitus called "the one" Zeus).

22. Schmitz, "Concept of 'God' in Aristeas," 706 (quoting Diog. Laert. vii 135, 136). See also Long, *Hellenistic Philosophy*, 111 ("That the cosmos is 'one' was asserted by Zeno").

23. Schmitz, "Concept of 'God' in Aristeas," 707 (One of Zeno's students, Cleanthes, expressed the idea that Zeus has many names).

24. See Wolfson, *Philo*, 1.15 ("Aristeas is presented as a . . . Stoic philosopher").

25. Cf. Let. Aris. 168 ("Nothing has been set down [in] Scripture . . . in the spirit of myth").

26. Though not actually the chief librarian for Ptolemy II, Demetrius of Phalerum is a historical figure, a philosopher taught by Aristotle's student Theophrastus. See

"The books of the Law of the Jews . . . should be given a place in your library, for their legislation is most philosophical and flawless, inasmuch as it is divine . . . [and] the views set forth in them have a certain holiness and sanctity."[27] Because Jewish law is "philosophical and flawless," the Jewish people can be presumed to be virtuous since Greek philosophers maintained that the practice of good actions is the result of habits acquired by adhering to good laws.[28] This point is succinctly stated when Eleazar says: "A good life . . . consists in the observance of the laws [of Moses], and this is attained by hearkening much better than by reading."[29] And Eleazar's reference to a "good life" means the type of life recognized as good in Greek culture because he is speaking to Aristeas.

In accordance with this point of view, the Letter emphasizes that Jewish morality is the same as Greek morality (or, at least, the same as the morality esteemed by Greek philosophers). In the first place, underlying moral conduct for the Greek philosopher Aristotle is the concept that a moral virtue is a mean between two extremes,[30] and the Jewish author of the Letter believed (or wanted others to believe) that underlying moral conduct for the Jews is the same concept of a moral virtue.[31] Therefore, he writes that after Aristeas became acquainted with the scholars chosen to translate Jewish laws into Greek, Aristeas noted that these scholars "zealously cultivated the quality of the mean (and that is the best course)."[32]

Moreover, the virtues mentioned by Aristeas and by Ptolemy as being most important for good governance are piety and justice,[33] and these exact same virtues are said by Eleazar to be prized by Moses, and the

---

Gruen, "Letter of Aristeas," 2717.

27. Let. Aris. 30–31.

28. See Aristotle, *Eth. nic.* 1103a15–1103b10. See also Hayes, *What's Divine*, 64–66, 106 (discussing Plato and asserting that the *Letter* echoes Plato, "according to which the best positive law conduces to virtue in two ways: by instructing . . . and by habituation").

29. Let. Aris. 127.

30. Aristotle, *Eth. nic.* 1106b10–25. Even before Aristotle, Plato repeatedly mentioned the doctrine of the mean. See Tirosh-Samuelson, *Happiness*, 467n85 (citing Plato, *Prot.* 345d; *Resp.* 602d; *Tim.* 36a; *Leg.* 691c, 679b, 701c, 728e, 792d).

31. Cf. chapter 7, sec. D, 2.

32. Let. Aris. 122. See also Let. Aris. 221 (One of the scholars teaches that "in all things moderation is a good principle").

33. See Let. Aris. 18, 24. In Greek culture, justice is the most important virtue, and piety is an aspect of justice—it is that part of justice having to do with right conduct directed toward the gods. See Plato, *Euthyphr.* 12b–e. See also chapter 7, sec. D, 6 (discussing Philo's understanding of piety).

prohibitions and commandments of Mosaic law are said by Eleazar to have been fashioned to instill these same two virtues.[34]

Not only does the Letter suggest that Jews and Greeks have a shared concept of what constitutes a moral virtue, and a shared understanding of the most important virtues, but it also suggests that Jews and Greeks share the same conception regarding the purpose of becoming virtuous—to achieve perfection as a human being. To self-actualize oneself as a human being was what constituted happiness for Aristotle and the Stoics,[35] and the Jewish author of the Letter has Eleazar assert that the laws of Moses "have all been solemnly drawn up for the sake of justice, to promote holy contemplation and the *perfecting of character*."[36]

To further evidence that the laws of the Jews are directed, as is the ideal Greek law, toward the perfecting of character, the Letter recounts a seven-day symposium that occurred when the seventy-two Jewish scholars arrived in Alexandria. The answers given by each of the seventy-two scholars to questions Ptolemy puts to them demonstrates their intellectual and moral virtue.[37] The scholars emphasize several key ideas of Stoic ethics—that virtue is more important than external goods such as wealth, fame, and luxurious living;[38] that one should avoid passions and be tranquil;[39] that one should be temperate;[40] that benevolence (or

---

34. Let. Aris. 131. See chapter 7, sec. B (For Philo, the Ten Commandments may be divided into two parts, one reflecting duties owed to God and the other reflecting duties owed to human beings).

35. See generally Aristotle, *Eth. nic.* 1097b20–1098a20; 1106a15–25 (The virtues are what enable human beings to fulfill their function excellently, to be all that they can be); Long, *Hellenistic Philosophy*, 173–74.

36. Let. Aris. 144 (emphasis added).

37. See Let. Aris. 187–294. See generally Aristotle, *Eth. nic.* 1103a 5–19 (distinguishing intellectual virtue, "virtue of thought," from moral virtue, "virtue of character").

38. See Let. Aris. 196, 211, 290. See also Long, *Hellenistic Philosophy*, 111 ("Throughout the history of the Stoa we find an emphasis on *indifference* to externals" [emphasis original]), 197 ("The Stoics claimed that virtue . . . is wholly constitutive of *eudaimonia*, happiness, welfare or well-being; in order to fare well a man needs nothing but virtue" [emphasis original]).

39. See Let. Aris. 216, 222, 232, 254, 256, 260. See also Long, *Hellenistic Philosophy*, 206 ("The Stoic sage is free from all passion. Anger, anxiety, cupidity, dread, elation, these and similar extreme emotions are all absent from his disposition").

40. See Let. Aris. 237, 278. See also Long, *Hellenistic Philosophy*, 200 (Temperance or moderation is one of the Stoics' four primary virtues).

humanity) and friendship are important;⁴¹ and that one should act in accord with nature and accept whatever befalls you.⁴²

Ptolemy is moved to exclaim, "I think the virtue of these men is extraordinary and their understanding very great," and the Greek philosopher Menedemus of Eretria (ca. 339–265 BCE) agrees.⁴³ A noteworthy point mentioned by Aristeas is that in their conduct and discourse the Jewish scholars "were far in advance of the [Greek] philosophers, for they made their starting point from God."⁴⁴ It is also noteworthy that when the king asked one of the Jewish scholars, "What is the teaching of wisdom?," the scholar mentions the admonition in Lev 19:18, saying, "Just as you do not wish evils to befall you . . . so you should deal with those subject to you."⁴⁵

The author of the Letter acknowledges real or imagined criticism that Jewish law and practices (especially Jewish dietary laws) are peculiar and set Jews apart from others.⁴⁶ It is argued, however, that all peculiarities in Jewish law have an important moral motive and, therefore, should be praised, not criticized. Eleazar explains that Moses, who "taught that God is one," deemed it necessary to separate Jews from those who worship "many gods," including those who worship "idols of stone and wood," and those, such as the Egyptians, "who have put their reliance in wild beasts . . . and worship these."⁴⁷ People who worship many gods concern themselves only with "food and drink and raiment" and "their whole disposition has recourse to these things."⁴⁸ For Jews, however,

> these things are reckoned as of nothing worth, but throughout the whole of life their contemplation is of the sovereignty of

---

41. See Let. Aris. 225, 228, 231, 290. See also Long, *Hellenistic Philosophy*, 200n1 (The Stoics' primary virtue of justice "embraces" kindness and fellow-feeling); Winston, "Philo's Ethical Theory," 391–94 (Linked to the concept of justice are the virtues of benevolence and friendliness).

42. See Let. Aris. 239, 244. See also Long, *Hellenistic Philosophy*, 165 ("The Stoics held that this is the best of all possible worlds," so one should be content with all that happens); n60 in this chapter.

43. Let. Aris. 200–1. See Gruen, "Letter of Aristeas," 2749 (identifying Menedemus).

44. Let. Aris. 235. See also Wolfson, *Philo*, 1.19.

45. *Let. Aris.* 207. See n82 in this chapter.

46. See Gruen, "Letter of Aristeas," 2740.

47. See Let. Aris. 132–38. See also Wolfson, *Philo*, 1.13–17 ("All the Hellenistic Jewish writers . . . denounce the heathenism of their new environment, its polytheism, its mythology, and its mysteries").

48. Let. Aris. 140–41.

God. And therefore, so that we should be polluted by none nor be infected with perversions by associating with worthless persons, he [i.e., Moses] has hedged us about on all sides with prescribed purifications in matters of food and drink and touch and hearing and sight.[49]

Eleazar further explains that such "purifications" have "a profound logic" (a symbolic meaning) intended to perfect the character of the Jewish people.[50] He points out, for example, that Jews are forbidden to eat "winged creatures" that are "wild and carnivorous and . . . oppress the rest and procure their food with injustice."[51] This may appear strange, but the dietary restriction is intended to serve as a symbol that Jews "must practice righteousness in spirit and oppress no one . . . but must guide their lives in accordance with justice."[52] Other dietary laws, such as those discriminating between animals with clefts through their hoofs (which may be eaten) and those with true hoofs (which may not be eaten),[53] are similarly explained as having symbolic meaning aimed at instilling the ability "to do all things with discrimination and with a view to righteousness," thereby perfecting character.[54] Some of these same dietary restrictions have the further benefit, according to Eleazar, of symbolizing the importance of intellectual virtues such as the virtue of a good memory which is reinforced by other practices (such as practice of attaching fringes to the four corners of garments) which are intended to continually remind people of God, "the ruler and preserver."[55] Aristeas is forced to concede that Eleazar made an excellent defense of the Jewish dietary laws which are all "directed toward justice and just intercourse among men."[56]

The author of the Letter also mentions that transgressions of Jewish law are punished, and he says that the law makes clear "the discomfitures

---

49. Let. Aris. 141–42.

50. Let. Aris. 143–44. See generally Svebakken, *Philo of Alexandria's Exposition*, 201–6, 216–17 (comparing the Letter of Aristeas, which interprets the dietary laws as having symbolic meaning, and Philo, who regards the dietary laws as a form of *askesis*); chapter 7, sec. C.

51. Let. Aris. 145–46. See Lev 11:13–19; Deut 14:11–17.

52. Let. Aris. 147.

53. See Lev 11:2–8; Deut 14:6–8.

54. See Let. Aris. 150–51.

55. See Let. Aris. 153–60.

56. Let. Aris. 168–70.

and visitations that would be inflicted by God on the guilty."⁵⁷ Punishment, in other words, is not restricted to human sanctions. Rather, the law teaches "that nothing done by men on earth secretly escapes [God's] notice, but that all that anyone does and all that is to be is manifest to him."⁵⁸ Moreover, Eleazar asserts that the law specifies that even evil intentions that are not carried out will be punished.⁵⁹

Significantly, neither the problem of moral evil nor the idea of a reward and punishment in an afterlife are mentioned. This, perhaps, is because the Letter seems to be comparing the Jewish concept of God and Jewish morality to the theological and ethical ideas of the *Stoic* philosophers, and, in contrast to *Platonists* (exemplified by Pseudo-Phocylides), Stoics neither believed in an afterlife nor were troubled by the problem of moral evil.⁶⁰

B. The *Sentences* of Pseudo-Phocylides sought to integrate Jewish and Greek moral norms, and adopted the Platonic idea of a soul rewarded in an afterlife for virtuous behavior.

The Hellenized Jewish author of a short didactic poem, written in old Ionic Greek dialect between about 50 BCE and 50 CE, attributed the work to Phocylides, a Greek gnomic poet of Miletus. Phocylides, born about 560 BCE, was "famous throughout antiquity as a great authority in matters of ethics and correct behavior."⁶¹ After scholars identified the Jewish authorship of the work, it was dubbed "the *Sentences* of Pseudo-Phocylides."⁶² The Jewish author, who possibly lived in Alexandria, attributed the work to Phocylides "because he wanted to integrate Jewish and Greek culture" and "to make clear that biblical and Greek ethics are

---

57. Let. Aris. 131.

58. Let. Aris. 132. Cf. Let. Aris. 210 (God "has knowledge of all things" and no man "working evil can escape his notice").

59. Let. Aris. 133.

60. See Long, *Hellenistic Philosophy*, 213n13 ("No Stoic postulated unlimited survival or immortality"), 180 ("From the perspective of the whole [advocated by the Stoics] nothing which befalls a man is disadvantageous. . . . Nature does not ordain suffering for its own sake, but it is necessary to the economy of the whole").

61. Van der Horst, "Pseudo-Phocylides, *Sentences*," 2353. See Collins, *Jewish Wisdom*, 159 (Phocylides was cited as an authority in ethical matters by Plato, Aristotle, and Isocrates; Greek gnomic poetry is analogous to the proverbial wisdom found in Proverbs and Ben Sira).

62. See generally Collins, *Jewish Wisdom*, 158.

not incompatible."[63] He may have also sought to reduce the teaching of the Torah to a limited number of moral principles, and to show Jews immersed in Hellenistic culture that an ancient Greek moralist recognized these same moral principles.[64] In any event, it was easy to harmonize biblical and Greek moral norms because both cultures had undergone a similar moral development—from a time when qualities and conduct having competitive value were the most highly esteemed to a time when qualities and conduct having cooperative value were the most highly esteemed—and fundamental biblical moral norms were not significantly different than fundamental Greek moral norms.

Greek philosophers had identified four cardinal virtues—*phronesis* (wisdom or prudence), *dikaiosune* (justice), *sophrosune* (temperance, moderation, or self-control), and *andreia* (courage or fortitude),[65] and the first part of Pseudo-Phocylides is "structured according to the canon of [the Greek] cardinal virtues."[66] The opening two verses of Pseudo-Phocylides are striking. They assert that the moral teaching "made known by Phocylides," which is purported to constitute the verses that follow the opening two verses, are the "commandments of God in his holy judgments."[67] In other words, "the author regarded pagan [moral] precepts as derived from or in essential accordance with the Torah," and he presents pagan moral precepts "as God's commandments."[68]

---

63. Van der Horst, "Pseudo-Phocylides, *Sentences*," 2353. See also Van der Horst, "Pseudo-Phocylides Revisited," 16 (Scholars assume that "the author wrote a kind of compendium of *miṣvot* for daily life which could help Jews in a thoroughly Hellenistic environment to live as Jews without having to abandon their interest in Greek culture").

64. See Van der Horst, *Sentences*, 45 (describing an article written by the Israeli scholar G. Alon).

65. See Wilson, *Mysteries of Righteousness*, 42–63; Long, *Hellenistic Philosophy*, 68 ("Prudence, justice, moderation and courage [are] the traditional four 'moral virtues' of Greek philosophy"); Plato, *Phaed.* 69b; *Resp.* 427e; *Leg.* 631c.

66. See Wilson, *Mysteries of Righteousness*, 75–119. Collins disputes this contention but acknowledges that the first part of the work deals, in turn, with the virtues of justice, moderation, and wisdom. See Collins, *Jewish Wisdom*, 160–61.

67. Ps-Phoc. 1–2.

68. Van der Horst, "Pseudo-Phocylides, *Sentences*," 2353. See also Van der Horst, "Pseudo-Phocylides Revisited," 16 (suggesting that the author "tried to provide a 'pagan' text that could be used safely in Jewish schools to satisfy Jewish parents who wanted their children to be trained in the classical pagan authors"). But see Collins, *Jewish Wisdom*, 175–76 ("The suggestion that Pseudo-Phocylides sentences were intended for schoolroom instruction is almost certainly right," but "in advertising his teachings under the name of Phocylides, the author surely hoped to attract pupils regardless of their adherence to Judaism").

After these opening verses, the author does not immediately refer to the Greek cardinal virtues. Rather, verses 3 to 8 set forth the moral commandments contained in the Decalogue—do not commit adultery, do not steal, do not murder, do not bear false witness, do not covet what belongs to your neighbor, and honor your father and mother.[69] Specifically, the reader is admonished: do not "commit adultery"; do not be "unjustly rich";[70] do not "defile your hands with blood"; do not "tell lies"; "abstain from what is another's"; and, "first and foremost honor God, and thereafter your parents."[71]

Only after mention of the moral norms of the Decalogue does Pseudo-Phocylides focus on the Greek cardinal virtues. Moreover, as noted by Collins, the author's discussion of these Greek virtues has "biblical overtones."[72] Indeed, Van der Horst comments that although "both Jewish and Greek parallels" can be found for most of the verses in the *Sentences*, there are a number of verses having "typically Jewish, sometimes very un-Greek themes," for which only Jewish parallels can be found.[73] Such verses include, according to Van der Horst, those expressing the great value of manual labor, strong concern for the poor and needy, concern for strangers, and a severe sexual ethics, as well as one admonishing the reader not to speak ill of a slave to his master.[74]

Pseudo-Phocylides considers the virtue of justice in verses 9 to 21. These verses can be associated with laws in the Torah about false testimony, deposits, and the need for just weights and measures.[75] Justice in Pseudo-Phocylides "is tempered [in verses 22 to 41] with mercy and kindness."[76] Presumably, the tempering of justice with mercy and kindness is because the Hebrew Bible associates *mishpat* (justice) with *hesed*

---

69. See Collins, *Jewish Wisdom*, 161–62; Van der Horst, "Pseudo-Phocylides Revisited," 17 (Not only are verses 3 to 8 a "summary of the Decalogue" but they also have "parallels in Delphic precepts").

70. Cf. Sir 5:8; 1 En. 97:8.

71. Ps-Phoc. 3–8.

72. Collins, *Jewish Wisdom*, 163. See also Van der Horst, "Pseudo-Phocylides Revisited" 15, 17 (Niebuhr "sees in these verses Jewish traditions in which Leviticus 19 and the Decalogue have been intertwined," Lev 19 being "regarded in early Judaism as a central chapter of the Torah").

73. Van der Horst, *Sentences*, 65.

74. Van der Horst, *Sentences*, 65.

75. Collins, *Jewish Wisdom*, 163.

76. Collins, *Jewish Wisdom*, 163.

(kindness).⁷⁷ Pseudo-Phocylides makes specific mention of "the duty of charity, in the sense of almsgiving . . . [grounded] in the common lot of human beings."⁷⁸ Although Collins sees biblical overtones in verses 22 to 41, he claims that the "most striking parallels" are Greek.⁷⁹ An alleged duty to be kind to strangers, for example, "is grounded in enlightened self-interest,⁸⁰ and, this "anthropocentric character," according to Collins, "is typical of Greek thought."⁸¹ Van der Horst contends, however, that verses 9 to 41 presents a great part of the precepts of Lev 19. He explains this by assuming that for Pseudo-Phocylides Lev 19 was "a kind of summary of the Torah or a counterpart of the Decalogue."⁸²

After an admonition that "love of money is the mother of all evil" and an elaboration of this statement,⁸³ the text turns to a discussion of the virtue of temperance, or moderation.⁸⁴ According to Collins, the sayings regarding moderation are, to a great extent, "Hellenistic commonplaces . . . [but] ancient Near Eastern wisdom also counseled moderation."⁸⁵ Discussion of the cardinal virtues concludes, in verses 122 to 131, with an affirmation of the virtue of wisdom. Collins comments that while certain of the statements made in these verses "can also be found in traditional Hebrew wisdom . . . the theme of these verses is commonplace in Greek literature."⁸⁶ He adds: "Distinctively

---

77. See chapter 4, nn38, 123. But see Long, *Hellenistic Philosophy*, 200n1 (The Stoics' primary virtue of justice "embraces" kindness and fellow-feeling).

78. Collins, *Jewish Wisdom*, 163.

79. Collins, *Jewish Wisdom*, 163-64.

80. Collins, *Jewish Wisdom*, 164. See Ps-Phoc. 40-41 (The duty exists because "we all experience the poverty that makes one wander; and the land has nothing constant for men").

81. Collins, *Jewish Wisdom*, 164. Cf. Exod 22:20 (In admonishing Israelites not to mistreat resident aliens the Hebrew Bible relies primarily on sympathy, reminding the Israelites that they "were strangers in the land of Egypt").

82. Van der Horst, *Sentences*, 66-67 (noting several other sources which take a similar view of Leviticus 19, including rabbinic sources, and tentatively concluding that "at the beginning of our era [Leviticus 19] was regarded as a central chapter in the Torah"). See also chapter 9, n107 and accompanying text; chapter 10, n11 and accompanying text; chapter 11, nn54-55, nn211-13 and accompanying texts.

83. See Ps-Phoc. 42-54.

84. See Ps-Phoc. 55-69, 76. See also Ps-Phoc. 193 ("Do not yield yourself wholly to unrestrained passion for a woman.").

85. Collins, *Jewish Wisdom*, 164-65.

86. Collins, *Jewish Wisdom*, 166.

Greek is the statement that when God allotted every creature a weapon he gave reason to man as his protection (vv. 125–28)."[87]

What is most significant in the first part of Pseudo-Phocylides, however, is not the author's consideration of the cardinal Greek virtues but his positing of a reward in an afterlife for possessing these virtues and all other virtues. The relevant verses state:

> Let the unburied dead receive their share of the earth.
>
> Do not dig up the grave of the deceased, nor expose to the sun what may not be seen as to incite divine anger.
>
> It is not good to disintegrate the human frame.
>
> For we really hope that the remains of the departed will soon come out of the earth to the light again; and thereafter they will be gods.
>
> For the souls remain unharmed in the deceased.
>
> For the spirit is a loan from God to mortals, and is his image.
>
> For we have a body out of earth, and when hereafter we are resolved again into earth, we are but dust; but the air has received our spirit. . . .
>
> All the dead are alike, and God rules over the souls.
>
> Our common eternal home and fatherland is Hades,
>
> A common place for all, both poor and kings.
>
> We humans do not live for a long time; but only briefly.
>
> But our immortal and ageless soul lives forever.[88]

These lines "are notoriously difficult" and most scholars "find it very difficult, if not impossible," to interpret them "as a systematic exposition of a consistent view."[89] Among other problems, the author "expresses confidence that the righteous deceased will be [physically] resurrected,"[90] and also asserts a belief in the immortality of the soul when, in the first century

---

87. Collins, *Jewish Wisdom*, 166.

88. Ps-Phoc. 99–115.

89. Van der Horst, "Pseudo-Phocylides on the Afterlife," 70. See Van der Horst, *Sentences*, 44 (Lewis claims that no attempt is made to reconcile the following three afterlife theories: (1) bodily resurrection; (2) the spirit proceeds to Hades; (3) the body is turned to dust, and the spirit is released into the upper elements).

90. See Van der Horst, "Pseudo-Phocylides, *Sentences*," 2357. But see Van der Horst, "Pseudo-Phocylides on the Afterlife," 72 (mentioning Collins' view that the author's acceptance of physical resurrection is not confident or certain but tentative).

CE, these beliefs were quite distinct in the Jewish community, with Jews in Judea primarily adopting a belief in bodily resurrection and Hellenized Jews in Alexandria primarily adopting the Greek idea of an immortal soul.[91] Nor does the author clarify his understanding of what a "soul" (*psyche*) is and how it is different, if at all, from a "spirit" (*pneuma*).[92] Rather, these verses "present a jumble of Hebrew and Greek anthropology."[93] Nevertheless, there is no question that the author accepted the Platonic view[94] that humans have a soul (*psyche*), that the soul is immortal, and (based, inter alia, on verse 11 which refers to God's judgment upon the wicked "thereafter") that the souls of the righteous are rewarded and the souls of the wicked are punished in an afterlife.[95]

The second part of Pseudo-Phocylides provides instruction on social relationships.[96] These verses have an affinity with "the kind of practical wisdom taught by Ben Sira."[97] Wilson divides this part into three subsections. The first subsection concerns how to deal with social outsiders "with an emphasis on how . . . to deal with evil persons."[98] The second subsection advises on the usefulness and importance of work. The third subsection deals with marriage and household relationships, including relationships with wives, other women, children, and slaves.

---

91. See Van der Horst, "Pseudo-Phocylides, *Sentences*," 2357 ("The author proclaims both the specifically Jewish idea of resurrection of the body . . . and the Greek conception of immortality of the soul"); Collins, *Jewish Wisdom*, 165 ("The idea of physical resurrection is exceptional in Jewish literature that is written in Greek"). See generally Starr, *Toward a History*, 33-90. But see Davies, *Paul and Rabbinic Judaism*, vii-x (In the first century, lines between Palestinian Judaism and Hellenistic or diaspora Judaism were "very fluid").

92. See generally Van der Horst, "Pseudo-Phocylides on the Afterlife," 73-74 (controversy whether the author understood the "soul" to be something distinct from the "spirit"). Cf. Starr, *Toward a History*, 72 (discussing the indiscriminate use of *psyche* and *pneuma* in the Greek text of the Epistle of Enoch).

93. Collins, *Jewish Wisdom*, 165.

94. Plato (but neither Aristotle, the Stoics, nor the Epicureans) advanced the view that there is reward and punishment of an immortal soul in an afterlife. For a discussion of Plato's views on the soul, see Robinson, *Plato's Psychology*, 3-157.

95. See Collins, *Jewish Wisdom*, 163. Cf. Josephus, *Ag. Ap.* 2.218-19 (Josephus supports his ethical code with an affirmation of a postmortem reward). See generally Starr, *Toward a History*, 86-90.

96. See Collins, *Jewish Wisdom*, 166-73.

97. Collins, *Jewish Wisdom*, 166.

98. Wilson, *Mysteries of Righteousness*, 119.

Much of what is said about marriage in the third subsection "is concerned with behavior in accordance with natural law."[99] A reason for why one should marry, for example, is to "give nature her due, beget in turn as you were begotten."[100] In other cases, advice as to what is natural is based on analogies with animals, as found elsewhere in Greek thought.[101] The third subsection also admonishes to avoid "violent sex with maidens; bestiality; or sex with one's stepmother, father's second wife (or concubines), sister, or brother's wives."[102] Van Horst notes: "Many of the warnings [contained in these verses] not to engage in deviant sexual behavior are inspired by passages in the Torah."[103] Prohibitions against "homosexuality and of abortions and infanticide" contained in the third subsection "stand out as trademarks of Jewish ethical teaching in the Hellenistic world."[104] Homosexuality "was an issue on which there is a clear contrast between Greek and Jewish ethics . . . [and the] prohibition of abortion and infanticide was also distinctive."[105]

The *Sentences* of Pseudo-Phocylides ends with an epilogue stating:

> Purifications concern the purity of the soul, not of the body.
>
> These are the mysteries of righteousness [*dikaiosune*]; living according to them you may complete a good life until the threshold of old age.[106]

Thus, the author uses the Greek term *dikaiosune* (which when narrowly construed refers to the specific virtue of justice) to connote *all* virtues and *all* virtuous behavior that is set forth in the body of the text. In this way, the *Sentences*, in effect, links the Greek term *dikaiosune*

---

99. Collins, *Jewish Wisdom*, 169.

100. Ps-Phoc. 176 (as translated by Collins). See Collins, *Jewish Wisdom*, 169 ("This is in accordance with Stoic teaching").

101. See Collins, *Jewish Wisdom*, 169. See, e.g., Ps-Pho. 190–91 ("Do not transgress the natural limits of sex. . . . Even animals are not pleased by intercourse of male with male").

102. Ps-Phoc. 179–183, 198.

103. Van der Horst, "Pseudo-Phocylides, *Sentences*," 2358 (citing Lev 18:8, 11, 20, 23; 20:15–16; 22:16; Exod 22:19; Deut 27:21). See also Collins, *Jewish Wisdom*, 169–70.

104. Collins, *Jewish Wisdom*, 170–71. See Ps-Phoc. 184–85 ("A woman should not destroy an unborn babe in her womb nor after its birth throw it away as prey for dogs and vultures"), 190–91.

105. Collins, *Jewish Wisdom*, 171–72. Cf. Let. Aris. 152 (Eleazar says that, contrary to Jewish practice, "most of the rest of mankind . . . have intercourse with males, [and] they even defile mothers and daughters").

106. Ps-Phoc. 228–30.

with the Hebrew term *tzedakah* since, in the Hebrew Bible, *tzedakah* similarly connotes all virtues and all virtuous conduct commanded by God.[107] The identification of *dikaiosune* with *tzedakah* is strengthened by the fact that Pseudo-Phocylides intends the epilogue to refer back to the opening lines of the poem, and so associates the "mysteries of righteousness (*dikaiosune*)" with the "commandments of God in his holy judgments (*dikai*)."[108] Finally, the claim that purifications "concern the purity of the soul, not the body" suggests the Platonic notion that living virtuously (or righteously) enables the soul to get free of the body and be rewarded in the afterlife.[109]

C. The Wisdom of Solomon identifies righteousness with the Greek cardinal virtues, links righteousness with wisdom, and argues that both righteousness and wisdom are more profitable in the long run than external goods because they lead to vindication in a judgment after death.

The Wisdom of Solomon, the "most important wisdom writing from the Hellenistic diaspora," was written in Greek by a learned and thoroughly Hellenized Jew of Alexandria probably after that city's conquest by Rome in 30 BCE and before 70 CE.[110] The anonymous author of this wisdom text identifies himself with King Solomon and so is conventionally referred to as "Pseudo-Solomon."[111] Pseudo-Solomon, as

---

107. Cf. chapter 1, sec. B, 1. See also Wolfson, *Philo*, 2.220 ("In native Judaism the view has been expressed that 'the commandment of [*tzedakah*] is balanced against all the commandments together'" [citing b. B. Bat. 9a]); Kugel, "*Testaments*," 1741 ("*Dikaiosune* [translated as 'righteousness'] was sometimes used as a kind of shorthand among Greek-speaking Jews for 'keeping the commandments of the Torah'"); Kugel, *Traditions of the Bible*, 310 (same).

108. Van der Horst, "Pseudo-Phocylides, *Sentences*," 2360. Van der Horst also notes that the phrase "*mysteries* of righteousness" is used to suggest "the revelatory nature of Pseudo-Phocylides's admonitions" stressed in the opening lines of the Sentences. Van der Horst, "Pseudo-Phocylides, *Sentences*," 2360.

109. See Plato, *Gorg.* 523–25; *Phaed.* 112–14; *Resp.* 614–21. See also Van der Horst, "Pseudo-Phocylides, *Sentences*," 2360; Van der Horst, "Pseudo-Phocylides Revisited," 27–29.

110. Collins, *Jewish Wisdom*, 178. See Enns, "Wisdom of Solomon," 2155 ("A date during the reign of the Roman emperor Gaius Caligula (37–41 CE) can be defended"); Winston, *Wisdom of Solomon*, 20–25.

111. See Enns, "Wisdom of Solomon," 2155 ("It is a commonly attested literary device in the ancient world to attribute one's work to a famous figure from the past").

Pseudo-Phocylides, uses the Greek term *dikaiosune* to broadly refer to all virtues and all virtuous behavior.¹¹² But Pseudo-Solomon is less interested than Pseudo-Phocylides in delineating what specific traits and conduct constitutes *dikaiosune*. Pseudo-Solomon does, however, specifically identify *dikaiosune*, and by implication the Hebrew term *tzedakah*, with the four Greek cardinal virtues. He writes:

> And if anyone loves righteousness [*dikaiosune*], [Wisdom's] labors are virtues; for she teaches self-control [*sophrosune*] and prudence [*phronesis*], justice [*dikaiosune*] and courage [*andrea*]; nothing in life is more profitable for mortals than these.¹¹³

The profitability of righteousness is the central concern of the work. Related to the profitability of righteousness is the profitability of wisdom (*sophia* and *phronesis*), for, as indicated in the passage just quoted, Pseudo-Solomon considers righteousness and wisdom to be linked.¹¹⁴ Collins explains Pseudo-Solomon's concept of "wisdom" as follows:

> It is a cosmic principle that "holds all things together" and is the link between God and the universe. As such, it clearly stands in a tradition with Prov 8 and [Ben Sira] 24, but the portrayal of Wisdom here is far more developed and makes extensive use of Greek philosophical terminology. While reference is made to the "laws" of Wisdom (6:18), [the Wisdom of Solomon] does not endorse the claim of Ben Sira that Wisdom is identical with the Laws of Moses.¹¹⁵

---

112. See, e.g., Wis 1:1 ("Love righteousness (*dikaiosune*)"); 5:15 ("The righteous (*dikaioi*) live forever").

113. Wis 8:7. See Winston, *Wisdom of Solomon*, 154 (Pseudo-Solomon follows the Platonic tradition in using the word *phronesis* to denote both a theoretical and a practical virtue, in contrast to Aristotle "who allotted theoretical knowledge to *sophia*" and "eventually confined *phronēsis* to the practical sphere"). Cf. 4 Macc 1:6, 18; 5:22–24.

114. See Enns, "Wisdom of Solomon," 2175 ("Righteousness can only be met in wisdom"); Nickelsburg, *Jewish Literature*, 209–10 (Wisdom "is closely connected with righteousness").

115. Collins, *Jewish Wisdom*, 196. See also Nickelsburg, *Jewish Literature*, 209–10 ("Wisdom is here not identified with Torah, as she is in [Ben Sira] and Baruch, and Torah is only of marginal importance in this work.... At the same time, the descriptions of Wisdom ... employ language most likely drawn from the praises of Isis ... [and other] characteristics of Wisdom, notably her permeation of the cosmos and her ordering of all things, are beholden to Stoic conceptions"); Kraus, "Wisdom of Solomon," 394 (Pseudo-Solomon's portrayal of wisdom "shows the influence of Greek ideas"). But see Wis 9:9 (Wisdom knows "what is pleasing in [God's] sight and what is right according to [God's] commandments"); Tirosh-Samuelson, *Happiness*, 81 (Although Pseudo-Solomon "never explicitly identifies Wisdom and Torah ... he implies [in

Not only does Pseudo-Solomon's description of wisdom make use of Greek philosophical terminology, but his understanding of wisdom is likened by scholars to the Greek concept of *Logos* found in Stoicism and Middle Platonism.[116] Pseudo-Solomon describes wisdom in detail in verses 7:15 to 8:1. Here wisdom, personified as a feminine figure,[117] is said to permit one "to know the structure of the world and the activity of the elements . . . the cycles of the year and the constellations of the stars; the natures of animals and . . . the reasonings of men."[118] Wisdom is here further said to be "a pure emanation of the glory of the Almighty . . . a spotless mirror of the working of God, and an image of his goodness."[119] As the pervading force in the universe, wisdom is God's agent. Consequently, "God is operative [in the world] through intrinsic, natural phenomena and causation rather than through extrinsic, transcendent intervention . . . [and] uses nature as a means of effecting divine judgment."[120] The section closes with the sentence: "She reaches mightily from one end of the earth to the other; and she orders all things well."[121]

Notwithstanding an association between Pseudo-Solomon's concept of wisdom and Greek philosophical concepts, an association also exists between Pseudo-Solomon's concept of wisdom and the Hebrew concept of *hokhmah*; and Pseudo-Solomon's linking of wisdom and righteousness may be compared with the biblical linking of *hokhmah* and *tzedakah*.[122] This is to say that Pseudo-Solomon's understanding of wisdom is consistent with the biblical view that there is a natural

---

chapters 10 to 19] that Wisdom is the archetypical Torah of which Mosaic Law is an image"); Winston, *Wisdom of Solomon*, 43 ("Very likely he believed with Philo that the teachings of the Torah were tokens of the Divine Wisdom, and that they were in harmony with the laws of the universe").

116. See generally Collins, *Jewish Wisdom*, 196–202; Winston, *Wisdom of Solomon*, 33–43, 59–60. See also Winston, *Wisdom of Solomon*, 178 (In verses 7:22b–24, wisdom is described in a series of twenty-one epithets "borrowed largely from Greek philosophy").

117. Cf. Prov 1:20–33; Wis 6:14.

118. Wis 7:17–20.

119. Wis 7:25–26.

120. Nickelsburg, *Jewish Literature*, 210.

121. Wis 8:1.

122. See chapter 1, sec. C, 2, n121 and accompanying text. See also Enns, "Wisdom of Solomon," 2174–75 (Although the terminology used to describe wisdom in verses 7:24–8:1 "is Greek . . . the personification and exaltation of wisdom is hardly limited to Greek thought, but is also seen in Proverbs"); Kraus, "Wisdom of Solomon," 394 (comparing *sophia* and *hokhmah*); Sandmel, *Two Living Traditions*, 282 (same).

and moral order inherent in the world that God established at the time of creation, which may be discerned by human beings;[123] and Pseudo-Solomon's view that righteousness is linked with wisdom is consistent with the biblical view that to attain *hokhmah* is to have knowledge of the moral order established by God (knowledge of God's will) and to adjust one's behavior to be in accord with God's moral order (in accord with God's will), that is, to be righteous.[124]

In comparing Pseudo-Solomon's views with biblical views, it should be noted that Pseudo-Solomon accepts Jeremiah's outlook that righteousness requires one to have an undivided heart.[125] It seems likely that Jeremiah's outlook would have been seen as comparable to the outlook of Aristotle. Aristotle distinguishes virtuous people, whose souls are integrated in that the irrational part of the soul "agrees with reason in everything," from continent persons, whose souls are divided in that the irrational part of the soul clashes and struggles with reason.[126]

Returning to the issue of the profitability of righteousness and wisdom, Pseudo-Solomon's position is ambivalent. On the one hand he claims that nothing is more profitable than righteousness, and that wisdom is to be preferred over wealth, health, beauty, or anything else,[127] suggesting that righteousness and wisdom are primarily intrinsically good. Yet, on the other hand, he claims that wisdom is good because it enables one to attain "all good things," including "uncounted wealth,"[128] suggesting that wisdom and righteousness are primarily instrumentally good as the means to material well-being. This ambivalence is clearly seen in chapter 7. Here, with a likely allusion to the life of the real King Solomon (described in 1 Kgs 3:1–15), Pseudo-Solomon says that he prayed to God for wisdom, and relates:

---

123. See Winston, *Wisdom of Solomon*, 154.

124. See chapter 1, sec. C, 2–3. Cf. Wis 9:9–18 (Through wisdom people may discern what God wills and understand what is right according to God's commandments).

125. See chapter 4, sec. D; Wis 1:1 (admonishing rulers to seek the Lord "in singleness of heart" or with an integrated [undivided] heart [*haplotete kardias*]). See generally Winston, *Wisdom of Solomon*, 101. Cf. sec. E in this chapter (discussing the pervasive emphasis in the Testaments on *haplotes* [integrity] and their mention of the "integrity (or singleness) of heart").

126. Aristotle, *Eth. nic.* 1102b15–25. See also chapter 7, n133 and accompanying text.

127. See Wis 7:8–10; 8:7.

128. Wis 7:11. See also Wis 8:18 (Wisdom brings "unfailing wealth").

> I preferred her [i.e., wisdom] above scepter and throne, and held riches as nought by comparison. I reckoned no priceless gem her equal.... I loved her above health and shapeliness.... But all good things came to me with her together, and wealth past counting in her hands; and I rejoiced in all since Wisdom leads them forth, yet I was unaware [at the time] that it was she who bore these things.[129]

Winston's comment on this passage merits attention. He writes:

> Solomon preferred Wisdom above all external goods, but subsequently discovered that the latter were ultimately attained along with her. There appears to be a faint echo of the well-known philosophical debate between the Peripatetics [Aristotelians] and the Stoics as to the relative importance of external goods (such as health, beauty, honor, and wealth . . .) for the happy life. The Stoics had placed special stress on the notion that virtue is self-sufficient for happiness . . . and the only good properly speaking.[130]

In contrast to the Stoics, Aristotle had argued that *complete* happiness required external goods in addition to virtue.[131] According to Winston, a "compromise" was adopted by Antiochus of Ascalon "who distinguished the *vita beata* [the phrase used by Cicero for "the good life" in his Latin explanation of Antiochus], which depends only on virtue, from the *vita beatissima* [most blessed life], which requires also the possibility of using external goods."[132] Winston claims that Philo of Alexandria "seems to follow the compromise adopted by Antiochus of Ascalon" and that Pseudo-Solomon "seems to reflect to some extent Philo's position."[133]

Winston errs in describing the view of Antiochus of Ascalon as a "compromise" between the positions of the Stoics and the Peripatetics. As explained by Allen, "[Antiochus'] position was that virtue is the chief good [and sufficient for a happy life (*vita beata*)], but not the sole good [because the *completely* happy life (*vita beatissima*) requires external

---

129. Wis 7:8–12.
130. Winston, *Wisdom of Solomon*, 167–68.
131. Aristotle, *Eth. nic.* 1099a25–1099b9.
132. Winston, *Wisdom of Solomon*, 168 (citing Cicero, *Acad. post.* 1.22; 2.22; 1.134). See generally Allen, "Antiochus of Ascalon," sec. 4 (citing Cicero, *Fin.* 5.71, 95; *Tusc.* 5.22).
133. Winston, *Wisdom of Solomon*, 168 (citing Philo, *Rewards* 104).

goods]; *and this is the Peripatetic view.*"[134] More importantly, Winston fails to mention Epicurus. This is a serious omission because Epicurus opposed the view that virtue is *intrinsically* good.

In the view of Epicurus, *pleasure* is the only thing intrinsically good,[135] and the virtues are merely instrumentally good—they are good as a means to achieving pleasure.[136] While Pseudo-Solomon does seem to advance the Peripatetic view that in this life external goods are required for complete happiness, he is, arguably, closer to the position of Epicurus than to that of either the Stoics, the Peripatetics, or Antiochus of Ascalon (who all held that virtue is *intrinsically* good). This is so because, like Epicurus, Pseudo-Solomon considered virtue (righteousness) to be primarily *instrumentally* good, good because he believed that righteousness was the means to enjoying a blissful immortality.[137] The claim that Pseudo-Solomon saw virtue (righteousness) as primarily *instrumentally* good is based upon Pseudo-Solomon's discussion of the problem of moral evil.

Pseudo-Solomon's discussion of this problem begins with a challenge posed to righteous people by the "godless" people. The godless argue that righteousness is not profitable, and, therefore, they opt to forgo it and, instead, opt "to enjoy the good things that exist" and to "oppress the righteous poor man" and any disadvantaged and weak member of society.[138] In response, Pseudo-Solomon, having adopted a modified Platonic notion of an immortal soul that is rewarded in an afterlife,[139] claims that the ungodly "were led astray" because they did not understand that there is an afterlife in which the souls of the righteous will enjoy a blissful immortality "with the Lord," but the wicked would become "dishonored corpses."[140]

In other words, the ungodly wrongly assume that there are no rewards for righteousness and no punishments for wickedness because they wrongly assume that there is no afterlife.[141] Pseudo-Solomon does

---

134. Allen, "Antiochus of Ascalon," sec. 4 (emphasis added).

135. Cf. chapter 5, secs. B, 2 and C (Both Qoheleth and Ben Sira maintain that pleasure is intrinsically good).

136. Epicurus, *Ep. Men.* 132.

137. Although agreeing with Pseudo-Solomon that virtue is instrumentally good, Epicurus dismissed notions of an afterlife. See Epicurus, *Ep. Men.* 125.

138. Wis 2:1–12.

139. See Starr, *Toward a History*, 64–69.

140. Wis 2:21–5:16.

141. See Nickelsburg, *Jewish Literature*, 205–7.

not argue that righteousness (virtue) is intrinsically good and sufficient without more for complete happiness, as the Stoics claimed; but neither does he argue that righteousness is intrinsically good and *together with external goods* sufficient for complete happiness, as the Peripatetics (and Antiochus) claimed. Rather, he argues that righteousness is *profitable* because it results in a blissful immortality with the Lord, denied to the unrighteous. Neither the Stoics nor the Peripatetics made such an argument; in fact, both groups rejected the idea of any afterlife.[142] But the argument is crucial for Pseudo-Solomon. In the words of Collins, who divides the Wisdom of Solomon into three parts, the "book of eschatology," the "book of wisdom," and the "book of history":

> Unlike the loosely structured book of Ben Sira, or gnomologion-like sayings of Pseudo-Phocylides, [the Wisdom of Solomon] presents a coherent argument to advocate a course of action and show that it is expedient and good. The subject of the exhortation is love of righteousness (1:1) and wisdom (6:9). The "book of eschatology" shows what is at stake by presenting the arguments of the opponents and showing their inadequacy. It also presents *the author's most basic argument for the value of righteousness: it leads to vindication in a judgment after death*. The "book of wisdom" describes the origin and nature of wisdom and the manner in which it is attained.... Finally, the "book of history" elaborates the theme by well-known examples. Biblical history, especially the exodus story, is expounded to show that the efficacy of righteousness is guaranteed by the universe itself.[143]

---

142. Later, in the second and third centuries, Aristotelian commentators such as Alexander of Aphrodisias "interpreted Aristotle in such a way that supported the immortality of what was called the 'acquired intellect.'" Starr, *Toward a History*, 178–79.

143. Collins, *Jewish Wisdom*, 181 (emphasis added). See Wis 5:1–23. See also Winston, *Wisdom of Solomon*, 146 ("The author envisages the future royal [splendor] of the just and the simultaneous annihilation of the wicked"); Enns, "Wisdom of Solomon," 2155, 2156 (The work is intended to show "persecuted Alexandrian Jews" that, "even if they die a martyr's death," the righteous will "live forever"); Nickelsburg, *Jewish Literature*, 207 (The author asserts the validity of immortality and appeals to his audience to accept it as a means of proving that "God's justice is a fact, all appearances to the contrary"); Tirosh-Samuelson, *Happiness*, 81 ("The ultimate reward for righteousness... [is] entrance into a life of blessed eternity").

D. The author of 4 Maccabees identified wisdom with education in the law, understood the cardinal virtues to be a part of wisdom, and justified adherence to the law and virtuous behavior on the grounds that they are rewarded by immortality.

Fourth Maccabees is another work written in Greek by a thoroughly Hellenized Jew who intertwined Jewish law and morality with ideas derived from Greek philosophers. Scholars disagree about the work's date and place of composition, but it was probably written in Asia Minor (maybe in Antioch) in the first century CE.[144] The anonymous author "is clearly well educated, both in Jewish literature and traditions and in Greek philosophy and rhetoric."[145]

Eusebius and Jerome called the work "On the Supremacy of Reason," and justifiably so; the stated aim of the author is to prove that reason (*logismos*) can control one's emotions,[146] and the author argues that such self-mastery enables one to acquire the virtues of justice, temperance, courage, and piety.[147] *Logismos* is defined as "the mind that with sound logic prefers the life of wisdom," and wisdom (*sophia*) is defined as "the knowledge of divine and human matters and the causes of these."[148] The belief that reason can control desires, passions, and emotions, and the understanding that wisdom is knowledge of divine and human matters, were commonplace among Greek philosophers.[149]

What distinguishes the author of 4 Maccabees from his pagan counterparts is his association of *sophia* with *nomos*, an association not made by any Greek philosopher.[150] Specifically, the author of 4 Maccabees states

---

144. See DeSilva, "4 Maccabees," 2363; Zurawski, "4 Maccabees," 500; Nickelsburg, *Jewish Literature*, 258; Redditt, "Concept of *Nomos*," 266-69.

145. Zurawski, "4 Maccabees," 500.

146. 4 Macc 1:13. In contrast to the Stoic position that one should be free of all passion, the author of 4 Maccabees states that passion should be controlled but not eliminated, presumably because passion has been implanted into human beings by God. See 4 Macc 1:6; 2:21; 3:5. Cf. chapter 7, sec. B. See also Wolfson, *Philo*, 2.270-71.

147. See 4 Macc 5:22-24. See also 4 Macc 1:3-4 (Reason "rules over" (1) "glutton and lust" (which hinder temperance); (2) "malice" (which hinders justice); and (3) "anger, fear and pain" (which hinder courage)); Zurawski, "4 Maccabees," 499, 500.

148. 4 Macc 1:15-16.

149. See Redditt, "Concept of *Nomos*," 260; Nickelsburg, *Jewish Literature*, 256; DeSilva, "4 Maccabees," 2366.

150. See Redditt, "Concept of *Nomos*," 255-56, 260 ("This identification of wisdom with *nomos* has its roots in Israel's wisdom literature"); DeSilva, "4 Maccabees," 2366

that *sophia* "is education in the Law (*nomos*), by which we learn divine matters reverently and human affairs *to our advantage*."[151] He goes on to state that there are four kinds of *sophia*—"rational judgment [*phronesis*], justice, courage, and self-control."[152] By equating the law of Moses with wisdom, and by saying that the four cardinal virtues are kinds of wisdom, the author of 4 Maccabees essentially makes the law of Moses the source of the cardinal virtues. And since acquisition of the cardinal virtues are also said to be the result of reason's ability to control the emotions, the law of Moses is linked as well to reason's ability to control the emotions in ways discussed in the following paragraph.[153] In any event, in contrast to the Stoics (who do not associate *nomos* with the commands of a divine legislator), for the author of 4 Maccabees it is education in the law of Moses (that is, divine commands constituting both *nomos* and *sophia*) which enables us to arrange human affairs "to our advantage."[154]

The author of 4 Maccabees may additionally be distinguished from his pagan counterparts by his belief, shared with Philo Judaeus,[155] that the law of Moses provides the training or practice (*askesis*) that enables one to acquire the self-control (*enkrateia*) needed to restrain the emotions.[156] For instance, according to 4 Maccabees, the law enables one to acquire the virtue of temperance because the law forbids Jews from eating certain pleasurable foods [Lev 11; Deut 14:1–21], and the tenth commandment of the Decalogue prohibits Jews from coveting their neighbors' wives, and these laws can be adhered to only when "reason is able to rule over appetites."[157] Similarly, the law enables the virtue of justice to be acquired because, when one "adopts a way of life in accordance with the Law, even

---

(The claim that "Torah observance is the path to such wisdom . . . is entirely in keeping with the extracanonical Jewish wisdom tradition" [citing Sir 1:26; 19:20; Wis 6:17–20]); Nickelsburg, *Jewish Literature*, 256.

151. 4 Macc 1:17 (emphasis added).

152. 4 Macc 1:18–19 (*Phronesis* is said to be "supreme" since it is by means of *phronesis* that *logismos* rules over the emotions).

153. See Redditt, "Concept of *Nomos*," 252 ("*Nomos* functions to enable rational living").

154. 4 Macc 1:17.

155. See chapter 7, sec. C.

156. See Zurawski, "4 Maccabees," 500; DeSilva, "4 Maccabees," 2263 (The author "presents the regimen of the Torah-observant life as a training program that fits reason to gain the upper hand over the passions, and thus to nurture the (Greek) cardinal virtues of justice, courage, self-control, and wisdom"). See also 4 Macc 1:17; 2:23.

157. See 4 Macc 1:33—2:6.

though a lover of money, one is forced to act contrary to natural ways and to lend without interest to the needy [Exod 22:24; Deut 23:20–21] and to cancel the debt when the seventh year arrives [Exod 21:2; Deut 15:1–3]."[158] The work ends with an exhortation to the "seed of Abraham" to continue to "obey this Law and exercise piety in every way, knowing that devout reason is master of all emotions."[159]

Among the examples of reason's mastery of all emotions proffered by the author is that of the Jewish martyrs who were tortured and killed by Antiochus IV Epiphanes. It is related that Antiochus, seeking to end Torah observance, ordered his guards "to seize each and every Hebrew and to compel them to eat pork and food sacrificed to idols."[160] Then the story is told of the martyrs who refused to comply with the demands of Antiochus because compliance required conduct prohibited by divine law, and who were tortured and killed because of their refusal. The first martyr mentioned, the aged priest Eleazar, justified his refusal as rational, proclaiming before he was killed:

> You scoff at our philosophy as though living by it were irrational, but it teaches us self-control, so that we master all pleasure and desires, and it trains us in courage, so that we endure any suffering willingly; it instructs us in justice, so that in all our dealings we act impartially, and it teaches us piety, so that with proper reverence we worship the only living God.[161]

After the account of Eleazar, the text tells the story of the seven martyred brothers, all of whom were "ready to die rather than transgress [their] ancestral commandments,"[162] and were prepared to suffer torture "for the sake of virtue,"[163] "for the sake of the Law,"[164] and "for the sake of God."[165] These martyrs were able to endure painful torture even though

---

158. 4 Macc 2:8. See also 4 Macc 2:9 ("If one is greedy, one is ruled by the Law through reason so that one neither gleans the harvest nor gathers the last grapes from the vineyard").

159. See 4 Macc 18:1.

160. 4 Macc 5:2.

161. 4 Macc 5:22–24. That Eleazar sees the Law primarily as the means to becoming virtuous is supported by his assertion that he would not transgress the Law even if it "were not truly divine." 4 Macc 5:17–18.

162. 4 Macc 9:1.

163. 4 Macc 11:2.

164. 4 Macc 10:20.

165. 4 Macc 13:9.

they obviously desired to avoid pain.[166] Therefore, says the author of 4 Maccabees, his thesis has been established:

> Everyone must concede that devout reason is sovereign over the emotions. For if they had been slaves to their emotions and had eaten defiling foods, we would say that they had been conquered by these emotions. But in fact it was not so. Instead, by reason, which is praised before God, they prevailed over their emotions.[167]

Granting, for argument's sake, that the thesis has been proved—reason *can* control the emotions—important questions remain. An obvious question is: why is control over emotions a good thing? One response might be: if reason can control emotions, one can become virtuous (courageous, just, prudent, and temperate). Consistent with this response, one might think that the goal of these martyrs, as portrayed by the author of 4 Maccabees, was to become virtuous; and one might also think, based on the defense given of the dietary laws, that the law of Moses was, for the martyrs, the means chosen to become virtuous through *askesis*.

If it were true that the goal of the martyrs was to become virtuous, another question arises: why is being virtuous a good thing? The response of a Stoic to this question would be that being virtuous means acting in accord with nature, and acting in accord with nature is intrinsically good; it constitutes happiness.[168] But it is inconceivable that a pagan Stoic would submit to the pain of torture rather than to enjoy the pleasure of eating pork—there is nothing unnatural about eating pork. This, in fact, is the argument Antiochus makes to Eleazar—that Eleazar is not acting in accord with nature as would a Stoic philosopher. Antiochus says:

> It does not seem to me that you are a philosopher when you observe the religion of the Jews. When nature has granted it to us, why should you abhor eating the very excellent meat of this animal? It is senseless not to enjoy delicious things that are not shameful, and wrong to spurn the gifts of nature.[169]

---

166. 4 Macc 13:1 (They "despised sufferings").
167. 4 Macc 13:1–3. See also 4 Macc 6:31, 35; 7:16; 16:1.
168. See Long, *Hellenistic Philosophy*, 179, 187–88.
169. 4 Macc 5:7–9. See Redditt, "Concept of *Nomos*," 256 ("Antiochus argues that it is both virtuous and reasonable to live in harmony with *physis*. Thus the understanding of *physis* placed on the lips of Antiochus ... appears to be Stoic").

The reason the author of 4 Maccabees believed that Jews *would* submit to extremely painful torture rather than to eat pork is because, in his view, to act in accord with nature meant something different than it did to the Stoics. The Stoics conceived of nature (*physis*) as immanent, eternal, and unchangeable, and they considered it "a moral principle that the purpose of man is to live *kata physin*, i.e., harmoniously with nature."[170] They also accepted that this "nature" is the foundation for law (*nomos*).[171] But for the Stoics, "neither the term *nomos* nor the term *physis* appears to be the invention of a divine legislator. Attributing them to God is a notion distinctively Jewish in origin."[172]

In contrast to the Stoics, "*physis* is understood by the author of 4 Maccabees as an immanent principle or world order built into creation by God himself, according to which mankind ought to live. Moreover, the key to understanding that world order is *nomos* itself."[173] Put differently, for the author of 4 Maccabees divine law cannot be opposed to nature. Therefore, he has Eleazar respond to Antiochus that "in the nature of things [literally, "according to nature"] the Creator of the World in giving us the law has shown sympathy toward us [and] has permitted us to eat what will be most suitable for our lives [i.e., what accords with our nature], but has forbidden us to eat meats that would be contrary to this."[174]

Because the author of 4 Maccabees understood the Stoic admonition to act in accord with nature as an admonition, not only to act virtuously (that is, with prudence, justice, temperance, and courage) but to act in accord with the laws of Moses and to obey the will of the Creator, acting in accord with nature entailed for the author of 4 Maccabees, but not for the Stoics, refusing to eat pork. He writes that the martyrs were prepared to suffer torture "for the sake of virtue," "for the sake of the Law," and "for the sake of God," and he has the martyrs claim, "We revere the Creator of all things and live according to his virtuous Law,"[175] which

---

170. Redditt, "Concept of *Nomos*," 255.
171. Redditt, "Concept of *Nomos*," 255.
172. Redditt, "Concept of *Nomos*," 255–56.
173. Redditt, "Concept of *Nomos*," 257.
174. 4 Macc 5:25–26. See Zurawski, "4 Maccabees," 509. See also Urbach, *Sages*, 1.292.
175. 4 Macc 11:5. See also 4 Macc 5:16 (Eleazar claims: "We . . . who have been persuaded to govern our lives by the divine Law, think that there is no compulsion more powerful than our obedience to the Law"), 30 (Eleazar is said to have "died nobly in his tortures; even in the tortures of death he resisted, by virtue of reason, for the sake

"virtuous Law" prohibited them from eating pork. Notwithstanding that the author of 4 Maccabees had a different understanding of acting in accord with nature than did the Stoics, he could still claim, as the Stoics claimed, that acting in accord with nature is *intrinsically* good. Yet, the author of 4 Maccabees never explicitly says this.

Rather, like Pseudo-Solomon and Pseudo-Phocylides, the author of 4 Maccabees implies that acting in accord with nature (and being virtuous) is only *instrumentally good*. He focuses on the reward and punishment meted out for being virtuous, Torah-observant, and obedient to the will of the Creator, and particularly on the reward received by the martyrs—immortality.[176] So, after his death, Eleazar is described as a "skillful pilot" who "steered his ship of religion over the sea of emotions, and though buffeted by the stormings of the tyrant and overwhelmed by the waves of torture," did not turn the ship's rudder "until he sailed into the haven of immortality."[177] In like fashion, the seven brothers are said to have been rewarded with the "prize [of] endless life," and are described after their death as standing "before the divine throne and [living] the life of eternal blessedness."[178] In addition, before their torture and deaths, the brothers jointly proclaim: "If we so die, Abraham and Isaac and Jacob will welcome us, and all the fathers will praise us," which is a clear reference to the soul's immortality.[179]

Conversely, it is repeatedly said that Antiochus would be punished in his present life and in an afterlife for his persecution of the Torah-observant Jews.[180] The martyrs say to him, "You . . . will deservedly undergo from divine justice eternal torment by fire";[181] "You . . . will undergo

---

of the Law"); 13:13 (The seven brothers say: "Let us . . . consecrate ourselves to God").

176. See generally Starr, *Toward a History*, 73–74; Nickelsburg, *Jewish Literature*, 258 ("Eternal life is God's reward for obedience to the Torah"). By way of contrast, the Stoics could not claim that acting in accord with nature was instrumentally good as the means to immortality because they denied that the soul is immortal.

177. 4 Macc 7:1–3.

178. 4 Macc 17:12, 18. See also 4 Macc 9:8 (Brothers declare that they "shall have the prize of virtue and shall be with God"), 22 (One brother is said to be "as though transformed by fire into immortality"); 15:3.

179. 4 Macc 13:17. Cf. 4 Macc 18:23 (The martyrs are "gathered into the chorus of the fathers and have received pure and immortal souls"). See Starr, *Toward a History*, 82 (discussing that "returning to the fathers" refers to the soul's immortality).

180. See 4 Macc 9:9, 32; 10:11; 12:12, 18; 18:5, 22.

181. 4 Macc 9:9.

unceasing torments";[182] "Justice has laid up for you intense and eternal fire and tortures, and these throughout all time will never let you go";[183] and, "On you [God] will take vengeance both in the present life and when you are dead."[184] And the narrator adds that Antiochus was, in fact, "both punished on earth and is being chastised after his death."[185] Moreover, there is a reference to the afterlife punishment of *anyone* who violates the law: "Great is the struggle of the soul and the danger of eternal torment lying before those who transgress the commandment of God."[186]

Paralleling the author's view that wisdom ("education in the Law") enables one to navigate human affairs *to one's advantage*, DeSilva argues that the martyrs saw adherence to the Law (even if resulting in torture and death) not as intrinsically good but as instrumentally good—good as the means to eternal life, and so *to one's advantage* in the long run:

> The martyrs' commitment to the covenant is empowered by their firm anticipation of postmortem reward and punishment. They are certain that, if they die for the sake of preserving God's honor, God will vindicate their honor in endless life. . . . In light of eternity, only faithfulness unto death could be considered advantageous. . . .
>
> The belief in an afterlife in which the pious are rewarded with endless life before God and the impious punished in ways that, perhaps, they escaped during life is essential to the author's understanding of the well-functioning mind informed by "religion." Those who are able to take the long view in regard to virtue's rewards are better able to embrace temporal loss and hardship for virtue's sake.[187]

The author views martyrdom as not only advantageous to the martyrs individually but as potentially advantageous to the nation of Israel collectively. Three of the martyrs call upon God "to be merciful" to "our nation," to "your people," and Eleazar asks that their "punishment suffice for [the rest of the people]."[188] Eleazar elaborates: "Make my blood

---

182. 4 Macc 10:11.
183. 4 Macc 12:12.
184. 4 Macc 12:18.
185. 4 Macc 18:5.
186. 4 Macc 13:15.
187. DeSilva, "4 Maccabees," 2382, 2390 (citing numerous comparisons in other related materials).
188. 4 Macc 6:28; 9:24; 12:17.

their purification, and take my life in exchange for theirs."[189] Commenting on this passage, DeSilva writes:

> The author evokes the language of the Greek version of Lev 17:11, where the blood of a sacrificial animal atones for a life (*anti tēs psychēs*), to interpret the significance of the martyrdom as the life-in-exchange (*antipsychon*) offered to satisfy God's honor, affronted by the revolt against God's covenant (see also 4 Macc 17:21–22). The particular combination of this interpretation of the death of an obedient, righteous person with the expectation that a display of covenant loyalty would reconcile God to God's people ... would also be brought together in Paul's reflection on the execution of Jesus as an act of atonement.[190]

E. The author of the Testaments of the Twelve Patriarchs is influenced by both Greek and Jewish sources; emphasizes the importance of integrity of heart to conquer evil impulses; and justifies righteousness on the grounds that it leads to well-being in this life.

The Testaments of the Twelve Patriarchs is a collection of "last wills and testaments" allegedly written by Jacob's twelve sons. They are not "property wills" but "ethical wills," in which "the dying person seeks to pass on to his descendants some of the wisdom he has amassed in his lifetime."[191] Although written in Greek, the Greek text may be a translation or a reworking of an original Hebrew text that has been lost.[192] The Greek text was written by a Hellenized Jew sometime after 250 BCE,

---

189. 4 Macc 6:29. See Nickelsburg, *Jewish Literature*, 257 (describing these words as "an appeal that God accept his death as an expiation for the sins of the nation").

190. DeSilva, "4 Maccabees," 2377. See also DeSilva, "4 Maccabees," 2383.

191. Kugel, "*Testaments*," 1697. See Kee, "Testaments," 775 ("Just prior to his death, each of the sons is depicted as gathering around him his offspring, reflecting on aspects of his life, confessing his misdeeds, exhorting his family to avoid his sins and exemplify virtue").

192. See generally Kugel, "*Testaments*," 1697–701 (discussing authorship, history, and language of composition); Kee, "Testaments," 775–78 (identifying various texts of the work in a variety of languages, discussing whether the original language of the work was Hebrew, and commenting on the date and provenance of the work); Kee, "Ethical Dimensions," 268–69 (arguing that the Testaments are Greek in origin, "the product of a Judaism which is thoroughly hellenized," although the author may have drawn on Hebrew or Aramaic traditions).

probably during the Maccabean period.[193] As explained by Kugel, the author explored the following ethical questions: "What makes people sin? What is it that prevents us ... from doing the right thing all the time? Most important: what do we need to do to avoid the usual pitfalls and strive for moral perfection?"[194] The author's answers to these questions are ambiguous. As Kugel puts it:

> On these fundamental issues the *Testaments* do not speak with one voice.... Some parts of the book seem to attribute human evil to outside sources, Spirits ... who can enter people's minds and cause them to go astray. Other parts seem to treat human evil as a mainly internal affair: an urge ... inside us spurs us to do what we know to be wrong. (Sometimes, this evil urge is depicted as being at war with an opposite urge, much as in later Rabbinic Judaism.)[195]

A good example of the point of view that humanity has two urges that are at war with each other is found in the Testament of Asher. Asher instructs his sons:

> God has given two paths to humanity, and two impulses, and two kinds of actions, and two ways of life, and two ends.... There are [thus] two ways, of good and evil, and along with them two impulses[196] within our breasts that differentiate them. Thus, if the soul chooses the good [impulse], everything it does will be [done] in righteousness, and [even] if it sins, it will repent right away. For when a person's thoughts are set on righteous things, and he rejects wickedness, he immediately overthrows what is evil.... But if [the person's soul] opts for the [evil] impulse, then its every action will be in wickedness, and ... it will [eventually] be ruled by Beliar. [Then,] even if [the person] does something good, he [Beliar] will convert it into something bad.[197]

---

193. See Kee, "Testaments," 777–78. See also Kugel, "*Testaments*," 1698 (dating the work at the end of second or the start of the first century BCE); Kee, "Ethical Dimensions," 269 (A likely date is 100 BCE).

194. Kugel, "*Testaments*," 1703.

195. Kugel, "*Testaments*," 1703. See chapter 9, sec. C (discussing rabbinic views on the evil *yetzer*).

196. The Greek word translated "impulses" is *diaboulia*, which Kugel presumes was used to translate the Hebrew *yetzerim*. See Kugel, "*Testaments*," 1810.

197. T. Ash. 1:3–8. See Kugel, "*Testaments*," 1810–11. See also T. Levi 19:1 (directing sons to choose between "light or darkness, the Lord's Torah or the works of Beliar"); Kee, "Testaments," 779 (discussing dualism).

This passage suggests that at some point in a person's life they choose to follow either the good impulse or the bad impulse, and that the choice made at that point determines which impulse prevails for the rest of the person's life, so that, thereafter, they will either be among the righteous or among the wicked. The difference between the righteous and the wicked, then, is a matter of one's free choice.

This choice to follow the good or the bad impulse is elsewhere referred to as a choice to follow "the Spirit of goodness" or "the Spirit of deceit," a choice made by the "mind's understanding."[198] According to Kee, "The Stoic concept of conscience [as arbiter between good and evil] is unmistakable" in [this] view that people freely choose to follow one of the two "spirits."[199] Yet Kee acknowledges that the Stoic notion of conscience as arbiter between good and evil does not appear "fully developed" until Seneca (in the first century CE).[200] In any case, even if Kee is correct in seeing Stoic influence here, the idea that one must choose between good and evil (life and death) is, of course, also biblical, and was emphasized by Ben Sira.[201]

Kee further states that the "counterpart to the doctrine of the Two Spirits ... is the pervasive emphasis [in the Testaments] on [*haplotes*]," a term whose basic meaning is simplicity or sincerity but which gains a special connotation when it is correlated with "the effects of the Two Spirits on human behaviour," for then "[*haplotes*] becomes something more like 'integrity' or integration, since it is a quality which enables a person to overcome the polarities of existence. It is the only way to overcome a divided mind and competing loyalties."[202]

Therefore, there is a direct correlation between possessing the virtue of "integrity" and being righteous (obeying the Lord's commands).[203]

---

198. T. Jud. 20:1-2. See Kee, "Ethical Dimensions," 264-66. But see Kugel, "*Testaments*," 1765 (distinguishing the view in the Testament of Judah from the view in the Testament of Asher because the latter "sees the two 'impulses' as inherent in every human," not as outside forces).

199. Kee, "Ethical Dimensions," 264. Kee further argues that this view "is strikingly similar to the Middle Stoic teaching on freedom of the will." Kee, "Ethical Dimensions," 265. See Kee, "Ethical Dimensions," 266 ("Good deeds are done where the will ... is inclined or disposed to the good" [citing T. Ash. 1:8]).

200. Kee, "Ethical Dimensions," 264 (claiming that the notion was "anticipated" by Posidonius of Apamea, born 135 BCE).

201. See chapter 5, n151 and accompanying text.

202. Kee, "Testaments," 265 (citing T. Reu. 4:1; T. Sim. 4:5; T. Levi 13:1; T. Iss. 5:1).

203. See T. Levi 13:1; T. Iss. 5:1. See also T. Ash. 3:1-4:1 (contrasting "two-sided people," people of goodness and wickedness, with "undivided people," people of only

Indeed, according to Kee, it is only through possessing the virtue of integrity (or singleness) that "the divisive effects of the spirit of evil are overcome, and divine wisdom as embodied in the Law is united with moral commitment."[204]

For the author of the Testaments, then, integrity is "the highest virtue," and Kee sees in this view further evidence of Stoic influence.[205] But yet again, the view that an integrated personality is required to be righteous (obey the Lord's commands) is also reminiscent of Jeremiah's teaching that obedience to God can only be achieved by one who possesses an undivided, or integrated, heart.[206] The influence Jeremiah's teaching on the author of the Testaments seems clear because the latter calls those who are righteous "undivided people,"[207] and speaks not just of integrity, but of "integrity (or singleness) *of heart*."[208]

Unless a person has an integrated (or undivided) heart, they will be overtaken by passion and led to commit evil acts. For example, the reader is cautioned to keep the passion of jealousy far away from themselves, for jealousy "can make the soul [go] wild.... It brings anger and conflict to the soul's disposition and provokes it even to bloodshed."[209] Another passion to be avoided is lust or licentiousness.[210] A third passion which is particularly dangerous, according to the Testaments, is greed.[211]

---

goodness).

204. Kee, "Ethical Dimensions," 266.

205. Kee, "Ethical Dimensions," 266. See also Kugel, "*Testaments*," 1711("Simplicity... is a crucial concept in the *Testaments*").

206. See chapter 4, sec. D.

207. T. Ash. 4:1.

208. See T. Reu. 4:1; T. Iss. 3:8; 4:1. See also T. Sim. 5:2 ("Make your hearts good"); T. Jud. 23:4 ("Turn to the Lord with [your] whole heart"). See generally Kugel, "*Testaments*," 1774, 1775 (associating "simplicity of heart" with the Hebrew *tom-lev*, and referring to Prov 10:9 which advocates "walking in simplicity"). But see Kugel, "*Testaments*," 1811 (The good and evil impulses "sit, as it were, on top of the soul"). See also chapter 4, n102.

209. T. Sim. 4:7-8. See T. Sim. 2:13-3:6 ("Jealousy takes over a person's whole mind and will not allow him to ... do anything good. [Rather,] it is always pushing him to kill the person of whom he is jealous").

210. See T. Reu. 3:3; 3:10-4:2; 5:3-4; 6:1; T. Sim. 5:3; T. Levi 9:9; T. Jud. 18:2-3 (Licentiousness causes one to turn from God's Torah); T. Iss. 7:2; Kugel, "*Testaments*," 1709 (Licentiousness is one of the "great villains" in the Testaments).

211. See T. Jud. 17:1; 19:1-2; T. Iss. 4:1 ("The person of simplicity does not covet gold").

According to Kee, although stress is placed on obedience to the Law, "the ethical appeal rarely refers to specific legal statutes of the Torah, [but rather,] universal virtues are presented in a manner strongly reminiscent of Stoicism."[212] Kee identifies these universal virtues as integrity, piety, uprightness, honesty, generosity, compassion, hard work, and self-control.[213] He adds that one of the highest virtues presented in the Testaments is brotherly love, which, he says, was given attention by the Stoic Panaetius.[214] Once again, however, though these virtues may be strongly reminiscent of Stoicism, they are strongly reminiscent of the Hebrew Bible as well. This is unremarkable since qualities and conduct having cooperative value had been extolled in both Greek and Jewish cultures since the seventh century BCE, if not earlier. The Testaments' advocacy of a simple, peaceful life (as a means of achieving an undisturbed soul or peace of mind),[215] similarly reflects Greek and Jewish influence. Both the Greek philosopher Epicurus and the authors of Jewish wisdom literature advocated this type of life.[216]

That the author of the Testaments was influenced by both Greek and Jewish sources is further evidenced by the fact that the Law in the Testaments is treated as "a virtual synonym for wisdom," and "is equated with natural law."[217] So that, for example, homosexuality is

212. Kee, "Testaments," 779. See Kee, "Ethical Dimensions," 263 ("The virtues that are extolled are expressed not in terms of legal precepts quoted from the Torah, but in the moral commonplaces of Stoicism").

213. Kee, "Testaments," 779.

214. Kee, "Testaments," 779; Kee, "Ethical Dimensions," 263, 267 ("Love of humanity seems to be grounded in a common humanity rather than an explicit concept of a covenant people"). See T. Iss. 5:2 ("Love the Lord and your neighbor"); T. Gad 7:7 ("Love one another"); T. Benj. 3:3 ("Fear the Lord and love your neighbor"); T. Sim. 4:7 ("Love each one his brother"); T. Dan 5:3 ("Love the Lord with all your heart and each other with a true heart").

215. See T. Sim. 4:7-9 (Jealousy brings anger and conflict which disturbs the soul and throws the mind into disorder and confusion); T. Iss. 4:1-5 ("The person of simplicity does not covet gold. . . . He does not hunger for complicated delicacies; he does not want different [sorts of] clothing. . . . Envy does not . . . take over his disposition, nor ill will melt his soul, nor does he think insatiably about making money").

216. See T. Gad 7:6 ("Someone who is poor and [yet] does not envy . . . is richer than all men, because he does not have the annoyances of [other] men"); Kugel, "*Testaments*," 1775 ("The theme of being satisfied with very little and eschewing earthly pleasures . . . [is found] in ancient Near Eastern wisdom literature, including the biblical book of Proverbs. . . . Prominent in biblical wisdom are the themes of not coveting gold or material possessions" [citing Prov 15:16; Qoh 5:10]); Epicurus, *Ep. Men.* 130-31; chapter 5, nn76, 78, 160 and accompanying texts.

217. See Kee, "Testaments," 780; Kee, "Ethical Dimensions," 261 (citing

condemned, not because it is prohibited in the Torah, but because it is incompatible with the law of nature.[218] There is no word in Hebrew that is a real equivalent for the Hellenistic term "nature," so what has taken place in the community for which the author of the Testaments is writing, in Kee's analysis, "is that the Jewish term for 'law,' in its Greek translation [*nomos*], is being interpreted under the perspective on universal law developed by the Stoics."[219]

Finally, neither the Stoics, the Epicureans, nor the authors of Jewish wisdom literature rely on reward and punishment in an afterlife to justify virtue or righteousness—and the author of the Testaments similarly eschews this justification.[220] Rather, he relies on the supposed beneficial consequences of virtue or righteousness *in this life*. So, for example, Levi instructs his children to "sow good things in [their] souls, so that [they] may find them in [their] life," and he warns them that "if [they] sow evil things, [they] will harvest every trial and tribulation."[221] Likewise, Dan tells his children that if they "keep the Lord's commandments . . . and turn aside from anger and despise lying"; if they refrain "from every evil deed, and cast aside all anger and lying, and love truth and patience"; if they "turn aside from all wickedness and cling to the righteousness of God's Torah," then "no war will overcome [them]," and they "will be safe forever."[222] Naphtali's admonition assumes that it is to one's advantage to have others bless you, the Lord love you, and the devil flee from you; and that it is to one's detriment to have others curse you, the Lord despise you, and the devil draw near to you. He says:

> If you do that which is good, my children, men and angels will bless you . . . and the Devil will flee from you . . . and the Lord will love you. . . . But whosoever does not do what is good, men

---

T. Levi 13:1—19:3).

218. Kee, "Testaments," 780 (citing T. Naph. 3:3–4); Kee, "Ethical Dimensions," 262 (same).

219. Kee, "Ethical Dimensions," 262. Cf. nn170–73 in this chapter and accompanying text.

220. Kee, "Testaments," 780 ("There is no clear evidence of a hope of an afterlife. . . . In some passages, however, the resurrection of the faithful is affirmed" [citing T. Jud. 25:1–4; T. Zeb. 10:2). But see T. Gad 7:5 (referring to punishment "for eternity," although one wonders if this is an insertion by a later redactor).

221. T. Levi 13:6.

222. T. Dan 5:1–2; 6:8–10.

and angels will curse [him] . . . the Devil will make him a household implement of his . . . and the Lord will despise him.[223]

The problem of moral evil is not addressed in the Testaments because the author saw no such problem. For example, he says if someone becomes rich out of evil doings, you should not be envious but should "wait for the time of the Lord" because "He takes away those things [acquired] wrongfully, or He forgives those who repent."[224] The author attributes the cause of all calamities to wrongful conduct.[225]

---

223. T. Naph. 8:4–6.

224. T. Gad 7:4–5. See Kugel, "*Testaments,*" 1809 ("To wait for the time of the Lord" is "probably not meant here in any eschatological sense"). Cf. chapter 5, n111 and accompanying text.

225. See T. Levi 14:5—15:4; T. Jud. 22:1—23:4; T. Iss. 6:1–2; T. Zeb. 9:5–6.

CHAPTER 7

Philo of Alexandria subsumed all the Greek virtues within biblical law and justified both on the basis that they were conducive to individual and societal well-being.

PHILO JUDAEUS OF ALEXANDRIA has been called "the most important representative of Hellenistic Judaism."[1] Born into a wealthy and prominent Jewish family in Alexandria at the end of the first century BCE, he became a leader of the Jewish community there and, after the anti-Jewish mob violence in 38 CE, headed a delegation of Alexandrian Jews to protest to the Roman Emperor Gaius Caligula.[2] Philo was well versed in both the Greek translation of the Hebrew Bible—the Septuagint—and Greek philosophy.[3] He was a prolific author, and almost fifty treatises that he wrote, all in Greek, have survived.

Most of Philo's treatises concern the five books that comprise the Pentateuch, which he believed to be divinely revealed and authored by Moses.[4] Runia states: "Philo is convinced that these books, if read properly,

---

1. Runia, "Writings of Philo," 11.

2. See generally Nickelsburg, *Jewish Literature*, 212–21 (providing information on the life and works of Philo).

3. Philo, who was almost certainly unable to read Hebrew, believed that the Septuagint "is an exact translation of the original Hebrew text," and the divine authority of the Septuagint "was for him an article of faith." Runia, "Writings of Philo," 14.

4. See Runia, "Writings of Philo," 13; Sandmel, *Two Living Traditions*, 281.

contain all the wisdom and guidance that one needs to know in order to lead a good life, devoted to God."[5] Because of this conviction, and because any teaching about how to achieve the good life was understood by him to be a "philosophy," Judaism to Philo was a philosophy.[6] And, while maintaining the superiority of Jewish philosophy, Philo was also convinced that Jewish teaching and Greek teaching about the good life were compatible. In fact, for Philo, "Jewish ethics and . . . [Greek ethics] tend to become virtually identical."[7]

In a group of Philo's treatises concerning the Pentateuch's teaching on the good life, referred to as the *Exposition of the Law*, Philo offers an exegesis of the Pentateuch centered around three topics—creation, history, and legislation.[8] To Philo, it is relevant in a treatment of Pentateuchal teaching about the good life to discuss creation because, for him, the biblical account of creation lays the philosophical basis for biblical law.[9] Therefore, the *Exposition* commences with Philo's treatise *On the Creation of the World*. The *Exposition* next considers (in *On Abraham*, *On Joseph*, and additional works which have not survived) the early Israelite history found in the patriarchal narratives, the patriarchs being viewed by Philo as living embodiments of the law.[10] Philo directly addresses the Pentateuch's legal codes in *On the Decalogue*, *On the Special Laws*, and *On the Virtues*. Citing language found in Deut 30:10–11, he claims that adherence to these laws is "not burdensome."[11]

---

5. Runia, "Writings of Philo," 13.

6. See Cohen, "Greek Virtues," 11 ("The conceptualization of Judaism in philosophic terms was almost certainly taken for granted . . . on the part of Greek speaking Jewry in the first century CE"), 13 ("'Philosophy' was looked upon as '*the acquisition of that knowledge which leads to the good life*'" [emphasis original]); Sterling, "Queen of Virtues," 123 (Philo presented Judaism "as a form of philosophy"). See also Neusner, *From Politics to Piety*, 8.

7. Sandmel, *Two Living Traditions*, 287.

8. See Philo, *Rewards*, 1; Runia, "Writings of Philo," 12; Svebakken, *Philo of Alexandria's Exposition*, 2–3. See also Philo, *Moses* 2.46–49; Wilson, "Virtues," 2447–48.

9. Runia, "Writings of Philo," 12.

10. See Svebakken, *Philo of Alexandria's Exposition*, 3n7 (Philo claims "that the patriarchs themselves represent unwritten counterparts to the written laws"); Sandmel, *Two Living Traditions*, 285–86 (explaining that the law of nature is unwritten but may be grasped by "philosopher-kings," and that "Abraham, Isaac, and Jacob were philosopher kings who, by virtue of their ability to live by nature, are exponents of the law of nature"); Wolfson, *Philo*, 2.181; Hayes, *What's Divine*, 120–24.

11. Philo, *Rewards* 79–80.

The *Exposition* concludes with *On Rewards and Punishments*. Here, having accepted the Platonic notion of a soul,[12] Philo contends that the highest good, and the source of happiness, is a well-ordered soul, that is, a soul in which its several parts are performing their proper function, with the rational part of the soul controlling immoderate desires. Philo believes that conduct in accordance with biblical law requires that one have a such soul. So, a well-ordered soul is the functional equivalent of Jeremiah's undivided heart. Philo argues that a person possessing such a soul is rewarded with material well-being in this life and with immortality in an afterlife. Conversely, Philo believes that conduct violative of biblical law is due to a soul that is not well-ordered, immoderate desires having overstepped the dictates of the rational part of the soul, which is the functional equivalent of Jeremiah's divided, uncircumcised heart. A person possessing such a soul, according to Philo, is deprived of material well-being in this life and denied immortality in an afterlife.

A. *On the Creation of the World.*

In *On the Creation of the World*, Philo asserts that Moses "did not want immediately to state what should be done and what not" but wanted to precede his pronouncement of the law by an account of the making of the cosmos because "the cosmos is in harmony with law and the law with the cosmos, and the man who observes the law is at once a citizen of the cosmos, directing his actions in relation to the rational purpose of nature, in accordance with which the entire cosmos is also administered."[13] This is to say that the law Moses prescribes for humanity is in accord with the order and structure that God, through the rational principle that Philo calls "the divine Logos," imposed on the cosmos.[14] Runia puts it this way: "[Philo] argues that before we are

---

12. In Plato's *Republic* he describes the human soul as having three parts—a rational part, an appetitive part, and a spirited part. Plato, *Resp.* 435b–442d. For a complete discussion of Plato's views on the soul, see Robinson, *Plato's Psychology*, 3–157.

13. Philo, *Creation* 2–3.

14. See Philo, *Creation* 15–20. Philo's interpretation of the biblical account of creation is modeled on the Platonic conception that there is both an eternal, immutable, and immaterial (or intelligible) world (Plato's World of Being) and a non-eternal, changing, and material world (Plato's World of Becoming), and on the Platonic account of creation found in Plato's *Timaeus*. See Runia, "On the Creation," 884 ("Philo's reading of the Genesis account is heavily influenced by his own reading of Greek philosophical texts, such as Plato's *Timaeus*"), 888 (Philo's distinction between the intelligible world

ready to understand the Law as it applies to human beings, we must first have an understanding of the Law in its cosmic context, since there is a direct correlation between the Law of God for humanity and the law of nature for the cosmos as the totality of the physical world."[15]

Elsewhere Philo explains that Moses put the "commands and the prohibitions" after an account of the creation of the world in order to show "two most essential things," first that the "Father and Maker of the world" is also its "Lawgiver," and second, that observing the Mosaic laws is equivalent to following nature by living "in accordance with the ordering of the universe."[16] Philo is here, essentially, adopting the belief, espoused by Greek philosophers from Plato to the Stoics, that to live in accordance with virtue is to live in accordance with reason, and to live in accordance with reason is to live in accordance with the nature of man and the rational nature of the cosmos.[17] According to this conceptual scheme, if wise legislators enact laws on the basis of reason, they are enacting "laws in accordance with nature [*physis*]."[18] Nevertheless, the Greek philosophers recognized that enacted laws [*nomos*], being the work of men and not nature, "differ from the work of nature in that they are not universal, they are not eternal, and they are not immutable."[19]

At this point, writes Wolfson,

> Philo steps in with his contention that, if it is law in accordance with nature that is sought after, then philosophers might as well give up their effort to devise such a law by their own reason.

---

and the sense-perceptible world "came from Plato's *Timaeus*"). See also Sandmel, *Two Living Traditions*, 283–84, ("Logos . . . is the whole complex of data that the reasoning mind can get to," and, just like *hokhmah*, "has a separate existence"), 286–87 ("The logos is the highest aspect of the godhead which the mind can get to").

15. Runia, "On the Creation," 882. See Wolfson, *Philo*, 2.210 ("The story of the creation of the world is meant to show that, since God is the creator of the world and the founder of the laws of nature, the Law for human guidance . . . is in harmony with these laws of nature").

16. Philo, *Moses* 2.47–48.

17. See Wolfson, *Philo*, 2.165–200; Winston, "Philo's Ethical Theory," 381–88; Long, *Hellenistic Philosophy*, 108.

18. Wolfson, *Philo*, 2.179 (briefly describing how Plato, Polemo, Aristotle, and the Stoics understood "in accordance with nature"). See also Sandmel, *Two Living Traditions*, 285 ("Putatively, there is a body of law which is perfect, and that is the law of nature. . . . A philosopher-king is able to let his mind range into the realm of ideas to encounter there the law of nature, unwritten, and then he turns the law of nature into the best possible written specific statutes").

19. Wolfson, *Philo*, 2.179.

> Only a law which was revealed by God, who is the creator of nature, can be in accordance with nature in the true sense of the term, for such a law, being the work of God, is like nature itself, and like nature it is universal and eternal and immutable.[20]

Only the laws of Moses, says Philo, are "in the true sense of the term [laws] in accordance with nature" because only the laws of Moses are modeled after laws implanted by God into the natural world.[21] In other words, the laws of Moses are not arbitrary decrees but are "the truest reflection of the Logos which is embodied in the physical universe and constitutes its immanent natural law."[22] As Wolfson explains:

> According to [Philo], before the creation of the [material] world, God created the Logos. Upon the creation of the [material] world, the Logos was implanted in it by God to act as its law. Then later, when God revealed the Law to guide men in their conduct in the world, that Law was the application to human conduct of the same law which He had previously implanted in the world for the regulation of the natural order. God is thus the true legislator of the laws for both nature and men, and the laws of Moses, though enacted laws, are still in the true sense of the term in accordance with nature, inasmuch as God who is their true legislator enacted them in harmony with those laws of nature of which He is also the legislator. . . .
>
> When philosophers speak of living in accordance with nature or reason or right reason, they mean thereby that man is to live in accordance with such principles discovered by human reason as would not bring him into conflict with his own nature or with the nature of the world around him. To Philo, however, it means to live in accordance with the revealed law which God himself has implanted in man and in the universe.[23]

---

20. Wolfson, *Philo*, 2.180.

21. Wolfson, *Philo*, 2.180. See Sandmel, *Two Living Traditions*, 286 ("The Laws of Moses, according to Philo, are the best possible imitation of and substitute for the law of nature. They are . . . immutable and eternal"). See also Hayes, *What's Divine*, 112–20 (arguing that Philo demonstrates that "the Torah is the natural law," and, as a consequence, is true, eternal, and unchanging, "not the arbitrary expression of a sovereign will").

22. Winston, "Philo's Ethical Theory," 381. See Long, *Hellenistic Philosophy*, 108 (For the Stoics, cosmic events and human actions are both consequences of *logos*, the rationality embodied in the universe).

23. Wolfson, *Philo*, 2.190, 194. See also Redditt, "Concept of *Nomos*," 256 ("*Physis* [for Philo] is no longer the nature of things, but 'the nature of God who stands in direct opposition to the world of existing things and imposes his *nomos* upon them.'

In short, as Philo sees it, all moral norms are based on an eternal, unchanging natural law. Scholars who claim that in adopting this view Philo was attempting to attribute the "properties and qualities of Greek natural law" to "biblical divine law" (which does not actually have such properties and qualities)[24] ignore that Philo may well have reasonably believed that biblical law *did* have such properties and qualities. This is because the notion that the moral norms commanded by God are based on a rational, immutable moral order that God imposed at the time of creation, and that this moral order is coordinate with the physical order that God imposed, *is* a genuine biblical notion.[25]

That Philo was indeed influenced by this biblical notion is suggested by the imagery he uses to describe the order God imposed on the world—it resembles the imagery used by biblical authors to describe the same thing. Specifically, in emphasizing the importance of cleaving to God's commandments, Philo says that these commandments are the means by which "the world itself continues constantly in the same nature without ever changing," and he compares the constancy imposed by the moral commandments to the constancy imposed by the *boundaries* God imposed on the physical world.[26] He says that every changing thing in the physical world, including the sea, "is still fixed within the same boundaries as those within which it was originally created, when it was first disposed of in regular order."[27] Furthermore, the Greek word that Philo adopts to denote the rational order inherent in the world—*logos*—may fairly be compared to the Hebrew word used in Proverbs to denote knowledge of the moral order associated with the will of God—*hokhmah*.[28]

B. *On the Decalogue.*

The essence of the Pentateuch's teaching concerning the good life is, for Philo, found in the *deka logoi* (the "ten words"), that is, the Decalogue. Philo believed the Decalogue is unique because God revealed its commands *directly* to all Israelites, in contrast to all other commands which

---

Moreover, this *nomos* is nothing other than the Torah itself" [quoting Koester]).

24. Hayes, *What's Divine*, 111, 112.
25. See chapter 1, sec. B, 4.
26. Philo, *Spec. Laws* 1.300. Cf. chapter 1, sec. B, 3–4.
27. Philo, *Spec. Laws* 1.300.
28. See chapter 1, sec. C, 2. See also Sandmel, *Two Living Traditions*, 282–83; Cohen, *From the Maccabees*, 78–79; Tirosh-Samuelson, *Happiness*, 84–85.

were revealed through a mediator, Moses.²⁹ Philo believed the Ten Commandments to be fundamental—the universal, eternal, and unchanging principles under which all other laws contained in the Pentateuch are subsumed.³⁰ He separately discusses each of the Ten Commandments in his treatise *On the Decalogue*. This is followed by his discussion of all other commandments in *On the Special Laws*.

He begins *On the Decalogue* by considering several preliminary issues, including why Moses promulgated the laws in the desert, not in a city. Among the reasons for this, according to Philo, is that Moses thought it best to provide the Israelites with rules to "regulate their civic life," and to allow them to "gain practice" in the rules, *before* entering cities so that they could then "settle down . . . in harmony and fellowship of spirit and rendering to every man his due."³¹ This explanation indicates that Philo realized that the laws of Moses inculcated qualities and conduct having cooperative value, and further realized that such qualities and conduct were important for successful urban life. He then makes the distinction between laws that are fundamental and laws that are not fundamental, and states that the laws revealed by God directly to all Israelites serve as "heads summarizing the [other] particular laws" so that the other particular laws, those revealed indirectly through Moses, may be subsumed under the "heads."³²

Saying that he would first discuss the laws "which are rather of the nature of summaries,"³³ Philo proceeds to addresses each of the Ten Commandments, dividing them in two groups of five, both of which groups, he says, are "profitable for life."³⁴ However, he also says that the

---

29. See Svebakken, *Philo of Alexandria's Exposition*, 5; Philo, *Spec. Laws* 2.189 (The "general laws" are the most "profitable" because they "came from the mouth of God, not like the particular laws, through an interpreter"); *Decalogue* 175.

30. See Pearce, "On the Decalogue," 990 (Philo considers the Ten Commandments of the Decalogue to be "general principles," and "he presents [all] other laws of the Torah as 'species' of each of the 'general principles'"); Svebakken, *Philo of Alexandria's Exposition*, 5–7 (Each of the Ten Commandments "functions as the 'head' . . . or 'summary' of an entire category of particular laws" in the relationship of "genus to species") (citing Philo, *Decalogue* 154; *Spec. Laws* 1.1; 4.132). See also Philo, *Decalogue* 155–74.

31. Philo, *Decalogue* 14.

32. Philo, *Decalogue* 18–19.

33. Philo, *Decalogue* 20.

34. Philo, *Decalogue* 50. Philo's division of the Decalogue into two groups of five probably reflects the Greek division of justice (proper conduct) into proper conduct toward the gods and proper conduct toward men. See Sterling, "Queen of Virtues," 112 ("Plato's *Euthyphro* [at 12e] is probably Philo's source"). See also Wolfson, *Philo*,

first group of five is the one in which "the most sacred injunctions are given"[35] and is "superior" to the second group of five.[36] The first group of five are: "You shall have no other gods before me"; "You shall not worship images"; "You shall not take the name of God in vain"; "You shall observe the seventh day and keep it holy"; "Honor your parents."[37] The first group is superior and most sacred because, as Philo understands them, they all concern "service to God" rather than proper conduct toward human beings.[38]

The Decalogue's second set of five commandments "contains the actions prohibited by our duty to fellow men,"[39] namely "adultery, murder, theft, false witness, desire."[40] Philo's discussion of these prohibitions makes clear that he saw each prohibition as essential for an orderly, harmonious, and prosperous society. The prohibition against adultery, for example, is required in order to prevent disharmony in family life and disputes about the paternity of children. Not only does the adulteress become estranged from her husband but, says Philo, adultery

> makes havoc of three families: of that of the husband who suffers from the breach of faith, stripped of the promise of his marriage vows and his hopes for legitimate offspring, and of two others, those of the adulterer and the woman, for the infection of the outrage and dishonor and disgrace of the deepest kind extends to the family of both....
>
> Very painful, too, is the uncertain status of the children, for ... there will be doubt and dispute as to the real paternity of the offspring ... [and] the poor children who have done no

---

2.200–1 (Philo's division of the laws into those "containing 'duties to God' and [those containing] 'duties to men' ... corresponds to the traditional Jewish division of the laws" [citing m. Yoma 8:9]).

35. Philo, *Decalogue* 106.
36. Philo, *Decalogue* 51.
37. Philo, *Decalogue* 51. See Pearce, "On the Decalogue," 990.
38. See Philo, *Decalogue* 108. See also Philo, *Decalogue* 110 (referring to those who concern themselves primarily with the first five commandments as "lovers of God" and contrasting them with those who concern themselves primarily with the second five commandments, called "lovers of men"). The commandment to honor your parents concerns service to God because "parents are the servants of God for the task of begetting children, and he who dishonors the servant dishonors also the Lord." Philo, *Decalogue* 119. See also Philo, *Decalogue* 107 ("The act of generation assimilates [parents] to God"); *Spec. Laws* 2.225; Pearce, "On the Decalogue," 1018.
39. Philo, *Decalogue* 121. See also Philo, *Decalogue* 106 ("The second set ... contains the duties of man to man").
40. Philo, *Decalogue* 51.

wrong will be . . . unable to be classed with either family, either the husband's or the adulterer's.⁴¹

Similarly, Philo presents murder "as an evil that [negatively] affects society as a whole."⁴² He says that it is in accord with nature for man "to be gregarious and sociable" and to "show fellowship and a spirit of partnership,"⁴³ and that nature has endowed man with reason, "the bond which leads to harmony and reciprocity of feeling."⁴⁴ Therefore, anyone who commits murder "is subverting the laws and statutes of nature so excellently enacted for the well-being of all."⁴⁵ Stealing likewise affects not just the victim of a particular theft but society in general because, though a thief may be able to steal from only some, "his covetousness extends indefinitely," and, thus, he is "the common enemy of the State."⁴⁶ Regarding the prohibition against being a false witness, Philo takes it for granted that an orderly, harmonious, and prosperous society requires the just resolution of disputes. Therefore, he condemns false testimony as corrupting truth and forcing judges to make unjust decisions.⁴⁷

The last commandment of the Decalogue, as abbreviated by Philo, states, "You shall not desire" (*ouk epithumeseis*), "indicating that in his view the [principal] concern of this Commandment is desire itself [*epithumia*], not desire's object."⁴⁸ Desire is one of four passions/emotions (*pathe*) identified by the Stoics and Middle Platonists, the others being pleasure, grief, and fear.⁴⁹ Thus, after mentioning the prohibition

41. Philo, *Decalogue* 124–30.
42. Pearce, "On the Decalogue," 1023.
43. Philo, *Decalogue* 132.
44. Philo, *Decalogue* 132.
45. Philo, *Decalogue* 132.
46. Philo, *Decalogue* 135.
47. Philo, *Decalogue* 138–40.
48. See Svebakken, *Philo of Alexandria's Exposition*, 1–2 (citing *Spec. Laws* 4.78), 9–11 (explaining the reason for Philo's abbreviated version). See also Sandmel, *Two Living Traditions*, 280–1 (Philo "interprets, 'You shall not covet' . . . by the word 'desire'"; unlike coveting which "implies that aggressive action results from coveting . . . desire itself can be limited and contained"); Pearce, "On the Decalogue," 1026 (The Septuagint "uses *epithumein* to represent two different Heb. verbs: 'You shall not covet' (*lo tachmod*) (Exod 20:14; Deut 5:20) and 'You shall not crave' (*lo tit'aveh*) (Deut 5:18) . . . In contrast to the biblical prohibitions, Philo does not address the objects of desire [your neighbor's wife, etc.], but the emotion of desire (*epithumia*) itself"); Wolfson, *Philo*, 2.226–28 (discussing "the special character of this commandment as dealing with pure emotion . . . in native Jewish literature," the Septuagint, and Philo).
49. See Svebakken, *Philo of Alexandria's Exposition*, 57. See also Svebakken, *Philo of*

against desire, Philo immediately seeks to explain why the other three *pathe* are not prohibited.

His explanation is that no moral culpability may be ascribed to the other *pathe* "since they originate from without and compel the moral agent to experience their effects involuntarily."[50] For example, pleasure occurs *involuntarily*, says Philo, when the mind is presented with something *from outside the self* "considered to be good," and grief occurs *involuntarily* when the mind is presented with something *from outside the self* considered to be "evil, the opposite of good."[51] In contrast, says Philo, desire occurs *voluntarily* when the mind *itself* "conceives an idea of something good ... and strains" to obtain "the desired object."[52] Philo contrives this distinction to provide the explanation he needs as to why only desire is prohibited, and the distinction is not that important.[53]

What *is* important is Philo's views about *epithumia* and the reason for its prohibition. Reflecting "the views of his Middle-Platonic contemporaries,"[54] Philo sees *epithumia* as a component of the nonrational part of the soul which provides motivation for human activity.[55] In particular, Philo understands *epithumia* as a nonrational appetite, or impulse, for pleasurable things such as food, drink, sex, victory, honor, or fame.[56] As a motivating force *epithumia* is neither problematic nor bad.[57] A desire may, however, become problematic or bad if it oversteps the dictates of the rational part of the soul, the dictates of reason, and opposes them.

When a desire, or any impulse, oversteps the dictates of reason, Philo and other Middle Platonists label the impulse "excessive," meaning that it has exceeded its proper limits. When this happens, "an otherwise

---

Alexandria's Exposition, 11n33.

50. Philo, *Decalogue* 142.

51. Philo, *Decalogue* 143–44.

52. Philo, *Decalogue* 146. See Pearce, "On the Decalogue," 1027 ("Desire begins with a person conceiving an idea of something that is not present; this forces the soul to chase what it can never reach"); Svebakken, *Philo of Alexandria's Exposition*, 156–59.

53. But see Wolfson, *Philo*, 2.232–35.

54. Svebakken, *Philo of Alexandria's Exposition*, 41. But see Wolfson, *Philo*, 2.230, n24.

55. See Svebakken, *Philo of Alexandria's Exposition*, 58, 69.

56. See Svebakken, *Philo of Alexandria's Exposition*, 58–64.

57. See Svebakken, *Philo of Alexandria's Exposition*, 119 ("Desire may pursue its aim of pleasure, *as long as* that pursuit serves a rational end and bears rational justification" [emphasis original]).

benign impulse . . . becomes a *passion*, a morally problematic, injurious force within the soul . . . an excessive *quantity* of a *nonrational* impulse."[58] When reason fails to impose proper limits on *epithumia*, the desire becomes "immoderate" and is called an *"ametros epithumia"* (a passionate or immoderate desire) or an *alogos epithumia* (an irrational desire).[59] Worse yet, *epithumia* may fully usurp the power of the rational part of the soul to direct a person's activity. Plato described such a situation in his portrayal of the "tyrannical soul."[60] Plato believed that *eros* (love) "can operate as a consuming, injurious, relentless desire for a single beloved object,"[61] and in *Phaedrus* Socrates defines *eros* as an *epithumia* that usurps reason and becomes tyrant.[62] Philo incorporated Plato's notion of a tyrannical desire (*eros*) to describe the ultimate victory of nonrational desire (*alogos epithumia*) over reason (*logos*).[63]

So, what Philo understood to be prohibited by the tenth commandment is not desire per se but immoderate desire. And the reason immoderate desires are prohibited, according to Philo, is because such desires are not in accord with nature,[64] and, thus, are detrimental to individual and societal well-being. Individuals are adversely affected by immoderate desires because, when ruled by such desires, individuals suffer "the punishment of Tantalus"—their unrelenting desire can never be satisfied so they exist in a state of constant frustration and anguish— which Philo compares to being "stretched upon a [torturer's] wheel."[65]

58. Svebakken, *Philo of Alexandria's Exposition*, 82–84 (emphasis original) (distinguishing the analysis of Middle Platonists from the analysis of Stoics). See Philo, *Spec. Laws* 4.79 ("Every unmeasured and excessive impulse, and every irrational and unnatural emotion of the soul is . . . faulty and blameworthy"). But see Wolfson, *Philo*, 2.234 (noting that *Special Laws* 4.95 urges, as one alternative, that desire be done away with entirely, which is the Stoic teaching).

59. See Svebakken, *Philo of Alexandria's Exposition*, 85–86. See also Philo, *Heir* 245 ("Irrational desires" [*alogoi epithumiai*] generated by "excessive impulse" are "implacable enemies" of the soul).

60. Plato, *Resp.* 572C–576B. See also Svebakken, *Philo of Alexandria's Exposition*, 87–88.

61. Svebakken, *Philo of Alexandria's Exposition*, 87.

62. Plato, *Phaedr.* 238B.

63. Svebakken, *Philo of Alexandria's Exposition*, 88. See also Svebakken, *Philo of Alexandria's Exposition*, 98 ("Tyrannical desire [*eros*] signals the complete defeat of reason by nonrational desire, in which desire enslaves reason, compelling the entire soul to pursue desire's single aim of pleasure.").

64. See Philo, *Decalogue* 150 ("All life's affairs will be necessarily distorted from what nature prescribes").

65. Philo, *Decalogue* 146, 149. See also Philo, *Spec. Laws* 4.80–82 (Immoderate

Societies are adversely affected by immoderate desires because individuals ruled by such desires impede the maintenance of societal order, harmony, and prosperity. His supporting argument in *On the Decalogue* takes the form of two rhetorical questions and two claims:

> Consider [an immoderate desire] for money or a woman or glory or anything else that produces pleasure: are the evils which it causes small or casual?
>
> Is [immoderate desire] not the cause of why kinsmen become estranged and change their natural goodwill to deadly hatred, why great and populous countries are desolated by internal factions, and land and sea are filled with ever-fresh calamities wrought by battles on sea and campaigns on land?
>
> For all the wars of Greeks and barbarians between themselves or against each other ... are sprung from one source, [immoderate] desire, the [immoderate] desire for money or glory or pleasure. These it is that bring disaster to the human race.[66]

Elsewhere Philo asserts that virtually all wrongdoing is due to immoderate desire:

> [Immoderate desire] is the source of all evils. For from what other source do all thefts, and all acts of rapine, and repudiation of debt, and all false accusations, and acts of insolence, and ... adulteries, and murders, and in short, all mischiefs, whether private or public, or sacred or profane, take their rise? ... And the most holy Moses appears to me to have had a regard to all these circumstances, and on that account to have commanded that men should discard this passion, detesting it as the most disgraceful thing and the cause of most disgraceful actions; and, therefore, to have prohibited above all other feelings as an engine for the destruction of the soul.[67]

Philo ends *On the Decalogue* with an explanation as to why God pronounced these ten laws "without laying down any penalty [for their

---

desire is said to produce "grievous anxieties" resulting in "Tantalus-like punishment" in which a person is "racked by the torture even to death"), 95 (Immoderate desire is "an engine for the destruction of the soul"); *Heir* 269. Cf. Plato, *Gorg.* 493d–94a (comparing a man with unrestrained desire to trying to carry liquids in a perforated jar); chapter 5, n78 and accompanying text.

66. Philo, *Decalogue* 152–53.

67. Philo, *Spec. Laws* 4.84; *Decalogue* 95. See Svebakken, *Philo of Alexandria's Exposition*, 171 ("All moral ills stem from [*epithumia*]").

violation], as is the way of legislators."[68] The explanation Philo offers is that it would go against God's nature to do so as the Lord is good, "the cause of good only and of nothing ill."[69] But Philo adds: "He did not thereby grant immunity to evil-doers, but knew that justice, His assessor, the surveyor of human affairs, in virtue of her inborn hatred of evil, will not rest, but take upon herself as her congenital task the punishment of sinners."[70] Philo goes on to equate "justice, [God's] assessor" with "generals in wartime" who are tasked by a king to "bring vengeance upon deserters," thereby suggesting that "justice" brings vengeance upon those who "desert" God,[71] and, presumably, the vengeance Philo has in mind includes the "punishment of Tantalus" and the destruction of the sinners' souls. So that just punishment is the natural consequence of immoderate desire, and direct divine intervention is not required.[72]

C. *On the Special Laws*, Books 1 to 4.

By "special laws" Philo means "the specific Mosaic regulations which in the Bible come immediately after the Decalogue."[73] Philo regards these laws as mere expansions of the Decalogue's ten universal and eternal principles.[74] This is made clear in *On the Decalogue* which states that "the Ten Commandments are the heads of all the particular and special laws . . . related in the sacred scriptures," and goes on to describe in general terms the special laws subsumed under each of the Ten Commandments.[75] For example, Philo takes the fourth commandment (observe the Sabbath) to be "a summary of all the laws relating to festivals, and of all purificatory rites enjoined to be observed by them . . . [as well as

---

68. Philo, *Decalogue* 176.

69. Philo, *Decalogue* 176.

70. Philo, *Decalogue* 177. See Pearce, "On the Decalogue," 1029 ("Philo often represents divine justice in these terms" [citing Philo, *Migration* 225; *Joseph* 48]). Cf. 4 Macc 4:21.

71. See Philo, *Decalogue* 178.

72. Cf. chapter 1, sec. C, 4.

73. Sandmel, *Two Living Traditions*, 281.

74. See Sandmel, *Two Living Traditions*, 281–82; Wolfson, *Philo*, 2.201.

75. Philo, *Decalogue* 154–75. The idea that "the Ten Commandments contain all the laws of the Torah" can be found in rabbinic literature. Wolfson, *Philo*, 2.201 (citing *Canticles Rab.*). But see Urbach, *Sages*, 1.361 (disputing Wolfson's reading of *Canticles Rab.*).

other laws] conducing to the production of gentleness and fellowship among men."[76]

The project of relating all the particular and special laws to one of the universal and eternal principles of the Decalogue is more fully pursued in the four books which constitute *On the Special Laws*. Book one considers those special laws subsumed under the first two commandments; book two considers those subsumed under the third, fourth, and fifth commandments; book three considers those subsumed under the sixth and seventh commandments; and book four considers those subsumed under the remaining three commandments.

A brief discussion of the special laws falling under the rubric of the tenth commandment will be undertaken to illustrate that Philo believes that the special laws falling under the last five of the Ten Commandments are commanded in order to instill moral virtues, the character traits people must possess to live the good life and maintain an orderly, harmonious, and prosperous society[77]—that is, to achieve "happiness" (*eudaimonia*). As Philo states near the end of the *Special Laws*, "the Jewish nation . . . lives under exceptional laws which are necessarily grave and severe because they inculcate the highest standard of virtue."[78] According to Wolfson: "Following . . . Aristotle's statements that 'moral virtue comes about as a result of habit,' that habits are formed by practice, and that the practice of good actions is the purpose of the laws, Philo tries to show that the laws of Moses have for their purpose the inculcation of the moral virtues."[79]

The relevant virtue that the tenth commandment is intended to inculcate is temperance (*sophrosune*), and one becomes temperate through exercising self-control (*enkrateia*), that is, by restraining desire whenever it tries to oppose or usurp the dictates of reason.[80] *Enkrateia*,

---

76. Philo, *Decalogue* 158–62.

77. See Wolfson, *Philo*, 2.221. Moral virtues are to be distinguished from intellectual virtues. The later include right opinions about God and God's creations. Philo claims that the first four commandments, and the special laws which fall under them, inculcate such right opinions—that God exists, is one, exercises providence, created the world, and revealed a Law which is eternal. See Wolfson, *Philo*, 2.208–11.

78. Philo, *Spec. Laws* 4.179.

79. Wolfson, *Philo*, 2.221 (citing Aristotle, *Eth. nic.* 1103a15–17, 31; 1103b2–6).

80. See Svebakken, *Philo of Alexandria's Exposition*, 99–100; Winston, "Philo's Ethical Theory," 399–405 (A higher ethical level than that of the ordinary man is symbolized by Isaac who achieved "perfect virtue without toil" and doesn't have to "struggle to make rational decisions," whereas Aaron "practices only *metriopatheia*, or moderation of passion," where reason must struggle to control passion). See also Wolfson, *Philo*,

which is akin to but distinguishable from *sophrosune*, is very important if one is to live the good life, and Philo "gives it a prominent role in his ethical theory."[81] For Philo and other Middle Platonists, one gains the ability to exercise self-control through practice (*askesis*). What distinguishes Philo is that he sees certain biblical laws as constituting a deliberate effort on Moses' part to promote *enkrateia* through *askesis*.[82] Included among such biblical laws are those falling under the universal principle "Do not desire."

The particular and special biblical laws that fall under this principle are primarily the dietary laws of Lev 11 and Deut 14:1–21. This is to say that Philo understands the dietary laws to be ascetic precepts designed to inculcate *enkrateia* with respect to the desire for food. According to Philo, though these laws inculcate self-control only with respect to the desire for food, once this desire is brought under control, it is easy to bring all other desires under control.[83] But before Philo begins his discussion of the dietary laws, he mentions the biblical law of first fruits (Deut 14:22–29), which he sees as having the same purpose as the dietary laws. He says that Moses forbids eating anything before separating off the first fruits in order to inculcate control of not just the desire to eat immediately, but all other desires as well.[84]

2.222n170, 235–36 (Philo "constantly uses [the term *enkratia*] as synonymous with 'temperance'" and *enkratia* is considered by him to be a virtue); 2.274–76 (For Philo, "an emotion when controlled by reason becomes transformed into a virtue, to which he gives the special name of [*eupatheia*]"). See generally Arnim, *Fragments*, 3.264 (Moderation or temperance is the primary virtue but "subordinate" to temperance is self-control)(Stobaeus).

81. See Svebakken, *Philo of Alexandria's Exposition*, 101 (citing *Spec. Laws* 1.173; *Contempl. Life* 34), 106–11 (distinguishing *enkrateia* and *sophrosune*). See generally Svebakken, *Philo of Alexandria's Exposition*, 101–38. For Aristotle, to exercise self-control means that you must struggle to control your desire and thus have not acquired the virtue of *sophrosune*. See Aristotle, *Eth. nic.* 1102b15–29. Cf. chapter 9, nn167–68 and accompanying text.

82. Svebakken, *Philo of Alexandria's Exposition*, 132–33 ("In the law regarding a year of Sabbath rest for the land (Lev 25:2–7; Exod 23:10–11), the law regarding fasting on the Day of Atonement (Lev 16:29–31; Num 29:7–11), and the law regarding marrying female prisoners of war (Deut 21:10–13), Philo recognizes deliberate efforts on Moses' part to promote [*enkrateia*] through [*askesis*]").

83. Philo, *Spec. Laws* 4.96. See Svebakken, *Philo of Alexandria's Exposition*, 178 ("Management of 'the desire having to do with the belly' ... serves as the paradigmatic model for managing *all* corruptible desires, since that one desire is fundamental" [emphasis original]).

84. Philo, *Spec. Laws* 4.99.

Turning to specific dietary laws, Philo says that the animals which Jews are prohibited from eating are those animals "which are most fleshy and fat" and, thus, are the ones most likely to excite "treacherous pleasure."[85] The prohibited animals include the pig and scaleless fish because they are supposedly the most delectable.[86] Moses also prohibits eating the fat of an animal because, Philo says, it is the most succulent part.[87] By prohibiting such delicacies, as Philo understood it, Moses intended to train the people to eat for physical well-being, not purely for pleasure. Philo believed that the Mosaic legislation strikes the perfect balance between two extreme lifestyles—the overly austere and the overly indulgent.[88]

Other dietary prohibitions help cultivate important qualities in addition to the control of immoderate desire. For example, Moses forbids the eating of any carnivorous animal because the eating of them is inappropriate for a "gentle soul."[89] He forbids the eating of dead animals to teach hunters, through practice with animal opponents, not to battle human opponents for unjust gain, but only for just causes.[90]

Philo closes his discussion of the special laws that fall under the rubric of the tenth commandment with mention of the narrative of Num 11:4–34 and the words of Moses in Deut 11:8. To Philo, the people in the narrative with "gluttonous craving"[91] represent people who believe that the pursuit of pleasure constitutes happiness or the highest good, and the narrative teaches that punishment befalls such people. The narrative also teaches that immoderate desire is incompatible with concern for other people (*philanthropia*) and with devotion to God (*eusebeia*). This is so because when people are obsessed with achieving pleasure, nothing, not even concern for others or devotion to God, is more important than the satisfaction of their desire.[92] Accordingly, Philo refers to the words of Moses in Deut 11:8, which Philo says

---

85. Philo, *Spec. Laws* 4.100.

86. Philo, *Spec. Laws* 4.101.

87. See Svebakken, *Philo of Alexandria's Exposition*, 225 (translating Philo, *Spec. Laws* 4.124).

88. See Philo, *Spec. Laws* 4.102.

89. Philo, *Spec. Laws* 4.103–4.

90. See Philo, *Spec. Laws* 4.119–21; Svebakken, *Philo of Alexandria's Exposition*, 220–24.

91. Num 11:4.

92. See Philo, *Spec. Laws* 4.129; Svebakken, *Philo of Alexandria's Exposition*, 231–32.

are equivalent to saying "let each person seek to please God, and the world, and nature, and wise men, repudiating self-love, if he would become a good and virtuous man."[93] In this way, Philo reiterates the claim made at the beginning of his discussion of the dietary laws that Moses intended the special laws subsumed under the tenth commandment to teach people to curb their desire for pleasure in order "to lead them to [not only to] temperance [but, in addition] to [the virtue of] humanity (*philanthropia*), and to the greatest of all virtues, piety (*eusebeia*)."[94]

Philo's belief that immoderate desire for pleasure prevents one from being humane and pious is not unlike Jeremiah's claim that having a hardened, uncircumcised, divided, and unintegrated heart (whose decision-making function is affected by conflicting desires) prevents one from being righteous and obedient to God's will.[95] Although Philo does not expressly name Jeremiah as a source of his beliefs about the effects of immoderate desire, Jeremiah clearly was a source. Two facts point to Jeremiah's influence. First, Philo says that circumcision is a symbol for the excision of immoderate desire,[96] and second, Philo associates immoderate desire with a thickening of the heart and a heart that is "uncircumcised." Specifically, Philo claims:

> Men who have ... [not] feasted on and luxuriated among justice and equality ... are uncircumcised in their hearts ... and by reason of the hardness of their hearts they are stubborn ... whom the Lord reproves, saying, "Be ye circumcised as to your hardheartedness"; that means, "do ye eradicate the overbearing character of your dominant part, which the immoderate impulses of the passing hour have sown and caused to grow within you, and which the wicked husbandman of the soul, folly, planted."[97]

---

93. Philo, *Spec. Laws* 4.131. See Svebakken, *Philo of Alexandria's Exposition*, 232–34 ("To indulge in one's own desire ... Philo suggests, amounts to a reprehensible love of self").

94. See Philo, *Spec. Laws* 4.97. See sec. D, 5–6 in this chapter (discussing *philanthropia* and *eusebeia*).

95. See chapter 4, sec. D.

96. Philo, *Spec. Laws* 1.9 (Circumcision symbolizes "the excision of excessive and superfluous pleasure").

97. Philo, *Spec. Laws* 1.304–5. See also Philo, *Spec. Laws*, 1.6 (The practice of circumcision "assimilates the circumcised member to the heart"); 4.137 ("We must set the rules of justice [that is, the biblical commandments] in the heart.").

While Philo agreed with Jeremiah about the impediment to acting virtuously—an uncircumcised heart, an unintegrated personality[98]—he disagreed with Jeremiah about how that impediment could be removed. Jeremiah believed that we had to wait for God to transform human nature by circumcising the human heart; Philo believed that practices inherent in biblical law itself could circumcise the heart—that is, "eradicate the overbearing character" of irrational desires—making it possible for human beings to transform themselves. As Winston describes Philo's viewpoint: "The focus is not upon God's activity and gifts of grace, but upon man's own effort. In the struggle for moral progress, passively waiting for God's help is a vice, and [askesis] is the key to ethical achievement."[99]

After closing his discussion of the special laws associated with each of the Ten Commandments, Philo says that "we must not fail to know that . . . *there are some things common to all*, which fit in not with some particular numbers such as one or two but with all the ten Great Words."[100] Then he writes:

> These are the virtues of universal value. For each of the ten pronouncements separately and all in common drill and inculcate wisdom and justice and godliness and the rest of the company of virtues. . . . Of the queen of the virtues, piety (*eusebeia*), or holiness,[101] we have spoken earlier, and also of prudence (*phronesis*) and temperance (*sophrosune*). Our theme must now be she whose ways are akin to them, that is, justice (*dikaiosune*).[102]

When Philo says that *phronesis* and *sophrosune* were spoken of earlier, he is referring to *On the Special Laws* "as a whole."[103] Believing that he had adequately discussed *phronesis* and *sophrosune*, he goes to

---

98. That Philo believes an integrated personality is required for well-being, or happiness, is supported by his claim that if our words, thoughts, and actions are "bound up with each other, reciprocally preceding and following each other through the indissoluble bonds of harmony . . . then happiness prevails." Philo, *Rewards* 81. See also Philo, *Virtues* 183–84 (Happiness consists in the integration and harmony of speech, thoughts, and actions); *Spec. Laws* 4.134; *Moses* 1.29; 2.48. See generally Cohen, "Greek Virtues," 19–23.

99. Winston, "Philo's Ethical Theory," 376.

100. Philo, *Spec. Laws* 4.133–34 (emphasis added).

101. See Sterling, "Queen of Virtues," 112–13 ("Philo used the two terms [piety and holiness] as virtual synonyms to refer to the human response to and perception of God"); Cohen, "Greek Virtues," 10, 18 (Philo uses the locution "piety and holiness," a hendiadys, as a synonym for *theosebeia*, "the worship of God").

102. Philo, *Spec. Laws* 4.134–35.

103. Cohen, "Greek Virtues," 15.

discuss *dikaiosune* and then briefly mentions courage (*andreia*), which he more fully discusses at the beginning of *On the Virtues*.[104] Thus, in his discussion of the special laws Philo addresses all four of the Greek cardinal virtues.[105]

According to Cohen, the phrase "some things common to all . . . the Ten Great Words," quoted above, may not be a reference *solely* to the Greek virtues, as some scholars have maintained.[106] Rather, Cohen argues, "very often Philo did not mean *either/or*," and here too, "he is not referring to *either* 'the Greek virtues' *or* to 'the Mosaic Laws,' but wished at one and the same time to allude *both* to the 'virtues of universal value' . . . which is clearly a Hellenistic idiom, *and* the Mosaic Laws, artfully equating the two."[107] According to Cohen, the ambiguous locution "served as the vehicle for Philo's didactic/homiletic message that since the commandments [separately and collectively] 'drill and inculcate . . . the whole company of (Greek) virtues,' the 'virtuous life' in terms of the Greek frame of reference is to be achieved by ordering one's life in accord with the precepts of the Mosaic revelation."[108] In other words, biblical law subsumes within it the entire complement of Greek virtues, evidencing the superiority of biblical law.[109]

---

104. See Philo, *Virtues* 1–50.

105. See also Philo, *Moses* 2.216; *Virtues* 180; *Alleg. Interp.* 2.18. See also Long, *Hellenistic Philosophy*, 200 (The four primary virtues are practical wisdom [or prudence], justice, moderation [or temperance], and courage); Arnim, *Fragments*, 3.264.

106. See Cohen, "Greek Virtues," 10.

107. Cohen, "Greek Virtues," 10 (emphasis original). See also Cohen, "Special Laws," 1104.

108. Cohen, "Greek Virtues," 11. See Runia, "Virtues," 2447 ("Philo says that it is possible to show that the Law in its entirety accords with 'the virtues of universal value,' by which he means piety, wisdom, temperance, justice, courage, and humanity."); Wolfson, *Philo*, 2.200 ("Philo undertakes to show that the commandments which constitute the laws of Moses are identical with the virtues upon which the ideal philosophic law is to be based"), 202 (For Philo, the special laws can be classified "under the headings of cardinal virtues" as well as under the headings of the Ten Commandments).

109. See Cohen, "Greek Virtues," 12, 14. See also Aristotle, *Eth. nic.* 1103b3–7 ("The legislator makes the citizens good by habituating them [to be virtuous]. . . . Correct habituation distinguishes a good political system from a bad one"); 1130b23–25 ("Most lawful actions . . . are those produced by virtue as a whole; for [correct] law prescribes living in accord with each virtue, and forbids living in accord with each vice"); Wolfson, *Philo*, 2.202 ("The conception that laws are to implant virtues is Platonic," and "Philo's contention is that the laws of Moses are the ideal laws which do actually implant all virtues").

D. *On the Virtues*.

Sterling speculates that after having completed his analysis of the special laws under the headings of the Ten Commandments, at *Special Laws* 4.132, Philo wanted "to organize the laws that spanned more than one of the Ten Commandments under the headings of specific virtues"[110] and "that Philo wrote treatments of the virtues in much the same way that he organized the legal material in [*On the Special Laws*], i.e., just as each of the Ten Commandments served as a heading for miscellaneous laws, so each virtue served as a heading for various laws."[111] Sterling believes that there were originally four separate treatises which may fairly be considered to have been appendices to the *Special Laws*: one on *dikaiosune* (presently existing in *Special Laws* 4.135-238), one on *andreia* (presently existing in *On the Virtues* 1-50), one on *philanthropia* (presently existing in *On the Virtues* 51-227), and one on *eusebeia* (that has been lost, with only fragments surviving).[112] We need not be concerned with this textual issue but only with a brief account of the cardinal virtues—*phronesis*, *sophrosune*, *dikaiosune*, and *andreia*—as well as with certain additional virtues that were important to Philo—*philanthropia*, *eusebeia*, and *metameleia*. Philo repeatedly remarks that virtues may be acquired in three ways: by nature, learning, and practice.[113]

1. *Phronesis* (Prudence).

Philo differentiates "prudence" (*phronesis*) from "wisdom" (*sophia*); he uses *sophia* "as a designation of the teachings contained in the revealed Law," and, as the Stoics, he uses *phronesis* in his various enumerations of the four cardinal virtues.[114] Being prudent is having good

---

110. Sterling, "Queen of Virtues," 107. See also Wolfson, *Philo*, 2.202 ("The Ten Commandments of Moses as well as the special laws included under them are 'the virtues of universal value,'" and, consequently, "the laws can be classified, according to [Philo], under the headings of the various virtues which they are meant to implant in men").

111. Sterling, "Queen of Virtues," 111.

112. See Sterling, "Queen of Virtues," 107-12.

113. See Philo, *Rewards* 64-65; Wolfson, *Philo*, 2.196-97; Winston, "Philo's Ethical Theory," 409-10.

114. Wolfson, *Philo*, 2.212 (citing Philo, *Posterity* 128). See also Philo, *Rewards* 81 ("Wisdom has reference to the service of God, and prudence to the regulation of human life"). Unlike the other three cardinal virtues, *phronesis* is an intellectual virtue, not

judgment—making a proper assessment of all the facts and circumstances concerning any moral decision. Being prudent does not mean doing what is profitable (advantageous) to you because it gratifies your desires; it means doing what is profitable to you because it is "the good"—it is what reason dictates you should do under all the relevant facts and circumstances.[115] The Stoics made clear that what is "good" and what is "profitable" are logically equivalent—whatever is denoted by "good" may also be denoted by "profitable."[116]

2. *Sophrosune* (Temperance).

Sophrosune has already been dealt with in connection with its importance regarding Philo's analysis of the tenth commandment. *Sophrosune* exemplifies Philo's adoption of the Aristotelian definition of virtue as the mean between two extremes.[117] Temperance is the mean between the extremes of pursuing too much pleasure ("profuse extravagance") and pursuing too little pleasure ("illiberal stinginess").[118] Because Philo believed that biblical law is intended to inculcate the moral virtues, and because the moral virtues constitute means between two extremes, Philo believed that the biblical laws are themselves means between two extremes.[119] This corresponds with Aristotle's statement that "the law is the mean."[120] Thus, for example, as previously mentioned, Philo understood the dietary laws to constitute a middle path between an extravagant diet and an austere diet.[121]

---

a moral virtue. See Aristotle, *Eth. nic.* 1103a5–19 (distinguishing intellectual virtue or "virtue of thought" from moral virtue or "virtue of character").

115. See generally Aristotle, *Eth. nic.* 1140b5–7 (Prudence is the state of using reason to grasp the truth about actions that are "good or bad for a human being"), 1142b1–35 (discussing deliberation). See also Arnim, *Fragments*, 3.262, 264 ("Prudence is the science of what should and should not be done. . . . To prudence are subordinated good sense, good calculation, quick-wittedness, discretion, resourcefulness")(Stobaeus).

116. See Long, *Hellenistic Philosophy*, 138, 193. Possessing the virtue of *phronesis* is comparable to being a *hokem*. See ch. 1, n135 and accompanying text.

117. See, e.g., Philo, *Unchangeable* 162–65; *Migration* 146–47; *Spec. Laws* 4.101–2; *Posterity* 101–2. Cf. Aristotle, *Eth. nic.* 1106a15–1107a25. See generally, Wolfson, *Philo*, 2.272–73.

118. Philo, *Unchangeable* 164. Cf. Aristotle, *Eth. nic.* 1117b24–1119b20.

119. See Philo, *Posterity* 101–2 (The "word of God is identical with the royal road," i.e., the "middle way"); Wolfson, *Philo*, 2.273.

120. Aristotle, *Pol.* 1287b4–5.

121. Philo, *Spec. Laws* 4.101–2.

3. *Dikaiosune* (Justice).

Philo distinguishes a concept of justice that is "concerned with law courts and judges" from a more general concept of justice.[122] Under the former concept of justice he subsumes, inter alia, laws from Exod 23—the laws prohibiting judges from accepting "idle hearing," outlawing judges from taking bribes, and admonishing judges not to show "pity to the poor."[123] He associates "idle hearing" with hearsay evidence which, being unreliable, may not be relied upon by a judge. Bribes "to do injustice" obviously must be banned as they undermine the judicial process, but bribes to do that which justice demands are also banned, says Philo, for two reasons: they habituate judges to be "covetous of money," and they injure those who deserved to be benefitted without having to "pay a price for justice."[124] Last, Philo sees the admonition not to show pity to the poor as teaching that judges must judge objectively, according to the truth, and not be swayed by emotion. Philo hastens to add, however, that there are other laws requiring that aid be given to the poor, and that "it is only on the judgment seat that we are forbidden to show them compassion."[125] He closes this part of his discussion on justice by alluding to the general principle of the fourth commandment prohibiting the giving of false testimony.

The special laws falling under the more general concept of justice include obvious ones such as the law requiring merchants to use just balances, weights, and measures, and the law commanding workers' wages to be paid promptly.[126] But they also include laws whose relation to justice is tenuous, such as the laws enjoining breeding animals of different species, sowing vineyards with two types of seed, ploughing fields with an ox and an ass together, and wearing garments woven of both wool and linen (Lev 19:19; Deut 22:9). Philo sees all four of these laws as related, and subsumes them under the virtue of justice because, to him, they prohibit actions that are unnatural and cause an unfair burden in some way; and, in the case of sowing fields to bear two crops, it allows people

---

122. See Philo, *Spec. Laws* 4.136; Kugel, *Traditions of the Bible*, 310 (*Dikaiosune* in *Special Laws* 4.135–36, and elsewhere, functioned as shorthand for "observance of the divine commandments," as it did generally among Greek-speaking Jews).

123. See Philo, *Spec. Laws* 4.59–78; Cohen, "Special Laws," 1098–103 (citing Exod 23:1, 3, 8; Lev 19:15).

124. Philo, *Spec. Laws* 4.60–65.

125. Philo, *Spec. Laws* 4.76.

126. Philo, *Spec. Laws* 4.193–96. See Deut 24:15; 25:13–15.

to give vent to "lawless desire."[127] He also includes under the rubric of general justice laws that relate to the proper conduct of rulers vis-à-vis their subjects and to the proper conduct of the nation of Israel vis-à-vis other nations at war with Israel.[128]

Philo concludes his discussion of justice by asserting that "the principle of equality . . . [is] the mother of justice."[129] No doubt, this is because the principle of equality is "to assign to every man his due according to his deserts."[130] Thus, because anything complex becomes harmonious and well regulated when each of its parts is assigned its due—performs its proper function—all things that are harmonious and well regulated "are the work of equality."[131] He adds that that which is best regulated in terms of the body results in health, and that which is best regulated in terms of the soul results in virtue.[132] That virtue is the result of a well-ordered soul in which each part of the soul performs its proper function is a Platonic idea; and, presumably, Philo, as Plato, took it as self-evident that it's to everyone's advantage to have a well-ordered soul, just as its self-evident that it's to everyone's advantage to have a well-ordered (i.e., healthy) body.[133]

Also, often coupled by Philo with the virtue of justice is the virtue of *philanthropia* (discussed below), and, through the virtue of *philanthropia*, the virtues of fellowship, concord, grace, and mercy.[134] Similarly, the Stoics held that the primary virtues admit of subdivisions, and "justice," for them, embraced kindness, honesty, fellow feeling, and fair dealing.[135]

---

127. See Philo, *Spec. Laws* 4.203–18. See also Levinson, "Deuteronomy," 395 ("These laws attempt to maintain specific boundaries between categories"); Schwartz, "Leviticus," 242.

128. See Philo, *Spec. Laws* 4.183, 219–29.

129. Philo, *Spec. Laws* 231.

130. Philo, *Moses* 2.9.

131. Philo, *Spec. Laws* 237.

132. Philo, *Spec. Laws* 237. See also Philo, *Alleg. Interp.* 1.68–73.

133. See generally Plato, *Resp.* 441c–445b. When Plato argues that the just man is one who has brought the various parts of his soul into "harmony and has made himself one man instead of many," and thereby has come to be "at peace with himself" (Plato, *Resp.* 443e), he is essentially agreeing with Jeremiah that men cannot be righteous unless they have a single (or integrated and undivided) heart. See also chapter 6, n126 and accompanying text.

134. See Wolfson, *Philo*, 2.218–19.

135. Long, *Hellenistic Philosophy*, 200n1; Arnim, *Fragments*, 3.264 ("Some virtues are primary, but others are subordinate to these")(Stobaeus).

4. *Andreia* (Courage).

Philo defines *andreia* as "the knowledge of what ought to be endured,"[136] which is the same definition the Stoics used.[137] Philo also says that *andreia* is "highly profitable to life," and explains, using Aristotelian language, that *andreia* is the mean between the extremes of rashness (too little fear) and cowardice (too much fear).[138] Again mimicking Aristotle, Philo cautions against adding or taking away anything from the mean of courage.[139] *Andreia* was understood to include more than knowledge of what ought to be endured in a military context, and so Philo states:

> There is also no small number of other things in human life which are confessed to be very difficult to endure, such as poverty, and want of reputation, and mutilation, and various kinds of diseases, by which weak spirited men are broken down . . . through their want of courage; but those men who are full of high thoughts and noble spirits, rise up to struggle against these things, and contend against them with fortitude.[140]

As Philo sees it, the inability to endure such adversity results from "insatiable and unappeasable appetites"; and so "the virtuous man wants but little."[141] More particularly, the virtuous man's ability to endure adversity is due to "the sound health of [his] soul" which condition consists in each part of the soul performing its proper function with "the reasoning power having predominance."[142] Then Philo states that "the proper name [for] this healthy state of the soul is moderation [i.e., temperance]," for moderation prevents "the thinking part" of the soul from "being overwhelmed

---

136. Philo, *Spec. Laws* 4.145.

137. See Long, *Hellenistic Philosophy*, 200 (citing Arnim, *Fragments*, 3.285). See generally Cicero, *Tusc.* 4.53 (providing numerous Stoic definitions of courage including that it is "a tenor of the soul obedient to the supreme law in matters requiring endurance").

138. Philo, *Spec. Laws* 4.145–46; *Unchangeable* 164 ("The middle between temerity and cowardice is courage"). Cf. Aristotle, *Eth. nic.* 1104a20–24; 1115a8–1116a16.

139. Philo, *Spec. Laws* 4.146. Cf. Aristotle, *Eth. nic.* 1106b12 (The mean in every science is such "that nothing could be added or subtracted").

140. Philo, *Virtues* 5.

141. Philo, *Virtues* 9.

142. Philo, *Virtues* 13. Cf. Philo, *Alleg. Interp.* 1.68–73.

by the impetuosity of the passions."[143] It is moderation, then, and a "very [well-regulated] soul"[144] which makes courage possible.

Since immoderation is caused by an excessive desire for bodily pleasure and for the pleasure of what Aristotle called "external goods,"[145] Philo says that there are many passages in the law "persuading" people "to despise all things which affect the body and all external circumstances."[146] Elsewhere he states that the highest good consists in the good of the soul (particularly in the good of its "dominant and most important part"), not "in any external thing, nor in any of the things which belong to the body."[147]

5. *Philanthropia* (Humanity or Benevolence).

The literal meaning of the Greek word *philanthropia* is "love of man." The Latin term *humanitas*, as used by Cicero, includes *philanthropia*, and *philanthropia* is typically translated into English as "humanity." Winston suggests that Philo's emphasis on this virtue is related to developments in Greek moral philosophy. *Philanthropia* is mentioned by neither Plato nor Aristotle; it only became an important virtue among Greek philosophers when "an all-embracing doctrine of human unity took shape."[148] Winston states: "Going beyond the negative formulation of justice which forbids one man to injure another, [the Stoic philosopher Panaetius] advances the positive definition of [justice] as an active beneficence, which forms the bonds of society."[149]

The notion of a fellowship among all human beings became linked by the Stoics to kindliness, benevolence, friendliness, and other qualities of the same sort which stem from the concept of justice.[150] The term

143. Philo, *Virtues* 14.
144. Philo, *Virtues* 17.
145. See Aristotle, *Eth. nic.* 1098b12-14 (distinguishing three types of goods), 1119a1-2 (The intemperate person has an appetite for all pleasant things). See generally Wolfson, *Philo*, 2.297-99.
146. Philo, *Virtues* 15.
147. Philo, *Virtues* 187. But see Winston, "Philo's Ethical Theory," 404-14 (discussing Philo's "divided statements as to what constitutes the proper attitude towards the human body and its needs" and Philo's attitude concerning "the various pursuits for external goods"); sec. E in this chapter. See also Wolfson, *Philo*, 2.202-4, 297-303.
148. See Winston, "Philo's Ethical Theory," 391-92.
149. Winston, "Philo's Ethical Theory," 392 (citing Cicero, *Off.* 1.20).
150. Winston, "Philo's Ethical Theory," 393.

philanthropia came into philosophical prominence after Panaetius, Antiochus, Musonias Rufus, and Plutarch used it to refer to this complex of qualities.[151]

According to Winston, we find this "same conceptual development" in Philo, and relevant statements made by Philo are similar to statements made by Stoic philosophers; in particular, Winston says, Philo follows Panaetius in emphasizing the positive aspect of justice as an active beneficence, and in encapsulating the quality of active beneficence in the word *philanthropia*.[152] Other statements made by Philo about *philanthropia* that Winston finds to be "in line" with Stoic views are that *philanthropia* requires both a benign attitude toward slaves and a preference for peace over war, and that, in practicing *philanthropia*, man is imitating God.[153]

Of course, in emphasizing the virtue of *philanthropia* Philo was influenced by the Hebrew Bible as well as by Greek philosophy. Indeed, for Philo a main purpose of the biblical narratives and laws was to train and instruct the people "in the precepts of fellowship."[154] He specifically mentions the treatises he wrote on Moses, who Philo claims loved *philanthropia* more than any other human being, and whose life, Philo says, serves "as an archetypical model" of this virtue.[155] After discussing the humanity that Moses exhibited in his life,[156] Philo goes on to discuss "the precepts which [Moses] left behind . . . commanding . . . [the exercise of] gentleness and humanity."[157] These commandments include those requiring that one act humanely towards fellow Israelites, such as the prohibition against lending on usury, the requirement that employers "pay the wages of the poor man the same day that they are earned," the directive "to leave a portion of the field unreaped," and the "enactments about the seventh year" and the "fiftieth year."[158] The commandments falling under the rubric of *philanthropia* also include laws commanding the Israelites to "love and cherish a stranger in the same degree with

---

151. Winston, "Philo's Ethical Theory," 394.

152. See Winston, "Philo's Ethical Theory," 393-94 (citing Philo, *Virtues* 166, 169).

153. See Winston, "Philo's Ethical Theory," 392-93, 396-97.

154. Philo, *Virtues* 51. See also Philo, *Virtues* 121 (Regulations are intended to "engender gentleness and humanity").

155. Philo, *Virtues* 51-52.

156. See Philo, *Virtues* 52-79.

157. Philo, *Virtues* 80-81. See Philo, *Virtues* 82-174.

158. See Philo, *Virtues* 82-101. See also Deut 23:20; 24:15, 19, 20; Exod 22:24; 23:10-11; Lev 25:8-17.

himself," to respect sojourners, to treat slaves humanely, to seek peace with enemies, and to show compassion for any persons captured after battle.[159] More than this, says Philo, Moses "extends his principles of humanity and compassion even to the race of irrational animals."[160] In fact, according to Philo, "*the whole of [Moses'] code of laws*" is aimed at creating "unanimity, and fellowship, and agreement" so that "the whole human race may be conducted to the very highest happiness."[161]

Wolfson argues that Philo's use of the Greek concept of *philanthropia* actually stems from the Septuagint's translation of the Hebrew concept *tzedakah*, writing:

> In the Septuagint the Greek word for justice [*dikaiosune*] translates the Hebrew word [*tzedakah*], and the same term [*tzedakah*] is also translated there by the Greek term for "mercy" or "alms" [*eleémosuné*], which ... is treated by Philo as a virtue akin to the virtue of humanity. Thus the Hebrew term [*tzedakah*] means both justice and philanthropy or humanity, the latter in the sense of giving help to those who are in need of it. Now in native Judaism the view has been expressed that "the commandment of [*tzedakah*] is balanced against all the commandments together." Philo's statement that justice and humanity are the leaders among the [moral] virtues is probably only another way of expressing the same traditional view.[162]

6. *Eusebeia* (Piety).

Philo calls *eusebeia* the "queen of the virtues."[163] Although he sometimes linked *eusebeia* with *philanthropia*, calling them together "the queens of

---

159. See Philo, *Virtues* 102-24. See also Exod 21:26-27; 23:9; Lev 19:33-34; Deut 15:12; 20:10-14; 21:10-14.

160. Philo, *Virtues* 125. See Philo, *Virtues* 125-47. See also, e.g., Exod 23:10 ("You shall not boil a kid in its mother's milk").

161. Philo, *Virtues* 119 (emphasis added). See Winston, "Philo's Ethical Theory," 399-400 (commenting that this "eschatological vision of human unity was ... already intimated ... by Cicero" [citing Cicero, *Leg.* 1.10.28-30]).

162. Wolfson, *Philo*, 2.220 (quoting b. B. Bat. 9a).

163. Philo, *Spec. Laws* 4.147. Philo sometimes refers to "piety and holiness" as the "queen of all the virtues." Philo, *Spec. Laws* 4.135. See also Philo, *Decalogue* 119. However, Cohen argues that "piety and holiness" is a hendiadys expressing essentially the same idea as piety. Cohen, "Greek Virtues," 10, 18. See also Sterling, "Queen of Virtues," 112-13 (Philo used the two terms, "piety" and "holiness," "as virtual synonyms"). See generally Wolfson, *Philo*, 2.212-18 (discussing Philo's use of "piety,"

the virtues,"[164] he repeatedly insisted on the priority of *eusebeia*.[165] This can be explained by the fact that piety refers to the perception and knowledge of God, which results in the commitment to serve and obey God.[166] It is precisely piety—the devotion to God—that Philo said is the ultimate "source of [all] the [moral] virtues."[167] In fact, Philo believed the acquisition of the moral virtues necessarily follows giving "due honor to the living God," just as viciousness necessarily follows "forsak[ing] the holy laws of God."[168] As Sterling puts it: "The physical and the moral worlds are both the creation of God. . . . Everything, including ethics, begins with a proper belief in the existence of God and the divine governance of the kosmos."[169] Therefore, moral virtue begins with piety.

Piety is an intellectual or a "divine virtue," meaning that it has God as its object.[170] According to Wolfson, divine virtues include having "right opinions," specifically the right opinions "which to [Philo] constitute the religious teachings of Scripture: (1) that God exists, (2) that He is one, (3) that He exercises providence, (4) that He created the world, (5) that the world which He created is one, (6) that He created incorporeal ideas, (7) that He revealed a Law, and (8) that the Law He created is eternal."[171]

Many of the laws of Moses have as their purpose, Philo believed, the inculcation of these right opinions. Such laws include the first four of the Ten Commandments as well as all the special laws that fall under the rubric of these commandments. The Greek word *sophia* (wisdom) "becomes with Philo a designation of the intellectual or divine virtues together with the actions corresponding to them."[172] While praising *sophia*, Philo decries *tuphos* (pride), a word which "combines notions of

---

"godliness," "holiness," and "faith").

164. Philo, *Virtues* 95. *Eusebeia* and *philanthropia* are linked because the former term is associated with the first group of the Ten Commandments and the latter term with the second group.

165. Sterling, "Queen of Virtues," 112.

166. See Philo, *Spec. Laws* 4.147; Sterling, "Queen of Virtues," 113; Wolfson, *Philo*, 2.213–14.

167. Philo, *Decalogue* 52. See Sterling, "Queen of Virtues," 120–23.

168. See Philo, *Virtues* 181–82.

169. Sterling, "Queen of Virtues," 121.

170. Wolfson, *Philo*, 2.208.

171. Wolfson, *Philo*, 2.209. See also Sterling, "Queen of Virtues," 114–18.

172. Wolfson, *Philo*, 2.212.

arrogance and mental confusion," and "is one of Philo's favorite words for the 'vanity' of false opinions that lead people away from God.[173]

7. *Metameleia* (Repentance).

Philo believed that a main cause of error is failing to recollect instruction that was given to you in "earliest infancy,"[174] and that "a recollection which ensues after forgetfulness . . . is repentance."[175] Never to err, he says, is "a peculiar attribute of God"; but "when one has erred, then to change so as to adopt a blameless course of life for the future is the part of a wise man."[176] Philo claims that such change is not difficult, requiring only that you integrate your personality by bringing your thoughts, words, and actions (symbolized by your heart, mouth, and hands) into harmony, and he further claims that "happiness consists" in this harmony.[177]

In addition, he gives assurance that the punishments God gives to those "who have despised the sacred laws of justice and piety" aims not at the destruction of the sinners but only at their "admonition and improvement."[178] If sinners "feel shame . . . and change their ways, reproaching themselves for their errors, and openly avowing and confessing all the sins that they have committed . . . they will then meet with a favorable acceptance from their merciful savior, God."[179]

E. On Rewards and Punishments.

The arguments Philo offers in his *Exposition of the Law* to justify being obedient to biblical law are varied. Philo accepted that all biblical laws were God-given, and he believed that the literal observance of these laws "has an intrinsic value."[180] Nevertheless, "there is no indication that . . . the laws were considered by him as being arbitrary commands

173. Pearce, "On the Decalogue," 993. See Philo, *Decalogue* 4–9.
174. See Philo, *Virtues* 176; *Rewards* 162.
175. Philo, *Virtues* 176.
176. Philo, *Virtues* 177. See generally Wolfson, *Philo*, 2.252–59.
177. Philo, *Virtues* 183–84.
178. Philo, *Rewards* 162–63.
179. Philo, *Rewards* 163.
180. Wolfson, *Philo*, 2.223. See generally Philo, *Migration* 89–93; Wolfson, *Philo*, 1.55–71 (discussing Philo's acceptance of both allegorical and literal interpretations of Scripture).

of God without any [intellectual or moral] purpose."[181] Nor is there any indication that the laws were considered by him as justified by the Divine Command Theory or any other deontological ethical theory.[182] Rather, every attempt is made to justify adherence to biblical law by the *consequences* of compliance or noncompliance—consequences for society and consequences for individuals—which is say that Philo adopted a teleological ethical theory.

The *Exposition* begins with Philo expressing the view, in *On the Creation of the World*, that biblical law is in accord with nature, constituting rational principles God built into the social world that are no less universal, eternal, and immutable than rational principles God built into the natural world. To live in accordance with biblical law, therefore, is to live in accordance with the rational purpose inherent in the world; and it was believed by the Stoics that to live such a life was intrinsically good, constituting *eudaimonia* (happiness or well-being). Yet, Philo seems to have deemed this argument, without more, insufficient to justify obedience to biblical law, or, perhaps, insufficient to convince the average person, just as Plato deemed the arguments he offered to prove the intrinsic worth of the moral virtues, without more, insufficient to convince the average person to acquire them.

In any event, the entire historical section of the *Exposition* is specifically intended to show, through the lives of the patriarchs, that mankind should live in accordance with biblical law (and should be virtuous) because human beings are *rewarded* for living in accord with biblical law (and for being virtuous) and are *punished* for living in opposition to biblical law (and for being vicious).[183] And the rewards and punishments Philo mentions relate to material well-being. So, for example, Abraham, described as being perfectly virtuous, is said to be extremely affluent, having an "abundance of gold and silver, and having numerous herds of cattle and flocks of ship."[184]

181. Wolfson, *Philo*, 2.223.

182. Philo argues that those who reject a literal acceptance of Scripture are defying public opinion, impairing their reputation, ignoring established customs of great antiquity, and disregarding the importance of the outward observance of the law for the preservation of its inner meaning—not that they defy, ignore, or disregard God. See Wolfson, *Philo*, 1.66–67.

183. See Wolfson, *Philo*, 2.210.

184. Philo, *Abraham* 208–9. While thus recognizing that external goods have importance, Philo almost immediately thereafter asserts that external goods are "spurious good things" and goods of "the lowest rank," while the goods of the soul are "genuine"

In the closing treatise of the *Exposition*, *On Rewards and Punishments*, Philo writes: "The historical part [of Scripture] is a record of the lives of different wicked and virtuous men, and of the rewards, and honours, and punishments set apart for each class in each generation."[185] He notes that these rewards and punishments pertain not only to the virtuous and vicious individuals themselves but to "houses, and cities, and countries, and nations."[186] The argument here seems to be that living in accord with biblical law is the means to achieving, and is justified by, beneficial consequences in this life for both society and the individual virtuous person.

Similarly, in *On the Decalogue*, he argues that the fundamental moral principles of biblical law—the second group of the Ten Commandments—are justified because they are needed for individual and collective well-being. Adultery, murder, theft, being a false witness, and having immoderate desires are all shown to impede an orderly, harmonious, and prosperous society. Immoderate desire is singled out as especially detrimental to societal well-being, and also as especially detrimental to individual well-being. This argument may be seen as elaborating the nature of the rewards and punishments promised in the historical section for living, respectively, virtuously and in accord with biblical law or viciously and in opposition to biblical law.

When Philo focuses on the special laws and the virtues, he claims that the special laws are justified because they teach people the right opinions (i.e., foster intellectual virtue) and train people to be temperate, just, courageous, and humane (i.e., foster moral virtue), inextricably intertwining intellectual and moral virtue with adherence to the special laws. However, fostering intellectual and moral virtue is, in turn, justified as leading to collective and individual well-being. Individual well-being is especially emphasized. When you possess intellectual and moral virtue (which the special laws inculcate) your soul is well regulated and you achieve *eudaimonia*. Viciousness, particularly excessive desire, corrupts the soul by undermining its proper regulation; but, if a man's desire is not excessive and he obeys the commanding authority of reason, his life will be "filled with peace, order, and genuine prosperity, resulting in perfect happiness."[187]

---

and "principal and dominant." Philo, *Abraham* 217–22.

185. Philo, *Rewards* 2.
186. Philo, *Rewards* 7.
187. Philo, *Spec. Laws* 4.95. See Svebakken, *Philo of Alexandria's Exposition*, 180.

In *On Rewards and Punishments* Philo distinguishes between three kinds of good things: the goods of the soul, the goods of the body, and external goods.[188] The goods of the soul are intellectual and moral virtue. As previously discussed, these goods make the soul well regulated so that all parts of the soul perform their proper function and passions are controlled by reason. Those who have become virtuous through practice or "meditation" are said by Philo to receive "the torpor of breath" as their "prize," meaning that these people have gained the ability to restrain and limit their impulses "so that the immoderate violence of the passions" become "enfeebled" and "breath" is given "to the better part of the soul."[189] To have a healthy soul is seen to be self-evidently advantageous or profitable—*intrinsically* good. As Philo puts it, the thoughts, words, and actions of one possessing such a soul become integrated, and "then happiness prevails."[190]

But more than this, Philo accepts the Platonic idea that the rational part of the soul is incorporeal, and Philo believes that if one lives virtuously, that is, according to biblical law, the incorporeal part of the soul will be granted immortality by God, and, after death, it will ascend to heaven to join the host of God, the "incorporeal and happy souls" which are the angels.[191] Philo hints at this when he says that "the meditator on and practiser of virtue . . . receives as his especial reward the sight of God."[192] Therefore, having a healthy soul is not only intrinsically good but is *instrumentally* good as well.

Philo sees the goods of the soul, especially the grant of immortality to the soul, as having the highest value. Having the goods of the soul is more important for individual well-being than having either the goods of the body or external goods. But this is not to say that the goods of the body and external goods are unimportant.[193] These goods, however, are likewise said to be rewards for (a favorable consequence of) being

---

188. Cf. Aristotle, *Eth. nic.* 1098b13–14. See generally Wolfson, *Philo*, 2.299–303 (discussing Philo's classification of goods and his claim that bodily and external goods are "given by God as a reward for the observance of the Law").

189. Philo, *Rewards* 47–48.

190. See Philo, *Rewards* 81.

191. See Starr, *Toward a History*, 77–85 (quoting Philo, *Sacrifices* 5). See also Philo, *Rewards* 110; Wolfson, *Philo*, 2.302–3.

192. Philo, *Rewards* 36. In contrast to the immortality of the virtuous, the wicked must endure "an undying and never ending death." Philo, *Rewards* 70.

193. See generally Winston, *Wisdom of Solomon*, 168.

virtuous and obeying biblical law, further indicating that virtue and obedience to biblical law are *instrumentally* good.

Regarding the nature of the external goods, Philo refers to the blessings promised in chapter 30 of Deuteronomy and chapter 26 of Leviticus, and specifically mentions military victory followed by peace, authority, wealth, honor, and numerous offspring.[194] Wealth includes food, clothing, and housing; and Philo urges that wealth is "very easily provided" if you avoid "superfluous and excessive extravagance."[195] Regarding the nature of the goods of the body, Philo claims that a "perfect freedom from disease in every respect" is allotted to the virtuous and those who adhere to biblical law, and that all parts of their body will remain in good condition, perfectly performing their function; and, if any infirmity should affect them, it is only to remind them of their mortality and, thereby, "eradicate overbearing pride."[196]

Philo is more graphic in describing the punishments inflicted on those who are vicious and transgress biblical law. Referring to the curses contained in the Torah, he says that Moses condemns the transgressors to experiencing "a want of all necessary things, and a participation in every kind of destitution," including defeat and enslavement by their enemies, every manner of disease, and mental torment "night and day."[197]

Two additional matters concerning rewards and punishments merit attention. First, there are several passages asserting that virtue is its own reward (urging "virtue for its own sake").[198] These passages do not contradict Philo's belief that virtue is rewarded with material well-being. As Wolfson points out, "In Philo, as in Judaism, [the phrase 'virtue for its own sake'] means [only] that the worship of God out of love will bring the highest reward."[199] Therefore, despite any urging that man should practice virtue for its own sake, "Philo believes that the practice of virtue

---

194. See Philo, *Rewards* 79–118.

195. Philo, *Rewards* 99. See also Winston, "Philo's Ethical Theory," 406n109 ("Philo . . . frequently emphasizes the need to be content with little"); 408 (The body is not to be neglected but "neither is it to be allowed to become the central focus of human concern"). Cf. chapter 6, nn215–16 and accompanying text.

196. Philo, *Rewards* 119.

197. Philo, *Rewards* 127–51.

198. Philo, *Spec. Laws* 2.259; *Alleg. Interp.* 2.167. See generally Wolfson, *Philo*, 2.294–97.

199. Wolfson, *Philo*, 2.295–96.

is to be rewarded by a good that is a real good, and that real good is what philosophers call happiness and what Scripture calls blessings."[200]

Second, in the several passages where Philo mentions the problem of moral evil, he dismisses it. For example, he states with certainty that "persons who, by reason of their impiety or unrighteousness, have no heavenly inheritance, have also no abundant possession or share of the good things upon earth," and then offhandedly adds, "and even if any such thing should come to them, it quickly departs again, as if it had originally happened to them, not for the advantage of the immediate recipients, but in order that a more vehement sorrow may overwhelm them."[201] Similarly, he admonishes that one should never "think any wicked man is happy, even though he may be richer than Croesus . . . more powerful than Milo of Crotena, and more beautiful than Ganymede," for such men are really slaves to their passions and "can never possibly be happy" even though the masses, "corrupted by . . . pride and vain opinion" and ignorant of what is truly good, may think that they are happy.[202] On the other hand, if one considered to be virtuous suffers, this is because, in reality, they are not virtuous.[203]

In the final analysis, despite overtones of utilitarianism, the ethical theory that best characterizes Philo's position is ethical egoism. He was convinced that the highest good is the good of the individual soul. Although he believed that having a well-regulated soul is intrinsically good (constituting true happiness), he more emphatically emphasizes that it is instrumentally good in that a person possessing such a soul is rewarded with material well-being in this life, and with immortality in an afterlife.[204]

---

200. Wolfson, *Philo*, 2.297. See also Philo, *Spec. Laws* 2.259 (Truth is "its own recompense and reward, affording as it does happiness to all who practice it, and blessings of which they cannot be deprived").

201. Philo, *Rewards* 105.

202. Philo, *Providence* 2.7–10.

203. Philo, *Providence* 2.54 ("The criteria by which God judges are far more accurate than any of the tests by which the human mind is guided").

204. See generally Wolfson, *Philo*, 2.291.

CHAPTER 8

The Tannaim and their predecessors, the Pharisees, promulgated and developed new rules of conduct that were handed down from generation to generation and eventually collected and organized in the Mishnah and the Tosefta.

IN THE SECOND CENTURY BCE, the Jews of Judea were divided by a variety of divergent points of view that led to the formation of sects.[1] Schiffman argues that "Jewish law was at the heart of the manifold controversies,"[2] and that the sects disagreed as to "how to incorporate . . . extrabiblical traditions and teachings into the legal system, and how to justify them theologically."[3] The disputes also concerned who had legitimate authority to adopt extrabiblical rules of conduct. Such disputes arose, or dramatically intensified, after the investiture of Simon as high priest in about 142 BCE. The investiture of Simon constituted a revolution, according to Rivkin, because it ended the hegemony of

---

1. See Rivkin, *Hidden Revolution*, 34n1 (analyzing the term "sect"); Cohen, "Significance of Yavneh," 29–30 (same). See generally Cohen, *From the Maccabees*, 111–13, 120–22, 138–66; Sanders, *Paul and Palestinian Judaism*, 425–26.

2. Schiffman, "Qumran and Rabbinic Halakhah," 139. See also Blenkinsopp, *Wisdom and Law*, 139–40 ("The seeds of sectarianism" are sown in different groups claiming to be "the true Israel").

3. Schiffman, "Qumran and Rabbinic Halakhah," 141–43.

Aaronide-Zadokite priests[4] in Judea and legitimized the authority of scribes to adopt extrabiblical rules of conduct.[5]

From the time of Moses, the priests were the only ones granted divine authority to teach God's "torah."[6] Then, beginning in the fourth century BCE, Ezra, the "priest-scribe," granted scribes permission to teach the laws of Moses to the people, and the supremacy of the priest was slowly compromised.[7] Scribes were not permitted, however, to adopt extrabiblical rules of conduct. Writing in 180 BCE, Ben Sira "accords to the Aaronide priests, *and to them exclusively*, the control of the Law."[8] Ben Sira considers the scribes of his day to be students and teachers of the law, but not legislators. As known by Ben Sira, the scribe "was not free to interpret the Law or to tamper with its meaning."[9]

But matters changed after the appearance of those scribes called Pharisees (shortly before Simon's investiture as high priest),[10] for the Pharisees *did* interpret the Law and *did* tamper with its meaning. This innovation was not without controversy. Indeed, as the Jewish historian Josephus (ca. 37–100 CE) tells it, after the rise of the Hasmoneans, a major issue among the sects which then formed was whether the extrabiblical rules of conduct adopted by the Pharisees were valid. Josephus identifies three sects—the Pharisees, the Sadducees, and the Essenes[11]—and he describes a controversy between the Pharisees and the Sadducees in the time of the Hasmonean ruler John Hyrcanus (r. 135–104 BCE):

---

4. The Zadokites traced their ancestry through Zadok, a priest in the time of King David, back to Phinehas, the son of Eleazar (Aaron's oldest son), to whom Aaron's priesthood had been transferred. de Vaux, *Ancient Israel*, 2.396. See also de Vaux, *Ancient Israel*, 2.372-76 (discussing Zadok and the descendants of Zadok), 2.394-97 (discussing the sons of Zadok and the sons of Aaron), 2.397-403 (discussing the office of high priest).

5. See Rivkin, *Hidden Revolution*, 211-95.

6. See Deut 33:10. See also Jer 2:8; 18:18. See generally de Vaux, *Ancient Israel*, 2.353-55.

7. See chapter 5 (quoting Bickerman, *From Ezra*, 17-18).

8. Rivkin, *Hidden Revolution*, 197 (emphasis added).

9. Rivkin, *Hidden Revolution*, 200 (The scribe's "provenance was not the Law but Wisdom").

10. The Pharisees are associated in the Gospels with scribes. See Rivkin, *Hidden Revolution*, 104-21; Moore, *Judaism in the First Centuries*, 1.66 (Most of the scribes were Pharisees).

11. Josephus, *Ant.* 13.171-3, 293-98; *J.W.* 2.162-67; *Life* 7-13. But see Cohen, "Significance of Yavneh," 30-31 (noting that some scholars question whether the Pharisees may technically be called a sect).

The Pharisees have passed on to the people certain regulations handed down by former generations [*nomima ek paradoseōs tōn paterōn*] and not recorded in the Laws of Moses, for which reason they are rejected by the Sadducaean group, who hold that only those regulations should be considered valid which were written down [in Scripture], and that those which had been handed down by former generations [the non-scriptural law] need not be observed.[12]

From the beginning of the Common Era and thereafter, non-scriptural regulations were also adopted by persons having the title of "rabbi." At a later time, these rabbis were referred to as the Tannaim (the "repeaters" or "teachers"). The non-scriptural regulations of the Tannaim were eventually collected in a work called the Mishnah (the "repetition" or "teaching"). The Mishnah is assumed to have been redacted in its final version by Rabbi Judah the Patriarch in around 200 CE, and the "Tannaitic period" is generally defined as spanning from 10 BCE to 220 CE. Although Tannaitic literature encompasses material other than the Mishnah,[13] the Mishnah is the most important Tannaitic work and is central to that form of Judaism which became normative after 70 CE—Rabbinic Judaism.

This chapter and chapter 9 will focus on the historical background and relevant thought of the Tannaim and their predecessors, the Pharisees,[14] including a discussion of the nature, arrangement,

---

12. Josephus, *Ant.* 13.293–98 (as translated by Neusner, *From Politics to Piety*, 58). See generally Rivkin, *Hidden Revolution*, 31–75 (discussing all references made by Josephus to the Pharisees); Novick, "Tradition, Scripture, Law, and Authority," 65–66 (stating that "terminology associating religious law with [traditions of] fathers or ancestors becomes prominent in Jewish circles in the Hellenistic context of the late Second Temple period," and commenting that references in 2 Maccabees to "ancestral laws" (*patrioi nomoi*), "rules" (*nomima*), and "customs from [the] forebears" (*ta epi tōn progonōn autōn ethē*) "belong to the world of Greek thought").

13. See Rivkin, *Hidden Revolution*, 127–29 (describing the "array . . . of highly diverse writings" constituting Tannaitic literature); Moore, *Judaism in the First Centuries*, 1.132–73 (dividing Tannaitic literature into three categories: *halakhot* ("rules of traditional law"), *midrash* ("juristic exegesis of the biblical laws"), and *midrash haggadah* ("collections of sermonic materials"); Sanders, *Paul and Palestinian Judaism*, 76 (Although the Mishnah is "the halakic work *par excellence*," surviving Tannaitic literature includes the Tosefta and "commentaries on the legal books of the Bible—Exodus, Leviticus, Numbers and Deuteronomy," called *midrashim*); Przybylski, "Meaning and Significance," 74.

14. See Cohen, "Significance of Yavneh," 36–38 (stating that "virtually all modern scholars agree that the rabbis of the Mishnah are closely related to the Pharisees," and providing a brief analysis of the relevant evidence of the connection); Rivkin, *Hidden*

substance, and sources of the Mishnah. Although the Pharisees exercised considerable legal authority over all the Jews in Judea at various times from the mid-second century BCE until the first century CE,[15] their authority was not unchallenged. In addition to the Sadducees, two other sects—the Essenes and the proto-Christians—opposed Pharisaic authority. They also espoused apocalyptic ideas.

Accordingly, chapter 10 will describe several influential Jewish apocalyptic works written from about 250 BCE until about 100 CE. These works expound a dualistic worldview, regard the present world as hopelessly corrupt and wicked, and envision a time when God will create a new world order, including a transformed humanity having undivided hearts. Chapter 11 will then describe the views of the Essenes and Jesus of Nazareth (whose followers may be called proto-Christians). The Essenes and the proto-Christians accepted the apocalyptic vision of a new world order and a transformed humanity; rejected, in whole or in part, the extrabiblical laws of the Pharisees and Tannaim because, they said, such rules of conduct were merely man-made; and accepted the extrabiblical laws adopted by their own leaders, claiming that these extrabiblical laws were divinely inspired.[16]

A. The relevant historical events leading to the creation of the Mishnah.

Palestine was reconquered by the Seleucidan ruler Antiochus III in 200 BCE. The district of Judea, called "the nation of Jews," was then a very small part of the province of Syria.[17] The term "Jew" applied "only to those 'who lived around the Temple of Jerusalem.'"[18] Judea was a

---

Revolution, 234–35 ("The Pharisees-*Soferim* [scribes] are linked together with . . . the schools of Shammai and Hillel, and with the individual *tannaim* as the teachers of a non-Pentateuchal system of authoritative law and doctrine" [emphasis original]).

15. See Rivkin, *Hidden Revolution*, 252–53, 261–69, 276. See also Schiffman, "Qumran and Rabbinic Halakhah," 140–41 ("The *Miqṣat Ma'asei Torah* (4QMMT) . . . lends credence to the Tannaitic assertion that the Pharisees were actually able to bring about adherence to their views in the Jerusalem Temple").

16. See generally Cohen, "Significance of Yavneh," 30 (Although we may assume that "there were many . . . sects on the Judean landscape during the last centuries of the Second Temple period, only two sects are well documented," the Essenes and the Christians).

17. Bickerman, *From Ezra*, 55.

18. Bickerman, *From Ezra*, 55 (quoting a Greek historian).

self-governing entity with a ruling body called the "council of Elders";[19] the intermediary between the royal government and the Jews was the high priest, appointed by the king.[20] The population was diverse, and Greek influence had undermined traditional Jewish practices.[21] Bickerman writes:

> There was a mixture of population and language and a diffusion of foreign (Hellenic) culture unparalleled in the Persian period. To begin with there were now Hellenic cities in Palestine. The Jewish territory was practically in the midst of Hellenic cities.... In Trans-Jordan there was a mixed settlement of Jewish and Greek soldiers under the command of a Jewish sheikh....
>
> The Jewish territory itself was crowded with Greek officers, civil agents and traders.... Another important factor was that now a foreign language, Greek, became that of business and administration....
>
> The influence of a new, foreign and technologically superior civilization acted ... as a powerful dissolvent which destroyed the traditional discipline of life. The author of the Book of Jubilees gives insight into the moral situation of Palestinian Jewry after one and a half centuries of intensive contact with the Greeks. He fulminates against the evil generation who forgot the commandments and sabbaths. He repeatedly warns against associating with the pagans or eating with them.... Another contemporary writer, Ben Sira, speaks of the Jews who are ashamed of the Torah and its regulations....
>
> As it often happens, in order to uphold traditional values, their apologists themselves propose the most radical innovations. The author of the Book of Jubilees outdoes later Talmudic teaching in his severity as to observance of ritual prescriptions.

---

19. Bickerman, *From Ezra*, 56–57. See also Wolfson, *Philo*, 2.349 (The Jewish governing body "during the Hellenistic and Maccabean periods, is known in Greek sources as *gerusia*, council of elders"); Moore, *Judaism in the First Centuries*, 1.30, 261 (The *gerusia* was replaced by the *sanhedrin*). It is unclear what relationship existed, if any, between the *gerusia* and the *Kennesset ha-Gedolah* ("Great Synagogue") referred to in m. 'Abot 1:1, the *synagoge megale* ("great assembly") referred to in 1 Macc 14, the *bet din*, or the *sanhedrin*; nor are the sources clear as to their composition, functions, and regularity of meeting. See generally Moore, *Judaism in the First Centuries*, 1.31n1, 85; Wolfson, *Philo*, 2.348–52; Cohen, *From the Maccabees*, 102–3, 150; Urbach, *Sages*, 1.592; Goodblatt, "Sanhedrin," 602–4.

20. Bickerman, *From Ezra*, 56–57. See de Vaux, *Ancient Israel*, 2.400 (Once the monarchy had disappeared, "the high priest became the head of the nation").

21. See generally Bickerman, *From Ezra*, 102–11 (discussing the corrosive influence of Hellenic culture); Moore, *Judaism in the First Centuries*, 1.48–49.

But to assert the everlasting validity of the Torah, this traditionalist places his own composition beside and even above Scripture, claims for his book a divine origin, and gives precepts which differ widely from those set forth in the Torah....

But the most important result of the Greek impact on Palestinian Judaism was the formation of a Jewish intelligentsia, different from the clergy and not dependent on the sanctuary. The new class was known as "scribes." "Scribe" ... was the technical term for a public official who entered the civil service as a profession.... Since all Jewish law and legal customs were derived from the Torah, the scribe became the authority as to the Law of Moses.... On the other hand, the scribe is not only counselor of kings and assemblies, but also wise man and teacher. "Turn to me, you ignorant," says Ben Sira, "and tarry in my school." ... So his scribe and his school of wisdom prepare the way for the coming of the Pharisaic scholar in the next generation.[22]

1. Mattathias, patriarch of the Hasmoneans, interpreted the Torah to make violation of the Sabbath permissible in order to defend against attackers.

An example of the "radical innovations" to which Bickerman refers occurred at the time of the Maccabean revolt engendered by the Antiochian persecutions.[23] After Antiochus IV became king of the Seleucid dynasty in 176 BCE, he appointed to the position of high priest in Judea men—specifically, Jason and Menelaus—who were willing to abandon those characteristics of their ancestral religion which "smacked of separation" from the dominant Greek culture.[24] Accordingly, "[all] the requirements of the law concerning the sacrificial ritual were rescinded"; and because the prohibition of using the pig for sacrifice or food "had seemed the most striking mark of Jewish separatism," the pig was "approved as a sacrificial

---

22. Bickerman, *From Ezra*, 58–71. See also Cohen, *From the Maccabees*, 11 (The scribes' authority derived from his erudition in the sacred scriptures and traditions).

23. See generally Bickerman, *From Ezra*, 93–111 (describing the "persecutions of Antiochus Epiphanes"); Moore, *Judaism in the First Centuries*, 1.48–55 (same).

24. Bickerman, *From Ezra*, 108–9. See Rivkin, *Hidden Revolution*, 213–14; Moore, *Judaism in the First Centuries*, 1.49–53; de Vaux, *Ancient Israel*, 2.401–2. Menelaus was particularly objectionable because he was not only a more enthusiastic devotee of Greek culture than Jason, but he was not even a legitimate priest of the Aaronide-Zadokite stock.

animal."²⁵ After December of 167 BCE sacrifices were conducted according to the new ritual and the festivals of Dionysus were celebrated in Jerusalem.²⁶ The high priest Menelaus even "procured a decree from the King *prohibiting* the Mosaic law and ordering the introduction of pagan customs."²⁷ Eating pork was *required*. Few openly transgressed these orders; those who did "were seized, scourged, martyred, and slain."²⁸ More numerous were those who sought to evade the orders.

The following year agents of Antiochus IV charged with enforcing the king's decree discovered a group of Jews who had hidden in the wilderness. The royal agents planned to attack the Jews on the Sabbath because they knew that observance of the Sabbath precluded the Jews from mounting any resistance. Mattathias, a priest from Modin, realizing that the Jews would be destroyed if they observed the Sabbath in accordance with Mosaic law, "ventured to interpret the law upon his own authority" to make it permissible to violate Sabbath observances when necessary to defend against attackers.²⁹ So, as Bickerman says, the defenders of traditional values ended up initiating a radical innovation—interpreting God-given, eternally valid law in a way that altered that law's Sabbath requirements.

2. The Hasmoneans ultimately obtained emancipation from Seleucidan rule, marking the start of the "Pharisaic Revolution."

After the death of Mattathias, his descendants (referred to as the Maccabees or Hasmoneans) continued to resist the introduction of pagan practices and waged a guerrilla war against the "new pagans of Jerusalem."³⁰ Although an agreement was reached with Antiochus in early 164 BCE permitting the Jews "to use their own food and to observe their own laws," the Maccabees determined to wrest power from Menelaus, and four years later they conquered Jerusalem.³¹ The Maccabees ultimately

---

25. Bickerman, *From Ezra*, 110.
26. See Moore, *Judaism in the First Centuries*, 1.51–53.
27. Bickerman, *From Ezra*, 110 (emphasis added).
28. Bickerman, *From Ezra*, 95–96.
29. Bickerman, *From Ezra*, 99. See 1 Macc 2:32–41; Josephus, *Ant*. 12.274–76. This is probably the earliest attestation for the rabbinic idea of *piqquach nephesh* (the idea that the preservation of human life overrides other rules).
30. Bickerman, *From Ezra*, 114.
31. Bickerman, *From Ezra*, 117–19. See Moore, *Judaism in the First Centuries*,

obtained emancipation from Seleucidan rule in 142 BCE and governed Judea until the Roman conquest in 63 BCE. According to the apocryphal book of 1 Maccabees, shortly after the emancipation from Seleucidan rule, one of Mattathias' sons, Simon, was proclaimed by all the people, in what is referred to as the "*synagoge megale*" ("great assembly" or "great synagogue"), to be "their leader and high priest forever."[32] The great assembly then directed Simon to "take charge of the sanctuary and appoint officials over its tasks and over the country," and commanded that Simon "should be obeyed by all."[33]

Rivkin argues that the investiture of Simon as high priest is the "first decisive datum" marking the beginning of the "Pharisaic Revolution."[34] It is a revolution, asserts Rivkin, because neither Simon nor his brother Jonathan, who had been serving as high priest immediately before Simon, "had a right to be High Priest, since they were not the direct descendants of Zadok, Phineas, Eleazar, and Aaron."[35] In other words,

> the High Priesthood was no longer the prerogative of the Aaron-Eleazar-Phineas-Zadok line. It was now vested in the Hasmonean family.... A priestly dynasty which had exercised unbroken hegemony from the time of the promulgation of the Pentateuch until the ousting of Onias III [by Jason in 175 BCE] was dissolved. The commands of the Pentateuch had been superseded by the decision of the Great Synagogue which God had not mandated and Moses had not ordained....
>
> A Great Synagogue is thus the ultimate authority, elevated above the High Priesthood and over the written Law of Moses. But whence this hegemony?... The answer is to be found in that class which was rejected by the Zadokites/Sadducees because it did not recognize the binding character of the *written* Law of Moses exclusively. It was a class which felt free to legitimate a new High Priest line on the basis of *laws not written down in the law of Moses*. In a word, the Scribes-Pharisees was such a class. They would convoke a Great Synagogue ... to serve

---

1.53–54.

32. 1 Macc 14:25–49. See also Blenkinsopp, *Wisdom and Law*, 146 (The fact that Jason and Menelaus had attained to the high priesthood by paying the gentile ruler prepared the way for Jonathan, the brother and successor of Judah Maccabee, to accept the offer of being high priest from Alexander Balas, usurper of the Seleucid throne, and for Jonathan's brother and successor, Simon, to be confirmed in the office).

33. 1 Macc 14:41–44.

34. Rivkin, *Hidden Revolution*, 215.

35. Rivkin, *Hidden Revolution*, 217.

as a constituent assembly to formalize the transfer of the High Priesthood from the Zadokite family to the Hasmonean family and from the Aaronides to themselves. They had this right because they affirmed that the laws *not* written down in the laws of Moses were binding laws.[36]

Rivkin further argues that at the time of the transfer of power to the Hasmoneans and the Pharisees,

> urbanization had so altered the structure and experience of merchant, shopkeeper, artisan, and peasant alike that the Pentateuch no longer resonated with their deepest needs and their innermost yearnings. For the Pentateuch had been designed for a relatively simple agricultural-priestly society and not a highly complex urban-agricultural society embedded within a world of *poleis*—a world in which each individual was stirred on the one hand by feelings of loneliness, alienation, and insignificance, and on the other by intimations of personhood, self-worth, and immortality. When, therefore, a crisis of leadership occurred with first Jason and then Meneleus violating the Law by buying the High Priestly office from Antiochus IV, the people were ripe, not merely for rebellion, but for revolution.[37]

3. The Pharisees were a dominant political party during the reign of John Hyrcanus.

It was at the beginning of the Hasmonean hegemony in about 160 BCE that the Pharisaic sect emerges.[38] It emerges primarily as a political party "which sought, and for a time evidently won, domination of the political institutions of the Maccabean kingdom."[39] During the reign

---

36. Rivkin, *Hidden Revolution*, 219–20 (emphasis original). Blenkinsopp argues that (1) the group of pietists called the Hasidim, who had "joined forces with Mattathias and his sons," and from whom, he speculates, "the Essenes probably originated," "would have rejected [the investiture of Simon] out of hand," and (2) the investiture of Simon "was the decisive issue leading to the schism [between the Hasidim and the Maccabees] and the formation of sects." Blenkinsopp, *Wisdom and Law*, 145, 146, 148.

37. Rivkin, *Hidden Revolution*, 206–7.

38. Josephus testifies to the existence of the Pharisees as a school of thought (*haeresis*) in the time of Jonathan, the Hasmonean who ruled from 160–144 BCE. Josephus, *Ant.* 13.163–73.

39. Neusner, *From Politics to Piety*, 49. See also Glatzer, *Hillel the Elder*, 18; Blenkinsopp, *Wisdom and Law*, 149 (The Pharisees "constituted a predominately lay movement which emerged from the matrix of Hasidim during the early Hasmonaean period,

of John Hyrcanus (grandson of Mattathias),[40] the Pharisees constituted the country's legislative and judicial body, the *bet din*.[41] But conflict between the Pharisees and Hyrcanus arose, according to Josephus,[42] when the Pharisees urged Hyrcanus to give up the high priesthood. In response, Hyrcanus joined the Saducean party and forbade observance of Pharisaic regulations.[43]

Suppression of the Pharisees continued during the reign of Hyrcanus' son, Alexander Jannaeus (r. 103–76 BCE). When Jannaeus suffered a significant military defeat in 90 BCE the Pharisees deemed it a propitious moment to overthrow him; a civil war raged for six years but the attempted coup was ultimately quashed.[44] Then, during the reign of Salome Alexandra (76–67 BCE), the widow of Alexander Jannaeus, a "Grand Compromise was put into effect—Salome Alexandra recognizing Pharisaic hegemony over the Law and the Pharisees, in turn, recognizing the legitimacy of the Hasmonean dynasty."[45] The government was put in

---

though probably later than the Essenes").

40. See Bickerman, *From Ezra*, 112–52 (summarizing the relevant historical events). See also Neusner, *From Politics to Piety*, 48–49.

41. See Rivkin, *Hidden Revolution*, 235–36. But see Moore, *Judaism in the First Centuries*, 1.85–86 (The *bet din* only came into existence at Yavneh, succeeding the *sanhedrin*). See also Goodblatt, "Sanhedrin," 602 ("It is likely that the two names [*bet din* and *sanhedrin*] describe the same institution"); n19 in this chapter.

42. Although the picture of the Pharisees provided herein accords with the scholarly consensus, such consensus relies on rabbinic literature and the historical works of Josephus, both of which are subject to historical challenge. See Goodblatt, "Place of the Pharisees," 12; Sanders, *Jesus and Judaism*, 194–98, 315–16. Josephus' account of events is neither completely coherent nor entirely reliable. See Neusner, *From Politics to Piety*, 64–66; Cohen, *From the Maccabees*, 141; Goodblatt, "Place of the Pharisees," 12–13, 16–21. Nevertheless, the scholarly debate on Josephus concerns primarily his characterizations of the degree of power and influence that the Pharisees had; it isn't disputed that Josephus provides an accurate depiction of the main points of controversy between the Pharisees and the Sadducees, which is what is most important for present purposes.

43. Josephus, *Ant.* 13.288–98. See Rivkin, *Hidden Revolution*, 35–42; Bickerman, *From Ezra*, 167–68. The Pharisees' break with the Hasmoneans is also recounted in the Babylonian Talmud, but in the talmudic version the Hasmonean ruler is identified as Alexander Jannaeus. See b. Qidd. 66; Neusner, *From Politics to Piety*, 57–60.

44. See Bickerman, *From Ezra*, 168–69; Moore, *Judaism in the First Centuries*, 1.63–64.

45. Rivkin, "Defining the Pharisees," 247n1. See Rivkin, *Hidden Revolution*, 256 ("Following on the accession of Salome Alexandra as Queen . . . the Pharisees were restored to power and their unwritten laws were reinstated"); Moore, *Judaism in the First Centuries*, 1.64–66, 70–71, 261 (During the reign of Salome Alexandra the Pharisees "demanded and obtained the abrogation of the Asmonean-Sadducean code of civil and criminal law and the substitution of their own ordinances . . . which had been annulled

the hands of the Pharisees, and they exercised power high-handedly—they "killed many of their opponents, especially the aristocrats who had supported Jannaeus."[46] But when Salome Alexandra's son Aristobulus II (r. 67–63 BCE) assumed power he once again opposed the Pharisees and "slaughtered many of them."[47]

Pharisaism led to an estrangement of the people from the Maccabean dynasty, and an embassy of Jews met with the Roman general Pompey in Damascus just prior to his conquest of Jerusalem in 63 BCE to tell him that the people were opposed to their Maccabean rulers because they had "destroyed their ancestral constitution" and "enslaved the people."[48] The Pharisees were not averse to Roman rule so long as the Torah remained binding law. This position constituted not merely a religious claim but a political one since they maintained that they alone determined the substance of the Torah.[49] Rome stripped Hyrcanus II (r. 63–40 BCE) of the title of king. Later, after the death of Herod (r. 37–4 BCE), "who killed even more" Pharisees than Aristobolus II,[50] the Pharisees again petitioned Rome, asking "that none of the Herodians be named king, but that they be permitted to live without a king, according to the laws of their fathers."[51] Thereafter, "the Pharisees as a group no longer played a role in the politics and government of Jewish Palestine."[52]

Constituting what Josephus called a "*haeresis*" (a philosophical school),[53] the Pharisees believed (1) that the Mosaic law had to be developed "as time and circumstance demanded,"[54] (2) "that the ancestral tradition was as binding as the written Torah of Moses,"[55] (3) that "the

---

by John Hyrcanus").

46. Cohen, *From the Maccabees*, 139; Neusner, *From Politics to Piety*, 50–52, 60–63 (quoting Josephus, *J.W.* 1.107–14; *Ant.* 13.399–418); Bickerman, *From Ezra*, 169–70.

47. Cohen, *From the Maccabees*, 139; Neusner, *From Politics to Piety*, 66.

48. Bickerman, *From Ezra*, 174. See Moore, *Judaism in the First Centuries*, 1.72–73.

49. Neusner, *From Politics to Piety*, 50.

50. Neusner, *From Politics to Piety*, 66. See also Neusner, *From Politics to Piety*, 7–8 (quoting Josephus, *Ant.* 17:41–44).

51. Bickerman, *From Ezra*, 174.

52. Neusner, *From Politics to Piety*, 66. See also Cohen, *From the Maccabees*, 216–20 (discussing the end of sectarianism after 70 CE and commenting that the "Pharisees disappeared too, but transformed themselves into rabbis").

53. Josephus, *Ant.* 13:171–73. See Rivkin, *Hidden Revolution*, 34n1; Neusner, *From Politics to Piety*, 52–53.

54. Bickerman, *From Ezra*, 163.

55. Cohen, *From the Maccabees*, 155. Among the ancestral traditions that the

entire people [were obligated to] study Torah,"⁵⁶ (4) "that to act rightly or otherwise rests . . . for the most part with men, but that in each action Fate cooperates,"⁵⁷ and (5) that there is reward and punishment in an afterlife with the souls of the righteous passing "into another body."⁵⁸

Bickerman argues that these beliefs are mostly "alien to the Bible," and that "Pharisaism . . . is in part characterized precisely by the introduction of certain leading ideas of the Hellenistic period into the world of the Torah."⁵⁹ For example, he says, "the Pharisees adopted the Hellenistic idea of resurrection [that is, the idea that 'retribution would come after death'] but subsumed it under the principles of the Torah."⁶⁰ Also, according to Bickerman, the idea that the ancestral legal tradition (later referred to as the oral, or unwritten, law) is as binding as the "written

---

Pharisees accepted as binding, according to Cohen, were the observance of certain purity laws (especially laws concerning "table fellowship"), tithing, "and numerous details in the laws of oaths, Sabbath, and marriage," perhaps because the Pharisees believed "that the temple cult alone was no longer adequate." Cohen, *From the Maccabees*, 155–57. But see Neusner, *From Politics to Piety*, 66 ("We should not suppose that what is important about being a Pharisee is ritual behavior: keeping dietary laws, observing holy days and the Sabbath, and similar wholly unpolitical and unphilosophical matters. Yet . . . the Gospels' Pharisees, although including important politicians, primarily concerned themselves not with philosophy but with matters of religious ritual"); Rivkin, "Defining the Pharisees," 212, 226, 233, 244–46.

56. Bickerman, *From Ezra*, 162.

57. Neusner, *From Politics to Piety*, 52–53 (quoting Josephus, *J.W.* 2.162–66). Josephus' language is meant to indicate that the Pharisees believed that what happens to a person is not *solely* a matter of fate, in contrast to the Essenes who, while recognizing (to some extent) free will and choice, paradoxically believed that what happens to a person is *always* a matter of fate. See generally chapter 11, sec. A, 1.

58. Neusner, *From Politics to Piety*, 52–53 (quoting Josephus, *J.W.* 2.162–66). See generally Starr, *Toward a History*, 86–90 (discussing Josephus' depiction of the views about the afterlife held by the Pharisees, Sadducees, and Essenes).

59. Bickerman, *From Ezra*, 160–61. See also Neusner, *From Politics to Piety*, 53–54 (quoting Bickerman and asserting (1) that what is "Hellenistic in Pharisaic Judaism" is "the stress on tradition" which is not written down but "endured in the life of the masters and was learned from their precept and example," and (2) that the "concept of a truth outside of Scripture opened the way to accommodation of new ideas and values within the structure of inherited symbols"); Rivkin, *Hidden Revolution*, 242–43 ("Whereas the components of the Pharisaic Revolution are incongruent with Scriptures, they are congruent with Greco-Roman models. It would therefore follow that the Pharisaic Revolution was seeking to incorporate within Judaism major structural components and major conceptual notions prevalent in the Greco-Roman world").

60. Bickerman, *From Ezra*, 164.

law" of Moses "is again Greek," being based on "the [Greek] concept of the 'unwritten law' (*agraphos nomos*)."⁶¹

4. Pre-Tannaitic teachers mentioned in the Mishnah were Pharisees and, accordingly, they acknowledged the ancestral tradition as normative.

Certain pre-Tannaitic teachers mentioned in the Mishnah held the same basic beliefs as the Pharisees and appear on the scene at the same time as the Pharisees. They were among the so-called *zugot* (pairs) who date from about 150 to 4 BCE.⁶² The *zugot* were the coleaders of the *bet din*, the legislative, judicial, and administrative body which "may well" have been established "as a permanent institution" simultaneously with the investiture of Simon as High Priest.⁶³ These coleaders were called the *nasi bet din* and the *av bet din*, the former tasked with representing the *bet din*'s majority point of view and the later its minority point of view.⁶⁴ During the period of the *zugot*, "the laws were determined by a majority vote of the *Bet Din* and were the only laws deemed authoritative."⁶⁵ The last of the *zugot* were Hillel and Shammai. Following the death of Hillel in about 4 BCE, "the office of *Nasi* became hereditary for the

---

61. Bickerman, *From Ezra*, 163–64. But see Urbach, *Sages*, 1.291 (distinguishing *agraphos nomos* from the unwritten law of the rabbinic "Oral Torah"). See also Wolfson, *Philo*, 1.188–94; 2.174, 180–81 (describing the Aristotelean and Philonic understanding of *agraphos nomos* and supporting the view that Philo's unwritten law is most often used in the Greek sense of the term but in some instances has reference to the Jewish oral law). See generally Hayes, *What's Divine*, 54–89 (discussing Greco-Roman written and unwritten law).

62. See Rivkin, *Hidden Revolution*, 236; Rivkin, "Defining the Pharisees," 216; Cohen, "Significance of Yavneh," 36.

63. See Rivkin, "Defining the Pharisees," 216, 224; Rivkin, *Hidden Revolution*, 235–36, 257. See also Moore, *Judaism in the First Centuries*, 1.82, 85, 261.

64. See Rivkin, *Hidden Revolution*, 235, 257; m. Hag. 2:2. But see Moore, *Judaism in the First Centuries*, 1.45n3, 255n4 (Moore assumes that the *bet din* mentioned in m. Hag. 2:2 is really a reference to the *sanhedrin* and that the titles of *nasi bet din* and *av bet din* attributed there to the *zugot* are anachronistic). See also Goodblatt, "Sanhedrin," 603 (m. Hag. 2.2 "does not explain the meaning of these titles or the identity of the court in question").

65. Rivkin, *Hidden Revolution*, 238. See generally Goodblatt, "Sanhedrin," 602 (Rabbinic materials using the terms *sanhedrin* or *bet din* suggest "a two-tiered judicial/administrative system; every town with a certain minimum population could establish a 'small *sanhedrin*' or *bet din* of 23 scholars . . . while a 'great *sanhedrin*' or *bet din* of 71 members met in the Jerusalem Temple"); Cohen, *From the Maccabees*, 36, 102–3, 150 (discussing the *sanhedrin*).

descendants of Hillel,"[66] and Hillel's son Gamaliel became *nasi* and was given the title *Rabban* ("our teacher").[67]

While at least some, if not all, of the *zugot* were among the historical Pharisees, the compilers of the Mishnah do not refer to any of them as Pharisees.[68] According to Rivkin, this is because the term "Pharisee" was used by their adversaries, the Sadducees, as a term of derision; the term meant that you were a separatist, deviant, or heretic.[69] From the standpoint of the Sadducees, such a designation was appropriate because the Sadducees viewed the Pharisees' reliance on ancestral tradition as heretical. However, the Pharisees did not accept this derogatory name. Rather than referring to the *zugot* as Pharisees, the Mishnah refers to them as *hakamim* (sages) or *sofrim* (scribes);[70] Rivkin calls these pre-Tannaitic teachers Pharisees-*hakamim* or Pharisees-*sofrim*.[71]

One pair of coleaders, Judah ben Tabbai and Simon ben Shetach, lived during the reigns of Alexander Jannaeus and Salome Alexandra. In rabbinic literature ben Tabbai and ben Shetach are characterized as great legal scholars who opposed positions taken by the Sadducees.[72] Rivkin argues that because ben Tabbai and ben Shetach acknowledge the non-scriptural or ancestral law "as the normative law, binding on each of them," they were Pharisees.[73] As Pharisees, he says, they were part of a "scholar class, dedicated to the authority of the two-fold Law [the scriptural law, or Written Torah, and the non-scriptural law, or Oral Torah] and having as their spokesmen the *nasi* and the *av bet din*."[74]

The Mishnah's account of Alexander Jannaeus' break with the "*hakmey yisrael*" (sages of Israel) is seen by Rivkin as evidence that the

66. Rivkin, *Hidden Revolution*, 257–58.
67. Rivkin, *Hidden Revolution*, 238.
68. See generally Cohen, "Significance of Yavneh," 38–40.
69. See Rivkin, "Defining the Pharisees," 231–32, 236–38, 248. See generally Rivkin, *Hidden Revolution*, 130–79; Cohen, "Significance of Yavneh," 40–42; Moore, *Judaism in the First Centuries*, 1.60–62.
70. See Rivkin, "Defining the Pharisees," 212–33. See also Cohen, *From the Maccabees*, 151–52, 218–19 ("The rabbis were latter-day Pharisees who had no interest in publicizing the connection").
71. Rivkin, "Defining the Pharisees," 224, 225, 228, 229, 231.
72. See Rivkin, "Defining the Pharisees," 216–17.
73. Rivkin, "Defining the Pharisees," 217.
74. Rivkin, "Defining the Pharisees," 217–18. But see Neusner, "Rabbinic Traditions," 10 (We are entitled to conclude that the Pharisees possessed ancient traditions but "are not entitled to speak of Oral Torah"). See ch. 9, sec. D.

Pharisees-*hakamim* were "a class of legislators" who "possessed great power and influence" and who "determined the law," which, says Rivkin, was binding on everyone, "even the king."[75] Similarly, Rivkin interprets the Mishnah's account of the rejection by the Boethusians (Sadduceans) of the procedures to be followed in the cutting of the omer as evidence that the authority for those procedures rested with the *bet din*, and concludes that the Pharisees-*hakamim* "must have been active legislators."[76]

5. Hillel continued the legislative activity of the Pharisees by making changes to biblical law; he also transformed the Pharisees from a political party to a fellowship sect.

The most famous of the teachers/legislators mentioned in the Mishnah is Hillel the Elder. Hillel was born in Babylonia before the middle of the first century BCE, came to Jerusalem probably around 40 BCE to study with the *zugot* Shemaiah and Abtalion, and, according to Neusner, "transformed the Pharisees from a political party to a table-fellowship sect."[77] Glatzer speculates that "after leaving the college of Shemaiah and Abtalion," Hillel spent a "period of communion" near Jericho with sectarians (such as the Essenes) who "lived in the wilderness where they could dedicate themselves to [lives] of Torah and *hasidut* [piety]."[78] He shared with such sectarians an emphasis on learning, biblical exegesis, Sabbath observance, mercy and lovingkindness, the rights of the poor, and simplicity and quietude.[79]

But ultimately, Hillel rejected the claim of these sectarians that all nonmembers were wicked and unredeemable. The wicked could be redeemed, Hillel thought, because he "believed in the power of the Torah to change the heart of man."[80] Accordingly, unlike the sectarians who withdrew from the community,[81] "Hillel actively engaged in improving the

---

75. Rivkin, "Defining the Pharisees," 220.
76. Rivkin, "Defining the Pharisees," 223–24.
77. Neusner, *From Politics to Piety*, 13–14. Neusner's point of view has been challenged by some but is accepted by others. See Glatzer, *Hillel the Elder*, 24; Blenkinsopp, *Wisdom and Law*, 149–50. See generally Goodblatt, "Place of the Pharisees," 19–20.
78. Glatzer, *Hillel the Elder*, 29–33.
79. See Glatzer, *Hillel the Elder*, 43–44, 46–49, 89.
80. Glatzer, *Hillel the Elder*, 32. Cf. chapter 9, sec. C.
81. See chapter 11, sec. A (discussing the Essenes).

conditions of the community."[82] One of the many sayings that the Mishnah attributes to Hillel is "Keep not aloof from the congregation."[83]

Hillel is represented in rabbinic material "as a legislator who not only interpreted existing statutes but [who] made new and important changes in the laws."[84] For example, Hillel is said to have created a legal way out of the remission of debts required every seventh year pursuant to Deut 15:1–3.[85] A way to avoid the remission of debts was necessary, according to rabbinic sources, because the people "held back from lending to one another."[86] So, Hillel ordained a procedure whereby a lender could deposit a certificate, called a *prozbul*, with a local court transferring the debt to the court in the Sabbatical Year, and simultaneously declare to the court that he retained the right to collect the debt *after* the Sabbatical Year. The Mishnah states that "Hillel ordained the *prozbul* for the good order of the world [*tikkun ha'olam*]."[87]

Neusner has carefully analyzed the passage about the *prozbul* using a form-critical method. He determined that the passage conflates two different stories. The viewpoint of one story is that Hillel's action was "based upon sound exegesis of Scripture and did not represent a modification of the law merely to accommodate the law to historical circumstances"; while the second story "ignores the exegesis," represents that Hillel "*did* change the law to accommodate it to the needs of the day," and implies that others who issue ordinances "are similarly justified as circumstances require."[88] Neusner states that there is no "firm basis on which to formulate a theory of events"; Hillel may have "actually made such a decree" or Hillel may have merely "served as a convenient name

---

82. Glatzer, *Hillel the Elder*, 66. See Glatzer, *Hillel the Elder*, 66–68.

83. m. 'Abot 2:5. See Glatzer, *Hillel the Elder*, 49.

84. Neusner, *From Politics to Piety*, 14.

85. See Moore, *Judaism in the First Centuries*, 1.80, 259–60.

86. See Neusner, *From Politics to Piety*, 14 (quoting Sifre Deut. 113). See also Greengus, *Laws in the Bible*, 102 (quoting b. Giṭ. 36b).

87. m. Giṭ. 4:3. The "good order of the world" is engendered by loosening credit and increasing economic activity. See Urbach, *Sages*, 1.373 (citing m. Šeb. 10:3); Glatzer, *Hillel the Elder*, 67. See also Neusner, *From Politics to Piety*, 16–17.

88. Neusner, *From Politics to Piety*, 16 (emphasis original). See Urbach, *Sages*, 1.373 (The *prozbul* is an example of "innovations and amendments" that were required to fulfill "the basic reason of the commandment, whereas its literal observance nullified its original intent").

to hang Pharisaic acceptance of it, despite contravening Scriptural law."[89] Neusner continues:

> While historical considerations lead to an impasse, form-critical ones do not. The story represents the effort, first, to attribute the anonymous exegetical justification of the *prozbul* to Hillel, and then to combine both views of ordinances—a compromise between those who held that one may legislate to meet the needs of the day and those who held that legislation always depended upon Scriptural exegesis. The latter believed exegesis was possible for all needed legislation. The former may have thought otherwise, or, more likely, had no sufficiently rich exegetical tradition that permitted them to rely upon Scriptural exegesis for important matters.[90]

Another instance of legislating attributed to Hillel pertains to the sale of houses in a walled city. Lev 25:29–30 permits a seller of a house in a walled city to redeem it within a year after the sale, but, if not redeemed within a year, it would belong to the buyer in perpetuity (that is, it would be unaffected by the Jubilee Year). In Hillel's time "the social circumstances of the day mitigated against the biblical law's effectiveness" for buyers took measures to prevent the original owners from making their redemption payments.[91] Therefore, according to rabbinic literature, Hillel ordained that the original owners could deposit their redemption payments in a court of law and that such deposit would constitute redemption of the property.[92]

In addition to Hillel's legislating, Hillel is historically significant, according to Neusner, because he "transformed the Pharisees from

---

89. Neusner, *From Politics to Piety*, 16.

90. Neusner, *From Politics to Piety*, 17. See also Neusner, *Mishnah*, 204–20 (describing two traditions about the Mishnah which echoes the debate about whether it is permissible to legislate or whether legislation must depend upon scriptural exegesis). Neusner adds: "It was [Rabbi Akiva] and his associates at Yavneh who so enriched the exegetical tradition of the rabbis that they could find whatever they wanted in Scripture. Earlier, before *ca.* [90 CE], those who had to issue decrees without the [Akivan] method thought it reasonable merely because the times obviously required it." Neusner, *From Politics to Piety*, 17. But see Glatzer, *Hillel the Elder*, 54–55 (Rules of scriptural interpretation attributed to Hillel made it possible to apply the Torah to all new conditions so that it wasn't necessary to rely on "legal enactment").

91. Neusner, *From Politics to Piety*, 18. See Glatzer, *Hillel the Elder*, 67 (The buyers would, for example, absent themselves around the time when it was anticipated that the original owners would make their redemption payments).

92. Neusner, *From Politics to Piety*, 18–19 (quoting Sifra Behar 4:8 and opining that "the whole story is probably a fabrication"); Glatzer, *Hillel the Elder*, 67.

THE TANNAIM AND THEIR PREDECESSORS, THE PHARISEES

a political party to a table-fellowship sect."[93] Thus, the Pharisees are depicted in the Gospels of Mark, Matthew, and Luke (completed by about 80 CE) as persons primarily concerned with the observance of dietary laws.[94] Similarly, most of the nearly seven hundred pericopae in talmudic literature pertaining to the pre-70 CE Tannaim relate to two areas of the law: "first, agricultural tithes, offerings, and other taboos, and second, rules of ritual purity."[95] The rules of ritual purity, "which predominate in the Pharisaic corpus," were the focus of sectarian controversy.[96] Neusner explains:

> The Pharisees were Jews who believed one must keep the purity laws outside of the Temple. Other Jews, following the plain sense of Leviticus, supposed that purity laws were to be kept only in the Temple, where the priests had to enter a state of ritual purity in order to carry out such requirements as animal sacrifice. They likewise had to eat their Temple food in a state of ritual purity, while lay people did not. To be sure, everyone who went to the Temple had to be ritually pure. But outside of the Temple the laws of ritual purity were not observed, for it was not required that noncultic activities be conducted in a state of Levitical cleanness.
>
> But the Pharisees held that even outside of the Temple, in one's own home, the laws of ritual purity were to be followed in the only circumstance in which they might apply, namely, at the table. Therefore, one must eat secular food (ordinary, everyday meals) in a state of ritual purity *as if one were a Temple priest*. . . . At this time, only the Pharisees held such a viewpoint, and eating unconsecrated food as if one were a Temple priest at the Lord's table was one of the two significations that a Jew was a Pharisee. . . .
>
> The other sign was meticulous tithing. . . . Both the agricultural laws and purity rules in the end affected table-fellowship; that is . . . they were "dietary laws" [defining what, with whom, and under what circumstances one may eat].[97]

93. Neusner, *From Politics to Piety*, 14. See Neusner, *From Politics to Piety*, 90–92.

94. See Neusner, *From Politics to Piety*, 67–80 (describing the stories about the Pharisees in the Gospels and commenting that the "Gospels' Pharisees . . . are a table-fellowship sect").

95. Neusner, *From Politics to Piety*, 83.

96. Neusner, *From Politics to Piety*, 83.

97. Neusner, *From Politics to Piety*, 83–84 (emphasis original; food which had not been properly grown and tithed could not be eaten). See generally Neusner, *From Politics to Piety*, 83–90.

A contemporary of Hillel named Shammai, also a member of the Pharisaic sect, is depicted in rabbinic material as often taking positions that were opposed to those of Hillel. Similarly, Hillel's disciples (referred to as the house of Hillel) are depicted in rabbinic materials as often engaging in debates with Shammai's disciples (referred to as the house of Shammai). These debates were about "the laws of purity, Sabbath, festivals, and table fellowship (What is the proper procedure for the eating of a meal? Which blessing must be recited and in what order? What are the rules of etiquette that are to be observed? How should purity rules be implemented during a meal?)."[98] Most scholars view the two houses as factions within the Pharisaic sect.[99]

One dispute between the two houses concerned when fish become susceptible to uncleanness.[100] The house of Shammai took the position that since fish do not require slaughtering, they become susceptible to uncleanness immediately after they are caught, even while alive; the house of Hillel disagreed, saying that fish become susceptible to uncleanness only after they are dead.[101] Another dispute concerned when a man may divorce his wife. Although they relied on the same biblical passage, Deut 24:1, the house of Shammai allowed divorce only on grounds of unchastity, but the house of Hillel allowed for much more liberal divorce.[102]

6. After the destruction of the Second Temple, Rabbi Yohanan ben Zakkai founded the Yavneh academy.

The war with Rome of 66 to 70 CE resulted in Jewish defeat, the destruction of the Second Temple, the death or enslavement of hundreds of thousands of Jews, the devastation of Jerusalem, and the end of an autonomous Jewish government.[103] After 70 CE a leading figure among

---

98. Cohen, *From the Maccabees*, 150–51. See generally Neusner, *From Politics to Piety*, 100–21 (discussing disputes between the houses of Shammai and Hillel); Glatzer, *Hillel the Elder*, 56–63 (same).

99. Cohen, *From the Maccabees*, 151. See also Moore, *Judaism in the First Centuries*, 1.77–81.

100. m. ʿUq. 3:8.

101. See Neusner, *From Politics to Piety*, 121.

102. m. Giṭ. 9:10. See Neusner, *From Politics to Piety*, 113–15; Glatzer, *Hillel the Elder*, 58–59 ("Hillel felt that a rigid divorce would be detrimental to family life"); Moore, *Judaism in the First Centuries*, 2.123–24; chapter 11, sec. B, 2.

103. See Cohen, *From the Maccabees*, 207.

THE TANNAIM AND THEIR PREDECESSORS, THE PHARISEES

the successors to the Pharisees, the Tannaim (who adopted the title of "rabbi"), was Rabbi Yohanan ben Zakkai. He had been a disciple of Hillel and a vigorous opponent of the Sadducees.[104] According to rabbinic legend, during the siege of Jerusalem ben Zakkai appeared before the Roman general Vespasian, acknowledged Rome's sovereignty, and asked permission to maintain a school in Yavneh (near Yaffa), which request was granted.[105]

Rabbinic legend also informs us that when a fellow rabbi beheld the Temple in ruins and cried out "Woe unto us that this, the place where iniquities are atoned for, is laid waste!," ben Zakkai told him "Be not aggrieved; we have another method of atonement as effective as this.... It is acts of lovingkindness, as it is said: *For I desire mercy and not sacrifice* [Hos 6:6]."[106] With the destruction of the Temple and the establishment of the Yavneh academy, religious authority was indisputably transferred from the priests to the rabbis, animal sacrifices ended, the synagogue emerged as a characteristic institution of Jewish life, the study of Torah was placed at the center of Jewish life, and biblical religion was reorganized as Rabbinic Judaism.[107]

Ben Zakkai, no less than Hillel, issued decrees prescribing what he believed the times required, with or without scriptural proof.[108] Among the decrees he issued were ones to preserve for synagogue life the rites and rituals formerly conducted only in the Jerusalem Temple.[109] Joining ben Zakkai at Yavneh were the disciples of both Shammai and Hillel, and they began to record and preserve the traditions they had inherited.[110] The most outstanding figure of the generation after ben Zakkai was Rabbi Akiva (ca. 50–135 CE). Leaders at Yavneh were soon "regarded by their fellow Jews as the successors to the Jerusalem Sanhedrin," and "the Roman authorities appear to have acquiesced in this court's exercise of

---

104. See Rivkin, "Defining the Pharisees," 220–22. See also Moore, *Judaism in the First Centuries*, 1.84–85.

105. See ’*Abot R. Nat.* 4; Scheindlin, *Short History*, 51–53; Glatzer, *Hillel the Elder*, 84–86.

106. ’*Abot R. Nat.* 4.

107. See Scheindlin, *Short History*, 51–53. See also, Moore, *Judaism in the First Centuries*, 1.84–85.

108. See Neusner, *From Politics to Piety*, 17; Moore, *Judaism in the First Centuries*, 1.260.

109. Neusner, *From Politics to Piety*, 111.

110. See Neusner, *From Politics to Piety*, 97–103 (describing the traditions attested at Yavneh); Danby, "Introduction," xix.

some measure of control and supervision over their co-religionists," with its *nasi* serving as their representative.[111]

According to Neusner, the importance of the Yavneh academy cannot be overstated. He writes:

> The rabbis of Yavneh laid the foundations for the classical form of Judaism which predominated from the first century to the twentieth.... Their achievements include preservation of the pre-70 Pharisaic tradition and development of the legal corpus which guided Judaism thence-forward, and which was eventually redacted as the Mishnah of Judah the Patriarch. The Yavneans furthermore laid down the main outlines of the Judaic Prayerbook, the *Siddur*, used from then to now.... They are also credited with the final canonization of the Hebrew Scriptures.[112]

7. Bar Kokhba, Usha, and the creation of the Mishnah.

A second Jewish revolt against Rome broke out in 132 CE, led by a purported messiah popularly known as Bar Kokhba, meaning "son of a star," a name given to him by those who accepted his messianic status.[113] Ending in 135 CE, the revolt utterly devastated Judea; henceforth, the main centers of Jewish settlement would be in Galilee.[114] The Romans reestablished the loyalist patriarchate, placing power in Simeon b. Gamaliel II (a direct descendant of Hillel), who reassembled the rabbinical masters at Usha (about ten miles inland from Haifa) where the Hillelites were in complete control.[115] Succeeding Gamaliel II as patriarch was his son, Rabbi Judah (referred to in the Mishnah simply as "Rabbi"); he belonged to the sixth generation in direct descent from Hillel the Elder.[116]

Concerning the rabbis at Usha, Scheindlin writes:

---

111. Danby, "Introduction," xx. See Moore, *Judaism in the First Centuries*, 1.86 (Gamaliel II was able "to secure the recognition of all Jewry for the Bet Din at [Yavneh] and submission to its authority").

112. Neusner, *From Politics to Piety*, 97.

113. See Scheindlin, *Short History*, 54; Cohen, *From the Maccabees*, 25–26; Moore, *Judaism in the First Centuries*, 1.89–90.

114. See Moore, *Judaism in the First Centuries*, 1.93–94.

115. See Neusner, *From Politics to Piety*, 123–41 (describing the traditions attested at Usha).

116. Danby, "Introduction," xxi. The lineage is Hillel, Simeon I, Gamaliel I, Simeon ben Gamaliel I, Gamaliel II, Simeon ben Gamaliel II, Rabbi Judah.

For the first time, a body of rabbis had acquired government recognition as the central organization of Jewish life; this development was an important step toward making rabbinic Judaism the dominant form of the Jewish religion for all time. A landmark in this process was reached toward the end of the second century, when Rabbi Judah the Patriarch composed and promulgated the Mishnah.[117]

B. The nature, arrangement, substance, and sources of the Mishnah.

The Mishnah is essentially a law code that preserves and organizes certain of the traditional laws or teachings of the Pharisees and their successors, the Tannaim.[118] According to rabbinic sources, in compiling the Mishnah, Rabbi Judah made use of thirteen earlier collections of *halakhot* (precepts or laws).[119] The Mishnah itself refers to a "Mishnah of Rabbi Akiva," as well as to a "First Mishnah."[120] Later rabbinic sources refer to a Mishnah of Rabbi Eliezer ben Hyrcanus and a Mishnah of Rabbi Eliezer ben Jacob.[121] There is a "strong probability" that some, if not all, of these earlier law collections were in writing.[122] According to Danby, "the principal source used by Rabbi was the *Halakah* collection

---

117. Scheindlin, *Short History*, 56.

118. See generally Danby, "Introduction," xvi–xvii; Moore, *Judaism in the First Centuries*, 1.151–54. But see Moore, *Judaism in the First Centuries*, 1.96 (Although the Mishnah "is often described as a code of rabbinical law . . . it must be understood that it was not meant to be a legal code in the sense those words first suggest to us, a corpus of law systematized for practical use, but an instrument for the study of the law, an apparatus of instruction").

119. Danby, "Introduction," xxi (citing m. Ned. 41a). See also Moore, *Judaism in the First Centuries*, 1.87–88 ("To Akiba is commonly attributed the systemization of the Halakah . . . distributing the rules by subjects under six capital divisions with numerous subdivisions, thus giving the unwritten law the form of a code"), 94 ("Every principal school had its own Mishnah," ordering "the accumulated mass of traditional laws . . . upon Akiba's plan"), 151 ("There were numerous Mishnah collections"), 153 (Different parts of the Mishnah "are based on earlier works proceeding from different individual scholars or schools").

120. m. Sanh. 3:4.

121. Danby, "Introduction," xxin5 (citing b. Men. 18a and b. Yeb. 49b). Ben Hyrcanus and ben Jacob were contemporaries of Akiva. See also Moore, *Judaism in the First Centuries*, 1.96 (The Talmud refers to three "Large Mishnahs [which] amplified, explained, and sometimes corrected our Mishnah").

122. Moore, *Judaism in the First Centuries*, 1.154.

of Rabbi Meir, who had himself made use of the collection of his teacher, Rabbi Akiba," but Rabbi used numerous additional and probably earlier sources as well.[123] Danby states:

> It was Rabbi's task to bring together this mass of *Halakoth*, the work of many generations, handed down in the form of miscellaneous collections of oral teachings, stored in many memories, and growing ever more complicated and unwieldy by reason of controversy between rival teachers and contradictory traditions; to reassemble this material and present it as a single coherent whole, arranging it systematically, abbreviating arguments, summarizing discussions, rejecting what seemed to be superfluous, sometimes in disputed cases giving his own ruling, or adding arguments if these seemed called for. . . .
>
> Thus Rabbi did not aim at promulgating the Mishnah as an authoritative, definitive legal code, a final summary of Jewish law. . . . It was, simply, a compilation of the [non-scriptural, ancestral law] as it was taught in the many rabbinical schools of his time.[124]

Material that was excluded from the Mishnah came to be collected and preserved in a work that was called the Tosefta ("Supplement").[125]

Rivkin emphasizes that, by any measure, "the Mishnah is incongruent with the Pentateuch," and that "if we compare the Mishnah with the Prophets and the Hagiographa, the discontinuity is no less striking."[126] Rivkin notes that the Mishnah does not follow the Pentateuch "in the arrangement of laws," that the Mishnah does not articulate laws "as a direct command [from God]," that the Mishnah "is replete with nonbiblical vocabulary set within a nonbiblical syntax," and that the Mishnah is "incongruent with the Pentateuch on substantive issues" (as is revealed "in the large number of tractates dealing with whole categories of laws that are *not* in the Pentateuch at all") and in the expression of "non-Pentateuchal dogma" (such as the "belief in the world to come and the resurrection of

---

123. Danby, "Introduction," xxi. See also Moore, *Judaism in the First Centuries*, 1.94 ("The Mishnah of R. Meir was taken by the Patriarch Judah . . . as the basis of his own"), 96 ("Besides the Mishnah of R. Meir, Judah digested much material not only from other Mishnah collections but from the juristic Midrash").

124. Danby, "Introduction," xxii.

125. See Moore, *Judaism in the First Centuries*, 1.97, 155–56 ("The Tosefta treats the subjects more at large than the Mishnah, very often giving the biblical ground of the rule or the reason for it, which the Mishnah rarely does").

126. Rivkin, *Hidden Revolution*, 223–24.

the dead").[127] Underlying "all these discontinuities," says Rivkin, is that "a scholar class is sitting in Moses' seat even though Moses had never bestowed upon a scholar class any authority over God's Law."[128]

1. The Mishnah is divided into six sections, containing rules of conduct not necessarily derived from biblical law.

Neusner believes that the people living before about 70 CE whose ideas are expressed in the Mishnah may be categorized as "a cultic sect, a holiness order, expressing the aspirations of lay people to live as if they belonged to the caste of priests, and of priests to live as if the whole country were the Temple."[129] Accordingly, the topics dealt with in the Mishnah include those having to do with food (how it is grown, prepared, and consumed) and sex (who may marry whom).[130] After the two wars with Rome, on Neusner's account, "the entire framework of the Mishnah" underwent revision and the "range of topics so expanded that laws came to full expression to govern not merely the collective life of a small group but the political and social affairs of a whole nation."[131]

The Mishnah is divided into six main sections or *sedarim* (orders), with each section divided into *massektot* (subsections or tractates), and each tractate further divided into *perakim* (chapters). In total, there are sixty-three tractates comprising 531 chapters. Individual laws are sometimes attributed to a particular teacher but are often anonymous. The six orders of the Mishnah are: Zera'im (agriculture), Mo'ed (appointed times), Nashim (woman), Neziqin (damages), Qodashim (holy things), and Teharot (purities).[132] As indicated by their titles, most of the orders of the Mishnah concern matters of ritual, but the order of Neziqin is devoted to matters of civil law, especially to issues of property rights, torts, and the administration of justice.

The regulations contained in each order, for the most part, are not derived in any obvious way from the Torah. Neusner asserts that

---

127. Rivkin, *Hidden Revolution*, 224-30 (emphasis original).
128. Rivkin, *Hidden Revolution*, 231-32.
129. Neusner, *Mishnah*, 51.
130. See Neusner, *Mishnah*, 51.
131. Neusner, *Mishnah*, 51.
132. See Neusner, *Mishnah*, 54-60 (containing a brief description of the contents of each order); Moore, *Judaism in the First Centuries*, 1.152.

"Scripture plays little role in the Mishnaic system"; the Mishnah, he says, "rarely cites a verse of Scripture, refers to Scripture as an entity, links its own ideas to those of Scripture, or lays claim to originate in what Scripture has said."[133]

Nevertheless, according to Neusner, the Mishnah *is* related to Scripture, and there are three modes of this relationship. First, "there are tractates which simply repeat in their own words precisely what Scripture has to say"; second, "there are tractates that take up facts of Scripture but work them out in unpredictable ways"; third, there are tractates which either "take up problems in no way suggested by Scripture" or "begin from facts only slightly relevant to facts of Scripture."[134] So, Neusner concludes, some tractates "repeat what we find in Scripture," some "are totally independent of Scripture," and some "fall in between."[135]

Alternatively, the *halakhot* in the Mishnah can be placed in two categories: (1) "enactments (*takkanot*) and decrees (*gezerot*)" which "have no basis in the Written Law," and (2) "interpretations of the Written Law."[136] Danby describes the development of mishnaic materials as follows:

> The earliest manner of transmitting the [traditional or unwritten] Law was by means of *Midrash*; that is to say, the [traditional or unwritten] Law was taught in the form of an exposition or running commentary on the text of Scripture. . . . At some stage a more direct manner came into use, and the traditional laws . . . were taught and repeated independently of the Scriptural basis which was claimed for them . . . and arranged in whatever manner of grouping was found most convenient.[137]

---

133. Neusner, *Mishnah*, 201. See Cohen, "Judaean Legal Tradition," 123 ("One of the striking features of the Mishnah . . . is its relative independence from the Torah [Pentateuch]").

134. Neusner, *Mishnah*, 202–3.

135. Neusner, *Mishnah*, 203.

136. Wolfson, *Philo*, 1.189. See Moore, *Judaism in the First Centuries*, 1.159 (distinguishing laws based on a "more precise understanding and application of what Scripture enjoined or forbade" from "traditional laws . . . [that] had prescriptive authority independent of Scripture," including *takkanot* and *gezerot*). See also Moore, *Judaism in the First Centuries*, 1.29, 33 (The *takkanot* of Ezra and the authorities of latter generations formed "a body of legislation supplementary to the written law in the Pentateuch"), 258 (*Takkanot* are "ordinances of a positive character" and *gezerot* are "prohibitions").

137. Danby, "Introduction," xix.

THE TANNAIM AND THEIR PREDECESSORS, THE PHARISEES

2. Cases in which the Mishnah refers to Scripture, and the Mishnah's casuistic mode of reasoning.

There do exist cases in which the Mishnah quotes, interprets, or takes up problems found in the Torah. One such case is in the tractate Berakhot (Benedictions) at 1:3, which quotes a portion of Deut 6:4-9. The biblical text begins: "Hear (*Shema*), O'Israel! The Lord is our God, the Lord alone," and it directs the Israelites to "take . . . these instructions" [literally, "these words," probably referring to the Decalogue][138] to heart, and to "recite them . . . when you lie down and when you get up," a possible merism signifying that one should reflect upon the words all the time.[139] During the Second Temple period Deut 6:4-9, together with two other biblical passages and certain benedictions, had become part of an established liturgy referred to as the "*Shema*."[140]

Berakhot 1:3 records a dispute between the house of Shammai and the house of Hillel concerning the recitation of the *Shema*. The dispute hinged on an exegesis of the biblical language in Deut 6, "when you lie down and when you get up." Both groups assumed that the command to recite "these words" was a reference to the *Shema*, but the house of Shammai argued that the biblical language "when you lie down and when you get up" should be understood to mean that when the *Shema* is recited in the evening it should be recited in a reclining position and when it is recited in the morning it should be recited in a standing position. The house of Hillel disagreed, arguing that the biblical language referred not to the position of the reciter but to the time of recitation (that is, that the *Shema* must be recited in the evening, when you lie down, and in the morning, when you get up).[141]

Far more common in the Mishnah than cases like Berakhot 1:3, where there is a direct reference to a biblical passage, are cases where there is only an *indirect* reference to a biblical passage. For example, the tractate Kil'ayim (Diverse Kinds) at 8:1 states that (1) it is forbidden to sow diverse kinds of seed in a vineyard, and it is forbidden to make use of them; (2) it is forbidden to sow diverse kinds of seed (in a field), but

---

138. Levinson, "Deuteronomy," 362.
139. See Levinson, "Deuteronomy," 362.
140. See Idelsohn, *Jewish Liturgy*, 25; Millgram, *Jewish Worship*, 96-97.
141. See Cohen, "Judaean Legal Tradition," 123-24 (commenting that passages like this, directly quoting and interpreting biblical language, "are relatively rare in the Mishnah").

they are permitted as food, and it is permitted to make use of them; and (3) it is permitted to use diverse kinds of garments in all respects, but it is forbidden to wear them. Cohen writes:

> Why do these prohibitions differ so? The Mishnah does not explain, but the answer is obvious—so long as one knows the [biblical] verses that stand behind the Mishnah. The prohibition of sowing two kinds of seed is expressed in identical language for both vineyard and field: *you shall not sow your field with diverse kinds of seed* (Lev 19:19) and *you shall not sow your vineyard with diverse kinds of seed* (Deut 22:9). But only with reference to the vineyard does the Torah add *else the crop . . . and the yield of the vineyard may not be used* (Deut 22:9). Hence, concludes the Mishnah, the yield of mixed seed in a vineyard is prohibited from use, but not the yield of mixed seed in a field. Why the Torah should make such a distinction is not the Mishnah's concern. As to garments, the Torah says *you shall not put on cloth from a mixture of diverse kinds of material* (Lev 19:19) and *you shall not wear cloth combining wool and linen* (Deut 22:11). Hence, concludes the Mishnah, only wearing is prohibited; manufacture and profit are permitted. These mishnaic rulings cannot be understood without knowledge of the verses of the Torah that they tacitly interpret.
>
> The Mishnah is filled with such examples. . . . Other areas of [mishnaic] law, however, have little or no basis in Scripture.[142]

Although many, if not most, of the rules of conduct contained in the Mishnah are like the ones just discussed in that they involve religious practices, not social or commercial human interaction, a substantial number of rules concern civil law—contracts, property, and torts. Here too, rules may be restatements and amplifications of biblical law. A good example of this is the beginning of seder Neziqin in the tractate Bava Qamma. This tractate and the two subsequent tractates in Neziqin deal with various problems arising out of the ownership of property. Bava Qamma focuses on torts (that is, injuries) caused by one's property.[143]

The first paragraph of the first chapter states that there are four main categories of injury: the ox, the pit, the crop-destroying beast, and

---

142. Cohen, "Judaean Legal Tradition," 124–25 (emphasis original). See Greengus, *Laws in the Bible*, 253–56.

143. Bava Metziʾa concerns lost property, guardianship, usury, and the hire of laborers; Bava Batra concerns immovable property. See generally Neusner, *Mishnah*, 64–118 (discussing various chapters in these tractates).

THE TANNAIM AND THEIR PREDECESSORS, THE PHARISEES

the outbreak of fire.[144] This would be an odd classification of injuries if one did not realize that this *halakhah* is based on several biblical laws contained in the Covenant Code. These biblical laws concern liability in four instances: when one's ox gores someone, when one does not cover an open pit, when one lets their livestock loose to graze on another's land, and when one starts a fire.[145] The Mishnah then proceeds to build upon this fourfold classification, deriving a general principle, applying the general principle to new facts and circumstances, and altering the general principle as required by the new facts and circumstances. It also clarifies the biblical laws where necessary.[146]

In that same first paragraph, it is stated that each category of injury is distinct from each other but that they all have in common that it is "in the way of them to [cause] injury and that the care of them falls on thee," so that, if they do in fact cause injury, restitution must be made.[147] Next, implicitly relying on Exod 22:4, it is stated that restitution must be made "with the best of his land."[148] The next paragraph begins a lengthy series of extensive rulings that are developed based on the initial classifications.

First, it is stated that if one is only partially responsible for the injury caused by one's property, one must, nevertheless, make full restitution.[149] It is next stated that assessments of monetary damages must be made in a court of law based on witness testimony from those who are "freemen and Sons of the Covenant."[150] Next, apparently relying on the distinction found in Exod 21:29 and 35 between an ox known to be in the habit of goring and an ox *not* known to have gored, Bava Qamma asserts that

---

144. m. B. Qam. 1:1.

145. See Exod 21:28—22:5. See also Greengus, *Laws in the Bible*, 172–79, 247–53.

146. For example, Rabbi Meir ruled that when evidence has been presented that an ox has caused damage on three separate occasions the ox may be found to be "an attested danger," clarifying the biblical language—"a habitual gorer"—in Exod 21:29. See m. B. Qam. 2:4; Greengus, *Laws in the Bible*, 172n109.

147. m. B. Qam. 1:1.

148. m. B. Qam. 1:1. Exodus 22:4 provides that if a man lets his livestock graze on another's land and the field or vineyard is grazed bare, restitution from the best part of that field must be made. That is, "whatever the quality of the damaged field or crops, the damages are assessed as if they were of the highest quality." Tigay, "Exodus," 147. See generally Greengus, *Laws in the Bible*, 247–51 (interpreting "best of his field" in Exod 22:4 and providing subsequent rabbinic interpretations).

149. m. B. Qam. 1:2.

150. m. B. Qam. 1:3. See Greengus, *Laws in the Bible*, 223 (A slave's servile status and demeaned condition was associated with moral laxity).

there are certain types of injury caused by an animal that the animal's owner is *not* considered to have been forewarned of and certain types of injury that an animal's owner *is* considered to have been forewarned of. In cases in which owners are not considered to have been forewarned they are only responsible for half the damage caused.[151]

The second chapter of Bava Qamma considers several additional kinds of cases in which foreknowledge of potential damage is the issue. One such case concerns a dog jumping off a roof and breaking some vessels; the animal's owner is presumed to have had foreknowledge of the animal's action and is, thus, responsible for full damages.[152] The chapter continues: "If a dog took a cake [that was still hot from baking] and went to a stack of corn and ate the cake and set the stack on fire, its owner must pay full damages for the cake but only half damages for the stack."[153] The rule is presumably due to a belief that one could reasonably foresee that a dog would take a hot cake, but one could not reasonably foresee that after a dog took the cake, it would go to a stack of corn *and* that the cake would be hot enough to set the stack of corn on fire. In essence, this *halakhah* is early precedent for the famous decision of Judge Benjamin Cardozo in the New York Court of Appeals case *Palsgraf v. Long Island Railroad Co.*[154]

Chapter 6 of Bava Qamma considers at greater length cases of damage caused by fire. Among other things, it restates the law of Exod 22:5 (which concerns accidentally letting fire escape onto your neighbor's property which burns the neighbor's sheaves or standing grain) to clarify what is meant in Exod 22:5 by "or the field (itself) is consumed," explaining it "as scorched earth."[155] The same paragraph of Bava Qamma also instructs that if a man sent out something to burn in the hands of a deaf mute, an idiot, or a minor, and the fire that was subsequently started damaged someone else's property, the man is "not culpable by the laws of man, but he is culpable by the laws of Heaven."[156] Greengus

151. m. B. Qam. 1:4.
152. m. B. Qam. 2:3.
153. m. B. Qam. 2:3.
154. 248 N.Y. 339, 162 N.E. 99 (1928). In *Palsgraf* railroad employees were helping a passenger load a package; they dropped the package, it exploded, and the explosion caused a large coin-operated scale to fall on the plaintiff, causing her injury. Cardozo held that the railroad was not liable because the plaintiff's injury was not a reasonably foreseeable harm of aiding a passenger with a package.
155. See Greengus, *Laws in the Bible*, 252 (quoting m. B. Qam. 6:4).
156. m. B. Qam. 6:4. See Greengus, *Laws in the Bible*, 253 (noting that the

notes that this rule "raises the issue of a parent, master, or guardian taking responsibility for actions done by those under their authority or sway, who lacked full legal capacity or mature moral judgment," and it asserts the parent, master, or guardian is not legally responsible.[157] This ruling brings to mind a dispute between the Sadducees and Pharisees recorded in Yadayim 4:7 concerning whether a slave owner may be held responsible for damages caused by their slave. The position of the Sadducees was that the owner is fully liable for the damage, but the Pharisees argued that the owner is not responsible, liability resting only upon the slave who caused the damage.[158]

Yet another instance of the Mishnah's amplification of biblical law is chapter 2 of Bava Metzi'a. The relevant biblical law, Exod 23:4, concerns the return of lost property but is extremely specific and limited. It provides: "When you encounter your enemy's ox or ass wandering you must take it back to him." Deuteronomy 22:1–3 amplified this law by requiring the return of not only lost animals but lost garments and "anything [else] your fellow loses and you find."[159] Deuteronomy 22 also "answers questions that might have arisen in response to the shorter statement of Exod 23:4, such as: what if the animal has strayed far from home? What if the finder doesn't know the owner?"[160] According to Deut 22, if the owner of the lost property "does not live near you or you do not know who he is," you must bring the lost property home with you and hold on to it until it is claimed.[161] Similarly, chapter 2 of Bava Metzi'a answers questions that probably arose in response to Deut 22, such as whether there are any limits on the time that one is required to keep lost property and whether the finder may use the lost property until it can be returned. Chapter 2 of Bava Metzi'a also determines that certain found objects need not be returned, discusses which objects fall into this category, and considers the detail with which a purported owner of any lost property must identify it.[162]

"transmission of fire by using coals, embers, or a torch was . . . common").

157. Greengus, *Laws in the Bible*, 253.

158. m. Yad. 4:7; Greengus, *Laws in the Bible*, 224. See also m. B. Qam. 8:4; Greengus, *Laws in the Bible*, 224–26 (A slave, woman, deaf mute, idiot, and a child are free from liability if they injure others since they do not control assets).

159. Deut 22:3.

160. Greengus, *Laws in the Bible*, 233.

161. Deut 22:2.

162. See generally Greengus, *Laws in the Bible*, 232–35.

These examples of the biblically based rules of civil law contained in the Mishnah illustrate how the Tannaim and their predecessors arrived at the rules of conduct they advocated. Their mode of reasoning is casuistical. In casuistry decisions about proper conduct are *not* arrived at by articulating "eternal, invariable principles, the practical implications of which [are] free of exceptions or qualifications"; rather, decisions are made by paying close attention to "the specific details of particular moral cases and circumstances."[163] This mode of reasoning is still used today. Levi describes the process of contemporary legal reasoning as follows:

> The basic pattern of legal reasoning is reasoning by example. It is reasoning from case to case. It is a three-step process described by the doctrine of precedent in which a proposition descriptive of the first case is made into a rule of law and then applied to a next similar situation. The steps are these: similarity is seen between cases; next the rule of law inherent in the first case is announced; then the rule of law is made applicable to the second case.[164]

Levi further explains that the doctrine of precedent does not mean that general rules, once properly determined, remain unchanged and are then applied in later cases; on the contrary, "rules change from case to case and are remade with each case."[165] Such change, Levi says, is

> the indispensable dynamic quality of the law. It occurs because the scope of a rule of law, and therefore its meaning, depends upon a determination of what facts will be considered similar to those present when the rule was first announced. The finding of similarity or difference is the key step in the legal process.[166]

---

163. Jonsen and Toulmin, *Abuse of Casuistry*, 2 (distinguishing "two very different accounts of ethics and morality," one of which is known traditionally as "casuistry").

164. Levi, *Introduction to Legal Reasoning*, 1–2. Edward Hirsch Levi was dean of the University of Chicago Law School and the first Jewish attorney general of the United States. His father, grandfather, and maternal grandfather were rabbis.

165. Levi, *Introduction to Legal Reasoning*, 2.

166. Levi, *Introduction to Legal Reasoning*, 2.

3. When they interpreted the Torah, the Tannaim used certain recognized rules of interpretation.

In conjunction with their legal reasoning, the Tannaim relied on rules of interpretation which justified certain types of biblical exegesis. Seven rules of biblical interpretation are traditionally accredited to Hillel the Elder. These are (1) *qal ve-homer*, (2) *gezerah shavah*, (3) *binyan av mi-katuv echad*, (4) *binyan av mi-shenei khetuvim*, (5) *kelal u-ferat*, (6) *kayotze bo mi-mekom akhar*, and (7) *davar ha-lamad me-inyano*.[167] Regarding these "hermeneutic norms for juristic deduction and analogy," Moore writes:

> They are obvious principles of interpretation for a divinely revealed law every word of which was significant and authoritative, and had doubtless been thus applied by scholars before [Hillel's] time; but with Hillel they became a method, defining certain ways in which logically valid conclusions in the juristic field are derivable from the written law.[168]

Qal ve-homer (literally, "light and heavy") is an argument *a fortiori*. That is, it is an argument that what is the case in a "lighter" situation will certainly be the case in a "heavier" situation. For example, if it is fatal to drink an ounce of some substance, it follows that it is fatal to drink two ounces of that substance. Hillel used such an argument when the elders of Bathyra asked him if the Passover sacrifice may "override" (that is, be offered on) the Sabbath. The elders acknowledged that other community sacrifices are offered on the Sabbath; thus, *a fortiori*, said Hillel, the Passover offering may be offered on (override) the Sabbath since neglect of the Passover offering is punished more harshly than neglect of any other community sacrifice, presumably suggesting that the Passover offering is heavier or more important than other sacrifices.[169]

Gezerah shavah is an argument from analogy based on congruent biblical expressions. Neusner defines it as "an analogy between two laws established on the basis of the verbal likeness of the texts in which they occur; an argument by analogy."[170] Hillel used this type of argument in

---

167. See ʾAbot R. Nat. 37; t. Sanh. 7:5.

168. Moore, *Judaism in the First Centuries*, 1.77–78.

169. See Neusner, *From Politics to Piety*, 23–24 (quoting t. Pisha 4:13); Alexander, *Textual Sources*, 59 (citing b. Pesaḥ. 66a).

170. Neusner, *From Politics to Piety*, 158. See Alexander, *Textual Sources*, 59 ("An argument that what holds true in one law will hold true in another, on the ground that

further support of his claim that the Passover sacrifice may override the Sabbath. He points out that, concerning the continual offering, Num 28:2 uses the language *be mo'ado* (at its set time) and, concerning the Passover offering, Num 9:3 uses the exact same language (at its set time). Therefore, he argues, just as the continual offering may override the Sabbath, so may the Passover sacrifice override the Sabbath.[171]

Neusner distinguishes *heqqesh* from *gezerah shavah* but both are arguments from analogy. Neusner defines "*heqqesh*" as an "analogy between two laws which rests on a biblical intimation or on a principle common to both; a law derived by analogy."[172] So, since the continual offering and the Passover offering are analogous (both being a community sacrifice), the Passover offering must override the Sabbath because the continual offering overrides the Sabbath.[173]

Binyan av mi-katuv echad is a deduction of a rule or general principle [literally, "the construction of a father"] from *one* biblical verse. It permits deducing from one biblical passage a rule or general principle that is applicable to other biblical passages. *Binyan av mi-shenei khetuvim* is deduction of a rule or general principle from *two* biblical verses.[174] *Kelal u-ferat* (general and specific) is "when a general term or statement is followed by a specific term or statement, the general must be taken to include only what is contained in the specific."[175] *Kayotze bo mi-mekom akhar* is a deduction made from something similar in another passage, and *davar ha-lamad me-inyano* is a deduction made from the total context of a passage.[176]

Rabbi Akiva interpreted the Torah creatively, claiming that "no smallest peculiarity of expression or even spelling is accidental or devoid of significance and evolved certain new hermeneutic rules for the discovery of the meaning thus suggested by the letter."[177] Using his new rules of interpretation, Akiva "found in the written law many things for which theretofore it had been possible only to allege tradition."[178] In op-

---

a certain significant word or phrase occurs in both laws").

171. See Neusner, *From Politics to Piety*, 27–28 (quoting y. Pesaḥ. 6:1); Alexander, *Textual Sources*, 59 (quoting b. Pesaḥ. 66a).

172. Neusner, *From Politics to Piety*, 158.

173. Neusner, *From Politics to Piety*, 27–28 (quoting y. Pesaḥ. 6:1).

174. See Alexander, *Textual Sources*, 59–60.

175. Alexander, *Textual Sources*, 60 (providing examples).

176. See Alexander, *Textual Sources*, 60–61.

177. Moore, *Judaism in the First Centuries*, 1.88.

178. Moore, *Judaism in the First Centuries*, 1.88.

position to Akiva, his contemporary, Rabbi Ishmael, "held that the Torah speaks ordinary language; varieties in the mode of expression of which in common speech no notice would be taken are not to be forced to yield a hidden significance."[179] Ishmael expounded thirteen rules of interpretation prefixed to *Sifra* (the Tannaitic midrash on Leviticus) which overlap with the seven rules of Hillel and which "became the standard principles of juristic hermeneutics."[180] These various rules of interpretation functioned in the Jewish tradition as a logic, constituting the standards required for rational inquiry into the meaning of Scripture.[181]

4. Certain rules promulgated by the Tannaim were intended to "make a fence" around the Torah.

Part of the lawmaking engaged in by the Tannaim entailed enacting rules meant "to guard against any possible infringement of the divine statute."[182] Such guarding against infringement of the Torah was referred to as "making a fence" around it.[183] The very first chapter in the Mishnah is a good example of this practice. It teaches that things which by the letter of the law must be completed before morning must, by rabbinical rule, be done before midnight to "keep a man far from transgression."[184] The explicit prohibition in Deut 4:2 not to add anything to what God has commanded "was easily got over by the exegesis of the schools: in

---

179. Moore, *Judaism in the First Centuries*, 1.88–89.

180. Moore, *Judaism in the First Centuries*, 1.88. See Alexander, *Textual Sources*, 59–61 (citing *Mek. of Rabbi Ishmael*, Pisha 4).

181. See Moore, *Judaism in the First Centuries*, 1.88n4 ("For purposes of homiletic 'improvement' the strict logic of legal deduction is not insisted upon"); Kadushin, *Organic Thinking*, 202–11 (describing the role of logical thinking in the rabbinic tradition and stating that the rabbis "use logical procedures to interpret biblical texts"). See generally MacIntyre, *Whose Justice?*, 7–11 (arguing for "a conception of rational inquiry as embodied in a tradition, a conception according to which the standards of rational justification themselves emerge from and are part of a history").

182. Moore, *Judaism in the First Centuries*, 1.33.

183. See m. 'abot 1:1; Moore, *Judaism in the First Centuries*, 1.259 ("Making a fence" for the law means protecting it "by surrounding it with cautionary rules to halt a man like a danger signal before he gets within breaking distance of the divine statute itself"). But see Goldin, "Ecclesiastes," 141 (suggesting that the expression "making a fence around Torah" originally referred to the preservation of the text of the Torah). See also Przybylski, "Meaning and Significance," 172n47 (arguing that Goldin's opinion as to the original meaning of the expression does not negate the fact that the Tannaim made use of the principle "of setting up a barricade to keep a man far from sin").

184. m. Ber. 1:1. See Moore, *Judaism in the First Centuries*, 1.33.

[Deut 17:11] they found implicit confidence in the courts of each generation and obedience to them prescribed, and they extended the same authority to the decisions and decrees of the rabbinical *bet din*."[185]

5. Mishnaic rules are derived not only from the Torah but from the legal traditions of the ancient Near East, the common practices of Jewish society, and other sources.

As previously noted, in addition to rules of conduct that are derived in some way from the Torah, the Mishnah also contains rules of conduct that have no relationship to the Torah at all. According to Moore:

> The actual content of [the rules] was of diverse origin. Part of it was long established custom for which the schoolmen might seek an explicit or implicit scriptural warrant.... But an important part consisted, as they were well aware, of regulations or prohibitions issued or imposed by those in whom at different times such virtually legislative authority was vested....
>
> When the exigencies of the time seemed to them to demand it, the rabbis in council or individually did not hesitate to suspend or set aside laws in the Pentateuch on their own authority, *without exegetical subterfuges or pretense of Mosaic tradition*.[186]

Cohen identifies five sources of mishnaic rules in addition to the Torah. These sources are the legal traditions of the ancient world, the customary practice of Jewish society, the realia of Jewish institutions, the teachings of priests, and the teachings of pietists and sectarians.[187]

Regarding the first of these sources, Cohen provides examples where the Mishnah uses language or employs practices which have a history that goes back to a time "at least a millennium before the Mishnah" and correspond to "the legal traditions of the ancient Near East."[188] Going beyond these specific examples, Cohen claims that the Mishnah has "numerous parallels and points of intersection with the great law codes of ancient Mesopotamia."[189] Greengus makes the same argument

---

185. Moore, *Judaism in the First Centuries*, 1.259 (citing Sifre Deut. §154; Midrash Tannaim on Deut 17:11).
186. Moore, *Judaism in the First Centuries*, 1.258–59 (emphasis added).
187. Cohen, "Judaean Legal Tradition," 122.
188. Cohen, "Judaean Legal Tradition," 126.
189. Cohen, "Judaean Legal Tradition," 126 (citing Greengus, "Filling Gaps," 149–71).

but more expansively. He says that the Mishnah contains laws that are found in ancient Near Eastern sources but are lacking in the Hebrew Bible; further, he says that such mishnaic laws represent legal practices which existed (and were probably in force) in biblical times, but which "the biblical editors omitted."[190]

One of several such examples provided by Greengus is a law on negligence in an agricultural lease found in Bava Metzi'a. The law describes a situation where, after a man has contracted with another person to cultivate his field, the lessee, through negligence, lets the field lie fallow, breaching his contractual obligation. Bava Metzi'a provides that the damages the lessee must pay the lessor should be based on how much the field "was likely to yield" because in such leases "the lessee customarily stipulated" that damages should be paid according to the field's "best historic yield."[191] An expanded version of the law is contained in the Tosefta. The Tosefta affirms the practice of looking to the historic yield of the field and states that this method represents a better method of calculating damages than looking at yields in neighboring fields.[192] Greengus then discusses at great length provisions in several ancient Near Eastern law codes, including the Code of Hammurabi and the Laws of Urnamma, and in "Old Babylonian lease agreements" dealing with the same situation of negligence in an agricultural lease.[193] He notes that these laws employed "two methods . . . to calculate the penalty for negligence: neighbors' yields for cultivated fields but a fixed payment in produce for land not yet cultivated," and he views the laws in these ancient codes as "supplying a conceptual foundation for the 'best yield' metric that we find in the later Mishnah and Tosefta."[194]

Another example Greengus discusses is the problem of the impact of an unexpected natural disaster on the terms of an agricultural lease.[195] Such an occurrence is viewed in Bava Metzi'a 9:6 as potentially requiring an adjustment of the original agreement. Specifically, if the disaster was suffered by the entire region, "one shall deduct the loss from his agreed rental," but if not suffered by the entire region, "one shall not deduct the loss from his agreed rental." Bava Metzi'a then

---

190. Greengus, *Laws in the Bible*, 240.
191. See m. B. Metṣi'a 9:3; Greengus, *Laws in the Bible*, 240.
192. See t. B. Metṣi'a 9:12; Greengus, *Laws in the Bible*, 240–41.
193. Greengus, *Laws in the Bible*, 241–45.
194. Greengus, *Laws in the Bible*, 242, 244.
195. Greengus, *Laws in the Bible*, 245–46.

adds, "Rabbi Judah said: if he had leased for a fixed sum of money, one shall not deduct the loss in either case."[196] Greengus compares this *halakhah* to a provision dealing with natural disasters and agricultural leases found in Hammurabi Laws §§45–46.[197] Greengus concludes that the "long trail" of continuity between laws attested in the ancient Near Eastern collections and collections of rabbinic law from the second and third centuries CE "supports the postbiblical Jewish claim concerning the existence of ancient 'oral laws' that had been 'handed down' alongside of the written laws of the Pentateuch."[198]

The second source of mishnaic law mentioned by Cohen—common Jewish practices—also merits brief comment. As Cohen puts it, sometimes what the Mishnah prescribes is simply that which was already the practice among everyday people, what Cohen dubbed "common Judaism."[199] For example, "documents discovered in the Judaean desert reveal that most of the stipulations required by the rabbis for a marriage contract were, in fact, standard stipulations in Jewish marriage contracts"; "the divorce formula required by the rabbis for a bill of divorce was in fact the standard formula in Jewish bills of divorce"; and "clauses discussed by the Mishnah in connection with contracts for the sale of land were in fact standard clauses in such contracts."[200] In the realm of ritual, Cohen states that numerous Sabbath practices prescribed in the Mishnah—including to light lamps before the onset of the Sabbath, not to walk more than a prescribed distance from one's home or from the city, to circumcise a baby boy on the eighth day even if that day was the Sabbath, and not to engage in medical or healing activity—were all part of "common Judaism."[201]

---

196. Greengus, *Laws in the Bible*, 245 (quoting m. B. Metṣi'a 9:6).

197. Greengus, *Laws in the Bible*, 246. See also Greengus, *Laws in the Bible*, 202–6 (B. Metzi'a 7:8–10 "fills a gap" in biblical laws concerning animals hired to assist workers, and the mishnaic law corresponds to ancient Mesopotamian laws).

198. Greengus, *Laws in the Bible*, 282.

199. Cohen, "Judaean Legal Tradition," 127–28. See Moore, *Judaism in the First Centuries*, 1.252–53 ("The major part of the native law under which the Jews lived during the centuries of Persian and Greek dominion must have been an unwritten common law, the custom of the community, preserved particularly by the elders or judges before whom cases came.... Thus... there always existed beside the written law a much more extensive and comprehensive body of unwritten law... [the authority for which] was common consent or the prescription of long established usage").

200. Cohen, "Judaean Legal Tradition," 128.

201. Cohen, "Judaean Legal Tradition," 130.

CHAPTER 9

The Tannaim changed biblical law to achieve desirable communal ends and claimed that torah study could control the evil *yetzer*.

THE ETHICAL THEORY THAT best reflects the outlook of the Pharisees and the Tannaim is utilitarianism. This is to say that these groups promoted those moral norms and adopted those moral rules that they deemed to have, based on experience and reason, beneficial consequences for the community. They did not typically say that their moral rules had been divinely revealed or were divine commands. Nor does Josephus report any such claims being made.[1] Only later, in the tractate Avot (added to the Mishnah generations after the Mishnah was first compiled),[2] is the claim explicitly made that all the rules adopted by the Tannaim had been divinely revealed to Moses and orally handed down in an uninterrupted chain of tradition.[3] When that claim is explicitly

---

1. Josephus, *Ant.* 13.10.6 (Josephus says only that they "handed down to the people certain regulations from ancestral succession [that were] not recorded in the law of Moses"). See Hayes, "*Halakhah le-Moshe mi-Sinai*," 67–77 (Although the term *halakhah le-Moshe mi-Sinai* appears in three Tannaitic texts and two toseftan texts, the meaning of the term in such texts (1) differs from its meaning in post-talmudic texts, (2) is unclear, and (3) may be intended only to indicate a tradition of great antiquity); n180 in this chapter.

2. See Neusner, *Mishnah*, 54, 220; n186 in this chapter.

3. See sec. D, 2–3 in this chapter. See generally Neusner, "Rabbinic Traditions," 12–15 ("The picture of Moses' oral formulation and transmission of traditions" was not "certainly held by rabbinic masters" before "ca. AD 150").

made, the justification for adherence to mishnaic rules became a deontological one, the Divine Command Theory. That is, the justification became not the rules' beneficial consequences but their divine origin. The rules were now claimed to be divine commands that Jews had to follow regardless of their consequences.

Nevertheless, it had always been believed that God is omnipotent and just, so it had always been believed that obedience to God's commands necessarily resulted in beneficial consequences—justice required that God reward the righteous and punish the wicked.[4] With increasing individualism, the beneficial consequences of obedience came to be seen as accruing primarily to the individual rather than the community; and with the introduction of the concept of a meaningful afterlife, many people accepted the idea that rewards and punishments would be individually meted out by God in a world to come. To the extent that mishnaic rules were obeyed on account of the supposed postmortem benefits individuals would receive for obedience (and postmortem punishments they would receive for disobedience), the ethical theory justifying the rules became ethical egoism, not the Divine Command Theory.

Before directly considering these issues of ethical theory, this chapter will address the ways in which the Tannaim set aside or altered biblical law and will identify the moral norms and principles the Tannaim and subsequent rabbis deemed to be most important.[5] This chapter will also address the Tannaitic and rabbinic understanding of moral failure. The Tannaim and subsequent rabbis, no less than Jeremiah, Ben Sira, and Philo, were interested in explaining the cause of unrighteous conduct. In brief, they believed that moral failure was caused by what they called the "evil *yetzer*" ("*yetzer*" being the Hebrew word Ben Sira used to refer to human inclinations that had to be controlled for one to obey God's commands),[6] and they claimed that the evil *yetzer* could be controlled through torah study.

---

4. See Sanders, *Paul and Palestinian Judaism*, 117 ("The theme of reward and punishment is ubiquitous in the Tannaitic literature").

5. Viewpoints expressed in the rabbinic literature relied upon in this chapter were not necessarily expressed by the Tannaim since some of the rabbinic literature relied upon postdates the Tannaitic period. Accordingly, when post-Tannaitic literature is relied upon, the views expressed in the literature are said to be those of the "Tannaim and subsequent rabbis" or just the "rabbis."

6. See chapter 5, n150 and accompanying text.

A. Biblical law was set aside or altered to achieve what the Tannaim believed to be desirable ends for the community.

One of the primary reasons that the Tannaim set aside or suspended civil and criminal laws found in the Torah and promulgated rules of conduct not found in the Torah was to achieve what they deemed to be beneficial for society. Such was the case, for instance, with Hillel's *prozbul*. Strict adherence to the relevant biblical law was seen to interfere with lending to the poor and disadvantaged. The *prozbul* was, therefore, deemed to be necessary for "the good order of the world [*tikkun ha-olam*]."[7] Of course, in the case of the *prozbul*, what Hillel deemed to be beneficial for society (lending to the poor and disadvantaged) was something that the biblical legists had themselves deemed to be beneficial for society, and thus morally valued.[8] The issue here was not one of differing moral values but of how to best achieve what both morally valued. According to Fox, this was not always the case; rather, Fox contends, the regulations of the Torah and the Mishnah "often reflect strikingly different value orientations."[9]

Illustrative of Fox's contention are cases in which the Tannaim treated the same rules of scriptural law "in directly opposed ways" in different cases precisely because they were trying to achieve what *they* considered to be "desirable ends."[10] As an example, Fox considers how the biblical laws of evidence are interpreted in the case of *agunah* (the deserted wife) on the one hand, and in the cases of capital crimes on the other hand. The relevant laws of evidence to which Fox refers are those in Deut 17:6 and 19:15. These passages require the testimony of at least two witnesses "to establish a valid body of testimony."[11]

Consequently, since women lacking a valid divorce could remarry only if they proved that their husbands were dead,[12] for an *agunah* to remarry she needed two witnesses to testify that her husband had in fact died. This evidentiary requirement was relaxed by the Tannaim. The tractate Yevamot at 16:7 recounts that when certain men were

---

7. m. Giṭ. 4:3 (Danby translates "for the general good"). See Alexander, "Art, Argument, and Ambiguity," 105 (*Tikkun ha-olam* "refers to a restoration of *social* order" [emphasis original]).

8. See Exod 22:24; Tigay, "Exodus," 149 ("Charitable loans to countryman ... [was] a moral obligation").

9. Fox, "Reflections on the Foundations," 24.

10. Fox, "Reflections on the Foundations," 25.

11. Fox, "Reflections on the Foundations," 25. See Deut 17:6; 19:15.

12. Fox, "Reflections on the Foundations," 25.

killed at Tel Arza, Rabban Gamaliel the Elder permitted their wives to remarry on the evidence of just one witness. Thus, despite some opposition, "the rule was established to [permit] a woman to marry again on the evidence of one witness."[13] Moreover, just one witness was deemed sufficient even if this witness provided only hearsay evidence.[14] Concerning this loosening of the biblical evidentiary requirement in the case of the *agunah*, Fox opines that the Tannaim "could not accept as morally sound a situation in which women would lead lives of permanent solitude only because, based on the rigorous [biblical] rules of evidence, courts were forced to conclude that there was no legally certain knowledge of the death of their husbands."[15]

In sharp contrast to what was done by the Tannaim to *lessen* the evidentiary burden the Pentateuch placed on the *agunah*, the Tannaim *increased* the evidentiary burden the Pentateuch placed on authorities to prove wrongdoing in capital cases. Fox writes:

> The fear of God (literally) was put into the witnesses before they began their testimony. They were to be questioned about every detail, relevant or irrelevant, surrounding the event about which they bore witness. It is recorded that Rabban Yohanan ben-Zakkai once required witnesses in a murder case to give detailed descriptions of the stalks of the figs on the tree near which the murder was alleged to have been committed.[16]

This tightening of evidentiary practices was done to prevent the death penalty from being imposed.[17]

Regarding the different evidentiary requirements in the cases of an *agunah* and one accused of a capital crime, Fox concludes that the biblical laws "reflect a set of [moral] values different from those of the [Tannaim]."[18] Furthermore, he says, the Tannaim "seemed to adjust the

---

13. m. Yebam. 16:7.
14. m. Yebam. 16:7. See Fox, "Reflections on the Foundations," 25.
15. Fox, "Reflections on the Foundations," 25.
16. Fox, "Reflections on the Foundations," 27 (citing m. Sanh. 5:2).
17. Fox, "Reflections on the Foundations," 27. But see Fox, "Reflections on the Foundations," 28n10 ("There were circumstances under which capital punishment was freely imposed even without paying attention to the most elementary procedural safeguards that the Torah sets forth" [citing m. Sanh. 6:4]). See also Greenberg, "Some Postulates," 25–28 (explaining that the abolition of the death penalty for homicide was in accord with the "peculiar inner reason" of the biblical law requiring it, the "uniqueness and supremacy of human life").
18. Fox, "Reflections on the Foundations," 27.

rules and procedures of the law to the values which they were anxious to preserve," and, in the cases of an *agunah* and one accused of a capital crime, "humane concern for persons threatened by tragedy apparently dictated how the rules of evidence would be applied."[19]

A similar humane concern can be seen in changes made to the biblical law of talionic reprisal, *lex talionis*. Leviticus provides that if a man inflicts a permanent injury upon his neighbor, then "as he has done so shall be done to him: fracture for fracture, eye for eye, tooth for tooth."[20] But the Tannaim rejected *lex talionis*, arguing (contrary to the plain reading of the biblical text) "that the option of physical retaliation should never be taken literally, nor could such remedies be made available to an injured victim."[21] Accordingly, the Mishnah takes the position that only monetary compensation is allowed in cases of nonfatal injury. Specifically, it is ruled that one who has injured his fellow man is liable for injury as follows:

> If he blinded his fellow's eye, cut off his hand, or broke his foot, [his fellow] is looked upon as if he [were] a slave to be sold in the market: they [the judges] assess how much he was worth [before the injury] and how much he is worth now [after the injury].[22]

Greengus notes that the Tannaim "may have felt morally justified to reject talionic reprisal" because it is "a cruel form of justice" and because "a victim [is] better off with compensation than with revenge."[23] Balberg argues that the change from retribution to restitution is due to "an utter rejection of the practice of punitive injury,"[24] and also reflects a rejection

19. Fox, "Reflections on the Foundations," 27.

20. Lev 24:19–20. See Exod 21:23–25.

21. Greengus, *Laws in the Bible*, 131. See Balberg, "Pricing Persons," 181–82 ("The revolutionary rabbinic interpretation of the biblical *lex talionis* . . . [converted] the retributive biblical law into a restitutory law"). See generally Daube, *Studies in Biblical Law*, 102–53.

22. m. B. Qam. 8:1. See Balberg, "Pricing Persons," 181–85 (In instituting a system of monetary compensation based on an assessment of an injured person's "particular situation, place in society, and circumstances [specific capabilities and qualities before and after the injury]" the Tannaim were guided "by a premise of fundamental *difference* between individuals" in opposition to the biblical premise of an "essential identicality of all human beings" [emphasis original]).

23. Greengus, *Laws in the Bible*, 132–36. See Rivkin, *Hidden Revolution*, 39–40 (Pharisees were well known for leniency in criminal matters). See also Greengus, *Laws in the Bible*, 158–59; Daube, *Studies in Biblical Law*, 102–53.

24. Balberg, "Pricing Persons," 187.

of the belief that all human beings may be treated as essentially alike.²⁵ The consequences of treating all human beings as essentially alike were seen to be unacceptable because under such treatment individual differences of people due to status, abilities, physical characteristics, qualities, and the like would not be taken into account.²⁶

Then too, the Tannaim and subsequent rabbis limit the reach of Deut 21:18–21 (which subjects a wayward and defiant son to death), "essentially eliminating cases in which the penalty would apply."²⁷ They similarly narrowed the circumstances under which a kidnapper might be subject to the death penalty, contravening the plain meaning of Deut 24:7.²⁸ Again, they eliminated the death penalty for the owner of an ox that is a habitual gorer as is prescribed in Exod 21:29.²⁹ Presumably, the Tannaim and subsequent rabbis considered capital punishment to be inhumane, at least in certain circumstances, and believed that it was in the interests of the community to eliminate capital punishment in such cases.³⁰

Indeed, there are several passages in the Mishnah in which the Tannaim explicitly state that their rulings were being made because, as with Hillel's *prozbul*, they were needed for "the general good" (*tikkun ha-olam*), that is, because they were thought to have beneficial consequences for the community.³¹ So, for example, it is determined in the tractate Gittin that captives should neither be "ransomed for more than their value" nor "helped to escape" as a "precaution for the general good," and Danby explains that the "general good" in these cases is, respectively, the community's interest in not making kidnapping "a lucrative trade," and not causing those who are kidnapped to be "bound in chains."³² Then too, the same passage prohibits, "for the general good,"

---

25. Balberg, "Pricing Persons," 181–85.
26. See Balberg, "Pricing Persons," 184–85, 191–96.
27. Levinson, "Deuteronomy," 394 (citing m. Sanh. 8). See also b. Sanh. 71a; Hayes, *What's Divine*, 314–17.
28. See Greengus, *Laws in the Bible*, 184–87.
29. See b. Sanh. 15b ("One executes for homicide that he himself committed, not for a homicide committed by his ox"). See also Greengus, *Laws in the Bible*, 172–79.
30. See Rivkin, *Hidden Revolution*, 39–40 (Pharisees refrain from inflicting the death penalty on Eleazar due to their principles, "a natural leniency in matters of punishment and an especial regard for the taking of a human life"). See also Greenberg, "Some Postulates," 25–28 (quoted at n17 in this chapter).
31. See m. Giṭ. 4:1–9.
32. m. Giṭ. 4:6. Danby, *Mishnah*, 311nn9–10.

the purchase of scrolls of the law, phylacteries, or mezuzahs from gentiles for more than their fair value, and Danby explains that the "general good" in this case is the community's interest in not encouraging the theft of these items.[33] Indeed, "the Halakha itself [explicitly] ordains that the judge is not obliged to act according to 'the letter of the Law' [in those cases] in which the strict requirement of the Law is not consonant with, and even runs counter to, 'the public weal.'"[34]

B. The Tannaim and subsequent rabbis viewed torah study, *tzedakah, gemilut hasadim*, and repentance as especially important moral norms, and reduced the moral teaching of the Torah to the single principle of loving your neighbor as yourself.

The Tannaim and subsequent rabbis prized essentially the same qualities and conduct as the sages of the Israelite wisdom tradition had prized centuries earlier (viz., those having cooperative value and associated with "righteousness"), but they said that biblical law should be obeyed not because human experience and reason had shown it to be beneficial for the community, but because it had been commanded by God. So, for the Tannaim and subsequent rabbis, proper conduct consisted in obeying God's commandments and wickedness consisted in transgressing God's commandments.[35] Accordingly, they emphasized that one must be devoted to torah study (*talmud torah*) because torah study informed one of that which God had commanded. They also believed that torah study enabled one *to do* that which God had commanded.[36]

Yet, what God commanded you to do included for the Tannaim and subsequent rabbis more than obeying the specific commandments set forth in the Torah. It also included doing acts of *tzedakah* (charity)

---

33. m. Giṭ. 4:6; Danby, *Mishnah*, 311n13.

34. Urbach, *Sages*, 1.330 (citing m. Giṭ. 4:4; t. Ter. 2:1). Cf. Schremer, "'Times to Act,'" 1–10 (discussing the concern for the *consequences* of a ruling in halakhic decision-making).

35. See Moore, *Judaism in the First Centuries*, 1.494 (The righteous man is not "one who is guided by the principles of a rational ethics, but he alone who strives to regulate his whole life by the rules God has given"); Urbach, *Sages*, 1.484nn80–81 and accompanying text; Przybylski, "Meaning and Significance," 148–50.

36. See b. Qidd. 40b ("Study leads to doing").

and deeds of lovingkindness (*gemilut hasadim*).[37] *Gemilut hasadim* are righteous deeds "not explicitly required in the law," such as "visiting the sick, giving shelter to strangers, equipping poor couples at the start of their married life, sharing in the expense of weddings and funerals, consoling mourners, and so on."[38] In a saying attributed to Simon the Just (a high priest in the early third century BCE), *gemilut hasadim*, together with torah study and worship, constitute the three pillars on which the world rests.[39]

Then too, the Tannaim recognized that the entire body of biblical law was extensive, complex, and difficult to master. Therefore, they reduced the moral teaching of biblical law to a single principle—love your neighbor as yourself. Finally, the Tannaim and subsequent rabbis stressed the importance of repentance, recognizing that because it is inherent in human nature to transgress God's commandments, a remedy for transgression is required.[40]

1. For the Tannaim and subsequent rabbis, devotion to torah study is among the most important qualities, and studying the torah among the most important activities.

The Hebrew word "torah" has an extraordinarily wide range of meaning. In the book of Proverbs, where there is no mention of laws or a covenant, "torah" refers to "the teaching of the father, the mother, the sage, and the teacher, or to the counsels of Wisdom itself."[41] In the book of Deuteronomy, torah is understood as teaching and instruction coming from God, which is identified with wisdom.[42] Torah is also identified

---

37. The rabbis understood saintliness (*hasidut*) to consist in imitating the character and conduct of God (*imitatio dei*, in Latin). So, as God "clothed the naked, visited the sick, comforted the mourners, so do thou also." Moore, *Judaism in the First Centuries*, 1.441 (citing b. Soṭah 14a, and relating this idea to *gemilut hasadim*). See also b. Šabb. 133b (as God is gracious and compassionate, so should you be gracious and compassionate). See generally Schechter, *Aspects of Rabbinic Theology*, 199-204; Wolfson, *Philo*, 2.194-96.

38. Eichrodt, *Theology*, 2.347. See n37 in this chapter.

39. m. 'Abot 1:2.

40. See Moore, *Judaism in the First Centuries*, 2.94 (God "did not expect an impossible perfection of creatures in whom he himself implanted the 'evil impulse,' and, therefore... provided repentance as the remedy for their shortcomings").

41. Urbach, *Sages*, 1.287.

42. Daube, *Law and Wisdom*, 171. See 2 Kgs 22:8 (referring to the teaching in

with wisdom in the book of Ezra, but in Ezra the legal aspect of torah "is far more pronounced than in the case of Deuteronomy."[43] A significant development in the meaning of torah occurs in the book of Ben Sira. As Daube sees it, in Deuteronomy and Ezra, "Torah is the wisdom of the Israelites," but in Ben Sira, "wisdom consists in the Torah," and "there is now essentially no wisdom outside the Israelite wisdom, outside the Pentateuch and perhaps other books of the Bible at all."[44] In rabbinic literature, wisdom (*hokhmah*), and thus torah, takes on the meaning of what the rabbis called "*halakhah*"—"a detailed legal or religious rule in the narrowest sense."[45] In fact, for the rabbis, the individual precept or *halakhah* was the basic element of torah.[46]

Urbach asserts that "before the Maccabean Revolt, the word 'Torah' comprised the corpus of precepts, the teaching of the prophets, and the wisdom of the elders," but, at the same time, denoted "the Torah of Moses in all its parts and not just the section treating of the commandments and ordinances."[47] Thereafter, the threefold division of the Hebrew Bible (the Torah [Pentateuch], the Prophets, and the Writings) emerged and the meaning of "torah" in this connection is limited to the Hebrew Bible's first five books, the Pentateuch. Nevertheless, verses from the Prophets and the Writings are also referred to as "torah,"[48] and Schechter quotes a saying that "the Torah is a *triad*, composed of the Pentateuch, Prophets,

---

Deuteronomy as a "*sepher torah*," translated "scroll of the Teaching"). See generally Daube, *Law and Wisdom*, 26–55 (arguing that Deuteronomy is "halfway between legislation and wisdom").

43. Daube, *Law and Wisdom*, 171–72. See Ezra 7:6–25 (referring to a document containing the "Teaching of Moses" (*torat moshe*) and stating that the Persian king Artaxerxes instructed Ezra to govern Israel pursuant to the "Wisdom of thy God" (*hokhmat elahach*)).

44. Daube, *Law and Wisdom*, 172. See also Hogan, "Meanings," 530–32 (discussing the shift in meaning of *torah* from instruction—living in accord with the divinely ordained natural order of things—to law); Urbach, *Sages*, 1.287 (In Ben Sira "the two concepts of Torah—that of Moses and that of Wisdom—are merged into a single idea").

45. Daube, *Law and Wisdom*, 174–77. Daube claims that this usage of *hokhmah* "comes from a Hellenistic setting and is comparable to and in alignment with the Septuagintal use of *nomos*, law, for Torah, for teaching in general." Daube, *Law and Wisdom*, 174.

46. Urbach, *Sages*, 1.315

47. Urbach, *Sages*, 1.287.

48. Urbach, *Sages*, 1.287 (noting that it nevertheless was accepted that "no inference could be drawn concerning Torah laws from statements in the post-Pentateuchal books of the Bible").

and Hagiographa [Writings]."⁴⁹ In short, the Hebrew word "torah," as used by the Tannaim and subsequent rabbis, is ambiguous. Although typically used to refer only to the Pentateuch, "torah" could mean a teaching or an instruction of any kind, including an individual precept or general principle, whether found in the Pentateuch or in other parts of the Hebrew Bible, or even outside the Hebrew Bible.⁵⁰

Although the word "torah" is ambiguous, the Tannaim and subsequent rabbis unambiguously regarded the study of torah (*talmud torah*) "as one of man's primary duties."⁵¹ This emphasis on *talmud torah* was no doubt due to associations the word "torah" had with the commands and laws of God found in the Pentateuch. It was important to act in conformity with God's commands and laws, and acting in conformity with them required one to have knowledge of them.⁵²

But it was believed that *talmud torah* resulted in more than just knowledge of what God required. They believed that it had "practical efficacy, that study implicates conduct, forms character,"⁵³ that knowledge of God's laws and commandments "stimulates the individual to perform the laws and commandments he has learned."⁵⁴ Conversely, for the rab-

---

49. Schechter, *Aspects of Rabbinic Theology*, 121.

50. Schechter, *Aspects of Rabbinic Theology*, 117. See Kadushin, *Organic Thinking*, 141 ("To the Rabbis Torah meant not only definite commandments and laws but also guidance in those varied and innumerable situations in life calling for ethical discrimination. . . . In other words, Torah spelled not only disparate *mitzwot* but general ethics"). See generally Kadushin, *Organic Thinking*, 16-42 (discussing the concept of torah).

51. Kadushin, *Organic Thinking*, 42.

52. See Kadushin, *Organic Thinking*, 69 ("Knowledge of Torah means knowledge of the *mitzwot*—commandments and laws—contained in the Torah"); Moore, *Judaism in the First Centuries*, 1.282 ("Inasmuch as righteousness and wickedness are defined by man's conformity to the divinely revealed norms of character and conduct or disregard of them, the well-being of the individual after death as well as the realization of national hope demanded education in [torah]").

53. Kadushin, *Organic Thinking*, 96.

54. Kadushin, *Organic Thinking*, 69. See also Kadushin, *Organic Thinking*, 75 ("To the Rabbis Torah was *the* character-forming agency. By means of the study of Torah . . . a man not only learns to do what is right but becomes so tempered as to find it natural to do good and to avoid evil" [emphasis original]). Cf. chapter 7, sec. C (describing Philo's view that observance of biblical law enables one to acquire the virtue of temperance). But see Kadushin, *Organic Thinking*, 77-78 ("And yet, ordinary human experience made it equally plain to [the rabbis] that this pragmatic efficacy of Torah is not inevitable. It is not impossible, even, for a man to be learned in the Torah and act the scoundrel").

bis, ignorance of torah resulted in "bad character and evil conduct."[55] It was also believed that the knowledge of torah was efficacious in strengthening one against evil inclinations,[56] and that the study of torah had the power to purify one of any sins committed.[57]

Devotion to *talmud torah* entailed a certain degree of asceticism. Asceticism is not held up as an ideal "for its own sake" but is praised "only because it is a requisite to the intensive study of Torah."[58] The indulging of appetites, for example, was not encouraged because it was thought to result in "a loss of that self-control and self-discipline required by the rigid adherence to an intensive program of study."[59] Then too, the pursuit of excessive pleasure, great wealth, or other worldly things was not encouraged because it meant that less time could be spent in torah study. As Kadushin puts it, "Every purpose, then, behind the rabbinic advocacy of ascetic practices relates to Torah, be it in order to avoid distractions, to strengthen self-control or to dedicate all time and attention to Torah."[60]

Torah study was a cooperative effort which took place in the *bet ha-knesset* (synagogue) or in a *bet ha-midrash* (school), and these two institutions were greatly developed by the Tannaim and subsequent rabbis.[61] The synagogue, which may have had its antecedents "in spontaneous gatherings of Jews in Babylonia and other lands of their exile" as a surrogate for worship in the temple, ultimately "attained an independent position as the seat of a worship of different character, a rational worship without sacrifice or offering."[62] Moreover, "regular instruction in religion [readings from the Pentateuch and "methodological instruction in the Law"] had taken its place as an organic part of worship, and even as its

---

55. Kadushin, *Organic Thinking*, 73. But see Kadushin, *Organic Thinking*, 78 (The rabbis also believed that it was possible for a person without knowledge of torah to act properly).

56. Kadushin, *Organic Thinking*, 70–71. See sec. C in this chapter.

57. Kadushin, *Organic Thinking*, 71–72, 76 ("By studying Torah the one who repents thereby demonstrates a complete change of heart, since he has, as it were, thus embarked on a new career of good conduct").

58. Kadushin, *Organic Thinking*, 53. See also Satlow, "And on Earth," 205 (arguing that the rabbis "saw ascetic praxis as an essential component of *talmud torah*," that for the rabbis "*talmud torah* was the ascetic practice par excellence," and that "*talmud torah* is a perfect example of *askēsis* in the context of late antiquity"). Cf. chapter 7, sec. C.

59. Kadushin, *Organic Thinking*, 54.

60. Kadushin, *Organic Thinking*, 55.

61. See Kadushin, *Organic Thinking*, 60.

62. Moore, *Judaism in the First Centuries*, 1.283–84.

most prominent feature."[63] Organized schools, which emerged in about the second century BCE, were preceded by meetings of *soferim* for study and discussion, "the results of which were sometimes embodied in decisions or in rules promulgated by their authority."[64] The school was frequently adjacent to the synagogue and "ministered to the instruction of the whole educated part of the community," although elementary schools for the education of young boys were also established.[65]

2. The Tannaim and subsequent rabbis considered the doing of *mitzvot*, especially the giving of charity (*tzedakah*), as more important than torah study.

Torah study was important primarily because it was believed that torah study would result in the doing of the commandments (*mitzvot*).[66] Hence, the *doing* of the commandments was viewed as more important than the study of them.[67] Although the rabbis did not differentiate between ethical and ritualistic *mitzvot*, Kadushin argues that the rabbis were aware of "the ethical as such," and that this awareness can be gleaned from the concept of *mitzvah* itself.[68] Indeed, this word *mitzvah*, according to Kadushin, "is employed at times to denote ethical matters only."[69]

As evidence of the rabbis' awareness of "the ethical as such" Kadushin refers to two factors: "an almost rationalistic tendency on the part of the Rabbis to assign [ethical] functions to [ritualistic] *mizvot*,

---

63. Moore, *Judaism in the First Centuries*, 1.284-86.

64. Moore, *Judaism in the First Centuries*, 1.311-13.

65. See Moore, *Judaism in the First Centuries*, 1.314-19. See also Kadushin, *Organic Thinking*, 61-68.

66. See also Kadushin, *Organic Thinking*, 95-96.

67. See m. 'Abot 1:17 ("Not the expounding [of the Law] is the chief thing but the doing [of it]"). Cf. Aristotle, *Eth. nic.* 1103b27-30 ("The purpose of our examination is not to know what virtue is, but to become good"). But see Moore, *Judaism in the First Centuries*, 2.246-47 (discussing the difference of opinion between R. Tarfon, who said that doing is greater than studying, and R. Akiva, who said that studying is greater than doing, and asserting that "the decision was unanimous in [Akiva's] favor, on the ground that 'study leads to doing'" [citing b. Qidd. 40b]). See also Satlow, "And on Earth," 220 ("A famous rabbinic dispute about the precedence of fulfilling the *mitzvot* and studying Torah clearly prefers a combination of the two: they all are part of the same praxis"); Urbach, *Sages*, 1.608-11; Sanders, *Paul and Palestinian Judaism*, 217-19.

68. Kadushin, *Organic Thinking*, 107.

69. Kadushin, *Organic Thinking*, 98-99.

and [to the] tendency ... to make gradations in *miẓvot*."[70] Regarding the first factor, Kadushin asserts that when the rabbis "assign an ethical purpose to a ritualistic *miẓwah* by saying that [it] was given by God in order to serve ends of social and personal betterment, the ritualistic is definitely subordinated to the ethical."[71] Regarding the second factor, Kadushin points to the designation of some *mitzvot* as "grave" and others as "light"; notes that in Seder Eliahu the only *mitzvot* mentioned as "grave" are the acknowledgment of the sovereignty of God and the giving of charity; and claims that the high significance placed on the *mitzvah* of charity[72] shows that the rabbis "were deeply aware of the ethical aspect of life" and "that this awareness was among the dominant factors making for gradations in *miẓwot*."[73]

Kadushin goes on to state that charity is not only a *mitzvah* but an "ethical *Derek Ereẓ*,"[74] an ethical act required of *all* human beings, including those not subject to God's commandments.[75] Acts of charity, he says, "should not be prompted merely by a sense of duty, an uninspired desire to fulfill a *miẓwah*, but should well out of love and tenderness and compassion for those in need."[76]

The Hebrew word translated "charity" is "*tzedakah*."[77] This is the same Hebrew word which, when found in the Hebrew Bible, is translated "righteousness." The rabbis use the word "*tzedakah*," an abstract noun,

---

70. Kadushin, *Organic Thinking*, 107–8. But see m. 'Abot 2:1 ("Be heedful of a light precept as of a weighty one"); Danby, "Introduction," xvii ("Israel's teachers had not the right to determine the relative importance of this or that injunction").

71. Kadushin, *Organic Thinking*, 108–9 (giving as examples the wearing of *tefillin* and Sabbath observance).

72. See Urbach, *Sages*, 1.484 (The Tannaim "indulged in many hyperboles in describing the importance, weighty character, and greatness of charity").

73. Kadushin, *Organic Thinking*, 109–10. See also sec. B, 4 in this chapter.

74. Kadushin, *Organic Thinking*, 131.

75. See Kadushin, *Organic Thinking*, 117–30.

76. Kadushin, *Organic Thinking*, 133. Cf. Kant, *Groundwork*, 60 (An action performed out of a sense of sympathy for others, and not because it is one's duty to help others, has "no genuinely moral worth"); Hume, *Inquiry*, 46–58 ("A concern for others" and for "everything which contributes to the happiness of society" is the principle "which accounts, in great part, for the origin of morality"). See also Daube, *Law and Wisdom*, 89–90 (The *Derek Eretz* treatises of the first few centuries CE "are the true inheritors" of the type of "idealistic wisdom" literature which teaches that one should "do better than required by the mere law").

77. See Przybylski, "Meaning and Significance," 158–59 (The "primary meaning" of *tzedakah* in Tannaitic literature is "almsgiving" and secondary meanings include "showing kindness by giving material benefits").

when they speak of charity in general and the word "*tzedakhot*," the plural, when they speak of specific acts of charity.⁷⁸ Interestingly, the rabbis never use the word "*tzedakah*" in the sense of righteousness "even when it occurs in the biblical verses they quote; to them it still means charity."⁷⁹

In Moore's etymological analysis, the "righteousness" of God is frequently shown in God's vindication of his people "by delivering them from their enemies or from other evils."⁸⁰ "Charity" is the equivalent of righteousness in this sense since the kindness of the giver of charity delivers the recipient of charity from the evil of poverty.⁸¹ Those who give charity are rewarded with life pursuant to the principle of "measure for measure" (as charity saves human life, the charity giver is rewarded with life), and those who have the wherewithal to give charity but don't are punished with death.⁸² In the Talmud, Rav Asi expresses the view that the *mitzvah* of *tzedakah* is equivalent to all the other *mitzvot* combined.⁸³

The rabbis set forth specific rules indicating those to whom priority should be given regarding private charity. First are one's parents; then one's siblings; then the poor members of one's own family; then the poor of one's neighborhood.⁸⁴ However, according to Moore, the biblical laws protecting the poor by means of private charity were inadequate under the conditions which prevailed in the age of the Tannaim.⁸⁵ Accordingly, the relief of the poor "was not left wholly to the benevolence of individuals; the community assumed its obligation to care for those

78. Kadushin, *Organic Thinking*, 131.

79. Kadushin, *Organic Thinking*, 132.

80. Moore, *Judaism in the First Centuries*, 2.171 (citing numerous biblical passages). See also Kadushin, *Organic Thinking*, 132 (Since *tzedakah* in the Bible means "righteousness," Jewish tradition "has looked upon the giving of charity as restoring justice to the poor," but "it is not very helpful to go back to the derivation of the word or to its usage in the Bible"), 135 (The giving of charity is "a manifestation . . . of tenderness and compassion, components of God's attitude toward man that the Rabbis epitomize as [*tzedakah*] . . . God's most distinctive attribute").

81. See Urbach, *Sages*, 1.484 (The name *tzadik* is applied to one who gives charity; such a man "imitates the deeds of his Creator and merits to be called by His name").

82. Kadushin, *Organic Thinking*, 136. Cf. m. Pe'ah 8:9. See Urbach, *Sages*, 1.438-39 ("The Mishna teaches: 'With what measure a man metes out it shall be meted out to him again'"); m. Soṭah 1:7.

83. See b. B. Bat. 9a. See also Wolfson, *Philo*, 2.220 ("Philo's statement that justice and humanity are the leaders among the virtues is probably another way of expressing the same traditional view").

84. See Moore, *Judaism in the First Centuries*, 2.170; Kadushin, *Organic Thinking*, 133-34.

85. Moore, *Judaism in the First Centuries*, 2.163.

permanently or temporarily in need."[86] The particulars of the system, found in the Tosefta, were probably "organized or reorganized under Simeon ben Gamaliel and the scholars who gathered around him in Galilee after the war under Hadrian."[87]

3. Associated with the concept of *tzedakah* is the concept of *gemilut hasadim*.

Yohanan ben Zakkai is attributed with teaching that after the destruction of the Second Temple and the end of animal sacrifice, acts of lovingkindness (*gemilut hasadim*) were to be the means of atonement.[88] The concept of *gemilut hasadim* is associated with the concept of *tzedakah*, the two terms even occurring together "as a stereotype phrase."[89] Moreover, as *tzedakah*, the practice of *gemilut hasadim* "is both an aspect of *Derek Erez* and a *mizwah*."[90] Then too, both terms are linked with the study of torah and "stand for Torah as conduct."[91] Deeds of lovingkindness are described by Kadushin as deeds done on behalf of one's fellow man "that an individual may do which are not specifically set down in any list of commands or duties but which are prompted solely by kindness of heart."[92] Such deeds, he adds, are "necessary for the welfare of others" and are "done out of love and kindness."[93]

---

86. Moore, *Judaism in the First Centuries*, 2.174.

87. Moore, *Judaism in the First Centuries*, 2.174. See Moore, *Judaism in the First Centuries*, 2.174-79 (describing the particulars of the system of public charity).

88. See chapter 8, sec. A, 6. See also Urbach, *Sages*, 1.348 (There exist homilies and sayings from the time of ben Zakkai and his disciples extolling charity and elevating it to the level of the Temple service); m. ʾAbot 1:2 (Deeds of lovingkindness are one of three things that sustain the world).

89. Kadushin, *Organic Thinking*, 131. See also Kadushin, *Organic Thinking*, 138-39 (The two concepts are so closely akin to one another that they may, on occasion, "be joined and act almost in the capacity of a single concept").

90. Kadushin, *Organic Thinking*, 136.

91. Kadushin, *Organic Thinking*, 139.

92. Kadushin, *Organic Thinking*, 137-38 (Deeds of lovingkindness are "not prescribed in detail by law"). See Herford, *Ethics of the Talmud of the Talmud*, 22 (*Gemilut hasadim* "denote unselfish benevolence in the fullest measure, to cover any good that one person can do to another"); Schechter, *Aspects of Rabbinic Theology*, 214 (The concept of *hasidut* (saintliness) developed from such general commandments as the one in Deut 6:18, "do that which is right and good in the sight of the Lord").

93. Kadushin, *Organic Thinking*, 137-38. See also n76 in this chapter and accompanying text; chapter 2, nn110, 113 and accompanying texts.

Moore states that *gemilut hasadim* is "a higher form" of *tzedakah* in that it does more than relieve bodily needs by private almsgiving or contributions to the organized charities of the community.[94] He refers to the following rabbinic teaching as evidence of the superiority of *gemilut hasadim* to *tzedakah*:

> Almsgiving and deeds of lovingkindness are equal to all the commandments of the Law. Almsgiving is exercised toward the living, deeds of lovingkindness toward the living and the dead; almsgiving to the poor, deeds of lovingkindness to the poor and the rich; almsgiving is done with a man's money, deeds of lovingkindness either with his money or personally.[95]

It may reasonably be assumed that both *gemilut hasadim* and *tzedakah* (which include conduct not explicitly commanded by God) were valued by the rabbis in part because they believed that acts of lovingkindness and charity, and qualities of compassion and mercy, were godlike and were required to attain a harmonious, just, and peaceful society.

4. Hillel and Rabbi Akiva reduced the moral teaching of the Torah to a single principle—love your neighbor.

Emphasis on the concepts of *tzedakah* and *gemilut hasadim* indicates a desire on the part of the Tannaim and subsequent rabbis to present the ethical teaching of the Torah and the Mishnah in a way that could be easily grasped by the average person. The biblical commandments are numerous,[96] and the Tannaitic rulings are even more numerous. It is impossible for anyone to be familiar with more than a small number of all the commandments and rulings. One way of dealing with this problem was to focus on the Decalogue (as Philo had done),[97] and, originally, the

---

94. Moore, *Judaism in the First Centuries*, 2.171.

95. Moore, *Judaism in the First Centuries*, 2.171–72.

96. Rabbi Simlai said that 613 precepts were given to Moses, 365 negative commandments and 248 positive commandments. See Urbach, *Sages*, 1.342–43 (quoting b. Mak. 23b).

97. See generally Wolfson, *Philo*, 2.201 ("In rabbinic literature, it is . . . said that the Ten Commandments contain all the laws of the Torah" [citing *Canticles Rab.* 5:14]).

Ten Commandments were emphasized in the Temple by reading them every day.[98] But this practice was ended.[99]

Another way of dealing with the problem was to distinguish certain commandments as being more important than others without regard to whether they were part of the Decalogue, and the "question of the relative value of the commandments found expression in many varied forms."[100] The view that certain commandments were of greater importance than others led to the distinction between "light commandments" and "weighty (or grave) commandments,"[101] but this distinction proved to be ineffective due to disagreement as to the criteria upon which to base the distinction and disagreement as to which commandments were "light" and which were "heavy."[102] Moreover, "we find dicta that proclaim the absolute equality of all the precepts."[103] Judah the Patriarch recognized the distinction between light and weighty commandments but minimized its importance in the following teaching: "And be heedful of a light precept as of a weighty one, for thou knowest not the recompense of reward of each precept; and reckon the loss through [the fulfilling of] a precept against its reward, and the reward [that comes] from transgression against its loss."[104]

---

98. See Urbach, *Sages*, 1.361; Urbach, "Role of the Ten Commandments," 162–67; Cohen, *From the Maccabees*, 60 ("centerpiece of priestly prayer in the temple was the recitation of the Ten Commandments . . . and the Shema").

99. See Urbach, *Sages*, 1.360–62; Urbach, "Role of the Ten Commandments," 168–82; Cohen, *From the Maccabees*, 61.

100. Urbach, *Sages*, 1.345. See generally Schechter, *Aspects of Rabbinic Theology*, 219–41 (asserting that "sin and disobedience are conceived as defiance and rebellion" against God and identifying three primary forms of such rebellion—"three cardinal sins"—which are idolatry, adultery, and shedding of blood); Urbach, *Sages*, 1.351 (The three offenses for which a man was required to give his life rather than transgress are "idolatry, incest, and murder"); Klawans, *Impurity and Sin*, 26 (Idolatry, sexual sins, and bloodshed are the only offenses that in ancient Israel bring about "moral impurity" (an impurity that *morally*—but not *ritually*—defiles the sinner, the land of Israel, and the sanctuary, and "leads to the expulsion of the people from the land of Israel") and are described in the Hebrew Bible as "abominations"), 118–35 (discussing moral impurity in Tannaitic literature).

101. See Wolfson, *Philo*, 2.271.

102. See generally Urbach, *Sages*, 1.345–60.

103. Urbach, *Sages*, 1.345. See Kadushin, *Organic Thinking*, 109–10 (There was a tendency to make gradations in the *mitzvot* by designating some as "grave" and others as "light," but both were "equally obligatory").

104. m. 'Abot 2:1. See Kadushin, *Organic Thinking*, 109.

The efforts of Hillel and Rabbi Akiva to condense all the Torah's ethical commandments to a single principle proved to be a more effective way of reaching the average person than distinguishing light from heavy commandments. The story is told in the Talmud about a pagan who asked Hillel to teach him the whole Torah while he stood on one foot. Hillel responded by saying that the whole Torah can be summed up in the general principle "What is hateful to you do not do to your neighbor."[105] Although Hillel believed that this general principle adequately captured the essence of the Torah's moral teaching, he did not think that grasping the essence removed the need for torah study since he immediately added, "The rest is commentary. Go and study it."[106]

Attributed to Rabbi Akiva is the saying that the most fundamental principle of the Torah is "Love your neighbor as yourself" [Lev 19:18].[107] In his discussion of Lev 19:18, Milgrom states:

> Most commentators (including myself) understand "as yourself" adverbially, modifying the verb: "Love (the good) *for* your fellow as you (love the good for) yourself," shortened to "Love your fellow as yourself." This interpretation is earliest attested in Jub. 30:24: "And among yourselves, my sons, being loving of your brothers as a man loves himself, with each man seeking for his brother what is good for him, and acting together on the earth, and loving each other as themselves."[108]

Milgrom emphasizes that "to love" your neighbor implies not only an emotional state or an attitude "but also deeds."[109] He believes that Akiva was fully justified in characterizing Lev 19:18 as the most fundamental principle of the Torah since it is, arguably, "the ethical summit ... in all

---

105. b. Šabb. 31a. See Milgrom, *Leviticus*, 233–35, 244 (Hillel is relying on Lev 19:18). The principle is also expressed in the apocryphal book of Tobit at 4:15. See Jacobs, "Tobit," 159 ("The negative form of the Golden Rule ... [is also attested] in Egypt, Greece, Rome, India, Persia, and China"). See also Philo, *Hypothetica* 7:6.

106. b. Šabb. 31a.

107. *Sipra Kedoshim* 4:12; *Gen. Rab.* 24:17. See Milgrom, *Leviticus*, 235; Moore, *Judaism in the First Centuries*, 2.85 (When Akiva declared Lev 19:18 "to be the most comprehensive rule in the Law, he was thinking of a rule of moral conduct"). See generally Moore, *Judaism in the First Centuries*, 2.85–88. See also chapter 6, n82 and accompanying text; chapter 10, n11 and accompanying text; chapter 11, nn54–55, nn211–13 and accompanying texts.

108. Milgrom, *Leviticus*, 234 (emphasis original).

109. Milgrom, *Leviticus*, 218, 234.

of Scripture."[110] According to Harvey, one loves their neighbor through acts of lovingkindness in imitation of God's acts of mercy and compassion toward Israel, so that "in *gemilut hasadim*, love of neighbor and *imitatio Dei* overlap."[111]

Still later, Rabbi Simlai, a Palestinian *amora* from the third century CE who claimed that 613 commandments had been given to Moses, said that these 613 had been reduced to eleven by David, to six by Isaiah, to three by Micah, and to one by Habakkuk ("The righteous person shall live by his faith," Hab 2:4).[112] Commenting on Simlai's statement, Urbach said: "It was not the purpose of these reductions to minimize the observance of the detailed mitzvot in which the general principles find expression."[113] The three principles attributed by Simlai to the prophet Micah come from Mic 6:8:

> He has told you, O man, what is good,
> And what the Lord requires of you;
> Only to do justice [*'asot mishpat*]
> And to love goodness [*ahavat hesed*],
> And to walk modestly with your God [or, to walk wisely with your God].[114]

The rabbis understood Micah's admonition "to love goodness" as an allusion to *gemilut hasadim*, doing deeds of lovingkindness.[115] Given that "loving" entails doing deeds, the rabbis' understanding is fully warranted. Micah's didactic saying "is one of the most influential and often quoted sayings in prophetic literature," and "was considered as a possible compendium of all the [*mitzvot*]."[116]

---

110. Milgrom, *Leviticus*, 218. See Schwartz, "Leviticus," 241 (This teaching serves as an "encapsulation of the Torah's ethics and as a blanket command covering all ethical duties not specifically mentioned"). See also Hobbes, *Leviathan*, 130 (The laws of nature "have been contracted into one easy sum . . . and that is *Do not that to another which you would not have done to yourself*" [emphasis original]).

111. Harvey, "Love," 8. See also n37 in this chapter.

112. See b. Mak. 23b–24a; Schechter, *Aspects of Rabbinic Theology*, 138–40; Moore, *Judaism in the First Centuries*, 2.83–84.

113. Urbach, "Role of the Ten Commandments," 175.

114. See Ben Zvi, "Micah," 1203.

115. See b. Mak. 24a.

116. Ben Zvi, "Micah," 1203. Micah's teaching may be seen as combining two principles—justice and love—that some contemporary philosophers see as being in conflict. See Frankena, *Ethics*, 56–59.

5. With the Tannaim, the importance and effectiveness of repentance became more pronounced than it was in ancient Israel.

While the Temple was still standing, sacrifice was the principle means of atonement—it was believed "that all kinds of [animal] sacrifice, public and private, propitiated God and worked the remission of sin."[117] The "sins" that required remission, however, were not primarily moral sins, but "the ignorant or inadvertent transgression of certain religious interdictions, or after childbirth, the restoration of a leper, the completion of a Nazirite's vow—without exception, things which have of themselves no moral quality."[118] Furthermore, the idea of repentance is not found in early biblical narratives. In neither the stories about the flood, the Tower of Babel, nor the people of Sodom is there a call to repent.[119] Similarly, "in the entire account of the [rebellions of the Israelites in the] wilderness there are admonitions against sin and warnings of the infliction of punishment, but no call to repentance."[120] And while a call to repentance appears in the prophetic books,[121] the importance and effectiveness of repentance becomes much more pronounced with the Tannaim.[122]

Indeed, the term for repentance—"*teshuvah*"—is coined by the Tannaim.[123] *Teshuvah* "calls for the abandonment of the way of sin and the inner resolve never to return to it, and not the outward acts that accompany it, such as fasting and prayer."[124] One mishnaic rule even permitted the disregard of what was required by a strict interpretation of property law "in order to encourage sinners to repent, and set right the wrong they

---

117. Moore, *Judaism in the First Centuries*, 1.497.

118. Moore, *Judaism in the First Centuries*, 1.461. See generally Moore, *Judaism in the First Centuries*, 1.497–506 (discussing ritual atonement).

119. Urbach, *Sages*, 1.462.

120. Urbach, *Sages*, 1.462.

121. See, e.g., Ezek 18:21–22.

122. See Urbach, *Sages*, 1.463–64; Cohen, *From the Maccabees*, 89 ("Rabbinic piety lays great store in the efficacy of repentance for the removal of sin and the restoration of favorable relations between God and the individual Jew"). See generally Moore, *Judaism in the First Centuries*, 1.507–34.

123. See Urbach, *Sages*, 1.462; Moore, *Judaism in the First Centuries*, 1.507–8.

124. Urbach, *Sages*, 1.464. See Moore, *Judaism in the First Centuries*, 1.507 (Repentance entails "a change in a man's attitude toward God and in the conduct of life, a religious and moral reformation"); Schechter, *Aspects of Rabbinic Theology*, 334–39 (Repentance requires "a strong determination . . . to break with sin," which "begins in thought" but is "further followed up by words of confession" and by appropriate conduct in the face of the opportunity to commit the same sin).

have committed.... Penitence is judged here to be of such high value in the established Jewish axiology, that it takes precedence over the strict interpretation of the laws of property rights."[125]

Teshuvah is, in fact, so important that the rabbis say it forms "one of the things which preceded creation, as a preliminary condition to the existence of the world."[126] This is because the nature of man was viewed as precluding the possibility of escaping sin, and, therefore, the rabbis reasoned, human existence would be "impossible without the remedy of repentance."[127] Moore puts it this way:

> Righteousness, in the conception of it which Judaism got from the Scriptures, had no suggestion of sinless perfection.... What distinguishes the righteous man who has fallen into sin is his repentance—a remedy which God, in knowledge of man's frailty and foresight of his sin, mercifully created before the world.[128]

C. The Tannaim and subsequent rabbis believed that sin is caused by the evil *yetzer* but that the evil *yetzer* could be controlled through torah study.

The belief that someone can repent and abandon the way of sin entails the belief that human beings have the ability to control their choices. Although for the most part the rabbis believed that human beings *did* have this ability, it could be limited to a greater or lesser degree by what they called the "evil *yetzer*" (the *yetzer ha-rah*). In Ben Sira, as in the Hebrew Bible, *yetzer* "is [no more than] the natural inclination of man,"[129] but the natural inclination of man was often seen to be evil, as

---

125. Fox, " Mishna," 91 (referring to the rule in m. Giṭ.5:5 which permits a person who used a stolen beam in the building of a house but then repented and wanted to make restitution to the owner of the beam to only pay the owner the value of the beam rather than to return the beam as the law of property required; to return the beam the penitent thief would have to dismantle the whole house, and this would discourage repentance).

126. Schechter, *Aspects of Rabbinic Theology*, 313–14.

127. Schechter, *Aspects of Rabbinic Theology*, 314.

128. Moore, *Judaism in the First Centuries*, 1.494-5.

129. Urbach, *Sages*, 1.472. See chapter 5, n150 and accompanying text; Collins, *Jewish Wisdom*, 83 (Recent scholarship "has been consistent in emphasizing the neutrality of the inclination in [Ben Sira], and its conformity to the biblical view," and the inclination in Ben Sira "is not an external, supernatural force"); Rosen-Zvi, "Two Rabbinic Inclinations," 519. See also Schofer, *Making of a Sage*, 57 (*Yetzer* "literally means

in Gen 8:21.[130] According to Collins: "Later, in rabbinic literature, the [*yetzer*] acquires a technical sense and is conceived as [an independent] force that determines behavior."[131]

In the rabbinic development of the term, the *yetzer* was most often referred to as the "evil *yetzer*" and was understood to be a malignant independent force that induces a person to sin—to do what God has prohibited or to fail to do what God has prescribed.[132] Occasionally, the independent force was conceived as being *external* to the human body (at times identified with Satan).[133] But most typically the independent force was conceived as being *internal*, a part of a person from birth, adversely impacting their decision-making.[134] The force was likened to a *"foolish old king* who accompanies man from his earliest youth to his old age" establishing "a certain government over man," and the "main activity" of the force was believed to consist in "seducing and tempting."[135]

Less often, the evil *yetzer* was directly identified with human passions and desires themselves, and, despite using the term "evil" *yetzer*,

---

'formation,' and . . . in some midrashic accounts, it represents the impulses that were placed in humans when God formed (*y.tz.r*) Adam").

130. Genesis 8:21 states that "the devisings of man's mind [or "inclinations of the human heart," "*yetzer lev ha- adam*"] are evil ["*rah*"] from his youth." See also Moore, *Judaism in the First Centuries*, 1.479–80 (citing Gen 6:5). But see Rosen-Zvi, "Two Rabbinic Inclinations," 519n20 (The biblical *yetzer* "is not conceived as *inherently* evil" [emphasis original]).

131. Collins, *Jewish Wisdom*, 82.

132. See Moore, *Judaism in the First Centuries*, 1.479 ("The impulses which prompt a man to do or say or think things contrary to the revealed will of God are comprehensively named *yeṣer ha-ra*"); Schofer, *Making of a Sage*, 85–86 ("Rabbis often present transgressive tendencies as emerging from the *yetzer*"). See generally Rosen-Zvi, "Two Rabbinic Inclinations," 517–20 ("According to the school of R. Akiva, the Torah always speaks to an undefined 'yetzer,' while the school of R. Ishmael specifies 'the evil yetzer'").

133. See Schechter, *Aspects of Rabbinic Theology*, 244, 251–52, 261–63; Urbach, *Sages*, 1.472; Moore, *Judaism in the First Centuries*, 1.492.

134. See Schofer, *Making of a Sage*, 87 (The evil *yetzer* is acquired from one's mother when one is in the womb); Moore, *Judaism in the First Centuries*, 1.481–82 (The evil *yetzer* "is present in the child from the earliest infancy" and is thought of as "maliciously seeking [one's] ruin"). See also Rosen-Zvi, "Two Rabbinic Inclinations," 520 (Although the force for R. Ishmael "is not a natural disposition or a simple embodiment of human desires," it is not an external force but is "an antinomian entity residing within men" which is "inciting them against the Torah"), 522 (Even though the evil *yetzer* resides within men, "it is in no way identical with them"; the *yetzer* influences one's "thoughts and reflections," as well as one's passions, and "cleverly tries to lead man astray" by "cogent legal arguments").

135. Schechter, *Aspects of Rabbinic Theology*, 244, 248, 254 (emphasis original).

it was accepted that human passions and desires could induce a person to do that which is good as well as that which is evil.[136] Indeed, it was said that without passions and desires, without the evil *yetzer*, "a man would neither build a house, nor marry, nor beget children, nor engage in commerce."[137] Human passions and desires "only become evil by the improper use man makes of them."[138] In particular, humans often make improper use of their passions by giving them unchecked rein.[139] Consequently, it was reasoned that opulence, wealth, gluttony, and all other manner of excessive gratifications of human desires needed to be avoided, such excessive gratifications being "auxiliaries to the *Evil Yezer*."[140]

On occasion, the evil *yetzer* was contrasted with the "good *yetzer*" (the "*yetzer ha-tov*"), a countervailing benign force.[141] Both malignant and benign forces were said to reside in the human heart.[142] Schechter writes:

---

136. Moore, *Judaism in the First Centuries*, 1.480, 482–83. See also Satlow, "And on Earth," 216 ("The evil inclination is not truly evil, for humans can avoid its sway"); Rosen-Zvi, "Two Rabbinic Inclinations," 515 (asserting that a "new scholarly consensus" has emerged in which "the evil *yetzer* is mainly a sexual bodily appetite" which is "not truly evil" and "can be tamed"); Urbach, *Sages*, 1.472 (In the teaching of the Tannaim the *yetzer* "sometimes denotes the power of thought, or serves as a synonym for the heart as the source of human desires").

137. Schechter, *Aspects of Rabbinic Theology*, 266–67. See Urbach, *Sages*, 1.474–75; Alexander, "Art, Argument, and Ambiguity," 101 (Some "textual evidence suggests a *positive* appraisal of the Evil Impulse, as the force that leads human beings to *righteous*, as well as sinful, deeds" [emphasis original]). See also Hogan, "4 Ezra," 1612 (quoted at n157 in this chapter).

138. Schechter, *Aspects of Rabbinic Theology*, 267. See Schechter, *Aspects of Rabbinic Theology*, 266–73.

139. Cf. chapter 7, sec. B (discussing Philo's account of *epithumia*).

140. Schechter, *Aspects of Rabbinic Theology*, 277. Cf. chapter 7, sec. C (For Philo it is important to control immoderate desire).

141. See m. Ber. 9:5; Moore, *Judaism in the First Centuries*, 1.483–85; Cohen, *From the Maccabees*, 91 (citing b. Ber. 61a; Qidd. 30b); Rosen-Zvi, "Two Rabbinic Inclinations," 515 ("All scholars, old and new, assume that according to the rabbis, human beings have two *yetzerim* (inclinations) inside of them: good and evil"); Schoffer, "Redaction of Desire," 48 (Chapter 16 of *The Fathers According to Rabbi Nathan* presents "a dualistic picture of competing good and bad forces within the self"). But see Rosen-Zvi, "Two Rabbinic Inclinations," 525 (arguing that the Tannaim posit only a single *yetzer*, and that the "entire Tannaitic corpus affords [but] a single exception to this rule"). See generally Rosen-Zvi, "Two Rabbinic Inclinations," 526–31 (discussing the origin of the "dual-*yetzer*" doctrine); Alexander, "Art, Argument, and Ambiguity," 115–16 (describing Boyarin's view that there were two partially conflicting psychologies within rabbinic culture, one dualistic and one monistic).

142. See Schofer, *Making of a Sage*, 86 ("Some sources locate the *yetzer* in the

> The seat both of the *Evil* and the *Good Yezer* is in the heart, the organ to which all the manifestations of reason and emotion are ascribed in Jewish literature. It is in this heart, with its manifold functions, that the *Evil Yezer* sets up his throne.... Somewhat different is the statement, "Two reins are in man: the one counsels him for good, the other for evil."... "The reins counsel and the heart understands (to decide for action)."[143]

The rabbinic view that the human heart's decision-making is influenced by opposing forces aligns perfectly with Jeremiah's belief that the heart is divided. Jeremiah believed that desires and emotions opposed to what God commanded competed in the heart with desires and emotions in accord with what God commanded. This resulted in moral failure because the desires and emotions opposed to what God commanded overrode those in accord with what God commanded. A person could love their neighbor and desire to adhere to God's command to treat their neighbor fairly, but because their opposing desires and emotions were stronger, they would disobey the command. Their desire for wealth or power or sexual satisfaction would override their desire to treat their neighbor fairly, and their emotions of hate, jealousy, or fear of their neighbor would override their emotions of love and compassion for their neighbor. Accordingly, Jeremiah maintained that moral failure could be prevented only if God gave humanity a new heart, one that was not divided by competing desires and emotions, but which was undivided, integrated, whole, or, as he understood it, circumcised.[144]

The rabbinic analysis of moral failure is essentially the same as Jeremiah's. The force of the evil *yetzer*—on some rabbinic accounts, simply uncontrolled human passions conflicting with righteous conduct—cause the heart to make the wrong decision. According to Rosen-Zvi: "The

---

heart"). Locating the *yetzer* in the heart stems from the biblical notion that the heart is the place of decision-making. See chapter 4, sec. D. Thus, when one has to decide between competing duties, the decision is conceived as being made in the heart. See Schechter, *Aspects of Rabbinic Theology*, 252 (quoting *Exod. Rab.* 36:8).

143. Schechter, *Aspects of Rabbinic Theology*, 255–57 (emphasis original). See Schechter, *Aspects of Rabbinic Theology*, 243. See also Wolfson, *Philo*, 2.230 (The evil *yetzer* and the good *yetzer* "are the rabbinic equivalent of what Greek philosophers call emotion and reason, and sometimes the [evil *yetzer*] is identified with 'desire'"), 279 (In both Greek philosophy and Judaism "it is assumed that in man there is a constant struggle between two motive forces," which in Judaism are called the evil *yetzer* and the good *yetzer*).

144. See chapter 4, sec. D.

yetzer creates a duality and division within the human heart, thus preventing the singularity that is necessary for serving God. One cannot serve the Lord with all his heart when the evil *yetzer* resides in it."[145]

Furthermore, at times the rabbis agreed with Jeremiah that moral failure (unrighteous conduct) could only be avoided by divine intervention.[146] It was said that God created human beings with the evil *yetzer*, so only God could remove it.[147] Thus, with reference to the biblical verse "May I wholeheartedly follow Your laws so that I do not come to grief" (Ps 119:80), the rabbis remark:

> David said, "Master of the world, when I am occupied in Thy Law, allow not the *Evil Yezer* to divide me ... that the *Evil Yezer* may not lead me astray ... *but make my heart one* [*'aseh levi echad*], so that I be occupied in the Torah [wholeheartedly] with soundness (perfection or fulness)."[148]

Notwithstanding the hope expressed in this passage that God would *immediately* integrate the heart (or make it one), it is elsewhere expressed that such divine intervention would not take place until the advent of the Messiah or in "the world to come."[149]

Many rabbinic prayers are like the petition ascribed to David. They adopt the view that the evil *yetzer* is a force that can only be removed by God, and they ask God to do just that. One example is:

> May it be thy will, O my God, and the God of my fathers, that thou breakest the yoke of the *Evil Yezer* and removest him

---

145. Rosen-Zvi, "Two Rabbinic Inclinations," 526. See also Schofer, *Making of a Sage*, 87–90 (referring to the "psychological dualism" of the bad *yetzer*, associated with "innate tendencies to transgress," and the good *yetzer*, associated with "the guidance of the traditional discourse").

146. See, e.g., Schofer, *Making of a Sage*, 103 (One teaching in *'Abot R. Nat.* "states in very strong terms that life is a constant struggle with the bad *yetzer*" and that "only God's eschatological judgment can remove it," and this view "is developed at length elsewhere in rabbinic literature" [citing, inter alia, b. Sukk. 51a–52b]).

147. God's removal of the evil *yetzer* from the heart can be compared to Jeremiah's vision of God's removal of the hardness encasing the heart. See chapter 4, n95.

148. Schechter, *Aspects of Rabbinic Theology*, 278 (emphasis added) (quoting *Exod. Rab.* 19:2).

149. See Schechter, *Aspects of Rabbinic Theology*, 282–83, 290–92; Moore, *Judaism in the First Centuries*, 1.482 ("Only in the world to come will [the evil *yetzer*] be extirpated by God"). See Schofer, *Making of a Sage*, 103–5. See also Alexander, "Art, Argument, and Ambiguity," 117 (R. Hiyya deduces that in the messianic era "only the Good Impulse will remain in the human heart, and so he states, 'the Evil Impulse has no sway in the time to come'" [discussing *Gen. Rab.* 48:11]).

from our hearts; for, thou hast created us to do thy will, and we are duty bound to do thy will. Thou art desirous and we our desirous. But who prevents it? The [evil *yetzer*]. It is revealed and it is known before thee that we have not the strength to resist him; but may it be thy will, O Lord my God . . . that thou wilt remove him from us, subject him, so that we may do thy will as our will, with a perfect heart.[150]

Another example is a prayer repeated several times on the Day of Atonement which alludes to Jeremiah's use of the notion of circumcision to describe the radical change that God had to bring about (altering an uncircumcised heart to a circumcised heart):

Our God and God of our fathers, forgive and pardon our iniquities on this day of Atonement. . . . Subdue our heart to serve thee, and bend our *Yezer* to turn unto thee; renew our reins to observe thy precepts, and circumcise our hearts to love and revere thy Name.[151]

Despite these petitions for divine intervention to remove the evil *yetzer* (viewed as an independent force beyond human control), the rabbis also emphasized a way to minimize the power of the evil *yetzer* which did *not* require divine intervention. This way was through *talmud torah*.[152] An emphasis on engaging in torah study to control the power of the evil *yetzer* is most clearly stated in *Sifre Deuteronomy* §45: "My children, I have created for you the Evil Inclination, (but I have at the same time) created for you the Torah as an antidote. As long as you occupy yourselves with Torah, he shall not have dominion over you."[153] It was believed that "he whose heart is absorbed in the words

---

150. Schechter, *Aspects of Rabbinic Theology*, 265–66 (emphasis original). See Satlow, "And on Earth," 210 (citing y. Ber. 4:2, 7d); Urbach, *Sages*, 1.480–81. See also Schechter, *Aspects of Rabbinic Theology*, 278–80.

151. Schechter, *Aspects of Rabbinic Theology*, 279–80. See Rosen-Zvi, "Two Rabbinic Inclinations," 526 ("The *Sifra* demands a removal of the *yetzer*, using the metaphor of circumcision"). See also chapter 4, n95.

152. See Rosen-Zvi, "Two Rabbinic Inclinations," 524 ("The most popular tool" that the Tannaim advocated "to extricate oneself from the *yetzer*'s wiles and exhortations . . . is Torah study"); Satlow, "And on Earth," 215 ("Torah's true value is as the ultimate weapon in the continuing struggle of the person against his (or her?) evil inclination"); Moore, *Judaism in the First Centuries*, 1.489 ("Most potent antidote for evil impulse is to occupy one's self with the word of God"). Cf. chapter 7, sec. C (Philo sees biblical law as offering a method of promoting *enkrateia* through *askesis*).

153. Urbach, *Sages*, 1.472 (quoting *Sifre Deut.* §45).

of the Torah removes thereby from himself all idle thoughts as well as thoughts insinuated by the *Evil Yezer*."[154]

Alternatively stated, the "new heart" that the rabbis believed was needed for human beings to act righteously (needed to subdue the force of the evil *yetzer*) was identified with "that quality of character" that could be "brought forth, nurtured and developed *only* by the study of Torah."[155] As Kadushin puts it, "To the Rabbis Torah was *the* character-forming agency"; through study of the Torah one "becomes so tempered as to find it natural to do good and to avoid evil."[156] When one is engaged in torah study, the rabbis argued, the influence of the evil *yetzer* is *minimized*—evil thoughts are blocked, and temptations and fears are allayed. The rabbis did not believe, however, that torah study would "uproot the Evil Inclination completely."[157]

Schofer identifies various tropes used by the rabbis to describe the process of ethical transformation ("the transformation of negative impulses") brought about by torah study.[158] Two of these tropes evidence the rabbis' reliance on Jeremiah. The first identifies the evil *yetzer* with stone or metal and describes the Torah as an active force which wears away the stone or metal.[159] This can be compared to Jeremiah's depiction of the heart as encased in a hard substance that must be removed. The second trope describes the transformative process in terms of a warrior conquering competing forces within a city. It compares torah study to "a movement from inner division to unity."[160] As Schofer puts it:

> The sage becomes one, after having experienced two or more forces contending within him....
>
> The self is at conflict with itself, with powerful forces on either side. After great struggle, eventually the stronghold is

---

154. Schechter, *Aspects of Rabbinic Theology*, 274 (emphasis original).

155. Kadushin, *Organic Thinking*, 115 (emphasis added). See also Kadushin, *Organic Thinking*, 69–71.

156. Kadushin, *Organic Thinking*, 75–76 (emphasis original).

157. Urbach, *Sages*, 1.472–73. See also Urbach, *Sages*, 1.475–76; Hogan, "4 Ezra," 1612 ("Torah observance... is understood to be a means of subduing the *yetzer ha-ra*, not eradicating it, because without it there would be no procreation or human striving" [citing b. Qidd. 30b; Sukk. 52a; B. Bat. 16a; *Sifre Deut.* 46]).

158. See Schofer, *Making of a Sage*, 90–103.

159. See Schofer, *Making of a Sage*, 95–96.

160. Schofer, *Making of a Sage*, 98.

brought down, the warrior comes to rule the city, and inner division is overcome.¹⁶¹

This trope captures Jeremiah's recognition that to achieve righteousness competing passions that affect the heart must be integrated or unified, thereby creating a "single [undivided] heart."¹⁶²

In analyzing the concept of *yetzer* in *The Fathers According to Rabbi Nathan* (a rabbinic ethical text that originates during the time of the Tannaim but undergoes substantial development thereafter), Schofer focuses on chapter 16. He concludes that this chapter

> (i) presents a dualistic picture of competing good and bad forces within the self, (ii) holds out the possibility that the negative impulses can be fundamentally transformed, and (iii) portrays this transformation as occurring through the study and practice of Torah, sometimes internalized through the good [*yetzer*]. God's role is twofold: giving the Torah, and showing compassion upon those who are unable to cultivate themselves.¹⁶³

Although chapter 16 holds out the possibility that the "bad forces within the self ... can be fundamentally transformed ... through the study and practice of Torah," certain parts of the chapter suggest an alternative point of view—they maintain that human beings "will never fully succeed in cultivating a righteous character that observes the divine commandments."¹⁶⁴ In these pessimistic parts of the chapter, eternal retribution is avoided only by "divine compassion."¹⁶⁵ *The Fathers According to Rabbi Nathan* also contains a pessimistic view of human transformation

---

161. Schofer, *Making of a Sage*, 98–100.

162. Jer 32:39.

163. Schofer, "Redaction of Desire," 28. The transformation brought about by the study and practice of Torah is analogized to the purification of metal brought about by fire, arguing that "one can re-form one's [*yetzer*] as an artisan shapes metal." Schoffer, "Redaction of Desire," 43–44.

164. Schofer, "Redaction of Desire," 46 (commenting on teaching attributed to Rabbi Simeon b. Yohai). See Schofer, *Making of a Sage*, 97–98 (b. Yohai uses a trope comparing humans to an unproductive piece of land to contend that, no matter how much effort [that is, torah study] they employ, "there are significant limits upon how much people can change themselves"). See also Schofer, "Redaction of Desire," 50–52.

165. Schofer, "Redaction of Desire," 46; Schofer, *Making of a Sage*, 97–98 (b. Yohai interprets the biblical statement that God "knows our formation (*yitzerenu*)" (Ps 103:14) through the construct of the evil *yetzer* to conclude that God knows the nature and power of our evil *yetzer* and that, therefore, God will show compassion, and "the descendants of Israel will not 'ever see the face of Gehenna'").

in a teaching attributed to R. Yose the Galilean. Schofer concludes his discussion of this teaching as follows:

> According to R. Yose, then, the students of the sages must struggle all their lives against the influences of the bad [*yetzer*], with no hope of resolution until the time of judgment. Torah is not sufficient to discipline, re-form, conquer, or govern their aggressive impulses....
>
> We see no sense that one should attempt to change the bad [*yetzer*] ... but rather that there is a constant fight with it until the decisive moment of divine intervention.[166]

Chapter 16 also distinguishes between those who struggle to overcome the force of the evil *yetzer* and those for whom righteous behavior is not a struggle. Specifically, narratives contrast Rabbi Tzadok and Rabbi Akiva, whose control of sexual desire is tested by a Roman general who offered both of them women for the night. Schofer describes the contrast:

> For R. Tzadok, Torah furnishes the direct means through which he eludes his own sexual desire. He fills his heart and mind with the words of tradition, studying all night ... and avoiding visual apprehension of the women. Why is R. Akiva greater than R. Tzadok? He ... does not need to engage in spiritual work to prevent being overcome by sexual desire. In contrast to R. Tzadok, his night is not one of struggle. R Akiva has no desire for the women at all ... [because] he has fully internalized the norms of Torah, such that his most fundamental instincts are channeled through its words.[167]

Schofer observes that the contrast here described is comparable to Aristotle's view—referred to by Schofer as the view in "virtue ethics"—that the man who is merely continent (and struggles to act properly) is distinguishable from the man of true virtue (for whom proper conduct is not a struggle but pleasurable).[168]

---

166. Schofer, "Redaction of Desire," 52. See Schofer, *Making of a Sage*, 103–5 (A teaching attributed to R. Yose is that "life is a constant struggle with the bad *yetzer*" which can be removed only by God's "eschatological judgment").

167. Schofer, "Redaction of Desire," 37–38. See Schofer, *Making of a Sage*, 106–15. See also Schoffer, "Redaction of Desire," 42 (Lesser figures "struggle" to resist temptations "while the greatest exhibit no signs of effort or internal struggle"); Urbach, *Sages*, 1.474 (distinguishing one who transforms "the evil into the good inclination" from one "who fights and refuses to surrender to [it]"). Cf. chapter 7, nn80–81 and accompanying text.

168. Schofer, "Redaction of Desire," 38n61. See Aristotle, *Eth. nic.* 1099a7–21,

Since the evil *yetzer* is extremely difficult to control, the rabbis believed that few human beings are completely righteous;[169] yet, since the evil *yetzer can be* controlled to a certain degree, the rabbis also believed that few human beings are completely wicked. Most people were considered to be *benonim* (middling or average).[170] The Talmud attributes to R. Yose the Galilean (a contemporary of R. Akiva) the view that "the righteous are ruled by the good inclination . . . the wicked are ruled by the evil inclination . . . average people are ruled by both."[171]

D. The ethical theory the Tannaim and their successors used to justify the moral norms and rules of conduct they promulgated changed over time.

Originally, the ethical theory justifying the moral norms and rules of conduct promulgated by the Pharisees and the Tannaim was utilitarianism. That is, the moral norms and rules of conduct were believed to have beneficial consequences for the community as a whole. However, sometime after its compilation, the Mishnah came to be called the "Oral Torah," and was purported to be the word of God revealed to Moses at Mount Sinai and orally handed down in an unbroken chain of tradition stretching from Moses to the disciples of Yohanan ben Zakkai. This "[Oral] Torah-myth," as Neusner calls it,[172] was adopted

---

1102b15–25, 1104b3–11. Cf. Kadushin, *Organic Thinking*, 97 ("Practice of the [*mitzvot*] of the Torah . . . should be accomplished with joy"); Schechter, *Aspects of Rabbinic Theology*, 148–50. See also Schofer, *Making of a Sage*, 111; Wolfson, *Philo*, 2.270 ("In rabbinic literature . . . the moral hero is not he who has extirpated his evil *yeṣer*, but rather he who has brought it under control" [citing m. ʾAbot 4.1; b. Yoma 69b]).

169. See Moore, *Judaism in the First Centuries*, 1.495 ("God was too good, too reasonable, to demand a perfection of which he had created man incapable"); Przybylski, "Meaning and Significance," 148 (The righteous man is not necessarily perfect).

170. Wolfson, *Philo*, 2.272. Cf. Starr, *Toward a History*, 197–98 (Maimonides, discussing "the three classes of persons delineated in rabbinic material," recognized that there are no wholly righteous nor wholly wicked persons).

171. b. Ber. 61b. See Schoffer, "Redaction of Desire," 50; Moore, *Judaism in the First Centuries*, 1.495.

172. Neusner, *Mishnah*, 204; "Rabbinic Traditions," 17. See generally Sigal, *Halakhah of Jesus*, 58 ("Oral transmission was always a means of teaching, but there was also always written transmission preserved in the archives of the academies and extracts recorded in students' notebooks and teachers' materials"), 58n81 ("The prohibition against writing oral torah was relatively late and without formal authority, for it is never mentioned in the Mishnah"); nn187–90 in this chapter and accompanying text.

in response to polemical attacks made by the Essenes and the proto-Christians. Both of these sects charged that the rules of conduct of the Tannaim and their predecessors were man-made and, thus, inferior to and less authoritative than their own rules of conduct which they claimed were divinely inspired.[173] These polemical attacks weakened the authority, power, and prestige of the Tannaim, and the Oral Torah myth was devised to counteract the attacks and, thus, strengthen the Tannaim's authority, power, and prestige.

When the Oral Torah myth was adopted, the ethical theory justifying the mishnaic moral norms and rules of conduct became the deontological theory called the Divine Command Theory. The mishnaic moral norms and rules of conduct were now said to be justified not because of their beneficial consequences for the nation of Israel, but because they constituted the revealed word of God. Or to state the matter more accurately, with the acceptance of the Oral Torah myth *both* utilitarian *and* deontological justifications of mishnaic moral norms and rules of conduct were maintained. This is the case because, despite teaching that one should obey the word of God without regard to consequences, the rabbis persisted in pointing out the beneficial consequences of obeying divine commands, including rabbinic *halakhah*.

Among the reasons offered for obeying God's commands was that God is just, and, accordingly, God rewards those individuals who are obedient and punishes those individuals who are disobedient. Once the masses were motivated to adhere to rabbinic *halakhah* primarily because they believed that, in an afterlife, an individual would be rewarded for obedience and punished for disobedience, the justification of the mishnaic moral norms and rules of conduct came to be, for the masses (if not the rabbis), neither utilitarianism nor the Divine Command Theory, but the theory of ethical egoism. This is to say that the moral norms and rules of conduct were viewed by the masses as justified because of their beneficial consequences for each of them as individuals.

1. The ethical theory justifying the moral norms and rules of conduct of the Tannaim was originally utilitarianism.

In modifying biblical rules of moral conduct and in adopting new rules of moral conduct, the Tannaim were guided by what they perceived to be

---

173. See chapter 11 (discussing the Essenes and the followers of Jesus of Nazareth).

"the good order of the world [*tikkun ha-olam*]."¹⁷⁴ They aimed to achieve beneficial consequences for the community—an orderly, harmonious, and peaceful society—and thus to establish the conditions for a satisfactory human life for the Jewish people.¹⁷⁵ In fact, the Mishnah records rules that explicitly state that they were "enjoined in the interests of peace,"¹⁷⁶ or that they were "instituted for the purpose of reducing conflict and maintaining peaceful and harmonious relationships among Jews and between Jews and gentiles."¹⁷⁷ Further, the Mishnah records rules that intentionally and explicitly circumvent the requirements of biblical law for "the good order of the world."¹⁷⁸ Similarly, biblical rules were circumvented for the purpose of achieving favorable financial consequences for a particular segment of society—farmers—presumably because it was in everyone's interests to assist this segment.¹⁷⁹

Therefore, the ethical theory justifying the rules promulgated by the Tannaim is the teleological (or consequentialist) theory of utilitarianism. Nowhere in the Mishnah is any specific rule justified on the grounds that it was a divine command directly communicated to any rabbi or group of rabbis.¹⁸⁰ Nor is any rule said to be enforced by God. Rather, enforcement

---

174. See sec. A in this chapter; Fox, "Mishna," 89–90 (citing m. Giṭ. 4:2, 5; ʿAbod. Zar. 1:7, and stating that this legislation aims at "protecting the general welfare").

175. According to Neusner, the concerns of Neziqin (the order of the Mishnah most directly dealing with moral rules of conduct) are to prevent "the disorderly rise of one person and fall of another," sustain "the status quo of the economy," and provide for "a system of political institutions to carry out the laws which preserve the balance and steady state of persons." Neusner, *Mishnah*, 16.

176. m. Giṭ. 5:8, 9.

177. Fox, "Mishna," 91.

178. See sec. A in this chapter.

179. See m. Maʿas. Š. 4:4; Tem. 5:1; Fox, "Mishna," 88.

180. See Rivkin, *Hidden Revolution*, 223–24 (The Mishnah does not articulate that its laws are "a direct command from God"), 232; Neusner, *Mishnah*, 202 ("The internal evidence of the Mishnah's sixty-two usable tractates (excluding Abot) . . . in no way suggests that anyone pretended to talk like Moses and write like Moses, claimed to cite and correctly interpret things like Moses had said, or even allege to have had a revelation like that of Moses"). There are, however, a handful of rules found in late Tannaitic material that may seem to be justified as a direct command of God, but probably aren't. See Moore, *Judaism in the First Centuries*, 1.30, 256 (stating that certain rules *from the time of Rabban Gamaliel* or from the school at Yavneh are specifically called a "Mosaic rule of law from Sinai" [emphasis added]); Hayes, "Halakhah le-Moshe mi-Sinai," 67–76 (identifying and discussing the three mishnaic and two toseftan texts in which the concept of *halakhah le-Moshe mi-Sinai* is found). In the mishnaic and toseftan texts identified by Hayes, the concept of a *halakhah le-Moshe mi-Sinai* is "posited as a source of a law, belief or practice whose authority is unstable because that law, belief or practice

was achieved through the power of the state.[181] The Mishnah is not even "interested in showing how its laws are to be attached to, or extracted from, the words of the Torah."[182]

The utilitarian focus of the Tannaim is also evident in the importance the rabbis placed on performing acts which, though not specifically commanded by God, benefited the community as a whole—*gemilut hasadim*—and in the rabbinic teaching that the conduct of each individual impacts the welfare of everyone else in the community.[183] Indeed, it was later taught that a single pious act might serve to maintain the entire world, and a single impious act might have the opposite effect.[184] Because "all Israel are surety one for another," it was deemed obligatory that one protest the commission of any immoral action of which one has knowledge:

> [All Israel are to be] compared to a company sailing in a ship, of whom one took a drill and began to bore a hole under his seat. When his friends protested, he said, "What does this concern you? Is not this place assigned to me?" They answered him, "But will not the water come up through this hole and flood the whole vessel?" Likewise the sin of one endangers the whole community.[185]

---

is exceptional [m. Pe'ah 2.6] or disputed by other Tannaim [m. Yad. 4.3; t. Yad. 2.7; m. 'Ed. 8.7] or by sectarians [t. Sukk. 3.2]." Hayes, "*Halakhah le-Moshe mi-Sinai*," 74. See also n1 in this chapter.

181. See Moore, *Judaism in the First Centuries*, 1.258; Rivkin, *Hidden Revolution*, 215–21, 236, 256.

182. Cohen, "Judean Legal Tradition," 124. See Schremer, "'[T]he[y] Did Not Read,'"124–26 (The *halakhah* encompassed in the tradition of the fathers was not necessarily rooted in the biblical text); chapter 8, nn126–27 and accompanying text.

183. See Schechter, *Aspects of Rabbinic Theology*, 191 (The judgment of heaven "makes the community responsible for the sins of the individual"). See also Schofer, *Making of a Sage*, 141 ("Teachings in *Rabbi Nathan* vary as to whether divine justice addresses specific people or a community or nation as a whole. Rabbinic interpretations of biblical accounts often focus on the latter.... Adam and Eve's transgression ... is a dramatic case in which the acts of individuals bring punishments for many").

184. See Schechter, *Aspects of Rabbinic Theology*, 189–91, 237–40.

185. Schechter, *Aspects of Rabbinic Theology*, 194 (citing *Seder Eliyahu*).

2. In the third century CE, certain of the Tannaim expressly adopted a deontological ethical theory.

In the third century CE, there is a clear change in the ethical theory relied on to justify the mishnaic rules of conduct. At that time, tractate Avot was added to the Mishnah.[186] Avot may be interpreted as stating that the mishnaic rules of conduct had *not* been arrived at by human experience and reasoning but by revelation, suggesting that they had to be obeyed as divine commands. According to a fair reading of Avot, all the mishnaic rules were originally revealed by God to Moses at Mount Sinai and passed down orally in an uninterrupted chain of tradition stretching to the sages whose decisions the Mishnah records.[187] The rules of conduct in this chain of orally transmitted tradition came to be called the "Unwritten (or Oral) Torah" to distinguish them from the rules of conduct found in Scripture, which came to be called the "Written Torah."[188]

---

186. Despite the fact that the tractate Avot is included in the Mishnah, it was actually composed "a generation or two later." Neusner, *Mishnah*, 54. See also Schofer, *Making of a Sage*, 7n15 (Avot "is a late addition to the Mishnah").

187. As discussed in sec. D, 3 in this chapter, the Oral Torah myth was adopted by a minority school of Tannaim in an attempt to legitimize mishnaic rules in light of polemical attacks. Another myth adopted to legitimize mishnaic rules in light of polemical attacks was that the Mishnah was the product of an authoritative *interpretation* of Scripture and, hence, proceeded from God derivatively. See Novick, "Tradition, Scripture, Law, and Authority," 69–70 (One of the responses to polemical attacks by Qumran sectarians that the *halakhah* of the Tannaim was man-made was that such *halakhah* emerges "from the interpretation of Scripture"); Schremer, "'[T]he[y] Did Not Read,'" 124–26 (Scriptural support for *halakhah* began to be emphasized in response to the "returning to the Torah of Moses" revolution initiated by the Qumran sect which emphasized that importance of using only the written text of the Torah to resolve halakhic issues); chapter 11, nn49–50, nn73–77 and accompanying texts. See also Kadushin, *Organic Thinking*, 33–35 (The rabbis claimed that the Bible "contained all [the laws of the Mishnah] implicitly"), 39, 95–96; Milgrom, *Leviticus*, 3 (asserting that the rabbis were certain "that the laws they proposed were not of their invention, but were derivable from Mosaic principles and, as such, connected up to the Bible's core values"). See generally Neusner, *Mishnah*, 204–20 (setting forth two positions that developed *after the Mishnah was published*—one deemed the Mishnah to be "autonomous of Scripture" but having "the same authority as that of Scripture," and the other deemed the Mishnah to be "dependent on Scripture").

188. Although the Pharisees relied upon laws handed down by their ancestors but not recorded in the law of Moses, they did not refer to these traditions as the "Oral Torah" and did not claim that these traditions had been revealed by God to Moses and orally transmitted in an unbroken chain of tradition. See Schiffman, *Halakhah at Qumran*, 20 (Neusner "is certainly right in stating that there is no evidence for oral transmission before Yavneh" [citing Neusner, "Rabbinic Traditions," 3f]); Schiffman, "Qumran and Rabbinic Halakhah," 142–43. In fact, according to Urbach, the term "Oral

Specifically, the tractate Avot states:

> Moses received Torah at Sinai and transmitted it to Joshua; Joshua to the elders; the elders to the prophets; the prophets transmitted it to the Men of the Great Assembly . . . [the high priest] Simeon the Righteous was one of the last of the Men of the Great Assembly . . . Antigonus of Sokho received [Torah] from Simon the Righteous . . . [four more links in the chain are given] . . . Hillel and Shammai received [Torah] from them . . . Rabban Yohanan ben Zakkai received [Torah] from Hillel and Shammai . . . Rabban Yohanan ben Zakkai had five disciples: R. Eliezer b. Hyrcanus, R. Joshua b. Hannaniah [and three others].[189]

Cohen notes that the reference to "Torah" in this excerpt from Avot is ambiguous:

> A minimal definition might be "rabbinic authority," so that Avot is saying that the mishnaic sages have the authority of Moses to teach and to issue legal decisions. . . . Or perhaps "Torah" here should be understood maximally. . . . In this conception, all of mishnaic law—indeed all of rabbinic law as explicated by the talmudic sages of Antiquity, and later by the interpreters and legal codifiers of the Middle Ages—was known to Moses. But whether minimal or maximal, the notion of Torah in Avot seems to adumbrate *the talmudic idea* of *"the Oral Torah,"* according to which Moses at Mount Sinai received two Torahs from God, the Written Torah, what we call the Five Books of Moses, the Pentateuch, Genesis through Deuteronomy, and

---

Torah" (*torah she-be-al-pe*) "first appears" only in the Babylonian Talmud (Šabb. 31a), and although the term is there said to have been used by Shammai, scholars claim that "'later Sages put [the term] into [Shammai's] mouth.'" Urbach, *Sages*, 1.290n19 (quoting J. H. Weiss). See also Novick, "Tradition, Scripture, Law, and Authority," 70 (The notion that there are two Torahs, one written and one oral, "is first attested [in a rabbinic commentary on Leviticus] as an interpretation of Lev 26:46"); Greengus, *Laws in the Bible*, 283n1 (noting other rabbinic texts in which the term "Oral Torah" appears).

189. m. 'Abot 1:1–2:10. See Cohen, "Judean Legal Tradition," 121; Danby, "Introduction," xvii (The "chain of tradition . . . maintains that the authority of those rules, customs, and interpretations which had accumulated [since the time of the Pentateuchal laws] was equal to the authority of those laws" and constitutes an "assertion . . . that side by side with a written code there exists a living tradition with power to interpret the written code, to add to it, and even at times to modify it or ignore it as might be needed in changed circumstances, and to do this authoritatively" [citing m. Sanh. 11:3]). See also t. Sukk. 3:1; Rivkin, *Hidden Revolution*, 152. The concept of a chain of tradition appeared in embryonic form in the mishnaic and toseftan texts in which the concept of *halakhah le-Moshe mi-Sinai* is found. See Hayes, "*Halakhah le-Moshe mi-Sinai*," 74–75.

"the Oral Torah," which supplemented and explicated the Written Torah. According to various passages in the Talmud, the contents of the Mishnah derive from the Oral Torah.¹⁹⁰

Once the contents of the Mishnah came to be understood as the revealed word of God (the "Oral Torah"), and once obedience to its rules came to be justified on the basis that they had been commanded by God, the dominant ethical theory justifying these rules was no longer the teleological theory the Tannaim had originally relied upon; it was now a deontological theory. In other words, the advantageous consequences of the rules for the community were no longer the primary basis on which they were justified. Moreover, unlike the Hellenized Jews of the diaspora, the rabbis never claimed that God's commands were *always* consistent with what human reason and experience determined to be beneficial.¹⁹¹

3. The claim that mishnaic moral rules had been divinely revealed was adopted by a minority school of Tannaim to guard against sectarian polemical attacks claiming that the Tannaitic rules of moral conduct, being merely man-made, lacked legitimacy.

According to Schremer, a "substantial part" of the tractate Avot does not reflect the teaching of "the rabbinic circles in Palestine who produced the Mishnah, but rather reflects the teachings of a different school that was most probably associated with R. Eliezer."¹⁹² In particular, Schremer speculates that the "chain of tradition" passage came from the school of R. Eliezer and "reflects *his* ideological investment in the Sinaitic status of rabbinic tradition," not that of the mainstream rabbinic circles in Yavneh that produced the Mishnah.¹⁹³ According to Schremer, the mainstream rabbinic circles actually rejected the Sinaitic status of Tannaitic rules of

---

190. Cohen, "Judean Legal Tradition," 121–22 (emphasis added). See Rivkin, *Hidden Revolution*, 269.

191. See generally Urbach, *Sages*, 1.290–93; Alexander, *Textual Sources of Judaism*, 17 ("Traditional Judaism" maintains that a *mitzvah* should be obeyed "whether or not we can see a reason for it"). See also Hayes, *What's Divine*, 286 ("For the most part, the rabbis locate the Law's authority in the sovereign will of God and accept the existence of nonrational decrees"). Cf. Hayes, "Halakhah le-Moshe mi-Sinai," 74 (A *halakhah le-Moshe mi-Sinai* was sometimes understood as "absolutely authoritative" and requiring "no logical justification").

192. Schremer, "*Avot* Reconsidered," 297. R. Eliezer ben Hyrcanus was a disciple of R. Yohanan ben Zakkai.

193. Schremer, "*Avot* Reconsidered," 289, 299–300 (emphasis added).

conduct.[194] Moreover, Schremer says, the relevant passage was not composed earlier than the first quarter of the second century.[195]

Most significant for present purposes, the idea that the mishnaic rules of moral conduct had a divine origin was not embraced because of any dissatisfaction with the utilitarian ethical theory underlying those rules. Rather, it was embraced to defend Tannaitic authority against the polemical attacks of the Tannaim's opponents, the Essenes (including the Qumran sectarians) and the proto-Christians.[196] These opponents claimed that the man-made regulations of the "tradition of the fathers" were inferior to their own rules which, purportedly, were divinely inspired.[197] The Essenes even accused the Tannaim and their predecessors of being "akin to idol worshippers because they treat[ed] the commandments of their human leaders with as much or indeed greater respect than the commandments of God."[198] As explained by Alexander, the purpose of the chain of tradition set forth in Avot "was to justify the claims of the Tannaim to be the authentic teachers of the Law, and its presence in the Mishnah serves to validate the Mishnah as a whole."[199] The claim that the

---

194. Schremer, "*Avot* Reconsidered," 311 ("The Yavnean sages ... needed to reject the Eliezeran claim that all of the halakhah has the status of 'Torah,' in order to pursue their grand project of adjusting both the law and the 'tradition of the fathers' to the new circumstances in which they lived").

195. Schremer, "*Avot* Reconsidered," 288 (quoting Halivni, *Mishnah, Midrash, and Gemara*, 47).

196. See Halivni, *Mishnah, Midrash, and Gemara*, 47 (The chain of tradition passage was composed by the disciples of ben Zakkai "for the purpose of strengthening their authority"); Schremer, "*Avot* Reconsidered," 288 (quoting Halivni, *Mishnah, Midrash, and Gemara*, 47); Novick, "Tradition, Scripture, Law, and Authority," 69–70 (Linking the traditions of the fathers to Sinai was a response used by the Pharisees "or their rabbinic successors" to the charge made by Jesus and the Qumran sectarians that "the Pharisees ignore what is properly divine—Scripture—in favor of traditions that do not enjoy explicit divine imprimatur"), 74 (The legal exegesis that arose among the Qumran sectarians "put pressure on the Pharisees and their successors, the rabbis, to justify their extra-scriptural traditions").

197. See chapter 11, sec. A, 2; Novick, "Tradition, Scripture, Law, and Authority," 66–67.

198. Novick, "Tradition, Scripture, Law, and Authority," 67.

199. Alexander, *Textual Sources of Judaism*, 18. See also Moore, *Judaism in the First Centuries*, 1.256 (Certain rules were said to have been given to Moses by God "to give the authentication of immemorial prescription and divine origin to traditional laws for which no biblical support could be adduced"); Neusner, "Rabbinic Traditions," 16–17 ("The claim of Mosaic 'authorship' for the Rabbinic Torah and its authentication by Moses constituted powerful propaganda. . . . The Roman support for the patriarchal-rabbinic government thus was made to seem incidental and unimportant. The authority of the rabbis derived from Moses, not from Rome").

Mishnah was the revealed word of God was also useful to those rabbis seeking to establish the rabbinical movement in Babylonia.[200]

Schremer concludes:

> The ideological claim that rabbinic halakhah is of Sinaitic origin and therefore has a divine status is defensive in its nature. It attempts to "guard" rabbinic teaching from a polemical attack, which purports to debunk its authority by emphasizing its human origin. Such attacks played a pivotal role in the anti-Pharisaic polemic of various sectarian groups of the Second Temple period.[201]

Schremer adds that despite the Yavnean sages' rejection of the Sinaitic origin of the Tannaitic rules of conduct, "the polemical horizon of the Pharisaic age lived on in attenuated form," and, therefore, one can find assertions in rabbinic tradition that rules "were said at Sinai" existing "side by side with the fundamental understanding of the human nature of rabbinic halakhah."[202] Ultimately, the understanding that the Mishnah constituted part of the so-called Oral Torah came to be generally accepted.

4. Although adopting a deontological ethical theory, the rabbis still sought to find reasons for God's commands in terms of their beneficial consequences.

The adoption of a deontological point of view did not stop the rabbis from seeking and finding *reasons* for God's commands in terms of their beneficial consequences.[203] In particular, an effort was made to assign to the ritualistic *mitzvot* reasons related to the end of social betterment.[204] Similarly, a completely deontological theory was precluded by the rabbis' recognition that gentiles as well as Jews were subject to moral obligations

---

200. See generally Neusner, *There We Sat Down*, 51–61. Cf. Hayes, "*Halakhah le-Moshe mi-Sinai*," 96 (The Babylonian Talmud uses the term *halakhah le-Moshe mi-Sinai* "in aggadic passages that explore and legitimize the . . . authority of the rabbis").

201. Schremer, "*Avot* Reconsidered," 310–11. See Schremer, "'[T]he[y] Did Not Read,'" 105–26; chapter 11, secs. A, 2 (discussing the polemical attack of the Essenes), and B, 2 (discussing the polemical attack of Jesus).

202. Schremer, "*Avot* Reconsidered," 311.

203. See Urbach, *Sages*, 1.365–99. See also Kadushin, *Organic Thinking*, 108–9.

204. See, sec. B, 2 in this chapter.

that were not divinely revealed in the Written Torah or the Oral Torah—the demands of an "ethical *Derek Erez*."²⁰⁵

The persistence of a teleological outlook underlying God's commands is highlighted by the fact that, in explaining the contradiction between Exod 20:5 and Deut 24:16, the rabbis postulated that Moses pointed out to God the deleterious *consequences* of visiting the sins of the father upon their children.²⁰⁶ Nevertheless, the ascertainment of a reason for a commandment was not a necessary condition for obedience to it.²⁰⁷ When no reason or utilitarian explanation could be found for a divine commandment, it still had to be obeyed.²⁰⁸

5. Since God's justice required that righteous individuals be rewarded and wicked individuals be punished, the masses were led to effectively accept the ethical theory of ethical egoism.

While emphasizing that rabbinic law is justified not teleologically but deontologically as divine commands, the rabbis, nevertheless, stressed the biblical conception that there is a moral order in the world and that a just and all-powerful God necessarily rewards those who obey divine commands and punishes those who transgress them.²⁰⁹ Indeed, one of

---

205. See Kadushin, *Organic Thinking*, 241; sec. B, 2 in this chapter..

206. See Schechter, *Aspects of Rabbinic Theology*, 185–87 (quoting *Num. Rab.* 19:33). See also n34 in this chapter. The appeal to consequences also suggests a standard of what is good or just other than that it is commanded by God. Cf. chapter 5, sec. A.

207. Urbach, *Sages*, 1.388. Cf. Eichrodt, *Theology*, 376 ("Where absolute command constitutes the fundamental basis of human living, something beyond the scope of discussion, the moral requirement cannot be justified by any calculations of results or considerations of expediency").

208. Urbach, *Sages*, 1.311 (citing opinion ascribed to R. Yohanan b. Zakkai). See also Urbach, *Sages*, 1.98–99, 377 (ben Zakkai purportedly "preferred not to search for reasons for the red heifer," claiming it is simply a decree of God). Cf. Fox, "Reflections on the Foundations," 28–29 (Fox contrasts Maimonides and Mendelssohn. Maimonides never confuses understanding the reasons for the commandments, in terms of their social utility, with a justification for accepting them—they are accepted only because "God is their source"; however, Mendelssohn argues that ethical principles are known to all men "through the independent operation of human reason").

209. See m. Qidd. 4:14; Moore, *Judaism in the First Centuries*, 2.89–90 (The rabbis "do not scruple" to appeal to reward and punishment as the motives for moral conduct); Sanders, *Paul and Palestinian Judaism*, 117–18. See generally Schofer, *Making of a Sage*, 121–65 (discussing divine reward and punishment in *'Abot R. Nat.* and noting that many passages depict a causal connection between an act and a consequence with no explicit mention of divine activity, indicating that "God's judgment includes and

the primary explanations given as the reason for the commandments was "that of reward."[210] Belief in reward and punishment is enshrined in the mishnaic principle of "measure for measure."[211] The Tannaim taught that specific afflictions suffered by an individual were the result of specific divine commands which that individual had transgressed, "measure for measure." For example, they taught that if a woman transgressed the laws of menstruation, that woman would be punished by dying in childbirth.[212] The principle of measure for measure was applied to an individual's adherence to or transgression of the moral norm of *tzedakah*,[213] and was applied collectively to the world for seven classes of transgressions.[214]

According to Kadushin, rewards and punishments were to be received primarily in this life, as is expressed in the Hebrew Bible, not in an afterlife, and included the reward of material well-being.[215] But Kadushin ignores the fact that once the problem of moral evil could no longer be explained away (that is, after beliefs in collective and intergenerational reward and punishment were abandoned, and after the persecutions of Antiochus IV and Hadrian), the notion of an individuated reward and punishment meted out in an afterlife (to a resurrected body or an immortal soul) came to be widely accepted as necessary to confirm God's power and justice.[216] Indeed, according to Rivkin, the "non-Pentateuchal dogma of the world

---

subsumes a natural causality" which is part of the moral order inherent in the world).

210. Urbach, *Sages*, 1.366.
211. See Sanders, *Paul and Palestinian Judaism*, 119.
212. m. Šabb. 2:6. See Urbach, *Sages*, 1.437.
213. See n82 in this chapter and accompanying text.
214. m. 'Abot 5:8. See Urbach, *Sages*, 1.438.
215. See Kadushin, *Organic Thinking*, 82–94, 111. See also Urbach, *Sages*, 1.440 (The belief in reward and punishment in this life "was so widespread and had so many adherents that it could not be ignored even by those Sages who personally were inclined to transfer the entire subject of reward and punishment to the hereafter, or who had reached the conclusion that the precept was its own reward and transgression its own punishment").
216. See Starr, *Toward a History*, 119 ("Rabbinic material is replete with references to obedience to Torah as a means of achieving a reward after death"); Sanders, *Paul and Palestinian Judaism*, 125 ("With the combination of belief in the resurrection and the observation of the suffering of the righteous in this world, especially between 70 and 135 CE . . . the view arose that the righteous would be rewarded and the wicked punished in the world to come"); Rivkin, *Hidden Revolution*, 229–31, 296–303; m. 'Abot 6:4 (*Talmud torah* advocated as a means to achieving not only happiness in this world but well-being in the world to come); Schofer, *Making of a Sage*, 126 ("God's punishment is not only in this world but also in the world to come"), 132–33, 140. See generally Starr, *Toward a History*, 33–122.

to come and resurrection is a core teaching of the Mishnah . . . [and] the cornerstone of the entire *halakhah* system."[217] An individuated reward and punishment was spurred on by the individualism fostered by changing political, economic, and social circumstances.[218]

To the extent that Jews adhered to mishnaic rules primarily because they desired a postmortem individual reward, and/or feared a postmortem individual punishment, they adopted the ethical theory of ethical egoism.[219] But here it may be useful to refer to a distinction made by Frankena. Frankena distinguishes between a *justification* for a moral point of view and a *motivation* for doing what is morally right.[220] Since Frankena asserts that one is taking the moral point of view only if, among other things, "one is not being egoistic" and "one considers the good of everyone alike," for Frankena a moral position can never be justified by its being in one's own self-interest.[221] When one says they are doing some act because it is in their own self-interest, on Frankena's view, one cannot be offering a valid justification for their conduct but only a motivation for it. Leaving the merit of Frankena's view aside, it is possible to argue that when the rabbis assert that individuals will be rewarded (in this life or an afterlife) for obeying God's commands and punished for transgressing them, they are only offering a *motivation* for adherence to the Torah, not a *justification* for it.[222] The justification remained that God had commanded it.

217. Rivkin, *Hidden Revolution*, 230.

218. See Rivkin, "Pharisaism," 35-51; Rivkin, *Hidden Revolution*, 206-7, 244; Moore, *Judaism in the First Centuries*, 1.113-14, 119-21, 501-2; Sanders, *Paul and Palestinian Judaism*, 237; chapter 5, sec. B. Individualism is reflected in the teaching that one cannot rely on the merit of one's ancestors to "diminish the extent of [one's own] responsibility." Urbach, *Sages*, 1.258. See generally Schechter, *Aspects of Rabbinic Theology*, 170-98.

219. See Schofer, *Making of a Sage*, 147 ("At one level, the dual system of rewards and punishments appeals to a fairly simple psychology of self-interest centered upon desire and fear. Rabbis link this self-interest to norms for right action"). Cf. chapter 5, sec. A. See generally Starr, *Toward a History*, 104-9.

220. See Frankena, *Ethics*, 95-116. See also Daube, *Law and Wisdom*, 56-65 (distinguishing "authentication or legitimation" and "motivation" in biblical law and wisdom literature).

221. Frankena, *Ethics*, 113.

222. See Wolfson, *Philo*, 2.287 (When the rabbis say "that man should not serve God in expectation of receiving a reward . . . what they mean thereby is that, even though a reward, in some form, is sure to come, still one should not serve God in expectation of any reward"). See also m. Sanh. 10:1 ("All Israel has a share in the world to come," implying that members of the covenant community do not "earn" their

Arguably, something like this is what the rabbis had in mind. As Sanders says:

> Although the Rabbis emphasize repeatedly that the commandments carry rewards (or punishments for non-fulfilment), they also warn against fulfilling the commandments *in order to* earn payment. Rather, one should perform the required commandments without ulterior motive and because they are themselves [intrinsically] good ("for their own sake") or from love of God ("for the sake of Heaven").[223]

In support of this statement Sanders cites the teaching "Let all thy deeds be done for the sake of Heaven," attributed to R. Jose, and the teaching "Do the commandments (only) for the sake of doing them [and] speak of them for their own sake (alone)," attributed to R. Eleazar b. R. Zadok.[224] Schechter discusses this topic under the concept of "*Lishmah*," by which is understood "the performance of the Law for its own sake, or rather for the sake of him who wrought (commanded) it, excluding all worldly intentions."[225] According to Schechter, the subject of *Lishmah* played "a very prominent part" in rabbinic literature.[226]

Yet Schechter admits that while "the more refined and nobler minds in Israel" may have been able "to dispense utterly with the motives of reward and punishment . . . these lower motives may have served as

---

postmortem reward by good works).

223. Sanders, *Paul and Palestinian Judaism*, 120 (emphasis original). See m. ʾAbot 1:3 ("Be not like servants who serve their master for the sake of receiving a reward"); b. Roš. Haš. 17a; Pesaḥ. 50b. See generally Urbach, *Sages*, 1.400–19 (distinguishing fear of God due to reverence from fear of God on account of reward and punishment). See also Wolfson, *Philo*, 2.286–88.

224. Sanders, *Paul and Palestinian Judaism*, 120 (citing m. ʾAbot 2:12; *Sifre Deut.* §48). See Moore, *Judaism in the First Centuries*, 2.95–97.

225. Schechter, *Aspects of Rabbinic Theology*, 159–69. See Moore, *Judaism in the First Centuries*, 2.98; Hayes, *What's Divine*, 160–62.

226. Schechter, *Aspects of Rabbinic Theology*, 159. See Moore, *Judaism in the First Centuries*, 2.96 ("That the law of God and every commandment in it should be kept 'for its own sake,' not for any advantage to be gained by it among men or with God, is frequently emphasized"). See also Schofer, *Making of a Sage*, 154–60 ("Rabbi Nathan stakes out a middle ground regarding the role of self-interest in ideal motivation. The editors . . . soften Antigonus of Sokho's claim that one should not act for any reward, maintaining that one should not act based on desire for reward in this world, but also implying that it is acceptable to maintain a limited and deferred self-interest, in which hopes for [reward] are postponed until the next world. In this context, the notion of 'the world to come' is . . . a motivational concept that influences desire").

concurrent incentives to a majority of believers."[227] Indeed, it seems likely that these so-called "lower motives" provided the "majority of believers" with their primary basis for adhering to the Torah. In this regard, it should be noted that the *Shema* prayer, which goes back to the Second Temple period, and which was recited by worshipers at least twice a day, includes the language of Deut 11:13–21, which emphasizes the rewards and punishments which will be divinely granted for, respectively, obedience to or transgression of God's commands. With such constant emphasis on reward and punishment, it may reasonably be supposed that for most believers it was the consequences of obedience and disobedience, reward and punishment, which justified adherence to the Torah, not the belief that the commandments were God-given.[228]

---

227. Schechter, *Aspects of Rabbinic Theology*, 169. See Moore, *Judaism in the First Centuries*, 2.89.

228. See Maimonides, *Commentary on Tractate Sanhedrin*, 139 (Commenting on the Mishnah's promise of reward in m. Sanh. 10:1, Maimonides opines that "the Sages ... knew that this matter (of serving God out of love) is extremely difficult.... Therefore, in order to strengthen the faith of the masses [that is, in order that masses obey the commandments], the Sages permitted them to perform meritorious acts with the hope of reward, and to avoid doing evil things out of fear of punishment"); Moore, *Judaism in the First Centuries*, 2.89 ("Reward and punishment are the motives to which the mass of mankind is most amenable").

CHAPTER 10

Jewish apocalyptic works emphasized the influence of demonic forces on human conduct, the irremediable evil nature of human beings, the need for the righteous to separate themselves from the wicked, the promise of an individual reward and punishment, and the transformation of human nature at an end time.

THE MISHNAH AND OTHER Tannaitic texts are not the only Jewish texts relevant to law, morality, human nature, and ethical theory being composed in Judea during the Second Temple period. Among these other texts are those classified as apocalypse. An apocalypse "is a literary work that has an angel or some inspired worthy revealing a secret or unraveling a mystery."[1] The origin of this literary device (the revelation of hidden knowledge) is found in a passage in Deuteronomy. In describing the law as divine wisdom revealed by God to Israel, Deuteronomy claimed that there was a portion of divine wisdom, an esoteric knowledge, which

---

1. Cohen, *From the Maccabees*, 187. See also Blenkinsopp, *Wisdom and Law*, 173 (An apocalypse "treats of mysteries, concerned primarily with the course of the future and supramundane world, as revealed by God to chosen intermediaries"); Fried, "4 Ezra," 345 (An apocalypse "is a revelation to a human form from an otherworldly being, one who describes supernatural worlds, some that exist currently and some that will exist only in the future"); Collins, *Apocalypse, Prophecy, and Pseudepigraphy* 1–22 (discussing definitions of the genre of apocalypse).

God kept hidden.² The writers of apocalyptic tracts claimed to be privy to this hidden portion of divine wisdom.³

In pre-Maccabean times the secrets and mysteries that such writers claimed had been revealed to them related to natural phenomena.⁴ But then, in response to the subjugation of the Jewish people by foreign powers, the persecution of Jewish practices by Antiochus IV, and the destruction of the Second Temple, the content of apocalypses shifted to dealing with "the secrets of history and eschatology."⁵ The mysteries unraveled now explained the existence of evil in the world and the domination of Jews by gentiles; and the secrets revealed now included the advent of a future time when righteousness would triumph over evil and the Jewish people (or righteous Jews) would be rewarded, and all others would be destroyed.⁶ This chapter will discuss four apocalyptic works: 1 Enoch, Jubilees, the biblical book of Daniel, and 4 Ezra.⁷

None of these works, except to some extent Jubilees, discuss modifying and extending biblical law to meet present-day challenges, developing new rules of conduct, or improving the general welfare and material well-being of the Jewish community. This is because their authors were not primarily concerned with regulating life in this world. Rather, they sought to describe a future world, expected to be imminently created by God, which would be radically better than this world.⁸ Regarding the future world envisioned by these authors, Cohen writes: "The end time is not merely some undetermined day in the future, as the prophets had said, but is the end of history itself, the end of normal existence. It is a new creation in which evil has no place."⁹

---

2. Blenkinsopp, *Wisdom and Law*, 152 (citing Deut 29:29, "The secret things belong to Yahweh"; 30:11–14).

3. Blenkinsopp, *Wisdom and Law*, 153.

4. Cohen, *From the Maccabees*, 187.

5. Cohen, *From the Maccabees*, 187.

6. See generally Moore, *Judaism in the First Centuries*, 2.323–95 (discussing messianic expectations and eschatology in the Judaism of the Second Temple period); Cohen, *From the Maccabees*, 92–97 (same).

7. Collins says that Jubilees is a hybrid work, only partially apocalyptic. See Collins, *Apocalypse, Prophecy, and Pseudepigraphy* 89–107 (discussing the genre of Jubilees).

8. See generally Saldarini, "Apocalyptic and Rabbinic Literature," 353 ("The Pharisees taught halakah to consecrate and guide people's daily lives . . . and apocalyptic books had a different purpose and tended to undermine the Pharisees' whole position") (citing Herford and Zeitlin).

9. Cohen, *From the Maccabees*, 96.

Although having a different temporal focus than the prophets, the apocalyptic authors valued the same qualities and conduct as the prophets—qualities and conduct having cooperative value.[10] The apocalyptic authors praised righteousness (associated with adhering to God's laws) and they condemned wickedness (associated with transgressing God's laws). And although they did not dwell on describing the content of God's law, or developing new law, they agreed with the Tannaim (and others) that the essence of God's moral commands had to do with loving your neighbor as yourself.[11]

The authors of these works also agreed with the Tannaim that the cause of human wickedness was a hardened or uncircumcised heart, a heart that was divided or defective. But in regard to other matters, including how a heart becomes defective and how a defective heart could be cured, the authors of these texts diverged from Tannaitic thought. In discussing 1 Enoch, Jubilees, Daniel, and 4 Ezra, five ways in which the thought of apocalyptic authors differed from Tannaitic thought will become clear.

First, most apocalyptic texts are more resolute than Tannaitic sources in attributing the hardening of the human heart (and human wickedness) to demonic forces. This outlook stemmed from a dualistic worldview which saw the distinction between good and evil as part of the basic structure of the cosmos.[12] According to Brand, "Dualism . . . is particularly prominent in apocalypses . . . where evil is attributed to demonic forces that conflict with the will of God."[13] The authors of these apocalypses saw gentiles as being entirely ruled and controlled by demonic forces, and thus as completely wicked. Although it was claimed that Jews were ruled *solely* by God, and thus capable of righteousness,

---

10. See generally Davies, *Christian Origins*, 19–30 (arguing that there was no "sharp separation of Apocalyptic from Pharisaism," and that "in its attitude to the Torah Apocalyptic was at one with Pharisaism"); Saldarini, "Apocalyptic and Rabbinic Literature," 354 ("We must not assume that sharp lines defined various groups"); Kirschner, "Apocalyptic and Rabbinic Responses," 31 ("Apocalyptic and rabbinic speculations often coincide in content," and it "is now widely assumed" that 4 Ezra and 2 Baruch "originated in circles close to the Tannaim").

11. See chapter 6, n82 and accompanying text; chapter 9, n107 and accompanying text; chapter 11, nn54–55, nn211–13 and accompanying texts.

12. See Brand, "Evil and Sin," 645; Cohen, *From the Maccabees*, 86 (A dualistic system "entered Judaism from Platonism and Zoroastrianism").

13. Brand, "Evil and Sin," 645. See chapter 11, n37.

it was nevertheless accepted that Jews, too, were impacted by demonic forces, explaining their transgressions of God's law.[14]

Second, due to their dualistic worldview, the apocalyptic authors were more pessimistic than the Tannaim about the ability of most humans to act righteously, and they saw little, if any, possibility for gentiles or wicked Jews to cure their defective hearts. The human condition is described in the apocalypses as hopelessly wicked and corrupt due to demonic influence, and no improvement in this condition is envisioned until the coming of a Messiah and a day of judgment sometime in the future when, it was said, God would destroy the demonic forces (and the wicked human beings) and create a new world order, including a transformed humanity without defective hearts.

In particular, no mention is made of *talmud torah* as a practice that could transform a human being and minimize the unrighteous conduct caused by the evil *yetzer*, such as the Tannaim believed. Indeed, except for a couple of instances in which "medicine" is mentioned as a means of counteracting demonic forces,[15] no hope is expressed for significant human transformation in the absence of divine intervention at the end time. And although those Jews who transgressed God's law were urged to repent, it is unclear how the authors of these apocalypses believed true repentance could occur, since repentance requires a significant transformation of one's conduct.

Third, the apocalypses instruct righteous Jews to segregate themselves from gentiles and from wicked and apostate fellow Jews to as great an extent as possible.[16] Association with those who are wicked was said to result in becoming wicked yourself, perhaps suggesting that association with those who are righteous might be a way to become righteous.[17] This

---

14. See Cohen, *From the Maccabees*, 93 ("For some Jews ... the injustice of the status quo was caused not only or not chiefly by the gentiles but by their fellow Jews. ... In this conception, the polarity of Jew versus gentile is accompanied, if not replaced, by the polarity of the righteous (that is, the sect) versus the wicked (all other Jews and, apparently, the gentiles as well). ... Alienated from the rest of society, they imagine an ideal world that in the end time would be realized on earth and vindicate them in the eyes of their opponents"); chapter 11, sec. A (discussing the Essenes).

15. See Brand, "Evil and Sin," 646-7 (mentioning the medicinal "cure" prescribed by the angel Raphael in Tobit and the teaching of medicine to Noah in Jubilees).

16. The idea that Jews need to separate from gentiles appears earlier in the biblical books of Ezra and Nehemiah, where gentiles are viewed as being inherently morally impure. See Klawans, *Impurity and Sin*, 43-46.

17. Cf. chapter 11, nn13-16 and accompanying text; Boström, *Sages*, 132 ("The notion that the person who associates with evil will be overcome by it may be called

instruction was a development of ideas found in Third Isaiah distinguishing "the chosen ones" of Yahweh from the wicked of the Israelite community, and envisioning an imminent judgment at which time the chosen ones would be rewarded and the wicked would be punished.[18] The teaching for the righteous to separate from the wicked (and the emphasis on Messianism) stands in sharp contrast to the teaching of Hillel who urged his disciples *not* to segregate themselves from the community and to improve conditions in the here and now, although most of the community were recognized to be less than completely righteous.[19]

Fourth, there are differences between the Tannaim and the apocalyptic authors with regard to the ethical theories they relied upon to justify moral norms and rules of conduct. Unlike the Tannaim and subsequent rabbis, apocalyptic authors never suggest acceptance of a deontological ethical theory. They never mention that one should be righteous irrespective of consequences. Their texts always indicate a preference for a teleological or consequentialist ethical theory. And although a *utilitarian* teleological position is sometimes expressed (as when Noah and Abraham instruct their descendants to be righteous because it will result in a harmonious, peaceful, and prosperous society, or when Israelite society is seen as suffering from foreign domination as a consequence of the community's sin), the apocalyptic authors most often express an *egoistic* teleological position. Postmortem rewards and punishments are meted out to individuals. Adopting the Greek concept of a soul, several apocalyptic authors envisioned postmortem rewards and punishments being meted out to individual souls or to souls rejoined with their resurrected bodies.[20]

---

a theme of the book [of Proverbs]"), 133 ("The sages may have thought of evil and good as almost contagious, as something that automatically had an influence upon any person who came into close contact with it").

18. See chapter 5, sec. D.

19. See Glatzer, *Hillel the Elder*, 66 (Unlike the sects "who forsook the community of Israel at large, we find Hillel actively engaged in improving the conditions of the community"), 69 (The "field of action" was to Hillel "not the future—the great theme of Messianism—but the present and its transfiguration"), 80 ("Hillel . . . opposed the individual's separation from the community"), 89 (Hillel opposed the apocalypse's "radical view of the just *versus* the wicked, good *versus* evil and advocated a middle line. . . . His religious outlook removed him from the ardent and urgent Messianism of the sects' pronounced individualism; instead, Hillel tried to revive the true and just community" [emphasis original]). See also chapter 8, sec. A, 5.

20. See generally Starr, *Toward a History*, 62–77.

Fifth, the apocalyptic authors did not believe that *all* Jews would be rewarded at the end time because they believed many, if not most, Jews were irredeemable sinners. They saw two groups of Jews—the apostate, wicked Jews and the righteous Jews who were the elect of Israel.[21] Only individuals among the elect of Israel would be rewarded at the end time. The Tannaim, however, taught that *all* Israel, most of whom were *ben-omin*, would have a share in the world to come.[22] Both apocalyptic and Tannaitic materials agree, however, that postmortem rewards would be due in large part to God's compassion and mercy.[23]

Apocalypses (except for the book of Daniel) were ignored by the Tannaim and "have never been recognized by [Rabbinic] Judaism."[24] These writings and the type of eschatology they espoused were, however, appreciated by certain segments of the Jewish population, including the Essenes and proto-Christians. In particular, Christians appropriated and preserved Jewish apocalyptic texts, and also recast similar material for themselves as in the Revelation of John.[25]

A. The Book of Enoch.

The book of Enoch, also called 1 Enoch, is comprised of several different apocalyptic works purported to have been authored by the biblical Enoch, who, in Gen 5:18-24, is described as having walked with, and been taken by, God.[26] These works, written in Judea, essentially recount mysteries that are claimed to have been revealed to Enoch by various archangels, including Raphael and Uriel. The Astronomical Book, thought to be the earliest of the compositions in 1 Enoch, advocates use of the solar

---

21. See Sanders, *Paul and Palestinian Judaism*, 361 (In 1 Enoch there is a conception of "true Israel" and their opponents, the "condemned apostates and/or heathen"; only "rarely are any others mentioned besides the wicked and the righteous"), 362 (The author of Jubilees distinguishes between "the faithful, covenant-keeping Israelites on the one hand and the apostates and gentiles on the other"), 418 (In 4 Ezra "only the perfectly righteous, who are few, will be saved by God").

22. See m. Sanh. 10:1; chapter 9, nn170-71 and accompanying text.

23. See Sanders, *Paul and Palestinian Judaism*, 422 ("The theme of God's mercy as being the final reliance even of the righteous appears in all [the Palestinian literature from 200 BCE to 200 CE] except 4 Ezra").

24. Moore, *Judaism in the First Centuries*, 1.127-28.

25. Moore, *Judaism in the First Centuries*, 1.128.

26. See generally Brand, "1 Enoch," 1359-64.

calendar and rebukes those who do not accept it.[27] Since the Tannaim did *not* adopt the solar calendar, this book reflects the views of people who were at odds with the Tannaim and their predecessors. This calendar-related disagreement led to "an ongoing argument regarding the dating of the festivals between those who supported a solar calendar and those who followed the lunisolar calendar."[28]

The remaining works which comprise 1 Enoch are the Book of the Watchers (dated to 250-200 BCE), the Epistle of Enoch (dated to the early second century BCE), the Book of Dream Visions (dated between 163 and 160 BCE), and the Parables of Enoch (dated to the turn of the Common Era).[29] These works attribute past calamities and defeats to evil forces inherent in the world and/or to the wickedness inherent in human nature. The Book of Dream Visions "is remarkable because it concentrates on the wicked within Israel rather than Israel's enemies" and promises their destruction.[30] The second parable in the Parables of Enoch (also called the Similitudes) envisions a "Chosen One" (the Messiah) who will usher in a new age when all evil forces will be defeated, the righteous few will be rewarded, and the earth will be transformed.[31] The other works which comprise 1 Enoch — the Book of Watchers and the Epistle of Enoch — deserve a more extended analysis.

1. The Book of Watchers.

The work begins with the blessing of Enoch in which he refers to "the day of distress [which is appointed] for the removal of all the wicked and impious."[32] At that time "the Eternal God . . . will appear with his host," there will be fear and trembling, "everything that is on the earth will be destroyed," and judgment will be rendered "upon all."[33] Those

27. See 1 En. 72-82; Brand, "1 Enoch," 1362 (dating a fragment of this book found at Qumran to the end of the third century BCE).

28. Brand, "1 Enoch," 1360.

29. Brand, "1 Enoch," 1360-61. But see Sanders, *Paul and Palestinian Judaism*, 347-48 (suggesting a "post-Christian" origin for the Parables and noting that at least one scholar dates the Parables as late as 270 CE).

30. Sanders, *Paul and Palestinian Judaism*, 351.

31. See 1 En. 45:1-6; 50:1-4.

32. 1 En. 1:1. See generally Brand, "1 Enoch," 1364-65 (comparing the opening chapters to Moses' blessing in Deut 33:1).

33. 1 En. 1:2-7.

who Enoch is addressing are directed to contemplate the unchanging order of the natural world—how "the lights in heaven . . . do not transgress their law"—and to perceive how everything is done "as God has decreed."[34] It is then stated that, in contrast to the natural order, "you have not . . . observed the law of the Lord" because you are "hard of heart."[35] What precisely is meant by the "law of the Lord" (and what specific conduct that law requires) is not specified but, given the comparison to the unchanging order of the natural world, it seems possible that the author could be referring to an inherent order of the social world rather than to the Torah.

In any case, the author (speaking in the name of the biblical Enoch) contends that at the end time, while the wicked will be destroyed, "the chosen . . . will inherit the earth."[36] Then "the righteous" (who, one must infer, are the same as "the chosen") will experience "joy and peace," while the "impious" will be cursed.[37] Who, precisely, are the righteous, or chosen, is not stated. Since they are contrasted with "the wicked and impious" who transgress the law of the Lord, it would seem that the righteous, or chosen, *do not* transgress the law of the Lord.[38] Yet, they cannot be *completely* without sin because it is stated that at the end time the chosen will be transformed in a manner that will prevent them from ever again doing wrong, "either through forgetfulness, or through pride."[39] Brand comments that "the chosen" may include all of Israel "or may specifically refer to the righteous within Israel."[40] Sanders states that the questions "who are the elect, what does one obey, and how obedient does he have to be to be considered among the righteous" are, in 1 Enoch, difficult to answer.[41]

---

34. 1 En. 2:1—5:3.

35. 1 En. 5:4. Cf. chapter 4, sec. D; chapter 9, sec. C. It is not clear whether the "you" in this passage includes all those to whom Enoch is speaking or just the wicked.

36. 1 En. 5:7. Cf. Ps 37:29; Matt 5:5; chapter 11, n23 and accompanying text.

37. 1 En. 5:7–9.

38. See Sanders, *Paul and Palestinian Judaism*, 350 ("The righteous will escape destruction on the day of judgment when the wicked are destroyed (10.17), but one is left to infer who they are only from the definition of the wicked").

39. 1 En. 5:9. See Brand, "1 Enoch," 1367 (It is "clear that the chosen are not completely righteous"). That the chosen transgress due to forgetfulness suggests inadvertent error but transgression due to pride suggests hardness of the heart.

40. Brand, "1 Enoch," 1365.

41. Sanders, *Paul and Palestinian Judaism*, 348.

Sanders does not doubt, however, that according to the author of 1 Enoch the wicked will receive no mercy at the end time and will be denied salvation.[42] Conversely, the righteous will be forgiven for whatever sins they have committed, and will "receive mercy, peace, forbearance and salvation."[43] Sanders also comments that

> it is not just the transgression of commandments which makes the sinners "sinners"—the righteous elect also transgress (it is a change when after the judgment they transgress no more). It is rather that the sinners have "turned away" and spoken against God. Their turning away, like their hard-heartedness . . . may well indicate a refusal to turn to God, that is, to repent. Those who reject God remove themselves from the sphere of his mercy, and consequently find no forgiveness.[44]

Next, the work relates the story of the "Watchers." Based on an interpretation of Gen 6:1–4, the Watchers were understood to be angels who had sexual intercourse with human women, producing "large giants" who were murderous and "lawless."[45] In addition, one of the Watchers, identified as "Azazel," is said to have taught human beings the art of warfare (leading to bloodshed and destruction), as well as the crafts necessary for female seduction (leading to sexual wrongdoing and impiety).[46] In short, the Watchers were responsible for the corruption of the earth, prompting God to order that they be prohibited from entering heaven for all eternity and be bound in the earth without peace.[47] It is then recounted that the Watchers enlist Enoch to petition God on their behalf for forgiveness but

---

42. Sanders, *Paul and Palestinian Judaism*, 360 (citing 1 En. 5:4–6).
43. Sanders, *Paul and Palestinian Judaism*, 360 (citing 1 En. 5:6).
44. Sanders, *Paul and Palestinian Judaism*, 360.
45. 1 En. 6:1—7:6. See Brand, "1 Enoch," 1359, 1369; Jub. 4:15, 22 (describing the watchers as "angels of the Lord . . . [who] descended to earth to teach humankind and to practice judgment and uprightness on earth" but who became defiled after mingling with "earthly women"); Goff, "Jubilees," 16 (The word "watchers" is derived from the Aramaic word for "angels").
46. 1 En. 8:1–2. See Brand, "1 Enoch," 1370.
47. See 1 En. 9:1—10:9. See also Klawans, *Impurity and Sin*, 56–57 (The Book of the Watchers "articulates the idea of moral defilement" in that the "watchers engage in sexually defiling behavior, which leads to their permanent degradation and their exile from Heaven").

that this petition is denied.[48] This mythology is probably presented to explain why there is the evil in the world.[49]

The work concludes with two accounts of Enoch's journey around the heavens in which secrets are revealed to him about the structure of the natural and moral world orders, and he is shown four places where human souls are stored until "the great day of judgment" (the notion of a soul having been adopted from the Greeks).[50] Three of the four places where human souls are stored are places for the souls of the wicked—one for sinners who failed to receive any punishment during their lifetime (and thus are subjected to torments *before* the final judgment day), one for sinners who *were* punished during their lifetime (and, therefore, do *not* receive further punishment prior to the final judgment day), and one for those who, according to Brand, are "more sinn'd against than sinning."[51] The fourth place is for the souls of the righteous. Sanders notes that "righteous" and "pious" are used synonymously; that these terms correspond to the Hebrew *tzaddakim* and *hasidim*, respectively; and that "whereas God pays the wicked their just deserts, he is considered to show mercy to the righteous."[52]

Enoch is then shown a place with seven magnificent mountains. He is told that the mountain in the middle will be the throne of God when "he comes down to visit the earth for good" on the day of final judgment.[53] This middle mountain is surrounded by fragrant trees, one of which is more fragrant than the others and has leaves, flowers, and wood which never wither.[54] It is explained to Enoch regarding this fragrant tree:

> No [creature of flesh] has authority to touch it until the great judgment when he will take vengeance on all and will bring [everything] *to a consummation* forever—this will be given to the righteous and humble. From its fruit life will be given to the

---

48. See 1 En. 12:1—16:3.

49. See generally Brand, "Evil and Sin," 646 (discussing the myth recounted in the Book of Watchers as disconnecting "both physical evil and the cause of sin from God").

50. See 1 En. 17:1—19:3, 21:1—33:1. See also Starr, *Toward a History*, 60–62, 69–72, 75–76. Cf. sec. D in this chapter (A similar depiction of souls being stored until the day of judgment is found in 4 Ezra).

51. Brand, "1 Enoch," 1383–84. See 1 En. 22:1–14.

52. Sanders, *Paul and Palestinian Judaism*, 350–51 (citing 1 En. 27:3f.).

53. 1 En. 24:1—25:3.

54. 1 En. 25:4.

> chosen.... Then they will rejoice with joy and be glad in the holy [place]; they will each draw the fragrance of it into their bones, and they will live a long life on earth, as your fathers lived, and in their days sorrow and pain and toil and punishment will not touch them.[55]

Near the end of his journey Enoch is shown a location full of trees that had what Enoch calls an "accursed valley in the middle of them."[56] It is explained to him that the accursed valley "is for those who are cursed forever... and here [will be] their place of judgment."[57] Commenting on this passage, Brand suggests that the accursed valley is the Valley of Hinnom, which in biblical times was the site of idol worship and child sacrifice and which was the focus of two prophesies of destruction in Jeremiah "that foresee its future as a valley of slaughter and is possibly alluded to as the site of the eternal torment of the wicked in Isa 66:24."[58] Brand asserts: "In Enoch [the Valley of Hinnom] is portrayed as an otherworldly counterpart to Zion, where the wicked will receive their punishment in the final era."[59]

2. The Epistle of Enoch.

The Epistle of Enoch is written as Enoch's testament to his son Methuselah. It begins with Enoch admonishing Methuselah to "walk in righteousness" and to avoid associating "with those of a double heart."[60] Thus, the Epistle associates righteous conduct with having a single, undivided heart, and, presumably, understands having such a heart to mean that the person has no desires or passions inconsistent with, or interfering with, adherence to God's will.[61] On the importance of an undivided heart for adherence to God's will, the view in the Epistle is consistent with the Tannaitic view.

---

55. 1 En. 25:4–6 (emphasis original).
56. 1 En. 27:1.
57. 1 En. 27:2.
58. Brand, "1 Enoch," 1387.
59. Brand, "1 Enoch," 1387.
60. 1 En. 91:1–4. See also 1 En. 97:4 (decrying association with sinners), 104:6 ("Do not be associated with [sinners], but keep far away from their wrongdoing").
61. See chapter 4, sec. D. See also 1 En. 96:4 ("Woe to you sinners, for your riches make you appear righteous, but your hearts prove to you that you are sinners"); 100:8 ("Woe to you, you perverse of heart").

The view in the Epistle is also consistent with the Tannaitic view in identifying God's will with the laws and moral norms of the Torah which the Epistle calls the "measure and the eternal inheritance of [the people's] fathers."[62] Conduct which Enoch specifically decries as wicked is, therefore, similar to conduct decried as wicked by the Tannaim—disproportionate or unjust acquisition of wealth,[63] lying,[64] giving false testimony,[65] and using one's power to oppress and persecute others, especially the righteous.[66] Moreover, Enoch accepts a notion of justice which includes the principle of "measure for measure," also accepted by the Tannaim.[67] Yet, the author of the Epistle probably would not have accepted the Tannaim's (or the Pharisees') interpretations, modifications, and expansions of biblical law because Enoch specifically condemns those who "amend the words of the Torah."[68]

Nevertheless, the views in the Epistle again coincide with the views of the Pharisees and Tannaim with respect to, at least, three further matters. First, the author of the Epistle agrees that God is not responsible for evil but, rather, that "man himself created it,"[69] and that, accordingly, it is up to man to "choose" the "paths of righteousness" rather than the "paths of wrongdoing."[70] No mention is made, however, as to how one may be

---

62. 1 En. 99:14; Brand, "1 Enoch," 1440 ("The measure and the eternal inheritance of their fathers" is the Torah).

63. 1 En. 94:7 ("Those who acquire gold and silver will quickly be destroyed in the judgment"); 97:8 ("Woe to you who acquire silver and gold, but not in righteousness").

64. 1 En. 99:1 ("Woe to you who . . . honor lying words").

65. 1 En. 95:6 ("Woe to you, lying witnesses").

66. 1 En. 95:7 ("Woe to you sinners, because you persecute the righteous"); 96:8 ("Woe to you, you powerful, who through power oppress the righteous"). See Sanders, *Paul and Palestinian Judaism*, 352-55 (opining that "the wicked are both the apostate and traitorous Israelites who collaborate with the rulers, thus gaining the right to become rich at the expense of loyal Jews, and the 'carpet-bagging' gentiles who are in league with them," while the "righteous and pious" obey the law and "are urged not to complain of their troubles and persecutions").

67. See 1 En. 95:5-6 (Those who repay their neighbors with evil will be repaid according to their deeds, and those who persecute the righteous will themselves be persecuted); Sanders, *Paul and Palestinian Judaism*, 356 (citing 1 En. 98:5); chapter 9, n82, nn211-14 and accompanying text.

68. Brand, "1 Enoch," 1439 (interpreting 1 En. 99:2 where Enoch decries those who "alter the words of truth [and] distort the eternal law"). See Sanders, *Paul and Palestinian Judaism*, 353 ("The wicked are here (99.2) apostate Jews who appeal to an erroneous (from the point of view of the author) interpretation of the law").

69. 1 En. 98:4.

70. 1 En. 94:1-5. See Brand, "1 Enoch," 1436 ("This passage, commonly known

trained to make the right choice, and, more specifically, no mention is made of *talmud torah* as the means of subduing one's evil inclination.[71] Second, the author of the Epistle, as the Tannaim, claims that the "evil deeds" of sinners "are revealed in heaven" and that their wrongdoing "is not covered or hidden" (so that their punishment is assured),[72] and that the good deeds of the righteous are remembered "in heaven" (so that, ultimately, they will be rewarded).[73] Third, there is partial agreement with respect to repentance and God's mercy. The Tannaim believed that all, or nearly all, Jews would repent of their transgressions and/or be forgiven by God.[74] The author of the Epistle, however, believed that the wicked (including apostate Jews) would receive no mercy but rather, on the basis of strict justice, would be destroyed at the appointed time.[75] On the other hand, the righteous, though not completely free of sin, have the ability to repent, and, if they did, would be shown mercy by God, enabling them to be rewarded on the day of judgment.[76]

With further regard to differences, Enoch's advice to keep away from people who are wicked (that is, people with a double heart)[77] differs from the teaching of Hillel who instructed his disciples *not* to dissociate themselves from other members of the congregation.[78] In addition, a significant difference concerns the emphasis placed on individual reward and punishment to justify adherence to rules of conduct,

---

as the 'Two Ways,' echoes the basic Deuteronomic principle of choosing the path of righteousness over the path of iniquity; one is life, the other is death (Deut 30:15–19)"); Sanders, *Paul and Palestinian Judaism*, 355–56 (The exhortation to choose righteousness and life "corresponds to the constant exhortations not to walk 'in the paths of wickedness' (94.3)").

71. See Sanders, *Paul and Palestinian Judaism*, 356–57 ("We are not told how an individual might *transfer* from the group of the unrighteous to the righteous" [emphasis original]).

72. 1 En. 98:6.

73. 1 En. 104:1. See Sanders, *Paul and Palestinian Judaism*, 355 ("The righteous are assured . . . that even though their plight goes unheeded here, the angels remember them before God (104.1), and they shall be vindicated").

74. See m. Sanh. 10:1 ("All Israelites have a share in the world to come").

75. 1 En. 100:7. See Sanders, *Paul and Palestinian Judaism*, 356.

76. See 1 En. 92:4 (God "will show mercy to the righteous man"); Sanders, *Paul and Palestinian Judaism*, 356–57.

77. See nn60–61 in this chapter.

78. See m. ʾAbot 2:5; chapter 8, sec. A, 5. See also Glatzer, *Hillel the Elder*, 89 ("Hillel appears in opposition to the sects: he rejected their radical view of the just *versus* the wicked, good *versus* evil" [emphasis original]).

and a corresponding difference in ethical theory. As discussed in the preceding chapter, although the Tannaim mention individual reward and punishment (including *postmortem* reward and punishment), their energies were devoted to devising rules of conduct to make the *present* world better *for the community as a whole,* and so the ethical theory that reflects their viewpoint is utilitarianism. Adherence to the rules of conduct they promulgated were justified because they had beneficial consequences *for the community.*

In sharp contrast, the author of the Epistle relies entirely on an *individual* reward and punishment *on the day of the final judgment* to justify adherence to rules of conduct. Adherence is justified because the righteous individual is rewarded, and the wicked individual punished, after death. No interest is shown in devising rules to make the present world better for the community as a whole. Rather, Enoch expresses extreme pessimism about the ability for the human condition to improve. He laments that "the state of wrongdoing will continue on the earth," and that even after "a great punishment will be carried out [alluding to the flood described in Genesis] . . . the deeds of wrong and of wickedness will prevail for a second time."[79] In fact, he warns, after the flood "iniquity and sin and blasphemy and wrong and all kinds of [evil] deeds [will] *increase.*"[80] Each subsequent generation will continue "to do wrong until a generation of righteousness shall arise, and wrongdoing shall be destroyed, and sin shall depart from the earth, and everything good shall come upon it."[81]

Furthermore, he acknowledges that sinners will be able to ridicule the righteous on account of their not having benefitted from their righteousness. The sinners (who are "content to eat and drink, and strip men naked and steal and sin, and acquire possessions and see good days") can say about the righteous when the righteous die:

> As we die, the righteous have died, and of what use to them were their [good] deeds? Behold, like us they have died in sadness and in darkness, and what advantage do they have over us? From now on we are equal, and what will they receive? . . . For behold, they too have died, and from now on they will never again see light.[82]

79. 1 En. 91:5–6.
80. 1 En. 91:7 (emphasis added).
81. 1 En. 107:1.
82. 1 En. 102:6–9. Cf. Wis 2:1–12. See also Nickelsburg, *Resurrection, Immortality,*

Enoch counters this argument of the sinners by appealing to the mysteries revealed to him. He assures Methuselah "that all good and joy and honor have been made ready and written down for the spirits of those who have died in righteousness, and [that] much good will be given you in recompense for your toil, and [that] your lot [will be] more excellent than the lot of the living."[83] The righteous will ultimately "shine like the lights of heaven . . . and the gate of heaven will be opened to [them]."[84] And even though sinners may have "died in prosperity and wealth" without any judgment having been executed on them, Enoch assures Methuselah, based on the same revealed mysteries, that after death their souls will descend to Sheol and "they will be wretched, and their distress [will be] great."[85] In addition, "in darkness and in chains and in burning flames [their] spirits will come to the great judgment, and the great judgment will last for all generations forever."[86]

In short, the problem of moral evil is resolved in the Epistle by an appeal to individual reward and punishment in the afterlife, displaying an underlying ethical theory of ethical egoism.

B. The Book of Jubilees.

The book of Jubilees was written in the second century BCE.[87] As 1 Enoch, Jubilees endorses a solar calendar as having been revealed to Enoch and as being in harmony with how God created the natural order; it explicitly condemns the lunar calendar as erroneous.[88] Jubilees purports to be an account of the people of Israel that God revealed to Moses on Mount Sinai at the time of the giving of the law. This account is described as including "both what had happened previously and what will take place [in the future]."[89] God tells Moses to write down all that he

---

and Eternal Life, 157-62.

83. 1 En. 103:1-4. Cf. Wis 2:21-23.

84. 1 En. 104:2. Cf. Dan 12:2-3. See Starr, *Toward a History*, 69-72 (discussing 1 Enoch and astral immortality).

85. 1 En. 103:6.

86. 1 En. 103:8.

87. See Kugel, "*Jubilees*," 272 ("sometime early in the 2nd century BCE"); Goff, "Jubilees," 3 ("the second half of the second century BCE"). See generally Kugel, "*Jubilees*," 272-82; Goff, "Jubilees," 1-5; Moore, *Judaism in the First Centuries*, 1.193-200).

88. Jub. 4:18; 6:36-37. See Goff, "Jubilees," 20.

89. Jub. 1:4.

is being told because the descendants of the then-current generation of Israelites would be "captured and fall into the hand of the enemy because they have forsaken my statutes, my commandments, the festivals of my covenant, my sabbaths," and God wants this future generation of Israelites to know "that I have not abandoned them on account of all the evil they have committed by straying from the covenant."[90]

Moses pleads with God not to deliver the Israelites over to the gentiles and not to permit the gentiles to rule over them.[91] He also pleads with God not to let "the spirit of Belial" [a wicked angel, or demon][92] "rule over" the Israelites "as to bring accusations against them before [God] and cut them off from every path of righteousness," but, rather, to "create for them a pure heart and a holy spirit."[93] God seeks to assuage Moses' concern by saying that at a future time the Israelites "will return to me with all righteousness," adding that: "I will cut off the foreskin of their heart.[94] . . . I will create for them a holy spirit and purify them so that they will never turn away from me, from that day until eternity. . . . They will keep my commandments."[95]

This exchange between Moses and God indicates that the author of Jubilees, as the author of the Epistle of Enoch, understood the cause of the Israelites' sinful behavior to be their defective, hardened, and uncircumcised hearts. But, whereas the author of the Epistle believed that the Israelites themselves were responsible for their defective hearts, it is unclear whether the author of Jubilees believed the same.[96] Both authors assumed, however, that if an Israelite transgressed, they could repent and would be pardoned and forgiven by God.[97]

---

90. Jub. 1:5–10 (The author is referring to the Babylonian exile). See Kugel, "Jubilees," 285; Goff, "Jubilees," 6. God further relates that at that same future time he will "send witnesses to warn them, but they will not listen"; rather, they "will kill the witnesses and also persecute those who investigate the law." Jub. 1:12.

91. Jub. 1:19

92. See Goff, "Jubilees," 7, 38 (Belial "should perhaps be equated with Mastema"); Kugel, "Jubilees," 287.

93. Jub. 1:20.

94. Cf. Jer 9:25 ("All the House of Israel are uncircumcised of heart").

95. Jub. 1:23–24. See generally Kugel, "Jubilees," 275 (The principal purpose of the book was to combat the view that because Israel had violated the covenant it had been rejected by God and fallen into God's disfavor).

96. Israelite hearts may have become hardened as a result of internal, human forces or external, demonic forces.

97. See, e.g., Jub. 41:23–25 (Judah committed an act that was evil when he slept with his daughter-in-law, but he lamented and implored God for forgiveness. "There

Most of the account set down in Jubilees is backward-looking, constituting a retelling of the narratives in the biblical books of Genesis and Exodus. The purpose of the retelling, according to Goff, is not to supplant the biblical account but rather "to offer a version of scriptural stories which functions as an interpretive lens conveying how the stories should be understood."[98] Several episodes of this retelling are relevant for present purposes.

1. The Flood Episode.

The first relevant episode is Jubilees' account of the flood in chapter 5. Here it is explained that prior to the flood the earth had been corrupted due to unions between earthly women and the "angels of the Lord" (the watchers).[99] After the birth of the children of these unions (the "giants") "violence [or injustice] increased" and "all mortal creatures corrupted their ordinances [or their way],"[100] and "every human's mind was evil all the time."[101] Only Noah "found favor" in God's sight.[102] Accordingly, God destroyed everything, except for what Noah brought onto the ark.

Presumably to explain how God could promise Noah in Gen 8:21 not to send another flood, Jubilees states that after the flood, God "made a new and righteous nature for all his creatures so that they would not sin in accordance with their whole nature forever," but would be righteous.[103] Yet, after the flood human beings were still sinning, so Jub. 5:13–19 was added by a later Interpolator to explain this fact.[104]

---

was forgiveness for him because he turned away from his sin").

98. Goff, "Jubilees," 1. See also Kugel, "*Jubilees*," 272 (The retelling "is accompanied by all sorts of new information designed to answer questions about the biblical narrative"). But see Saldarini, "Apocalyptic and Rabbinic Literature," 352 ("If Zeitlin is correct, [Jubilees] was even written in conscious opposition to the Pentateuch").

99. Jub. 5:1–2.

100. Jub. 5:2–3. Cf. Jub. 7:20–21 (The flood came about because of "fornication, impurity, and all violence [or, injustice]").

101. Jub. 5:2. Cf. Jub. 7:24 ("Every inclination and desire of humankind was without purpose and evil all the time").

102. Jub. 5:5. See Jub. 5:19 (Noah's "heart was righteous in all his ways" and he "did not depart from anything that was ordained for him").

103. Jub. 5:12. See Goff, "Jubilees," 17; Kugel, "*Jubilees*," 308 (God "retooled human nature—previously judged by God to be 'nothing but evil all the time' (Gen 6:5)—so that all of humanity would never again sin as it had before the Flood and so require the same punishment"). Cf. 1 En. 10:16–21.

104. See Kugel, "*Jubilees*," 278–81, 308.

As modified by the Interpolator, Jubilees is *not* asserting that after the flood, human nature was transformed in a way which completely prevented sin; it is only asserting that sin would now be less likely to occur due to automatic punishments imposed for sinful behavior.[105] That sin would not be completely prevented is underscored by the claim that after the flood, it was "written and ordained" that the sins of the Israelites would be forgiven and pardoned if they repented and turned away from their guilt "once each year."[106]

2. The Post-Flood Episode.

The second relevant episode relates to Noah's activity *after* the flood. Noah builds an altar, makes numerous sacrifices, and offers "a pleasant aroma acceptable before the Lord."[107] Immediately upon smelling the sweet aroma of Noah's sacrifice God makes a covenant with Noah.[108] Noah and his sons swear an oath requiring "that they would not eat any blood that was in any flesh."[109] In return for Noah's oath, God promises "that for all the days of the earth, seedtime and harvest would never cease; that cold and heat, summer and winter, day and night would not change their ordained arrangements and never cease."[110] This is meant to indicate that the natural order of the world (that human beings rely upon for their survival) would continue unabated. More directly, God also

---

105. Kugel, "*Jubilees*," 308.

106. Jub. 5:17-19 (referring to the Day of Atonement). See Kugel, "*Jubilees*," 309 ("For the Interpolator . . . in common with other Second Temple period sources (see also M. *Yoma* 8:9) atonement required the worshiper to turn aside from past sins and not repeat them"). See generally Sanders, *Paul and Palestinian Judaism*, 375-80 (discussing God's mercy and man's repentance and atonement). Cf. chapter 9, sec. B, 5.

107. Jub. 6:1-3.

108. Commenting on these verses, Kugel states: "In Genesis . . . God's promises never to bring another flood required nothing of Noah. . . . But by introducing the word 'covenant' *before* God's undertaking never to bring another flood, *Jubilees*' author implies that God's promise was made in the context of a mutual agreement that called on Noah's descendants never to eat blood—because the life of the flesh is in the blood. . . . Thus, the whole biblical narrative from Gen 8:20 to 9:17 became, for *Jubilees*' author, one great covenant ceremony, the first in a series of covenants and promises that bound Israel and God long before the Sinai revelation." Kugel, "*Jubilees*," 311 (emphasis original).

109. Jub. 6:10.

110. Jub. 6:4.

assures Noah that he and his descendants would have food to eat.[111] In other words, God is required, under the terms of the covenant, to provide the conditions for human material well-being.

Shortly thereafter it is related that Noah "began to instruct his grandsons in ordinances and commandments—every law that he knew," specifically mentioning that they should "cover the shame of their flesh, bless the one who created them, honor father and mother, love one another, and protect themselves from fornication, impurity, and all violence [or injustice]," the last three being said by Noah to be the offenses that caused the flood.[112] These "ordinances and commandments," which Noah associates with "righteousness,"[113] are said by Goff to "echo the Ten Commandments."[114] They are distinguishable from the Ten Commandments, however, in that the conduct required is not required by God, only by Noah. Indeed, according to Kugel, this passage is but one instance of the desire of Jubilees' author "to attribute divine laws to human initiatives."[115]

But what is the basis for these human initiatives? How are moral norms justified if they are not the commands of God? It appears that Noah's justification is teleological. He believes that the material well-being of his grandsons depends on their adherence to moral rules, and he is fearful that his grandsons are transgressing them. Specifically, he tells his grandsons that they have not been "walking in righteousness" and that, consequently, they will become separated from one another, envious of one another, and disunited.[116] He fears that after he dies, they will even kill each other.[117] In other words, Noah believes that righteousness is required for there to be unity, harmony, and peace. He pleads with his grandsons to "act with justice and righteousness so that [they] may be planted with righteousness on the surface of the whole earth."[118]

---

111. See Jub. 6:6 ("Behold, I have given you all wild animals, livestock, everything that flies, everything that creeps upon the ground, and the fish in the waters—everything for food, like the green plants. I have given you everything so that you may eat").

112. Jub. 7:20-21.

113. Jub. 7:20. See also Kugel, "*Jubilees*," 364 (To "'do 'righteousness' . . . suggested to . . . Second Temple period authors, to 'keep the commandments'").

114. Goff, "Jubilees," 22.

115. Kugel, "*Jubilees*," 320.

116. Jub. 7:26.

117. Jub. 7:27.

118. Jub. 7:34. See Jub. 1:16 (God promises to transform the Israelites "into a plant of righteousness");16:26 (From Abraham there was to be "a plant of righteousness");

Yet, despite finding fault with his grandsons for their unrighteous conduct, Noah also expresses the view they are not to blame. They are blameless because they have been led astray by "demons."[119] Noah petitions God to imprison these "spirits" just as God had imprisoned the watchers, but the chief of these spirits, identified as "Mastema" or "Satan," protests.[120] Mastema requests that God permit a tenth of the spirits to remain free, under Mastema's rule, and to permit Mastema to "execute the power of [his] will on humankind"; *and God grants this request!*[121] Accordingly, after Noah died, his descendants

> began to fight against each other, take captives, kill one another, shed human blood upon the earth, eat blood, build powerful cities, walls, and towers, consider (one) man superior to the people, establish the beginning of kingdoms, and go to war—people against people, nations against nations, and city against city.[122]

In short, due to Mastema's influence on human desire and conduct, once again everyone "began to do evil."[123]

3. The Abraham Episode.

The third episode to be considered is the saga of Abram/Abraham. After the flood, we are told, everyone was wicked except for Abram who "was perfect with the Lord in all deeds and pleasing in righteousness all the days of his life."[124] We are not told how Abram came to be pleasing in righteousness all the days of his life, but only that when he was

---

36:6 (Isaac admonishes Esau and Jacob to remember God so that God may "establish [them] in the earth as a plant of righteousness"); Goff, "Jubilees," 7 ("A plant of righteousness" is "a common phrase in late Second Temple literature that denotes the elect" [citing 1 En. 10:16; 1QS 8.5-6]).

119. See Jub. 7:27. See also Jub. 10:2; Kugel, "*Jubilees*," 321 ("For *Jubilees*' author (but not the Interpolator), demons and wicked angels are a constant danger, since they can enter the mind and mislead people").

120. See Jub. 10:3-11.

121. See Jub. 10:8-11.

122. Jub. 11:2. See Goff, "Jubilees," 30 ("Violence, slavery, and idolatry . . . are ascribed to the influence of demons on Noah's sons," these demons "carrying out the arrangement between God and Mastema stipulated in 10:5-10").

123. Jub. 11:2, 5 (Mastema "would convey to those under his control the desire to carry out every kind of iniquity and sin").

124. Jub. 23:9.

seventy-five, he prayed to God to deliver him from the influence of "evil spirits who have power over the thoughts of the human mind" and to prevent them from leading him away from following God,[125] and that God granted Abram's request.[126]

Twenty-five years later, God made a covenant with Abram, changing his name to Abraham. The covenant required Abraham and his descendants to "keep the covenant" in exchange for receiving the land of Canaan, which they would "rule over forever."[127] However, except for circumcising their foreskins as a sign of the covenant, the details of what Abraham and his descendants were obligated to do under the covenant are not mentioned. It *is* stated, though, that God "chose Israel to be his people," distinguishing them from all other people. Significantly, this choice meant that

> he gave spirits dominion over everyone to lead them astray from following him. But he did not give dominion over Israel to any angel or spirit at all since he alone is their ruler. He will protect them and assert authority over them instead of his angels, his spirits.[128]

This suggests that demonic forces would not be able to lead the Israelites astray. And yet, it is immediately foretold that some Israelites *would* go astray—they would not properly circumcise their sons—and that this transgression would be caused by Belial.[129] So, God's dominion over, and protection of, the Israelites did not entail the complete elimination of demonic influence.[130] Indeed, according to Jubilees, transgressions

---

125. Jub. 12:20.

126. See Jub. 12:22–27.

127. See Jub. 15:3–14.

128. Jub. 15:31–32. See also Jub. 16:17–18 ("From a son of Isaac one will become a holy offspring. He will . . . become the portion of the Most High. All his descendants have fallen into the lot that God possesses so that they may become . . . a holy nation"); Deut 32:8–9; Levinson, "Deuteronomy," 419; Exod 19:5–6; Kugel, "*Jubilees*," 353–54, 416. See generally Sanders, *Paul and Palestinian Judaism*, 362–63 ("One of the main concerns of the author of Jubilees was to establish the basic distinction between the faithful, covenant-keeping Israelites on the one hand and the apostates and gentiles on the other. . . . The special status of Israel as God's elect is a theme of which the author never tires").

129. Jub. 15:33–34 (referring to the transgressors as "sons of Belial"). See Goff, "Jubilees," 38 (commenting that the phrase "sons of Belial" means that "those who do not practice circumcision are under the influence of demonic powers"). But see Kugel, "*Jubilees*," 349 ("[Belial] here is not . . . a Satanic figure").

130. See also Jub. 19:28 (Abraham's blessing of Jacob includes the wish that "the

were likely to occur if the Israelites associated with gentiles, especially Canaanites, and thus the Israelites were admonished to separate themselves from the gentiles.[131] After any transgression, however, an Israelite could repent and would be forgiven.[132]

Abraham instructs his children and grandchildren "to observe the way of the Lord," to "conduct themselves with righteousness," to "act with justice and righteousness," to "conduct [themselves] with righteousness and integrity," to avoid straying "to the right or to the left from all the paths which the Lord has commanded us," and to "keep [God's] ordinances, commandments, and judgments."[133] Other than expressing concern about circumcision, however, few specifics are provided. The main reference to a moral norm is the admonition "that each . . . love his neighbor."[134] But the ethical theory of the author is clear. He believes that righteous conduct is justified because, if the children of Abraham are righteous, God will be "pleased with [them], grant his favor, and send down the rain upon [them]," suggesting that they will be rewarded with material well-being.[135] Moreover, all the nations of the earth will be pleased with them, suggesting that they will enjoy peaceful relations with other peoples.[136]

In addition to instructing his descendants that righteousness is required to reach the goal of material well-being and peace, Abraham instructs his descendants that the way to achieve righteousness includes separating themselves from other people.[137] He says that "all the deeds

---

spirits of Matsema not rule over [Jacob] or [his] offspring," a wish which wouldn't be necessary if demonic influence had been eliminated).

131. See Jub. 22:16. See n138 in this chapter and accompanying text.

132. For some transgressions, such as the failure to practice circumcision, there is no "pardon or forgiveness." See Jub. 15:34; Sanders, *Paul and Palestinian Judaism*, 368–70 (discussing commandments, the transgression of which "was regarded by the author as forsaking the covenant and thus forfeiting one's status as a member of Israel").

133. Jub. 20:2, 9; 21:5.

134. Jub. 20:2. See also Jub. 36:8–11 (Anyone who "seeks evil against his brother" will be destroyed, together with his descendants); Sanders, *Paul and Palestinian Judaism*, 364–65 (The only moral commandment "which is especially emphasized . . . is the commandment to love one's brother" [citing Jub. 36:8–11]).

135. Jub. 20:9. See also Jub. 21:23 ("Do [God's] will and be successful in all things"); Goff, "Jubilees," 48 ("Abraham teaches Isaac that his prosperity is contingent on following God's commandments").

136. See Jub. 20:10.

137. See Jub. 21:21–22; 22:16–18. See also Klawans, *Impurity and Sin*, 46–48 ("As in Ezra and Nehemiah, the moral impurity of gentiles is deemed [in Jubilees] to be

of humankind are sin and wickedness," and suggests that, unless his descendants separate themselves from other people, they too would become "impure, contaminated, and perverted."[138] If that happened, God would "cut [them] off from the land."[139] The separation that Abraham recommends is extreme. He advises his descendants to neither eat nor associate in any way with others.[140] Subsequently, Moses is instructed to command the Israelites not to marry non-Israelites because to do so "is repulsive before the Lord."[141] Israel, we are told, "is holy to the Lord,"[142] and, if even a single Israelite has a gentile wife or "closes his eyes to those who commit impure acts . . . then the entire community will be punished together."[143]

4. The Esau-Jacob Episode.

A fourth episode to be considered is the account of the relationship between Esau and Jacob. Esau is described as having an inclination (*yetzer*) that is evil.[144] There is "no righteousness in [Esau]," says Isaac, "since all his ways are violent and wicked."[145] In sharp contrast to Esau, Jacob is described as "perfect and upright . . . because there is no evil in him but only goodness."[146] In addition to the personality difference, there is also a difference in divine guardians. Kugel writes: "Esau is protected by a mere guardian angel, whereas Jacob is protected directly by God, as Deut 32:8–9 states."[147] Because Rebekah is fearful that Esau, being evil, might harm Jacob, she requests that Esau and Jacob "love each other, and

---

inherent").

138. See Jub. 21:21–22 (God would "hide his face from [them] and give [them] over to the influence of [their] transgressions").

139. Jub. 21:22. Cf. chapter 3, secs. A, C.

140. See Jub. 22:16.

141. Jub. 30:11.

142. Jub. 30:8. See also Jub. 16:17–18.

143. Jub. 30:13–15. Cf. Jub. 26:3–8 (mandating collective punishment for one individual's transgression).

144. Jub. 35:9. See Goff, "Jubilees," 74–75.

145. Jub. 35:13. See also Jub. 35:15 (Esau would not abide by any oath; he "would not do good but only evil").

146. Jub. 35:12.

147. Kugel, "*Jubilees*," 416.

that neither seeks evil against his brother but only mutual love alone."[148] Significantly, she adds that, if they love each other, then they will prosper and be honored.[149] Esau swears to do as Rebekah requests.

A few years later, Isaac summons Esau and Jacob. He commands them

> to practice righteousness and uprightness on the earth so that the Lord may bring upon you the full extent of everything the Lord said that he would do for Abraham and his descendants. My sons, [among yourselves] love one another as brothers as one loves himself,[150] with each one seeking what is good for his brother and by working together on the earth. May each love the other as himself. . . . No one is to desire evil for his brother from now on and forever,[151] all the days of your lives, so that you may prosper in all your deeds and not be destroyed.[152]

Esau and Jacob swear an oath to abide by Isaac's commands.

Unfortunately, after Isaac's death, Esau's sons learn that Isaac (through Jacob's guile) had given Jacob the birthright that should have gone to Esau, and they prepare to go to war against Jacob, and to kill both Jacob and his sons.[153] Esau initially protests, mentioning the oath he had sworn to Isaac.[154] But Esau's sons cajole and manipulate him, going so far to threaten to kill him if he did not lead them in battle against Jacob.[155] So, Esau forgets about the oaths he had sworn to Isaac and Rebekah, and remembers "all the evil things that were hidden in his heart against Jacob,"[156] and leads the military forces his sons had

---

148. Jub. 35:20. See Kugel, "*Jubilees*," 416 ("This is Lev 19:18 . . . followed by the 'negative Golden Rule,' a common interpretation of the same verse").

149. Jub. 35:20.

150. See Kugel, "*Jubilees*," 417 (referring to Lev 19:18 and asserting that the wording used by Isaac "is intended to limit the scope of this commandment, much as the Qumran community and others sought to limit it: it did not necessarily mean loving all humanity, nor even all Israel, but only some subsection thereof . . . so that God will plant them (Isaac's descendants) 'as a righteous planting'").

151. See Kugel, "*Jubilees*," 418 ("This is again the so-called 'negative Golden Rule,' a common interpretation of Lev 19:18: do not do to anyone what you would not want done to you").

152. Jub. 36:3-8.

153. See Jub. 37:1-11.

154. Jub. 37:4.

155. Jub. 37:11.

156. Jub. 37:13.

mustered against his brother. Upon learning that Esau was coming for battle, Jacob goes out to meet him and reminds Esau about the oaths they had sworn to love one another. Esau replies with a proverb comparing human beings to snakes and suggesting that all humans have an evil *yetzer* and are evil by nature, so that one cannot expect human beings to keep oaths or to be loving toward one another—it would be like expecting wolves to be peaceful with lambs.[157]

Commenting on this encounter, Goff writes:

> The heinous nature of Esau's sons, who are worse than their father, reinforces an important lesson in Jubilees—that one should not marry among the Canaanites (as Esau does), because they are evil. . . . Esau is from the line of Jubilees's favorite patriarch Abraham, suggesting he has a measure of righteousness (38:1), but he also has an evil inclination (35:9). He attempts to keep his oath to be kind toward Jacob but, prodded by malicious sons, his "yetzer" prevails.[158]

Comments by Kugel are along similar lines:

> Esau is the son of the good Isaac and grandson of the even better Abraham; he must have had good instincts, even if . . . he did not respect his own vows. . . . Esau's waffling and ultimate transformation can only be understood in light of the author's genealogical view of the world . . . the son of Isaac and Rebecca could not be altogether bad—indeed, he had been a loving brother until now. His sons, however, are half-breeds; they have no innate goodness.[159]

Once Esau attacked, Jacob killed him. Then Jacob's sons killed most of the non-Israelite forces that Esau's sons had mustered, including Aramaeans, Moabites, Ammonites, Philistines, Edomites, and Horites. Only six hundred warriors were not killed; these fled with four of Esau's sons, leaving Esau on the hill where he had been slain (suggesting, perhaps, eternal torment). Jacob's sons captured the remaining sons of Esau, but they didn't kill them. Rather, at Jacob's direction, his sons made peace with the sons of Esau. They did, however, place "the yoke of servitude upon them so that they would pay tribute to Jacob and his sons for all

---

157. See Jub. 37:18–23. See Goff, "Jubilees," 79; Kugel, "*Jubilees*," 422. Cf. Jer 13:23.
158. Goff, "Jubilees," 78.
159. Kugel, "*Jubilees*," 417, 421.

time."[160] The moral of the episode is that Jacob's righteousness had beneficial consequences for him while Esau's unrighteousness had, for him, consequences that were extremely deleterious.

5. The Eschatology of Jubilees.

Notwithstanding Jubilees' claim that righteousness has beneficial consequences for the Israelite community and individual Israelites *in this life*,[161] the work stresses that this life is essentially miserable for everyone on account of the wickedness of humanity in general. This is evidenced by the assertion that *after the flood* the human lifespan began to decrease. After the flood, humans, it is said, "grow old quickly and have their days finished sooner because of much affliction and through the wickedness of their ways."[162] Even Abraham, who was perfect, had his lifespan shortened "because of evil."[163] The author of Jubilees continues (in words purportedly spoken by an angel to Moses, revealing to him future events):

> All the generations that arise from now [the time of Moses] until the great day of judgment will become old quickly.... Their knowledge will cease because of their old age.... There will be no peace, for there will be blow after blow, tumult after tumult, distress after distress, evil report after evil report, disease after disease, and every other punishment like this, one with another: disease, stomach illness, snow, hail, frost, fever, chills, torpor, famine, death, sword, and exile—every kind of scourge and affliction.[164]

As the quoted language indicates, a great day of judgment is envisioned. This great day occurs at an end time; it is, in other words, a day of *eschatological* judgment. Preceding this day of eschatological judgment, according to Jubilees, a particularly evil generation will arise. As the author of Jubilees puts it: "Everyone is evil and there is no peace in

---

160. Jub. 38:12.

161. See Sanders, *Paul and Palestinian Judaism*, 366-67 ("The author of Jubilees holds the traditional view that there is [individual and collective] reward for obedience and punishment for transgression" and "maintains the old view of the collective punishment of the entire people because of the unatoned sin of an individual").

162. Jub. 23:9.

163. Jub. 23:10. See Kugel, "*Jubilees*," 375 ("Once sinfulness caused humans to live shorter life spans, even the righteous shared in their punishment").

164. Jub. 23:11-13.

the days of that evil generation.... All their deeds are impure and detestable. All their ways are defiled, impure, and detestable."¹⁶⁵ The Israelites, too, will abandon "the edicts which the Lord established between them and him"; they will fight with one another "concerning the law and the covenant because they have forgotten [or neglected] ... every ordinance"; each will seek to take "everything that belongs to another"; and they will even "defile the holy of holies with impurity, with the corruption of their pollution."¹⁶⁶

As envisioned by the author of Jubilees, the appearance of "that evil generation" will usher in the "great day of judgment," after which day demonic forces will no longer exist to "cause destruction," with the concomitant circumstance that "the Lord will heal his servants," the Israelites will "study the commandments, and turn to the way of righteousness" and, therefore, they will "see great peace," and "their spirits will have much joy."¹⁶⁷ The book closes with a reference to this period; the author writes:

> Israel will be purified from all sexual transgression, impurity, pollution, sin, and iniquity. They will live in all the land while being faithful. *It will no longer have any satan or evil person.* The land will be pure from that time until eternity.¹⁶⁸

As Goff interprets this passage, it describes an "idyllic epoch"—an epoch in which the Israelites "are in the land of Canaan, without enemies and practicing full obedience to God"—and this epoch "represents a template for the eschatological future."¹⁶⁹ In sum, demonic forces, and the wickedness of human beings, it seems, was understood to preclude Israelite society from being one which achieved either true righteousness or complete well-being. Only when demonic forces and human

---

165. Jub. 23:15–17.
166. Jub. 23:16–21.
167. See Jub. 23:26–31. See Goff, "Jubilees," 52 ("Jub. 23:11–32 ... prophetically proclaims that an apostate generation will arise and that after this, God will send a 'great punishment' ... [followed by] a utopian existence characterized by long life, peace, and correct obedience to God"), 53 ("After divine punishment, an idealized existence is envisioned *for the righteous*," an existence without satanic (demonic) forces to lead them astray [emphasis added]).

168. Jub. 50:5 (emphasis added). See also Jub. 23:29 ("There will be no satan or evil person at all who will cause destruction").

169. Goff, "Jubilees," 96.

wickedness were eliminated in a new idyllic epoch would the Israelites be truly righteous and achieve complete well-being.

C. Book of Daniel.

As previously mentioned,[170] chapters 7 to 12 of the book of Daniel, written at the time of the Seleucid persecution of 167 to 164 BCE, are seen as a theological response to the crises of that persecution and of the martyrdom of those who refused to violate any of the Torah's laws. The author of Daniel "could see no salvation for the people other than through the direct intervention of God."[171] In chapter 11, the author describes a vision concerning what will happen at the end of days, saying "a contemptible man," a foreign king [in reality Antiochus IV] will be determined to do harm to "the holy covenant."[172] Reflecting the tension in the reign of Antiochus between Jews who resisted Antiochus' attempt to end Torah observance and Jews who embraced Hellenization and sympathized with Antiochus, Daniel states that the foreign king would "have regard unto them that forsake the holy covenant" but that "the people devoted to their God will stand firm."[173]

The author soon moves to describing the "time of the end" itself. He says that the patron angel of Israel, Michael, would confront the wrongdoers. Michael is both the warrior chieftain of the heavenly armies and God's appointed agent to render judgment. Michael would strike down the demonic power behind the foreign king and his kingdom, and render judgment separating the righteous and wicked of Israel.[174] At that time, recently departed Israelites would be resurrected to receive divine reward or punishment. Resurrected Israelites who had suffered for their righteousness while alive would enter "eternal life"; resurrected Israelites who had been wicked while alive, and who had inflicted suffering on others, would receive "reproaches" and "everlasting abhorrence."[175]

170. See chapter 5, sec. D.
171. Bickerman, *Ezra to Maccabees*, 94.
172. Dan 11:21, 28.
173. Dan 11:30–32.
174. See Starr, *Toward a History*, 42–43.
175. Dan 12:2–3. See Starr, *Toward a History*, 43–44. See also Cohen, *From the Maccabees*, 95 (Daniel "omits (or takes for granted) many . . . elements that were standard features in the eschatological speculations of his contemporaries and successors: the renewal of Jerusalem . . . the ingathering of the exiles, the reestablishment of the

D. 4 Ezra.

Fourth Ezra is an apocalypse in which the author, purporting to be the biblical Ezra, recounts seven visions or revelations he is said to have received concerning a messiah, a messianic age, and an end time.[176] As set forth in the book's opening lines, these visions were received in Babylon in 556 BCE, thirty years after the Babylonian exile.[177] In reality, scholars believe that the work was written around 100 CE as a response to the destruction of the Second Temple by the Romans and mass deportation of Judeans from Judea in 70 CE.[178] The author begins the work with a lament (that Zion is desolate and Babylon is well off), followed by a brief recapitulation of biblical history (not unlike the one that Jubilees provides, centering on God's choosing of, and covenant with, Abraham), and then a theodicean question (How could God's justice be reconciled with giving Babylon dominion over the people of Israel?).

Fourth Ezra's historical recap emphasizes the "evil heart" of humanity that began with "the first Adam" and that is the cause of sin and suffering in the world.[179] Just as Adam, burdened with an evil heart, transgressed, all people and nations that descended from Adam "walked after [their] own will," did "ungodly things," and rejected God's "commands."[180] Then, just as Adam was punished with death,[181] God brought the flood to punish

---

Davidic kingship, the veneration of God by the gentiles . . . and the renewed creation of the cosmos").

176. See generally Fried, "4 Ezra," 345–84; Hogan, "4 Ezra," 1607–68.

177. 4 Ezra 3:1. This date is about a century before the biblical Ezra actually lived.

178. See Hogan, "4 Ezra," 1607. See also Fried, "4 Ezra," 346 (The composition "is usually dated to the reign of Domitian (81–96 CE) or Nerva (96–98 CE), but the period of the failed Bar Kokhba revolt (132–35 CE) in the reign of Hadrian is also possible").

179. 4 Ezra 3:20–21. See Hogan, "Meanings," 536 (An "evil heart" is "probably equivalent to [*yetzer ha-rah*] from rabbinic literature").

180. 4 Ezra 3:7–8. The claim that Adam's immediate descendants transgressed God's commands seems to presuppose the existence of a moral order capable of being discerned by all people and constituting divine commands. This is supported by 4 Ezra 7:20 ("The Lord strictly commanded those who came into the world, when they came, what they should do to live, and what they should observe to avoid punishment"). See Collins, "Idea of Election," 86 (7:20 "would seem to require, in effect, some kind of natural law, as the law of Moses is not known to all those who come into the world"). But see Fried, "4 Ezra," 347. See generally Hogan, "Meanings," 533–52 (demonstrating that 4 Ezra "maintains a very broad understanding of [*torah*], as divine 'instruction' in various forms . . . [including an] abstract entity that is closely allied with divine wisdom, the order of creation, and 'the way[s] of the Most High,'" which ways include "what we would call the natural order or laws of nature").

181. See Hogan, "4 Ezra," 1611 ("The author interprets Gen 3:19 to mean that

all of Adam's descendants, save for "Noah with his household, and all the righteous who have descended from him."[182] But these descendants eventually "began to be more ungodly than were their ancestors"[183] because all descendants of Adam had the same evil heart as Adam.[184]

Although not explicitly stated, Abraham was, presumably, able to subdue his evil heart and act righteously, because it is recounted that God loved Abraham and covenanted with him, promising to "never forsake his descendants."[185] Thereafter, at Mount Sinai, God gave "the law to the descendants of Jacob," but God "did not take away their evil heart from them, so that [God's] law might produce fruit in them."[186] The text continues: "Thus the disease became permanent; the law was in the hearts of the people along with the evil root; but what was good departed, and the evil remained."[187] Accordingly, after David built the city of Jerusalem, its inhabitants transgressed "just as Adam and all his descendants had done, for they also had the evil heart."[188] In other words, the giving of the law did not make the Israelites' actions any more righteous than those of the gentiles. As Collins states: "Herein lies one of the central problems of the book: Jews and gentiles suffer alike because of . . . the evil heart that afflicted Adam from the start."[189]

After this brief historical account, the fictional Ezra wants God to explain why Babylon was permitted to defeat, and exile, the inhabitants of Zion even though God had promised not to forsake the descendants of Abraham (God's people). True, the Israelites had transgressed the law God had commanded them to obey, but this was only because God had failed to take away their evil hearts. Moreover, the Babylonians also had evil hearts and acted ungodly. Ezra asks:

---

human mortality is the result of Adam's transgression").

182. 4 Ezra 3:9–11.
183. 4 Ezra 3:12.
184. 4 Ezra 3:20.
185. 4 Ezra 3:13–16 (also stating that God gave to Abraham both Isaac and Jacob, and that their offspring "became a great multitude"). It is later acknowledged by God's angel that God "loves" Israel. See 4 Ezra 5:33.
186. 4 Ezra 3:19–20.
187. 4 Ezra 3:22. See Hogan, "Meanings," 537n24 ("The idea of the law being 'in the hearts of the people' may derive from Jer 31:31–34").
188. 4 Ezra 3:25–26.
189. Collins, "Idea of Election," 85.

Are the deeds of those who inhabit Babylon any better [than the deeds of the Israelites]? Is that why it has gained dominion over Zion? For when I came here [to Babylon] I saw ungodly deeds without number, and my soul has seen many sinners during these thirty years. And my heart failed me, because I have seen how you endure those who sin, and have spared those who act wickedly, and have destroyed your people and protected your enemies, and have not shown to anyone how your way may be comprehended. Are the deeds of Babylon better than those of Zion? Or has another nation known you besides Israel? Or what tribes have so believed the covenants as these tribes of Jacob? Yet their reward has not appeared and their labor has borne no fruit. For I have travelled widely among the nations and have seen that they abound in wealth, though they are unmindful of your commandments.[190]

At this point the angel Uriel appears to Ezra, and in a series of seven revelations makes known to Ezra the *future* reward the righteous shall receive and the *future* punishment in store for the wicked.[191] Accepting the Greek concept of an incorporeal/incorruptible soul that, at death, separates from a corporeal/corruptible body, the author of 4 Ezra envisions that the souls of the righteous will be stored in an underground chamber or treasury (in Hebrew, *otzar*) "guarded by angels in profound quiet" and shall "rejoice that they have now escaped what is corruptible and shall inherit what is to come."[192] The souls of the wicked, however, "shall not enter into habitations, but shall immediately wander about in torments, always grieving and sad, in seven ways," which the text describes, including that they shall "waste away in confusion and be consumed in shame, and shall wither with fear at seeing the glory of the Most High . . . in whose presence they are to be judged in the last times."[193]

---

190. 4 Ezra 3:28–33. See also 4 Ezra 4:23 (Ezra asks about "why Israel has been given over to the gentiles in disgrace; why the people whom you loved has been given over to godless tribes"); 5:28 ("Why have you handed the one over to the many, and dishonored the one root beyond the others, and scattered your only one among the many?"); 6:55–59 ("If the world has indeed been created for us, why do we not possess our world as an inheritance?").

191. See Hogan, "Meanings," 539 (Ezra "readily accepts Uriel's teaching that the rewards of [*torah*] observance are not to be sought in this world, but rather in the world-to-come" (7:17–18; cf. 7:10–16)").

192. See 4 Ezra 4:35; 7:32, 75–101. See also Starr, *Toward a History*, 48–49, 74–75; Hogan, "4 Ezra," 1615.

193. 4 Ezra 7:80–87.

The "last times" refers to a final time period. The period of time in which Ezra was then existing (the "first age"), Uriel tells him, "is hurrying swiftly to its end."[194] As Ezra has already described it, and as Uriel acknowledges, the first age is one of evil ("full of sadness and infirmities"), but, says Uriel, it will be followed by a future age (he calls it "the age which follows") in which all who acted righteously in the first age will be rewarded and all who were wicked in the first age will receive the punishment they deserve.[195] Using an agricultural metaphor, Uriel says:

> For the evil about which you ask me has been sown, but the harvest of it has not come. If therefore that which has been sown is not reaped, and if the place where the evil has been sown does not pass away [that is, if the first age does not end], the field where the good has been sown [that is, the age which follows in which there will be no evil—no sadness or infirmity—and in which all the righteous from the first age will enjoy immortality] will not come. For a grain of evil seed was sown in Adam's heart from the beginning.[196]

The age which will follow the first age is described as idyllic. In keeping with the point of view originally voiced by Jeremiah and Ezekiel (that unless human nature is radically transformed human beings will continue to disobey God's moral commands),[197] the most significant feature of the new age is that "the heart of the earth's inhabitants shall be changed and converted to a different spirit," and, consequently, "evil shall be blotted out . . . [and] faithfulness shall flourish."[198]

This future age is to be preceded by the appearance of a messiah and a messianic age lasting four hundred years, after which time "the world

---

194. 4 Ezra 4:26; 6:7. Ezra repeatedly pleads with Uriel to reveal exactly when the first age will end. See 4 Ezra 3:33; 6:7; 8:63. Uriel reveals the signs that will precede the end but adds nothing more precise than that the first stage is hurrying swiftly to its end.

195. See 4 Ezra 4:27–30; 6:7; 7:113.

196. 4 Ezra 4:28–30. See Hogan, "4 Ezra," 1615.

197. See chapter 4, sec. D.

198. 4 Ezra 6:26–28. See also 4 Ezra 7:113 (The age to come will be "an immortal age . . . in which corruption has passed away, sinful indulgence has come to an end, unbelief has been cut off, and . . . truth has appeared"); 8:52–54 ("The root of evil is sealed up from you, illness is banished from you, and death is hidden; Hades has fled and corruption has been forgotten; sorrows have passed away, and . . . immortality is made manifest"). Cf. 2 Bar. 73:1–74:3 (In the age to come "passions, and envy, and hatred, and whatever things are like these shall go into condemnation and be removed," for they were the things "which have filled this world with evils, and on account of these the life of man has been greatly troubled").

shall be turned back to primeval silence for seven days, as it was at the first beginnings, so that no one shall be left."[199] After the seven days of primeval silence, the bodies of the dead shall be resurrected (that is, "the earth shall give up those who are asleep"), and the souls of the dead shall be rejoined with these bodies (that is, "the chambers shall give the souls that have been committed to them"), and God will appear "on the seat of judgment" to pass sentence on all these resurrected persons.[200] This day of judgment is graphically described:

> The pit of torment shall appear, and opposite it shall be the place of rest; and the furnace of hell shall be disclosed, and opposite it the paradise of delight. Then the Most High will say to the nations that have been raised from the dead, "Look now, and understand whom you have denied, whom you have not served, whose commandments you have despised. Look on this side and on that; here are the delight and rest, and there are fire and torments."[201]

According to Uriel, God will show no compassion for the wicked on the day of judgment; only God's attribute of justice will be evident.[202] Nor will any human prayers for mercy on others or other attempts by the righteous to intercede on behalf of the unrighteous and ungodly (including fathers for sons or sons for parents) be effective, but rather each "shall bear their own righteousness and unrighteousness."[203] Ezra understandably claims that Uriel's depiction of the day of judgment—in which only God's attribute of justice is displayed—ignores the fact that God "is gracious to those who turn in repentance to his law," and leaves no room for God's well-known attributes of mercy, patience, and compassion,[204] but Uriel insists that God "made . . . the world to come for the sake of

---

199. See 4 Ezra 7:28–30. See Fried, "4 Ezra," 360 ("All who are alive at the advent of the messiah [who are the righteous remnant of Israel] shall rejoice with him for four hundred years and then, with him, die. . . . No person and no animal will be alive, including the messiah himself"). See also 4 Ezra 12:32 (The Messiah "will arise from the offspring of David").

200. 4 Ezra 7:32–33. See Hogan, "4 Ezra," 1630 (7:32 "describes the resurrection of the dead that will precede the final judgment"). See also Fried, "4 Ezra," 360 ("The bodies of the dead in their graves shall disappear" and the "souls will stand up in incorruptible bodies").

201. 4 Ezra 7:34–38.

202. See 4 Ezra 7:33.

203. 4 Ezra 7:102–5.

204. See 4 Ezra 7:132–40.

only a few."²⁰⁵ Thus, it is clear that on the day of judgment repentance will not help those who have been unrighteous.²⁰⁶

But who exactly are the "righteous," and who the "unrighteous?" The righteous certainly includes some, but not all, Israelites—those few Israelites who have perfectly obeyed the Torah. But is anyone else included? Some scholars have argued that the righteous also includes gentiles, one scholar citing Paul's claim (in Rom 2:12-14 and 3:1) that it is not the hearers of the law who are justified but the doers of the law.²⁰⁷ But this argument is weakened by the fact that these scholars fail to address the passage from 4 Ezra 7:34-38 which states that "the nations" who have "despised" God's commandments are consigned to the pit of torment. It has also been argued, with justification, that the final visions in 4 Ezra present a different view of the end time than is found in 4 Ezra 7, a view in which God is merciful and the remnant of the people of Israel God saves is not determined by its righteousness.²⁰⁸ But, if this interpretation is correct, then it is likely that these visions served merely as a "'saving' appendix to make [4 Ezra] more palatable in Jewish circles."²⁰⁹

Leaving aside scholarly debate concerning how to interpret 4 Ezra and its theology,²¹⁰ it will be useful to compare certain clearly discernible views regarding human nature and ethical theory in 4 Ezra to the views of the Tannaim. First, the author of 4 Ezra unquestionably agrees with the Tannaim that human beings are born with an inherent tendency to sin—that it is human nature to disobey God's commandments and to be wicked—and that this is due to the evil heart (or *yetzer ha-rah*) that God

---

205. 4 Ezra 8:1. See also 4 Ezra 7:20-21.

206. See Sanders, *Paul and Palestinian Judaism*, 414-16 ("It is better for transgressors to perish than for the glory of the law to be besmirched by having mercy on them").

207. See Sanders, *Paul and Palestinian Judaism*, 415 (There is no indication "that the few are Israel and the multitude the gentiles"); Collins, "Idea of Election," 86 (Admission to eternal life "would seem to be on an individual basis" and the rules "for those who belong to the covenant community are no different than for those who do not"), 91-92 (citing Hogan for the proposition that the whole from which a remnant is saved need not be Israel).

208. See 4 Ezra 12:34 ("In mercy [God] will set free the remnant of my people"); Collins, "Idea of Election," 92; Sanders, *Paul and Palestinian Judaism*, 418. But see Hogan, "4 Ezra," 1625, 1656 (The "remnant" referenced in 12:34 are the "righteous few"). See also Hogan, "Meanings," 549n208 (In the final episode, called the epilogue (14:1-50), Ezra "maintains his belief that God will show mercy at the judgment").

209. Sanders, *Paul and Palestinian Judaism*, 418.

210. For discussion of the scholarly debates with regard to 4 Ezra, see Hogan, *Theologies in Conflict*, 1-40.

gave to Adam, not to external demonic forces.[211] There is also agreement that it *is possible* for one to be righteous and to obey God's commandments by struggling with, and subduing, one's evil heart.[212]

Nevertheless, there is sharp disagreement as to the role played by *talmud torah* in overcoming the evil heart. As discussed in the previous chapter, the Tannaim viewed *talmud torah* as the *only* way to subdue the evil *yetzer*.[213] The author of 4 Ezra, however, appears to view *talmud torah* as wholly ineffective in subduing the evil heart. He writes that when God gave the descendants of Jacob the law, it was unable to produce fruit because God did not take away their evil heart.[214] But when the heart of the earth's inhabitants will be changed the "truth (that is, the law), which has been so long without fruit, shall be revealed (that is, it shall bring forth fruit)."[215]

Exactly how one can subdue the evil heart (before it is changed on the day of judgment) is nowhere explained by the author of 4 Ezra,[216] but he doesn't think that it is easily achieved or that many people can do it.[217] Indeed, Ezra complains that "the world to come will bring delight to few, but torments to many," for the evil heart has brought to perdition

---

211. See Hogan, "4 Ezra," 1612.

212. See 4 Ezra 7:89 (It is possible to withstand danger so that you "keep the law ... perfectly"), 92 (The righteous are those who "have striven with great effort to overcome the evil thought that was formed with them, so that it might not lead them astray from life into death"), 14:34 (One is kept alive by ruling over their minds and disciplining their hearts).

213. See chapter 9, sec. C.

214. 4 Ezra 3:20. See Hogan, "Meanings," 546 (Ezra "persists in counting himself (and presumably all Israel, since he does not mention that there any exceptions) among those who have sinned and will therefore perish (9:36), implying that he still does not believe that it is possible to save oneself by [*torah*]-observance").

215. 4 Ezra 6:26–28. See also 4 Ezra 9:30–37 (The fruit of the law did not perish after it was received by the Israelites despite the fact that it wasn't observed). See Hogan, "4 Ezra," 1625 ("The description of the truth as being 'so long without fruit' recalls the struggle between the Torah and the 'evil heart' (3:20–22; cf. 9:31–33).").

216. He does, however, suggest that it is a matter of willpower or choice. See 4 Ezra 7:129 (referring to the admonition of Deut 30:19 to "choose life ... so that you may live"). Cf. chapter 5, sec. C (For Ben Sira adherence to the law is a matter of choosing or willing).

217. See 4 Ezra 8:3 ("Many have been created, but only a few shall be saved"); 35 ("In truth there is no one among those who have been born who has not acted wickedly; among those who have existed there is no one who has not done wrong"); Sanders, *Paul and Palestinian Judaism*, 418 (4 Ezra views sin "as a virtually inescapable power" [citing 4 Ezra 3:20]).

"almost all who have been created."²¹⁸ Uriel explains to Ezra that things which are precious and desirable are always rare.²¹⁹ In short, according to the understanding expressed in 4 Ezra, not all Israelites will be saved to participate in the world to come. In fact, most will not. This is another instance in which 4 Ezra differs from the view of the Tannaim. The position expressed in the Mishnah is that *all* Israelites have a share in the world to come.²²⁰

Yet a further difference between 4 Ezra and the Tannaim relates to ethical theory. The ethical theory of the Tannaim is utilitarianism or, later, the Divine Command Theory.²²¹ Although an egoistic justification for adherence to rules may also be found in Tannaitic material, it is not the dominant position. Nor were the Tannaim greatly concerned about *postmortem* consequences. They were focused on improving conditions in the here and now. The ethical theory of the author of 4 Ezra, however, is ethical egoism. He is entirely focused on consequences *for the individual*, and he is concerned about *postmortem* consequences. Nowhere in 4 Ezra is it claimed that adherence to laws is required to achieve beneficial consequences for the community, or that one should obey the law regardless of consequences.

---

218. 4 Ezra 7:47-48. See also 4 Ezra 7:62-69 ("All who have been born are entangled in iniquities, and are full of sins and burdened with transgressions," so that, if they were not to be punished after death for their wickedness, "perhaps it would have been better for [them]"), 116-26 (What good is it that God will reward the righteous if everyone is wicked?); 132-40 (If God does not pardon the wicked, "not one ten-thousandth of humankind could have life").

219. See 4 Ezra 7:52-57.

220. m. Sanh. 10:1.

221. See chapter 9, sec. D.

CHAPTER 11

The Essenes and the followers of Jesus of Nazareth criticized the tradition of the fathers on the grounds that its rules of conduct were man-made, not divine; and they believed that an end time was imminent.

THE CREATION OF SECTS during the late Second Temple period was related, in large part, to differences concerning the incorporation of extrabiblical regulations and teachings into the legal system. Having discussed the relevant views of one of these sects—the Pharisees/Tannaim—attention is now turned to the relevant views of two other sects—the Essenes and the proto-Christians. Both the Essenes and the proto-Christians, like the Sadducees, attacked the regulations and teachings which the Pharisees/Tannaim incorporated into the legal system, the so-called tradition of the fathers.[1] In the view of the Essenes and proto-Christians, the tradition of the fathers consisted of merely man-made regulations, and were, therefore, inferior to their own regulations which, they claimed, represented the divine will.[2]

The Essenes derived regulations solely from the text of the Torah. They distinguished between "revealed" laws—laws in the Torah that were clearly mentioned and known to all the people—and "hidden"

---

1. See chapter 8, n12. The tradition of the fathers was called in Greek texts the *nomima ek paradoseōs tōn paterōn* (Josephus, *Ant.* 13.298) or the *patroi nomoi* (2 Macc 6–7). See Novick, "Tradition, Scripture, Law, and Authority," 65–66.

2. See Novick, "Tradition, Scripture, Law, and Authority," 66–68.

laws—laws not explicit in the biblical text but derived from it through, purportedly, divinely inspired exegesis undertaken by the sect's priestly leaders.³ The Essenes' unwillingness to rely on the tradition of the fathers was likely related to the fact that the Pharisees were predominately laymen who rejected priestly authority, while the leaders of the Essenes were Zadokite priests.

Jesus of Nazareth similarly criticized the tradition of the fathers. He, as the Essenes, claimed that the regulations constituting that tradition were man-made regulations and, therefore, lacked divine authority. In contrast to the Pharisaic regulations, regulations promulgated by Jesus were, in the view of his followers, the proto-Christians, derived from an intuitive awareness of the will of God and, thus, had divine authority. Despite criticizing the tradition of the fathers, Jesus relied on the very same exegetical methods used by the Pharisees/Tannaim, and, paradoxically, told his followers that the Pharisees "sit on Moses' seat."⁴

Both the Essenes and the proto-Christians may also be distinguished from the Pharisees/Tannaim in several other respects. First, both the Essenes and the proto-Christians believed that an end time, in an "eschatological form," was imminent.⁵ This is a belief with roots in apocalyptic literature. While the Pharisees/Tannaim also came to accept the idea of an end time, referred to as the *Olam Ha-Bah* (the "world, or age, to come"), they did not teach that the world to come was imminent and did not adopt the eschatological form of the end time.

Second, the Essenes and proto-Christians sharply distinguished between the members of their respective sects (whom they considered to be the righteous) and all other Jews (whom they considered to be among the wicked). And they interpreted Ps 37's assertion that the righteous would "inherit the land" but that the wicked would be "cut off" to mean that the members of their sect would receive eternal life at the end time but that nonmembers of the sect would be condemned to eternal torment.⁶ This emphasis on an individual reward and punishment, like the eschatological form of the end time, had roots in apocalyptic literature. In contrast to such beliefs, the Pharisees/Tannaim focused on the well-being of the entire Jewish community in the here and now, emphasized that one

---

3. See sec. A, 2 in this chapter.
4. Matt 23:1–4.
5. See nn226–27 in this chapter and accompanying text.
6. See chapter 3, sec. C (discussing Ps 37).

should *not* separate themselves from the rest of the Jewish community, and taught that "all Israelites have a share in the world to come."[7]

Third, because the Pharisees/Tannaim justified the rules of conduct they adopted primarily on the basis of their beneficial consequences for the Jewish community as a whole, their ethical theory was utilitarianism. Conversely, because the Essenes and the proto-Christians justified their rules of conduct on the basis of beneficial consequences for the individual members of their sect, their ethical theory was ethical egoism.

There are also important points of agreement among all three sects. First, all three sects promoted qualities and conduct having cooperative value, despite disagreeing on matters of cult and ritual purity.[8] Second, all three sects understood the essence of qualities and conduct having cooperative value to be summed up by the biblical command to love thy neighbor as thyself, or, as it was alternatively stated, to do unto others as you would have them do unto you. Third, all three sects essentially agreed that humanity's failure to obey God's commands was the result of people having divided hearts, but the Essenes and proto-Christians did not agree with the Pharisees/Tannaim that the problem of a divided heart could be mitigated by *talmud torah*.

A. The Qumran community and other Essenean communities developed written law codes that they deemed authoritative because they purportedly were divinely revealed, and they rejected the regulations constituting the tradition of the fathers because they were merely man-made.

The Qumran community is the name scholars have given to a Jewish sectarian group living in the Judean desert near the place where the Dead Sea Scrolls were discovered, Khirbet Qumran.[9] Collins argues that the Qumran community was one of many similar communities associated with a Jewish sect called the Essenes,[10] and the Dead Sea

---

7. m. Sanh. 10:1.

8. For example, the Essenes (unlike the Tannaim) adopted the solar calendar and prohibited marriage between an aunt and nephew.

9. See generally Vermes, "Introduction," 1–24 (discussing the discovery of the Dead Sea Scrolls and subsequent scholarly research).

10. Collins, *Beyond the Qumran Community*, 10, 122–56, 209 ("The scholarly consensus that identifies the sectarian movement known from the Scrolls with the Essenes is most probably correct, even if not indisputable"). See Baumgarten, "Jewish

Scrolls reflect similarities and differences among these Essenean communities. In particular, the communities described in the texts called the Community Rule and the Damascus Rule "correspond to the two orders of the Essenes (celibate and marrying)" and "should be viewed as complementary, in a harmonious relationship, not the result of a schism in the Essene movement."[11]

The Qumran community was founded in about the middle of the second century BCE and existed until 68 CE, when the site was permanently abandoned.[12] It is likely that this group, as well as other Essenean groups, separated themselves from the rest of Israel because they believed the members of the Essenean sect to be righteous (and, thus, pure and holy) and they viewed all others to be sinful (and, thus, a source of ritual as well as moral impurity).[13] Since something ritually impure defiles whatever comes in contact with it,[14] the group deemed it advisable that its members avoid contact with those outside the sect to prevent defilement.[15] Klawans writes:

War," 2889 (The Dead Sea covenanters were "an offshoot" of a "Pre-Qumran Essene movement"). See also Blenkinsopp, *Wisdom and Law*, 146, 148 ("The Essenes probably originated as a branch of the [Hasidim] who broke with the Maccabean leadership after Jonathan assumed the high priestly office," and several scholars "have identified either Jonathan or Simon with the Wicked Priest of the Qumran scrolls who opposed the Teacher of Righteousness, founder and leader of the sect").

11. Collins, *Beyond the Qumran Community*, 209. See also Collins, *Beyond the Qumran Community*, 1–11 (distinguishing the community reflected in the Damascus Rule from the one reflected in the Community Rule and arguing that both "should be seen as complementary branches of a larger movement"), 12–13 (distinguishing the Damascus Document from the Damascus Rule), 52–65 (discussing the different forms of the Community Rule and the relationship of the Community Rule to the Damascus Rule), 79 (asserting that the "popular theory that the *Damascus Rule* represents an order that practiced marriage, while the [Community Rule] was the rule for celibates . . . is substantially correct" [emphasis original]); Vermes, "Introduction," 16, 34–35, 42–45 (arguing that "this was a single religious movement with two branches").

12. See Vermes, "Introduction," 49–66 (discussing the history of the Qumran community and related sectarian communities). See also Collins, *Beyond the Qumran Community*, 166–208 (discussing the scholarly debate regarding the Qumran site).

13. See Klawans, *Impurity and Sin*, 81–82, 88 (What was in the Hebrew Bible the independent concepts of ritual impurity and moral impurity became at Qumran "fully intertwined." This resulted in a conception of defilement "not unlike Zoroastrianism: What is evil is impure, what is impure is demonic"); Jassen, "Rule of the Community," 2932 (mentioning "the widespread conflation of ritual and moral impurity").

14. See Klawans, *Impurity and Sin*, 25.

15. See Cohen, *From the Maccabees*, 122–23 ("One Qumran document presents a 'we' group castigating a 'you' group for not properly observing some twenty laws in the areas of ritual purity, temple offerings, marriage, and the like," and stating '[You know

The idea of the ritually defiling force of sin necessitates, justifies, and reinforces the physical separation of the sectarians from the larger Jewish polity. If you believe in the maintenance of purity, and you believe that sin and sinfulness are defiling, you have little choice but to remove yourself from that society that you consider to be irredeemably wicked.[16]

The emphasis on separating that which is pure and holy from that which is defiling has obvious similarities to beliefs held by the priestly authors of Leviticus. Those priests believed that moral impurity defiled the land of Israel, and that defilement of the land resulted in the exile of all Israelites.[17] Accordingly, the Qumran sectarians (led by Zadokite priests) "viewed themselves as living in exile."[18] Further, because they believed that the period of exile would soon be ending, they accepted the call of Second Isaiah to "clear in the desert a road for the Lord,"[19]

> expounding it as a summons to dissociate themselves from their sinful contemporaries (1QS 8:12–16),[20] and to live in the desert as *Šbym ltwrh*—"returners to the Torah" (4QpPs 37 1, 1–2)—according to the laws which had been revealed to them (1QS 9:19–20). . . . They go into the desert for a season, to be

---

that] we have separated ourselves from the multitude of the people [and from their impurity] and from mingling with them'" (quoting *Some Precepts*, 7–8).

16. Klawans, *Impurity and Sin*, 90. This emphasis on separation from gentiles and wicked Jews is similar to the outlook found in the apocalyptic works discussed in chapter 10, and a number of such apocalyptic texts, including Jubilees and 1 Enoch, were unearthed at Qumran. Schiffman, *Halakhah at Qumran*, 10. See Collins, *Beyond the Qumran Community*, 40–43 (comparing the Damascus Rule to 1 Enoch and Jubilees); Klawans, *Impurity and Sin*, 46–48 (stating that the author of Jubilees is concerned with *moral* impurity more than with *ritual* impurity). See also Klawans, *Impurity and Sin*, 21–42 (discussing ritual and moral impurity in the Hebrew Bible), 56–57 (discussing moral impurity in the Book of Watchers).

17. See chapter 3, sec. B, 1, 3.

18. Klawans, *Impurity and Sin*, 89.

19. Isa 40:3. See Sommer, "Isaiah," 843 (Isaiah 40:1–11 introduces the main themes of Second Isaiah: God assures the nation "that their term of punishment in the Babylonian exile has ended, and promises that they will soon return to Zion").

20. The Community Rule states the "council of the community . . . shall atone for the land" and that "they shall separate from the habitation of unjust men and shall go into the wilderness to prepare there the way of him; as it is written, 'Prepare in the wilderness the way of [Yahweh] [Isa 40:3].'" 1QS 8:1–6, 13–14. See Jassen, 2955 ("The wilderness . . . allows the community to re-create the Israelite experience in the desert and thus receive anew the revelation of the Torah," and noting that "Isaiah 40:3 is widely employed in the New Testament to refer to the wilderness ministry of John the Baptist").

> born again as the New Israel, to enter into the Covenant of the last days.... The flight into the desert effected their secession from their sinful contemporaries.... Ultimately the "desert" became the locale of a period of purification and preparation for the achievement of a new goal. The goal is the conquest of the Holy Land, culminating in the seizure of Jerusalem, and the re-establishment in it of the supreme sanctuary of Israel.... The desert is a passage to this goal, not the goal itself.[21]

Talmon explains that these sectarians invested the motif of the fall of the wicked found in Ps 37 with "specific Sectarian eschatology."[22] They applied the language in verse 11—that "the *'anavim* ("lowly" or "meek") shall inherit the land and delight in abundant well-being"—to themselves, and understood it to mean that they would "inherit" not the land per se but the "Kingdom to Come."[23]

In short, the Qumran community, and related communities, viewed contemporary Jewish society as divided into two parts: the members of the sect who were the elect community constituting the true Israel, aligned with God and obedient to God's law, and the rest of Jewish society who they believed transgressed God's law and were steeped in wickedness. They believed that they lived in a predetermined period of wickedness that was to end *imminently* with the arrival of a messianic age. According to their way of thinking, the current ascendancy of the wicked was a result of God having relinquished control of the world to demonic forces; but the relinquishment to demonic forces was only for a predetermined period of time, which period of time was to soon end.[24] Thus, the Qumran community, and other Essenean communities, are seen by scholars as but one branch of the larger apocalyptically oriented Jewish movements deeply disturbed by what they saw as the large-scale Jewish abrogation of the Sinaitic covenant.[25]

---

21. Talmon, "'Desert Motif,'" 60–63.
22. Talmon, "'Desert Motif,'" 58.
23. Talmon, "'Desert Motif,'" 58. See Sanders, *Jesus and Judaism*, 84 (Psalm 37 was interpreted in the Dead Sea Scrolls to apply to "the redemption and reward of the sectarians and the final destruction of their enemies"); Berlin and Brettler, "Psalms," 1307 (The authors of the Dead Sea Scrolls wrote a commentary on Ps 37 in which they see themselves as the people who will inherit the land).
24. See IQS 4:18–20.
25. See Angel, "Damascus Document," 2978–79.

1. As set forth in the Community Rule, the Essenes considered themselves to be the true covenant community—the community of those fully devoted to the observance of God's precepts, correctly understood; they advocated qualities and conduct having cooperative value; and they attributed wickedness to both a human failing and to cosmic, demonic forces.

Among the Dead Sea Scrolls is a document called the Community Rule. This document is a collection of rules and ideals for life within the Qumran sectarian community.[26] In its preamble, the community is instructed "regarding the division of humanity into Sons of Light and Sons of Darkness."[27] The *maskil* (a community leader and expositor of the rules)[28] is directed to

> admit into the covenant . . . all those who have freely devoted themselves to the observance of God's precepts, that they may be joined to the counsel of God and may live perfectly before him in accordance with all that has been revealed concerning their appointed times, and that they may love all the Sons of Light, each according to his lot in God's design, and hate all the Sons of Darkness, each according to his guilt in God's vengeance. All those who freely devote themselves to his truth shall bring all their knowledge, powers, and possessions into the community of God [the *"yahad El"*]. . . . They shall not depart from any command of God concerning their times; . . . they shall stray neither to the right nor to the left of any of his true precepts.[29]

Commenting on this passage, Jassen states that (1) the idea of a new covenant "brokered between God and the sectarians is central to the

---

26. See Jassen, "Rule of the Community," 2923 (The Community Rule "further outlines many of the central theological and ideological bases of the sectarian community").

27. Jassen, "Rule of the Community," 2927.

28. Cf. Blenkinsopp, *Wisdom and Law*, 176 (discussing the *maskilim*—the wise or the teachers ("literally, those who impart wisdom")—in Daniel, and commenting that Daniel, to whom mysteries were revealed, "exemplified" the *maskilim*).

29. 1QS 1:7-15. See also Sanders, *Paul and Palestinian Judaism*, 243-44 (Non-sectarian Israelites are rarely called "the wicked" but are given such epithets as "the congregation of Belial"; similarly, members of the sect "are rarely called 'the righteous'. . . . They are rather the sons of light, the sons of truth, the sons of righteousness, the men of the lot of God who walk perfectly in all his ways, the elect of God's pleasure"), 247 (The sectarians "retained the consciousness of being a specially chosen part of Israel").

community's self-identity," and (2) "*yahad*" is the term used throughout the Community Rule as the name for the sectarian community.[30] The sectarians probably took the idea of a new covenant from Jeremiah,[31] but the sectarians altered the meaning of this idea. For Jeremiah, what was new in the new covenant was *not* the conduct God required of man, but the ability of man to act in accordance with conduct previously required.[32] For the Essenes, however, the new covenant supplemented conduct previously required with new interpretations of the original covenant, as well as with additional requirements, revealed only to, and understood only by, the sectarian community.[33] Collins speculates that the sectarian movement "was not organized into a structured association" until an individual called the Teacher of Righteousness (*moreh tzedek*) arrived who, it was believed, was able to properly interpret the divine will.[34] According to Collins, it was the Teacher of Righteousness "who inaugurated the 'new covenant,'" and the *yahad* was a later development of his activities.[35]

Following the preamble, the Community Rule sets forth a liturgy for a covenant ceremony used to initiate new members into the *yahad*. As part of the ceremony, the initiate is instructed to obey all God's commandments "so that they may not abandon him because of fear or terror or trial during the dominion of Belial."[36] Belial is the demonic figure, also known as Mastemah and the Angel of Darkness, "who rules over the world in the present pre-eschatological age."[37] Also set forth in the Community Rule is a liturgy for a covenant *renewal* ceremony that was

---

30. Jassen, "Rule of the Community," 2928, 2929.

31. See Jer 31:31 ("A time is coming—declares the Lord—when I will make a new covenant [*brit hadashah*] with the House of Israel").

32. See chapter 4, sec. D.

33. Sanders, *Paul and Palestinian Judaism*, 240 (The original covenant was supplemented by "hidden things understood only in the [sectarian] community"). See Vermes, "Introduction," 67–72 (The Essenes believed that they belonged to a community "which alone interpreted the Holy Scriptures correctly"); sec. A, 2 in this chapter.

34. See Collins, *Beyond the Qumran Community*, 37–39. See also CD 1:11–12; Angel, "Damascus Document," 2983 (The *moreh tzedek* "taught the community the proper observance of the Law and the true eschatological meaning of the words of the prophets").

35. See Collins, *Beyond the Qumran Community*, 37–39.

36. 1QS 1:16–18.

37. Jassen, "Rule of the Community," 2930. See generally Vermes, *Jesus the Jew*, 61 ("The idea that demons were responsible for all moral and physical evil had penetrated deeply into Jewish religious thought in the period following the Babylonian exile, no doubt as a result of Iranian influence").

required to be conducted annually for all current members of the *yahad* "for as long as the dominion of Beliel endures."[38]

The next section of the Community Rule, called the Treatise on the Two Spirits, articulates the community's "dualistic worldview" which encompasses both cosmic dualism ("the belief that conflicting spirits of good and evil exist in the world") and anthropological dualism ("the belief that spirits of good and evil compete within each human").[39] The Community Rule's dualism differed from pagan dualism in that it did not posit two preexisting, independent, autonomous forces; rather, it affirmed that there is only one creator God, but the one creator God was understood to be responsible for the existence of two competing spirits or cosmic entities—the Prince of Light (the spirit of truth and light) and the Angel of Darkness (the spirit of deceit and darkness).[40]

All "the children of righteousness" are said to be "ruled by the Prince of Light and walk in the ways of light," and all "the children of deceit" are said to be "ruled by the Angel of Darkness and walk in the ways of darkness."[41] The Angel of Darkness is not, however, without influence over the children of righteousness; specifically, the Community Rule states that the Angel of Darkness "leads all the children of righteousness astray, and until his end, all their sin, iniquities, wickedness, and all their unlawful deeds are caused by his dominion in accordance with the mysteries of God."[42] In fact, all human beings were understood to be ruled by both of the two competing cosmic entities and to "walk in (both) their ways."[43]

After the Treatise on the Two Spirits, the Community Rule sets forth rules for life in the sectarian community. These rules include instructions as to "the ways which all [members of the community] shall walk . . . in their dwelling places," which emphasizes the importance of studying the law.[44] Study of the law was, in fact, the community's *raison d'être* because

---

38. 1QS 2:19. Cf. Blenkinsopp, *Wisdom and Law*, 137 ("The Chronicler understood the covenant to be a public act . . . repeated at intervals").

39. Jassen, "Rule of the Community," 2923.

40. See 1QS 3:18–19, 25.

41. 1QS 3:20–21.

42. 1QS 3:21–23.

43. 1QS 4:15. See also 1QS 4:23–24 ("Until now the spirits of truth and deceit struggle in the hearts of men and they walk in both wisdom and folly"). Cf. b. Ber. 61b (The average person is ruled by both the good inclination and the evil inclination).

44. See 1QS 6:1–8. See also Jassen, "Rule of the Community," 2945 ("Collins connects the scattered communities in this passage with the 'camps' mentioned throughout

the purpose of the community's sojourn into the desert was to "make... a path for our God," and the community believed that such a path "is the study of the law which he commanded by the hand of Moses."[45] Accordingly, it is required that, wherever ten members of the sect formed a community, "there be perpetual study of the Law,"[46] and the members in each community are collectively directed to "read the book" and "study the law" for "a third of every night of the year."[47]

Schremer claims that it was because the "Qumran sect" appealed *exclusively* to the written text of the Torah for resolving "halakhic issues" that it "placed intensive study of the Torah at the center of its religious activities."[48] He argues that the Qumran sect actually initiated a "revolution" in using only the written text of the Torah to resolve halakhic issues; previously, "it was not customary to appeal to the book of the Torah as the deciding factor [in resolving such issues]."[49] It is in this light, he says, that the sect's requirement that members "'*return* to the Torah of Moses'" is best understood.[50]

The community rules also evidence that the community encouraged the development of qualities and conduct having cooperative value. It states that "the rule for the men of the community who have freely pledged themselves to be converted from all evil and to cling to all his commandments according to his will" was to "separate from the congregation of the men of deceit" and to practice "truth and humility in common, and justice and uprightness and charity in all their ways."[51]

---

the *Damascus Document*. The *yahad*, suggests Collins, is not the single sectarian community in the desert but rather a term for an umbrella organization of communities scattered throughout the land (including Qumran)" [emphasis original]).

45. 1QS 8:13-15. See Blenkinsopp, *Wisdom and Law*, 148 ("The principal activity of the [Qumran] group was the study of the law, which served as a substitute for participation in temple worship"; the Teacher of Righteousness "was above all a faithful interpreter of the law, and the task of authoritative legal exposition was continued by the Zadokite priests who formed the leadership").

46. Schiffman, *Halakhah at Qumran*, 32 (interpreting 1QS 6:6-8).

47. 1QS 6:7. See Jassen, "Rule of the Community," 2946; Schiffman, *Halakhah at Qumran*, 33; Schremer, "'[T]he[y] Did Not Read,'" 112 (translating 1QS 6:6-7 as "And where there are ten (members) there must not be lacking a man who studies the Torah day and night, constantly, one relieving another").

48. Schremer, "'[T]he[y] Did Not Read,'" 111-15.

49. Schremer, "'[T]he[y] Did Not Read,'" 113, 115.

50. Schremer, "'[T]he[y] Did Not Read,'" 110 (quoting 1QS 5:8-9 with added emphasis). See also Novick, "Tradition, Scripture, Law, and Authority," 75-78.

51. 1QS 5:1-4. See also 1QS 5:25 (emphasizing "truth, humility, and charity"), 8:2

Other virtues mentioned in the Community Rule include patience, mercy, goodness, understanding, intelligence, and discernment.[52] In addition, no one was to "address his companion with anger, or ill-temper, or obdu[racy, or with envy prompted by] the spirit of wickedness," and no one was to "hate him."[53] Arguably, all the qualities and conduct that the community valued were subsumed under the admonition to "love all the Sons of Light . . . and hate all the Sons of Darkness."[54] The Damascus Document more clearly alludes to Lev 19:18 by stating that all brought into the covenant are "to love each man his brother as himself, to support the poor . . . and to seek each man the peace of his brother."[55]

Conversely, the community condemned qualities and conduct that did not have cooperative value. The "the ways of the spirit of deceit" are said to be "greed, and slackness in the search for righteousness, wickedness and lies, haughtiness and pride, falseness and deceit, cruelty and abundant evil, ill-temper and much folly and brazen insolence, abominable deeds (committed) in a spirit of lust, and ways of lewdness in the service of uncleanness, a blaspheming tongue, blindness of eye and dullness of ear, stiffness of neck and heaviness of heart."[56]

The members of the Qumran community understood the cause of sinfulness to be a "stubborn," or a "wanton," heart,[57] a heart considered

---

(emphasizing "truth, righteousness, justice, lovingkindness, and humility").

52. 1QS 4:3-4.

53. 1QS 5:25-26. See Sanders, *Paul and Palestinian Judaism*, 312 (The children of righteousness should possess humility, pursue the truth, love their brothers, and exercise charity toward their fellow members of the covenant community; they should not acquire wealth unrighteously or be arrogant [citing the Community Rule and the Damascus Document]).

54. 1QS 1:9-10. See also 1QS 1:3-4 (". . . that they may love all that he has chosen and hate all that he has rejected"). Cf. Matt 5:43-44; ch. 5, n147 and accompanying text.

55. CD 6:12—7:1. See Angel, "Damascus Document," 2994. See also CD 14:14-15 (establishing a fund to provide for "the fatherless . . . the poor and the needy, the aged sick and the man who is stricken (with disease) . . . and the ma[id for] whom no man cares").

56. 1QS 4:9-11. See Vermes, "Introduction," 30-32 (discussing the Rule's "list of faults with their corresponding sentences" which faults included "any transgression, by commission or omission, of 'one word of the Law of Moses, on any point whatsoever,'" lying deliberately, bearing malice unjustly, taking revenge, and failing to care for a companion). See also CD 6:15-17 (Wickedness includes stealing from the poor and preying upon widows and orphans).

57. See, e.g., 1QS 2:14, 26; 3:3; 5:4; 7:19, 24; CD 2:17-18; 3:5, 11-12; 8:8, 19; 19:20, 33; 20:9-10.

to be uncircumcised and subject to an evil inclination. The Community Rule states:

> No man [in the *yahad*] shall walk in the stubbornness of his heart so that he strays after his heart and eyes and evil inclination, but shall circumcise in the community the foreskin of evil inclination and of stiffness of neck that they may lay a foundation of truth for Israel, for the community of the everlasting covenant.[58]

A stubborn or wanton heart suggests a heart which is unrestrained and which refuses to control thoughts, passions, and desires inconsistent with lawful conduct, adhering to immoderate human passions rather than the divine will. So, sinfulness was understood to be caused by a human failing.[59] Conversely, righteousness was seen to be the result of seeking God "wholeheartedly," that is with a "whole heart," a "single heart," or a "perfect heart," a *lev shalem*.[60] Such a heart, presumably, was understood to be like the undivided heart of Jeremiah, a heart in which a man's thoughts, passions, and desires are integrated with God's will.

Notwithstanding the outlook that sinfulness was caused by a human failing, the Treatise on the Two Spirits states at 3:21–23 that *all* the unlawful deeds of the children of righteousness are caused by an uncontrollable external power, the Angel of Darkness, a power that, according to 4:15, jointly rules the children of righteousness, together with the Prince of Light. Commenting on 4:15, Jassen contends that this aspect of the "two-spirits doctrine" comes closest to the rabbinic

---

58. 1QS 5:4–5. See Jassen, "Rule of the Community," 2938, 2941. See also 1QS 9:10. Cf. Deut 10:16.

59. See also CD 3:2 (Abraham "did not choose (that which) his (own) spirit desired" but "kept God's ordinances"). This passage evidences the widespread belief that disobedience is caused by one's own "spirit" desiring something other than that which God has willed. See Brand, "Evil and Sin," 649 ("The *Damascus Document* . . . presents a history of sinners who went astray due to following their own 'will,' that is, their evil inclination (CD 2.14—3.12)" [emphasis original]).

60. See CD 1:10 (The righteous remnant sought God "wholeheartedly"); 1QS 1:2 (Seeking God with a "whole heart and soul" is associated with doing "what is good and right before him as he commanded through Moses"); Jassen, "Rule of the Community," 2928 (The use of the expression "whole heart and soul" to express the observance of the commandments draws on Deuteronomic usage; providing examples of similar usages in Second Temple literature and the New Testament); Davies, *Sermon on the Mount*, 44 (translating CD 1:10 as seeking God "with a perfect heart"). See also Angel, "Damascus Document," 2983 (comparing the term "wholeheartedly" in the Damascus Document to language in 1 Chronicles which speaks of a *lev shalem*, a "single heart" or a "whole heart"); 1 Chr 28:9; 29:9, 19.

explanation for the nature of sin and evil, which posits a good inclination and an evil inclination, but that, despite similarities, there is a significant difference between the rabbinic doctrine and the two-spirits doctrine: "The Rabbinic doctrine presumes humans can choose to follow either [the good or evil] inclination," but the "two-spirits doctrine is based on a principle that each person is *predetermined* to be either in the lot of God or the lot of Belial."[61]

While it is correct that for the Qumran community one's lot is *predetermined*, Jassen errs in suggesting that such predetermination precluded one's ability to choose to follow either the good or evil inclination. That members of the sect could *choose* to act sinfully is suggested by the fact that the Community Rule sets forth a list of punishments designed to get the offending sectarian to alter their behavior.[62] If the predetermination of human behavior precluded human choice, punishments intended to alter behavior would make no sense.[63] Brand is more accurate than Jassen when she states:

> Qumran community members ... bemoan their own tendency to sin and attribute this tendency *either* to an evil inclination *or* to demonic entities that have entered their physical frames and "do battle" with God's laws *in their hearts*. ... At the same time, members of the Qumran community frequently perceive that others ... are under the direct influence of demons.[64]

In using the correlative conjunction "either/or" Brand presumably means that the Qumran community members paradoxically believed *both* that their tendency to sin was due to their own choice (as influenced

---

61. Janssen, "Rule of the Community," 2938 (emphasis added). See Josephus, *J.W.* 2.8.14 §§164–65 (The Essenes believed that "fate is mistress of all things, and that nothing befalls men unless it be in accordance with her decree").

62. See Vermes, "Introduction," 30–32. The offenses punished include deliberately lying, being impatient with others, deliberately insulting others, deliberately deceiving others, and unjustly bearing malice against others. See 1QS 6:24—7:25. See Jassen, "Rule of the Community," 2949 (The penal code in the Rule "closely parallels" other Dead Sea Scroll penal codes and "experienced constant reworking").

63. See Amihay, "Law and Society," 19–20 (The sectarians "manifest not only a disdain for their compatriots, but also a sincere concern and an attempt to change their ways" and "by implication disclose an assessment that ... there is hope for change").

64. Brand, "Evil and Sin," 649 (emphasis added). See also 1QS 10:21 ("I will not keep Belial within my heart").

by their evil inclination) *and* to an external force, the demonic entity called the Angel of Darkness.⁶⁵

Sanders assumes a similar inconsistency in comparing what he says are the sect's belief in freedom of choice and the sect's acceptance of predetermination (the belief that God chooses those who will be among the elect). He contends that there was an emphasis "on *both* God's choice of the elect and man's individual responsibility to choose."⁶⁶ With specific reference to Community Rule 3:21-23, Sanders claims: "Here, although the sins are obviously misdeeds, they are said to be caused by the Angel of Darkness, which means that their basis is not stubbornness of heart, but a power *which even being in the community cannot break*."⁶⁷ Yet, he continues, "saying that transgressions are caused by the Angel of Darkness is not intended as a denial that they are the result of man's will . . . [but] an attempt to explain why one in the community continues to sin."⁶⁸ A different explanation for the same problem, says Sanders, "attributes man's continued sin even in the covenant [community] to (if we may use the phrase) human nature."⁶⁹

2. The Qumran Community, and other Essenean communities, believed that they alone properly interpreted the Torah.

The Dead Sea Scrolls demonstrate that the Qumran community, and other Essenean communities, were no less interested in enacting laws than were the Tannaim and their predecessors, and several of the scrolls—including the Community Rule, the Damascus Document, the Temple Scroll, and the War Scroll—contain law codes.⁷⁰ Vermes states that the code of law laid down in the Damascus Document contains laws that are to a large extent identical with laws found in the Community Rule insofar as they

---

65. See also Amihay, "Law and Society," 16-20 (discussing the "tension" between the view that the members of the sect have "chosen to live righteously" and their understanding that they live righteously because "their fate has destined them to be among the Sons of Light").

66. Sanders, *Paul and Palestinian Judaism*, 266. See also Sanders, *Paul and Palestinian Judaism*, 257-70 (discussing "election and predestination" in the Dead Sea Scrolls), 320 ("God's predestining election was not perceived as excluding human choice"): Amihay, "Law and Society," 17-19.

67. Sanders, *Paul and Palestinian Judaism*, 282 (emphasis original).

68. Sanders, *Paul and Palestinian Judaism*, 282.

69. Sanders, *Paul and Palestinian Judaism*, 282.

70. See generally Schiffman, *Halakhah at Qumran*, 4-9.

relate to communal discipline, but that the Damascus Document "differs in content" from the Community Rule because it contains "a more detailed sectarian reformulation of scriptural laws regulating Jewish life as such."[71] Notwithstanding any differences, however, the Community Rule and the Damascus Document, as well as other Dead Sea texts, "reflect—for the most part—a shared [legal] tradition."[72]

The shared legal tradition entailed incorporating extrabiblical regulations into the legal system *entirely* through biblical exegesis.[73] Thus, the Damascus Document directs everyone in the community "to *return* to the Torah of Moses, *for in it everything is specified*."[74] Similarly, the author of the Temple Scroll, at 56:3–4, adapting and expanding on the language of Deut 17:8–13, wrote: "You must act according to the instruction that they [that is, the priest or judge deciding any case] relate to you ... from the book of the Torah." The author added "from the book of the Torah" to the wording in Deuteronomy in order to emphasize "the importance of establishing halakha on the written text of the Torah alone, thus excluding the 'tradition of the fathers' as a legitimate halakhic source."[75]

Schremer characterizes the return to the Torah as "a revolution," arguing that it "stood in contrast to a different mode of religiosity that had been in existence at that time, that is, 'tradition-based observance,' which emphasized ... the tradition of the fathers."[76] He writes further:

> I am suggesting that with respect to halakha ... Qumran's bibliocentricity was an innovation. Prior to that "revolution" it was not customary to appeal to the written text of the Torah in order to draw halakhic guidance from it. This can be shown ... by the very fact that there is almost no reference to Scripture in the early halakhic dicta of the Second Temple era....

71. Vermes, "Introduction," 37.

72. Amihay, "Law and Society," 2–3. See Angel, "Damascus Document," 2977 ("The laws of the *Damascus Document* are often in accordance with other legal works discovered at Qumran," and there is a "common legal tradition underlying these texts" [emphasis original]).

73. See Schiffman, *Halakhah at Qumran*, 134 (The "Dead Sea sect ... lack[s] an oral law concept. Scripture, then, becomes the sole source of *halakhah*").

74. CD 16:1 (emphasis added). Cf. 1QS 5:7–10. The author of the Damascus Document considered the sect to have "rediscovered" the Torah and to have innovated the practice of appealing to the Torah as the "source of halakhic guidance." Schremer, "'[T]he[y] Did Not Read,'" 110.

75. Schremer, "'[T]he[y] Did Not Read,'" 111.

76. Schremer, "'[T]he[y] Did Not Read,'" 113.

> Urbach has suggested that . . . in those days halakhic decisions were not derived from Scripture. Rather institutional authority was their main source of legitimacy.[77]

The *halakhah* of the Pharisees/Tannaim consisted of traditional regulations handed down to them, and new regulations added to that tradition, that were not typically based on biblical exegesis nor (before the Yavnean period) claimed to be divinely revealed. Therefore, the Essenes considered the regulations of the Pharisees/Tannaim to be based on "false legal exegesis,"[78] and they considered such regulations to be "lies or falsehoods."[79] So, they called the Pharisees/Tannaim "*dorshei halakot*" (lying interpreters).[80] In sharp contrast to the *halakhot* of the Pharisees/Tannaim, the Essenes claimed that the regulations they promulgated had been derived exclusively from divinely revealed biblical exegesis.[81] They "also believed that successive revelations of inspired interpretation would allow the law to change with the times."[82] The community was instructed to live "according to the Torah" and its sectarian interpretation.[83]

The Essenes distinguished laws that were "revealed" in the biblical text from laws that were "hidden" in the biblical text, called, respectively,

---

77. Schremer, "'[T]he[y] Did Not Read,'" 115-16. See also Schremer, "'[T]he[y] Did Not Read," 122 ("The evidence indicates not only that Qumran's appeal to Scripture should be seen as a reforming innovation but also that it marks the beginning of this new fashion").

78. Schiffman, "Pharisees," 621.

79. See Angel, "Damascus Document," 2984 (explaining the phrase "smooth things" in CD 1:18). See also Novick, "Tradition, Scripture, Law, and Authority," 66-67 (discussing a sectarian text from Qumran that attacks the Pharisees as being "akin to idol worshippers because they treat the commandments of their human leaders with as much or indeed greater respect than the commandments of God, and so divinize their human leaders").

80. Schiffman, "Pharisees," 621. See Angel, "Damascus Document," 2984 ("It puns on the Hebrew *dorshei halakhot* (interpreters of the laws), apparently a protest against Pharisaic traditions not having a firm source in Scripture").

81. The sectarians believed that the correct understanding of biblical laws that were too nebulous to be beyond dispute could be obtained by "divinely guided" biblical exegesis and that such exegesis was known only to the members of the sect. Schiffman, *Halakhah at Qumran*, 19, 32, 48, 68, 75-76; Angel, "Damascus Document," 2978. See Amihay, "Law and Society," 13 (For the Essenes "the law is divine in origin"), 16 ("Law is conceived as the true manifestation of the will of God, part and parcel of the natural order").

82. Schiffman, *Halakhah at Qumran*, 76.

83. CD 7:7-9 (referring to Num 30:17). See Num 30:17 ("Those are the laws that the Lord enjoined upon Moses"); Schiffman, *Halakhah at Qumran*, 46.

"*niglot*" and "*nistarot*." According to Schiffman, "the *niglot* are those [laws] stated in clear terms about which there is no doubt as to meaning and manner of implementation," whereas "*nistarot* are commandments worded in general or vague terms lacking detailed instructions as to how to carry out the law."[84] Put differently, the *nigleh* "is nothing more than Scripture, while the *nistar* is sectarian interpretation of it."[85]

Another important terminological distinction made by the sectarians with regard to biblical exegesis is that between *perush* and *midrash*. Through the exegetical method of *perush*, laws could be derived from biblical verses without the use of prooftexts. Laws derived in this manner were distinguished, according to Schiffman, from *midrash*, *midrash* being sectarian laws derived from one biblical verse on the basis of another biblical verse.[86] The term "*mishpatim*" was used by the sectarians to mean all "the regulations derived through sectarian exegesis."[87] Schiffman contends that *mishpatim* could be "determined at public legislative sessions during which disputes were also settled."[88]

Because the sectarians believed that *only they* knew God's will, they considered God to have, in essence, established a new covenant with them, and the Damascus Document recounts how and when this renewed divine relationship came about. The recounting begins by asserting that Abraham "kept God's ordinances and did not choose (that which) his (own) spirit desired,"[89] that Abraham "transmitted (his way) to Isaac and Jacob; and they observed (them) and were registered as lovers of God and parties to (his) covenant forever."[90] Thereafter, however, the "sons of Jacob strayed"; they "walked in the wantonness of their heart(s),

---

84. Schiffman, *Halakhah at Qumran*, 23. See also Angel, "Damascus Document," 2978 ("'Revealed' laws are those clearly mentioned by Scripture and known to all the people of Israel, who nevertheless violate them. 'Hidden' laws, on the other hand, are not explicit in Scripture and known only to the members of the sect"); Schiffman, *Halakhah at Qumran*, 22–32 (discussing *nigleh* and *nistar*).

85. Schiffman, *Halakhah at Qumran*, 32.

86. See Schiffman, *Halakhah at Qumran*, 60, 76 ("*Perush* refers to an exegesis of the text that which does not involve the citation of corroborative material from elsewhere in Scripture. The *midrash* is an exegetical form in which a passage is interpreted in light of a second passage").

87. Schiffman, *Halakhah at Qumran*, 43.

88. Schiffman, *Halakhah at Qumran*, 68.

89. CD 3:2.

90. CD 3:2–4.

plotting against the ordinances of God, each man doing what was right in his own eyes."[91] The text continues:

> But out of those who held fast to God's ordinances . . . God established his [new] covenant with Israel forever, revealing to them hidden things [*nistarot*] in which all Israel had strayed: his holy Sabbaths, the glorious appointed times, his righteous testimonies, and the desires of his will, which a person shall do and live by them.[92]

This passage indicates that the new covenant included regulations with regard to the keeping of the Sabbath and the observance of festivals.[93] Numerous sectarian Sabbath rules are included in the Damascus Document.[94] These rules mandate, inter alia, that the Sabbath begin on Friday night. They also prohibit walking in the field to do business, eating anything other than what had already been prepared, making any decision in matters of money and gain, walking more than one thousand cubits beyond the town, bringing anything in or out of the house, opening a sealed vessel, and lifting an animal out of a cistern or pit that it may have fallen into.[95]

In contrast to the Pharisees/Tannaim, but like the extremist Sabbath rules found in Jubilees,[96] the Qumran sectarians "reached a peak in restrictiveness" in their Sabbath rules.[97] For example, the Qumran

91. CD 3:4-6. Cf. Judg 17:6; 21:25; chapter 1, n18 and accompanying text.

92. CD 3:12-16.

93. See Schiffman, *Halakhah at Qumran*, 77 ("The sect felt that Israel had gone astray in its Sabbath observance, not possessing the correct interpretation (*nistar*) of the Sabbath law. The sect [also] had calendar differences with the Jerusalem establishment as to the correct days for the observance of the festivals"), 136 (Qumran used a solar calendar); See Vermes, "Introduction," 78-80 (The Qumran sect adhered to a solar calendar, a practice also attested in Jubilees and 1 Enoch, and consequently "its feast-days were working days for other Jews and vice versa"); Angel, "Damascus Document," 2988 ("The failure of Israel to observe the proper calendrical cycle is also a concern in Jubilees. . . . In fact, a number of texts discovered at Qumran promote the 364-day calendar"). Cf. Jub. 1:14-15; 6:36-37 (Those who follow the lunar calendar "corrupt the temporal order and make a day of testimony an abomination, and a profane day a festival").

94. See CD 10:14—11:17. See also Schiffman, *Halakhah at Qumran*, 77-133 (discussing CD 10:14—11:17).

95. See Schiffman, *Halakhah at Qumran*, 77-133.

96. Jub. 2:17-33; 50:6-13 (Sabbath *halakhah*). See Sigal, *Halakhah of Jesus*, 174-80 (discussing Jubilees' Sabbath *halakhah*); Moore, *Judaism in the First Centuries*, 1.98 (Interpretation and expansion of biblical laws in Jubilees is "stricter" than in the Mishnah).

97. Sigal, *Halakhah of Jesus*, 181. See also Schremer, "'[T]he[y] Did Not Read,'" 112

community's rules and the rules in Jubilees do not allow one to eat *anything* that was not prepared in advance of the Sabbath, and this represents "a more ancient and rigorous *halakhah* than that of the Tannaim."[98] Neither do the Qumran community's rules nor the rules in Jubilees allow for deviations from Sabbath restrictions to save a human life, while the Tannaim permitted such deviations pursuant to the concept of *piqquach nephesh* (saving a life), which holds that the preservation of human life overrides virtually any other rule of conduct.[99]

The Essenes also differed from the Pharisees/Tannaim in their interpretation of other biblical laws. For example, using the hermeneutical principle of *heqqesh*, the sectarians expanded the biblical law prohibiting a man from marrying an aunt (Lev 18:12–13) to prohibit any sibling of a parent from marrying any of that parent's children.[100] Thus an uncle was prohibited from marrying his niece, something *not* prohibited by the Pharisees/Tannaim.[101] Then too, the sectarians strenuously objected to the Tannaim's permissive attitude to divorce and polygamy. Relying on Gen 1:27 ("male and female he created them"), the author of the Damascus Document claims that a man's "taking two wives in their lives" is a type of "unchastity" (*zenut*) and is a sin.[102] This claim is interpreted

---

(referring to Qumran's "tendency to halakhic stringency"); Schiffman, *Halakhah at Qumran*, 97 ("From Josephus [J.W. 2; 8:9] it is clear that the Essenes were quite strict in their Sabbath code"); Blenkinsopp, *Wisdom and Law*, 149 (The members of the sect "committed themselves not just to Torah in general but to a particular interpretation of the laws.... The sect's interpretation is in general stricter than that of the Pharisees, especially with regard to sabbath and ritual cleanliness"). See generally Sigal, *Halakhah of Jesus*, 181–85 (comparing what Sigal takes to be "the stringent halakhah of Qumran and Jubilees," which had "no options for leniency or humanitarian concerns," with what he takes to be the less restrictive approaches of the "proto-rabbis" and Jesus).

98. Schiffman, *Halakhah at Qumran*, 99.

99. See CD 11:16–17; Sigal, *Halakhah of Jesus*, 177, 182–85; Schiffman, *Halakhah at Qumran*, 125–27 (While noting that other possible interpretations of CD 11:16–17 are possible, Schiffman opines that it is "most probable that the sect did not accept the doctrine of *piqquaḥ nefesh*").

100. See CD 5:7–8; Sigal, *Halakhah of Jesus*, 84.

101. See Angel, "Damascus Document," 2991 (CD 5:7–8 is a "likely polemic against the practice of the Pharisees," who permitted uncle-niece marriages "and even praised them"). See also Novick, "Tradition, Scripture, Law, and Authority," 75 ("The Qumran sectarians insist that the Bible intends for the incest prohibitions to be read in a gender-symmetric way").

102. See CD 4:19–20. Reliance on Gen 1:27 suggests a belief in natural law. See Novick, "Tradition, Scripture, Law, and Authority," 80–81 (The sectarian law against polygamy (or remarriage) "follows from the nature of the created world"). See also Amihay, "Law and Society," 13–14 (quoted at n106 in this chapter). Cf. Mark 10:2–9.

by scholars as prohibiting polygamy and a second marriage after divorce, both of which were permitted by the Pharisees/Tannaim.[103]

3. The ethical theory the Essenes used to justify their laws is ethical egoism.

The Community Rule directs the *maskil* to instruct the members of the community about punishments that are inflicted by divine powers. He must tell them that the punishments to be visited upon all who walk in the spirit of deceit and darkness include "a multitude of plagues by the hand of all the destroying angels, everlasting damnation by the avenging wrath of the fury of God, eternal torment and endless disgrace together with shameful extinction in the fire of the dark regions."[104] Conversely, the *maskil* instructs that "the [divine] visitation of all who walk in [the spirit of truth and light] . . . shall be healing, great peace in a long life, and fruitfulness, together with every everlasting blessing and eternal joy in life without end, a crown of glory and a garment of majesty in unending light."[105]

While many of the moral rules set forth in the sectarian texts—such as never addressing another in anger, never hating another, and never acquiring wealth by unrighteous means—are conducive to an orderly, harmonious, and just society, no individual law or collection of laws is ever said to be justified on such utilitarian grounds.[106] Similarly, even

---

103. See Klawans, *Impurity and Sin*, 52–53; Sigal, *Halakhah of Jesus*, 136–37; Jassen, "Damascus Document," 2990. Cf. Mark 10:6–10 (quoted in sec. B, 2 in this chapter); Matt 19:3–9. See generally Klawans, *Impurity and Sin*, 52–56 (discussing CD 4:12–5:11 and arguing that the sin of unchastity, in contrast to the sins of incest and contact with a menstruant, was not understood to defile the sanctuary).

104. 1QS 4:12–13. The Community Rule further teaches regarding all who walk in the spirit of deceit, "The times of all their generations shall be spent in sorrowful mourning and in bitter misery and in calamities of darkness until they are destroyed without remnant or survivor." 1QS 4:13–14. Cf. CD 6–7; Jub. 24:30. See also 1QS 2:4–8; 5:12–13.

105. 1QS 4:6–8. See Jassen, "Rule of the Community," 2937 ("Visitation" is here used "in a positive sense to describe the bountiful rewards awaiting the Sons of Truth in the end-time").

106. But see Amihay, "Law and Society," 13–14 (arguing that a "version of natural law" is reflected in the texts of Essene law, and that "laws concerning time or place reflect natural phenomena and attributes that the creator imbued in them. As a result, any transgression of the law entails a disruption of balance in the world, and causes a physical reality [presumably having adverse consequences for the community]").

though the extrabiblical laws of the Essenes were considered by them to be divine (and thus authoritative), nowhere is it stated that one should adhere to the law for that reason alone, regardless of consequences. Rather, appeal is primarily made to the beneficial consequences for the individual of obedience and the adverse consequences for the individual of transgression. So, the ethical theory the Essenes used to justify their laws is ethical egoism.

4. There are significant differences between the Essenes and the Pharisees/Tannaim.

Five differences between the Essenes and the Tannaim are worth reiterating. Most important, there is a difference in the source of and means of transmitting extrabiblical law. The Essenes rejected the man-made, non-scripturally based laws constituting the tradition of the fathers relied upon by the Pharisees/Tannaim, and they rejected reliance on the oral transmission of law, later embraced by those Tannaim who created the Oral Torah myth. Instead, the Essenes purported to derive their own regulations exclusively from the written text of the Torah, and they put their legal traditions in writing.[107] The Essenes considered the *halakhah* of the Pharisees/Tannaim to be non-authoritative and illegitimate. They believed that only their own rules had authority and legitimacy, as these rules, they claimed, represented God's will.

Second, there is a difference with regard to the acceptance of dualism. The Essenes, but not the Pharisees/Tannaim, accepted both cosmic and anthropological dualism. According to the Essenean worldview, Jews were divided into two separate and distinct groups controlled by two separate and distinct cosmic forces. The righteous, who knew God's will and walked with God, were controlled by the Prince of Light. The wicked, who transgressed God's will, were controlled by Belial, the Angel of Darkness. Although the Pharisees/Tannaim distinguished righteous Jews from wicked Jews, they did not postulate that these constituted two separate and distinct groups controlled by two separate and distinct cosmic forces.

---

107. See Schiffman, *Halakhah at Qumran*, 20 ("It is definite that the sectarians had no compunctions about putting their legal traditions into writing. This practice is in marked contrast to the later Rabbinic dicta discouraging or prohibiting the writing of *halakhot*. In Rabbinic tradition, the prohibition of the use of written halakhic texts was designed to reinforce the doctrines of oral Law and oral transmission").

Indeed, they believed that the vast majority of Jews were neither wholly righteous nor wholly wicked but *benonim* (middling).[108]

Third, there was disagreement about the potential for human nature and human society to be transformed absent divine intervention. More specifically, there was disagreement about (1) the ability of human beings to become righteous through a transformative process of their own doing, (2) whether torah study could transform human behavior, and (3) the degree to which human society could be improved by laws promulgated for the general good. The Pharisees/Tannaim believed that human beings could mitigate the power of the evil *yetzer*, that this could be achieved through *talmud torah*, and that human society as a whole could be improved by laws promulgated for "the general good" [*tikkun ha-olam*] without the need for supernatural intervention.[109]

The Essenes were far less sanguine than the Pharisees/Tannaim about the ability of human beings to transform themselves or human society. Rather, they believed the present world was irredeemably evil and that all human beings (except for members of their sect) were irredeemably wicked. Although they stressed the importance of torah study, there is no indication they believed that torah study could transform human nature. And although they promulgated rules for their own communities, there is no indication they believed their rules could transform wicked communities into righteous communities. Indeed, any such beliefs would undermine their view that God was *imminently* going to create a new world in which evil and wickedness would be eradicated. For the Essenes, then, absent divine intervention, neither human nature nor human society could be meaningfully transformed.

Fourth, there is a difference in their views about segregation of the righteous from the wicked. The Essenes believed that all members of their community (who constituted the righteous) had to segregate themselves as much as possible from all other Jews (who were among the wicked). In sharp contrast to this outlook, the Pharisees/Tannaim taught that one

---

108. See ch.9, n170 and accompanying text. See also Glatzer, *Hillel the Elder*, 89 ("Hillel appears in opposition to the sects: he rejected their radical view of the just *versus* the wicked, good *versus* evil and advocated a middle line" [emphasis original]).

109. See also Levenson, "Messianic Movements," 628 ("Messianic themes represent only a small fraction of rabbinic literature"; rather, "most rabbinic literature focuses on sanctifying this world by studying and keeping the commandments and repenting for sin by deeds of mercy and piety," and rabbinic texts "state that these, and not supernatural intervention, are the acts that will bring redemption").

should *not* separate themselves from the rest of the community.¹¹⁰ As Cohen puts it, the "dominant ethic" in the Mishnah "is not exclusivity but elasticity."¹¹¹ Subsequent rabbinic teaching went so far as to say that "those who separate themselves from the ways of the community" would be punished in hell "for generations."¹¹²

Fifth, there are differences in ethical theory. The Essenes justified biblical law and their own extrabiblical regulations on the bases of their purported beneficial consequences for the individual at the end time, so the ethical theory justifying their laws is ethical egoism, while the Pharisees/Tannaim justified their *halakhah* on the bases of its beneficial consequences for the community as a whole, so the ethical theory justifying their *halakhah* is utilitarianism.

B. Jesus of Nazareth was a teacher and lawmaker who used exegetical methods identical to those of the Tannaim to pronounce laws that differed from theirs but which were deemed authoritative by his followers.

As depicted in the Gospels (written in Greek), Yeshua, or Jesus,¹¹³ was a teacher and lawmaker who "participated in Pharisaic-type fellowship meals."¹¹⁴ Vermes contends that there was no "fundamental disagree-

---

110. See m. ʾAbot 2:5 ("Hillel said: Sever not thyself from the congregation"); Herford, *Ethics of the Talmud*, 45 (stating with regard to m. ʾAbot 2:5: "It is probable that Hillel had in mind the Essenes, who felt drawn to a life of secure seclusion"). See also Glatzer, *Hillel the Elder*, 89 (comparing Hillel to the "sectarian Dead Sea movements" and stating that he rejected "the withdrawal into the desert and the sects' pronounced individualism," opting, rather, to encourage all members of the community to be "true and just").

111. Cohen, "Significance of Yavneh," 29. Cohen argues that, after Yavneh, opposing points of view were for the first time preserved by Jews for the specific purpose of ending the need for sectarianism. He points to one Tannaitic midrash which remarks "ʾ*loʾ titgodedu* [Deut 14:1]. Do not make separate factions (ʾ*agudot*) but make one faction all together." Cohen, "Significance of Yavneh," 29.

112. Moore, *Judaism in the First Centuries*, 2.387 (citing t. Sanh. 13:4–5; b. Roš Haš. 17a).

113. The name "Jesus" is a Latin form of the Greek "*Iesous*," which, in turn, is a Greek form of the Hebrew "*Yehoshua*" (meaning "Yahweh is salvation"), which was abbreviated as "Yeshua." Swidler, *Yeshua*, 1.

114. Swidler, *Yeshua*, 65. See generally Neusner, *From Politics to Piety*, 87–96 (In the Gospels and in rabbinic traditions deriving from pre-70 CE times, the Pharisees are depicted as a "table-fellowship sect within Judaism" concerned primarily with "the laws of tithing and ritual purity, defining what and with whom one may eat").

ment between Jesus and the Pharisees";[115] Pawlikowski concludes "that it would not be wrong 'to consider Jesus as a part of the general Pharisaic movement, even though in many areas he held a distinctive viewpoint'";[116] and Sigal, who associates the Pharisees of the Gospels with "separatists" (such as the Essenes), not with the Tannaim's predecessors,[117] calls Jesus a "proto-rabbi."[118] In addition to his teaching and lawmaking, Jesus was an eschatological preacher and a charismatic.[119]

Jesus was born in about 4 BCE and began teaching in Galilee in the second decade of the first century CE.[120] He gathered around him followers who called him "Rabbi,"[121] suggesting a relationship to Jesus similar to the relationship that the Tannaim had with their followers,[122] i.e., Jesus' followers considered him to be an authority on, and teacher of, the law.[123] Jesus' followers accepted his modifications and expansions of biblical law (his "*halakhah*"), as the followers of the Tannaim accepted Tannaitic *halakhah*. And Jesus derived his *halakhah* on the basis of the very same exegetical techniques used by the Tannaim.[124]

---

115. Vermes, *Jesus and Judaism*, 11.

116. Swidler, *Yeshua*, 65–66 (quoting Pawlikowski, *Christ*, 92). See generally Swidler, *Yeshua*, 57–71.

117. See Sigal, *Halakhah of Jesus*, 3–8. There are problems with Sigal's argument which, except for one comment, are not addressed herein. See n146 in this chapter.

118. Sigal, *Halakhah of Jesus*, 192. Sigal even speculates that Jesus and Yohanan b. Zakkai "were colleagues in Galilee," and that Jesus "probably studied at both the schools of Hillel and Shammai." Sigal, *Halakhah of Jesus*, 192n13.

119. See Davies, *Sermon on the Mount*, 131–34; Vermes, *Jesus the Jew*, 58–82 (discussing "Jesus and charismatic Judaism" and comparing Jesus to Honi the Circle-Drawer and Hanina ben Dosa); Swidler, *Yeshua*, 71–73.

120. See generally Vermes, *Jesus the Jew*, 42–47 (discussing "Jesus and Galilee").

121. John 1:38, 39; 4:31; 6:25; 9:2; 11:8; 20:16; Matt 26:25; Mark 9:5. See also Matt 23:7-8 (Jesus told his followers, "You are not to be called rabbi"). See generally Davies, *Sermon on the Mount*, 134–38.

122. See also Sigal, *Halakhah of Jesus*, 31 (That Jesus' disciples called him "rabbi" enhances the probability "that he was considered a proto-rabbi in his day").

123. See Reinhartz, "Gospel According to John," 188; Davies, *Sermon on the Mount*, 119 ("The title 'Rabbi' as applied to Jesus . . . bore the connotation of 'teacher'"), 135 ("Much of his time with his disciples went into the exposition of the Law"); Rivkin, *Hidden Revolution*, 275 ("Jesus was, like the Pharisees, a *didaskalos*, a teacher. He taught by word of mouth and example, even as did the Pharisees. . . . [He] is addressed . . . as Teacher (*didaskalos, rav*)").

124. See Gale, "Gospel According to Matthew," 10 ("Matthew's Jesus is . . . depicted as utilizing Jewish exegetical methods to create new authoritative rulings"). See also Sigal, *Halakhah of Jesus*, 78–87.

Sigal argues that the *halakhah* of Jesus, as the *halakhah* of the Tannaim, was guided by the principle of *lifnim meshurat ha-din* (going beyond the requirements of the law) and was much more "lenient" than the "stringent halakhah" of the "pietists and separatists" responsible for the book of Jubilees and the Damascus Document.[125] As Sigal sees it, for both Jesus and the later-day rabbis, the principle of *lifnim meshurat ha-din* and the tendency toward leniency "derive ultimately from the love command [Lev 19:18]"—that is, from the importance they placed on the quality of mercy and on "humanitarian considerations" such as protecting the underprivileged, elevating the status of women, and promoting domestic harmony.[126] Klawans asserts: "Virtually all of the statements attributed to Jesus on 'the law' fit within ancient Jewish thought and practice."[127]

In addition, the qualities and conduct that Jesus said God required were, essentially, the same qualities and conduct that the Tannaim said God required, namely, those qualities and conduct having cooperative value. Both Jesus and the Tannaim also taught that such qualities and conduct included, fundamentally, the moral requirements contained in the Decalogue and were encapsulated in the rule "Do unto others as you would have them do unto you."

Jesus was at odds with the Tannaim, however, on several important issues. First, in some instances, Jesus' interpretations of biblical law differed from those of the Tannaim, and in such instances Jesus' followers believed that Jesus' interpretations were authoritative. Second, Jesus based several of his differing interpretations and modifications of biblical law on a concept of natural law not used by the Tannaim. Third, although Jesus agreed with the Tannaim that wickedness was caused by an

---

125. See Sigal, *Halakhah of Jesus*, 29, 58, 87–89, 93–97, 155, 170, 177, 183–84, 191. See generally Amihay, "Law and Society," 7–8 (objecting to characterizing law from Qumran as "*halakhah*").

126. See Sigal, *Halakhah of Jesus*, 29, 69–75, 87–97. For the rabbinic principle of *lifnim meshurat ha-din*, see b. B. Meṣi'a 30b ("R. Johanan [ben Zakkai] said: 'Jerusalem was destroyed only because they ... did not act above and beyond the strict requirements of the law [*lifnim meshurat ha-din*]'"); Fonrobert, "Ethical Theories in Rabbinic Literature," 57–58; Korn, "Legal Floors," 2–19; Barer, "Law, Ethics, and Hermeneutics," 1–14.

127. Klawans, "Law," 656. See generally Sanders, *Jesus and Judaism*, 245–69 (discussing "Jesus and the law" and concluding that although Jesus "looked to a new age, and therefore ... viewed the institutions of this age as not final," we "find no criticism of the law which would allow us to speak of his opposing or rejecting it"). Paul of Tarsus, however, was later to teach gentiles who joined the original Jewish followers of Jesus that adherence to Jewish law was not important to achieve salvation or well-being. It is with Paul, therefore, that something outside of Judaism begins.

undivided heart, Jesus never said, as did the Tannaim, that righteousness could be achieved through torah study. Fourth, in contrast to the Tannaim, Jesus taught that the end time was imminent. Fifth, nowhere does Jesus justify his interpretations of biblical law on the utilitarian grounds of *tikkun ha-olam*, as did the Tannaim; rather, the ethical theory that best reflects the justification offered by Jesus is ethical egoism.

1. Jesus interpreted, modified, and expanded biblical law by means of the same exegetical techniques used by the Tannaim.

In the Sermon on the Mount, Jesus is purported to have taught his followers to fully accept the first two sections of the Hebrew Bible (the Torah, or Law, and the Prophets) that, by that time, had been compiled. Jesus said:

> Do not think that I have come to abolish the law or the prophets; I have come not to abolish but to fulfill. For truly I tell you, until heaven and earth pass away, not one letter, not one stroke of a letter, will pass from the law until all is accomplished. Therefore, whoever breaks one of the least of these commandments, and teaches others to do the same, will be called least in the kingdom of heaven; but whoever does them and teaches them will be called great in the kingdom of heaven.[128]

Despite fully accepting biblical law, Jesus did not hesitate to modify or expand it.[129] Jesus described six of his modifications or expansions of biblical law as constituting a heightened level of righteousness. These are the six "antitheses" (oppositions) pronounced immediately after admonishing his disciples that "unless [their] righteousness exceed[ed] that of the scribes and Pharisees,[130] [they would] never enter the kingdom

---

128. Matt 5:17-19. See Klawans, "Law," 655 ("'Law' and 'prophets' likely refers to the first two sections of the Hebrew Bible"); Gale, "Gospel According to Matthew," 20. Cf. Luke 16:17 ("It is easier for heaven and earth to pass away, than for one stroke of a letter in the law to be dropped").

129. See Klawans, "Law," 656 ("Because 'the Law' (i.e., the written Torah) is not the only or final word on what Jews deem authoritative, it becomes clear why Jesus asserts that he comes to 'fulfill the law' and simultaneously asserts the written Torah's insufficiency.... The Torah's literal sense does not define Jewish law, whether for the rabbis, the Dead Sea sectarians, or for Jesus and his followers").

130. See also Sigal, *Halakhah of Jesus*, 5 (Sigal argues that "the *Pharisaioi* [the Greek translation of the Hebrew *perushim*, "Pharisees"] of the New Testament represent a complex, inchoate, mass of pietists and separatists . . . [that] were rigid in their halakhah . . . and were therefore at serious odds with Jesus"), 57 ("The *Pharisaioi* of the New Testament are not the proto-rabbis of the Hillel and Shammai circles or of the

of heaven."¹³¹ Each antithesis entails using the Tannaitic exegetical technique of building a fence around the law.

In the first antithesis, Jesus instructs:

> You have heard that it was said . . . "You shall not murder"; and "whoever murders shall be liable to judgment." But I say to you that if you are angry with a brother or sister, you will be liable to judgment.¹³²

Although it has been argued that this antithesis constitutes an *abrogation* of the Torah, it is properly understood as an attempt to *build a fence around* the Torah.¹³³ The second and fourth of the antitheses are also clear attempts to build a fence around the Torah. Jesus instructs:

> You have heard that it was said, "You shall not commit adultery." But I say to you that everyone who looks at a woman with lust has already committed adultery with her in his heart. . . . Again, you have heard that it was said . . . "You shall not swear falsely, but carry out vows you have made to the Lord." But I say to you, Do not swear at all.¹³⁴

---

school of Yoḥanan b. Zakkai"), 59 ("The term *perushim* encompasses a variety of extremists, including Essenes, Qumranites, Zealots, among others").

131. Matt 5:20. See generally Przybylski, "Meaning and Significance," 247–56, 176 ("The righteousness that is to exceed that of the scribes and Pharisees is a righteousness that is representative of an extremely meticulous observance of the law"), 181 ("By the greater righteousness Matthew really points toward perfection," as stated in Matt 5:48), 185 (The greater righteousness Jesus demanded of his disciples did not mean that they were to live according to a different law, but that they were "to live according to a different interpretation of the law, namely, an extremely meticulous and strict interpretation"). Sigal associates the greater righteousness demanded by Jesus with the principle of *lifnim meshurat ha-din*. See Sigal, *Halakhah of Jesus*, 95.

132. Matt 5:21–22.

133. See Gale, "Gospel According to Matthew," 18, 20; chapter 8, sec. B, 4. Cf. Schechter, *Aspects of Rabbinic Theology*, 212–13 (Building a fence around the prohibition against killing, the rabbis prohibited "other kinds of shedding blood, as, for instance, to put a man to shame in public, which causes his blood to leave his face. Hence to cause this feeling is as bad as murder"). See also Vermes, *Authentic Gospel*, 204–5 ("The underlying aim is the prevention of murder by eliminating its root cause, inward hostility. . . . In fact what we encounter here is not the abrogation but a counterinterpretation of the Torah"); Davies, *Sermon on the Mount*, 29 ("In none of the Antitheses is there an intention to annul the provisions of the Law but only to carry them out to their ultimate meaning").

134. Matt 5:27–28, 33–34. Cf. Schechter, *Aspects of Rabbinic Theology*, 214 (According to the rabbis, Job 24:10 and Num 15:39 "teaches us that an unchaste look or even an unchaste thought are also to be regarded as adultery'" [quoting *Lev Rab.* 23:11]), 225 (The teaching of the rabbis was that adultery "includes every . . . unchaste

The remaining three antitheses may also be understood as attempts to build a fence around biblical law.[135]

Another clear example of Jesus using one of the same exegetical techniques used by the Tannaim is when Jesus defends his disciples who, on the Sabbath, "began to pluck heads of grain and to eat."[136] Since plucking grain could be considered harvesting, and since harvesting was forbidden on the Sabbath,[137] Jesus was asked why he let his disciples do "what is not lawful to do on the sabbath."[138] Jesus responded:

> Have you not read [in 1 Sam 21:1–6] what David did when he and his companions were hungry? He entered the house of God and ate the bread of the Presence, which it was not lawful for him or his companions to eat, but only for the priests. Or have you not read in the law that on the sabbath the priests in the temple break the sabbath and yet are guiltless? I tell you, something greater than the temple is here.[139]

The first part of this response is an argument from analogy (*heqqesh*), such as was used by the Tannaim.[140] If hunger permitted David and his

---

thought"); Vermes, *Authentic Gospel*, 206–7 (According to Philo and Josephus, the Essenes abstained from oaths).

135. See Gale, "Gospel According to Matthew," 20 ("Some interpreters incorrectly understand the antitheses to be abrogations of Torah. This is not the case. . . . Rather, the antitheses *intensify* the Law, or in Jewish terms, 'build a fence around Torah'" (see m. 'Abot 1.1), that is, mandate observing a law well beyond its minimum requirements to ensure that the law itself is observed" [emphasis original]). See generally Przybylski, "Meaning and Significance," 169–85 (arguing that "the principle of making a fence around Torah underlies Matt 5:21–48").

136. Mark 2:23–28; Matt 12:1–6; Luke 6:1–5. See Vermes, *Authentic Gospel*, 44–49, 174–76; Sigal, *Halakhah of Jesus*, 155–65 (Jesus employs "proto-rabbinic methodology that was . . . in full agreement with the later rabbis").

137. See m. Šabb. 7:2; Vermes, *Authentic Gospel*, 45; Gale, "Gospel According to Matthew," 33. But see Sigal, *Halakhah of Jesus*, 157–59 ("The activity of the disciples . . . falls into at least two permissible spheres").

138. Matt 12:2. See Mark 2:24; Luke 6:2. Sigal argues that Jesus' interlocutors are not "proto-rabbis" but sectarian pietists who maintained stringent interpretations of biblical law, including stringent Sabbath requirements, in opposition to Jesus and the "proto-rabbis" whose humanitarian concerns led them to advance lenient interpretations. See Sigal, *Halakhah of Jesus*, 163, 165.

139. Matt 12:5–6. See Mark 2:25–26

140. See chapter 8, sec. B, 3. See also Wills, "Gospel According to Mark," 75–76 ("The argument form, familiar in both Greek philosophic and rabbinic legal material, is from the lesser to the greater; if David could supersede law to meet human needs . . . so could Jesus' disciples," and noting that, in rabbinic law, "Sabbath restrictions could be set aside if a life was in danger").

companions to do something which was not otherwise lawful, then, by analogy, hunger justified the disciples doing something which was not otherwise lawful.[141] The second part of the response is a *qal ve-homer*.[142] If the priests are permitted to do acts otherwise forbidden on the Sabbath that are required for sacrificial worship (such as butchery and cooking), then, *a fortiori*, the disciples should be allowed to do acts otherwise forbidden on the Sabbath that are required for them to live because preserving life is "greater" than—that is, heavier or more important than—sacrificial worship.[143] This is in keeping with Jesus' teaching that ethical conduct is more important than ritual—a teaching of the prophets as well.[144]

Another *qal ve-homer* argument is used by Jesus to justify curing a man with a withered hand on the Sabbath.[145] His interlocutors acknowledged that, if their sheep fell in a pit on the Sabbath, they would retrieve it.[146] Then Jesus says: "How much more valuable is a human being than a sheep! So it is lawful to do good on the sabbath."[147] *Qal ve-homer* is again used in Matt 6:25–26.[148] Jesus also makes use of the *binyan av mi-shenei khetuvim* argument, the deduction of a rule or general principle

---

141. See Vermes, *Authentic Gospel*, 45. See also Sigal, *Halakhah of Jesus*, 160 ("Matt 12:3–4 constitute a combined *heqqēsh* and an implied *qal waḥomer*"). But see Vermes, *Authentic Gospel*, 175 ("Such a proof based on an example recorded outside the Law of Moses conflicted with rabbinic methodology, which considered the Pentateuch as the only authoritative source for legal rulings"); Gale, "Gospel According to Matthew," 33 (questioning the appropriateness of the analogy on the grounds that David's men, but not the disciples, were in a dangerous situation).

142. See Sigal, *Halakhah of Jesus*, 160–61; chapter 8, sec. B, 3.

143. See Vermes, *Authentic Gospel*, 45, 175–76. See also Mark 2:27 ("The sabbath was made for humankind, and not humankind for the sabbath"). Cf. m. Yoma 8:6 (Danger to life "overrides the Sabbath"); b. Yoma 85b ("The Sabbath is given over to you, not you to the Sabbath").

144. See, e.g., Matt 9:13; 12:7 ("I desire mercy and not sacrifice" [quoting Hos 6:6]). See also Sigal, *Halakhah of Jesus*, 87, 161–62 ("It is the view of Jesus that one must consider *ḥesed* above cult, of which the Sabbath is an integral part, and that despite its status of *qodesh* it is secondary to the preservation of human life and health").

145. See Sigal, *Halakhah of Jesus*, 165–72.

146. Matt 12:11. See Gale, "Gospel According to Matthew," 33 ("Rabbinic law permitted alleviating an animal's distress on the Sabbath" [citing t. Šabb. 15:1; b. Šabb. 128b]). This passage raises a problem for Sigal's identification of Jesus' interlocutors with "separatists" since the separatists did not permit retrieving animals from a pit on the Sabbath. See n95 in this chapter and accompanying text.

147. Matt 12:12. See Vermes, *Authentic Gospel*, 46–49 ("Jesus demonstrates the legitimacy of his action with a cogent *a fortiori* argument"). Cf. Luke 13:10–17; 14:1–5. See also Sigal, *Halakhah of Jesus*, 168 (Jesus is here "rejecting *perushite* stringency").

148. See Gale, "Gospel According to Matthew," 10.

from two biblical verses,[149] when he uses Gen 1:27 and 2:24 to deduce that divorce is prohibited by God.[150] In short, "Jesus expressed his own halakhic viewpoint based upon his own interpretation and application of *traditional* hermeneutics and principles."[151]

2. Jesus' followers believed that his interpretations of biblical law, which were based in part on a concept of natural law, were more authoritative than the interpretations of anyone else.

At times, Jesus' interpretations or modifications of biblical law conflicted with the interpretations or modifications of the same biblical law offered by the Tannaim.[152] One example of such disparity is Jesus' rejection of the biblical law of divorce, Deut 24:1.[153] The biblical law provides:

> A man takes a wife and possesses her. She fails to please him because he finds something obnoxious ['erwat dabar] about her, and he writes her a bill of divorcement, hands it to her, and sends her away from his house.[154]

Relying solely on the language of this biblical passage (specifically on the phrase "something obnoxious"), the houses of Hillel and Shammai came to different opinions about what, specifically, a woman had to do in order for her husband to be permitted to write her a bill of divorcement. The house of Shammai ("exegeting 'erwat dabar ... as any *dabar* [thing] that can be defined as 'erwat," and interpreting 'erwat to mean "sexual indecency, although not necessarily adultery"[155]) opined that a woman

---

149. See chapter 8, sec. B, 3.

150. See Matt 19:3-6; Gale, "Gospel According to Matthew," 10, 46; Sigal, *Halakhah of Jesus*, 122.

151. Sigal, *Halakhah of Jesus*, 152 (emphasis added).

152. Three instances in the Gospel of Matthew where Jesus' differing interpretation of biblical law "arises with special force" is Matt 12:1-14 (concerning the observance of the Sabbath), 15:1-20 (dealing with the laws of purity), and 19:1-19 (dealing with divorce); in all three instances, "Matthew makes it clear that the teaching of Jesus is not in antithesis to the written Law of Moses, though it is critical of the [tradition of the fathers]." Davies, *Sermon on the Mount*, 29-30. Another example is Jesus' interpretation of the biblical law of *lex talionis* which he claimed requires one to "turn the other cheek" (Matt 5:38-39; cf. Lam 3:30), in contrast to the mishnaic interpretation (m. B. Qam. 8:1) which requires only monetary damages. See chapter 9, sec. A.

153. See Sigal, *Halakhah of Jesus*, 105-27.

154. Deut 24:1.

155. Sigal, *Halakhah of Jesus*, 111.

had to be sexually indecent for her husband to divorce her; the house of Hillel (interpreting ʿ*erwat* more broadly) opined that anything the husband found to be obnoxious (ʿ*erwat*) was grounds for divorce.[156] Rabbi Akiva, relying on the phrase "she fails to please him," opined that even if the woman had done *nothing* obnoxious, her husband could divorce her merely because "he found another fairer than she."[157]

The liberal attitudes toward divorce favored by the house of Hillel and by Akiva were unacceptable to Jesus.[158] Jesus went so far as to teach, according to two Gospel accounts (that of Mark and Luke), that divorce is *never* permissible. According to these accounts, Jesus said that "whoever divorces his wife and marries another commits adultery against her; and if she divorces her husband and marries another, she commits adultery."[159] Jesus could not base his opposition to divorce on an interpretation of Deut 24:1 because that passage clearly *permits* divorce.[160] So, Jesus appealed "to the order of creation itself . . . to what was *prior* to the Law of Moses in time and rooted in the act of creation."[161] Jesus appealed, that is, to a concept of natural law.[162]

This appeal to natural law appears in the Gospel of Mark at 10:2-9, where the following incident is recounted:

---

156. See m. Giṭ. 9:10; Moore, *Judaism in the First Centuries*, 2.123-24; Neusner, *From Politics to Piety*, 114. See also Sigal, *Halakhah of Jesus*, 110-11 ("We cannot determine what the author of Deuteronomy meant by ʿ*erwat dabar*," but the Targums render it ʾ*aberat pitgam* (translated "some sinful deed") and the Septuagint renders it *aschēmon pragma* which signifies "indecorous" and "indecent" and may "include sexual indecency but need not").

157. m. Giṭ. 9:10. See Neusner, *From Politics to Piety*, 115 (Akiva "stands well within the Hillite tradition, extending the ruling to a more extreme case than is given to the Hillites").

158. See Sigal, *Halakhah of Jesus*, 140, 142 (suggesting that Jesus' opposition to liberal divorce was due to a concern for protecting the rights of women).

159. Mark 10:10. See Luke 16:18. But see Matt 5:32 (Here Jesus permits divorce but only in cases of unchastity (*porneia*)); Matt 19:9. See Gale, "Gospel According to Matthew," 46; Sigal, *Halakhah of Jesus*, 112, 114 (Jesus "exegeted ʿ*erwat dabar* to mean *porneia*").

160. See Moore, *Judaism in the First Centuries*, 2.124.

161. Davies, *Sermon on the Mount*, 144 (emphasis added). See Sigal, *Halakhah of Jesus*, 114, 122.

162. See Sigal, *Halakhah of Jesus*, 122 ("Jesus lays before his questioners the principle that the natural state of humanity . . . as described by Gen 1:27 and 2:24, was to brook no marital severance"); Hayes, *What's Divine*, 284 (Jesus "believes that human nature was created in such a way as to dictate the practice of monogamy").

> Some Pharisees came [to Jesus and] . . . they asked, "Is it lawful for a man to divorce his wife?" He answered them, "What did Moses command you?" They said, "Moses allowed a man to write a certificate of divorce and to divorce her." But Jesus said to them, "Because of your hardness of heart he wrote this commandment for you. But from the beginning of creation, 'God made them male and female' [Gen 1:27]. 'For this reason a man shall leave his father and mother and be joined to his wife, and the two shall become one flesh.' [Gen 2:24]. So they are no longer two, but one flesh. Therefore what God has joined together, let no one separate."[163]

According to this account, at the time of creation, God brought into being a single male and a single female, and made them inseparable, "one flesh." From this Jesus deduced, says Vermes, "that the primordial divine project did not include divorce and consequently it should not be imposed by men."[164] But, if this is so, "Why then," Jesus is asked, "did Moses command us [in Deut 24:1] to give a certificate of dismissal and to divorce her?"[165] Jesus responded: "It was because you were so hard-hearted that Moses allowed you to divorce your wives, but from the beginning it was not so."[166] Interpreting this response, Vermes asserts that divorce was permitted by Moses because "the fall of Adam and Eve corrupted the heart of man."[167] In other words, the fall of Adam and Eve affected the indivisibility of the human heart, so that human passions, centered in the heart, were now able to prevent a person from choosing to adhere to

---

163. Mark 10:2-9. Cf. Matt 19:3-9.

164. Vermes, *Authentic Gospel*, 55. A similar argument based on Gen 1:27 was used by the Qumran community "to demonstrate the divine purpose of monogamous marriage, and possibly also of the prohibition of divorce." Vermes, *Authentic Gospel*, 55-56 (citing CD 4:19-5:2). See also Davies, *Sermon on the Mount*, 145 (Jesus' appeal to the "created order" of the world may also be found "in the Zadokite Fragments, which probably belonged to the Dead Sea Sect. . . . And again in the Book of Jubilees laws are constantly based on the history of creation"); n102 in this chapter and accompanying text; Angel, "Damascus Document," 2990.

165. Matt 19:7.

166. Matt 19:8.

167. Vermes, *Authentic Gospel*, 55. See generally Brand "Evil and Sin," 648 (The idea that human beings are given an "evil heart" at birth because of Adam's sin is found in 4 Ezra and 2 Baruch and "is used to underscore the inevitability of sin for all humankind," although 2 Baruch "argues against it"); cf. Schechter, *Aspects of Rabbinic Theology*, 188n2 ("There can be little doubt that the belief in the disastrous effects of the sin of Adam on posterity was not entirely absent in Judaism, though the belief did not hold such a prominent place in the Synagogue as in the Christian Church.").

the will of God, resulting in the sin of adultery, among other sins.[168] And since adultery severs the marriage union, after the fall of Adam and Eve, for the Matthean Jesus, divorce became permissible.[169]

More generally, Davies argues that the ethical teaching of Jesus is presented in "a context of creation."[170] In support of this argument, Davies mentions Mark 10:2-9, quoted above, Matt 5:43-5, and Matt 6:26-32, and states that the same appeal to the created order of the world "is implied in the parables of Jesus."[171] In Matt 5:43-5 Jesus admonishes his followers to love their enemies so that they may be "children of their Father in heaven; for he makes his sun rise on the evil and the good, and sends rain on the righteous and the unrighteous."[172] In Matt 6:26-32 Jesus tells his followers not to worry about what they will eat or drink, or what they will wear. He advises them to look at the "birds of the air" and to consider that God feeds the birds; to look at the "lilies of the field" and to consider that God clothes the lilies; and to trust that their "heavenly Father" will feed and clothe them, for he knows "that you need all these things."[173]

Jesus' rejection of the biblical law relating to divorce implied the rejection of all interpretations of that law which liberally permitted divorce and which permitted polygamy.[174] In fact, Sigal argues, "the Matthean Jesus has a wholly independent viewpoint [on the subject of divorce

---

168. See Sigal, *Halakhah of Jesus*, 121 ("The 'hardheartedness' of 19:8 refers to the fact that they have not transcended the sin of adultery"), 122 ("Conditions have changed since the sin of Adam" and "adultery is a fact of life").

169. See Vermes, *Authentic Gospel*, 179-81 ("While the Jesus of Mark and Luke tolerates no second union, Matthew's Jesus twice introduces into the passage the exception clause of unchastity. . . . The reason for this is that the wife's sexual misbehavior has already destroyed the unity of 'one flesh'"); Sigal, *Halakhah of Jesus*, 122 ("Because adultery is in itself a severance of the unity of flesh envisioned by Gen 2:24, divorce was allowed in order to give the innocent party a new opportunity at a sacred marriage"), 125 (Jesus "prohibits all divorce except where the marriage has already been severed by adultery").

170. Davies, *Sermon on the Mount*, 143. According to Davies, the context of creation is one of three contexts in which Jesus' ethical teaching is presented, the other two contexts being "a context of Law" and a "context of doom." Davies, *Sermon on the Mount*, 143.

171. Davies, *Sermon on the Mount*, 144-45.

172. Matt 5:43-5.

173. Matt 6:26-32. See Luke 12:31.

174. See Sigal, *Halakhah of Jesus*, 114-16 (By exegeting *'erwat dabar* to mean *porneia* Jesus "abrogated the halakhah of polygamy, denying a man's right to have more than one wife"), 190, 191.

and polygamy]" that stands apart from the many other viewpoints existing in Second Temple Judaism, including the viewpoints of Ben Sira, the Qumran community, and Philo.[175] In particular, the Matthean Jesus "differed considerably from what ultimately became rabbinic halakhah, embodied in both the Tosefta and the Mishnah, which continued to recognize the validity of [liberal divorce and] polygamy."[176] The rejection of Tannaitic interpretations of biblical law which differed from the way in which Jesus interpreted biblical law is consistent with Jesus' assertion that he did not accept the "tradition of the elders."[177] He did not accept the "tradition of the elders" because he deemed the regulations constituting that tradition to be merely man-made.[178]

Yet, despite his refusal to accept "the tradition of the elders," Jesus explicitly instructed his followers to do what the scribes and Pharisees told them to do; indeed, he says, the scribes and Pharisees "sit on Moses' seat," meaning, presumably, that they had authority to promulgate rules of conduct.[179] The conflict between rejecting the "tradition of the elders," on the one hand, while instructing his followers to do what the scribes and Pharisees tell them, on the other hand, is hard to explain, but, perhaps, Jesus can be understood as instructing his followers to do what the scribes and Pharisees say to do whenever their rules of conduct did not conflict with those promulgated by Jesus.

In any case, the scribes and Pharisees could not have had divine authority to promulgate rules because, according to the Gospels, only Jesus "taught . . . as one having [divine] authority."[180] The "scribes" are

175. Sigal, *Halakhah of Jesus*, 191. See Sigal, *Halakhah of Jesus*, 123, 127–43.

176. Sigal, *Halakhah of Jesus*, 143.

177. See Matt 15:1–19; Mark 7:1–13. See also Davies, *Sermon on the Mount*, 139 (The force of Jesus' criticism of the Pharisees in chapter 7 of Mark is that "the very tradition which they sponsored, as Jesus saw it, had ceased to express the spirit of the Law around which it had grown, and had, indeed, come even to annul its intention. . . . He rejected their kind of tradition"); Novick, "Tradition, Scripture, Law, and Authority," 66 (quoted at n178 in this chapter).

178. See Mark 7:6–13; Novick, "Tradition, Scripture, Law, and Authority," 66 ("The problem with the tradition of the elders . . . is that it is human, not divine, presumably because it is independent from Scripture"); Hayes, *What's Divine*, 228–29 (Jesus regards the Pharisaic traditions "as mere human law" and mocks "their elevation of a purely human legal device over a divine commandment").

179. Matt 23:1–4. See Gale, "Gospel According to Matthew," 52 ("Jesus acknowledges the Pharisees' Torah interpretation"); Moore, *Judaism in the First Centuries*, 1.262 (Jesus recognizes the "Scribes and Pharisees . . . as the legitimate interpreters of the law, and bids his disciples obey their injunctions").

180. Matt 7:28. See Mark 1:21–22, 27. See generally Novick, "Tradition, Scripture,

expressly said *not* to have taught with [divine] authority.¹⁸¹ According to Davies, Jesus' authority was based on his "intuitive awareness of the will of God in its nakedness."¹⁸² In addition, judging from the account of Jesus' teaching at a synagogue in Capernaum, Jesus' authority was based on his charismatic acts of exorcism and healing. As recounted in the Gospel of Mark, when Jesus entered the synagogue in Capernaum and taught, the worshipers "were astounded at his teaching, for he taught them as one having authority."¹⁸³ At that moment, a man with an "unclean spirit" entered the synagogue and Jesus exorcized the unclean spirit.¹⁸⁴ After this, the people are said to have been amazed and to have kept on asking each other, "'What is this? A new teaching—with authority! He commands even the unclean spirits, and they obey him,'" and immediately "his fame began to spread."¹⁸⁵ As Sanders argues, "It is entirely reasonable to assume that Jesus' following . . . saw [the miracles that Jesus performed] as evidencing his status as true spokesman for God, since that sort of inference was common in the Mediterranean."¹⁸⁶

3. The qualities and conduct that Jesus said were demanded by God are those having cooperative value, and he taught that these qualities and conduct could be summed up by the Golden Rule.

According to Przybylski, the concept of righteousness in the Gospel of Matthew "refers to right conduct, namely, conduct that corresponds to

---

Law, and Authority," 72–73 (Just as the contrast between Torah and rabbinic *halakhah* "highlights the authority of the latter" because "it is not bound" by the former, so the antitheses, because they go beyond the requirements of the Torah, highlight the authority of Jesus).

181. Matt 7:28; Mark 1:22.
182. Davies, *Sermon on the Mount*, 148.
183. Mark 1:21–22.
184. Mark 1:23–26.
185. Mark 1:27. See Wills, "Gospel According to Mark," 72 ("Jesus' *teaching* includes not just his words, but also his *authority* to rebuke spirit[s]. . . . Authority (Gk 'exousia'), the freedom to express one's powers by teaching without referring to other teachers or scribes while successfully commanding unclean spirits" [emphasis original]). See Vermes, *Authentic Gospel*, 400 ("People commented that he introduced a new form of teaching, one 'with authority,' in subjugating the forces of evil through the spirit of God").

186. Sanders, *Jesus and Judaism*, 172. See Vermes, *Authentic Gospel*, 339 (Jesus' teaching "was accompanied and validated by charismatic acts, mostly healing and exorcism").

the will of God as expressed in [biblical] law."[187] But Przybylski goes on to explain that such right conduct was insufficient for the followers of Jesus since the followers of Jesus were required to attain a higher level of righteousness—their conduct had to correspond to the will of God as expressed not in biblical law alone, but in biblical law as modified and expanded by Jesus' interpretations of biblical law. So, for example, refraining from murder (as required by biblical law) was "righteous," but it insufficiently corresponded to the will of God since Jesus' interpretation of this law required that one refrain from anger as well as from murder. For this reason, in Matthew, followers of Jesus are not referred to as "righteous" but as "disciples," a disciple being one whose conduct conformed to "the righteousness of God."[188]

Because, at a minimum, Jesus expected his followers to act in accordance with biblical law, the qualities and conduct he most esteemed were, ipso facto, those having cooperative value, those constituting "righteousness" in the Torah.[189] So, among the so-called Beatitudes (Matt 5:3-12), Jesus told his followers to "hunger and thirst for righteousness."[190] Righteousness, says Gale, is "a Matthean theme" that "was linked to justice, ethics, and Torah observance."[191]

The specific virtues Jesus endorsed in the Beatitudes are humility,[192] meekness,[193] being merciful,[194] being a "peacemaker,"[195] and being "pure in heart."[196] These virtues, according to Vermes, "are common virtues

187. Przybylski, "Meaning and Significance," 11.

188. See Przybylski, "Meaning and Significance," 12, 192-94, 247 ("Those who are properly religious in a Christian sense are not righteous. They are disciples. The essence of discipleship is not expressed as righteousness but as doing the will of God"), 249.

189. See generally Przybylski, "Meaning and Significance," 161-256. In the Septuagint the Greek word *dikaiosune* is used to translate the Hebrew word *tzedakah*. See Przybylski, "Meaning and Significance," 163.

190. Matt 5:6.

191. Gale, "Gospel According to Matthew," 12 (citing Matthean and biblical passages).

192. Matt 5:3 ("Blessed are the poor in spirit"). See Gale, "Gospel According to Matthew," 19 (equating the "poor in spirit" with the "humble" [citing Isa 63:1; 66:2; Zeph 2:3]).

193. Matt 5:5. See Gale, "Gospel According to Matthew," 19 (The meek are "people who do not take advantage of their position" [citing inter alia, Isa 49:13; Ps 22:27; Prov 16:19]).

194. Matt 5:7.

195. Matt 5:9.

196. Matt 5:8.

of Jewish piety," and "are prominent in the books of the Old Testament, attested in the Dead Sea Scrolls, and again and again praised by Jesus elsewhere in the Gospels."[197]

Those who possess the virtues endorsed in the Beatitudes are told by Jesus that "theirs is the kingdom of heaven."[198] Elsewhere in the Gospel of Matthew—in the parable of the last judgment—conduct said to merit entry into "the kingdom" includes feeding the hungry, clothing the naked, caring for the sick, and welcoming the stranger.[199] These activities all have cooperative value and are extolled in the Torah and the Prophets.[200] Vermes comments that the parable of the last judgment is based on "an original Jewish parable," and is influenced by the doctrine of *imitatio Dei*, which, he says, "is an essential concept in the teaching of Jesus."[201] The "ultimate source" of the doctrine is Lev 19:2, "You shall be holy, for I, the Lord your God, am holy."[202] Vermes adds that in the parable of the last judgment, under the influence of the *imitatio Dei* doctrine, "man's behavior towards his fellow man is employed as the moral yardstick by which good and evil actions are ultimately distinguished."[203]

Two other behaviors having cooperative value were particularly important to Jesus—almsgiving and eschewing wealth. Almsgiving is implied by instructing his followers to feed the hungry and clothe the naked, but Jesus also specifically refers to the giving of alms using the Greek word *eleēmosunē*.[204] According to Przybylski, the Matthean use of *eleēmosunē* is "equivalent" to the way *tzedakah* is used in Tannaitic literature.[205] Jesus cautions that one's motive in giving alms should not be to earn the praise of others, so one should give alms "in secret."[206] Jesus also teaches that one should not strive for wealth, or even worry about "what you will eat or what you will drink, or about your body, what you

197. Vermes, *Authentic Gospel*, 312.
198. See Matt 5:3. With a clear reference to Ps 37:11, Jesus also says that the meek shall inherit the earth.
199. See Matt 25:34–46.
200. See, e.g., Isa 58:6–7; Ezek 18:5–9.
201. Cf. Matt 5:48; Luke 6:36.
202. Vermes, *Authentic Gospel*, 149–51, 353.
203. Vermes, *Authentic Gospel*, 151.
204. See Matt 6:2, 3, 4. See generally Przybylski, "Meaning and Significance," 212–15; Gale, "Gospel According to Matthew," 22 ("Almsgiving is an increasingly valued practice in Hellenistic and rabbinic Judaism"); chapter 9, sec. B, 2.
205. Przybylski, "Meaning and Significance," 215.
206. Matt 6:2–4.

will wear."²⁰⁷ Rather, he instructs his followers to sell their possessions and use the proceeds to give alms,²⁰⁸ and he famously proclaimed that "it easier for a camel to go through the eye of a needle than for someone who is rich to enter the kingdom of God."²⁰⁹

Jesus was no less interested than the Tannaim in reducing the moral teaching of the Torah to as few principles as possible.²¹⁰ When Jesus was asked which commandments one had to keep in order to gain eternal life, Jesus referred to the ethical portion of the Decalogue and to Lev 19:18.²¹¹ On two other occasions, Jesus reduced the moral teaching of the Torah and the Prophets to just Lev 19:18. He was asked on one of those occasions, "Which of the Torah's commandments was the greatest?," and he answered:

> "You shall love the Lord your God with all your heart, and with all your soul, and with all your mind" [Deut 6:5]. This is the greatest and first commandment. And a second is like it: "You shall love your neighbor as yourself" [Lev 19:18]. On these two commandments hang all the law and the prophets.²¹²

On the second occasion, he put Lev 19:18 into a form similar to the form adopted by Hillel, the so-called "Golden Rule." He said: "In everything do to others as you would have them do unto you; for this is the law and the prophets."²¹³

207. Matt 6:24-25. See Luke 12:22-34; 16:13.

208. See Matt 19:21; Luke 12:33.

209. Matt 19:24. See also Glatzer, *Hillel the Elder*, 43 (Philo describes the Essenes as being "'without money and without possessions,'" and the "early Judeo-Christians who followed the Jerusalemite Christian community called themselves *ebionim*, Ebionites, the poor ones" [citing Philo, *Prob.* 12]).

210. See chapter 9, sec. B, 4.

211. See Matt 19:16-19.

212. Matt 22:37-40. See also Mark 12:28-34; Luke 10:25-28; Rom 13:8-10; Davies, *Sermon on the Mount*, 146-47 ("The concept of love is undoubtedly the best summation of the ethical teachings of Jesus"); chapter 6, n82 and accompanying text; chapter 9, n107 and accompanying text; chapter 10, n11 and accompanying text; nn54-55 in this chapter and accompanying texts.

213. Matt 7:12. Cf. Luke 6:31; chapter 9, n105 and accompanying text. In the sixth of the antitheses, Jesus is purported to have taught, "You have heard it said, 'You shall love your neighbor and hate your enemy.' But I say to you, Love your enemies and pray for those who persecute you." Matt 5:43-44. Cf. Luke 6:27, 32-35. See Davies, *Sermon on the Mount*, 147 ("By extending the term neighbor to include everybody [Jesus] universalized the demand of love"). However, "no biblical text records [the] saying [love your neighbor and hate your enemy]" (Gale, "Gospel According to Matthew," 21). Moreover, Proverbs specifically taught that if your enemy is hungry, you should give

4. Jesus agreed with the Tannaim that righteousness requires an undivided heart but he never clearly stated how such a heart might be achieved.

When a group of Pharisees saw Jesus' disciples failing to wash their hands before eating, they asked Jesus why his disciples failed to live "according to the tradition of the elders" which required one to wash their hands before eating. In response, Jesus accused the Pharisees of abandoning the moral commandments of God in order to adhere to traditions regarding proper ritual, and he argued that matters of ritual impurity are far less important than matters of moral impurity.[214] What is most significant about this incident for present purposes is that Jesus quotes the prophet Isaiah, who said: "This people honors me with its lips, but their hearts are far from me [Isa 29:13]."[215] The quote suggests that proper moral conduct is associated with the human heart being close to God, which is to say, being in accord with the divine will. Then Jesus says to the crowd: "It is not what *goes into* the mouth that defiles a person, but it is what *comes out of* the mouth that defiles."[216] When he is asked to explain what he means, Jesus makes clear that it is the defective condition of the human heart that causes immoral conduct. He says:

> Do you not see that whatever goes into the mouth enters the stomach, and goes out into the sewer? But what comes out of the mouth proceeds from the heart, and this is what defiles. For *out of the heart come evil intentions, murder, adultery, fornication, theft, false witness, slander.*[217]

To better understand why Jesus contends that evil intentions, murder, adultery, fornication, theft, false witness, and slander come out of the heart it is useful to reexamine the antitheses. Several of the antitheses suggest that Jesus associated transgressions of God's commands with

---

him bread. Prov 25:21. See also Prov 24:17–18; Deut 10:19. See generally Fagenblat, "Concept of Neighbor," 645–48.

214. See Matt 15:1–21; Mark 7:1–15; Vermes, *Authentic Gospel*, 51–53.

215. Matt 15:8; Mark 7:6. See also Vermes, *Authentic Gospel*, 53 (Jesus was concerned with the opposition between internal and external piety).

216. Matt 15:11 (emphasis added). See Mark 7:16.

217. Matt 15:18–19 (emphasis added). Cf. Mark 7:20–23 ("For it is from within, from the human heart, that evil intentions come: fornication, theft, murder, adultery, avarice, wickedness, deceit, licentiousness, envy, slander, pride, folly. All evil things come from within, and they defile a person"); Luke 6:45. See Vermes, *Authentic Gospel*, 53 ("Defilement is caused not by the fact that something is intrinsically unclean, but by man's failure to obey God").

THE ESSENES AND THE FOLLOWERS OF JESUS OF NAZARETH

human passions, and in order that his followers avoid transgressions he instructs them to eliminate the passion relevant to the transgression being considered.[218] So, for instance, murder is often committed because the murderer is angry at the person murdered. Accordingly, Jesus teaches that "if you are angry with a brother or sister, you will be liable to judgment" for murder.[219] Again, adultery is committed when a man has lust for a woman. Accordingly, Jesus teaches "that everyone who looks at a woman with lust has already committed adultery with her in his heart."[220] Because the passions of anger and lust were believed to originate in the heart and affect the heart's decision-making function, Jesus asserts that murder and adultery come out of the heart.

The claim that transgressions of God's commandments come out of the heart is similar to the teaching of Jeremiah that there cannot be obedience to God's commandments until human beings are given an undivided heart, that obedience to God's commandments is a matter of possessing an undivided heart. Anger and lust are to be avoided for the reason that they divide the heart and, thus, impede a person from doing what God has commanded. This understanding of Jesus' meaning is supported by his teaching in the Beatitudes that "the pure in heart . . . will see God,"[221] for Vermes tells us that "purity of heart" means a heart with "simplicity and integrity" (that is, "wholeness"),[222] and such a heart is essentially the same as Jeremiah's *"lev 'echad"* (single or undivided heart).

But how does one acquire a pure heart, an undivided heart? How does one eliminate anger, lust, or any other passion that prevents a person from acting in accord with God's commands? How does one become righteous? Nowhere is a clear answer provided by Jesus. He probably thought that it was a matter of using willpower to control passions, but he never explicitly says this. After the death of Jesus, however, Christianity adopted the conception that "the power of sin can be overcome only through faith in Christ."[223]

---

218. See Vermes, *Authentic Gospel*, 356-57.

219. Matt 5:22. See Vermes, *Authentic Gospel*, 356 ("The saying typifies Jesus' tendency to go straight to . . . the inward motivation of the moral action").

220. Matt 5:28. See Vermes, *Authentic Gospel*, 357 ("To prevent sin actually happening, the eschatological ethics of Jesus enjoins resistance to adultery's inward motive, the thought of lust").

221. Matt 5:8. See Gale, "Gospel According to Matthew," 19 (The heart "represents the center of thought and conviction" [citing Isa 35:4; Prov 27:11]); chapter 4, sec. D.

222. See Vermes, *Authentic Gospel*, 314.

223. Cohen, *From the Maccabees*, 92.

In any case, Jesus may be distinguished from the Tannaim on this issue in that the Tannaim taught that an undivided heart, and righteousness, could be achieved through *talmud torah*,[224] and this was not taught by Jesus.[225] It is also clear that Jesus may be distinguished on this issue from the Essenes, for they claimed that righteousness was predetermined by God, and nowhere does Jesus make a similar claim.

5. Jesus believed that a day of judgment was near, and he warned sinners that they needed to repent.

From at least as early as the second century BCE, Jews expected the coming of an end time, which expectation took two basic forms that were not, at first, clearly distinguished: a "national form," conceived as the "coming of a golden age for the Jewish people," and an "eschatological form," conceived as the "final catastrophe of the world as it is and the coming in its place of a new world."[226] According to Moore:

> The national, or as we might call it the political, expectation is an inheritance from prophecy. Its principal features are the recovery of independence and power, an era of peace and prosperity, of fidelity to God and his law, of justice and fair-dealing and brotherly love among men, and of personal rectitude and piety. The external condition of all this is liberation from the rule of foreign oppressors; the internal condition is the religious and moral reformation or regeneration of the Jewish people itself....
>
> By the side of this political ideal of the promised golden age there was another conception of larger scope and more religious character, a time to come when all men would own and serve the one true God.... For this supremacy of God the familiar Jewish phrase is Malkut Shamaim, "the kingdom of Heaven," by which is to be understood not the realm over which God rules, but his *kingship*, his character of king....

---

224. See chapter 9, sec. C.

225. The apostle Paul was explicit about the inefficacy of torah study, claiming that it cannot bring about a change in human nature and character. See Urbach, *Sages*, 1.424 (citing Rom 8:3). See also Kugel, *Traditions of the Bible*, 310 (Paul saw in Gen 15:6 "an argument against the view that carrying out the commandments of the Torah was what would bring God to 'find in one's favor'").

226. Moore, *Judaism in the First Centuries*, 2.323.

> In its original conception the national golden age inaugurated by the coming of the Messiah was of unmeasured duration. The newer eschatology with its general resurrection, last judgment, and final and endless Age to Come, did not supersede it; and, when the two were more clearly distinguished, could find a place only beyond it. Consequently... the Messianic Age became an interim, which in Esdras is to last four hundred years....
>
> Jewish eschatology is the ultimate step in the individualizing of religion, as the messianic age is the culmination of the national conception. Every man is finally judged individually, and saved or damned by his own deeds.... Besides this it offered a solution of a tormenting problem, how to reconcile the facts of human experience, in which both the good and the bad often fare far otherwise than, as everybody sees, they deserve, with belief in divine providence.[227]

The teaching of Jesus stands within the end time tradition that Moore calls "Jewish eschatology."[228] This is to say that Jesus did not envision a political or military restoration of Israel;[229] rather, he envisioned that the present order would soon give way (through a miraculous event, without the use of force) to a new social order called "the kingdom of God" or "the kingdom of heaven."[230] The exact nature of the new social

---

227. Moore, *Judaism in the First Centuries*, 2.324, 371-72, 375-77 (emphasis original). See also Levenson, "Messianic Movements," 622-28.

228. See Sanders, *Jesus and Judaism*, 326 (It is "virtually certain" that "Jesus shared the world-view... called [by Sanders] 'Jewish restoration eschatology'"). The main themes of Jewish restoration eschatology include "the redemption of Israel (whether politically or in a new world), a new or renewed temple, repentance, judgment." Sanders, *Jesus and Judaism*, 335.

229. See Sanders, *Jesus and Judaism*, 231 ("It is hard to imagine that many of those who followed Jesus around Galilee... expected military victory.... It is now virtually universally recognized that there is not a shred of evidence which would allow us to think that Jesus had military/political ambitions").

230. See Mark 9:1; Luke 9:27; Sanders, *Jesus and Judaism*, 326 (It is "virtually certain" that while Jesus "preached the kingdom of God," he did not think "the kingdom would be established by force of arms," but "looked for an eschatological miracle"), 231 (The expectation was that a miraculous event would so transform the world that arms would not be needed); Davies, *Sermon on the Mount*, 143 ("The Gospels present Jesus as labouring under the conviction that the present order was to pass away either immediately or soon."). This teaching is similar to that of the Essenes and those responsible for the Jewish apocalyptic literature. Cf. Schechter, *Aspects of Rabbinic Theology*, 65-115 (discussing the rabbinic understanding of the kingdom of God/kingdom of heaven in its universal and national aspects and noting that, in its national aspect, it includes the faith that the Messiah will restore the kingdom of Israel in this world; the notion that a last terrible battle will take place with the enemies of God; the belief

order envisioned by Jesus cannot be determined with certainty but he probably believed that everyone in the new order would show their loyalty to God by obeying God's law.[231]

According to Sanders, Jesus expected that there would be a selection made of those allowed entry into the kingdom of God, and, Sanders says, selection "implies a judgment."[232] But the judgment and selection would be of individuals among the people of Israel, not of Israel among the nations of the world, and Jesus' call for repentance[233] was a call for *individual Jews* to repent, not a call for the nation of Israel to repent. Sanders writes:

> He did not, however, address a message to Israel to the effect that at the end there would be a great assize at which Israel would be vindicated and the nations rebuked and destroyed; and it seems that he did not make thematic the message that Israel should repent and mend their [sic] ways so as to escape punishment at the judgment....
>
> The parables of selection may reasonably be taken as implying a call to repentance, but there is no explicit evidence that Jesus was a preacher of *national* repentance.... There is a clear implication that hearers can act in such a way as to be among

---

that all the nations will accept the unity of God and seek instruction from God's law; and the conviction that it will be an age of material happiness when further death will disappear and the dead will revive).

231. See Sanders, *Jesus and Judaism*, 335–36. See also Sanders, *Jesus and Judaism*, 228–37 (discussing the nature of the kingdom that Jesus looked for and that his followers understood him to be promising and concluding that "Jesus had in mind an otherworldly-earthly kingdom" in which God would "provide a new temple, the restored people of Israel, and presumably a renewed social order" in which God's law would be obeyed). Sanders argues that, for Jesus, the kingdom would include a certain number of unrepentant sinners. Sanders, *Jesus and Judaism*, 174, 200–7. But if the kingdom was to include unrepentant sinners, how would they be able to obey God's law? Perhaps God would give sinners new, undivided hearts, as Jeremiah envisioned, but this isn't expressed in the Gospels. But see Cohen, *From the Maccabees*, 96–97 (For Jews in the early Christian communities "the 'kingdom of heaven' was to be realized by individual transformation on earth").

232. Sanders, *Jesus and Judaism*, 115.

233. After John the Baptist was arrested, Jesus withdrew to Galilee and, from that time on, is said to have begun to proclaim, "Repent, for the kingdom of heaven has come near." Matt 4:12-17. See Mark 1:14-15. Thereafter, the activity of Jesus is repeatedly described as "going about all the cities and villages, teaching in [the] synagogues, and proclaiming the good news (in Greek, *euangellion*) of the kingdom." Matt 9:35. See Matt 4:23.

the select group—i.e., repent. But there is equally clearly the implication that the selection will be *of individuals*.[234]

All those selected for entry into the kingdom would be granted "eternal life," while all those denied entry would be destroyed or would receive "eternal punishment."[235] So, it was crucial to repent and become righteous. Even if you had been a sinner your entire life, repentance before the day of final judgment would enable you to participate in the kingdom equally with someone who had been righteous their entire life.[236] Accordingly, Jesus' priority was to associate with sinners. He said, "'Those who are well off have no need of a physician, but those who are sick. . . . I have come to call not the righteous but sinners [to repentance].'"[237] In this he may be contrasted with the Essenes who believed that the wicked were irredeemable and that the righteous should hate, and completely disassociate themselves from, the wicked.

6. The ethical theory justifying the proto-Christians' adherence to biblical law (and extrabiblical interpretations and modifications of biblical law) is ethical egoism.

While the Tannaim were primarily concerned with the well-being of the Jewish community as a whole, in this world and the next,[238] the proto-Christians were primarily concerned with the well-being of the *individual* Jew in the kingdom to come. Therefore, neither Jesus nor those who followed him justified obedience to biblical laws by their beneficial

---

234. Sanders, *Jesus and Judaism*, 115 (emphasis added).

235. See, e.g., Matt 13:24-30, 36-43 (the parable of the weeds); Vermes, *Authentic Gospel*, 141 ("We are shown in this allegory the destruction of the wicked and the salvation of the righteous at the final judgment"). See also Matt 25:31-46 (The wicked "will go away into eternal punishment, but the righteous into eternal life").

236. See Matt 20:1-16 (parable of the laborers in the vineyard); Vermes, *Authentic Gospel*, 146 ("The generous master . . . is attracted to less meritorious late-comers, the tax-collectors and sinners"). See also Matt 21:28-32. Cf. chapter 5, nn48-52 and accompanying text (discussing Ezekiel).

237. Matt 9:11-13; Mark 2:17; Luke 5:31-32. See Vermes, *Authentic Gospel*, 76 ("The message conveyed [in this passage] epitomizes the mission of Jesus: as a healer, appointed by God, he is also the man commissioned to bring sinful Jews to repentance and set them on the way to the kingdom of heaven"). See generally Sanders, *Jesus and Judaism*, 174-211 ("The one distinctive note which we may be certain marked Jesus' teaching about the kingdom is that it would include the 'sinners'").

238. See m. Sanh. 10:1 ("All Israel has a share in the world to come").

consequences for the community. And despite humanitarian concerns underlying some of Jesus' *halakhah*, he did not argue that his extrabiblical interpretations and modifications of biblical law were necessary to improve the general welfare of the community. Indeed, given the belief that a new social order would imminently be coming into existence, concern with improving conditions in the then-current social order was unnecessary. Thus, the ethical theory justifying Jesus' normative judgments could not reasonably be said to be utilitarianism. Nor does Jesus ever explicitly offer a deontological justification of righteousness.[239]

Rather, Jesus justified adherence to biblical law and the incorporation of extrabiblical regulations and teachings into the legal system by their beneficial consequences *for the individual*. He predicted the imminent coming of a new social order—the kingdom of God—in which, not the community as a whole, but only certain chosen members of the community would be selected to participate.[240] And he taught that it was in your individual self-interest to possess whatever qualities and perform whatever acts would ensure your selection. For example, in the Beatitudes, Jesus says that only those having the requisite moral virtues would be included in the kingdom of heaven, that their "reward [will be] great in heaven."[241] Continuing in the Sermon on the Mount, Jesus instructs his followers to concern themselves only with the individual reward they will receive "in heaven."[242] He tells them:

> Do not store up for yourselves treasures on earth, where moth and rust consume and where thieves break in and steal; but store up for yourselves treasures in heaven, where neither moth nor rust consumes and where thieves do not break in and steal.[243]

---

239. See also Moore, *Judaism in the First Centuries*, 2.90n1 (Just like "the Jewish teachers," reward and punishment as motives for moral conduct were "freely employed by Jesus in the Gospels").

240. See Matt 22:14 ("Many are called, but few are chosen"). Cf. 4 Ezra 8:3.

241. Matt 5:3, 10, 12.

242. Matt 6:1. Jesus assures his followers that "your Father who sees in secret will reward you" for your piety. Matt 6:4. See also Matt 6:6, 18.

243. Matt 6:19. See Matt 19:21 ("Sell your possessions, and give the money to the poor, and you will have treasure in heaven").

Then, he tells them that only those individuals who adhered to the will of God "will enter the kingdom of heaven,"[244] and that, if they wished "to enter [eternal] life," they had to "keep the commandments."[245]

Although the parable of the final judgment in Matt 25 is considered by some to be "inauthentic,"[246] the emphasis there on individual reward for obedience and individual punishment for transgression expresses Jesus' true outlook. In the parable it is said that the "righteous" (those who feed the hungry, clothe the naked, welcome the stranger, and visit the sick) will "inherit the kingdom" and be granted "eternal life," while the "accursed" (those who do the opposite of the righteous) will be excluded from the kingdom and condemned to "go away into eternal punishment."[247]

Thus, the justification offered by Jesus for obeying God's will is individual reward and punishment to be received in the kingdom of heaven, not in the present life.[248] The reference in Matt 25 to the righteous "inheriting the kingdom," and the accursed being excluded from it, is an allusion to Ps 37.[249] In Ps 37 the "righteous," and those who "keep to His way" (and, therefore, are "blessed by Him"), are told that they will "inherit the land and delight in abundant well-being," while the wicked will be "cut off."[250] The Gospel of Matthew transposes Ps 37's promise of individual reward and punishment in this world to the world to come. But the justification for righteousness is otherwise the same—beneficial consequences for righteous individuals and disastrous consequences for unrighteous individuals, which is ethical egoism.

244. Matt 7:21.
245. Matt 19:17.
246. See Vermes, *Authentic Gospel*, 412; Sanders, *Jesus and Judaism*, 111.
247. Matt 25:31-46. See Gale, "Gospel According to Matthew," 58 ("Salvation is based on works of compassion" [citing Matthean passages]).
248. There is one passage in the Gospel of Matthew that suggests that the righteous would be rewarded in *this* life, as well as in the kingdom to come, at least to the extent that God would provide for their basic needs. See Matt 6:25-33. See also Mark 10:30; Luke 12:22-31; 18:29-30. But, according to Vermes, passages promising reward in this life are inauthentic. See Vermes, *Authentic Gospel*, 272 ("Jesus is unlikely to have promised recompense in this world *before* the imminently expected onset of the Kingdom")(emphasis original).
249. Cf. n6, nn22-23 in this chapter and accompanying texts.
250. Ps 37:9, 11, 22, 29, 34. See chapter 3, sec. D. Reference to Ps 37 also appears in the Sermon on the Mount where Jesus says that the meek are blessed "for they will inherit the land." Matt 5:5. See Gale, "Gospel According to Matthew," 19 (Matt 5:5 is "based on Ps 37:11 [LXX]").

Bibliography

English Translations

Berlin, Adele, and Marc Zvi Brettler, eds. *The Jewish Study Bible*. 2nd ed. Oxford: Oxford University Press, 2014.
Danby, Herbert, trans. *The Mishnah*. Oxford: Oxford University Press, 1933.
Feldman, Louis H. et al., eds. *Outside the Bible: Ancient Jewish Writings Related to Scripture*. 3 vols. Philadelphia: Jewish Publication Society, 2013.
Klawans, Jonathan, and Lawrence M. Wills, eds. *The Jewish Annotated Apocrypha: New Revised Standard Version*. Oxford: Oxford University Press, 2020.
Levine, Amy-Jill, and Marc Zvi Brettler, eds. *The Jewish Annotated New Testament: New Revised Standard Version*. 2nd ed. Oxford: Oxford University Press, 2017.

Secondary Sources

Adkins, Arthur W. H. *Merit and Responsibility: A Study of Greek Values*. Oxford: Clarendon, 1960.
———. *Moral Values and Political Behaviour in Ancient Greece*. New York: Norton, 1972.
Alexander, Elizabeth Shanks. "Art, Argument, and Ambiguity in the Talmud: Conflicting Conceptions of the Evil Impulse in *b. Sukkah* 51b–52a." *Hebrew Union College Annual* 73 (2002) 97–132.
Alexander, Philip S., ed. *Textual Sources for the Study of Judaism*. Chicago: University of Chicago Press, 1984.
Allen, James. "Antiochus of Ascalon." *Stanford Encyclopedia of Philosophy*, August 6, 2020. Edited by Edward N. Zalta. https://plato.stanford.edu/archives/fall2020/entries/antiochus-ascalon/.
Amihay, Aryeh. "Law and Society in the Dead Sea Scrolls: Preliminary Remarks." *Diné Israel* 29 (2013) 1–32. https://www.academia.edu/5043013/Law_and_Society_in_the_Dead_Sea_Scrolls_Preliminary_Remarks.
Angel, Joseph L. "Damascus Document." In *Outside the Bible: Ancient Jewish Writings Related to Scripture*, edited by Louis H. Feldman et al., 3:2975–3035. Philadelphia: Jewish Publication Society, 2013.

BIBLIOGRAPHY

Arnim, Hans von. *Stoicorum Veterum Fragmenta (Fragments of the Early Stoics)*. 4 vols. Indexes by Maximilian Adler. Leipzig: Teubner, 1924.

Assmann, Jan. *The Mind of Egypt: History and Meaning in the time of the Pharaohs*. Translated by Andrew Jenkins. New York: Henry Holt, 1996.

Balberg, Mira. "Pricing Persons: Consecration, Compensation, and Individuality in the Mishnah." *The Jewish Quarterly Review* 103.2 (2013) 169–95.

Barer, Deborah. "Law, Ethics, and Hermeneutics: A Literary Approach to Lifnim Mi-Shurat Ha-Din." *Journal of Textual Reasoning* 10.1 (2018) 1–14.

Barton, John. *Ethics in Ancient Israel*. Oxford: Oxford University Press, 2014.

———. *Understanding Old Testament Ethics: Approaches and Explorations*. Louisville: Westminster John Knox, 2003.

Baumgarten, Albert I. "Jewish War: Excursus on Jewish Groups." In *Outside the Bible: Ancient Jewish Writings Related to Scripture*, edited by Louis H. Feldman et al., 3:2888–919. Philadelphia: Jewish Publication Society, 2013.

Ben Zvi, Ehud. "Micah." In *The Jewish Study Bible*, edited by Adele Berlin and Marc Zvi Brettler, 1193–206. 2nd ed. Oxford: Oxford University Press, 2014.

Berlin, Adele, and Marc Zvi Brettler. "Psalms." In *The Jewish Study Bible*, edited by Adele Berlin and Marc Zvi Brettler, 1263–435. 2nd ed. Oxford: Oxford University Press, 2014.

Bickerman, Elias. *From Ezra to the Last of the Maccabees: Foundations of Post-Biblical Judaism*. New York: Schocken, 1962.

Blenkinsopp, Joseph. *Wisdom and Law in the Old Testament: The Ordering of Life in Israel and Early Judaism*. Rev. ed. Oxford: Oxford University Press, 1995.

Boström, Lennart. *The God of the Sages: The Portrayal of God in the Book of Proverbs*. Stockholm: Almqvist and Wiksell, 1990.

Botta, Alejandro F. "The Babylonian and Persian Period: History and Culture." In *The Jewish Annotated Apocrypha: New Revised Standard Version*, edited by Jonathan Klawans and Lawrence M. Wills, 529–35. Oxford: Oxford University Press, 2020.

Brand, Miryam T. "1 Enoch." In *Outside the Bible: Ancient Jewish Writings Related to Scripture*, edited by Louis H. Feldman et al., 2:1359–452. Philadelphia: Jewish Publication Society, 2013.

———. "Evil and Sin." In *The Jewish Annotated Apocrypha: New Revised Standard Version*, edited by Jonathan Klawans and Lawrence M. Wills, 535–42. Oxford: Oxford University Press, 2020.

Bremmer, Jan N. *The Early Greek Concept of the Soul*. Princeton, NJ: Princeton University Press, 1983.

Bright, John. *A History of Israel*. 3rd ed. Philadelphia: Westminster, 1981.

Buber, Martin. *Moses: The Revelation and the Covenant*. New York: Harper & Row, 1958.

Cohen, Naomi. "The Greek Virtues and the Mosaic Laws in Philo: An Elucidation of *Specialibus Legibus IV* 133–135." *The Studia Philonica Annual* 5 (1993) 9–23.

———. "On the Special Laws 1–4." In *Outside the Bible: Ancient Jewish Writings Related to Scripture*, edited by Louis H. Feldman et al., 1:1033–133. Philadelphia: Jewish Publication Society, 2013.

Cohen, Shaye J. D. *From the Maccabees to the Mishnah*. 2nd ed. Louisville: Westminster John Knox, 2006.

———. "The Judaean Legal Tradition and the *Halakhah* of the Mishnah." In *The Cambridge Companion to the Talmud and Rabbinic Literature*, edited by Charlotte

Elisheva Fonrobert and Martin S. Jaffe, 121–43. Cambridge: Cambridge University Press, 2007.

———. "The Significance of Yavneh: Pharisees, Rabbis, and the End of Jewish Sectarianism." *Hebrew Union College Annual* 55 (1984) 27–53.

Collins, John J. *Apocalypse, Prophecy, and Pseudepigraphy: On Jewish Apocalyptic Literature*. Grand Rapids: Eerdmans, 2015.

———. *Beyond the Qumran Community: The Sectarian Movement of the Dead Sea Scrolls*. Grand Rapids: Eerdmans, 2010.

———. "The Idea of Election in 4 Ezra." *Jewish Studies Quarterly* 16.1 (2009) 83–96.

———. *Jewish Wisdom in the Hellenistic Age*. Louisville: Westminster John Knox, 1997.

Critias. *Sisyphus*, fragment 25. In *Sextus Empiricus: Against Physicists. Against Ethicists*, translated by R. G. Bury, 28–33. Cambridge, MA: Harvard University Press, 1936.

Danby, Herbert. "Introduction." In *The Mishnah*, translated by Herbert Danby, xiii–xxxii. Oxford: Oxford University Press, 1933.

Daube, David. *The Deed and the Doer in the Bible*. Edited by Calum Carmichael. West Conshohocken, PA: Templeton, 2008.

———. *Law and Wisdom in the Bible*. Edited by Calum Carmichael. West Conshohocken, PA: Templeton, 2010.

———. *Studies in Biblical Law*. Cambridge: Cambridge University Press, 1947.

Davies, William David. *Christian Origins and Judaism*. Philadelphia: Westminster, 1962.

———. *The Sermon on the Mount*. Cambridge: Cambridge University Press, 1966.

DeSilva, Daniel A. "4 Maccabees." In *Outside the Bible: Ancient Jewish Writings Related to Scripture*, edited by Louis H. Feldman et al., 3:2362–98. Philadelphia: Jewish Publication Society, 2013.

de Vaux, Roland. *Ancient Israel*. 2 vols. New York: McGraw Hill, 1965.

Eichrodt, Walter. *Theology of the Old Testament*. 2 vols. Translated by John A. Baker. Philadelphia: Westminster, 1967.

Enns, Peter. "Wisdom of Solomon." In *Outside the Bible: Ancient Jewish Writings Related to Scripture*, edited by Louis H. Feldman et al., 3:2153–207. Philadelphia: Jewish Publication Society, 2013.

Fagenblatt, Michael. "The Concept of Neighbor in Jewish and Christian Ethics." In *The Jewish Annotated New Testament: New Revised Standard Version*, edited by Amy-Jill Levine and Marc Zvi Brettler, 645–50. 2nd ed. Oxford: Oxford University Press, 2017.

Falk, Ze'ev W. *Hebrew Law in Biblical Times: An Introduction*. 2nd ed. Provo, UT: Brigham Young University Press, 2001.

Fonrobert, Charlotte Elisheva. "Ethical Theories in Rabbinic Literature." In *The Oxford Handbook of Jewish Ethics and Morality*, edited by Elliot N. Dorff and Jonathan K. Crane, 51–70. Oxford: Oxford University Press, 2013.

Fox, Marvin. "The Mishna as a Source of Ethics." In *Marvin Fox: Collected Essays on Philosophy and on Judaism*, edited by Jacob Neusner, 3:75–93. Lanham, MD: University Press of America, 2003.

———. "Reflections on the Foundations of Jewish Ethics and Their Relation to Public Policy." *Selected Papers from the Annual Meeting (Society of Christian Ethics), Twenty-First Annual Meeting* (1980) 23–62. https://www.jstor.org/stable/23559842.

Fox, Michael V. "Proverbs." In *The Jewish Study Bible*, edited by Adele Berlin and Marc Zvi Brettler, 1437–87. 2nd ed. Oxford: Oxford University Press, 2014.

———. "Wisdom in Qohelet." In *In Search of Wisdom: Essays in Memory of John G. Gammie*, edited by Leo G. Perdue et al., 115–32. Louisville: Westminster John Knox, 1993.

Frankena, William Klaas. *Ethics*. 2nd ed. Upper Saddle River, NJ.: Prentice Hall, 1973.

Frankfort, Henri. *Ancient Egyptian Religion*. New York: Columbia University Press, 1961.

Fried, Lisbeth S. "4 Ezra." In *The Jewish Annotated Apocrypha: New Revised Standard Version*, edited by Jonathan Klawans and Lawrence M. Wills, 345–84. Oxford: Oxford University Press, 2020.

Gale, Aaron M. "The Gospel According to Matthew." In *The Jewish Annotated New Testament: New Revised Standard Version*, edited by Amy-Jill Levine and Marc Zvi Brettler, 9–66. 2nd ed. Oxford: Oxford University Press, 2017.

Ganzel, Tova. "Ezekiel." In *The Jewish Study Bible*, edited by Adele Berlin and Marc Zvi Brettler, 1033–123. 2nd ed. Oxford: Oxford University Press, 2014.

Glatzer, Nahum M. *Hillel the Elder: The Emergence of Classical Judaism*. Rev. ed. New York: Schocken, 1956.

Goff, Matthew. "Jubilees." In *The Jewish Annotated Apocrypha: New Revised Standard Version*, edited by Jonathan Klawans and Lawrence M. Wills, 1–97. Oxford: Oxford University Press, 2020.

Goldin, Judah. "The End of Ecclesiastes: Literal Exegesis and Its Transformation." In *Biblical Motifs: Origins and Transformations*, edited by Alexander Altmann, 135–58. Cambridge, MA: Harvard University Press, 1966.

Goodblatt, David. "The Place of the Pharisees in First Century Judaism: The State of the Debate." *Journal for the Study of Judaism in the Persian, Hellenistic, and Roman Period* 20.1 (1989) 12–30.

———. "The Sanhedrin." In *The Jewish Annotated New Testament: New Revised Standard Version*, edited by Amy-Jill Levine and Marc Zvi Brettler, 602–4. 2nd ed. Oxford: Oxford University Press, 2017.

Goodman, Martin. "Jewish History, 331 BCE–135 CE." In *The Jewish Annotated New Testament: New Revised Standard Version*, edited by Amy-Jill Levine and Marc Zvi Brettler, 583–89. 2nd ed. Oxford: Oxford University Press, 2017.

Gordis, Robert. *Koheleth, the Man and His World: A Study of Ecclesiastes*. 3rd augmented ed. New York: Schocken, 1968.

Greenberg, Moshe. "Some Postulates of Biblical Criminal Law." In *The Jewish Expression*, edited by Judah Goldin, 18–35. New Haven, CT: Yale University Press, 1976.

Greengus, Samuel. "Filling Gaps: Laws Found in Babylonia and in the Mishna but Absent in the Hebrew Bible." *Maarav* 7 (1991) 149–71.

———. *Laws in the Bible and in Early Rabbinic Collections: The Legal Legacy of the Ancient Near East*. Eugene, OR: Cascade, 2011.

Greenstein, Edward L. "The Heart as an Organ of Speech in Biblical Hebrew." In *Semitic, Biblical, and Jewish Studies in Honor of Richard C. Steiner*, edited by Aaron J. Koller et al., 206–18. Jerusalem: Bialik Institute, 2020.

———. "Job." In *The Jewish Study Bible*, edited by Adele Berlin and Marc Zvi Brettler, 1489–556. 2nd ed. Oxford: Oxford University Press, 2014.

Gruen, Erich S. "The Letter of Aristeas." In *Outside the Bible: Ancient Jewish Writings Related to Scripture*, edited by Louis H. Feldman et al., 3:2711–68. Philadelphia: Jewish Publication Society, 2013.

Halberstam, Chaya. "Law in Biblical Israel." In *The Cambridge Companion to Judaism and Law*, edited by Christine Hayes, 19–47. Cambridge: Cambridge University Press, 2017.

Halivni, David Weiss. *Mishnah, Midrash, and Gemara: The Jewish Predilection for Justified Law*. Cambridge, MA: Harvard University Press, 1986.

Harvey, Warren Zev. "Love: The Beginning and the End of Torah." *Tradition: A Journal of Orthodox Thought* 15.4 (1976) 5–22.

Hayes, Christine Elizabeth. "*Halakhah le-Moshe mi-Sinai* in Rabbinic Sources: A Methodological Case Study." In *The Synoptic Problem in Rabbinic Literature*, edited by Shaye J. D. Cohen, 61–117. Providence, RI: Brown Judaic Studies, 2020.

———. *Introduction to the Bible*. New Haven, CT: Yale University Press, 2012.

———. *What's Divine About Divine Law? Early Perspectives*. Princeton, NJ: Princeton University Press, 2015.

Henrich, Joseph. *The WEIRDest People in the World: How the West Became Psychologically Peculiar and Particularly Prosperous*. New York: Farrar, Straus and Giroux, 2020.

Herford, Robert Travers. *The Ethics of the Talmud: Sayings of the Fathers*. New York: Schocken, 1962.

Heschel, Abraham Joshua. *God in Search of Man: A Philosophy of Judaism*. New York: Harper & Row, 1955.

———. *The Prophets: An Introduction*. 2 vols. New York: Harper & Row, 1962.

Hesiod. *Works and Days*. Translated and edited by Glenn W. Most. Cambridge, MA: Harvard University Press, 2018.

Hillers, Delbert R. *Covenant: The History of a Biblical Idea*. Baltimore: John Hopkins University Press, 1969.

Hobbes, Thomas. *Leviathan Parts I and II*. Indianapolis: Bobbs-Merrill, 1958.

Hogan, Karina Martin. "4 Ezra." In *Outside the Bible: Ancient Jewish Writings Related to Scripture*, edited by Louis H. Feldman et al., 2:1607–68. Philadelphia: Jewish Publicatio Society, 2013.

———. "The Meanings of tôrâ in 4 Ezra." *Journal for the Study of Judaism* 38.4/5 (2007) 530–52. https://www.jstor.org/stable/24670025.

———. *Theologies in Conflict in 4 Ezra: Wisdom Debate and Apocalyptic Solution*. Leiden: Brill, 2009.

Holtz, Shalom E. "Reading Biblical Law." In *The Jewish Study Bible*, edited by Adele Berlin and Marc Zvi Brettler, 2201–7. 2nd ed. Oxford: Oxford University Press, 2014.

Hume, David. *An Inquiry Concerning the Principles of Morals*. Indianapolis: Bobbs-Merrill, 1957.

Hyatt, J. Philip. *Exodus*. Vol. 2 of *The New Century Bible Commentary*. Rev. ed. Grand Rapids: Eerdmans, 1980.

Idelsohn, Abraham Z. *Jewish Liturgy and its Development*. New York: Schocken, 1972.

Jacobs, Naomi S. "Tobit." In *The Jewish Annotated Apocrypha: New Revised Standard Version*, edited by Jonathan Klawans and Lawrence M. Wills, 149–75. Oxford: Oxford University Press, 2020.

Janzen, Waldemar. "ʾAŠRÊ in the Old Testament." *The Harvard Theological Review* 58.2 (1965) 215–26.
Jassen, Alex P. "Rule of the Community." In *Outside the Bible: Ancient Jewish Writings Related to Scripture*, edited Louis H. Feldman et al., 3:2923–74. Philadelphia: Jewish Publication Society, 2013.
Johnson, Aubrey Rodway. *The Vitality of the Individual in the Thought of Ancient Israel*. 2nd ed. Cardiff: University of Wales Press, 1964.
Jonsen, Albert R., and Stephen Toulmon. *The Abuse of Casuistry: A History of Moral Reasoning*. Berkeley, CA: University of California Press, 1988.
Josephus, Flavius. *The Works of Flavius Josephus*. Translated by William Whiston. Buffalo: John E. Beardsley, 1895.
Kadushin, Max. *Organic Thinking: A Study in Rabbinic Thought*. New York: Bloch, 1938.
Kant, Immanuel. *Groundwork of the Metaphysics of Morals*. Translated by Herbert James Paton. New York: Harper & Row, 1964.
Kaufmann, Yehezkel. *The Religion of Israel: From Its Beginnings to the Babylonian Exile*. Translated and abridged by Moshe Greenberg. Chicago, IL: University of Chicago Press, 1960.
Kee, Howard Clark. "The Ethical Dimensions of the Testaments of the XII as a Clue to Provenance." *New Testament Studies* 24.2 (1978) 259–70.
———. "Testaments of the Twelve Patriarchs." In *The Old Testament Pseudepigrapha*, edited by James H. Charlesworth, 1:775–828. Garden City, NY: Doubleday, 1983.
Kirschner, Robert. "Apocalyptic and Rabbinic Responses to the Destruction of 70." *The Harvard Theological Review* 78.1/2 (1985) 27–46.
Klawans, Jonathan. *Impurity and Sin in Ancient Judaism*. Oxford: Oxford University Press, 2000.
———. "Jewish Theology and the Apocrypha." In *The Jewish Annotated Apocrypha: New Revised Standard Version*, edited by Jonathan Klawans and Lawrence M. Wills, 640–44. Oxford: Oxford University Press, 2020
———. "The Law." In *The Jewish Annotated New Testament: New Revised Standard Version*, edited by Amy-Jill Levine and Marc Zvi Brettler, 655–58. 2nd ed. Oxford: Oxford University Press, 2017.
Koehler, Ludwig. *Old Testament Theology*. Translated by A. S. Todd. London: Lutterworth, 1957.
Koester, Helmut. "*Nomos physeōs*: The Concept of Natural Law in Greek Thought." In *Religions in Antiquity: Essays in Memory of E. F. Goodenough*, edited by Jacob Neusner, 524–42. Leiden: Brill, 1968.
Korn, Eugene. "Legal Floors and Moral Ceilings: A Jewish Understanding of Law and Ethics." *The Edah Journal* 2.2 (2002) 2–19.
Kosmin, Paul J. "The Hellenistic Period: History and Culture." In *The Jewish Annotated Apocrypha: New Revised Standard Version*, edited by Jonathan Klawans and Lawrence M. Wills, 535–42. Oxford: Oxford University Press, 2020.
Kraus, Matthew. "The Wisdom of Solomon." In *The Jewish Annotated Apocrypha: New Revised Standard Version*, edited by Jonathan Klawans and Lawrence M. Wills, 391–425. Oxford: Oxford University Press, 2020.
Kugel, James L. "Jubilees." In *Outside the Bible: Ancient Jewish Writings Related to Scripture*, edited Louis H. Feldman et al., 1:272–469. Philadelphia: Jewish Publication Society, 2013.

———. "Testaments of the Twelve Patriarchs." In *Outside the Bible: Ancient Jewish Writings Related to Scripture*, edited Louis H. Feldman et al., 2:1697–855. Philadelphia: Jewish Publication Society, 2013.

———. *Traditions of the Bible: A Guide to the Bible as It Was at the Start of the Common Era*. Cambridge, MA: Harvard University Press, 1998.

Laertius, Diogenes. *Lives of the Eminent Philosophers*. Translated by R. D. Hicks. 2 vols. Cambridge, MA: Harvard University Press, 1925.

Levenson, David B. "Messianic Movements." In *The Jewish Annotated New Testament: New Revised Standard Version*, edited by Amy-Jill Levine and Marc Zvi Brettler, 622–28. 2nd ed. Oxford: Oxford University Press, 2017.

Levi, Edward Hirsch. *An Introduction to Legal Reasoning*. Chicago: University of Chicago Press, 1949.

Levinson, Bernard M. "Deuteronomy." In *The Jewish Study Bible*, edited by Adele Berlin and Marc Zvi Brettler, 339–428. 2nd ed. Oxford: Oxford University Press, 2014.

Lewis, Naphtali. "Solon's Agrarian Legislation." *The American Journal of Philology* 62.2 (1941) 144–56.

Lipschits, Oded. "The History of Israel in the Biblical Period." In *The Jewish Study Bible*, edited by Adele Berlin and Marc Zvi Brettler, 2107–18. 2nd ed. Oxford: Oxford University Press, 2014.

Long, Arthur A. *Hellenistic Philosophy: Stoics, Epicureans, Sceptics*. 2nd ed. Berkeley, CA: University of California Press, 1986.

Machinist, Peter. "Ecclesiastes." In *The Jewish Study Bible*, edited by Adele Berlin and Marc Zvi Brettler, 1599–618. 2nd ed. Oxford: Oxford University Press, 2014.

MacIntyre, Alasdair. *Whose Justice? Which Rationality?* Notre Dame, IN: University of Notre Dame Press, 1988.

Madigan, Kevin J., and Jon D Levenson. *Resurrection: The Power of God for Christians and Jews*. New Haven, CT: Yale University Press, 2008.

Maimonides, Moses. *Maimonides' Commentary on the Mishnah Tractate Sanhedrin*. Translated by Fred Rosner. New York: Sepher-Hermon, 1981.

Meyers, Carol. "Joshua." In *The Jewish Study Bible*, edited by Adele Berlin and Marc Zvi Brettler, 462–507. Oxford: Oxford University Press, 2004.

Milgrom, Jacob. *Leviticus: A Book of Ritual and Ethics*. Minneapolis: Fortress, 2004.

Mill, John Stuart. *Utilitarianism*. Edited by Ben Eggleston. Indianapolis, IN: Hackett, 2017.

Miller, Patrick. D. Jr. "The Place of the Decalogue in the Old Testament and Its Law." *Interpretation* 43.3 (1989) 229–42.

Miller, Stuart S. "Torah, Law and Commandments." In *The Jewish Annotated Apocrypha: New Revised Standard Version*, edited by Jonathan Klawans and Lawrence M. Wills, 620–25. Oxford: Oxford University Press, 2020.

Millgram, Abraham. *Jewish Worship*. Philadelphia: Jewish Publication Society of America, 1971.

Mittleman, Alan L. *A Short History of Jewish Ethics: Conduct and Character in the Context of Covenant*. West Sussex: Wiley-Blackwell, 2012.

Moore, George Foot. *Judaism in the First Centuries of the Christian Era: The Age of the Tannaim*. 2 vols. New York: Schocken, 1958.

Morenz, Siegfried. *Egyptian Religion*. Translated by Ann E. Keep. London: Methuen, 1973.

Neusner, Jacob. *From Politics to Piety: The Emergence of Pharisaic Judaism*. Englewood Cliffs, NJ: Prentice-Hall, 1973.

———. *The Mishnah: An Introduction*. Northvale, NJ: Jason Aronson, 1989.

———. "Rabbinic Traditions about the Pharisees Before AD 70: The Problem of Oral Transmission." *Journal of Jewish Studies* 22 (1971) 1–18.

———. *There We Sat Down: Talmudic Judaism in the Making*. Nashville: Abingdon, 1972.

Nickelsburg, George W. E. *Jewish Literature Between the Bible and the Mishnah: A Historical and Literary Introduction*. 2nd ed. Minneapolis: Fortress, 2005.

———. *Resurrection, Immortality, and Eternal Life in Intertestamental Judaism and Early Christianity*. Expand. ed. Cambridge, MA: Harvard University Press, 2006.

Novak, David. *Natural Law in Judaism*. Cambridge: Cambridge University Press, 1998.

Novick, Tzvi. "Tradition, Scripture, Law, and Authority." In *The Literature of the Sages: A Re-Visioning*, edited by Christine Hayes, 64–92. Leiden: Brill, 2022.

Orlinsky, Harry M. *Ancient Israel*. 2nd ed. Ithaca, NY: Cornell University Press, 1960.

Pawlikowski, John T. *Christ in the Light of the Christian-Jewish Dialogue*. New York: Paulist, 1982.

Pearce, Sarah Judith. "On the Decalogue." In *Outside the Bible: Ancient Jewish Writings Related to Scripture*, edited Louis H. Feldman et al., 1:989–1032. Philadelphia: Jewish Publication Society, 2013.

Perdue, Leo G. *Wisdom and Cult: A Critical Analysis of the Views of Cult in the Wisdom Literature of Israel and the Ancient Near East*. Missoula, MT: Scholars, 1977.

Pope, Marvin. *Job*. Vol. 15 of *The Anchor Bible*. Garden City, NY: Doubleday, 1965.

Przybylski, Benno. "The Meaning and Significance of the Concept of Righteousness in the Gospel of Matthew: With Special Reference to the Use of This Concept in the Dead Sea Scrolls and the Tannaitic Literature." PhD diss., McMaster University, 1975.

Redditt, Paul L. "The Concept of *Nomos* in Fourth Maccabees." *The Catholic Biblical Quarterly* 45.2 (1983) 249–70.

Reed, Annette Yoshiko. "Canon." In *The Jewish Annotated Apocrypha: New Revised Standard Version*, edited by Jonathan Klawans and Lawrence M. Wills, 570–75. Oxford: Oxford University Press, 2020.

Reinhartz, Adele. "The Gospel According to John." In *The Jewish Annotated New Testament: New Revised Standard Version*, edited by Amy-Jill Levine and Marc Zvi Brettler, 168–218. 2nd ed. Oxford: Oxford University Press, 2017.

Rivkin, Ellis. "Defining the Pharisees: The Tannaitic Sources." *Hebrew Union College Annual* 40/41 (1969–70) 205–49.

———. *A Hidden Revolution: The Pharisees' Search for the Kingdom Within*. Nashville: Abingdon, 1978.

———. "Pharisaism and the Crisis of the Individual in the Greco-Roman World." *The Jewish Quarterly Review* 61.1 (1970) 27–53.

Robinson, Thomas M. *Plato's Psychology*. Toronto: University of Toronto Press, 1970.

Rodd, Cyril S. *Glimpses of a Strange Land: Studies in Old Testament Ethics*. Edinburgh: T. & T. Clark, 2001.

Rom-Shiloni, Dalit. "Jeremiah." In *The Jewish Study Bible*, edited by Adele Berlin and Marc Zvi Brettler, 901–1032. 2nd ed. Oxford: Oxford University Press, 2014.

Rosen-Zvi, Ishay. "Two Rabbinic Inclinations? Rethinking a Scholarly Dogma." *Journal for the Study of Judaism in the Persian, Hellenistic, and Roman Period* 39.4 (2008) 513–39.

Runia, David T. "On the Creation of the World." In *Outside the Bible: Ancient Jewish Writings Related to Scripture*, edited by Louis H. Feldman et al., 1:882–901. Philadelphia: Jewish Publication Society, 2013.

———. "The Writings of Philo." In *Outside the Bible: Ancient Jewish Writings Related to Scripture*, edited by Louis H. Feldman et al., 1:11–17. Philadelphia: Jewish Publication Society, 2013.

Saldarini, Anthony J. "Apocalyptic and Rabbinic Literature." *The Catholic Biblical Quarterly* 37.3 (1975) 348–58.

Sanders, Ed Parish. *Jesus and Judaism*. Philadelphia: Fortress, 1985.

———. *Paul and Palestinian Judaism: A Comparison of Patterns of Religion*. Philadelphia: Fortress, 1977.

Sandmel, Samuel. *Two Living Traditions: Essays on Religion and the Bible*. Detroit: Wayne State University Press, 1972.

Sarna, Nahum M. *Understanding Genesis*. New York: Schocken, 1966.

Satlow, Michael L. "'And on Earth You Shall Sleep': Talmud Torah and Rabbinic Asceticism." *The Journal of Religion* 83.2 (2003) 204–25.

———. "Ben Sira." In *The Jewish Annotated Apocrypha: New Revised Standard Version*, edited by Jonathan Klawans and Lawrence M. Wills, 427–98. Oxford: Oxford University Press, 2020.

Schechter, Solomon. *Aspects of Rabbinic Theology*. Woodstock, VT: Jewish Lights, 1993.

Scheindlin, Raymond P. *A Short History of the Jewish People From Legendary Times to Modern Statehood*. Oxford: Oxford University Press, 1998.

Schiffman, Lawrence H. *The Halakhah at Qumran*. Leiden: Brill. 1975.

———. "Pharisees." In *The Jewish Annotated New Testament: New Revised Standard Version*, edited by Amy-Jill Levine and Marc Zvi Brettler, 619–22. 2nd ed. Oxford: Oxford University Press, 2017.

———. "Qumran and Rabbinic Halakhah." In *Jewish Civilization in the Hellenistic-Roman Period*, edited by Shemaryahu Yalmon, 138–46. Philadelphia: Trinity Press, 1991.

Schmitz, Barbara. "'. . . using different names, as Zeus and Dis' (Arist 16). Concepts of 'God' in the Letter of Aristeas." In *Die Septuaginta—Orte und Intentionen*, edited by Siegfried Kreuzer et al., 703–16. Tübingen: Mohr Siebeck, 2016.

Schofer, Jonathan Wyn. *The Making of a Sage: A Study in Rabbinic Ethics*. Madison, WI: University of Wisconsin Press, 2005.

———. "The Redaction of Desire: Structure and Editing of Rabbinic Teachings Concerning Yeṣer ('Inclination')." *The Journal of Jewish Thought and Philosophy* 12.1 (2003) 19–53.

Schremer, Adiel. "*Avot* Reconsidered: Rethinking Rabbinic Judaism." *Jewish Quarterly Review* 105.3 (2015) 287–311.

———. "'[T]he[y] Did Not Read the Sealed Book': Qumran Halakhic Revolution and the Emergence of Torah Study in Second Temple Judaism." In *Historical Perspectives: From the Maccabees to Bar Kokhba in Light of the Dead Sea Scrolls*, edited by David Goodblatt et al., 105–26. Leiden: Brill, 2001.

———. "'Times to Act for the Lord': Rulings in Contrast to the Law in Jewish Legal Tradition." *Interpretation and Legal Change: A Comparative Perspective*. Jerusalem, Israel, 2015.

Schwartz, Baruch J. "Leviticus." In *The Jewish Study Bible*, edited by Adele Berlin and Marc Zvi Brettler, 193–266. 2nd ed. Oxford: Oxford University Press, 2014.

Scolnic, Benjamin Edidin. "Circumcision and Immortality." *Conservative Judaism* 64.4 (2013) 6–29.
Sigal, Phillip. *The Halakhah of Jesus of Nazareth According to the Gospel of Matthew*. Lanham, MD: University Press of America, 1987.
Smith, Morton. "Palestinian Judaism in the First Century." In *Israel: Its Role in Civilization*, edited by Moshe Davis, 67–81. New York: Harper & Row, 1956.
Sommer, Benjamin D. "Isaiah." In *The Jewish Study Bible*, edited by Adele Berlin and Marc Zvi Brettler, 763–899. 2nd ed. Oxford: Oxford University Press, 2014.
Speiser, Ephraim, A. *Genesis*. Vol. 1 of *The Anchor Bible*. Garden City, NY: Doubleday, 1964.
Sterling, Gregory E. "The Queen of the Virtues: Piety in Philo of Alexandria." *The Studia Philonica Annual* 18 (2006) 103–23.
Starr, Zachary Alan. *Toward a History of Jewish Thought: The Soul, Resurrection, and the Afterlife*. Eugene, OR: Wipf & Stock, 2020.
Swidler, Leon. *Yeshua: Jesus the Jew a Model for Everyone*. 3rd ed. Mesa, AZ: iPub Global Connection, 2020.
Svebakken, Hans Richard. *Philo of Alexandria's Exposition of the Tenth Commandment*. PhD diss., Loyola University Chicago, 2009. http://ecommons.luc.edu/luc_diss/244.
Talmon, Shemaryahu. "The 'Desert Motif' in the Bible and in Qumran Literature." In *Biblical Motifs: Origins and Transformations*, edited by Alexander Altmann, 31–63. Cambridge, MA: Harvard University Press, 1966.
Theognis. *Theognidea*. In *Greek Elegiac Poetry*, edited and translated by Douglas E. Gerber. Cambridge, MA; Harvard University Press, 1999.
Tigay, Jeffrey H. "Exodus." In *The Jewish Study Bible*, edited by Adele Berlin and Marc Zvi Brettler, 95–192. 2nd ed. Oxford: Oxford University Press, 2014.
Tirosh-Samuelson, Hava. *Happiness in Premodern Judaism: Virtue, Knowledge, and Well-Being*. Cincinnati: Hebrew Union College Press, 2003.
Urbach, Ephraim E. "The Role of the Ten Commandments in Jewish Worship." In *The Ten Commandments in History and Tradition*, edited by Ben-Zion Segal and Gershon Levi, 161–89. Jerusalem: Magnes, 1990.
———. *The Sages: Their Concepts and Beliefs*. 2 vols. Translated by Israel Abrahams. 2nd enlarged ed., revised. Jerusalem: Magnes, 1987.
Van der Horst, Peter W. "Pseudo-Phocylides on the Afterlife: A Rejoinder to John J. Collins." *Journal for the Study of Judaism in the Persian, Hellenistic, and Roman Period* 35.1 (2004) 70–75.
———. "Pseudo-Phocylides Revisited." *Journal for the Study of the Pseudepigrapha* 2.3 (1988) 3–30.
———. "Pseudo-Phocylides, Sentences." In *Outside the Bible: Ancient Jewish Writings Related to Scripture*, edited by Louis H. Feldman et al., 3:2353–61. Philadelphia: Jewish Publication Society, 2013.
———. *The Sentences of Pseudo-Phocylides: With Introduction and Commentary*. Leiden: Brill, 1978.
Vermes, Geza. *The Authentic Gospel of Jesus*. New York: Penguin, 2004.
———. "Introduction." In *The Complete Dead Sea Scrolls in English*, 1–90. 50th ann. ed. New York: Penguin, 2011.
———. *Jesus the Jew: A Historian's Reading of the Gospels*. Philadelphia: Fortress, 1973.
———. *Jesus and the World of Judaism*. Philadelphia: Fortress, 1983.

Von Rad, Gerhard. *The Message of the Prophets*. Translated by David M. G. Stalker. New York: Harper & Row, 1962.
———. *Wisdom in Israel*. Translated by James D. Martin. London: SCM, 1972.
Weinfeld, Moshe. "The Origin of the Humanism in Deuteronomy." *Journal of Biblical Literature* 80.3 (1961) 241–47.
———. *Social Justice in Ancient Israel and the Ancient Near East*. Jerusalem: Magnes, 1995.
———. "The Uniqueness of the Decalogue and Its Place in Jewish Tradition." In *The Ten Commandments in History and Tradition*, edited by Ben-Zion Segal and Gershon Levi, 1–44. Jerusalem: Magnes, 1990.
Wills, Lawrence M. "Daniel." In *The Jewish Study Bible*, edited by Adele Berlin and Marc Zvi Brettler, 1635–59. 2nd ed. Oxford: Oxford University Press, 2014.
———. "The Gospel According to Mark." In *The Jewish Annotated New Testament: New Revised Standard Version*, edited by Amy-Jill Levine and Marc Zvi Brettler, 67–106. 2nd ed. Oxford: Oxford University Press, 2017.
Wilson, Walter T. *The Mysteries of Righteousness: The Literary Composition and Genre of the Sentences of Pseudo-Phocylides*. Tübingen: Mohr, 1994.
———. "On the Virtues (51–174)." In *Outside the Bible: Ancient Jewish Writings Related to Scripture*, edited Louis H. Feldman et al., 3:2447–80. Philadelphia: Jewish Publication Society, 2013.
Winston, David. "Philo's Ethical Theory." In *Aufstieg und Niedergang der romischen Welt II*, 372–416. Berlin: Walter de Gruyter, 1984.
———. *The Wisdom of Solomon*. New York: Doubleday, 1979.
Wolfson, Harry Austryn. *Philo: Foundations of Religious Philosophy in Judaism, Christianity, and Islam*. 2 vols. Cambridge, MA: Harvard University Press, 1968.
Wright, Benjamin G. III. "Wisdom of Ben Sira." In *Outside the Bible: Ancient Jewish Writings Related to Scripture*, edited by Louis H. Feldman et al., 3:2208–352. Philadelphia: Jewish Publication Society, 2013.
Zurawski, Jason M. "4 Maccabees." In *The Jewish Annotated Apocrypha: New Revised Standard Version*, edited by Jonathan Klawans and Lawrence M. Wills, 499–525. Oxford: Oxford University Press, 2020.

www.ingramcontent.com/pod-product-compliance
Lightning Source LLC
Chambersburg PA
CBHW071237300426
44116CB00008B/1067